THE THEOSOPHICAL MOVEMENT

THE THEOSOPHICAL MOVEMENT

1875-1925 A HISTORY AND A SURVEY

GYAN

Published by

Gyan Publishing House
5, Ansari Road
Daryaganj, New Delhi-110002
Phone: 011-47034999, 9811692060
E-mail: books@gyanbooks.com

Distribution Network
gyanbooks.com
India, USA, Canada, UK, Australia

ISBN: 978-93-7169-419-3 (PB)

First Published, 1925

2nd Impression 2025

Printed at: Gyan Press, Delhi.

THE THEOSOPHICAL MOVEMENT

THE THEOSOPHICAL MOVEMENT

THE THEOSOPHICAL MOVEMENT

1875-1925

A HISTORY AND A SURVEY

NEW YORK
E. P. DUTTON & COMPANY
681 FIFTH AVENUE

"To all true Theosophists, in every country and of every race, for they called it forth, and for them it was recorded."

PREFACE

There exists nowhere a collected and authentic recital of the Theosophical Movement of the nineteenth century. Yet, although a scant half century has elapsed since the foundation of The Theosophical Society at New York City, the work there begun has spread into all portions of the civilized world, until the word Theosophy is a familiar term to every educated mind. The teachings known under that name have been more or less investigated and adopted by millions, while its more earnest students who have accepted it as a complete and satisfactory explanation of all the problems of life, here and hereafter, are numbered by thousands in every country and of every race.

In an indirect but none the less powerful manner the teachings of Theosophy have profoundly affected the ideas and ideals of the race on the great questions of ethics, of morality, of religion, philosophy and science, so that today it may be truly said that there is nothing worthy of the consideration of the human mind that has not been leavened by the injection of Theosophical leaven. It is not too much, therefore, to affirm that the direct and indirect influence of Theosophy upon humanity in the course of a single generation has been greater than that of any other system ever promulgated, during as many centuries as the Theosophical Movement numbers decades. And the Movement can as yet scarcely be said to have passed the stage of its germinal impulsion.

The record of the Theosophical Movement is scattered through thousands upon thousands of pages of books, magazines, newspapers, pamphlets and other documents. Many of these are extremely controversial in character, many inaccurate, many contradictory and confusing. The attempt to study, digest, collate and compare the immense literature of the subject is a monumental undertaking. The writers have spent many years in connection with the work of the Theosophical Movement, and their opportunities and facilities have been greater than most. Yet they know only too well the impossibility of doing anything like justice to the subject, or of affording satisfactory replies to all questions of the sincere student of its complexities. The very nature of the subject forbids. For Theosophy, the Theosophical Movement, and the real and true Theosophical Society have, each of them, an esoteric as well as an exoteric side, and the latter can never be fully grasped and understood but through the former.

Some of this hidden side can be touched upon, some documents referred to, some indications submitted, some deductions offered for the consideration of the reflective mind, but for by far the most important portion of the esoteric aspect the student must rely upon his own intuition: for the hidden side of Theosophy can only be arrived at through the hidden nature of the student himself.

Still another difficulty that confronts alike the writers and the sincere student is the fact that many of those who were active in the lifetime of the parent Theosophical Society are still living and now prominent, both in the public eye, and as leaders and exponents of the many conflicting theosophical and occult societies that have sprung up in the past twenty-five years, since the death of the original society. All these antagonistic organizations have their devoted adherents, their own particular tenets and claims of pre-eminence and successorship. The situation exactly parallels that of the early centuries of Christianity. Rival pretensions to apostolic succession, to knowledge, to authority, and to the possession of the keys to the teachings of the Founders confront the inquirer. The danger is imminent that if a better knowledge and understanding of the real teachings of Theosophy, the real mission of the Theosophical Movement, and the real facts in connection with the history of the Parent Theosophical Society, are not made available for all those who may become interested, the fate that has long since overtaken Brahminism, Buddhism and Christianity will inevitably befall the great Message of H. P. Blavatsky.

For all the reasons expressed and implied, an accessible record of the facts, as accurate a survey of their significance and bearing on the present and on the future as possible, is of the utmost moment to all sincere students and to all earnest enquirers. Themselves members of none of the existing organizations, but profoundly convinced of the surpassing value of the noble philosophy of Theosophy, the writers are moved to this attempt to aid the unimpeded flow of the great stream of the Theosophical Movement, not so much by any belief in their own especial ability as by the conviction that that flow is being impeded and corrupted by the partisanship and pretensions of the leading exponents of the existing societies. It is therefore addressed, not to any society or societies, but to all true Theosophists, whether members of any of the existing organizations or of none, and to all true enquirers everywhere, who may be willing to accept truth wherever it may be found, and to defend it, even looking popular prejudice—and their own—straight in the face.

For the rest, it may be added that the SYLLABUS which precedes the text will, it is hoped, be found, both by the general reader and the serious student, to be more satisfactory than an index. The abundant direct citations and the collateral references included in the text render superfluous a separate bibliography and will, it is thought, enable those so minded to verify at first hand every minor as well as major subject discussed.

CONTENTS

CHAPTER		PAGE
I.	Channels of the Theosophical Movement	1
II.	The Parent Theosophical Society	13
III.	"Isis Unveiled"	26
IV.	Early Days of the Theosophical Society	42
V.	The S.P.R. and the Theosophical Phenomena	59
VI.	The Report of the S.P.R.	75
VII.	Divisions among Theosophists—New Publications	94
VIII.	Esoteric and Exoteric Aspects of the Theosophical Movement	110
IX.	H.P.B., Olcott, and Judge	127
X.	The Formation of the Esoteric Section	144
XI.	The Work of the Esoteric Section	163
XII.	Mabel Collins and Professor Coues	178
XIII.	The Coues-Collins Charges and Their Aftermath	195
XIV.	*The New York Sun* Libel Case	211
XV.	Olcott Versus H.P.B.	226
XVI.	Olcott's Attempt to Centralize All Authority	244
XVII.	H.P.B. Takes Charge of the T.S. in Europe	267
XVIII.	Death of H.P.B.—Her Last Messages	275
XIX.	The Crisis in the Society	293
XX.	Attempts to Supersede H.P.B.'s Influence	302
XXI.	Growing Divergences—Olcott Resigns as President	321

CHAPTER		PAGE
XXII.	Convention of 1892—Olcott Withdraws His Resignation	334
XXIII.	H.P.B.'s "Successors"—The Publication of "Old Diary Leaves"	351
XXIV.	Controversy over H.P.B.'s Status as Agent of the Masters	380
XXV.	Annie Besant in America, 1892-1893	405
XXVI.	Beginnings of the "Judge Case"	425
XXVII.	Mrs. Besant Changes Sides	441
XXVIII.	The American Section Supports Judge	468
XXIX.	The "Judicial Enquiry" in London	493
XXX.	British Convention Dismisses Case against Judge	519
XXXI.	The "Eastern Division" and "Western Division"	559
XXXII.	*Westminster Gazette* Attacks the Society	574
XXXIII.	Mrs Besant Tries to Drive Judge Out of the Society	596
XXXIV.	The American Section Declares Its Autonomy and Elects Judge Its Life-President	622
XXXV.	Judge's Death and the Tingley "Successorship"	653
XXXVI.	Present and Future of the Theosophical Movement	689

ANALYTICAL TABLE OF CONTENTS

PAGE

CHAPTER I. CHANNELS OF THE THEOSOPHICAL MOVEMENT 1

The Theosophical Movement the story of Spiritual and Intellectual evolution—Religions and systems of thought, governments, sects and parties, landmarks of its cyclical progression through the ages—The Reformation, Free Masonry, the American Republic, the abolition of human slavery, all steps—the "divine right" of God and the "divine rights" of kings alike obstacles to progress—all physical evolution preceded and accompanied by intellectual and moral growth—upward impulses due to the inspiration of higher evolved Intelligences—they work through appropriate channels—modern signs of the Theosophical Movement abundantly in evidence—Western interest in oriental philosophy and religion—the great influence of the "Light of Asia"—the tremendous effect of Darwin's "Origin of Species" on prevailing religious ideas of "creation," God and Nature—Buckle's intuitive perception of the rise of new religions and philosophies—the great work of iconoclasts like Ingersoll and Bradlaugh, of liberal preachers like Kingsley and Channing—the Bastilles of orthodoxy no longer impregnable—Spiritualism an index of the transitional state of mind in religion—phenomena and forces ignored by Science—the writings of Allan Kardec—Spiritualism devoid alike of morality and philosophy—becomes in a generation the faith of millions—due to awakening psychic faculties—Madame Blavatsky enters the Western arena—her exhibition of powers exercised at will—her totally unknown philosophy of Life—her first efforts made with the Spiritualists.

CHAPTER II. THE PARENT THEOSOPHICAL SOCIETY . . . 13

Madame Blavatsky comes to New York in 1873—meets Col. H. S. Olcott in 1874 at the Eddy farmhouse—she controls the exhibition of phenomena unknown to the spectators—Olcott a prominent lawyer and newspaper writer, a life-long Spiritualist—becomes greatly interested in H.P.B.'s powers and knowledge—introduces her to Wm. Q. Judge, a young lawyer—Olcott and Judge become pupils of H.P.B.—Olcott's book, "People from the Other World," draws public attention to the phenomenal powers of H.P.B.—her apartment dubbed "the Lamasery" becomes the scene of a never ending throng of visitors and marvel seekers—Olcott proposes a "Miracle Club," which falls through—the Theosophical Society established in November, 1875, by H.P.B., Olcott and Judge—other early members—most of them Spiritualists who turn enemies—teachings of H.P.B. entirely opposed to the theories of Spiritualism—many European and Indian Fellows join the new Society—The Arya Somaj and *Swami* Sarasvati—the original Society democratic in organization—no restrictions on freedom of conscience or liberty of

PAGE

thought—the "Three Objects" of the Parent Theosophical Society—H.P.B. writes "Isis Unveiled," published in 1877—goes with Col. Olcott to India, leaving Judge in America—rapid growth of the Society in the Orient—early publications and formation of new "Branches," East and West.

CHAPTER III. "ISIS UNVEILED" 26

"Isis Unveiled" a Master Key to the mysteries of science and religion, modern and ancient—dedicated to the Theosophical Society with whose "Three Objects" its teachings are in correlation—discusses the roots of all religion, the negations of science, and the phenomena of Spiritualism—declares all three before a blank wall only to be penetrated by recourse to the wisdom of the ancient sages—affirms the existence of the Wisdom-Religion as the true Source of the Theosophical Movement in all ages—H.P.B. avows her own intimate acquaintance with living Adepts—phenomenal powers over space, time and matter—proves the fallacies of "exact" science by the testimony of its own exponents—all claims of religious "infallibility" mere theological dogmas—raises her voice for spiritual freedom and enfranchisement from all tyranny whether of Science or Theology—postulates a double evolution, spiritual and intellectual—the Wisdom-Religion the only philosophy which can reconcile faith and knowledge—Metempsychosis, in its esoteric sense—the solution of the "missing links" in Science and the mysteries that baffle religionists—ancient *Magic* a Divine Science—Cyclic Law, or *Karma,* the explanation of the rise and fall of civilizations—the periodic destructions and renovations of Nature—every problem of existence solved by the Wise Men of old—the secret and unbroken chain of the Adepts of the Great Lodge—the great propositions of Occultism—there is no miracle, everything under Law (Karma)—Spirit, Mind and Matter the evolving Trinity in Nature and in Man—Adeptship versus Mediumship—the Trinity of Nature the lock of Magic—the Trinity of Man the Key that fits it.

CHAPTER IV. EARLY DAYS OF THE THEOSOPHICAL SOCIETY 42

The Theosophical Society an attempt to form a human association on the basis of the Lodge of Adepts, pure *Altruism*—H.P.B. not deceived in regard to the obstacles to be met—sectarian religious prejudices, the great barrier to true Fraternity—the Second Object of the T.S.—the idea of "miracles" and materialistic hypotheses of modern science the great enemies of true knowledge, hence the Third Object—Man inherently perfectible, not a mortal fallible being—Adepts the living proof of the divinity inherent in every man—the Wisdom-Religion can be known and its Adepts found by any sincere man—the real enemies of human welfare—bound to array themselves against H.P.B., her Society and her mission—who those enemies are—orthodox religions, materialistic science, pseudo-scientists, pretended *authorities*—the mercenaries and parasites of the press—"Isis Unveiled" neither a revelation nor an arbitrary theory—a statement of verifiable facts, physical and metaphysical—rests upon its own inherent worth—the Theosophical Society a body of students—dependent upon self-induced and self-devised efforts to study and apply the teachings of Theosophy—rejected and opposed by the Spiritualists, its natural allies, because of its

PAGE

teachings on after-death states and conditions—greatly helped in the East because of the natural mysticism of the inhabitants —*Swami* Sarasvati and his Arya Somaj originally sympathetic —Buddhist and Hindu friends gained for the Society in India—Sumangali, Damodar Mavalankar and Subba Row, powerful allies—A. P. Sinnett and A. O. Hume influential friends among the English—*The Theosophist* founded in 1879—Olcott's "Buddhist Catechism" published—this and his lecturing tours gain many adherents—Missionary hostility aroused at the success and propaganda of the Society—H.P.B. charged with being a Russian spy and an immoral woman with Col. Olcott for her dupe —other calumnies—charges recanted by enemies—first internal disturbance in the London Lodge—Dr. George Wyld's defection —Dr. Anna Bonus Kingsford's "Perfect Way"—her pamphlet assault on Mr. Sinnett's "Esoteric Buddhism"—Mr. Subba Row replies—Mr. C. C. Massey precipitates further troubles—the "Kiddle charges" of plagiarism by the Master—the storm raised in England and France in 1884—H.P.B. and Col. Olcott go to Paris and London—meet Mr. Solovyoff—Judge comes to Paris, goes to India, and returns to America *via* London—H.P.B. and Col. Olcott meet leading members of the Society for Psychical Research while in London—the S.P.R. plans to investigate the "Theosophical phenomena."

Chapter V. The S.P.R. and the Theosophical Phenomena 59

The Society for Psychical Research preceded by the Dialectical Society—that Society investigates Spiritualism in 1869—publishes its Report in 1870—concludes phenomena of Spiritualism are genuine—transcend all known laws—should be investigated scientifically—criticisms of the Report by London papers—Professor Crookes investigates Spiritualism—publishes his results in 1872—Mr. Crookes assailed as savagely as Darwin—no advance in understanding of Spiritualistic phenomena during next ten years—the "Unseen Universe"—the Society for Psychical Research established in 1882—its chief sponsors Spiritualists—some of them members of the Theosophical Society also—many well-known men and women join the S.P.R.—it begins its investigation of the "Theosophical phenomena" in the summer of 1884—Olcott, Sinnett, Chatterji and others examined—H.P.B. interviewed—many other witnesses to the phenomena of H.P.B. give testimony—Preliminary Report of the S.P.R. issued in the fall of 1884—admits the *prima facie* genuineness of the phenomena—reservations due to the charges just made in India by the Coulombs against the good faith of H.P.B.—declares a further investigation necessary in India—appoints Mr. Richard Hodgson for that purpose—the story of the Coulomb charges of fraud against H.P.B.—H.P.B. shipwrecked in 1871—goes to Cairo—meets Madame Coulomb—is succored by her—starts a society to investigate Western Spiritualism—the attempt a failure—H.P.B. returns to Russia in 1872—goes to Paris and then to New York in 1873—Madame Coulomb marries in Egypt—meets with reverses—is living in poverty in Ceylon when H.P.B. and Col. Olcott come to India—the Coulombs appeal for aid—go to India—join the Theosophical Society in 1880—are given employment at headquarters—Madame Coulomb a bigoted Christian and Spiritualist medium—becomes jealous of H.P.B.'s successful mission—tries to extort money from members—circulates

PAGE

slanders about H.P.B.—is brought to "trial" by the members of the Council during absence of H.P.B. and Olcott in Europe in the summer of 1884—the Coulombs communicate with Madras missionaries—are expelled from the Theosophical Society—are supported by the missionaries—the Coulomb charges published in the *Christian College Magazine* and in a pamphlet—the outburst occasioned.

CHAPTER VI. THE REPORT OF THE S.P.R. 75

Madame Blavatsky resigns from Theosophical Society when Coulomb charges made public—resignation refused by Olcott under pressure—H.P.B. writes London *Times* and *Pall Mall Gazette* pronouncing charges a conspiracy—H.P.B. and Olcott return to India at end of 1884—H.P.B. insists charges must be met by court proceedings against the Coulombs—Olcott and the Hindus oppose legal action—the Adyar Convention declines to defend H.P.B. while affirming belief in her *bona fides*—Olcott and Sinnett already mistrust H.P.B.—she resigns from the Society and leaves India early in 1885—Mr. Hodgson in India during the Convention and desertion of H.P.B. by Theosophists—powerfully affected by the lukewarmness and doubts of leading Theosophists—returns to England and submits his report to Committee of S.P.R.—Hodgson's findings adopted by Committee in June, 1885—Report of the S.P.R. published following December—Conclusions reached—H.P.B.'s phenomena fraudulent—in a long-continued conspiracy to deceive public—Coulomb letters and *Mahatma* letters written by H.P.B.—declare H.P.B. "one of the most accomplished, ingenious, and interesting impostors in history"—the Report of the S.P.R. examined critically shows it to be wholly *ex parte*—no safeguards employed to ascertain and render justice—the investigation that of a rival society controlled by Spiritualists—the S.P.R. not interested in philosophy or ethics—avid for phenomena—ignorant of Occultism—contradictions and inconsistencies of S.P.R. Committee shown from its own Report—Committee relies wholly on Mr. Massey's suspicions, the Coulomb charges, and the opinions of the London handwriting experts—Mr. Massey's suspicions shown to be without tangible foundation—the Coulombs shown out of their own mouths to be lying tricksters—the handwriting experts shown as first declaring the *Mahatma* letters could *not* have been written by H.P.B. —then, at Hodgson's solicitation, changing their opinion to the contrary—the expert Netherclift shown to have sworn positively in the Parnell case to the opposite of the facts—the motives of all adverse witnesses shown to have been culpable and their testimony impeached—more than one hundred responsible witnesses affirm the genuineness of phenomena witnessed by them —the S.P.R. Committee declares these to have been victims of "hallucination"—Hodgson's findings examined—a mass of suspicions and contradictory conjectures to account for facts testified to—Hodgson recognizes necessity for showing a motive sufficient to account for H.P.B.'s alleged fraud during twenty years —rejects supposition that she was influenced by greed or ambition—submits theory that H.P.B. was a Russian spy—her Society and her phenomena a cloak to conceal her designs against British rule in India.

PAGE

CHAPTER VII. DIVISIONS AMONG THEOSOPHISTS—NEW PUBLICATIONS 94

Effect on Theosophists of Coulomb-S.P.R. "exposure"—Olcott goes to Burmah—H.P.B. desperately ill—attempt to unseat Olcott, who returns to Adyar—H.P.B. supports him—but tells him in deserting her the Theosophists have deserted the Masters—H.P.B. resigns and leaves India for Europe—Damodar leaves Adyar and goes to the Masters—the Society in India languishes and falls into public contempt—H.P.B. finds friends and supporters in Europe—Olcott and Indians find they cannot continue without H.P.B.—Convention at close of 1885 invites her to resume her office of Corresponding Secretary—refuses resignation of Olcott who is ready to retire as President—temporary restoration of harmony among Theosophists—H.P.B. in Europe, first in Italy, then Germany, then Belgium—her sickness, poverty, courage, good temper and unremitting exertions—visited by many noted Theosophists—her physical condition desperate for two years—carried to London by Countess Wachtmeister and the Keightleys in summer of 1887—her presence a great stimulus to Theosophy in England—new publications, the *Sphynx*, the *Lotus* and *Lucifer*—the "Blavatsky Lodge" formed at London—Sinnett publishes "Incidents in the Life of H. P. Blavatsky" as an offset to S.P.R. *Report*—new books—"Light on the Path"—"Five Years of Theosophy"—"Man: Fragments of Forgotten History"—revival of Theosophical spirit and work—in Asia—in Europe—in America—Judge the heart of the Movement in America—rebuilds the Society—Judge begins *The Path* in 1886—secures the establishment of the American "Board of Control" by Olcott—new Branches and Lodges in the United States—Judge forms the "American Section of the T.S."—first really democratic organization in the Society—Judge becomes its General Secretary—the work now in three streams—Judge in America—H.P.B. in Europe—Olcott in India—all in outward concord.

CHAPTER VIII. ESOTERIC AND EXOTERIC ASPECTS OF THE THEOSOPHICAL MOVEMENT 110

The "Esoteric Section of the T.S."—the Theosophical *Movement* has an esoteric as well as an exoteric aspect—the Theosophical *Society* merely the public experimental aspect of the Movement and its Third Section—the First Section the Lodge of Masters—the Second Section composed of *accepted*, lay and probationary Chelas or Disciples—the Masters or First Section never publicly known—the Second Section kept secret, but probationers accepted privately—Judge and Olcott the earliest members of the Second Section known—first public notice of the Three Sections in India in 1880—hints and articles on Chelaship thereafter appear at intervals in *The Theosophist*—difference between Occultism and Spiritualism—Chelaship and mediumship opposed courses—reasons for secrecy in connection with "Chelaship of the Second Section"—the immense change in the work of H.P.B. and Judge after 1886—shown in contents of *Lucifer* and *The Path*—illustrative articles cited—"the ordeals of Chelaship"—practically exemplified in case of Mrs. Cables and Mr. W. T. Brown—Mrs. Cables a Spiritualist Christian with mystical tendencies—begins publication of *The Occult Word*—W. T. Brown a "probationary Chela"—becomes a "Rosicrucian"—joins Mrs. Cables—they seek for "communications from the

PAGE

Mahatmas"—receive no "signs"—publish a "manifesto"—H.P.B. replies—shows dangers and requirements of Chelaship—cites Brown's own case in illustration without naming him—Mrs. Cables and Brown leave the Society—failures frequent among candidates for Chelaship—out of hundreds "one only" achieves full success—seven years successful probation the minimum requirement before "communication with Masters" possible on both sides—failure of Theosophists to *lead the life.*

CHAPTER IX. H.P.B., OLCOTT AND JUDGE 127

H.P.B. the Messenger of the Masters—Judge next to her in importance esoterically—Olcott the public head and front of the *exoteric* work—Olcott's limitations and obstacles—his own letter quoted—Olcott, the probationary *Chela,* fails often and upsets his work as President—his attitude toward H.P.B. and Judge—his friendship and intimacy with those who afterward became enemies or traitors—Massey, Prof. Coues—Olcott's slights to H.P.B.—his partiality for Subba Row—friction between Subba Row and H.P.B. over the "Sevenfold Classification"—the contentions in *The Theosophist*—Judge intervenes in the controversy—internal frictions cause of all external troubles—failure of Theosophists to adhere to First Object and of probationary Chelas to keep their Pledges—could not endure correction at hands of H.P.B. or Judge—"Pledge Fever" real cause of stormy course of the Society—necessity for restoration of the Movement to true lines—Judge advises formation of "Esoteric Section"—draws up its Rules—Olcott torn by fears and doubts—the battle between the "Three Founders" prior to the formation of the "Esoteric Section"—not disclosed till long afterwards in "Old Diary Leaves"—neither H.P.B. nor Judge ever wrote anything personal—never "washed Theosophical dirty linen in public"—story of friction between the Founders unknown to Theosophists at the time—disclosed long afterward by Olcott—"Old Diary Leaves" not a history but an autobiography.

CHAPTER X. THE FORMATION OF THE ESOTERIC SECTION . 144

The "critical period" preceding the formation of the "Esoteric Section" of the T.S.—H.P.B. discusses Olcott's nature in a letter to Dr. Franz Hartmann in 1886—Olcott and others never understood either Masters or H.P.B.—Olcott sincere but "lacks in the psychological portion of his brain"—H.P.B.'s story of her difficulties—trying to aid others to perception of the facts—Olcott tells his story at length in "Old Diary Leaves"—thinks H.P.B. wise, foolish and fanatic—opposes establishment of *Lucifer* and of "Blavatsky Lodge"—offended at H.P.B.'s course in the Subba Row controversy—discusses H.P.B.'s nature—calls her "insulted and misunderstood Messenger"—then says she "frets and worries over mares' nests"—calls the Judge-Coues controversy a "personal quarrel"—gives his version of the storm preceding the "Esoteric Section"—calls H.P.B. a "mad person," "hyperexcited hysterical woman"—discloses that H.P.B. was prepared to leave the T.S. and form a new Society of her own if he does not reform—the Hindu "Council" frightened at H.P.B.'s stand—more trouble in the Paris Branch—Olcott makes it an excuse to go to Europe in 1888—to "fight it out" with H.P.B.—first overrules her then rescinds his action—confirms H.P.B.'s "interference" as within her

PAGE

''Constitutional rights''—Olcott receives a letter on shipboard in 1888 direct from the Master—wrongly relates it in ''Old Diary Leaves'' to the visit in 1884—the Master's letter a phenomenon indeed—it reproaches Olcott for his attitude and conduct towards H.P.B.—declares that it is she who is their *direct agent*—affirms that ''*with occult matters she has everything to do*''—warns Olcott to attend to his own business—tells him he will have to suffer for his injustice to H.P.B.—the letter effective for the time being—Judge goes to London and the Three Founders effect a reconciliation—H.P.B. issues public notice of the Esoteric Section, accompanied by an ''official authorization'' from Olcott—joint note of H.P.B. and Olcott to all Theosophists—Olcott afterwards takes credit to himself for the outcome—''pacifies H.P.B.''

CHAPTER XI. THE WORK OF THE ESOTERIC SECTION . . 163

''Old Diary Leaves'' tells the story of Olcott's return to India late in 1888 for the ''Adyar Parliament''—his Address to the Convention—never set himself up as a competent teacher—the Esoteric Section H.P.B.'s sole responsibility—glosses the European events to show himself the leading actor—the Convention of the American Section in April, 1889, following—a letter read from H.P.B.—Judge's respect and reverence for H.P.B. in contrast with Olcott's attitude—H.P.B.'s letter refers to the Esoteric Section—formed to *work for Theosophy under her direction*—gives a warning direct from Masters—Altruism Their object—Theosophists must strive for true fraternity—Preliminary Memorandum to candidates for the Esoteric Section—the Pledge required—secrecy, service and study—the Esoteric Section necessary because the T.S. had proved after thirteen years a ''dead failure'' and a ''sham''—the Esoteric Section not for ''practical occultism''—for brotherly union, mutual help, and the salvation of the T.S.—other extracts from the Preliminary Memorandum and Book of Rules.

CHAPTER XII. MABEL COLLINS AND PROFESSOR COUES . 178

The Esoteric Section promptly brings about Pledge Fever in the T.S.—the great storm of 1889-90—Mabel Collins and Prof. Coues the conscious and unconscious instruments—Mabel Collins joins London Lodge in 1884—a ''psychic'' with no knowledge of Occultism—medium for ''Light on the Path'' and ''The Gates of Gold''—becomes Associate Editor of *Lucifer* with H.P.B.—acquires great Theosophical reputation—suddenly dropped from *Lucifer* in February, 1889—Prof. Coues of Catholic descent and training—highly educated—noted scientific authority and writer—interested in ''psychical research''—joins T.S. at London in 1884—becomes member of American Board of Control—establishes the Gnostic Branch of the American Section T.S., at Washington, D. C.—aids in establishing an American Society for Psychical Research—tries to control T.S. in United States—Judge's cautions—Coues corresponds with H.P.B., Judge and Olcott, trying to set them at odds with each other—Olcott nearly succumbs—letter from Olcott to Coues—Coues made Chairman at American Section Convention of 1888 at Chicago—gives the Chicago *Tribune* a spurious ''Mahatma message''—admits it to Judge—denies it to H.P.B.—his letters to Judge and H.P.B.—his hypocrisy and thirst for notoriety

PAGE

and power—H.P.B. replies to him—speaks plainly—refuses to countenance his "messages" or his ambitions—he demands to be made head of the American Section as the price of his allegiance—his offer rejected—not present at the Convention of April, 1889.

CHAPTER XIII. THE COUES-COLLINS CHARGES AND THEIR AFTERMATH 195

Coues sends a letter to the *Religio-Philosophical Journal* of May 11, 1889—Bundy, Coleman, Michael Angelo Lane and Mabel Collins enlisted in Coues' campaign to ruin Judge and H.P.B.—Coues' letter jeers at the "Theosophical mahatmas" —quotes a letter from Mabel Collins—says he never met Miss Collins personally—wrote her first in 1885 asking real source of "Light on the Path"—she replied that it was "dictated to her by one of the adepts" of H.P.B.—no intervening communication—now "unexpectedly" he receives letter which he gives —Miss Collins declares her original statement false—knows nothing of existence of any Master—made her false statement because H.P.B. "begged and implored" her to—the Coues-Collins' charges critically examined—show Coues a conscienceless schemer and Mabel Collins a mediumistic dupe of Coues—their combined testimony proved false from their own evidence—collateral and chronological facts show baselessness and impossibility of allegations in regard to H.P.B.—aftermath of events—Mabel Collins sues H.P.B. for libel—her own attorneys dismiss the suit on being shown a letter of Mabel Collins in H.P.B.'s possession—the real mysteries involved in the origin of Collins' "inspired" books—Mabel Collins a "failure in occultism"—dismissed, with M. A. Lane, from the Esoteric Section—Coues never a member of the Section—admission refused him.

CHAPTER XIV. *The New York Sun* LIBEL CASE . . . 211

Professor Coues' case taken up by Judge—the Executive Committee of the American Section expels Coues from the T.S.—the Convention in April, 1890, approves the expulsion—the Gnostic Branch dischartered—Coues plans revenge—the New York *Sun* joins in the fray—calls H.P.B. an "impostor," lauds Coues for exposing her "humbug religion"—followed by full-page interview with Coues—he rehashes all the old slanders on H.P.B.—charges Judge with duplicating in America H.P.B.'s frauds in England—the "mahatmas" a hoax and their "messages" invented by H.P.B. and Judge—charges H.P.B. with immorality—Judge brings suit for libel against *Sun*—H.P.B. follows—her letter in *The Path*—no evasion of the issues—the *Sun* fights the case for two years—no evidence obtainable to support the charges made—the *Sun* publishes in 1892 a full retraction and repudiates Coues—retraction accompanied by publication in *Sun* of a long article by Judge in defense of H.P.B.—*Sun* says editorially "Mr. Judge's article disposes of all questions regarding Madame Blavatsky as presented by Dr. Coues"—the *Sun* libel case a complete vindication of H.P.B. —infamy of subsequent reiteration of exploded slanders by Count Witte and Margot Tennant—Coues disgraced by outcome of suits—retires to obscurity—importance of the Coues-Collins-*Sun* battle—should be familiar to all students.

PAGE

CHAPTER XV. OLCOTT VERSUS H.P.B. 226

Esoteric aspect of the Coues struggle—cycles in Theosophical Movement—the Three Founders the personification of the Three Sections of the Movement—a breach between the Sections in the first ten years—Olcott and others' failure to defend H.P.B. in 1885 the sign of the rupture—first doubts—then dissent and dissimulation—then temporising—then repudiation of the Occult status of H.P.B.—the long list of "failures in occultism" in the first thirteen years—Coues counted on Olcott's support—Olcott becomes frightened at possible consequences to Society and himself—refuses to align himself with his colleagues—but does not openly support Coues—blinded by jealousy and vanity —"Old Diary Leaves" discloses Olcott's inner attitude and struggles—his "pitched battle" with H.P.B. in 1888 over the Esoteric Section—due to his inner doubts and fears—thought H.P.B. and Judge were engaged in "the building up of a new structure of falsehood, fraud and treachery in which to house new idols"—takes Richard Harte back to India with him—Olcott's comments in "Old Diary Leaves" on the events from 1888 to 1890—obsessed with the importance of the *Society*—of himself as its President-Founder—changes in the Constitution and articles in *The Theosophist*—engineered by Olcott to make himself supreme—tries to relegate H.P.B. and Judge to "their proper place"—"Revised Rules" adopted by the "Adyar Parliament"—Judge and H.P.B. oppose—supported by the American and British Sections.

CHAPTER XVI. OLCOTT'S ATTEMPT TO CENTRALIZE ALL AUTHORITY 244

1888-1890—the long campaign waged by Olcott and his lieutenant Richard Harte—coincident with the Coues' assaults—the uproar in the Society—H.P.B. and Judge the target for attacks within and without the Society—*The Theosophist* wages war on the independence of the Sections—belittles the Esoteric Section—threatens the dissolution of the American and British Sections —lauds "Adyar" as "the centre of the Movement"—long series of derogatory articles—*The Theosophist* the sole source of information in India—attempts of H.P.B. and Judge publicly and privately to restore harmony—Bertram Keightley's foolish letter to Harte—Judge writes direct to Olcott—re-affirms the issues at stake—declares H.P.B. the heart of the Society as well as the Movement—Olcott refuses to publish Judge's letter —gives extracts and defends Harte—declares himself the head and front of the Society and the cause—H.P.B. takes action—her article in *Lucifer*, August, 1889—"A Puzzle from Adyar" —she reprints some of Harte's fulminations—"Pure nonsense to say that she is 'loyal to the Theosophical Society and to Adyar'"—"loyal to death to the Theosophical *Cause*"—"There is no longer a 'Parent Society'"—"It is abolished and replaced by an aggregate body of Theosophical Societies, *all autonomous*"—will leave the Society at the first sign of disloyalty to the *Cause*—and will lead those who remain true.

PAGE

CHAPTER XVII. H.P.B. TAKES CHARGE OF THE T.S. IN EUROPE 267

Esoterically, the great storm of 1888-90 due to the clash between human and divine nature—the Objects of the Movement practical, not theoretical—the gulf between the views of Olcott and his party and those personified by H.P.B. and Judge—Olcott once more sobered by "A Puzzle from Adyar"—realizes he has gone too far—fears for his beloved Society—determines to go once more to England—realizes that to rise in rebellion means to ally himself with Coues—arrives in England late in 1889—met as always by H.P.B. with affection and charity—heart warmed by the treatment accorded him—his fears allayed for the moment—makes a tour of the British Isles—issues an "Order" delegating his Presidential powers for Europe to H.P.B. and an "Advisory Council"—"Bombay Conference" adopts stirring resolutions in support of H.P.B. during Olcott's absence—fresh Paris troubles after Olcott's return to India—he once more interferes and issues Presidential ukases—the British and Continental Theosophists rise up in arms—Mrs. Annie Besant joins the Society—becomes associate editor of *Lucifer* and President of the "Blavatsky Lodge"—she heads the insurrection against Olcott's papal actions—unanimous demand that H.P.B. take direction of affairs in Europe—H.P.B. bows to the will of the European Theosophists—issues a Notice in *Lucifer* assuming full authority and responsibility for Society in Europe—names it "The Theosophical Society in Europe" and declares for democracy, August, 1890—cables Olcott of her action—Olcott saves his face by accepting the facts and repudiating the factors.

CHAPTER XVIII. DEATH OF H.P.B.—HER LAST MESSAGES 275

H.P.B. dies May 8, 1891—Her life an open book to friend and foe—remains today as much a mystery as then—Theosophists never studied her life in the light of her teachings—regarded personally even by her most devoted followers—judged at second hand on hearsay and opinion by the world and by Theosophists—weighed by trifles—her teachings and her works the true evidence of her Mission and her nature—no fact adduced by her ever overthrown by counter-evidence—her theories as unimpeachable as ever—her life and her message absolutely consistent—her followers and detractors weighed in same scale make a sorry showing—her Messages to the American Theosophists prove her sage and prophet—her "dying declaration"—"My Books"—"Isis Unveiled" a *Message from the Masters*—every word of her teachings from the Masters of the Wisdom—no charge against her ever substantiated—her inexhaustible philanthropy—the price she paid to serve mankind.

CHAPTER XIX. THE CRISIS IN THE SOCIETY 393

The great crisis following the death of H.P.B.—in the exoteric Society—in the Esoteric Section or School—how the crisis was met—Judge goes to London—summons a meeting of the "Council of the Esoteric Section"—the Council meets May 27, 1891—considers documents left by H.P.B.—affirms Judge H.P.B.'s representative—H.P.B.'s last words "Keep the Link unbroken" Council goes on record Esoteric School should be continued

PAGE

on lines laid by H.P.B.—Judge and Annie Besant to conduct the School—Council issues confidential circular to all members of the E.S.T., signed by all—Council resigns—address of Mrs. Besant and Judge as Outer Heads to the School—claim no authority over the members save such as delegated by H.P.B.

CHAPTER XX. . ATTEMPTS TO SUPERSEDE H.P.B.'S INFLUENCE 302

Position of the Exoteric Society following H.P.B.'s death—Olcott comes to London to attend Convention of British-European Section—great gathering of leading Theosophists—London Lodge not represented at Convention but sends letter——London Lodge declares its independence—action tacitly accepted by Convention—speeches of Col. Olcott—Mrs. Besant—Mr. Judge—entire harmony and concord—*Lucifer* memorial articles—the workers scatter—Mrs. Besant takes charge of *Lucifer*—her great work publicly—Judge returns to America—Olcott to India—his "triumphal procession"—Mrs. Besant's proclamation of the nature and status of H.P.B. in *Lucifer*, 1890-91—her famous speech in St. James' Hall, August 30, 1891—"A Fragment of Autobiography"—declares she has received messages from the Mahatmas since the death of H.P.B.—the furore aroused—Olcott "views with alarm" the declarations made—his Address to the "Adyar Parliament" December, 1891—H.P.B. "not as perfect a channel as some others"—protests "against all attempts to create an H.P.B. school, sect or cult"—Judge sounds the true note for all Theosophists—"first, *Solidarity*, and second, *Theosophical education*"—"Jasper Niemand" publishes a message from the Masters in *The Path*, August, 1891—Olcott stirred up—writes Judge—Judge publishes article on "Dogmatism in Theosophy"—Society founded to destroy dogmatism—quotes H.P.B.—real object Universal Brotherhood—not dogmatism to study, teach and apply Theosophy—members have equal rights to affirm or reject any doctrines—but no right to impose their private views on others—or promulgate them as official tenets of the T.S.

CHAPTER XXI. GROWING DIVERGENCES—OLCOTT RESIGNS AS PRESIDENT 321

The old issues once more aroused—The Theosophical Movement one thing—the Theosophical Society quite another—the criteria applicable to Theosophical history—Altruism the self-professed Object of the Fellows of the T.S.—Altruism and Theosophy the self-pledged objectives of the members of the E.S.T.—Fellows of the T.S. must be weighed in the scales of their own conduct, not that of others—members of the Esoteric Section by their allegiance to their voluntary Pledges, not by worldly standards—the war of ideas within a year after H.P.B.'s death—official report of the Adyar Convention of 1891—Olcott's Presidential Address—great importance of Olcott's declarations—Judge meets the issue—publishes article on "The Future and the Theosophical Society"—quotes a letter of H.P.B.'s—her vision of the coming strife—"a few earnest Theosophists"—"in a death struggle with nominal and ambitious Theosophists"—the dangers now the same as always—the Society not a "School for Occultism"—must flourish on its

PAGE

moral worth not on phenomena—members must be "true to themselves"—Judge corrects Olcott's Presidential remarks on H.P.B.—Judge declares H.P.B. knew she was going—decries attempts to create bogies—a thunderbolt in the Society—Olcott resigns the Presidency—Judge publishes official correspondence and takes charge as Vice-President, March, 1892—secret of Olcott's sudden resignation a mystery to this day—the hidden facts disclosed—Olcott indiscreet at London in summer of 1891—charges of "grave immorality" made by Miss Müller—Mrs. Besant excited by the charges—comes to New York to see Judge—demands Judge force Olcott's resignation—Judge writes Olcott—suggests he resign *if charges are true*—Olcott denies charges but tenders resignation—Olcott's fatal blunder—proud and sensitive—cannot endure contumely and calumny—Judge writes him loyally.

CHAPTER XXII. CONVENTION OF 1892—OLCOTT WITHDRAWS HIS RESIGNATION 334

Convention of American Section held in April, 1892, immediately following Olcott's resignation—great growth of the Section—letters from Olcott read—Judge reviews the year since H.P.B.'s death—pays tribute to Annie Besant—convention resolutions in regard to Olcott—Olcott requested to withdraw his resignation—request cabled to Olcott—Olcott replies must wait to hear from all the Sections—Convention re-elects Judge General Secretary——votes for Judge for President in case Olcott adheres to his resignation—American Convention's recommendation to British Convention for July, 1892—advises same action in regard to Olcott's resignation as its own—Mrs. Besant gets out private circular urging Judge for President—Olcott writes to British Convention—intimates willingness to withdraw resignation—Convention nevertheless votes for Judge and to accept resignation—Olcott in a quandary—encouraged by Judge—Judge sends him message from Masters—Olcott decides to withdraw resignation and remain President—Judge publishes Olcott's notice and informs American Branches.

CHAPTER XXIII. H.P.B.'S "SUCCESSORS"—THE PUBLICATION OF "OLD DIARY LEAVES" 351

Adyar Parliament at end of 1892—Olcott's Presidential address—explains his resignation as due to ill-health—ready now to continue to the end as a "sacrifice demanded by the best interests of the Society"—names Judge as his successor—adverts once more to "Adyar" as the centre of the Movement—admits Adyar Convention merely an informal gathering—"only 5 Branches out of 145 really doing satisfactory work" in the Indian Section—Indian Branches mainly exist on paper—First Object makes no appeal to Indian membership—trouble in the E.S.T.—due to Mrs. Besant's private circular preceding Convention of British Section—Judge issues notice in the E.S.T.—the School has no connection officially with the T.S.—members free to act according to their own judgment—Mrs. Besant's private circular stirs up Olcott's friends—her action ascribed to Judge's influence—Mrs. Besant issues circular to the Esoteric School explaining her action—Judge's efforts to shield Mrs. Besant—and restore harmony in the Society and the E.S.T.—why the circular was jointly signed—members too prone to fol-

PAGE

low authorities—would not "cultivate self-reliance and develop the intuition"—the bane of "successorship"—H.P.B. declared in "Isis" that "apostolic succession is a gross and palpable fraud"—the "successorship" idea among Theosophists after H.P.B.'s death—Duchesse de Pomar hailed as H.P.B.'s "successor"—then Annie Besant in England and Judge in America —Judge tells the reporters "H.P.B. was *sui generis*"—"she can have no successor"—claims of mediums and "Occultists" to be H.P.B.'s "successor"—the case of Henry B. Foulke—Judge's two letters on the subject to the Wilkes-Barre *Times*—Mrs. Besant reprints Judge's letters in *Lucifer*—Olcott declares himself on "successorship" claims—"*Blavatsky nascitur, non fit*" —Olcott begins the publication of "Old Diary Leaves" in *The Theosophist* for March, 1892—their effect on the Society and the Movement—"Old Diary Leaves" ostensible purpose to give a "true history of the Theosophical Society"—the actual motive to pull down H.P.B. to the common level—the real animus not disclosed till 1895—contradictory views of H.P.B. held by Olcott and others—the "real H.P.B." unknown to Olcott—some hints for the intuitional-minded on "our *Brother*, H.P.B."

CHAPTER XXIV. CONTROVERSY OVER H.P.B.'S STATUS AS AGENT OF THE MASTERS 380

Constant belittlement of H.P.B. publicly and privately—emanates from Olcott and Sinnett—could not endure her preeminence—Judge's difficult situation—bound to defend H.P.B. —realizes must antagonize prominent leaders—steps taken in the E.S.T.—"We have not been deserted"—"Authorship of the 'Secret Doctrine'"—other articles in *The Path*—the old controversy between Mr. Sinnett and H.P.B.—"The earth chain of globes"—London Lodge lectures—W. Scott Elliott claims "inspiration"—Alexander Fullerton's *faux pas*—Judge disclaims responsibility for Fullerton—corrects misconceptions in *The Path*—Judge quotes Masters' certificates on the "Secret Doctrine"—letter from Masters to Francesca Arundale—shows conditions in London Lodge as far back as 1884—Miss Arundale's letter unknown to members at time—the controversy becomes violent—Judge writes on "Masters, Adepts, Teachers and Disciples"—Sinnett comes out in the open—declares H.P.B. "under other influences" than Masters—affirms he is still in communication with Mahatmas—Judge and Mrs. Besant try to quiet the storm while upholding H.P.B.—Olcott speaks in praise of Sinnett—the situation by the early fall of 1893—a sharp and sheer cleavage over teachings—and over status of H.P.B. as agent of the Masters.

CHAPTER XXV. ANNIE BESANT IN AMERICA, 1892-3 . . 405

Mrs. Besant invited to visit India again in fall of 1892—goes to America instead—her American tour a great success—returns to England loud in praise of Mr. Judge—Olcott writes the American Convention in April, 1893—raises the "hero worship" bogy once more—Judge speaks as General Secretary American Section—disclaims all hero worship and dogmatism—but insists those who reverence H.P.B. have perfect right to express their views—warns against official promulgations on matters of individual opinion—Mrs. Besant upholds members' rights to freedom of individual belief and expression—W. Scott Elliott's claims to

PAGE

"inspiration" discussed—"authority" in the T.S.—no doctrines "authoritative"—all must stand on their own merit—Mrs. Besant quotes H.P.B. on freedom of opinion in the T.S.—E. T. Sturdy takes a hand—Sturdy a member of the E.S.T.—objects to claims of "messages from Masters"—Mrs. Besant writes on "Gurus and Chelas"—opposes Sturdy's views—the whole subject of "Mahatma messages" once more to the fore—claims of "Jasper Niemand" in *The Path* article—claims of Mrs. Besant to recent "messages" from Masters—Mrs. Besant now the foremost figure in the Society—Olcott and Sinnett worried over Mrs. Besant's championship of Judge and H.P.B.

CHAPTER XXVI. BEGINNINGS OF THE "JUDGE CASE" . 425

Mrs. Besant publishes in *Lucifer* for April, 1893, Judge's letter to Olcott in 1891 about the "Jasper Niemand" message—Sturdy's article really a reply to Judge's letter to Olcott—Olcott joins in the fray—"N.D.K." writes in *The Theosophist*—challenges Judge's statements in the letter to Olcott—Olcott reprints Sturdy's article including paragraphs omitted by Mrs. Besant—Walter R. Old and S. V. Edge—Old a member of the "E.S.T. Council"—Edge assistant on *The Theosophist*—they write in *The Theosophist* on "Theosophic Freethought"—the article a veiled attack on Judge—they tell of the "Mahatma Message" at the "E.S.T. Council" meeting of May 27, 1891—they question the *bona fides* of Judge and the genuineness of the "message"—Old and Edge undoubtedly inspired by Olcott—the question of "Master's seal"—the whole subject of "messages from Masters" discussed—H.P.B.'s statement—"Occult phenomena can never be *proved*"—The publication of "Theosophic Freethought" a violation of the E.S.T. pledges of Old and Edge—taken up by Mrs. Besant in the Esoteric Section—Old and Edge suspended from membership in the E.S.T. in August, 1893—the circular issued to members of the E.S.T. by Mrs. Besant and Judge—Olcott follows up the attack on Judge and H.P.B.—the White Lotus Day meeting at Adyar, May 8, 1893—the quandary of Olcott and his allies—can Judge be unseated in confidence of members?—H.P.B. cannot be "buried" while Judge lives—Judge invincible with Mrs. Besant's support—the problem to win over Mrs. Besant against Judge and H.P.B.—beginnings of the conspiracy against Judge.

CHAPTER XXVII. MRS. BESANT CHANGES SIDES . . . 441

Judge and Olcott personify the opposing issues—the First and Second Sections *versus* the Third Section—esoteric aspects of the Movement *versus* the exoteric—"The Judge case" the external phase of the battle—the momentous year of 1893—Bertram Keightley the unconscious agent in the subornation of Mrs. Besant—Keightley originally a staunch supporter of H.P.B.—gets in trouble with Mabel Collins—sent by H.P.B. to America in 1890—poses as her "representative"—H.P.B. issues famous Notice of August 9, 1890—disavows Bertram Keightley's "teachings"—says Judge her "sole representative"—recalls Keightley to Europe—sends him to India—he becomes General Secretary Indian Section—becomes an adherent of Olcott's—falls under influence of G. N. Chakravarti—Chakravarti a

PAGE

"psychic"—poses as a "Chela"—Keightley comes to America in spring of 1893—attends American Section Convention—invited by Judge to select Brahmin and Buddhist Delegates to World's Parliament of Religions at Chicago Fair—Chakravarti chosen—Judge's efforts to allay Brahminical hostility to the T.S.—he warns of "A plot against the Theosophical Society"—Keightley a close friend of Mrs. Besant—he goes to England from America—works on Mrs. Besant—she begins to grow suspicious of Judge—Chakravarti comes to London—Mrs. Besant becomes one of his worshippers—adopts "ascetic" practices—her intimacy with Chakravarti—Mrs. Besant, Miss Müller, and Chakravarti come to America to attend the "Parliament of Religions"—the great success of the Parliament—Mrs. Besant and Chakravarti share honors as the great feature of the "Parliament"—Mrs. Besant succumbs to the lures held out—goes to India in the fall of 1893—her visit there a regal triumph—how Olcott set the stage—his contemptuous review of Judge's *Ocean of Theosophy*—prepares the "Adyar Convention," Christmas, 1893—his Presidential Address—laudations of Mrs. Besant—sees in Mrs. Besant a messiah from the Masters—the epiphany of Mrs. Besant—intimates a coming storm—understood to refer to Judge—the secret meeting behind the public address—the Christmas night conclave at Adyar in 1893—Mrs. Besant, Col. Olcott, Walter R. Old, and others plan the assault on Judge—the meeting unknown to the members—Mrs. Besant chosen to hurl the thunderbolt prepared—she writes a formal letter to Olcott Feb. 6, 1894—makes charges against Judge—demands investigation—next day Olcott writes officially to Judge—demands he resign or stand trial for "misusing Mahatmas' names and handwritings."

CHAPTER XXVIII. THE AMERICAN SECTION SUPPORTS JUDGE 468

The real issue Theosophy or the Society—Chelas or mediums—Brotherhood or sectarianism—how Judge acted on receipt of Olcott's "ultimatum"—addresses a circular March 15, 1894, to all members of the T.S.—lays bare the facts—refuses to resign—announces his readiness to meet any charges—denies any wrong-doing—admits receiving and delivering messages from Masters—declares them genuine—never courted publicity—says no one but a genuine chela can determine what is or is not a "message"—the charges a distinct violation of Constitution of Society—make a dogma out of Masters and Messages—an assault on liberty of conscience—will meet his accusers—Judge's circular widely distributed—its frankness and fairness in meeting all issues—Bertram Keightley and George Mead receive copies of charges and Judge's reply—their sense of honor and fair play outraged—they address an open letter to Col. Olcott as General Secretaries of Indian and British Sections—charge Olcott with violation of Constitution and the principles of Brotherhood—declare the matter at issue one of personal opinion and barred from constitutional attack—Olcott follows up his first letter to Judge with another—invites Judge to "prove himself innocent" and suspends him from Vice-Presidency—sets the "trial" to be held at London in July, 1894—Mrs. Besant leaves India to return to England and carry the fight against Judge before the British Section Convention

PAGE

—the American Section Convention meets in April, 1894—unanimously votes confidence in Judge—re-elects him General Secretary—charges Olcott with violation of the Constitution—demands that if Judge's "messages" are investigated those of Sinnett, Mrs. Besant, Col. Olcott and others be also investigated at the same time—declares for freedom of opinion and belief in the Society—votes to reimburse Judge for the expenses he has been put to because of the charges against him.

CHAPTER XXIX. THE "JUDICIAL ENQUIRY" IN LONDON . 493

Olcott's position in spring of 1894—determined to "fight it out to the hilt" this time—feels master of the situation due to alliance with Mrs. Besant—his other aids—Walter Old's help—Old determines to return to England with Mrs. Besant—Old an astrologer and "psychic" with many English friends—Olcott's panegyrics on Mrs. Besant—his signed article in *The Theosophist* on Mrs. Besant—his attitude toward Judge contrasted with his deification of Mrs. Besant—makes Mrs. Besant his vice-regal agent—grants her *carte blanche* in Australasia—the significance of this—Olcott and Mrs. Besant natural autocrats—no idea of democracy—the bombshell of Keightley and Mead's rebellion—the situation reversed—Olcott now fearful of defeat—consults his advisers—sends out a new Official Notice—tries to explain situation—announces his decision to go to England—his "explanation" examined—the battlefield transferred to England—The "Judicial Committee" meets at London in July, 1894—Mrs. Besant, Olcott and others confer—the case thrashed out in Committee—Judge attends the session of the Committee—remains silent—Committee in hard case—points raised by Judge inescapable—Judge announces his readiness to be "tried"—the Committee controlled by Besant and Olcott—they fear Judge can "prove his innocence" if tried—they reverse themselves—Olcott makes a speech—declares case cannot constitutionally be tried—the Committee decides it has "no jurisdiction"—the action taken a complete exposure of the animus of the persecution—the "Enquiry" a farce.

CHAPTER XXX. BRITISH CONVENTION DISMISSES CASE AGAINST JUDGE 519

Effect of the decision of the "Judicial Committee"—Theosophists at London for the British Convention sense the wrong done Judge—Mrs. Besant and Olcott try to "save their face"—they demand a "Jury of honour"—Judge's reply—where are the competent "occultists"?—who can tell whether a "Message" is or is not genuine?—Mrs. Besant proposes the matter be placed before the British Convention as a "Jury"—Judge promptly consents—Mrs. Besant and Judge read Statements to the Convention—Mrs. Besant admits the charges due to "personal hatred" of Judge by "certain persons"—Old and Edge indicated as the "guilty persons"—Mrs. Besant denies responsibility—says she sponsored charges for "Judge's sake"—admits Judge is in communication with Masters—says the "messages" in the "Master's script"—but says she believes Masters did not "directly" precipitate them—acquits Judge of dishonorable intentions—apologizes for her share in the case—asks

PAGE

Judge's forgiveness "for wrongs done him"—Olcott adds a footnote to Mrs. Besant's Statement—says he asked her to make the charges—betrays himself—Judge makes his Statement—says he did not couple Mrs. Besant's name with the charges to save her—denies "forging the handwriting of Mahatmas"—admits having delivered Messages—affirms their genuineness—refuses to say *how* they were done—denies right of anyone to make unverifiable charges—says anyone can receive Messages who "lives the life"—never tried to influence others—says handwriting, seals and "precipitation" not a "proof" that Messages are from Masters—forgives his enemies—Mrs. Besant's and Mr. Judge's Statements analyzed and compared—the British Convention unanimously accepts the Statements made and declares the "Judge case" a "closed incident"—the "Occultism and Truth" circular distributed after adjournment of the Convention—Mrs. Besant's *Lucifer* article on the "Judicial Enquiry"—her evasions and misrepresentations—the signers of the "Occultism and Truth" circular—show who were behind the persecution of Judge—what "possessed" his defamers—were Mrs. Besant, Olcott and the rest deliberate malicious assassins of reputation of Judge?—they were "occult failures"—could not discriminate between truth and falsehood—moved by the same self-righteous relentlessness as religious bigots in all times—Olcott's Parthian shot after the Convention—his article on "T.S. Solidarity and Ideals."

CHAPTER XXXI. THE "EASTERN DIVISION" AND "WESTERN DIVISION" 559

The calm after the storm of the "Judicial Committee" in July, 1894—the lesson of the "Enquiry"—"occult phenomena cannot be proved"—no part of the business of the Theosophical Society—phenomena no evidence of morality or ethics—can be performed by mediums and "black magicians" as well as Chelas and Adepts—H.P.B.'s mission philosophical and ethical—not to supply a demonstration of the Occult Sciences—her phenomena incidental and unavoidable to her Mission—phenomena never made public by either H.P.B. or Judge in first instance—the "Judge case" a testing out of the "Esoteric Section"—further extracts from the *Preliminary Memorandum*—rules and purpose of the E.S.T.—conduct of Olcott, Besant, *et al.*, gross violation of their own Pledges in Occultism—clear evidence of their total failure as "probationary Chelas"—the warnings given to Mrs. Besant in the School—aftermath of the "Judicial Enquiry"—how the matter was settled for the time in the E.S.T.—the joint circular of Mrs. Besant and Mr. Judge to the Members, August, 1894—its history and re-organization recited—the agreement reached—Mrs. Besant to conduct the "Eastern Division" and Mr. Judge the "Western Division"—"time must be allowed" for the restoration of tranquillity—Mr. Judge the real Agent of H.P.B. in the School—Mrs. Besant "Recorder of the teachings"—her failure as "Recorder"—her corruption of the "Secret Doctrine"—her spurious Third Volume—her boldness in publishing misrepresentations of fact and philosophy—she puts an utter falsehood in the mouth of H.P.B.—declares H.P.B. "professed faith in the gods"—Mrs. Besant's loss of ethical balance whenever her statements questioned or her actions impugned.

PAGE

CHAPTER XXXII. *Westminster Gazette* ATTACKS THE SOCIETY 574

The situation in the early fall of 1894—Judge returns to America—Olcott and Keightley return to India—Mrs. Besant goes to Australia—Walter Old remains in England—renews the fight on Judge—evidences of collusion—Old provides Edmund Garrett with ammunition—Garrett opens a grand assault in the *Westminster Gazette*—ridicules Theosophy—pokes fun at Olcott and Mrs. Besant—calls them dupes of H.P.B. and Judge—Garrett an honest man—avows his animus—declares himself enemy of Theosophy—his purpose to destroy T.S.—his series of articles published in book form—their tremendous circulation and effect—Old writes the *Gazette*—admits his complicity—regrets to drag in Mrs. Besant and Olcott—exposes his enmity to Judge—confesses unwittingly the secret conference at Adyar, Christmas, 1893—the "Judge case" planned then by Old, Besant, Olcott and others—decries H.P.B. as well as Judge—the enemies of Judge moved by "pride and wounded vanity"—the steps taken by Judge after the *Westminster Gazette* attack—his letter to the New York *Sun* and the *Gazette*—his famous E.S.T. Circular of November 3, 1894—"By Master's Order" he tells the E.S.T. members the whole story—"black magic" *versus* "white magic"—Mrs. Besant the unconscious tool and victim of Chakravarti—the real issue between the Brahminism of the Orient and the Theosophy of H.P.B.—the Society will stand or fall by H.P.B.—deposes Mrs. Besant from her Co-Headship in the E.S.T.—Judge informs Mrs. Besant in Australia by cable of his action—Mrs. Besant's circular from Colombo, December 18, 1894, in reply to Judge's—defies Judge—misrepresents the facts of the Meeting of May 27, 1891—declares herself "H.P.B.'s Successor"—Mrs. Besant's circular analyzed—its falsity shown.

CHAPTER XXXIII. MRS. BESANT TRIES TO DRIVE JUDGE OUT OF THE SOCIETY 596

The war on Judge breaks out more fiercely than ever—Mrs. Besant proceeds to India—publishes long article in Madras *Mail*—sends violent attack on Judge to the London *Daily Chronicle*—attends the Adyar Convention at end of December, 1894—Olcott's Presidential Address—calls Judge a medium—Mrs. Besant introduces *Resolutions* against Judge—demands that Judge resign—her bitter speech—the whole proceedings plainly planned in advance—the long list of denunciatory speeches—Miss Müller's infamous remarks—not a voice raised in defense of Judge—not a demand made for fair dealing—Mrs. Besant's *Resolutions* unanimously adopted—next day's Indian Convention—more denunciation of Judge—Resolutions adopted demanding an "explanation" from Judge or his expulsion from the Society—coincident steps in England—George Mead first deprecates Old's and the *Westminster Gazette* articles—then hears from Mrs. Besant—then begins the "Clash of Opinion" in *Lucifer*—publishes letters from Old and others assailing Judge—prints Mrs. Besant's Indian attacks on Judge—Bertram Keightley follows suit—Alexander Fullerton like Mead is between two fires—first for Judge and then against—Mrs. Besant's former

PAGE

triumphal tour of India repeated—she returns to England in April, 1894—issues her pamphlet "The Case Against W. Q. Judge"—demands his expulsion from the T.S.

CHAPTER XXXIV. THE AMERICAN SECTION DECLARES ITS AUTONOMY AND ELECTS JUDGE ITS LIFE-PRESIDENT . 622

Proceedings in America—Judge writes the *Westminster Gazette* and New York *Sun*—deals with situation fully and frankly—publishes "The Prayag Letter" in *The Path* for March, 1895—declares it a genuine "message from the Masters"—the history of the "Prayag Message"—originally sent in 1881—from Masters to Brahmins—sent through H.P.B.—Judge throws down the gauntlet to his adversaries—says whole "case" against him due to his defense of H.P.B.—makes public that Olcott, Mrs. Besant, Sinnett and others have been making privately same charges against H.P.B.—invites Col. Olcott and Mrs. Besant to make public statement regarding "The Prayag Letter"—The "Message" in full—Mrs. Besant replies in *Lucifer*—"I do not regard the message as genuine"—Olcott comes out in the open—his "Postscript" in the *Supplement* to *The Theosophist* for April, 1895—"the message a false one"—"the simple theory of mediumship" accounts for H.P.B.—Sinnett says "I never in my life called Mme. Blavatsky a fraud"—the proof positive out of Sinnett's own mouth that he did just that—the original of the "Prayag message" in the handwriting of H.P.B.—the original was in Sinnett's hands all the time—published since his death in *The Mahatma Letters to A. P. Sinnett*—both Judge and H.P.B. vindicated completely by the text of the *Mahatma Letters*—the American Convention of April, 1895—The Convention adopts Resolutions to withdraw officially from the T.S. and become *The Theosophical Society in America*—adopts a Constitution—elects Judge President for life—draws up a Letter to the forthcoming British Convention—text of the Letter—the British Convention meets July 4, 1895—tables the Letter from the American Theosophists—split in the British Convention—Olcott issues another Executive Notice—admits legality of the action of the American Convention—cancels all diplomas and charter of Americans—refuses all official intercourse—expresses good-will—Judge's "Reply" to Mrs. Besant's "Case against W. Q. Judge"—the "Case" analyzed—never any *evidence* against Judge—the whole "Case" rests on suspicions and "psychic revelations."

CHAPTER XXXV. JUDGE'S DEATH AND THE TINGLEY "SUCCESSORSHIP" 653

After the split in 1895—Mrs. Besant alters the "Pledge"—puts her own and Leadbeater's writings on a par with H.P.B.'s—Judge holds true to the line—but sickens and dies March 21, 1896—The Tingley "Successorship" myth—E. T. Hargrove and others hold a "General E.S.T. Meeting," March 29, 1896—they announce to the members that "Judge left an occult heir"—the circular of April 3, 1896—the statements of the "Council" and the "Minutes" of the meeting of March 29—the identity of the "Successor" to be kept secret for one year—the whole claim rests on "messages" from the *dead* W. Q. Judge—not a scrap in the physical handwriting of the *living* W. Q. Judge produced then or since—the real explanation—the

PAGE

secret meeting at Mrs. Tingley's home on March 26, 1896—the American Theosophists accept the Tingley "Successorship"—the Convention of 1896—Mrs. Tingley disclosed as the "Successor"—the "Crusade"—frictions begin—Hargrove resigns—another secret meeting at Mrs. Tingley's home—the "Universal Brotherhood" planned—the Convention of February, 1898—Hargrove and his friends "bolt" the Convention—the war of recriminations—the members follow Mrs. Tingley—Hargrove's "E.S.T." circular—the degradation of both wings of the old Society—offshoots from Tingleyism—Hargrove's "T.S. in A."—the "Temple of the People"—the "T.S. of New York"—Dr. Buck and "The T.K."—Mrs. Alice L. Cleather and her "pupils"—the "Blavatsky Association"—the Besant-Olcott fragment—Leadbeater the "power behind the throne" of Mrs. Besant—Leadbeater admits infamous teachings to boys—resigns from the T.S.—Olcott dies—Mrs. Besant claims "Successorship" to President-Founder—More charges and counter-charges—Leadbeater invited back to the T.S.—the "Coming Christ"—the "Liberal Catholic Church"—complete reversion of the T.S.—its offshoots—Dr. Rudolph Steiner and the "Anthroposophical Society"—Max Heindel and his "Rosicrucian Cosmo-Conception"—other "Occult" societies.

CHAPTER XXXVI. PRESENT AND FUTURE OF THE THEOSOPHICAL MOVEMENT 689

Has the Theosophical Movement been a failure?—Cyclic Law—Centenary efforts since fourteenth century—H.P.B.'s mission the fifth—Mediumship and psychism inevitable concomitants of the public Movement—the Movement has not failed—spread of Theosophical ideas—they permeate religion, philosophy and science to-day—the signs and evidences—the real aim of H.P.B. achieved—the Masters never fail—what of the future of the Theosophical Movement?—1925 its nadir point—the first and Seconds Sections still active as always—signs of their work—*Nirmanakayas*—true Disciples known by their fruits—Edmond Holmes—"The Creed of Buddha"—the *Angarika* Dharmapala—B. P. Wadia—Julia H. Scott—Robert Crosbie—the United Lodge of Theosophists—the magazine *Theosophy*—the "changing *Buddhi-Manas* of the race"—due to incarnation of the pioneers of the "Sixth Sub-Race"—the destiny of the Movement until 1975.

THE THEOSOPHICAL MOVEMENT

THE THEOSOPHICAL MOVEMENT

CHAPTER I

CHANNELS OF THE THEOSOPHICAL MOVEMENT

IN its larger aspect the Theosophical Movement is the path of progress, individually and collectively. Wherever thought has struggled to be free, wherever spiritual ideas, as opposed to forms and dogmatism, have been promulgated, there the great Movement is to be discerned. Organized religions, systems of thought, governments, parties, sects—all have their origins in efforts for the better co-operation of men, for conserving energy and putting it to use. They all in time become corrupted and must change, as the times change, as human defects come out, and as the great underlying Spiritual and Intellectual evolution compels such alterations.

Luther's Reformation must be counted as a part of the Theosophical Movement. Masonry has played a great and important part in it, and still does to some extent, for however restricted in application, however its great symbolism may have been forgotten or obscured, Masonry none the less stands for tolerance, for religious and intellectual liberty, for charity. The formation of the American Republic with its noble Declaration of Independence, its equality of all men before the law, its ideals of brotherhood and freedom from sectarian religious partialities must be accounted a great forward step in the Theosophical Movement. And with the abolition of human slavery in all the great Western nations during the course of the nineteenth century, another great step in the emancipation of the race must be acclaimed. The "divine right" of an orthodox God speaking through a vested clergy was rebelled against in every voice raised against the Catholic hierarchy. The "divine right" of kings was overthrown by the American and French Revolutions. The "divine right" of one man or set of men to enslave another or others was the real issue involved in the American Civil War, and the emancipation of the serfs in Russia. Nationalism, socialism, universal suffrage, struggles between classes, between labor and capital, are all physical and metaphysical efforts toward freedom from bondage, however they may be mistaken, misguided, misled, perverted to selfish and destructive purposes and ends.

The principle of an underlying Spiritual and Intellectual evolution proceeding apace with its visible manifestation in physical effects, will disclose unerringly that the formation of the Society and the injection of the literature of Theosophy into the mind of the race must have been preceded and accompanied by collateral efforts and resultants. Those indirect preparations must necessarily be as varied as the varieties of human experience and belief regarding fundamental things. And those preparations do not issue in the first instance from any human invention or discovery, although the characters of certain individual human beings can be and must be the channels, conscious or unconscious, for the play of higher forces and the inspiration of higher Intelligence. The course of all evolution is first Spiritual, then Mental, then Personal to certain gifted individuals. From these latter it permeates gradually the race mind, impelling the whole mass forward and upward, in however slow or slight degree. "Evolution" appears as physical only to those who do not look beneath the surface of events. The real process of Nature is ever cyclic: from the highest to the lowest on the invisible side of Nature; correspondingly from the lowest to the highest on the visible side, as human vision is at present exercised in the fields of religion, philosophy and science.

Indirect but none the less potent and necessary concomitants of the spiritual and psychical aspects of the Theosophical Movement should therefore be looked for in all directions. One of these was and is the great tide of interest in Oriental religions and philosophies. Until the work of Madame Helena Petrovna Blavatsky was well under way none but the conqueror, the merchant, the missionary and the philologist, each immersed in his own especial objects, had any concern with the Far East. The mass of the populations of the Western world were farther removed from the living East with its immense but alien wealth of metaphysical acquisitions, than from the dead and by-gone stores of ancient Greece and imperial Rome. Generally speaking, it was unknown and unsuspected that the great leaders of early European civilization, no less than their modern successors, had in fact derived their inspiration and their learning from the exhaustless treasury of Oriental thought and practice.

Beginning with Wilkins near the close of the eighteenth century, a series of translations of the ancient and venerated "Bhagavad-Gita" had successively been brought out in England, in Germany, in France and in the United States. The riches of the Vedanta philosophy had thus to some extent become accessible to aspiring minds in the West. Copies came into the possession of Thoreau and Emerson. Emerson's fame as a lecturer and writer and the nobility of his character made of him one of the most potent vehicles for the dissemination of the great and timeless ideas of the East. Through his life and work countless younger minds were given a freer range and truer basis, and by so much freed from the sterile and narrow dogmas of sectarian Christianity. Religion was seen by many not to be confined nor due to sects or special revelations. The celebrated "Brook Farm Community" spread far and wide transcendental aspirations and increased the thirst for freedom from the bondage of prevailing ideas.

Sir Edwin Arnold's "Light of Asia" was published in 1879, and read by hundreds of thousands in Europe and America. Myriads of minds gained for the first time some true idea of the noble ethics and philosophy of Buddhism, and were amazed to find that for centuries antedating the time of Jesus his moral teachings had been imparted in their plenitude, coupled with a philosophy unknown to the Christian world at any time. Scholarly men began to give some heed other than purely scholastic to Oriental experience as embodied in its age-old literary remains. Despite the general contempt for "heathen" people and the exclusiveness of ignorance that had so long obtained, Western explorers began in earnest to adventure in search of the hereditary metaphysical possessions of the Orient, much in the same fashion as other Western adventurers had long exploited by conquest or by theft the physical treasures of the sacred East. Wilson's translation of the "Vishnu Purana" and Dr. Max Müller's edition of the "Sacred Books of the East," were part of the fruitage thus made accessible in the West.

When Charles Darwin's great work, "The Origin of Species by Means of Natural Selection," appeared in 1859, a powerful voice was raised against the deeply imbedded ideas of miracle and special creation by an omnipotent personal God, as engraved by centuries of dogmatic theologies. Mr. Darwin's work was not intended as an attack either on revealed religion or the dead-letter creeds, but was limited to the presentation of an immense accumulation of ascertained facts in natural history, and to the submission of inferences drawn with inescapable logic from the facts thus far amassed. It was perhaps the most brilliant example in history of sustained inductive reasoning. It showed and proved physical man to be no "special creation," but an evolutionary part of the "natural order of things." "The Origin of Species," and its supplement, "The Descent of Man," published in 1871, were purely scientific works in the best sense of the term. The "Darwinian theory" was received by the educated world with profound interest, followed by a tidal wave of revulsion as its bearing and effects upon current Christian dogmas and interpretations of the Bible were perceived. It was attacked on every hand and its author was subjected to every form of ridicule, slander and calumny that religious bigotry, ever the most fertile in malice and malevolence, could invent. Nevertheless, as scientific students verified its compilations of physical facts and tried conclusions with its logic, the theory gained headway in spite of all the storms of opposition. Its author lived to see his facts admitted, his conclusions accepted and adopted in whole or in part, even by his detractors. Corrupted and grotesquely distorted as the Darwinian theory has been in the intervening years, and however limited in its view of "evolution" from the standpoint of Occult philosophy, it none the less remains to this day the greatest advance in scientific hypotheses since the time of Newton, and aided largely in making possible the presentation of the triple evolutionary scheme outlined in the "Secret Doctrine." Whatever the defects of the Darwinian theory, they are due to no lack of honesty, zeal nor industry on the part of its great author, but rather to the limitations of his mode of research and to the inherent defect of all inductive reasoning. So immense has been the effect of the Darwinian theory of evolution on the ideas prevailing without question a generation ago, that it is very difficult for the average mind of today to realize how this theory of physical evolution could ever have been questioned, denied, opposed, vilified.

In his "History of Civilization in England," a work foremost among the contributory factors we are discussing, Mr. Henry T. Buckle sums up these lessons of the past which, in our opinion, are equally a prophecy of the future of Theosophy and the Theosophical Movement, however unconscious Mr. Buckle may have been of the immense reach of the spiritual and intelligent Agencies at work behind the scenes of human life. In the first volume of his work, which appeared in 1857, Mr. Buckle writes (p. 257):

> Owing to circumstances still unknown there appear from time to time great thinkers who devoting their lives to a single purpose are able to anticipate the progress of mankind, and to produce a religion or a philosophy by which important events are eventually brought about.

> But if we look into history we shall clearly see that, although the origin of a new opinion may be thus due to a single man, the result which the new opinion produces will depend on the condition of the people among whom it is propagated. If either a religion or a philosophy is too much in advance of a nation, it can do no present service, but must bide its time until the minds of men are ripe for its reception. . . . Every science, every creed has had its martyrs. According to the ordinary course of affairs, a few generations pass away, and then there comes a period when these very truths are looked upon as common-place facts, and a little later there comes another period in which they are declared to be necessary, and even the dullest intellect wonders how they could ever have been denied.

The student of Theosophy knows that the "circumstances still unknown" to Mr. Buckle, but which he intuitively recognized to exist, are in fact due to the *Karmic* provision of Spiritual and Intellectual evolution. Under Karmic Law, at transitional periods in the cyclic progression of Humanity, great Adepts restore to mankind through both direct and indirect channels some of the Wisdom once "known," but which in the lapse of time has become lost or obscured during the complexities of physical and personal evolution. For it must not be overlooked by the student that these Elder Brothers are themselves a part of the very stream of evolution in which we belong. As such, They take an active, albeit undisclosed and but too often unperceived, share in the government of the natural order of things. And although this part of the operation of cyclic law is often delayed and defied by the ignorance and prejudice of mankind in general, each rise and fall of civilizations is succeeded by a regeneration and further progression.

Other constructive factors in the preparatory work of the Theosophical Movement in our time may be seen in the great and sudden leap (from the standpoint of racial and national cycles) in invention, discovery, trade, the means and methods of transportation, manufacture, and utilization of all the raw materials in Nature—all making in one way and another for inter-dependence, inter-communication, inter-respect in the great human family, and the consequent breaking down of the barriers of Nature, of human insularity and separateness: a harrowing of the soil, whether by the means of war or peace, as a necessary prelude for once more sowing in that soil the seeds of Brotherhood. And in the political field the great careers of Abraham Lincoln, of John Bright, of Mazzini, and many others, all made for the Rights of Man, as opposed to the forces of reaction.

In an iconoclastic sense an equally necessary and valuable pioneer work in the breaking of the molds of fixed ideas into which human thought forever tends to crystallize, can be discerned in the work of such men as Robert G. Ingersoll in America, Charles Bradlaugh in England, and, in the church, by such men as Charles Kingsley and W. E. Channing. Whether apparently pursuing the path of agnosticism, of a purely socialistic and materialistic altruism, or of a liberalized orthodoxy, the efforts of all these commanded a wide following and broke to a large extent the hold of bigotry and intolerance. Philosophical speculations like those of Herbert Spencer, the esthetic spirit of men like Ruskin, the rebellious mind of Carlyle, the insubordination to the harrow of conventional ideas of writers like Dickens, George Eliot, Balzac, Tolstoy, Walt Whitman, and many others, all aided in the pioneer work of the Theosophical Movement. They may all be said to have fought for the unrestricted domain of the individual conscience, the larger outlook upon human life and human duty, as opposed to the *ipse dixit* of any "thus saith the Lord." All these individual and collective factors, some, perhaps, dimly conscious of the germinal force at work within themselves, others aware only of the travail without issue of human existence—all were of value. All that in any way has made, or that makes, possible the arousal of serious attention to the Second and Third Objects of the Parent Theosophical Society, all that facilitates the revolt of the mind and conscience from creedal exclusiveness, all that might turn men from the sordid materialism of a one-life existence devoted to the pursuit of physical well-being—all this is truly a concurrent part of the Theosophical Movement, and necessary to any attempt at the practical realization of its First Object—Universal Brotherhood, the life of service as opposed to the life for self.

The ideas represented by such terms as revealed religion, a favored people, a personal God, miracles, heaven gained by an "act of faith," a "vicarious atonement," selfish personal salvation—the fetters forged by many centuries of ecclesiastical usurpation of authority over the ignorant mind and conscience: all these veritable Bastilles of moral and mental tyranny were under assault or siege during a large part of the nineteenth century. Their *lettres de cachet* no longer sufficed to imprison or outcast the individual mind, to forfeit the reputable estate of the individual rebel against the "established order." If the mind of the race could not be said to have been in revolution against spiritual and mental intolerance, it was none the less true that everywhere could be found sincere and reverent-minded men in outspoken rebellion against the dominant and dominating ideas of centuries. The "millennium" of sectarian religion was drawing to a close. Agnosticism, infidelity, bold questioning of the foundations hitherto esteemed inviolate, were no longer branded with the brand of infamy by the all-powerful sects, because the sects were no longer all-powerful. A spirit of liberty, often of license mistaken for liberty, was abroad in Europe and America. Even in India the Brahmo-Somaj of Ramohun Roy and his successors had begun to undermine the ancient walls of creed and caste.

Spiritualism had perhaps more to do than any other single factor in producing among millions that transitional state of mind into which the granite ideas of centuries had begun to disintegrate. This Ishmael among faiths, under many names and proscriptions, is as old as the history and tradition of the race. In its modern form it began with the mediumistic manifestations of the Fox sisters at Rochester in New York State, U.S.A., in 1848. In the ensuing twenty-five or thirty years it spread, in spite of the most relentless opposition of the orthodox Christian sects, despite the ridicule of scientific students and the incredulity of the general public, despite also the real or pretended exposures of many of the most noted mediums, until its believers were numbered by millions in America, England, France, and in lesser numbers in other countries. Most celebrated of the mediums following the Fox sisters were the Americans, Andrew Jackson Davis, his disciple Thomas Lake Harris, P. B. Randolph, Daniel Dunglas Home, the Davenport brothers, Henry Slade, Mrs. Emma H. Britten, and the Eddy brothers. All these were accused of fraud times without number, and some of them were made the victims of persecution. Nevertheless, the genuineness, variety and extent of their phenomena were attested by numbers of famous investigators of the highest character. Notable among those who from sceptical experimenters became convinced believers in the reality of the manifestations were Dr. Robert Hare of Philadelphia, Epes Sargent, Judge Edmunds, the noted lawyer, Dr. Robert Chambers, Col. Olcott, and many other men of mark in America. In England Profs. William Crookes, Alfred Russel Wallace, Lodge, C. C. Massey, Lord Borthwick, Lord Lindsay, Sergeant Cox, and other men of the highest standing accepted the evidences after searching tests. In Germany the famous Prof. Zöllner held prolonged sittings with Slade and others and published his conclusions and theories in the work, "Transcendental Physics," dealing with the phenomena as a problem in the "fourth dimension." In France the Emperor Napoleon and his wife, and in Russia the Czar and his consort became the firm friends and followers of Mr. D. D. Home. The papers of the Russian savant, Dr. A. Aksakoff, show how profound was his interest in the new phenomena. Leon-Denizarth-Hippolyte Rivail, author of numerous popular and educational scientific texts for French schools, became so interested in the phenomena and so convinced of their value in establishing communication with discarnate intelligences, that he devoted his entire time to study and experiments. In order that the prejudices thus aroused should not interfere with his established writings and reputation he adopted the pseudonym of "Allan Kardec," by which he is now almost universally known. Contrary to the general supposition, Allan Kardec was not himself a medium. All his experiments were conducted at second hand. He published two books of enormous circulation, the "Book of Spirits," and the "Book of Mediums," both of which were translated into English. The French editions alone of "Le Livre des Esprits" attained a circulation of more than one hundred and twenty thousand copies in the twenty years following the publication of the "revised edition" in 1857. It was Allan Kardec who, more than any other, made systematic efforts to establish a philosophy of Spiritualism from the communications he obtained through carefully chosen mediums.

The spread of Spiritualism was greatly facilitated by a number of factors. It required no education, no study, no moral discipline, on the part either of the medium or the believer. Its phenomena were not essentially antagonistic to religion, and the communications received more often than otherwise repeated the platitudes of the churches. In fact nearly every noted medium or reputable proponent of the phenomena was still more or less orthodox in his acceptance of the fundamental dogmas of the Christian creeds. To the bereaved who might be more or less sceptical or indifferent to orthodox teachings regarding after-death states, Spiritualism made a profound appeal, for it offered the prospect of immediate assurance and consolation. To the materialistic and the curious-minded it offered a fascinating subject for facile experimentation. Nor can it be doubted that in the increasing dilemma of many, due to the Darwinian theory of physical evolution, Spiritualism offered an attractive middle ground of experimental evidence that enabled them, without too great sacrifice of cherished religious convictions or logical common-sense, both to hold on to hereditary Christian ideas and to accept the theory of "evolution." And in this compromise many were doubtless moved by the example of Prof. Wallace, co-originator with Mr. Darwin of his theory. Prof. Wallace was himself a Spiritualist and a believer in Christianity, even if not altogether orthodox in his faith.

In a single generation Spiritualism, from being a pariah both as to its phenomena and its many theories, became almost respectable. Modern science, hitherto deaf, dumb and blind towards everything but the empirical acquisition of physical facts and hypotheses based on them, began, reluctantly and suspiciously, but still began, to take note of the phenomena of the metaphysical, which, if true, compelled the admission of other factors than "force and matter" as the causative agencies of the phenomenal world. But the general attitude of scientific students towards Spiritualism affords a curious parallel to the attitude of the theologians toward Darwinism: first derision and contempt, then wholesale denial and opposition, then grudging acceptance in part.

Into this mighty arena of contending forces entered H. P. Blavatsky with her Theosophical Society and her first public exposition of Theosophy. Looking backwards from the safe distance of the intervening years, something of the significance of the mighty struggle between orthodox Christianity and modern materialistic science, between both these and the changeling, Spiritualism, can now be discerned in the light of history—a light necessarily denied all the active combatants except H.P.B. herself. That she saw and foresaw what was and was to be, and was herself under no illusions, is very clearly indicated in the Preface of "Isis Unveiled" alone, without going deeper into the abundant evidences. Bitterly as theology and science might be opposed to each other with spear and trident, each was, at the last quarter of the nineteenth century, equally hostile to the new combatant, Spiritualism, armed with its net of weird phenomena and strange theories. Alone, friendly to all the gladiators, but without a solitary understanding ally among them, H.P.B. came equipped with an unknown knowledge and an unknown purpose which must serve her for both sword and shield. It was too much for her to hope, however vast the reconstructive forces loosed by her in the world of public opinion, that those forces, their source, their scope and their significance, would be grasped by any but the very few. Nor did she expect that their effect on the mind of the race would be altogether and immediately constructive, however beneficent her purpose might be. Nor could she look for other than a hostile and retardative reception at the hands of vested and mercenary interests, the ignorant and the dogmatic, the predatory and contentious. Although her aim was to elevate the mind of the race, her method could only be to deal with that mind as she found it, by trying to lead it on, step by step; by seeking out and educating a few who, appreciating the majesty of the eternal Wisdom-Religion and devoted to "the great orphan—humanity," could carry on her work with zeal and wisdom; by founding a society which, however small its numbers might be, would inject into the thought of the day the ideas, the doctrines, the nomenclature of the Wisdom-Religion.

CHAPTER II

THE PARENT THEOSOPHICAL SOCIETY

THE Theosophical Movement of the nineteenth century was publicly inaugurated with the founding of the Theosophical Society at New York City.

By birth a Russian of noble family, Madame Blavatsky had been a wanderer for more than twenty years in many lands, oriental and occidental. She had twice or thrice been in the Americas, North and South, before coming to New York in July of 1873. She lived in retirement there and in Brooklyn for more than a year. In October of 1874 she journeyed to the Eddy farmhouse near Chittenden, Vermont, and there made the acquaintance of Col. Henry S. Olcott.

Colonel Olcott was an American and had acquired his title in the American Civil War. He had been agricultural editor of the *New York Tribune*, had written many articles for various publications on many subjects, had been admitted to the bar, and was at the time a well-known lawyer, with a very wide acquaintance among prominent men. For many years he had been a Spiritualist. Interested in an account he had seen of the manifestations taking place through the mediumship of the Eddy brothers, he had visited Chittenden in July and written an account of what he had witnessed for the *New York Sun*. This article was copied and commented on in many publications. In September Col. Olcott returned to the Eddy place under commission to investigate the phenomena and report on them to the *New York Graphic*. It was while he was engaged in this congenial work that Madame Blavatsky arrived at Chittenden.

Although Madame Blavatsky apparently took no part in the proceedings other than as a visitor and interested witness, Col. Olcott noted that the phenomena changed greatly in character and variety immediately after her arrival. He was so impressed by what he saw and by his conversations with Madame Blavatsky that he followed up the acquaintance after her return to New York.

At the request of Madame Blavatsky he introduced to her a young lawyer of his acquaintance named William Q. Judge. Mr. Judge was of Irish parentage, and had been brought by his family to America while still a boy. From his earliest years he had been markedly religious in temperament, and, as he grew older, had delved in religions, philosophies, mystical writings, Mesmerism, Spiritualism, and kindred subjects. He was many years younger than either Madame Blavatsky or Col. Olcott, who were born, respectively, in 1831 and 1832, while Mr. Judge's birth date was 1851. Both Col. Olcott and Mr. Judge became pupils of Madame Blavatsky and passed all their available time in her company.

In the winter of 1874-5 Madame Blavatsky was in Philadelphia, where she made the acquaintance of several noted Spiritualists. With them and Col. Olcott she attended the *séances* of Mr. and Mrs. Holmes and others. Certain sceptical investigators having attacked in the press the genuineness of the Eddy and Holmes phenomena, and questioned the *bona fides* of any mediumship, both Col. Olcott and Madame Blavatsky replied vigorously, defending the fact of mediumship itself, and urging the necessity for impartial investigation of the claims of Spiritualism, both as to its philosophy and its alleged facts. This was Madame Blavatsky's first appearance in print in the English language. The peculiarities of her style of expression, the boldness of her statements, the apparent range of her knowledge on the subject, all conspired to attract the attention of Spiritualists, investigators, and the public generally.

In January, 1875, Col. Olcott's book, "People From the Other World," was issued, describing in detail the Eddy and Holmes phenomena, and giving a curiosity-provoking account of Madame Blavatsky. Whatever opinion any reader may form of the marvels described, or of Col. Olcott's comments and conclusions, there can be no question of his good faith. Nor, as the book was written during the very period of the occurrences, can there be any question that it reflects accurately the opinions and state of mind of Col. Olcott at the time.

On Madame Blavatsky's return to New York from Philadelphia she took apartments at 46 Irving Place. The wonders recited by Col. Olcott and her own letters to the newspapers had drawn so much attention to her that her rooms became a center of attraction. Nearly every evening was given over to visitors. One of the newspaper reporters dubbed her apartment "the lamasery," and the name quickly became current as typifying the flavor of mystery surrounding her and the subjects discussed at her *soirées.* To these evening gatherings came Spiritualists, Kabalists, Platonists, students of modern science and of ancient mysteries, the profane, the sceptical, the curious and the seekers after the marvelous. Colonel Olcott and Mr. Judge were nearly always present, and, after the departure of the casual visitors, would remain far into the night immersed in study and discussion.

In their many conversations she told them more or less of her travels and their purpose. Amongst other experiences she had endeavored unsuccessfully to establish a group at Cairo, Egypt, in 1871, to investigate the rationale of mediumship and its phenomena. Moved by what he had seen and heard, no less than by his ardent desire to explore more deeply the phenomena which fascinated him, Col. Olcott had proposed, as early as May, 1875, to form a secret "miracle club" for the production and examination of phenomena. Colonel Olcott's own account, written many years after the event, states that the "miracle club" plan failed because the expected medium could not be obtained for the experiments he desired to conduct. The fact that he was so fascinated by the phenomena privately performed by Madame Blavatsky in exposition of her theories, that he thought her "infallible" and her Masters "miracle workers," would indicate that the "expected medium" was none other than Madame Blavatsky herself, and that the failure of his attempt was due to her refusal, then as thereafter throughout her career, to lend herself to the production of phenomena under his or anyone's directions, or for the purposes he and others desired.

On the evening of September 7, 1875, a talk was given in Madame Blavatsky's apartment by a Mr. G. H. Felt, who had been a student of Egyptian mysticism, and who professed to be able to control "elementals." While the assemblage was discussing the talk, Col. Olcott wrote on a slip of paper which he handed to Mr. Judge these words: "Would it not be a good thing to form a society for this kind of study?" Mr. Judge read the paper, passed it to Madame Blavatsky, who nodded assent, and then Mr. Judge proposed that the assemblage come to order and that Col. Olcott act as chairman to consider the proposal. Another meeting was arranged for the following evening at Madame Blavatsky's rooms and at that time sixteen persons gave in their names as being willing to join in founding a society for Occult study. Other meetings were held at Col. Olcott's law offices, and at the residence of Mrs. Emma Hardinge Britten in furtherance of the proposed society. On September 13 the name, The Theosophical Society, was chosen. On October 16 a preamble and by-laws were adopted. On October 30 additional names were added to the list of "Founders," and Officers and a Council were elected. The principal Officers were Col. Olcott as President, Madame Blavatsky as Corresponding Secretary, and Mr. Judge as Counsel. On the evening of November 17 a formal meeting was held at Mott Memorial Hall, 64 Madison Avenue. Colonel Olcott delivered an "Inaugural Address" and 500 copies of this address were ordered electrotyped "for immediate distribution."

Thereafter, stated meetings continued to be held from time to time; various talks and lectures were given, much discussion ensued and many plans for experimentation in phenomena were proposed. Neither Madame Blavatsky nor Mr. Judge took any active part in the meetings after the first few sessions. The former busied herself in correspondence, in communications to the press, in discussion with the steady stream of visitors to "the lamasery," and in the writing of "Isis Unveiled." Mr. Judge, occupied with the necessities of his daily living, gave his evenings to study under Madame Blavatsky's direction and instruction. Colonel Olcott alone was active in the meetings of the Society. Additional Fellows were admitted from time to time, both Active and Corresponding, and great efforts made to procure phenomena. Mr. Felt's promised revelations failed to materialize and after a time he left the Society, as did most of the other early members when it was found that the expectations aroused were not fulfilled. Very early in the history of the Society Mr. Felt had exacted a pledge of secrecy regarding the disclosures he had promised to make, and this was signed, at his and Col. Olcott's request, by most of the attendant Fellows. It was this pledge which was many years later published in the *New York Herald* as the original pledge of secrecy of the Theosophical Society, and afterwards incorporated in "Hours With the Ghosts," by Henry Ridgely Evans, published by Laird & Lee, Chicago, in 1897. The material for the *Herald* attacks was supplied by Mr. Henry J. Newton, one of the original Founders, who had been elected Treasurer of the Society at its inception. He was a well-known and ardent Spiritualist who became bitterly hostile to the Society after the publication of "Isis Unveiled." Others among the Founders were Mrs. Emma Hardinge Britten and her husband Dr. Britten. Both were Spiritualists and Mrs. Britten was herself a versatile medium, very widely known as the author or reputed author of "Ghostland," "Art Magic," "Nineteenth Century Occultism," and other writings. She had also been active in the investigations conducted by the London "Dialectical Society," a few years previously. Another Spiritualist Founder was Mr. C. C. Massey, an English barrister and well-known writer for British spiritualist publications. On his return to London after the formation of the Society, he interested a number of others, among them the famous

W. Stainton Moses ("M.A. Oxon."), and Miss Emily Kislingbury, at that time Secretary of the British Spiritualist Association. The British Theosophical Society was established in 1876, with Mr. Massey as its first President. The members of the British Society were accepted as "Corresponding Fellows" of the Parent Society, but were not formally recognized until the summer of 1878, when John Storer Cobb, the then Recording Secretary, journeyed to London for the purpose, under commission from the Parent Society. With the exception of Miss Kislingbury nearly all the original and early London Fellows later became antagonistic. Both in London and New York nearly the entire membership consisted of Spiritualists. As phenomena were not forthcoming, as the teachings of Madame Blavatsky came to be recognized as fatal to the theory that mediumistic communications are messages from departed human beings, the great majority of Spiritualist members either silently dropped out or became the most active enemies of the new Society.

Another early Fellow was Dr. Alexander Wilder, the learned Platonist, who remained friendly to the Society and its purposes throughout his life. It was he who read the manuscript of "Isis Unveiled" and recommended its publication to Mr. J. W. Bouton. He also wrote most of the prefatory article "Before the Veil," which precedes Chapter I of Volume 1 of "Isis." In other ways, also, he was helpful to Madame Blavatsky and her mission, and his services were often gratefully referred to by her. Other early members were Rev. J. H. Wiggin, a Unitarian clergyman, Dr. Seth Pancoast of Philadelphia, a lifetime student of the Kabbala, and Major-General Abner W. Doubleday, U. S. Army, retired. General Doubleday remained a consistent and devoted member of the Society to the day of his death. He became President *pro tem.* after the departure of Madame Blavatsky and Col. Olcott for India, and spent much of his time in correspondence and other activities in behalf of the Society. Some unique manuscripts and rare books given by him to the original library of the

New York Society are in the possession of the writers. One of his last services was to present the Society with a complete file of the first six volumes of *The Theosophist*, completely indexed in manuscript prepared and written out by himself.

Through the labors of Madame Blavatsky, Corresponding Fellows were obtained in many lands. In this way the Ionian Theosophical Society was established at Corfu in 1877. Other activities by correspondence resulted in an affiliation with the Arya Samaj, a Hindu association originally formed for the revival of interest in the ancient scriptures and philosophical systems of India. It was presided over by the Swami, Dayanand Sarasvati, well known in his native country. Joint diplomas were issued to many Fellows of the T.S. as members of "The Theosophical Society of the Arya Samaj of Aryavart" (the ancient designation of India). This alliance endured until 1881, when it was ruptured and the Swami and his partisans became violent opponents to the T.S. in India. A very full account of the various difficulties is contained in the "Extra Supplement" to *The Theosophist* for July, 1882.

As originally constituted the Theosophical Society was entirely democratic in its by-laws and organization. All Officers were elective. Changes in by-laws, whether by substitution or otherwise, had first to be submitted in writing at a stated meeting at least thirty days prior to a vote, and then ratified by the affirmative action of two-thirds of the Fellows present. All nominations for Fellowship were required to be in writing, to be endorsed by two Fellows in good standing, and approved by the Council. Three classes of Fellows were provided for: Active, Corresponding and Honorary, whose nature is sufficiently indicated by their designations. The earlier Societies established after the foundation of the Parent body adopted its preamble and made additional rules and by-laws not in conflict, to suit themselves. Intercourse between the various Societies was more or less desultory and informal, but all Fellows received their diplomas from the Parent Society until branch Societies began to be formed in India, when diplomas were signed by Col. Olcott and Madame Blavatsky. In America diplomas were signed after 1878 by Gen. Doubleday as President *pro tem.*, and by Mr. Judge as Recording Secretary, until 1883, after which date diplomas were signed in the first instance in India or America as exigency might require, until 1885, after which time H.P.B. being in Europe, Mr. Judge in America, and Col. Olcott in India, all regular diplomas were signed in the first instance by Col. Olcott as *de facto* President of all the Theosophical Societies. Diplomas, when issued, were recognized as valid certificates of Fellowship by all lodges wherever situated.

No formal Convention of all the Societies was ever held during the existence of the Parent body, but in India a species of gathering or "Anniversary Convention" was held as early as 1880, and thereafter annually at the end of each year. These were attended by delegates from the Indian and Ceylon Lodges and by occasional visitors from Europe and America. No Sections were organized during the first ten years of the Society's history.

The Parent Theosophical Society had three declared Objects, and these were formally adopted by all subsequently formed Societies except a few of the Indian branches. Those Objects were:

I. To form the nucleus of a Universal Brotherhood of Humanity, without distinction of race, creed, sex, caste, or color;

II. The study of ancient and modern religions, philosophies and sciences, and the demonstration of the importance of such study; and

III. The investigation of the unexplained laws of Nature and the psychical powers latent in man.

Assent to the First Object only was required of all Fellows, the remaining Objects being set forth as subsidiary and optional. Originally, and until as late as 1885, a form of initiation, several times changed, was used for the induction of new members, and the proceedings of the several Societies were quasi-private.

In the beginning the Parent Society and the other Theosophical bodies had no literature of their own. The Kabbala, translations of Plato, Oriental philosophies and religions, the Spiritualist publications, the numerous writings of Christian mystics, and the existent Western works on magic, hypnotism, mesmerism and related subjects supplied the only material for study.

Madame Blavatsky had begun the composition of "Isis Unveiled" in 1874, and this work she continued steadily, subject to the multifarious interruptions and activities occasioned by her increasing acquaintance and the labors incident to her work as Corresponding Secretary of the new Society. In order to be near at hand in the preparation of "Isis" for the press, Col. Olcott and his sister, Mrs. Mitchell, took rooms in the same building with Madame Blavatsky's apartment. Most of the proofs of "Isis" were read by him, and the arrangement of the text is his. Both Col. Olcott and H.P.B. were greatly hampered by the lack of works of reference, by attendant circumstances, and by special difficulties. English was a foreign tongue to H.P.B. and had never been acquired by her except in a colloquial sense in childhood. She was entirely unfamiliar with current literary usages or the exigencies of the printer's art. On his side Col. Olcott had but the slightest acquaintance with many of the subjects treated; was totally ignorant of most of the languages ancient and modern necessarily referred to, and the authors and authorities whose statements were quoted and discussed. The almost endless ramifications of theologies, philosophies and other writings referred to were for the most part unknown to him, and in many cases no exact equivalents or corresponding terms existed in English to convey the desired meanings and interpretations. A further difficulty developed in Madame Blavatsky's having occasion to rewrite large portions of the text, or to incorporate new matter in the proofs, even after the stereotype plates were cast. When the many obstacles are considered, it is remarkable that so few errors exist in the work as finally published by Mr. J. W. Bouton of New York in the early autumn of 1877. Two editions of "Isis" were immediately exhausted, and new editions followed from the original plates for many years. An edition of "Isis" was also issued many years later by Mrs. Tingley's Theosophical organization from the original Bouton plates, with additional matter. Still another edition of "Isis" reset throughout has been published by the same organization. An entirely new edition was also issued in London in 1907 by the Theosophical Publishing Society, affiliated with Mrs. Besant's Theosophical organization.

Some corrections of the more glaring errors in the original Bouton editions of "Isis" were made at various times by Madame Blavatsky, in *The Theosophist, The Path* and *Lucifer,* but the original plates, not being owned by her, could not be corrected.

"Isis Unveiled" having been completed and the Society in America being on as firm a footing as possible, active preparations began to carry its propaganda to other countries where beginnings had already been made. Accordingly, a little over a year after the publication of "Isis," Madame Blavatsky and Col. Olcott sailed for India as a "committee" of the Society. A fortnight's stay was made in London, arrangements were made at Paris for the immediate formation of "The Theosophical Society of French Spiritists," and the two Founders proceeded on their way, arriving at Bombay, India, February 16, 1879.

Almost at once accessions to the Society began in India, both among English residents and Hindus. Learned members of the various sects and castes, pundits, professors of the various schools of Hindu philosophy, Indian rulers, writers, lawyers, gave their adhesion to the Society. Among noted English Fellows in India were Major-General Morgan, British Army, retired, and his wife; Mr. A. O. Hume, late Secretary to the Government of India; and Mr. A. P. Sinnett, editor of the leading pro-Government organ, the Allahabad *Pioneer.* In October of 1879 Madame Blavatsky began the publication of *The Theosophist.* The magazine soon attained a wide circulation not only in India, but in Europe and America as well. In 1881 Mr. Sinnett's book, "The Occult World," was published at London. It was subsequently republished in America, and passed through many editions. It was followed in 1883 by "Esoteric Buddhism," which circulated as extensively. In India, "Hints on Esoteric Theosophy, No. 1," was issued in 1882, and "No. 2" a year later. In 1881 Col. Olcott published his "Buddhist Catechism," a work which was later adopted as accurate by both the Northern and Southern wings of the Buddhist faith, and which speedily passed through a score of editions and is still being published. In the period from 1879 to 1884 there were established in India and Ceylon an even hundred Theosophical Societies. For the first time in recorded history, some approach to fellowship in a common society with a common aim was brought about amongst members of sects and castes which from time immemorial had considered it a sin and a degradation to meet and mingle on equal terms.

Correspondence with the Parent, the British and the French Societies, and with H.P.B., resulted in the formation of several additional Societies in America and Europe in the first decade of the Movement. Thus the "St. Thomas" Society in the Danish West Indies was formed in 1881, the "Post Nubila Lux" Society at The Hague, Holland, the "Odessa Group" in Russia in 1883, the "Scottish" at Ayre, the "Germania" at Elberfeld, in 1884. The Queensland Society in Australia was formed in 1881. In the United States the first Society established after the Parent body was the Rochester T.S., organized in July, 1882, by the efforts of Mrs. J. W. Cables. The first publication in America devoted to Theosophical subjects was *The Occult Word,* the first number of which was issued by Mrs. Cables in April, 1884. The "Pioneer" T.S. was formed at St. Louis in the summer of 1883, and the "Gnostic" at Washington, D. C., in 1884.

Madame Blavatsky's first work was with the Spiritualists. When her powerful voice was raised in their defense, when she demanded that their wonders should be investigated with an open mind, their claims examined impartially, she was hailed as a friend, as an ally, as a champion of the new dispensation. When it was noised about through the indiscreet but well-meant laudations of Col. Olcott that she was herself a medium *par excellence,* she was acclaimed as a prophet. Her *soirées* and her Society were crowded with the rush of seekers demanding a sign. But when she refused to produce the hoped-for marvels; when in her conversations and letters to the press she hinted at other and truer explanations of the phenomena than "communications from the dead"; when she uttered veiled warnings regarding the dangers of mediumship, she was listened to with surprise, with incredulity, with suspicions. And when at last "Isis Unveiled" was issued, a fierce revulsion set in, increasing as the years went on. She was denounced by some Spiritualists as a traitor to the "cause," and slandered by others as a mere cheating trickster, not even an honest medium. Nearly every Spiritualist who had entered the Society departed from it, and she was generally regarded quite as much the foe of Spiritualism as of orthodox religion or materialistic science. It is of more than passing significance that in every case the chief enemies of H.P.B. and her teachings, both within and without the original Theosophical Society and the many organizations which still employ that name, have been persons who were Spiritualists, or whose natural tendencies have been in that direction. All the many attacks upon her name and fame throughout all the years can be traced back to their source either in Spiritualists or those addicted to mediumship and its practices.

What, then, were her earliest expositions of Theosophy, which sufficed on the one hand to provide the material for the growth and study of the members of the Theosophical Society, and, on the other hand, drew upon her devoted head from the very first, a series of attacks which, gradually increasing in range and intensity, culminated in the tremendous explosions of 1884-5? No student of the Theosophical Movement can afford to neglect the most painstaking examination of "Isis Unveiled." To a summary of its most important contents we may now turn our attention profitably, the collateral and accompanying circumstances having been outlined.

CHAPTER III

"ISIS UNVEILED"

"ISIS UNVEILED" is stated on its title page to be "*a* master-key to the mysteries of ancient and modern science and theology." In the body of the work there are said to be seven of these keys to the mysteries of Nature and of Man, of which one only is given. The volumes are dedicated to "The Theosophical Society which was founded to study the subjects on which they treat."

By correlating the work to the Three Objects of the Society a clear light may be had on the method of treatment employed. Volume 1 has for its general subject "Science," and in that respect relates strictly to the Third Object. Volume 2 is entitled "Theology," and relates to the Second Object. But as both science and theology relate to the great objects of human inquiry, the treatment is inter-woven and inter-blended throughout. As all inquiry presents two general poles, the ascertainment of facts and the consideration of their meaning and relations, so "Isis" takes up the acquisitions of modern scientific research and the theories and hypotheses built up to account for ascertained physical phenomena; the revelations and claims of the various religions, particularly the Christian, are examined, and their theologies (or theories to account for metaphysical phenomena) are analyzed.

The work is necessarily addressed to the most open-minded of the race, and the method pursued is necessarily adapted to the limitations of those minds. It is not so much the introduction of new evidence that is attempted, as the partial presentation of an entirely new (to Western minds) hypothesis to explain the evidence that already exists in the general fund of human experience.

In the course of the work it is demonstrated over and over again that the dogmas of the sects are not only mutually contradictory and destructive, but, as well, that sound philosophical principles, correct logic and the proved facts of modern science are in direct and overwhelming opposition to the claims and pretensions of theology. The same method of examination is also applied to the "working hypotheses" of modern science, and the various theories are tested out by comparison, one with another, all with the facts of experience. It is conclusively established that, no more than theology, can the philosophy of modern science stand the light of searching investigation. The believer in theology or science is furthermore shown by masses of indisputable testimony that certain facts exist and always have existed, which are in themselves absolutely destructive alike of the claims of orthodox religion and materialistic science; that these facts have been persistently overlooked, ignored or denied, both by the votaries of "revealed religion" and of modern "exact science"; yet that these disregarded facts have at all times been uniformly testified to by the noblest minds of the race no less than by the common belief of mankind. Side by side, therefore, with the introduction of the affirmative evidence of these facts is placed the testimony of the ages as to their bearing on the great subjects of religion, philosophy and science, and the inference is drawn that there has always existed, from the remotest times, a system whose teachings in regard to Nature and to Man are inclusive of all things and exclusive of nothing. This system Madame Blavatsky denominates the Hermetic philosophy, or Wisdom-Religion, and declares that her work and mission are a "plea for the recognition of the Wisdom-Religion as the only possible key to the Absolute in science and theology." The work itself is the evidence that she uses the word "plea" in its strictly legal and forensic sense. "Isis" contains the testimony, the analysis of the evidence, the arguments, and the citations of principles, laws and precedents. The work is "submitted to public judgment" upon its inherent reasonableness as to its conclusions, its verifiable accuracy as to the facts, and not upon any assumed authority.

Turning ever and anon from the purely inductive method which characterizes the work generally, Madame Blavatsky submits some of the principal tenets of the Wisdom-Religion, which she names THEOSOPHY, and shows that there is more than ample ground, from evidence accessible to the general student, to justify the statements she makes, that the Wisdom-Religion underlies and antedates every religion, every philosophy, every system of thought, every science known to mankind, and that all these have in point of fact sprung from periodical impartations of portions of the Secret Doctrines by its Adept custodians.

"Isis" is in no sense put forward by its writer as an inference, a revelation, or a speculation, although the burden of its mighty contents is necessarily largely assumed to prove that the existence of Adepts and a Wisdom-Religion is the unavoidable inference from the testimony; the prior missions and messages of great Adepts the indubitable source of the great religions and the common belief in gods, saviors and redeemers; their teachings regarding the "mysteries" the real fountain whence have been drawn the materials for the philosophical and ethical treatises of the great writers of all times. She shows that everywhere, from the remotest antiquity, there are abundant indications that the arts and sciences as re-discovered in our times, were known and practiced by the "wise men of old"; furthermore, that much was "known" to the ancients concerning certain sciences and arts now "unknown" even to the most advanced science and scientists of our day. And although popular religion, philosophy and science became in time polluted with purely human speculations and fancies, "Isis" shows that they all started originally as clear and unadulterated streams from the mother source. What was originally a teaching depending on knowledge and inspiration degenerated in time into mere dogmas and speculations; what was originally a Teacher of primeval truths became in time an object of veneration and worship as a god or a divine incarnation.

With these considerations in mind something may be grasped of the epochal importance of Madame Blavatsky's first great work, and of the leading statements of Occultism embodied in it. Although "Isis Unveiled" has been before the world for nearly half a century few, even among Theosophists, have as yet assimilated more than a few crumbs from this "storehouse of thought."

The plan of the work is early stated. The object is not to force upon the public the personal views or theories of the author, nor does it aim at creating a revolution in some department of thought:

> It is rather a brief summary of the religions, philosophies, and universal traditions of human kind, and the *exegesis* of the same, in the spirit of those *secret doctrines*, of which none—thanks to prejudice and bigotry—have reached Christendom in so unmutilated a form as to secure it a fair judgment. Hence the unmerited contempt into which the study of the noblest of sciences—that of the *spiritual* man—has gradually fallen.
>
> In undertaking to inquire into the assumed infallibility of Modern Science and Theology, the author has been forced, even at the risk of being thought discursive, to make constant comparison of the ideas, achievements, and pretensions of their representatives with those of the ancient philosophies and religious teachers. Things the most widely separated as to time have thus been brought into immediate juxtaposition, for only thus could the priority and parentage of discoveries and dogmas be determined. In discussing the merits of our scientific contemporaries, their own confessions of failure in experimental research, of baffling mysteries, of missing links in their chains of theory, of inability to comprehend natural phenomena, of ignorance of the laws of the causal world,

> have furnished the basis for the present study. Especially we will review the speculations and policy of noted authorities in connection with those modern psychological phenomena [Spiritualism] which began at Rochester and have now overspread the world. *We wish to show how inevitable were their innumerable failures, and how they must continue until these pretended authorities go to the Brahmins and Lamaists of the far Orient, and respectfully ask them to impart the alphabet of true science.*
>
> Deeply sensible of the Titanic struggle that is now in progress between materialism and the spiritual aspirations of mankind, our constant endeavor has been to gather into our several chapters, like weapons into armories, every fact and argument that can be used to aid the latter in defeating the former. Sickly and deformed child as it now is, the materialism of Today is born of the brutal Yesterday. Unless its growth is arrested it may become our master. To prevent the crushing of these spiritual aspirations, the blighting of these hopes, and the deadening of that intuition which teaches us of a God and a hereafter, we must show our false theologies in their naked deformity, and distinguish between divine religion and human dogmas. Our voice is raised for spiritual freedom, and our plea made for enfranchisement from all tyranny, whether of SCIENCE or THEOLOGY.

The work plunges forthwith into the comparison of the ancient Occult tenets both with modern theological dogmas and modern scientific theories. Some of the tenets laid down are as follows:

I. The pre-existence of *spiritual* man clothed in a body of ethereal matter, and with the ability to commune freely with the now unseen universes.

II. An almost incredible antiquity is claimed for the human race in its various "coats of skin," and the great doctrine of Cycles of Destiny (Karma) is emphasized, as well as that these Cycles do not affect all mankind at one and the same time, thus explaining the rise and fall of civilizations and the existence at one and the same time of the most highly developed races side by side with tribes sunk in savagery.

III. A double evolution, spiritual and intellectual as well as physical, is postulated whose philosophy alone can reconcile spirit and matter and cause each to demonstrate the other mathematically.

IV. The doctrine of the *Metempsychosis* of the spiritual and mental Man is given as the key which will supply every missing link in the theories of the modern evolutionists, as well as the mysteries of the various religions. The lower orders of evolution are declared to have emanated from higher spiritual ones before they develop. It is affirmed that if men of science and theologians had properly understood the doctrine of Metempsychosis in its application to the indestructibility of matter and the immortality of spirit it would have been perceived that this doctrine is a sublime conception. It is demonstrated that there has not been a philosopher of any note who did not hold to this doctrine of Metempsychosis as taught by the Brahmins, Buddhists, and later by the Pythagoreans and the Gnostics, *in its esoteric sense.* For lack of comprehension of this great philosophical principle the methods of modern science, however exact, *must end in nullity.*

V. The ancients knew far more concerning certain sciences than our modern savants have yet discovered. *Magic* is as old as man. The calculations of the ancients applied equally to the *spiritual* progress of humanity as to the physical. Magic was considered a divine science which led to a participation in the attributes of Divinity itself. "As above, so it is below. That which has been will return again. As in heaven, so on earth." The revolution of the physical world is attended by a like revolution in the world of intellect—the spiritual evolution proceeding in Cycles, like the physical one. The great kingdoms and empires of the world after reaching the culmination of their greatness, descend again, *in accordance with the same law by which they ascended;* till, having reached the lowest point, humanity re-asserts itself and mounts up once more, the height of its attainment being, by this law of ascending progression by cycles, somewhat higher than the point from which it had before descended.

> VI. Too many of our thinkers do not consider that the numerous changes in language, the allegorical phrases and evident secretiveness of old Mystic writers, who were generally under an obligation never to divulge the solemn secrets of the sanctuary, might have sadly misled translators and commentators. One day they may learn to know better, and so become aware that the method of extreme necessarianism was practiced in ancient as well as in modern philosophy; that *from the first ages of man, the fundamental truths of all that we are permitted to know on earth were in the safe keeping of the adepts of the sanctuary; that the difference in creeds and religious practice was only external; and that those guardians of the primitive divine revelation, who had solved every problem that is within the grasp of human intellect, were bound together by a universal freemasonry of science and philosophy, which formed one unbroken chain around the globe.*

The first chapter of Volume 1, from which we have extracted the several statements which we have here numbered for their better massing and comprehension, closes with a forecast, drawn from the study of the past:

> The moment is more opportune than ever for the review of old philosophies. Archaeologists, philologists, astronomers, chemists and physicists are getting nearer to the point where they will be forced to consider them. Physical sci-

ence has already reached its limits of exploration; dogmatic theology sees the springs of its inspiration dry. Unless we mistake the signs, the day is approaching when the world will receive the proofs that only ancient religions were in harmony with nature, and ancient science embraced all that can be known. Who knows the possibilities of the future? An era of disenchantment and rebuilding will soon begin—nay, has already begun. *The cycle has almost run its course; a new one is about to begin,* and the future pages of history may contain full evidence, and convey full proof that

> "If ancestry can be in aught believed,
> Descending spirits have conversed with man,
> And told him secrets of the world unknown."

If we turn now to the twelfth and last chapter of Volume 2 of "Isis," we shall be confronted with an introductory paragraph, also prophetic at the time of its writing, now all too truly a matter of both theosophical and profane history. She there says:

> It would argue small discernment on our part were we to suppose that we have been followed thus far through this work by any but metaphysicians, or mystics of some sort. Were it otherwise, we should certainly advise such to spare themselves the trouble of reading this chapter; for, although nothing is said that is not strictly true, they would not fail to regard the least wonderful of the narratives as absolutely false, however substantiated.

The chapter follows with a recapitulation of the principles of natural law, covered by the fundamental propositions of the Oriental philosophy as successively elucidated in the course of the work. She states them in numbered order as follows:

I. There is no miracle. Everything that happens is the result of law—eternal, immutable, ever-active. This "immutable law" is frequently referred to throughout the volumes under such terms as cycles, the "law of compensation," Karma, "self-made destiny," and so on. Its mode of operation is incessantly discussed in treating of the rise and fall of civilizations, successive races of men, earth transformations, the three-fold principle of evolution, Spiritual, Mental, and Physical; the compound nature of man and the universe; and in such terminology as pre-existence, metempsychosis, transmigration, reincarnation, evolution, transformation, permutation, emanation, immortality, and after-death states and conditions. Constant effort is made to keep before the reader the unvarying principle that spiritual and mental evolution proceeds apace with physical manifestations, and stands to physical evolution in the relation of cause to effect. This is all summarized in the second proposition.

II. Nature is triune: there is a visible, objective Nature; an invisible, indwelling, energizing Nature, the exact model of the other, and its vital principle; and, above these two, *spirit*, source of all forces, alone eternal and indestructible. The lower two constantly change; the higher third does not. This universal postulate is then applied specifically to human nature and evolution in the third proposition.

III. Man is also triune: he has his objective, physical body, his vitalizing astral body (or soul), the real man; and these two are brooded over and illuminated by the third—the sovereign, the immortal spirit. When the real man succeeds in merging himself with the latter, he becomes an immortal entity. The argument throughout the two large volumes of "Isis" is always that such mergence or union is possible and is the underlying purpose of all evolution; that such beings as Jesus, Buddha and others had in fact arrived at this consummation, and that the real mission of the Founders of all religions is to point mankind to the purpose of Mental and Spiritual evolution, and give the directions and conditions precedent to the "perfectibility of man." Such exalted beings are by H. P. Blavatsky variously called the sages, the Adepts, the Great Souls of all time. Their knowledge of Nature and of Nature's laws is called in its entirety the Wisdom-Religion, and its practical exemplification is summarized in the fourth proposition.

IV. and V. Magic, as a science, is the knowledge of these principles, and of the way by which the omniscience and omnipotence of the spirit and its control over Nature's forces may be acquired by the individual while still in the body. Magic, as an art, is the application of this knowledge in practice. Granting that great powers exist in Nature, and that the conscious control over these powers may be attained by the incarnated being through metaphysical means, it follows that such control may be exercised beneficently or maleficently. Arcane knowledge misapplied is sorcery, or "Black Magic"; beneficently used, true Magic or WISDOM. In either case it constitutes Adeptship, whether of the *Right-* or the *Left-hand* Path. This is the fifth proposition, and the text of the two volumes contains almost numberless direct and indirect references to celebrated characters in history, tradition and myth who exemplified the two characters of Adeptship.

VI. This proposition sets forth that Mediumship is the opposite of Adeptship. Whereas the Adept actively controls himself and all inferior potencies, the Medium is the passive instrument of foreign influences. There is no more important practical theorem in the whole work. Many, many pages are devoted to discussion of the characteristics, tendencies, practices and fruits of mediumship. Its phenomena, objective and subjective, are dealt with at length. Spiritualism, or mediumship, is shown to have been prevalent in all ages, no matter under what names known, and its recurrence, whether in individual cases or amongst masses of men, is shown to be subject to cyclic law, now more generally known to Theosophical students under its Sanskrit designation of Karma. In Mediumship, as in Adeptship, it is shown that there are two polar antitheses, dependent on the moral character of the medium for the quality and range no less than the effects, good or bad, of its exercise.

The remaining numbered propositions of the last chapter of Volume 2 will be considered in other connections later on,[1] but their essential nature and implications are contained in the following sentences, without the basic apprehension of which no inquiry into Theosophy and the Theosophical Movement can be fruitful of understanding, however it may afford information:

> To sum up all in a few words, MAGIC is spiritual WISDOM; nature, the material ally, pupil and servant of the magician. *One common vital principle pervades all things, and this is controllable by the perfected human will.* The adept can stimulate the movements of the natural forces in plants and animals in a preternatural degree. Such experiments are not obstructions of nature, but quickenings; the conditions of intenser vital action are given.
>
> The adept can control the sensations and alter the conditions of the physical and astral bodies of other persons not adepts; he can also govern and employ, as he chooses, the spirits of the elements. *He cannot control the immortal spirit of any human being, living or dead, for all such spirits are alike sparks of the Divine Essence, and not subject to any foreign domination.*

The restrictions with which the information conveyed in "Isis" is hedged about, both from the standpoint of the teacher endeavoring to impart and the inquirer endeavoring to learn, and the dangers, known or unknown to the latter, are indicated towards the close of the chapter:

[1] See Chapter XXXIII.

By those who have followed us thus far, it will naturally be asked, to what practical issue this book tends; much has been said about magic and its potentiality, much of the immense antiquity of its practice. Do we wish to affirm that the occult sciences ought to be studied and practiced throughout the world? Would we replace modern spiritualism with the ancient magic? Neither; the substitution could not be made, nor the study universally prosecuted, without incurring the risk of enormous public dangers.

We would have neither scientists, theologians nor spiritualists turn practical magicians, but all to realize that there was true science, profound religion, and genuine phenomena before this modern era. We would that all who have a voice in the education of the masses should first know and then *teach* that the safest guides to human happiness and enlightenment are those writings which have descended to us from the remotest antiquity; and that nobler spiritual aspirations and a higher average morality prevail in the countries where the people have taken their precepts as the rule of their lives. We would have all to realize that magical, *i.e.*, spiritual powers exist in every man, and those few to practice them who feel called to teach, and are ready to pay the price of discipline and self-conquest which their development exacts.

Many men have arisen who had glimpses of the truth, and fancied they had it all. Such have failed to achieve the good they might have done and sought to do, because vanity has made them thrust their personality into such undue prominence as to interpose it between their believers and the *whole* truth that lay behind. The world needs no sectarian church, whether of Buddha, Jesus, Mahomet, Swedenborg, Calvin, or any other. There being but ONE Truth, man requires but one church—the Temple of God within

> us, walled in by matter but penetrable by any one who can find the way; *the pure in heart see God. The trinity of nature is the lock of magic; the trinity of man the key that fits it.* Within the solemn precincts of the sanctuary the SUPREME had and has no name. It is unthinkable and unpronounceable; and yet every man finds in himself his god.
>
> Besides, there are many good reasons why the study of magic, except in its broad philosophy, is nearly impracticable in Europe and America. Magic being what it is, the most difficult of all sciences to learn experimentally—its acquisition is, practically, beyond the reach of the majority of white-skinned people; and that, whether their effort is made at home or in the East. Probably not more than one man in a million of European blood is fitted—either physically, morally, or psychologically—to become a practical magician, and not one in ten millions would be found endowed with all these three qualifications as required for the work. Unlike other sciences, a theoretical knowledge of formulae without mental capacities or soul powers, is utterly useless in magic. The spirit must hold in complete subjection the combativeness of what is loosely termed educated reason, until facts have vanquished cold human sophistry.

The concluding pages of "Isis" recite that those best prepared to appreciate Occultism are the Spiritualists, although, through prejudice, they have hitherto been the bitterest opponents to its introduction to public notice. She sums up thus:

> Despite all foolish negations and denunciations their phenomena are real. Despite, also, their own assertions they are wholly misunderstood by themselves. The totally insufficient theory of the constant agency of disembodied hu-

> man spirits in their production has been the bane of the *Cause*. A thousand mortifying rebuffs have failed to open their reason or intuition to the truth. Ignoring the teachings of the past, they have discovered no substitute. We offer them philosophical deduction instead of unverifiable hypothesis, scientific analysis and demonstration instead of undiscriminating faith. Occult philosophy gives them the means of meeting the reasonable requirements of science, and frees them from the humiliating necessity to accept the oracular teachings of "intelligences," which as a rule have less intelligence than a child at school. So based and so strengthened, modern phenomena would be in a position to command the attention and enforce the respect of those who carry with them public opinion. Without invoking such help, spiritualism must continue to vegetate, equally repulsed—not without cause—both by scientists and theologians. In its modern aspect it is neither a science, a religion, nor a philosophy.

With this outline of the teaching of Occultism as contained in "Isis Unveiled"; its overwhelming arraignment out of the mouths of their own exponents, of the religion, science and philosophy of the day; its outspoken treatment of dogmatic Christianity, of materialistic hypotheses, of the phenomena and theories of Spiritualism, the student can begin to comprehend the enormous difficulties faced by H.P.B. in gaining a foothold for the Theosophical Society and a hearing for her teachings of Theosophy. Her task was not that of a teacher in a kindergarten: to meet and lead plastic and unsullied minds eager with interest, unburdened with preconceptions, into new and delightful paths of occupation and learning. Far from it. Rather it was that of the alienist in a mad world, its unsane inhabitants soaked through and through with their several illusions, each profoundly certain of the truth of his own particular mania, profoundly convinced of the hallucination of all others; each looking at the phenomena of life through the distorted lenses of fundamental misconceptions. Regardless of names and forms, she had to reckon with the fact, from the standpoint of the teachings of Occultism, that everywhere, the men of the Western world were fast fixed in false beliefs, taking that to be the Eternal which is not eternal; that to be Soul which is not soul; that to be Pure which is impure; that to be Good which is evil. She had to destroy while seeming to create, to create while seeming to destroy.

Looking back from the present basis of tolerated if not accepted ideas, it is only by the contrast that the supreme miracle of her wisdom can be even faintly sensed. The *identity* of man with the Supreme Spirit; the doctrine of Cycles, the law of Compensation; Spiritual and Intellectual as well as physical evolution; *inherent* immortality, metempsychosis; the Spiritual Brotherhood of all beings, Adepts as the culmination of the triple evolutionary scheme in Nature; Spirit and Matter as the eternal dual presentment of evolving Consciousness, the polar aspects of the One Essence—all these great and supreme ideas she and none other restored to a vital place in human thought. The *words* existed—mummified forms from the by-gone Past, wrapped in the thousand cerements of the sects. As in the Talmudic legend, she breathed upon the clay, breathed into it the breath of life. Or, better, as in the story of Joseph, she made the dead come forth from the tomb, clothed in the habiliments in which the living dead had buried him against a far-off impossible resurrection.

Much has been written by Theosophists—those who owe their all to her and her work—that the H.P.B. of 1875 was not the H.P.B. of later days; that she, like themselves, was but a student, stumbling, halting, groping, finding her way through failures and mistakes; that it was only in later years that she came to learn of this, of that, of reincarnation among other matters; that many contradictions will be found in "Isis" when compared with her final teachings.

The inquirer into facts and philosophies has but to read "Isis," to annotate its teachings, to compare them with all her subsequent multifarious writings to see and know for himself that the teachings of "Isis" are her unchanging teachings; that not in jot or in tittle is there a contradiction or a disagreement in all she ever wrote; that in "Isis" are the foundational statements of Occultism. All her later writings are but extensions, ramifications, the orderly development and unfolding of what is both explicit and implicit in "Isis Unveiled." Study and comparison will do more: it will give the student a solid and impregnable standard from which to survey the real nature and character of the Avatar of the nineteenth century; a criterion by which, as well, truly to measure the understanding, the nature and the development of those disciples, students and followers of H.P.B. of whom she might well have repeated in the words of Blake on "certain friends":

> I found them blind; I taught them how to see;
> And now they neither know themselves nor me.

The facts being ascertained, and some faint perception of their significance being grasped, the student needs no interpreter to tell him that obstacles, opposition, misunderstanding, contumely, hatred and misrepresentation were unavoidable concomitants of every step in the progress of the Theosophical Society, no less than in the path of her whose mission it was to be its "presiding deity." The chief of these difficulties have now to be considered.

CHAPTER IV

EARLY DAYS OF THE THEOSOPHICAL SOCIETY

At first glance the Objects of the Theosophical Society might be assumed to be in themselves so manifestly beneficial and, negatively speaking, so entirely harmless as at once to commend them to the good-will if not to the active support of all men everywhere. To draw this conclusion, however, is unfortunately to be blind to the lessons of human history; is to be ignorant of the forces which dominate the operations of human consciousness. Selfishness, in one or another of its countless forms, is and at all times has been the prevailing keynote of human action. Many have been the attempts to form enduring associations having for their prime object the realization of an actual nucleus of universal brotherhood among men. To unite firmly a body of men in brotherly love bent on pure altruistic work has been the dream of many high-souled men and women. Whatever of progress and amelioration has been achieved for the race from time to time has been due to such efforts. But in their durable purpose they have all failed of the great object, and humanity is today waiting as vainly as ever for the accomplishment of the most holy and most important mission that has ever commanded the devotion of the savior, the philanthropist and the martyr. Disruptive pressures from without, disintegrating forces from within, have in the end made mock and havoc of every attempt to embody practically what all men reverence as the noblest of ideals. Yet the ideal persists, though its successive incarnations wither and decay.

It cannot, then, be supposed that H. P. Blavatsky was in ignorance or misconception of the gigantic task she set for herself in the endeavor to create among men a Society which should have for its primary purpose the formation of a nucleus of actual Brotherhood. Nor is it to be imagined that she was indifferent to or unacquainted with the causes of all former failures in that direction. The Second and Third Objects of the Society have their real foundation in her understanding of the causes of all failures among men to achieve their heart's ideal. So long as men find occasion for frictions and antagonisms, rather than grounds for union and harmony, in what they believe and practice in the name of religion, so long will they be fundamentally at variance. So long as their ideas of knowledge—of true science—are confined to mere bodily existence, so long will all attempts at brotherhood degenerate into sordid search for material well-being, for physical and intellectual progress and development only. Faith and knowledge, instead of being natural allies, will pursue opposed courses, religion and science take mutually destructive paths, the ideal and the practical seem to be separated by an impassable gulf.

All these things are clearly, if succinctly, indicated in the Preface to the first volume of "Isis Unveiled." Never in all her vast outpour of teaching and practical example did Madame Blavatsky place on record anything of more enduring and far-reaching worth than the propositions and implications of this Preface. After dedicating "these volumes to the Theosophical Society, which was formed in New York, A. D. 1875, to study the subjects on which they treat," her first words are an affirmation of the existence of Masters, of the Wisdom-Religion, of her own intimate acquaintance with Them and with Their philosophy:

> The work now submitted to public judgment is the fruit of a somewhat intimate acquaintance with Eastern adepts and study of their science.

Here is implied the existence of an actual Brotherhood of living men, of perfected human beings who have become such through self-induced and self-devised exertions; herein is affirmed the perfectibility of man, the possibility of a fraternity of peace and good-will through the means and the example afforded by acquaintance with and study of these Adepts and their science. Centuries of sectarian theological teachings that man is a poor miserable sinner, inherently imperfect and never by any possibility to become perfect save through an act of faith in a vicarious Saviour; centuries of materialism in thought and action on a one-life basis—over against these deeply imbedded and dominating ideas is set, sheer and clear, the *fact of Masters;* not as some far-off, remote abstraction, some longed-for but impossible ideal, some unique and special creation of a favoring God, but veritable Divine Beings who have reached physical and mental, no less than moral and spiritual, perfection *under Law.* Here is the tremendous assurance that the realization of Brotherhood is not an impossibility to any man who will follow the path They show, by creating in and of himself the conditions precedent to the acquisition of Their knowledge and nature.

What those conditions precedent are is indicated in the succeeding sentences:

> It is offered to such as are willing to accept truth wherever it may be found, and to defend it, even looking popular prejudice straight in the face. It is an attempt to aid the student to detect the vital principles which underlie the philosophical systems of old.

All men are willing to accept truth, but each is predisposed to determine for himself the terms and conditions upon which he will base his acceptance. Each man holds, consciously or unconsciously to himself, certain fundamental ideas as to Deity, Nature and Man. He will, by consequence, accept only so much of truth as may conform to those ideas, modifying or rejecting all else. As those fundamental conceptions proceed from human ignorance and partialities, the true vital principles which *underlie* the race-old systems of thought must be detected. That cannot be for any man so long as he clings to forms of religion and philosophy which separate instead of unite mankind in the bonds of true fraternity. The Second Object, the study for comparative purposes of the various religions and philosophies, will lead to the perception of the common vital principles upon which all faiths are founded. In this comparative study the searcher for truth must emulate the plan and purpose of "Isis," which is written "in all sincerity. It is meant to do even justice, and to speak the truth alike without malice or prejudice. But it shows neither mercy for enthroned error, nor reverence for usurped authority. Toward no form of worship, no religious faith, no scientific hypothesis has its criticism been directed in any other spirit. Men and parties, sects and schools are but the mere ephemera of the world's day. TRUTH, high-seated upon its rock of adamant, is alone eternal and supreme." Unless the inquirer adopts and maintains the spirit of "Isis," he cannot rid himself of prejudice, of preconception, of bias and self-interest—the real barriers to knowledge and to Brotherhood.

The Third Object runs current with the following clauses of the noble Preface:

> We believe in no Magic which transcends the scope and capacity of the human mind, nor in "miracle," whether divine or diabolical, if such imply a transgression of the laws of nature instituted from all eternity. Nevertheless, we accept the saying of the gifted author of "Festus," that the human heart has not yet fully uttered itself, and that we have never attained or even understood the extent of its powers. Is it too much to believe that man should be developing new sensibilities and a closer relation with nature? The logic of evolution must teach as much, if carried to its legitimate conclusions. If, somewhere, in the line of ascent from vegetable or ascidian to the noblest man a soul was evolved, gifted with intellectual qualities, it cannot be unreasonable to believe and infer that a faculty of perception is also growing in man, enabling

> him to descry facts and truths even beyond our ordinary ken.

He who would pass behind the "veil of Isis," and learn to fathom the mysteries of Nature and of Man, must boldly take his stand in advance of the science of our times and proceed to the study of the unexplained laws of Nature and the psychical powers latent in man. The quoted sentences postulate the omnipresent existence of immutable Law; do away with the idea of miraculous intervention in human or mundane affairs; affirm the inherent capacity of the mind of man for such development of its faculties as shall enable him to penetrate the arcana of being; to understand, and understanding, control the phenomena of Nature and of his own consciousness, without which true Brotherhood must forever remain a longed-for but inaccessible Utopia.

The Second and Third Objects thus constitute the ways and means by which alone the great First Object may be consummated. Viewed from the standpoint of religions which teach that enduring happiness is possible only beyond the grave, or from that of a science which inculcates that earthly existence and earthly knowledge are all that are accessible to man, all the Objects of the Theosophical Society are alike futile, because impossible of attainment. Considered from the basis of the ordinary man those Objects are equally useless or unsatisfactory, because they all imply and require the giving up of objects and possessions counted valuable; at best in exchange for something remote and intangible, yielding no personal or selfish benefit; at worst the loss of what one holds dear without any return but failure.

Here, then, the Preface predicates the true and enduring foundation for the seeker's faith and efforts. The philosophy of the Adepts is given:

> They showed us that by combining science with religion, the existence of God and immortality of man's spirit may be demonstrated like a problem of Euclid. For the first time we re-

> ceived the assurance that the Oriental philosophy has room for no other faith than an absolute and immovable faith in the omnipotence of man's own immortal self. We were taught that this omnipotence comes from the kinship of man's spirit with the Universal Soul—God! The latter, they said, can never be demonstrated but by the former. Man-spirit proves God-spirit, as the one drop of water proves a source from whence it must have come. *Ex nihilo nihil fit;* prove the soul of man by its wondrous powers—you have proved God!

Every attempt to establish a religion on the fundamental conception that man is inherently fallible and sinful, every attempt to understand Nature on the theory that man is inherently mortal and finite, must end in failure. But once the stand is taken that there is an *immortal self* in man, its limitless potentialities for knowledge and power (true religion and true science) follow; the Three Objects of H. P. Blavatsky seem no longer a vain attempt at hitching of the earthly wagon to the firmamental lights; a nucleus of Universal Brotherhood becomes the one thing to be striven for, because seen to be eternally possible and eternally desirable; the immortal is substituted for the mortal as basis and as structure, as object and as subject.

The fact of Adepts grasped, the fact of the Wisdom-Religion recognized, he only is in any real sense a Fellow of the real Theosophical Society who sets out to perform the work of clearance standing in the way of his own realization of both. By the study of the Wisdom-Religion of these Elder Brothers says H.P.B., "science, theology, every human hypothesis and conception born of imperfect knowledge, lost forever their authoritative character" in her sight. The same result must take place in the student, else the Second and Third Objects of the Society have been misconstrued in their purpose, will fail of their mission with him, and the First Object be as far off as ever from realization by him. Unless this position is assumed it will remain hidden from him, as she says it always has been hidden, "from those who overlooked it, derided it, or denied its existence." Encouragement is offered to prosecute the search and the effort, and the explanation made of her mission at this time in the words, "the day of domineering over men with dogmas has reached its gloaming. The drift of modern thought is palpably in the direction of liberalism in religion as well as in science. Each day brings the reactionists nearer to the point where they must surrender the despotic authority over the public conscience, which they have so long exercised and enjoyed."

Nevertheless, she well realized that all the forces of reaction, within as well as without the Society, would fight to the death against the hearing and the spread of the ideas she came to impart. So she says, prophetic at the time, facts of history now:

> To show that we do not at all conceal from ourselves the gravity of our undertaking, we may say in advance that it would not be strange if the following classes should array themselves against us:
>
> The Christians, who will see that we question the evidences of the genuineness of their faith.
>
> The scientists, who will find their pretensions placed in the same bundle with those of the Roman Catholic Church for infallibility, and, in certain particulars, the sages and philosophers of the ancient world classed higher than they.
>
> Pseudo-scientists will, of course, denounce us furiously.
>
> Broad Churchmen and Freethinkers will find that we do not accept what they do, but demand recognition of the whole truth.
>
> Men of letters and various *authorities,* who hide their real belief in deference to popular prejudices.
>
> The mercenaries and parasites of the Press,

who prostitute its more than royal power, and dishonor a noble profession, will find it easy to mock at things too wonderful for them to understand; for to them the price of a paragraph is more than the value of sincerity. From many will come honest criticism; from many—cant. But we look to the future. We repeat again—we are laboring for the brighter morrow.

Once a clear apprehension is gained of what is actually implied in the Three Objects of the Theosophical Society, and of what is involved in the attempt to apply them, the student will have no difficulty in determining how absolutely dependent the Society was for its life and sustenance on the teachings imparted by H. P. Blavatsky, if it were not to fail utterly as a vehicle of Brotherhood, whatever other success it might incidentally achieve. The same understanding will make plain that external and internal difficulties were inseparable from its every effort toward even a measurable and partial realization of those objects.

The effect upon the Spiritualists has already been foreshadowed in a general way. Convinced as they were of the reality of metaphysical phenomena; multitudinous, conflicting and oftentimes grotesque as were the theories formulated or accepted to account for them, the "forces of reaction," that is to say, of pre-conception and bias, had already ascribed all these phenomena to the agency of "disembodied human spirits." When, then, philosophical principles and logical deductions, as well as the uninterrupted line of teaching of all the sages of the past, were applied to the manifestations, and it was pointed out that they could not proceed from the rational moral elements of once-living men, the Spiritualists almost without exception rose in arms. They were all "looking for truth," but not in that direction.

One may soberly ask himself, after a careful study of "Isis Unveiled": What is there in that work but the conscientious, painstaking and stupendous presentation of facts, principles, arguments and analogies to explain consistently and irrefutably the source and rationale of the phenomena called Spiritualistic? What is there to arouse the opposition, the anger, the malevolence of anyone, let alone one seeking truth "wherever it may be found" in regard to mysterious and ill-explained happenings—happenings so recently brought to the attention of mankind in the mass that the three parts of that mankind reject as absurd and incredible the events themselves? Here is a metaphysical phenomenon worthy of the utmost consideration: the rejection of evidence and testimony from verifiable living sources in favor of the blind acceptance of unverifiable theories, speculations and "communications" at variance with the whole order of Nature and the whole history of human experience. Madame Blavatsky was assailed and pursued by Spiritualists with a persistency of misrepresentation equaled only by that of the religionists and pseudo-scientists of the day. Surely, if they had approached the séance room and the medium in the same spirit that H.P.B.'s communications were received, they would, according to their own unvarying experience, have received nothing at all; yet what she had to say, when contrasted with the best that has ever been recorded from any "spirit," was a thousand times more logical, more consistent, more philosophical, more explanatory and more easily verifiable.

In the earlier years of the Society in the West the bulk of the opposition to its teachings came from the Spiritualists. The teachings of H.P.B. were as yet so alien to rooted inherited ideas in religion and science that her Society attracted but little attention except among the Spiritualists and hence the weight of the opposition came from the same quarter.

In India, where the conditions were altogether different, the obstacles arose from another source. There, in spite of the rigid sects and castes, the religious faith and philosophy of the people (apart from the Mohammedan element of the population), was deeply akin to the message the Founders had to bring. For they but brought back to their source the ancient teachings, stripped of their outward, human garments, the accretions of the millenniums of interpreters and priests. What they had to say appealed alike to Brahmin, Buddhist, Jain and Parsi, once the barriers of creedal exclusiveness were passed. In the earlier and precarious days the alliance hitherto formed by correspondence with the Swami, Dayanand Saraswati, and his Arya Samaj, was of the utmost assistance in this respect. A visit was made to Ceylon and there the Buddhist high priest, Sumangala, a noble and enlightened man, received H.P.B. as a fellow devotee of the great founder of the Buddhist faith. He admitted Col. Olcott to membership in the Buddhist congregation and was at pains to favor their mission. A couple of years later Col. Olcott's "Buddhist Catechism" aided in producing a veritable revival of Buddhism and gained for him and his Society the enduring friendship, not only of enlightened Buddhists, but of the other faiths of the ancient East. Almost immediately after their arrival Col. Olcott began lecturing throughout India, and his clear expositions, his great tact, his intuitive understanding of and sympathy with the Oriental mind made the establishment of branches phenomenally successful.

Damodar K. Mavalankar, a native Brahmin youth of high caste, met H.P.B. and recognizing in her his *Guru,* forsook family, fortune and all worldly prospects to become her devoted follower, pupil and servant. *The Theosophist* was founded by H.P.B. within less than a year after the arrival in India. Contributions were invited and obtained from Hindu writers of ability and repute on the various subjects afforded by Eastern philosophy and religion, and these, with H.P.B.'s own articles, soon made of the magazine a forum which attracted attention far and wide. Shortly after the establishment of *The Theosophist,* H.P.B. made the acquaintance of T. Subba Row, an orthodox Brahmin, a lawyer, a man of ability, immense erudition and great influence. His friendship and attachment to the Society paved the way for many accessions. His contributions to the pages of *The Theosophist* were models of literary and philosophic excellence.

These activities quickly drew the notice and aroused

the ire of the missionaries of the various Christian sects established in India. Almost immediately rumors began to circulate that H.P.B. and Col. Olcott were disreputable characters, practically forced into exile from their own land. A sinister purpose was alleged to be behind their Society, and that purpose the overthrow of British rule in India. H.P.B. was said to be an immoral woman, a Russian spy, and Col. Olcott her dupe and her abettor. Nothing could have been better calculated to prejudice their mission, and nothing could have been more difficult to counteract and disprove. The Government set a watch upon their every movement and for months the spies of the secret service dogged their every step. In the end, however, nothing of an objectionable nature was discovered, and Col. Olcott was able to submit to the central authorities indubitable documentary proof of the antecedent good character and repute of himself and his colleague. Fortunately, also, within the first year, the Founders met Mr. A. P. Sinnett, editor of the Allahabad *Pioneer,* a strong pro-Government organ, and Mr. Allan O. Hume, late Secretary to the Government. Both of these gentlemen had been interested in spiritualistic manifestations, and learning something of the nature of H.P.B. and the scope of her teachings, became members of the Society and active in its behalf. They busied themselves in removing all misconceptions as to the nature and purpose of the Theosophical Society, the authorities became friendly, and the reaction speedily brought the Society to the favorable attention of many well-known English residents.

Other stories were circulated that H.P.B. and Col. Olcott were "godless," atheists as well as "infidels," and their purpose equally to destroy the Hindu religions as well as the Christian and make of India a land of materialism. The pages of *The Theosophist* as well as its "Supplements" during the earlier years show how unbrokenly and in what varied fashion the opposition to the Society and its teachings continued. One device was the importation of the Rev. Joseph Cook, then a widely known American clergyman and lecturer, who came to India ostensibly on a tour, but whose lectures were almost uniformly devoted to such misrepresentations of Theosophy, the Society and its Founders as would have done honor to a hired mercenary. He was repeatedly challenged to meet the Theosophists in debate, but always avoided any such direct issue. Finally, he was publicly denounced in a signed card published by a British army officer, and thereafter speedily departed the country. A similar stratagem was employed in the case of the Rev. Moncure D. Conway, who, while in India, visited the headquarters and was cordially received there by H.P.B. He afterwards published articles in leading magazines of America and England in disparagement of Theosophy and the work of the Society and declared that H.P.B. had admitted to him in his interview with her that her phenomena were all "glamour," hence fraudulent. Once or twice, in unguarded moments, the assailants of the Theosophists laid themselves open to proceedings which enforced public retractions, but in general the assaults were too cunningly made to permit of redress or rebuttal. So much for the general course of antagonism to the Society's progress.

The first serious ripple within the Society occurred when Dr. George Wyld, President of the London Lodge, resigned his Fellowship and became extremely antagonistic. Dr. Wyld was a well-known and highly educated man, a Christian and a Spiritualist. When he came to learn that the teachings of H.P.B. were opposed to the theories of "spirit communion," and to all ideas savoring of a "personal God," he attacked her, her "Masters" and her Theosophy with equal violence.

Dr. Anna Bonus Kingsford then became President of the British Society. Though she remained friendly to H.P.B. and sympathetic toward the general Objects of the Theosophical Society throughout her life, Dr. Kingsford had very pronounced ideas of her own. These are embodied in her work, "The Perfect Way, or the Finding of Christ," originally delivered as a series of lectures before a private audience during the summer of 1881, and published in book form in 1882. A "psychic" and strongly colored with Christian mysticism, it appeared to Mrs. Kingsford that the Society was devoting too much attention to purely oriental teachings, which she considered to be more or less anti-Christian and tainted with a materialistic bias. Together with Mr. E. Maitland (associated then as thereafter with her in her teachings), Dr. Kingsford issued in 1883 a pamphlet "Letter to the Fellows of the London Lodge," containing a severe arraignment of some of the statements embodied in Mr. Sinnett's "Esoteric Buddhism." A good deal of more or less acrimonious discussion followed and finally, very early in 1884, T. Subba Row published, with the approval of Madame Blavatsky, a pamphlet for private circulation among the Fellows. This pamphlet contained some "Observations" on the various questions raised and in it Subba Row discussed the general teachings outlined in "Esoteric Buddhism." He defended the book as a whole, while admitting the justice of some of the criticisms, which he explained by reciting Mr. Sinnett's unfamiliarity with the Occult tenets, and by correcting some of Mr. Sinnett's erroneous deductions and expositions. To Subba Row's pamphlet in turn Mr. C. C. Massey gave attention in a seventy-page booklet bearing the title, "The Metaphysical Basis of Esoteric Buddhism." Mr. Massey's booklet was on the whole an ably argued support of the position taken by Dr. Kingsford, and, in addition, embodied some criticisms and complaints on his own account of Madame Blavatsky's policy. He charged her with teaching, first one thing and then another on the same subject, and of countenancing opposing views propounded by her pupils and followers. In due sequence, also, Mrs. Kingsford and Mr. Maitland returned to the fray and published a "Reply" to Subba Row, reiterating and further fortifying their earlier criticisms and objections.

Mr. Massey's charges against H.P.B. really originated from an article in *The Theosophist*. As early as June, 1882, she had published certain questions addressed to her by "Caledonian Theosophist" on the apparent lack of consistency and uniformity in some of the statements in "Isis Unveiled" as compared with later articles in *The Theosophist* supposedly emanating from the same source. To these queries, published under the title of "Seeming Discrepancies," H.P.B. had replied in an Editorial Note, closing her explanation with the words: "But there never was, nor can there be, any radical discrepancy between the teachings in 'Isis' and those of this later period, as both proceed from one and the same source—the ADEPT BROTHERS." In the English Spiritualist publication *Light*, for July 8, 1882, "C. C. M." (C. C. Massey) took up "seeming discrepancies" and more or less directly charged H.P.B. with equivocation in her reply to "Caledonian Theosophist." He instanced that in "Isis" the subject of Reincarnation was treated in a manner not reconcilable with her later writings on the same topic. To this challenge H.P.B. replied in *The Theosophist* for August, 1882, denying any contradictions in teachings, but stating that much in "Isis" was preliminary only, therefore incomplete, but not in actual conflict with anything subsequently given out. Various other articles appeared thereafter in *Light*, in *The Theosophist*, and in other publications in English and in French on this mooted subject of the Theosophical doctrines on "reincarnation." Arguments, speculations, charges and counter-claims were adduced by different writers, but H.P.B. held her peace. Not until 1886 did she break silence on the much discussed passages in "Isis," Volume 1, pp. 346-51 *et circa*. This will be considered in its proper sequence.[1]

Another fruitful occasion for external attack and internal disturbance arose out of the publication of Mr. Sinnett's book, "The Occult World." This work contains extracts from letters of the Master "K. H." to Mr. Sinnett and an unnamed friend who was, in fact, Mr. A. O. Hume. In one of these letters the Master took occasion to refer to Spiritualistic ideas and theories. In 1883 Mr. Henry Kiddle, highly reputable and well-known American lecturer on Spiritualism, published in *Light* a communication in which he claimed and proved that Mr.

[1] See Chapter IX.

Sinnett's published extract was in large part made up of unacknowledged quotations from an address of Mr. Kiddle's delivered in the summer of 1880 (a year prior to the publication of "The Occult World") before a Spiritualist camp meeting at Mount Pleasant, New York. He published in "deadly parallel" the germane portions of his address as printed at the time in several papers, and the quotations from the Master's letter in "The Occult World." Mr. Kiddle's letter was, of course, very widely copied in Spiritualist publications and the secular press, and numerous Spiritualists and other commentators made merry over the discomfiture of the Theosophists. The vaunted "Adepts," it seemed, were not above stooping to "borrow" without credit from ordinary human exponents of doctrines these "Masters" professed to consider erroneous and false. In many quarters the episode was quite sincerely believed to be not only proof of plagiarism, but a complete exposure of H.P.B. and her pretended Adepts. The existence of Masters and of a Wisdom-Religion was derided; they were ascribed to the inventive imagination of Madame Blavatsky by some and by others called as much a plagiarism from the ideas of Eliphas Lévi as the "Master's letter" was a plagiarism from Mr. Kiddle. The trust of the Theosophists in the good faith of H.P.B., in the source of her teachings, and in her teachings, was considered to rest upon a basis more unsubstantial and more discreditable than the belief of the Spiritualists in their mediums, "guides" and "controls." Madame Blavatsky's phenomenal powers were either laughed at as mere humbugging devices or ascribed to the same character as mediumship. The defenders of the orthodox sects and the disbelievers in psychical manifestations of any kind made haste to avail themselves of the ammunition provided by Mr. Kiddle's "revelation," and used it with equal zeal to discredit both the Theosophists and the Spiritualists. Much feeling grew up out of the "Kiddle incident" and much of whatever amicable relations existed between the various Spiritualist and Theosophical exponents was dissipated by it. In the Theosophical Society, and among those friendly to it, a good deal of doubt sprang up, on the theory that where there was so much smoke there must be some fire. H.P.B. remained silent as the proverbial sphinx, but in time several cautiously worded articles appeared in *The Theosophist* and in other friendly publications, from Subba Row and others, defending the *bona fides* of Mr. Sinnett, of the Masters, and testifying from personal physical as well as psychical relations with them to the actual existence of Adepts as living and perfected men, with phenomenal powers over space, time and matter. Subba Row's article, in particular, contained some guarded statements on the subject of the precipitation of Occult letters. He also referred to the manifest discrepancies in the extracts published in "The Occult World," as indicating that in the process of "precipitation" some mistakes of omission or of commission had occurred. This article also was widely commented on, and the explanations hinted at were accepted of course by Theosophists with relief, a few others with reserve, but for the most part by antagonists with sarcastic comments on the *ex post facto* nature of the explanations. Finally, in 1884, in the fourth edition of "The Occult World," Mr. Sinnett added an Appendix containing the Master's own reply to his letter of inquiry on the subject. The explanation given was received by many as not only wholly satisfactory in itself, but as containing some most valuable hints on Occult processes; by others as merely a further effort on the part of the Theosophists to extricate themselves from an embarrassing situation. As the "Kiddle incident" the matter has long since been forgotten or has never been heard of by present-day students, but it has an important bearing on the "Coulomb case," on the "Report" of the Society for Psychical Research, on the charges made a decade later against Mr. Judge, and on the whole subject of the phenomena of "precipitation," and the so-called "Occult letters." We shall treat the matter more fully at a later period of the Theosophical Movement.[2]

The troubles over the Kiddle matter, the charges of

[2] See Chapters XXVI and XXX.

contradictory teachings on the subject of "reincarnation," the disputes existing in the London Lodge as a result of the broadsides of pamphlets on the materialistic trend of "Esoteric Buddhism," all occurred contemporaneously and were added to by sharp dissensions among the French Fellows. Practically all the members of the Society in France were Spiritualists, and believers in "reincarnation" and other subjects as developed by Allan Kardec. As the Theosophical teachings were at variance, both in theory and practice, with the Kardec philosophy, the zeal of the proponents of the respective views threatened to disrupt the Paris Lodge as well as the British. These and other reasons impelled H.P.B. and Col. Olcott to make a visit to Europe. They accordingly sailed from India early in 1884. The Paris difficulties were first adjusted and a new impetus given both to the Society and the Movement. It was while at Paris on this occasion that V. V. Solovyoff sought and made the acquaintance of H.P.B., became a Fellow of the Society and, for the time being, an assiduous worker and student. Mr. Judge had come over from America to meet the Founders. He spent some time with H.P.B. in France and then went on to India, returning to America *via* London, where he met Col. Olcott again, late in the year. After their Paris stay H.P.B. and Col. Olcott proceeded to London. Much time and effort were given to straightening out the difficulties in the London and Paris Lodges, to meeting the Fellows of the Society, and in receptions to inquirers. An immense interest was excited by the presence in England of H.P.B., and it was at this time—the summer of 1884—that the Society for Psychical Research began its investigations of the Theosophical phenomena. To this we must now turn our attention.

CHAPTER V

THE S.P.R. AND THE THEOSOPHICAL PHENOMENA

The first serious modern attempt to investigate metaphysical phenomena in a quasi-scientific spirit was that made by the London Dialectical Society. At a meeting of the Council of that Society in January, 1869, a Committee was appointed "to investigate the Phenomena alleged to be Spiritual Manifestations, and to report thereon."

The Committee, composed of thirty-four well-known persons, passed nearly eighteen months in its investigations. It held fifteen sittings of the full Committee, received testimony from thirty-three persons who described phenomena occurring within their own personal experience, and procured written statements from thirty-one others. The Committee also appointed from its membership six subcommittees who undertook first-hand investigations by experiments and tests. The Committee sent out letters inviting the attendance, co-operation, and advice of scientific men who had expressed opinions, favorable or adverse, on the genuineness of Spiritualistic phenomena.

On July 20, 1870, the full Committee rendered its unanimous Report to the Council, with request for publication of the Report under the approval of the Society. The Council received and filed the Report, discharged its Committee with a vote of thanks, but declined to accede to the request for publication of the Report. In consequence the Committee unanimously resolved to publish its Report on its own responsibility. Two editions of the Report were printed to supply the demand for copies, and at the time caused a very great discussion.

The Report is drawn with great conservatism. The

statement of facts ascertained and conclusions reached by the Committee is, condensed, as follows:

The Committee specially invited the attendance of persons who had publicly ascribed the phenomena to imposture or delusion. On this the Report says:

> Your Committee, while successful in procuring the evidence of believers in the phenomena and in their supernatural origin, almost wholly failed to obtain evidence from those who attributed them to fraud or delusion. A large majority of the members of your Committee have become actual witnesses to several phases of the phenomena without the aid or presence of any professional medium, although the greater part of them commenced their investigations in an avowedly sceptical spirit.

The Committee recites that the reports of the several subcommittees "substantially corroborate each other." The Report concludes:

> Your Committee, taking into consideration the high character and great intelligence of many of the witnesses to the more extraordinary facts, the extent to which their testimony is supported by the reports of the subcommittees, and the absence of any proof of imposture or delusion as regards a large portion of the phenomena, the large number of persons in every grade of society and over the whole civilized world who are more or less influenced by a belief in their supernatural origin, and the fact that no philosophical explanation of them has yet been arrived at, deem it incumbent upon them to state their conviction that the subject is worthy of more serious attention and careful investigation than it has hitherto received.

It has been fifty years since the above Report was issued. In that period unnumbered thousands have repeated the investigations of "the phenomena alleged to be spiritual manifestations," great numbers of books have been issued, arguments and theories pro and con have been multiplied, but no advance whatever in actual knowledge has been gained. It remains today, as it remained then, that *"no philosophical explanation of them has been arrived at"* outside the propositions advanced by H. P. Blavatsky in "Isis Unveiled."

Viewing the moderation, the accuracy and the dispassionateness of the Committee's report of facts ascertained and conclusions reached, it should be of interest to the student of human nature in the light of the teachings of Theosophy, to observe the reception accorded the Report of the Committee by the moulders of public opinion in press and science. The London *Times* called the Report "a farrago of impotent conclusions, garnished by a mass of the most monstrous rubbish it has ever been our misfortune to sit in judgment upon." The *Pall Mall Gazette* declared, "It is difficult to speak or think with anything else than contemptuous pain of proceedings such as are described in this report." The London *Standard* commented, with unconscious verisimilitude, as follows: "If there is anything whatever in it beyond imposture and imbecility, there is the whole of another world in it." The *Morning Post* swept the whole matter aside in one contemptuous sentence: "The Report which has been published is entirely worthless." The *Saturday Review* pronounced the subject "one of the most unequivocally degrading superstitions that have ever found currency among reasonable beings." The reviewer of the *Sporting Times* made these dispassionate remarks: "If I had my way, a few of the leading professional spiritualists should be sent as rogues and vagabonds to the treadmill for a few weeks. It would do them good. They are a canting, deceiving, mischievous lot. Some of their dupes are contemptibly stupid—insane, I should say." Professor Huxley, who had spoken slightingly of the manifestations, wrote, in reply to the Committee's invitation to participate: "It would be little short of madness for me to undertake an investigation of so delicate and difficult a character, the only certain result of which would be an interminable series of attacks from the side from which I might chance to differ. I hope that I am perfectly open to conviction on this or any other subject; but I must frankly confess to you that it does not interest me." Professor Tyndall's attitude is indicated by this quotation from his "Fragments of Science": "The world will have a religion of some kind, even though it should fly for it to the intellectual whoredom of Spiritualism."

While the Dialectical Society Committee was engaged in its investigation, Prof. William Crookes, later to become the most notable scientist of his generation but then just beginning to attract the attention of the Fellows of the Royal Society, had determined on his own account to study the phenomena privately. His bold and unqualified statements of the results achieved, his cautious discussion of the many theories to account for the phenomena he witnessed, were first printed in the numbers of the *Quarterly Journal of Science* for 1870-2, and published in book form in 1874, with the title, "Researches into the Phenomena of Spiritualism." His researches were undertaken in a truly scientific spirit, in the public interest, and his results described with a sincerity, a courage and candor that in any other field would have received, as they merited, the highest commendation. But upon his head, as in the case of Darwin, was heaped every abuse, and against his scientific repute every calumny was spread, that could be devised by the reactionists of religion and science.

In 1875 was published "The Unseen Universe," an attempt primarily to reconcile the Darwinian theory with the tenet of a "revealed religion," and containing a discussion of ancient religions, Spiritualism, and immortality in relation to the phenomena of the visible universe. In less than a year the work passed through four editions. Numerous other books and continuous discussion in the press throughout the period from 1870-80 marked the steady increase of interest in metaphysical phenomena, and betokened the growing unrest of the generation. The formation of the Theosophical Society and its rapid progress was like a Gulf stream in the vast ocean of public discussion. The teachings embodied in "Isis Unveiled" and *The Theosophist* and put in popular form in "The Occult World" and "Esoteric Buddhism" might be likened to the sudden upheaval of a new land in the midst of that ocean, offering its compelling attraction to adventurous explorers.

It was in such circumstances that the Society for Psychical Research was established early in 1882 by a number of well-known persons, among them Prof. F. W. H. Myers, Mr. W. Stainton Moses (M.A. Oxon), and Mr. C. C. Massey, all members of the London Lodge of the Theosophical Society. The preliminary announcement of the new Society declared that "the present is an opportune time for making an organized and systematic attempt to investigate that large group of debatable phenomena designated by such terms as mesmeric, psychical, and Spiritualistic." Committees were to be appointed to investigate and report upon such subjects as telepathy, hypnotism, trance, clairvoyance, sensitives, apparitions, etc. The announcement stated that "the aim of the Society will be to approach these various problems without prejudice or prepossession of any kind, and in the same spirit of exact and unimpassioned inquiry which has enabled science to solve so many problems, once not less obscure nor less hotly debated."

With such a broad and just prospectus and such an inviting field for its efforts, the new Society almost immediately attracted to its Fellowship some hundreds of men and women of reputation and ability in their several fields. By 1884 the Society had made numerous investigations, had begun the publication of the voluminous reports of its *Proceedings,* and was firmly established in the public confidence as a serious scientific body engaged in the methodical and unbiased investigation of the disputed phenomena.

Meantime Mr. Sinnett had removed to London, his published books had been read by thousands, he had been elected Vice-President of the London Lodge, and was the center and inspiration of eager investigations and experiments in the line of the Third Object of the Theosophical Society. Rumors and circumstantial stories were afloat regarding "astral appearances," "Occult letters" and other phenomena connected with the mysterious "Brothers" supposed to be the invisible directors behind the Theosophical activities. When Col. Olcott arrived in London early in the summer of 1884, followed a little later by H.P.B., interest rose to a genuine excitement. This excitement, coupled with the fact that a number of members of the Society for Psychical Research were also Fellows of the Theosophical Society, made it natural and plausible for the S.P.R. to turn its attention to the new and inviting possibilities at hand. Accordingly, on May 2, 1884, the Council of the S.P.R. appointed a "Committee for the purpose of taking such evidence as to the alleged phenomena connected with the Theosophical Society as might be offered by members of that body at the time in England, or as could be collected elsewhere." Out of this beginning grew the famous "exposure" that for a time threatened the ruin of the Theosophical Society.

The S.P.R. Committee as originally constituted consisted of Profs. E. Gurney, F. W. H. Myers, F. Podmore, and J. H. Stack. To these were subsequently added Prof. H. Sidgwick, Mrs. Sidgwick, and Mr. Richard Hodgson, a young University graduate.

The Committee held meetings on May 11 and 27 at which Col. Olcott was present and replied to numerous questions, narrating the details of various phenomena of which he had been witness during the years of his connection with H.P.B. Mohini M. Chatterji, a young Hindu who had accompanied the Founders from India, was questioned on June 10. On June 13 Mr. Sinnett repeated to the Committee his observations on the phenomena described in his "Occult World." During the summer the meetings of the Cambridge Branch of the S.P.R. were attended on several occasions, by invitation, by Col. Olcott, Chatterji, and Madame Blavatsky. On these occasions, says the preliminary Report, "the visitors permitted themselves to be questioned on many topics." Additional evidences were obtained by the Committee from many sources, testifying to a wide range and variety of phenomena through the preceding ten years, in America and Europe as well as in India. All the witnesses were persons of repute and some of them well known in England and on the Continent. In the autumn of 1884 the Committee published "for private and confidential use" the "first report of the Committee." This Report, now very rare, is a pamphlet of 130 pages. The first thirty-three pages are devoted to the formal recital of the basis and nature of the investigations made, the Committee's comments on the various questions raised, the conclusions tentatively arrived at, and two notes, one relating to the Coulombs and the other, by Prof. Myers, giving a brief digest of the Theosophical views and explanations of the phenomena enquired into. The remaining ninety-seven pages consist of XLII Appendices, giving the substance of the evidence obtained from the many witnesses.

The phenomena investigated by the Committee were chiefly (1) "astral appearances" of living men; (2) the transportation by "Occult" means of physical substances; (3) the "precipitation" of letters and other messages; (4) "Occult" sounds and voices. The appendices contain the details of numerous occurrences of the kinds indicated, the sources of the testimony and the names of the scores of witnesses, with comments of the Committee on the character and validity of the testimony as to its sufficiency and bearing, and not upon the good faith of the witnesses themselves, all of whom are regarded as reputable. In the earlier portion of the Report the Committee says that in considering evidences of abnormal occurrences it "has altogether declined to accept the evidence of a paid medium as to any abnormal event." It goes on to say, "in dealing with these matters, it is admitted that special stringency is necessary, and one obvious precaution lies in the exclusion of all the commoner and baser motives to fraud or exaggeration." But with regard to the Theosophical exponents it says, "we may say at once that no trustworthy evidence supporting such a view has been brought to our notice."

Although the witnesses expressly state that the Theosophical phenomena are not of the kind familiarly known as mediumistic, and although Madame Blavatsky expressly declined to produce any phenomena for the consideration of the Committee as her purpose was to promulgate certain doctrines, not to prove her possession of Occult powers, the Committee's basis of treatment of the phenomena, and its theories to account for them, were the familiar ones employed in Spiritualistic investigations. Nevertheless, the Committee recognized that there were three points calling for the greatest care on its part. The first of these is "that it is certain that fraud has been practiced by persons connected with the Society." This refers to the charges brought by the Coulombs, who were members of the Theosophical Society, against Madame Blavatsky; to the "Kiddle incident," and to certain "evidence privately brought before us by Mr. C. C. Massey." On this matter the Committee says that it suggests, "to the Western mind at any rate, that no amount of caution can be excessive in dealing with evidence of this kind."

The second point raised by the Committee is that "Theosophy appeals to Occult persons and methods." Accustomed to dealing with mediums and mediumistic manifestations, where the moral and philosophical factors have no bearing, accustomed to believe that where there is reticence there must be fraud, the Committee does not like the idea made plain at all times by H.P.B. that the subject of Occult phenomena, their production and laws, will not be submitted to scientific exploitation, but will only be made known to those who qualify themselves under the strictest pledges of secrecy and discipleship.

Finally, the Committee recognizes that

> Theosophy makes claims which, though avowedly based on occult science, do, in fact,

ultimately cover much more than a merely scientific field.

This, also, is not agreeable to the Committee, which remarks:

> The history of religions would have been written in vain if we still fancied that a Judas or a Joe Smith was the only kind of apostle who needed watching. . . . Suspicions of this kind are necessarily somewhat vague; but it is not our place to give them definiteness. What we have to point out is that it is our duty, as investigators, in examining the evidence for Theosophic marvels, to suppose the possibility of a deliberate combination to deceive on the part of certain Theosophists. We cannot regard this possibility as excluded by the fact that we find no reason to attribute to any of the persons whose evidence we have to consider, any vulgar or sordid motive for such combination.

These frank expressions of the Committee are illuminating as to its own basis and motives, and equally illuminating when contrasted with the fair promises made in the preliminary announcement of the formation of the S.P.R. They become still more clear when viewed in the light of the Preface to "Isis Unveiled," with its statement in advance of the kind of opposition its author would be called upon to face.

In spite of its suspicions, its doubts, its fears, its mental reservations occasioned by its own ignorance of the laws governing metaphysical phenomena; by the absolute refusal of H.P.B. to disclose the processes of practical Occultism; by the atmosphere of mystery surrounding the whole subject of the hidden "Brothers" and their powers; by the charges of fraud laid by the Coulombs at the door of H.P.B.; by the undisclosed "evidence privately brought before us by Mr. C. C. Massey"—in spite of all these disturbing equations, the testimony amassed by the Committee was so absolutely overwhelming as to the *fact* of the alleged phenomena that the Committee found itself compelled to make certain admissions, as follows:

> It is obvious that if we could account for all the phenomena described by the mere assumption of clever conjuring on the part of Madame Blavatsky and the Coulombs, assisted by any number of Hindu servants, we could hardly, under present circumstances, regard ourselves as having adequate ground for further inquiry. But this assumption would by no means meet the case. The statements of the Coulombs implicate no one in the alleged fraud except Madame Blavatsky. The other Theosophists, according to them, are all dupes. Now the evidence given in the Appendix in our opinion renders it impossible to avoid one or other of two alternative conclusions: Either that some of the phenomena recorded are genuine, or that other persons of good standing in society, and with characters to lose, have taken part in deliberate imposture.

Accordingly, the Committee expressed the following conclusions:

> On the whole, however (though with some serious reserves), it seems undeniable that there is a *prima facie* case, for some part at least of the claim made, which, at the point which the investigations of the Society of Psychical Research have now reached, cannot, with consistency, be ignored.

The Committee decided to send one of its members to India to investigate the charges made by the Coulombs, to interview the numerous witnesses to phenomena testified to by Hindus and Europeans in India, and report on the results of such examination. Mr. Richard Hodgson was the member chosen. His report is the foundation and superstructure of the celebrated "exposure" embodied in Volume 3 of the Proceedings of the Society for Psychical Research. Before considering Mr. Hodgson's report, it is necessary to review the antecedent and surrounding circumstances and events, the main features of which are wrapped up in the connection of the Coulombs with the Theosophical Society.

In the year 1871, Madame Blavatsky was voyaging on a vessel which was wrecked by an explosion. Along with other passengers she was landed in Egypt, destitute of money or belongings. She made her way to Cairo and there met Madame Coulomb, an English woman then unmarried and conducting a lodging house. Madame Coulomb was moved by the misfortunes and distress of the wanderer, received her into her house, supplied her necessities and advanced her funds until H.P.B. could communicate with her family.

Madame Coulomb was mediumistic, intensely interested in Spiritualism, and the more so because she had but recently lost a brother with whom she was anxious to "communicate." Finding that H.P.B. possessed a fund of lore and experience in matters Occult, Madame Coulomb besought her to aid in procuring the longed-for communications, as, from her experience, they could not consciously be obtained except through another. Finding that others in Cairo were also interested in the mysterious phenomena with which all the Western world was then dabbling in one way and another, H.P.B. took advantage of the opportunity, and endeavored to form a Society for investigation and experiment. It speedily developed that curiosity and the thirst for phenomena, not the desire for philosophy and understanding, were at the bottom of all the would-be investigators' zeal, and H.P.B. dropped the matter. The Society went to pieces as soon as she did so. H.P.B. was in Egypt in all nearly a year, returning to Russia in 1872. From there, in the spring of 1873, she went to Paris, and thence to New York, returning to India early in 1879.

Madame Coulomb married in Egypt. After a succession of misfortunes the Coulombs went to India, and then to Ceylon. Their misfortunes pursued them and they were living in direst penury when they heard of the arrival of H.P.B. and Col. Olcott in India and the interest attendant upon their activities. Madame Coulomb at once wrote to H.P.B., recalling the Cairo acquaintance, detailing her circumstances and asking for help. To this letter H.P.B. replied with expressions of sympathy, but stating that she herself was in little better plight personally than the Coulombs, and describing her mission and purposes in India. Madame Coulomb wrote again avowing the interest of herself and husband in the Society, and pleading for help. To this appeal H.P.B. answered that if the Coulombs so desired they could come to headquarters and share such fortunes as might befall the Founders. Accordingly, the Coulombs made their way to India, arriving early in 1880. They took the pledges of membership and entered the Theosophical Society. During the ensuing four years Madame Coulomb acted as housekeeper, and, as she was acquainted both with French and Italian, and the labors were great and the workers few, she assisted in translations and in foreign correspondence. M. Coulomb was made general utility man around the premises. He acted as gardener, as carpenter, as librarian, and also assisted in some of the correspondence. The Coulombs were made entirely free of the premises and the work at headquarters. At first they professed the utmost gratitude for the succors given them, and the liveliest interest and sympathy in the work of the Society. As affairs progressed, they became acquainted with numerous visitors and inquirers, European and Hindu, at headquarters. Dissatisfied and discontented with the comparatively insignificant and menial rôle played by themselves, they felt that they were not receiving their just dues. Greedy, weak by nature, and anxious to become financially independent, it appeared to them that Madame Blavatsky was receiving an attention and prominence to which she was no more entitled than themselves. In addition, the Coulombs were

Christians of the narrowest kind, superstitious to a degree, and in fact wholly out of sympathy and accord with the aims and teachings of the Founders.

Within a couple of years Madame Coulomb tried to extort or beg money from wealthy persons interested in the Society, notably from the native prince, Harrisinji Rupsinji. This coming to the knowledge of H.P.B., she reproved Madame Coulomb sternly. To others of the visitors and residents at headquarters Madame Coulomb whispered tales of her own powers and of her ability to find "hidden treasures." To others she intimated that Madame Blavatsky's powers were from the "evil one." The Coulombs were more or less constantly in communication with the establishments of the missionaries near by, and Madame Coulomb, in particular, was in constant frictions and disputes over religious matters and opinions with resident chelas and members of the Society. Col. Olcott took her to task for these needless difficulties on several occasions. In general, however, the Coulombs were looked upon as harmless meddlers, their misfortunes caused them to be viewed with charity, and the known gratitude of H.P.B. for help received from Madame Coulomb at a time of need reconciled the Theosophists to the annoyances and disturbances occasioned by their presence and officiousness at headquarters.

Just prior to the departure of H.P.B. and Col. Olcott for Europe in February, 1884, a Council was appointed to take charge of affairs at headquarters during the absence of the Founders. Among the Council were Dr. Franz Hartmann, Mr. St. George Lane-Fox, and Mr. W. T. Brown, with whom, particularly Dr. Hartmann and Mr. Lane-Fox, the Coulombs had been in almost constant wrangles. These desired to dispense with the Coulombs altogether, but on the prayers of Madame Coulomb H.P.B. permitted them to remain as hitherto, and, in order to remove sources of disagreement as much as possible, gave the Coulombs "authority" to do the housework, to have charge of the upkeep of the premises, and to keep her own rooms in order.

The Founders away, fresh fuel for the fires of discord was soon heaped on the ashes of discontent. The Coulombs refused to accept any orders or obey any instructions from the resident members of the Council; they refused all access to H.P.B.'s apartments and declared that H.P.B. had placed them in independent control of her quarters and the conduct of the household. On the other hand, the members of the Council living at headquarters, having no liking for the Coulombs and distrusting them utterly were more or less harsh and contemptuous towards them, communicating with them only by letter, and refusing to eat with them, or to eat the food provided by Madame Coulomb. They charged Madame Coulomb with extravagance, waste, and with personally profiting out of her handling of the domestic funds, and set about auditing and checking her daily expenditures. Vain, sensitive, and without doubt smarting under their grievances, real and imaginary, the Coulombs planned revenge in dual fashion. They wrote to H.P.B., reciting their wrongs, asserting their own loyalty and innocence of any wrong-doing, and making sundry charges against the Council members. At the same time the Council members were also writing the Founders their side of the disputes, and telling circumstantially the actions of the Coulombs and the insinuations being whispered about by them against the good faith of the Theosophists and H.P.B. While this war of charges and recriminations was going on by mail, the Coulombs were busy fortifying themselves for their ultimate treachery by constructing false doors and sliding panels in the so-called ' Occult room" in H.P.B.'s apartments so as to give such an appearance of mechanical contrivance as might support charges of fraud in the phenomena taking place at headquarters. To our mind, after weighing well all the circumstances of this unhappy period, there is no room for doubt that the Coulombs were already in active conspiracy with the missionaries and were carefully following able but sinister instructions in their course of conduct. By temporizing with the resident members of the Council, by their written denials and protestations to H.P.B. and Col. Olcott, they were gaining the time needed to perfect the *mise en scène* for their subsequent accusations.

Both H.P.B. and Col. Olcott wrote the Coulombs and the Council, endeavoring to patch up the rancors and bitternesses engendered, and appealing to all for the sake of the Society and its work, to exercise mutual forbearance and tolerance. But the evil forces at work were too favored of circumstance. The Council members at last forced their way to the quarters of H.P.B., discovered what had been going on there, talked severally with the Coulombs, and summoned them before the meeting of the Council to answer charges of bad faith, of treachery, of false stories about H.P.B. and the phenomena at headquarters. The Coulombs neither affirmed nor denied the statements made in the several affidavits read concerning their behavior, and declining to produce any evidence to support their allegations, were expelled from the Society and ordered to leave the premises. Legal proceedings were then threatened to eject them, and in the wrangling St. George Lane-Fox struck M. Coulomb, who had him arrested and fined for assault and battery. The Coulombs offered, during the disputes and negotiations, to leave the country and go to America if paid 3,000 rupees and given their passage. This was refused. Finally, on the direct approval of H.P.B., to whom both the Coulombs and the Council members had appealed, and after the Coulombs had threatened to her that if she did not support them in their contentions they would expose her, the Coulombs were compelled to leave the premises. This took place at the end of May, 1884.

The Coulombs went at once to the missionaries by whom they were received with open arms. They were given money and their living was provided them. In the ensuing three months the plans of battle were perfected for the assault which it was hoped would once and for all destroy the reputation of H.P.B., and in the ruin of her good repute, ruin the Theosophical Society. In the September and succeeding issues of the *Christian College Magazine* were published with extended comments a series of letters purporting to have been written by H.P.B. to Madame Coulomb which, if genuine, showed H.P.B. to have been a conscienceless and heartless swindler, her phenomena plain frauds, her Society a collection of dupes, her Masters a mere invention, her teachings a myth of the imagination.

The facts, so far as publicly disclosed, may be found as represented by the various interests involved, in the *Christian College Magazine* articles entitled "The Collapse of Koot Hoomi"; in Madame Coulomb's pamphlet issued at the time in India and republished in London by Elliott Stock "for the proprietors of the Madras *Christian College Magazine,*" under the title "Some Account of My Intercourse with Madame Blavatsky from 1872 to 1884, by Madame Coulomb"; in Dr. Franz Hartmann's pamphlet, "Observations During a Nine Months' Stay at the Headquarters of the Theosophical Society, Madras, India," published in the fall of 1884; in the "Report of the Result of an Investigation into the Charges against Madame Blavatsky," by the Committee of the Indian Convention; in the Report of the Indian Convention of the Theosophists held at the close of December, 1884; in Mr. Sinnett's book, "Incidents in the Life of H. P. Blavatsky"; in Col. Olcott's "Old Diary Leaves," and in numerous articles pro and con at the time and during succeeding years in many Theosophical, Spiritualist, Christian, and secular publications. The facts as herein given are those derived from the immense accumulation of literature on the subject, after the most careful and painstaking comparison and weighing.

We may now consider the effect of the Coulomb disclosures and the missionary use of them, both on the Theosophists and on the Society for Psychical Research.

CHAPTER VI

THE REPORT OF THE S.P.R.

The Preliminary Report of the Committee of the Society for Psychical Research was drawn up in the midst of the excitement occasioned by the Coulomb accusations and the missionary attacks in the *Christian College Magazine* of Madras, India.

Immediately the charges were cabled to England Madame Blavatsky took steps to protect the good name of the Theosophical Society. On September 27, 1884, she handed to Col. Olcott as President her resignation as Corresponding Secretary, but under pressure from leading members of the Society in England Col. Olcott refused to accept her withdrawal. At the same time H.P.B. addressed a letter to the London *Times* which was published in that paper in its issue of October 9. The letter follows:

> Sir,—With reference to the alleged exposure at Madras of a dishonourable conspiracy between myself and two persons of the name of Coulomb to deceive the public with occult phenomena, I have to say that the letters purporting to have been written by me are certainly not mine. Sentences here and there I recognise, taken from old notes of mine on different matters, but they are mingled with interpolations that entirely pervert their meaning. With these exceptions the whole of the letters are a fabrication.
>
> The fabricators must have been grossly ignorant of Indian affairs, since they make me speak of a "Maharajah of Lahore," when every

Indian schoolboy knows that no such person exists.

With regard to the suggestion that I attempted to promote the "financial prosperity" of the Theosophical Society by means of occult phenomena, I say that I have never at any time received, or attempted to obtain, from any person any money either for myself or for the Society by any such means. I defy anyone to come forward and prove the contrary. Such money as I have received has been earned by literary work of my own, and these earnings, and what remained of my inherited property when I went to India, have been devoted to the Theosophical Society. I am a poorer woman to-day than I was when, with others, I founded the Society. —Your obedient Servant,

H. P. BLAVATSKY.

On October 23, the *Pall Mall Gazette* published a long interview with H.P.B. in which her denial of the authorship of the letters attributed to her by the Coulombs is reiterated, the facts of the Coulombs' bad faith given and attention called to the further fact that two letters attributed by the Coulombs to Gen. Morgan and Mr. Sassoon had already been conclusively proved to be forgeries.

On the opposing side the attack was pressed with vigor and all possible capital made of the Coulomb accusations, with, of course, a renewal of every old and exploded charge against H.P.B., her teachings, and her Society. The Christian sects, the Spiritualist publications, the space writers in the daily press to whom any sensation was so much material for "copy," regardless of the merits of the case, all joined in the fray.

Immediate preparations were made by the Founders to return to India. Colonel Olcott arrived at headquarters in November. H.P.B. stopped off in Egypt to obtain information in regard to the Coulombs and did not reach India till December. On her arrival she was met and presented with an Address signed by some three hundred of the native students of the Christian College, expressing gratitude for what she had done for India, and disclaiming any part or sympathy in the attacks of the *Christian College Magazine*.

The Convention of the Society in India met at headquarters near the end of December. From the first H.P.B. had insisted that the Coulombs and the proprietors of the *Christian College Magazine* must be met in Court by legal proceedings for libel. The future of the Society, the *bona fides* of her teachings, she declared were wrapped up in the assaults made upon her own reputation, and if her good name were destroyed both the Society and Theosophy would suffer irreparable injury. For herself, she avowed, she cared nothing personally, but the fierce onset was in reality directed against her work, and that work could not be separated in the public mind from herself as its leading exponent. To destroy the one was to inflict disaster on the other.

Colonel Olcott was between Scylla and Charybdis, both in himself and in relation to the Society to which he was wholly devoted. His close and long personal friendship and spiritualistic relations with Mr. W. Stainton Moses and Mr. C. C. Massey, both of whom believed that H.P.B. had been the agency both for genuine and spurious phenomena, undoubtedly affected him powerfully. His relations with Mr. Sinnett were concordant in Theosophical views, and he knew that Mr. Sinnett had similar ideas to his own regarding the nature of H.P.B. On his return to India he found that Mr. A. O. Hume, formerly a responsible Government official and, next to Mr. Sinnett, the most influential friend of the Society in India, had become infected with doubts and suspicions and believed that, while some of H.P.B.'s phenomena were undoubtedly genuine, others had been produced by collusion with the Coulombs. Colonel Olcott speedily found, also, that the more prominent Hindu members of the Society, while willing to speak politely in favor of H.P.B., were a unit in opposition to legal proceedings in which religious convictions and subjects sacred to them would be dragged in the mire of merciless treatment by the defendants' attorneys in an alien Court. On every hand he was urged to consider that psychical powers and principles could be proved only by actual production of phenomena in Court—a thing forbidden alike by their religious training and the rules of Occultism. Others argued that a judgment, even if obtained, would be valueless before the world, since the mischief was already done; those who believed the phenomena fraudulent would still think so, judgment or no judgment; those who believed them genuine would continue to hold that view if the matter were allowed to drop; while an adverse judgment would forever brand H.P.B. and destroy the Society beyond any hope of resuscitation.

But H.P.B. stood firm for legal prosecution of the defamers, declaring her faith in Masters and her own innocence; that They would not countenance disloyalty and ingratitude, and that, if worst came to worst, it were better for the Theosophists to be destroyed fighting for what they held to be true than to live on by an inglorious and ignominious evasion of the issues raised. Torn by his fears and doubts, Col. Olcott took what was doubtless to him the only possible road. He proposed a compromise which was in effect a betrayal; he demanded that H.P.B. place the matter in the hands of the Convention and abide by its decision; threatening, if this were not done, that he himself and the others with him would abandon the Society and leave it to its fate. H.P.B. acceded to the demand made. Accordingly, at the Convention a Committee was appointed, and this Committee unanimously reported as follows:

> Resolved—That the letters published in the *Christian College Magazine* under the heading "Collapse of Koot Hoomi" are only a pretext to injure the cause of Theosophy; and as these letters necessarily appear absurd to those who are acquainted with our philosophy and facts, and as those who are not acquainted with those facts could not have their opinion changed, even by a

> judicial verdict given in favour of Madame Blavatsky, therefore it is the unanimous opinion of this Committee that Madame Blavatsky should not prosecute her defamers in a Court of Law.

The report of the Committee was unanimously adopted by the Convention. This action was received by the Indian press and that wedded to sectarian interests with prolonged jeers and contumely leveled against H.P.B., her followers and her Society. By the great majority of public journals and intelligent minds it was considered to be the tacit admission by Theosophists that the Coulomb charges were true.

The blow was well-nigh mortal to the body of H.P.B. Defenseless and undefended, her life was despaired of by her physician. During the succeeding three months she was rarely able to leave her bed. Finally, toward the end of March, yielding to the solicitations of the few who still remained devotedly loyal to her, she prepared to leave India and go to Europe. On the 21st of March she addressed a formal letter to the General Council, once more tendering her resignation as Corresponding Secretary, and closing her communication with these words:

> I leave with you, one and all, and to every one of my friends and sympathizers, my loving farewell. Should this be my last word, I would implore you all, as you have regard for the welfare of mankind and your own Karma, to be true to the Society and not to permit it to be overthrown by the enemy. Fraternally and ever yours—in life or death.
>
> H. P. Blavatsky.

Her resignation was accepted by the Council with fulsome compliments, even as the cowardly action of the Convention and its Committee had been accompanied with brave words.

Mr. Richard Hodgson, chosen by the Society for Psychical Research to continue in India the investigations begun in England, arrived at headquarters in December, passed three months in pursuing his inquiries and returned to England in April, 1885. He was, therefore, present in India during all the typhoons of fierce attack and all the period of wavering defense. He witnessed the bold confidence of the accusers and observed the timid, the cautious, the doubting and fearing attitude and actions of Col. Olcott and other leading Theosophists. Had there been no other influence at work upon his mind, these alone, we think, would have been more than ample to persuade him that Theosophy, the Theosophical Society, the "Adept Brothers" and their teachings were, with the phenomena of H.P.B., nothing but a vast fraud devised and perpetrated for some secret purpose.

Mr. Hodgson's report of his investigations was submitted to the Committee of the S.P.R., by them endorsed, and at the General Meeting of the Society on June 24, 1885, Prof. Sidgwick of the Committee read its Conclusions. Certain difficulties developing, the ensuing six months were spent by Mr. Hodgson in revising and re-vamping his report. In the interval it became common knowledge that the report of the Committee and the S.P.R. would be entirely adverse to the Theosophical phenomena. As in the Coulomb case, the machinery of assault was prepared in secrecy and silence. No opportunity was given the Theosophists to inspect Mr. Hodgson's report, no chance offered for correction, criticism, objection, or counter-statement, while during all the long interval the most injurious damage was being inflicted through the public knowledge of what the findings would be, and while the Theosophists could only await the production of charges of whose essential nature they knew nothing and to which, therefore, no reply was possible.

The Conclusions of the Committee and the full text of Mr. Hodgson's report were finally embodied in the *Proceedings* of the S.P.R., Volume 3, pp. 201-400, issued in December, 1885.

The essential conclusions of the Committee are embodied in the following extracts:

> After carefully weighing all the evidence before them, the Committee unanimously arrived at the following conclusions:
>
> (1) That of the letters put forward by Madame Coulomb, all those, at least, which the Committee have had the opportunity of themselves examining, and of submitting to the judgment of experts, are undoubtedly written by Madame Blavatsky; and suffice to prove that she has been engaged in a long-continued combination with other persons to produce by ordinary means a series of apparent marvels for the support of the Theosophic movement.
>
> (2) That, in particular, the Shrine at Adyar, through which letters, purporting to come from Mahatmas were received, was elaborately arranged with a view to the secret insertion of letters and other objects through a sliding panel at the back, and regularly used for this purpose by Madame Blavatsky or her agents.
>
> (3) That there is in consequence a very strong general presumption that all the marvelous narratives put forward as evidence of the existence and occult power of the Mahatmas are to be explained as due either (a) to deliberate deception carried out by or at the instigation of Madame Blavatsky, or (b) to spontaneous illusion, or hallucination, or unconscious misrepresentation or invention on the part of the witnesses.
>
> (4) That after examining Mr. Hodgson's report of the results of his personal inquiries, they are of the opinion that the testimony to these marvels is in no case sufficient, taking amount and character together, to resist the force of the general presumption above mentioned.

> Accordingly, they think it would be a waste of time to prolong the investigation.

With reference to Madame Blavatsky herself, the Committee say:

> For our own part, we regard her neither as the mouthpiece of hidden seers, nor as a mere vulgar adventuress; we think that she has achieved a title to permanent remembrance as one of the most accomplished, ingenious, and interesting impostors in history.

The preliminary and final reports of the Committee should be taken together. The former is to be found only in private collections and a few large libraries, but the *Proceedings* of the Society for Psychical Research, Volume 3, may be consulted in nearly every library of any consequence in England and America. Every student of Theosophical history ought to read, digest and collate this report for himself. Such a careful and first-hand examination and comparison will prove to him as nothing else can the monstrous injustice and infamy of the S.P.R. investigation and report.

Miscarriages of justice are frequent even in controversies involving only ordinary physical events, and where surrounded and safeguarded by all the jurisprudence, principles and practice embodying the accumulated experience of the race in the determination of moot and disputed issues. How much greater, then, the risk of mistaken or false judgment in cases not so protected, and where the issues to be decided not only do not lie within the general experience of the race, but by most men are believed to be impossible and therefore incredible; where the very facts themselves to be investigated, as well as the laws and principles by virtue of which alone their possibility can be assumed, lie outside the knowledge or experience of the investigators themselves; and where it is recognized that the admission or establishment of these laws, principles, and phenomena will work a revolution in every department of human thought and action. Bearing these considerations and the concomitant circumstances in mind the real facts and the real issues may be understood from a study of the reports of the Society for Psychical Research alone.

In the first place, the investigation was entirely *ex parte*. The Committee laid out its own course of procedure, determined its own basis, admitted what it chose, rejected what it chose, reported what it chose of the evidence—subject to no supervision, no correction, no safeguards to insure impartiality, or afford redress if bias were exercised. Of its own motion and decision it constituted itself court, judge, and jury; at its pleasure it finally took upon itself the rôle of prosecutor without allowing or permitting to those it thus constituted defendants to its proceedings any right of cross-examination or rebuttal. That which began ostensibly as a mere inquiry into the evidences available concerning the Theosophical phenomena degenerated into a criminal prosecution, in which a verdict of "guilty" was pronounced upon H. P. Blavatsky—without a hearing, without appeal, without recourse for the victim. Had the Committee been a duly and legally constituted Court, its procedure would have been without a parallel in English history save in the "bloody assizes" of the infamous Jeffreys.

But in fact the Committee was that of a rival society whose objects, methods, and purposes were diametrically opposed to the objects and principles proclaimed by H. P. Blavatsky and the Theosophical Society for ten years preceding the investigation. The Society for Psychical Research was interested in phenomena solely and only as phenomena; was moved by mere scientific curiosity. It specifically disclaimed any interest in philosophical research, any concern in Occult laws, any regard for the moral factor, in its equations. The Theosophical Society and H.P.B., on the contrary, specifically avowed the primary Object of its existence was the moral factor of Universal Brotherhood, its second Object the serious study and comparison of religions and philosophies, and its third object the investigation of *laws* and *powers* as yet unexplained and misunderstood; not phenomena at all, save as these might be incidental and illustrative.

These differences were recognized by the Committee. The preliminary report says:

> The difference between The Theosophical Society and the Society for Psychical Research is . . . almost diametrical. The Society for Psychical Research exists merely as a machinery for investigation. . . . The Theosophical Society exists mainly to promulgate certain doctrines already formulated, those doctrines being supported by phenomena which are avowedly intended and adapted rather for the influencing of individual minds than for the wholesale instruction of the scientific world.

What the Committee's attitude was in regard to the *moral factor,* and its attitude toward the "certain doctrines already formulated" for the promulgation of which the Theosophical Society "mainly exists" are shown by its own reports. In the preliminary report the statement is made, "The Theosophical Society was founded . . . for certain philanthropic and literary purposes, with which we are not now concerned." In the final report the statement is made: "The Theosophical Society was founded *ostensibly* for certain philanthropic and literary purposes . . . with these doctrines (or so-called 'Wisdom-Religion') the Committee have, of course, no concern."

It should be understood in connection with the use of the word "ostensibly" above, that not a shred of evidence is introduced or claimed to be introduced that the Theosophical Society ever had any other objects than its proclaimed ones.

The Committee took enough note of the Theosophical doctrines to recognize at the beginning their enormous import:

> The teaching . . . comprises a cosmogony, a philosophy, a religion. With the value of this teaching *per se* we are not at present concerned. BUT IT IS OBVIOUS THAT WERE IT WIDELY ACCEPTED A GREAT CHANGE WOULD BE INDUCED IN HUMAN THOUGHT IN ALMOST EVERY DEPARTMENT. TO TAKE ONE POINT ONLY, THE SPIRITUAL AND INTELLECTUAL RELATIONSHIP OF EAST TO WEST WOULD BE FOR THE TIME IN GREAT MEASURE REVERSED. "EX ORIENTE LUX" WOULD BE MORE THAN A METAPHOR AND A MEMORY; IT WOULD BE THE EXPRESSION OF ACTUAL CONTEMPORARY FACT.

Why was the Committee "not concerned in the value of this teaching?" Was it because the West or the Committee already possessed abundant knowledge as to the existence of superphysical phenomena and the laws and processes by which such phenomena are produced? Here is what was proclaimed in the prospectus of the S.P.R. in 1882:

> The founders of this Society fully recognize the exceptional difficulties which surround this branch of research; but they nevertheless hope that by patient and systematic effort some results of permanent value may be attained.

And the Committee itself admits in the preliminary report that the evidence for these phenomena "is of a kind which it is peculiarly difficult to disentangle or to evaluate. The claims advanced are so enormous, and the lines of testimony converge and inosculate in a manner so perplexing that it is almost equally hard to say what statements are to be accepted, and what inferences as to other statements are to be drawn from the acceptance of any."

To have concerned itself seriously with Madame Blavatsky's teachings, to have investigated and studied the principles and processes she inculcated would have called for a self-sacrificing devotion that no member of the

Committee had any zest for. There was advertising value in "investigating" H.P.B. and her phenomena; immediate and safe profit and advantage in arguing such opinions and speculations as accorded with their own preconceptions and theories and not in direct opposition to the "cosmogony, philosophy and religion" of the times, nor counter to prevailing ideas of the complete superiority of "the spiritual and intellectual relationship" of the *West* to the East. The Committee had no appetite in a direction that *might* result in making "*ex oriente lux*" something more than "a metaphor and a memory." What other rational inferences can be drawn from the Committee's own statements?

Realizing that the whole investigation was *ex parte*, and a farce as well, because it refused to enter into any study of the stated principles under which the phenomena were possible, the next question is concerned with the *competency of the Committee* to inquire into the Theosophical phenomena or weigh the value of the evidence amassed.

The whole history of Spiritualistic and allied phenomena without exception shows that the occurrences are *involuntary* on the part of the *medium*, both as regards their production and control, and that their rationale and processes are not understood either by mediums or investigators. On the other hand, absolutely every iota of evidence amassed by the Committee shows that the Theosophical phenomena were *voluntary,*—that is, consciously produced and consciously controlled by the operators, and those operators themselves claimed that the explanation of laws and processes could be acquired *only* through the Theosophical teachings. Nevertheless, the Committee and Mr. Hodgson steadfastly took the position that the Theosophical phenomena were of the same character as Spiritualistic manifestations, and were to be approached in the same way. Although the phenomena were admittedly *metaphysical* in causation, the Committee used only *physical* means of investigation, and rejected every hypothesis other than physical to explain them. Although in the preliminary report it was already aware of the Coulomb accusations in regard to phenomena in India, of the "Kiddle incident" in connection with one of the "letters" in the "Occult World," and of the nature of Mr. Massey's "private evidence" in regard to another "Occult letter," yet the testimony to numerous other phenomena was so overwhelming, so unquestioned, that the Committee say it is "impossible to avoid one or other of two alternative conclusions:—Either that some of the phenomena recorded are genuine, or that other persons of good standing in society, and with characters to lose, have taken part in deliberate imposture." In the final report not a scintilla of evidence can be found to controvert this testimony, nor to impeach the "persons of good standing in society, and with characters to lose." They, at least, are not charged with having "taken part in deliberate imposture."

How, then, does the Committee explain the phenomena so overwhelmingly testified to? It says they were due "to spontaneous illusion, or hallucination, or unconscious misrepresentation or invention on the part of the witnesses." For this wholesale "explanation," *nota bene*, not one particle of evidence is introduced or pretended to be introduced. It rests unequivocally, nakedly and unashamedly on the *ipse dixit* of the Committee; its only support their theories and speculations to account for phenomena that cannot otherwise be done away with. Where then was the "spontaneous illusion, or hallucination, or unconscious misrepresentation or invention"—"on the part of the witnesses," *or on the part of the Committee and Mr. Hodgson?*

It remains to be stated that neither the members of the Committee nor Mr. Hodgson were able themselves to produce any phenomena, nor were witness of any of the Theosophical phenomena. Nor did they claim for themselves any knowledge of their own as to how such phenomena could or could not be produced. All that they had originally set out to do was to secure the testimony of witnesses who had seen phenomena. The two reports show that with the single exception of the accusations of the Coulombs not a witness of the more than one hundred whose testimony was obtained, but testified unequivocally and positively to the occurrence of phenomena under circumstances that for him precluded any other conclusions but that the phenomena were genuine. So much for the competency of the Committee to adjudge the *facts as testified to.*

Upon what, then, did the Committee rely for its conclusions? Upon the Coulombs; upon the "Kiddle incident"; upon Mr. Massey's "private evidence"; upon the "expert opinions" of Mr. F. G. Netherclift and Mr. Sims on handwritings; most of all on the "opinions" of Mr. Hodgson and others. The Coulombs and their charges have already been discussed. By their own story they were knaves, cheats, and extortioners, "accomplices" with plainly evident evil motives, whose story had no independent corroboration whatever outside the suspicions of Mr. Hodgson and others, and which was denied point-blank by H.P.B., contradicted point-blank by the testimony of scores of actual independent witnesses and investigators. "The Kiddle incident" has been given,[1] and whatever opinion may be formed in regard to it, there is no evidence whatever of fraud in connection with it, or of any bad faith on the part of Mr. Sinnett or H.P.B. or any other Theosophist. Mr. Massey's "private evidence" is given at p. 397 of the Report and anyone who reads it can determine for himself that, whatever of the mysterious and the unexplained there may be in connection with the matter, there is *no evidence whatever of any fraud on H.P.B.'s part.* As in many, many other cases, something occurred which Mr. Massey could not understand; his doubts were aroused; H.P.B. denied absolutely any wrong-doing, but refused as absolutely to explain the mystery; hence she was "guilty of fraud."

Mr. Hodgson and the Committee reached the conclusion that the "Mahatma letters" to Mr. Sinnett and others were in fact written by Madame Blavatsky—a conclusion only, be it noted. To fortify this opinion some of the letters were submitted to Mr. Sims of the British

[1] See Chapter IV.

Museum and to Mr. Netherclift, a London handwriting expert, along with samples of the writing of H.P.B. *In the first instance both Mr. Netherclift and Mr. Sims independently reached the conclusion that the Mahatma letters were* not *written by H.P.B.* This is one of the "certain difficulties" already spoken of as confronting Mr. Hodgson and the Committee. For if the Mahatma letters were *not* written by H.P.B., *who wrote them?* After his return to England, therefore, Mr. Hodgson found himself in a quandary on this phase of his report. He thereupon took the matter up again with the experts, and agreeably they reversed their opinion and decided that the letters *were* written by H.P.B.! Incredible as this may appear it is the fact as derived from the report itself. One who is at all familiar with the course of "expert testimony" as to handwriting knows that, at best, such testimony is but opinion, and often erroneous, even where not formed to suit the desires of the client. An example is furnished of the fallibility of "expert opinion" by this very Mr. Netherclift himself, for, a few years later, he was called as an expert witness in the celebrated case of Charles Stewart Parnell against the London *Times* for libel. In that case Mr. Netherclift swore positively that the signature to the famous "Pigott letters" was the handwriting of Mr. Parnell. Later on in the case Pigott himself confessed in open court that he had forged the signatures.

The earliest known Mahatma letter was one handed to Madame Fadeef, aunt of H.P.B. and widow of a well-known Russian General, in 1870, long before H.P.B. was known in the world, and long before the formation of the Theosophical Society. According to the written testimony of Madame Fadeef, whose good character no one questioned, the letter was handed to her in Russia by an Oriental who *vanished before her eyes.* She stated that, at the time, H.P.B. had been absent for years, no one of the family knew of her whereabouts, all their inquiries had come to naught, and they were ready to believe her dead when the letter relieved their anxieties by saying that she was in the care of the Mahatmas and would rejoin her family within eighteen months. With regard to this first Mahatmic letter, which is given in the preliminary report, Prof. F. W. H. Myers, the leading member of the Committee, *himself certified as follows*: "*I have seen this letter, which certainly appears to be in the K. H.* (Mahatma) *handwriting.—F. W. H. M.*" Can anyone suppose that this Mahatma letter, written to relieve the pressing anxieties of loved and loving relatives, was "due to deliberate deception carried out by or at the instigation of Madame Blavatsky?" *If not, how account for it and the other Mahatma letters being in the same handwriting?*

Remains one more question for consideration: that of the "moral factor" of motive. The influences affecting the motives and conduct of the Committee, Mr. Hodgson, the Coulombs and others, have been indicated. In every case preconceptions, ignorance of Occult laws and processes; mysterious circumstances which they could not understand and which H.P.B. refused to elucidate; the baffling nature of the phenomena; self-interest; popular and sectarian pressures and prejudices—all combined to create uncertainties, doubts, suspicions, conjectures and inferences of fraud and deception. The *evidence,* that which was actually testified to, was overwhelmingly in support of the genuineness of the phenomena.

The motives of the *witnesses* are equally evident; they had nothing whatever to gain and everything to lose by their testimony. They were affirming the genuineness and reality of phenomena in which nine-tenths of humanity disbelieves, and which, if proved and accepted, would upset and destroy cherished and almost universally prevailing ideas in religion, science, and "almost every department of human thought and action." The most that could have been expected from the Committee in such circumstances was such a conclusion as that of the London Dialectical Society on the Spiritualistic phenomena. But the Theosophical principles and phenomena reach far deeper into the foundations of human consciousness. Unlike the Spiritualist manifestations and theories, there is no room for reconciliation or compromise between Theosophical teachings and phenomena and the "forces of reaction," the established interests in church and science and human conduct. Bitter as was the opposition to Darwinism, malevolent as was the antagonism to the spread of Spiritualism and to such investigators of it as Prof. Crookes, these were as nothing to the fear and hatred inspired by H.P.B., her teachings and her phenomena. In the one case compromise, a middle ground, was possible. In her case it was instinctively recognized by all that no compromise was possible. Hence, the conclusions of the Committee were in fact foregone from the beginning.

In no one thing, perhaps, is the weakness of the S.P.R. investigation more fatally self-betraying than in the motives they assign to account for the "long-continued combination and deliberate deception instigated and carried out by Madame Blavatsky." That anyone, let alone a woman, should for ten or more years make endless personal sacrifices of effort, time, money, health, and reputation in three continents, merely to deceive those who trusted her, with no possible benefit to herself; should succeed in so deceiving hundreds of the most intelligent men and women of many races that they were convinced of the reality of her powers, her teachings, her mission as well as her phenomena, only to be unmasked by a boy of twenty-three who, by interviewing some of the witnesses and hearing their stories, is able infallibly to see what they could not see, is able to suspect what they could find no occasion for suspecting, is able to detect a sufficient motive for inspiring H.P.B. to the most monumental career of chicanery in all history—this is what one has to swallow in order to attach credibility to the elaborate tissue of conjecture and suspicion woven by Mr. Hodgson to offset the solid weight of testimony that the phenomena were genuine.

"No crime without a motive." What, then, was the motive attributed by Mr. Hodgson and the Committee to make credible their conclusion that she was "one of the most accomplished, ingenious, and interesting impostors in history?" *She was a Russian spy, and her motive was to destroy British rule in India!*

It is interesting to observe the successive steps of the Committee's struggle with this question of the possible motive of H.P.B. In the preliminary report the Committee raises the question of "all the commoner and baser motives to fraud or exaggeration," and dismisses them: "*we may say at once that no trustworthy evidence supporting such a view has been brought under our notice.*" Next the Committee considers the possibility of "good" motives for bad conduct: "*Now we know, indeed, that the suspicions which the Anglo-Indian authorities at first entertained as to the political objects of the Theosophical Society have been abandoned as groundless.*" Next the Committee say, "But we can *imagine* schemes and intentions of a patriotic kind . . . we must be on our guard against men's *highest* instincts quite as much as their lowest."

In the final report Mr. Hodgson goes over the grounds of possible motives: "The question which will now inevitably arise is—*what has induced Madame Blavatsky to live so many laborious days in such a fantastic work of imposture?* . . . I should consider this Report *incomplete* unless I suggest what I myself *believe* to be an *adequate explanation of her ten years' toil on behalf of the Theosophical Society.*"

Was it egotism? "*A closer knowledge of her character would show such a supposition to be quite untenable.*"

Was she a plain, unvarnished fraud? "She is, indeed, *a rare psychological study,* almost as rare as a 'Mahatma'! *She was terrible exceedingly when she expressed her overpowering thought that perhaps her 'twenty years'' work might be spoiled through Madame Coulomb.*"

Was it religious mania, a morbid yearning for notoriety? "I must confess that the problem of her motives . . . caused me *no little perplexity.* . . . The sordid motive of pecuniary gain would be a solution still less satisfactory than the hypothesis of religious mania. . . .

But even this hypothesis I was unable to adopt, and reconcile with my understanding of her character."

What, then, *was* the compelling motive that induced the labors of a Hercules, the sacrifices of a Christ, to carry on a career of deception worthy of the Prince of Deceivers himself? "*At last a casual conversation opened my eyes.* . . . I cannot profess, myself, after my personal experiences with Madame Blavatsky, to feel much doubt that her *real object has been the furtherance of Russian interests. . . . I suggest it here only as a supposition which appears best to cover the known incidents of her career during the past 13 or 14 years.*"

H. P. Blavatsky lived and died a martyr, physically, mentally, and in all that men hold dear; she forsook relatives, friends, ease and high social standing, became an expatriate and naturalized citizen of an alien land on the other side of the globe; she founded a Society to which she gave unremitting and unthanked devotion; she wrote "Isis Unveiled," the "Secret Doctrine," the "Voice of the Silence," all of which were proscribed in Russia; she became a veritable Wandering Jew devoted to the propagation of teachings and ideas hateful to the world of "reactionary forces"; she eschewed all concern with political objects of any kind, all attachment to "race, creed, sex, caste, or color," and her lifeblood formed and sustained a Society sworn to the same abstentions; she lived and she died in poverty—slandered, calumniated, betrayed by followers and foes alike; misunderstood by all; she never, from 1873 to the day of her death, set foot on Russian soil, an exile from family and country.

Why did she do these things? "*In furtherance of Russian interests!*"

CHAPTER VII

DIVISIONS AMONG THEOSOPHISTS—NEW PUBLICATIONS

It will easily be understood that the opening of the year 1885 found the Theosophists in India in the utmost disorder and disarray—assailed on all sides from without by triumphant enemies; prey to confusion and recriminations within.

H.P.B. lay physically ill, wavering between life and death. Col. Olcott, availing himself of an invitation previously extended to him in recognition of his work for the revival of Buddhism, left almost immediately for a visit to the Burmese capital, Mandalay. On his arrival at Rangoon, *en route* to the court of Theebaw III, he was met by the leading Buddhist priests and dignitaries. Here he was cordially received and remained for a considerable time, holding conferences, giving lectures, and regaining his spirits in an atmosphere removed from the depressing situation at headquarters. Just as he was on the point of proceeding to Mandalay he received a telegram from Damodar urging his immediate return to India because of the apparently fatal turn in the condition of H.P.B.

It can scarcely be doubted that Col. Olcott's return to headquarters was impelled by what were to him still more urgent reasons, for he was at the same time in receipt of advices from his Hindu intimates that affairs were fast becoming desperate. He was advised that many Lodges were lapsing into dormancy, others threatening to dissolve; his General Council divided into two camps, with those opposed to him in the ascendant. The facts appear to have been that in addition to those few who had remained steadfastly loyal to H.P.B., numerous other European and some Hindu members had, by reaction, felt to some extent the monstrous injustice done H.P.B. and were in the mood to make the President-Founder the scapegoat for the timidity and the lukewarmness of all. The sense of present and impending loss caused many to realize the fatal error of deserting H.P.B. and all knew that the Convention's action was directly due to the sanction of Col. Olcott. A determined movement had gained headway to limit his autocratic control and direction of the society's affairs, by making the Council an actual executive and responsible governing body, instead of as hitherto the mere cloak and instrument of the President's wishes. This spontaneous feeling was placed before H.P.B., and she had given her signature of approval in the following words: "Believing that this new arrangement is necessary for the welfare of the Society, I approve of it, so far as I am concerned."

Colonel Olcott, who had been foremost in the belief that it was necessary to abandon H.P.B. "for the honor of the Society" and to preserve it from shafts aimed at it through H.P.B., now felt himself stung to the quick by these evidences of defection and disaffection on the part of the members towards himself. After consultation with his friends he went straight to the mortally stricken H.P.B., as all thought her, and besought her to restore him to his former status and function. Clouded and piecemeal as are the published fragments of information concerning the events of those trying months, certain facts seem clear in the light of subsequent history. It would appear that Col. Olcott recognized and admitted his faults, promised to take a more loyal and consistent course in the future, and agreed to pursue a less arbitrary policy in his management of the Society. Knowing that his devotion to the well-being of the Society was constant and unswerving, whatever his mistakes due to his vanity and self-sufficiency, and always tolerant and generous to the last degree toward friend or foe, it is clear that H.P.B. accepted his repentance and professions and once more lent him her powerful protection. She withdrew her authorization of the proposed changes, smoothed out the personal feelings aroused between Col. Olcott and his partisans and those opposed to his rulership, and left to him to make as of his own volition and accord the needful modifications of policy and conduct. This is the secret of the various notices in the "Supplement" to *The Theosophist* for May, 1885, concerning the "Formation of an Executive Committee," the "Special Notification," and the "Special Orders of 1885." Likewise in these events will be found the explanation of Col. Olcott's visit to Mr. Hodgson and his effort to get that gentleman to take a more impartial if not more friendly attitude toward the Theosophical evidences and explanations connected with the phenomena, which Mr. Hodgson was investigating almost entirely from the standpoint of the Coulombs and the missionaries. Sincere and well-intentioned as this move of Col. Olcott's undoubtedly was, it could but serve, in view of all the circumstances, to increase and confirm the already acute suspicions of Mr. Hodgson; and this, as we have seen, is what in fact occurred. Col. Olcott also, in his new zeal, made strenuous and partly successful efforts to procure the writing and publication of articles favorable to H.P.B. and her phenomena in various Indian papers.

But knowing well the weaknesses as well as the virtues of her colleague, H.P.B. was under no illusions as to the final outcome. She knew Col. Olcott's self-esteem, his doubts, jealousies and suspicions; knew only too well the personal ambitions, rivalries and animosities with which the headquarters were rife. As appeared many years later, she addressed on April 11, 1885, a letter to Col. Olcott, in which she told him that no parole loyalty would suffice to repair the mischief that had been done; that she had willingly borne and would continue to bear in her own person the evil Karma engendered by him and by the Society, but that in deserting her the Society and its leaders were in fact deserting the Masters whose Agent she was; that she had done her best for them all, but that she could not avoid for them the harvest of their own mistakes and ingratitude.

This letter was written by H.P.B. from Aden, after she had left India. Colonel Olcott suppressed this letter and in all his voluminous writings never referred to it. It was preceded by her formal letter of March 21, addressed to the General Council, submitting her resignation, which was accepted. The published inter-change assigned the illness of H.P.B. as the cause of her severance of relations officially with the Society in India, and the same cause was given for her departure. This was all true but the deeper reason, the Occult basis, was the desertion by Col. Olcott and his associates of the paramount objectives of her Masters. This is shown by the acceptance of her resignation; by the letter of April 11, 1885, as mentioned; by the report of a conversation with one of the Mahatmas,[1] which report was also suppressed by Col. Olcott and never referred to by him, though partially coming to light many years later; and by Col. Olcott's course immediately following the resignation and departure of H.P.B. He at once set actively to work to make the Society independent of H.P.B. The June number of *The Theosophist* was prefaced at the head of the text with an italic insert accompanied by a "printer's hand" and reading as follows:

> *The Theosophical Society, as such, is not responsible for any opinion or declaration in this or any other Journal, by whomsoever expressed, unless contained in an official document.*

In the same (June) number Col. Olcott published over his signature a leading editorial on "Infallibility," devoted to a disclaimer of any reliance by the Society on anyone's assumed powers, knowledge, or status, or that such reliance was in any way necessary for the Society's success or existence. This was all aimed at H.P.B. and her status as Agent of the Masters supposed to be behind the Theosophical Movement and the Theosophical Society. Indirectly, it was at the same time an assertion

[1] Some extracts from this letter and from the conversation mentioned are given in *The Theosophist* for October, 1907, pp. 9, 10, and 78.

of his own pre-eminence as the Head of the Society, since the only official documents were those issued by himself as President-Founder, or at his instructions.

Damodar K. Mavalankar, next to H.P.B., the most loved and the most envied of the Theosophists in India, and, aside from her, the only one of them generally known to be in constant active touch with the Masters, had been her faithful and devoted servant and indefatigable worker in the Cause. Much of her correspondence throughout the world had been carried on by him under her directions; visiting chelas at headquarters were largely cared for by him; the chief burden of the getting out of *The Theosophist* fell upon his shoulders; and he had shared with her the stigma of the Coulomb charges and Mr. Hodgson's investigating suspicions. He remained at Adyar for some time after the departure of H.P.B., doing what could be done for the few who possessed the elements of real loyalty and steadfastness. Towards the latter half of the year he left headquarters on a "pilgrimage," and was last publicly heard of near the Thibetan frontiers. By many he was thought to have perished of exposure, but there can be little doubt, from hints afterwards given by H.P.B. and Mr. Judge, that in fact he was called by the Masters into Their direct service and company. He thus received the reward of his undying devotion and his uncomplaining endurance of the tribulations consequent upon his human defects and mistakes. Of him the Master K. H. wrote, "Before he could 'stand in the presence of the Masters' he had to undergo the severest trials that a neophyte ever passed through." Damodar had first met H.P.B. early in 1879, had immediately forsaken everything that men hold dear to become her faithful servant and chela, and in the ensuing years of his probation had remained steadfastly loyal to her and her mission "without variableness or the shadow of turning." Of his subsequent fortunes, his present status, his future relations with the Theosophical Movement, the story remains untold; one of the unwritten chapters of the Second Section.

As the months went by it began to be apparent that the life of the Society in India could not be maintained by its venous circulation alone. The contents of *The Theosophist* deteriorated in quality; the circulation of the magazine diminished; numerous branches ceased to exist except on paper, the membership fell off in others; contributions and dues lessened; the Society was fast falling into mere discussion of the endless metaphysics of Hindu faiths and philosophies. On the other hand news began to permeate the Indian contingent that H.P.B. was being visited in her European retirement by staunch friends, corresponded with by an ever-increasing number of inquirers, supported by the adherence of new and notable persons. Colonel Olcott, who had ever a weakness for the acquaintance of the great and the near-great, began to take stock of the fortunes of war. Nor can it, we think, be doubted that as time went on, as her absence and his sense of loss of the old daily intimacy, the old strong and unfailing guidance of the "lion of the Punjab" grew more keen; as the truer and nobler side of his nature had opportunity to reassert itself—that side of his nature which had inspired him in the beginning to do as Damodar had done, to give up all to follow her in her unknown path—it cannot be doubted, we think, that Col. Olcott repented him of the mistakes and lukewarmness of the recent years, and endeavored so far as was in his power, short of a public disavowal of his erroneous course, to remedy his mistakes. And in this he was strengthened by the treatment accorded him by H.P.B. She chided him as little as might be; she continued unfailingly to send him articles for insertion in *The Theosophist*; she made a will bequeathing to him her entire interest in the magazine and making over its entire revenue to him; she encouraged by every means in her power every good effort, every good impulse that arose from him; she laughed at her own miseries and misfortunes, and made light of all obstacles in the way.

Colonel Olcott was supported and encouraged also by the good-will of those near at hand who had remained steadfast in devotion to H.P.B. without withdrawing their countenance from him. All these factors had their compelling influence, and at the Indian Convention at the close of 1885 his public Address as President to the assembled delegates and visitors was marked by the expression of strong feeling and sincere declarations in respect to H.P.B. In this mood he was willing to retire as President to promote the solidarity and renewed life of the Society. Says the Report of the Convention as published in the "Supplement" to *The Theosophist* for January, 1886:

> The President being called away temporarily on business, and Major-General Morgan occupying the Chair, the following resolutions . . . were carried by acclamation with great enthusiasm:
>
> *Resolved,* That in the event of the health of Madame H. P. Blavatsky being sufficiently restored, she be requested to resume the office which she has relinquished.
>
> *Resolved,* That the charges brought against Madame Blavatsky by her enemies have not been proven, and that our affection and respect for her continue unabated.
>
> *Whereas* the Convention has heard with great sorrow from the lips of the President-Founder, Col. H. S. Olcott, the expression of his desire to retire to private life on account of his competency for his present duty being questioned by some, the Convention unanimously
>
> *Resolve*: (1) That the President-Founder has by his unremitting zeal, self-sacrifices, courage, industry, virtuous life and intelligence, won the confidence of members of the Society and endeared himself to them throughout the world; and (2) that as this Convention cannot for one moment entertain the thought of his retiring from the Society which he has done so much to build up, and has conducted safely through vari-

> ous perils by his prudence and practical wisdom, they request him to continue his invaluable services to the Society to the last.

This approach to real union, this united aim, brotherly feeling, and mutual support in the spirit of the First Object, as manifested by the Convention, had its immediate beneficial effect, and for the ensuing three years the Society in India shared in the prosperity of the Movement throughout the world—the rising tide after the S.P.R., attempt to wreck the Society. It is worth while for students to note that every storm that ever raged about the Society had its inception in neglect of the First Object and its practical application, brotherly loyalty and devotion; every recovery from wounds and losses was due to a return to the fundamental basis of the Society and the fundamental precept of the Second Section—instant readiness to "defend the life or honour of a brother Theosophist even at the risk of their own lives." Had this been borne in mind by those who were "quick to doubt and despair, who had worked for themselves and not for the Cause," had the consistent example set, no less than the precepts given, by H.P.B. been made the rule of action by those responsible for the policy and conduct of the Third Section—the Theosophical Society proper—the "solidarity in the ranks" of the Society would not only "have enabled it to resist all external attacks, but also have made it possible for greater, wider, and more tangible help to have been given it" by the First and Second Sections, "who are always ready to give help when we are fit to receive it."

H. P. Blavatsky left the headquarters and sailed from India at the beginning of April, 1885. Such was her physical condition that she had to be carried on board the vessel. Accompanied by her physician and an attendant she voyaged to Naples, Italy, where she remained for some months in sickness, poverty, and isolation. From there she removed in the summer to Würzburg, Germany, where she was visited and sustained by the devoted Gebhards of Elberfeld. Thither also came the Countess Wachtmeister, widow of the late Swedish Ambassador to England. Countess Wachtmeister was an English woman by birth, a natural psychic who had been interested in Spiritualism and then in the Theosophical phenomena. She had become a member of the London Lodge and had met H.P.B. at London the year before. Hearing of the distress into which H.P.B. was plunged, and convinced by her own experiences that the phenomena of H.P.B. were genuine, the Countess came from Sweden to visit her. What she saw and felt caused her to remain, and from then onwards the Countess gave herself up to the service of H.P.B., as friend, as companion, as amanuensis, as voluntary servant. To Würzburg came also friends and correspondents of Dr. Franz Hartmann, whose experience and intuition of the real nature of H.P.B. were always strong enough to keep him loyal despite the frictions of personalities between himself and others. Here came Dr. Hubbe-Schleiden, the noted German savant, who had met H.P.B. the year before at the Gebhards and who, like Dr. Hartmann, had absorbed enough of her philosophy to keep him energized for the remainder of his life in channels akin to the work of the Theosophical Movement. Came also the Russian writer, Solovyoff the younger, who had met H.P.B. in Paris the year before, and whose evil Karma it was subsequently to become tool and victim of the forces opposed to her and her work. During her Würzburg residence H.P.B. was also visited by Mr. and Mrs. Sinnett and others from London and Paris. Here also came many others moved by sympathy, by gratitude, by curiosity, by all the motives that affect mankind.

H.P.B. lived at Würzburg for nearly a year, alternating between long relapses and brief partial recoveries. During the whole period her labors never abated. Articles for *The Theosophist*, miscellaneous contributions to Russian periodicals for her daily bread, and a correspondence that daily increased, kept her busy. Many of her letters at this period were written by her volunteer helpers at her dictation or direction. During the whole period, also, she was occupied with the vast burden of the composition of the "Secret Doctrine."

In May, 1886, her medical advisers once more insisted on a change of climate and surroundings if her life were to be prolonged. Accordingly, she removed to Ostend, Belgium, and here she lived in constantly increasing toil and turmoil. Dr. Anna Bonus Kingsford and her associate, Mr. E. Maitland, visited her here, and here came many English and French Theosophists for making or renewing personal touch with her. Late in the winter and in the early spring of 1887, the physical state of H.P.B. once more became so desperate that her life was despaired of. Miss Francesca Arundale, Miss Kislingbury, the two Keightleys, Archibald and Bertram, and other London Theosophists were anxious for her to remove to England where she could be better cared for. Madame Gebhard and Dr. Ashton Ellis, a young London physician and member of the London Lodge, were telegraphed for by Countess Wachtmeister. They came in all haste and were assiduous in their ministrations. This unstinted devotion once more pulled H.P.B. through the crisis. The Keightleys came over and urged the necessities of the English Theosophists for her presence among them. Yielding to the loving solicitations of these devoted friends and followers, the wanderer once more took ship, carried on board as before, and, physically a helpless and inert mass, was installed in a cottage in Norwood, where she passed the summer of 1887. In the autumn the house at 17 Lansdowne Road, Holland Park, West, was taken by her friends and thither H.P.B. was removed to quarters specially prepared for her in the midst of an atmosphere of good-will and watchful consideration.

Thus surrounded and sheltered, H.P.B. measurably regained strength, though her health never became such as to exempt her from continuous physical suffering or to enable her to take needful exercise. It is doubtful if during the last six years of her life she had a single waking hour of complete relaxation, and it is certain that she rarely was able to go outside her domicile unaided.

Yet these six years were the ones of her stormy career most filled, not only with the trials and tribulations incident to the many attacks upon her name and fame, not only with the press and demands of claimants upon her time and attention, not only with the correspondence and work of the Theosophical Movement from day to day, but they were, as well, the most fruitful of enduring results for all mankind. It was during this period that the "Secret Doctrine," the "Key to Theosophy," "The Voice of the Silence," and the "Theosophical Glossary" were written; *Lucifer* was begun with its first issue dated September 15, 1887, and its monthly contents during the succeeding years contained a steady stream from the inexhaustible fountain of her wisdom.

The presence of H.P.B. in Europe resulted from the first in a revival of courage, confidence, and action on the part of those who had remained steadfast during the Coulomb charges, the S.P.R. investigation and report, and the succeeding blasts in the press. Work began in Germany and France with fresh vigor and new Lodges were formed in addition to the existing ones. Many new Fellows entered the Society, some of them persons of considerable reputation in other fields of effort. *The Sphynx* was begun in Germany, *Le Lotus* in France, and the study and discussion of subjects within the lines of the Three Objects went on apace. After the removal of H.P.B. to England, additional Lodges were established in Ireland, Scotland, in the larger cities of England, and the Blavatsky Lodge was formed in London. Here H.P.B. herself replied to questions on the "Stanzas" of the "Secret Doctrine" at a number of sessions. These questions and answers were stenographically reported and, when revised, were published as "Transactions 1 and 2 of the Blavatsky Lodge."

When the S.P.R. *Proceedings,* Volume 3, were published late in 1885, Mr. Sinnett, then President of the London Lodge, wrote a pamphlet "Reply" which was published early in 1886. He also wrote a strong letter to *Light,* the leading Spiritualist publication in England. His clear statements and wide repute went far to stem the unfavorable tide of press comment consequent on the S.P.R. report. In the summer of 1886 his "Incidents in the Life of Madame Blavatsky" was published by Redway. This book, with its partial disclosures of personal matters, its anecdotes and narratives of the most astonishing phenomena, its mysterious hiatuses, its pervading atmosphere of sincerity, candor, and common sense in the midst of the well-nigh incredible marvels recited, and above all, with its pictures of the living H.P.B. as a most fascinating and human being steadily giving herself, soul, mind, and heart to a cause sacred to her; a good-natured, unrevengeful fighter undismayed and undaunted by the mountains of hatred and calumny heaped upon her—this book created a profound impression far and wide, and aroused a sympathy for this martyr to her convictions, and an interest in her teachings, that brought many into the ranks of the Society, and turned to good account the adverse findings of the S.P.R.

In the spring of 1885 was published "Light on the Path, written down by M. C." The initials stood for Mabel Collins, niece of the celebrated novelist. Mabel Collins was a psychic, a member of the London Lodge, and herself a novelist. "Light on the Path" was "written down" by its sponsor without previous knowledge or study of Eastern teachings. As originally published it was but a small pamphlet without the "Comments" subsequently published in *Lucifer* and incorporated in most of the later editions of "Light on the Path." The work created a veritable sensation and has probably been more widely circulated than any other single Theosophical publication. Its companion books, "The Idyll of the White Lotus," and "Through the Gates of Gold," have also been very widely read and studied. Many stories have been told, both by the reputed author and others, regarding the actual source of these writings. These will be discussed in their proper place.[2]

"Five Years of Theosophy," made up of articles reprinted from the first five volumes of *The Theosophist*,

[2] See Chapter XIII.

and "Man—Fragments of Forgotten History," by "Two Chelas of the Theosophical Society," were issued in 1885 by Reeves & Turner, London, and both passed through several editions. The "Two Chelas" are stated by Miss Francesca Arundale to have been Mohini M. Chatterji and Mrs. L. C. Holloway (*The Theosophist*, October, 1917).

Contemporaneously with the revival in India and the renaissance in Europe and England, the spiral upward path of the Movement produced a fresh and higher impulsion in the United States. Where in India the restrictions were such that practically the whole force of the Movement took the line of the Second Object, and in England and on the Continent the environment of thought and action naturally limited the major attention to the line of the Third Object, in America the chief stress from the beginning of the second decade was upon the great First Object.

In India the study and discussion of comparative religion and philosophy was the only possible open door to any arousal of interest among the members of the hitherto rigidly exclusive sects and castes. In England and Europe, given over to Christian sectarianism, scientific materialism, and Spiritualism, and with the binding fetters of caste and class exclusiveness hardly less rigid than in India, only the neutral ground of interest afforded by the Third Object gave a field in which to sow the seed of the Theosophical teachings. In America the Second and Third Objects had formed the magnet for the original organization and membership of the Society, and had been used by H.P.B. as the *raison d'être* for the writing and publication of "Isis Unveiled." Not till the second decade of the Society opened was it possible to re-start the work of the Movement in its direct public channel, the Society, on the real line, that of the First Object. The beginning of this was in the United States, at New York, in the Aryan Theosophical Society, the re-organization and re-incarnation of the parent Society of 1875. The presiding genius of the Aryan Society, and of the work of the Movement, esoteric and exoteric, in the United States was Mr. William Q. Judge. With the second decade the work fell into its three streams with Mr. Judge in America, H.P.B. in Europe, and Col. Olcott in India. As we shall all too soon see, that which was intended to be the three great natural branches of the work of the Society, metaphysically as well as geographically, broke into alien organizations as well as alien purposes.

Mr. Judge had kept up an unbroken communion with H.P.B. and an unbroken accord with Col. Olcott during all the years from the time of the separation of the three Founders at the close of the year 1878 when H.P.B. and Col. Olcott departed for India. In the early summer of 1884 he had gone to France and passed some time with H.P.B., proceeded thence to India where he formed acquaintance with the leading Hindu members, completed his touch with Damodar and others connected with the First and Second Sections, and had returned to America near the close of the year. During the year 1885 he was busied with the rejuvenation of the Aryan Lodge, with the revival of interest among the scattered Fellows and the few existing Lodges in the United States. In April, 1886, he issued the first number of *The Path*, the magazine of which H.P.B. said and wrote: "It is pure Buddhi." Thenceforth *The Path* was the organ *par excellence*, not only of the American members of the Theosophical Society, but of the Theosophical Movement and the practical, devotional applications of the teachings of Theosophy. Within a year from the commencement of its publication the number of branches had tripled, and active study and propaganda had created a widespread interest in the press and in the public mind. The Board of Control appointed in 1884 by Col. Olcott, the President, at Mr. Judge's suggestion, for the facilitation of the routine of the American Branches and membership, continued until the summer of 1886. October 30 of that year, again at Mr. Judge's request to H.P.B. and upon her suggestion to Col. Olcott, the Board of Control met at Cincinnati, together with delegates either in person or by proxy from the American Lodges and organized the "American Section of the Theosophical Society." In April, 1887, the first Convention of the newly formed Section met at New York City, a constitution and by-laws were adopted, officers chosen, and the first democratic organization embracing a number of independent Branches was effected in the Society's history. Mr. Judge was elected General Secretary of the American Section.

The American Section of the Theosophical Society was not an organization of the individual Fellows of the Society, but a federation of all the Branches, Lodges, or Societies in the United States. Each separate Society was autonomous in its own internal affairs, like the states of the American Union, but all were joined together in a single governing body with its own constitution, powers, and officers, similar to the Federal government, which was, in fact the model followed, both in the organization of the Parent Theosophical Society and of the American Section. The General Council in India was recognized, and the unity of the Society throughout the world in purpose and teaching was affirmed. At the same time the right to independence was placed on record in these words of Mr. Judge in his first formal Report, read at the second Convention at Chicago in April, 1888: "Of course the American Branches could have met together and formed themselves independently, but since we draw our real inspiration from India, it would seem unwise as well as disloyal to have failed to try and keep the orderly and regular succession." The prior *de facto* nature of the conduct of the Society's affairs, corresponding to that of the Confederation of the Thirteen Colonies before the adoption of the American Constitution, was also recorded in these words referring to the previously existing Board of Control:

> That Board was therefore in charge of the interests of the movement here, and was in fact a continuation of the system of somewhat paternal and unrepresentative government which had up to that time prevailed.

The "somewhat paternal and unrepresentative government" continued to mark the conduct of affairs in India throughout, and in Europe until 1890, but in America the conduct of the Society was henceforth strictly democratic.

This Convention of 1888, while the second chronologically, was really the first from the standpoint of organized activity in America. It was attended by delegates in person or by proxy from all the active Lodges in the United States, by that time twenty-two in number; was signalized by letters of greeting from India, from the Council of the London Lodge, and by the attendance of Dr. Archibald Keightley as a formal delegate from the Blavatsky Lodge and the London Lodge, in both of which he was an officer. Dr. Keightley was also acting as the special representative of Madame Blavatsky, from whom he bore a long and important Letter to the Convention. This Letter was read to the assembled delegates and afterwards printed in the published "Official Report of Proceedings" issued by the American Section.

The autumn of 1888, the beginning of the fourteenth year of the Society's career, was marked by the most important event in its history, next to the organization of the democratic American Section, and was, in fact, the outcome of that epochal point: the public announcement and inauguration of the Esoteric Section, which must now be traced.

CHAPTER VIII

ESOTERIC AND EXOTERIC ASPECTS OF THE THEOSOPHICAL MOVEMENT

Hitherto we have been concerned with the survey of the Theosophical Movement of the nineteenth century from its public aspects: the recital of a series of events more or less in relation with each other and with the sum of human activities, together with such reflections on their bearings and significance as to us appear logical and consistent. An attempt has been made to show clearly that the vicissitudes both of the Theosophical Society and Madame Blavatsky's teachings of Theosophy were inevitable and but a repetition of the varying fortunes which have attended every former effort to introduce a system of thought and action at variance with the ideas, customs, and practices still firmly entrenched in the mind of the race. So far, all that we have discussed is accessible in all its detail to any inquiring student, and the ordinary mind will find nothing beyond the range of common observation and experience. The student will have both the advantage and the disadvantage of the familiar multitude of conflicting testimony and opinion that attends every inquiry into human affairs. He will find nothing that transcends the possibility of reconciliation or explanation on his habitual lines of thought, without greatly deranging his fundamental preconceptions regarding God, Nature, Man, and the course of evolution.

But, as we have early intimated,[1] the Theosophical Movement has an esoteric as well as an exoteric side, and here the Western student is without guide, chart, or compass, either in his own memorial experience or in any ac-

[1] See Chapter III.

credited testimony of the race to which he belongs. Not only so, but he will find himself confronted, both in himself and in the race, with a deeply imbedded incredulity which derides and despises the very possibility, even, of intellectual and spiritual evolution within and behind physical evolution. The student of the esoteric side of the Theosophical Movement has then literally to take the position of a Columbus. He has to postulate the existence of the spiritual and mental world or worlds, independent of and superior to our familiar universe, yet inter-penetrating it at every point, standing in relation to it as a cause to an effect, and, in man, almost inextricably interwoven and interblended in his embodied existence. He has to admit the fundamental assumption that spiritual and intellectual evolution is as much under Law in its processes and resultants as physical evolution, and that the latter is but the shadow and the reflex of the mental, as the mental is of the spiritual. He has to recognize the inevitable corollary of these propositions, that Life, individual as well as collective, is *continuous,* and that the infinite course of spiritual, mental, and physical evolution has produced Beings as much superior to man as man is superior to a black beetle—as was once speculatively suggested by Prof. Huxley—and, finally, that these Beings take an active part in "the government of the natural order of things."

The student will find that Western religious history and Western tradition and myth do, indeed, present an immense literature dealing with gods, angels, demons, fairies, and so on, and with their relations to human beings and human affairs, but such beings and their interventions are regarded either as miraculous or fictitious, and belief in them rests either on the grounds of "revelation" or of mere opinions ingrained from childhood, or of some misunderstood personal psychological experience. Nowhere is there any philosophy, any scientific, any logical, any *historical* evidence or basis for the existence and action of superhuman and subhuman entities as the *product of evolutionary Law.* Such a theory or such a fact is as unknown or as derided in the West, as foreign to its basic concepts, as the ideas of pre-existence, metempsychosis, reincarnation, Karma, *continuous* immortality—all integral and inseparable parts of the fundamental assumptions connected with the esoteric aspects of the Theosophical Movement. Only when all these are recognized, at least as a working hypothesis, does the expression, "the esoteric side of the Theosophical Movement," become tolerable in any but a materialistic sense. The student is compelled to turn aside from the religion, philosophy, and thought of the day and familiarize himself with the recorded philosophy of Theosophy, if he is to view the facts of record in any other light than that of the well-nigh universal preconceptions of the Western race. It is only through the most careful and conscientious study and application of the teachings of Theosophy that the student can hope to penetrate beyond the visible aspects of the Theosophical Movement to the arcana of the intellectual and spiritual factors and forces which constitute the *Occult* side of that Movement.

The first direct affirmation of the existence of Adepts, Beings perfected spiritually, intellectually, and physically, the flower of human and all evolution, is, so far as the Western world is concerned, to be found in the opening sentence of "Isis Unveiled." From beginning to end that work is strewn with evidences, arguments, and declarations regarding Adepts and their doctrines. Theosophy is declared to be a portion of Their Wisdom; its teachings are presented for the examination and study of the world and of the Fellows of the Theosophical Society.

As subsequently appeared from the repeated testimony of all three, before the publication of "Isis," and even prior to the foundation of the Theosophical Society, H.P.B. had imparted many of her teachings to Col. Olcott and Mr. Judge, had convinced them of her phenomenal powers over matter, time, and space, and had accepted them as her pupils. More, through her intervention both of them had become assured of the existence of the Adepts, had received phenomenal visits from them, and had made their pledges under the rules of Occultism direct to the Masters of the Great Lodge of Adepts. They had reached the determination to follow the guidance and instruction of H.P.B. and it was under her inspiration that the Theosophical Society was formed. Again, from the subsequent repeated statements of all three as to the events and relations of those earliest days, it is apparent that the connection between H.P.B. and Mr. Judge was of a different and deeper nature than the relation established with Col. Olcott—as will develop in the due course of our study. Nor were Col. Olcott and Mr. Judge her only pledged associates, though the names, duties, and activities of the others have never been publicly disclosed. But mention of the fact occurs in the "Introductory" of the "Secret Doctrine," in *Lucifer*, Volume 3, p. 173, in various "E. S. T. Aids," and in other places in Theosophical writings. And something of the nature and widespread activities of the Adepts apart from the Theosophical Society, is plainly to be discerned in an article in *Blackwood's Edinburgh Magazine* for January, 1880. This was written by an English publicist and embodies a very remarkable letter written by an unknown individual named as a "Turkish Effendi," on the relations of Christianity and Islam.

The fact of these private teachings, of the intimate connection of the Adepts with the foundation and spread of the Theosophical Society, of an inner core of chelas or disciples as the active agents of the Adepts, both in the Society and the Movement, of the practical possibility of a direct connection with these Adepts and their chelas through Madame Blavatsky, was kept sedulously concealed until after the arrival of H.P.B. and Col. Olcott in India. A few Fellows suspected from occasional personal hints given them, or by inferences from the accessible teachings, that more might be learned. But H.P.B. turned a deaf ear to all prayers and entreaties in that direction, bidding the aspirants join the Society, to study the published literature, and apply themselves actively to the Objects of the Society.

In India the religious convictions of the inhabitants

are, quite in contrast with the West, the predominant factor in daily life. The spiritual and mental heredity of the populace is such that the teachings of Theosophy have in them nothing of the incredible or revolting to inherited ideas. Bound and fettered as they are by rigid castes and creeds, separated by alien tongues, crippled by an enormous percentage of illiteracy, abused by a priesthood which keeps them in subjection to gross idolatries and superstitions, ground by an ever-present poverty, the vast majority of the Indian populations are, nevertheless, deeply religious in feeling, of simple and kindly lives, imbued with the ideas of guardian spirits, of tutelary deities, of the near presence of the immortal and invisible, and of the sacredness of all life. The country is full of *Sannyasis, Sadhus,* and *Faquirs,* many of them men of the noblest and most self-sacrificing character who have exempted themselves from all restrictions of caste and worldly life and who wander the length and breadth of the land keeping alive the reverence and faith of the populace, practicing and inculcating the great virtues of all time. And among the educated classes are very many highly intelligent men profoundly versed in the philosophical teachings of the ancient sages, Rishis and Mahatmas.

Almost from the first moment of their entry the Founders met with a sympathetic and understanding reception from the Hindus, and in this kindly atmosphere of traditional appreciation it was natural that the first declaration should be made of the deeper import of the Theosophical Movement. In *The Theosophist* for March, 1880, the article relating to the "Turkish Effendi" was reprinted from *Blackwood's.* In the succeeding number appeared "The Theosophical Society or Universal Brotherhood." This directly identified the Society with its great First Object, and made the first public proclamation of the Superior Sections. The article is an official and authoritative announcement, is signed by Kharsedji N. Seervai, Joint Recording Secretary, and has for its subtitle, "Principles, Rules and By-Laws, as revised in General Council, at the meeting held at the Palace of

H. H. the Maharajah of Vizianagram, Benares, 17th December, 1879."

Thereafter references in the pages of *The Theosophist* become more and more frequent; the mysterious Brothers, or Mahatmas, are often spoken of; chelas and chelaship are discussed, Occultism and its rules are alluded to and, on rare occasions, the names and designations of various chelas in their differing degrees are guardedly and indirectly introduced.

Subba Row and Damodar became more and more known in this way both to Hindus and Europeans. Others mentioned from time to time in peculiar and particular ways in *The Theosophist* have remained unknown to the world and the references to them seem never to have aroused question or comment among Theosophical students. Amongst Europeans, Mr. A. P. Sinnett and Mr. A. O. Hume, both then resident in India, came into indirect contact with the Mahatmas through H.P.B.'s agency. These two were witnesses of many phenomenal occurrences, and wrote numerous letters to the hidden "Brothers." Although they never met the Adepts personally and were never themselves able to communicate with them directly, both Mr. Sinnett and Mr. Hume received lengthy communications from them, "Occult letters" amongst those sent and received in more prosaic fashion. In the summer of 1881 Mr. Sinnett's book, "The Occult World," was published in London. This contains long extracts from some of the letters of the Mahatma "K. H.,"[2] written in a script and with a name chosen for the purpose of communicating with lay and probationary chelas. In these extracts will be found much of permanent value concerning the real nature of the Theosophical Movement, the purpose of the exoteric Theosophical Society or Third Section, the rules and discipline of chelaship of the Second Section, the methods of the Adepts in dealing with humanity, and other Occult

[2] The complete unexpurgated text of these communications has recently been published under the title, "The Mahatma Letters to A. P. Sinnett," London, T. Fisher Unwin, Ltd.; New York City, Frederick A. Stokes Company.

matters. In 1882, "Hints on Esoteric Theosophy" was published and contains much matter bearing directly and indirectly on the existence and activity of the Second Section. The subject of the Superior Sections, their teachings, work, and the limitations imposed on and by them in dealing with the complex nature of Man, are largely discussed in the series of articles, "Fragments of Occult Truth," publication of which was begun in *The Theosophist* for October, 1881. In the number of March, 1882, was commenced "The Elixir of Life," with the parenthetical notation that it was "From a Chela's Diary," giving the physical discipline and scientific resultants of successful probationary chelaship, and setting out the conditions precedent to "Occult preferment." In January, 1883, "Chelas and Knowers" was printed, followed in the "Supplement" to the issue for July, 1883, by "Chelas and Lay Chelas." This, perhaps the most important article on Occultism ever published, sets forth the difference between accepted chelas and the pledged probationers and neophytes of every degree. It repeats in detail the risks and dangers of rushing prematurely into "practical Occultism," gives illustrative examples of failure, and specifies some of the iron conditions of self-discipline necessary. The same subject was first discussed in a general and guarded fashion toward the close of the last chapter in "Isis Unveiled." Finally, the leading article for July, 1884, entitled, "Mahatmas and Chelas," gave in clearest words the nature of Adeptship and the folly and futility of prevailing ideas among Theosophists in regard to Mahatmas and the means of approaching Them.

We have selected only a few of the numerous writings which gradually appeared bearing on the esoteric side of the Theosophical Movement during the first ten years of the Society's life. Only when these articles and the collateral circumstances of their appearance are understood can their relation to and bearing upon the incidents connected with the career of the exoteric Society be properly grasped and the behavior of various leading persons connected with it be comprehended. *To the "rush for chelaship" and to the failures of probationers in Occultism must the student look for the metaphysical and spiritual explanations of the internal storms which then and thereafter rent the original Theosophical Society and its Branches.*

The extensive circulation of "The Occult World" and "Esoteric Buddhism," the intense activity of the London Lodge in the pursuit of the Third Object after the return of Mr. Sinnett to London and his leading position in that Lodge, most of whose members were Spiritualists and avid for "phenomena," caused many to believe that the Masters could be reached *via* mediums, séances, and "psychic practices" of one kind and another, to the entire neglect of the First Object or the study of philosophy. The powerful currents that surrounded H.P.B. wherever she went; the impetus given to curiosity and ambition for "Occult" knowledge by the great amount of published tales and speculations concerning her and her mission; the preliminary investigations of the Society for Psychical Research into the Theosophical phenomena —all these produced a great danger for the selfish, the unwary, the venturesome Fellows of the Society who had profited spiritually not at all from "Isis Unveiled," from the Master's letters in "The Occult World," from the repeated instructions and warnings in *The Theosophist,* nor from the private communications from H.P.B. and the Mahatmas to numerous individuals most bent on forcing their way into the sphere of action of the Superior Sections without regard to the unknown laws and perils to be encountered. Not until late in 1884, when the independent and misguided energies of the London Lodge threatened the gravest danger both to its Fellows, to the Society, and to the Movement, was permission granted, at their petition, to Miss Francesca Arundale and others to form an Inner Group of the London Lodge as probationers of the Second Section. The signers pledged themselves to follow strictly the rules and instructions given them. All this remained secret for many years, but in the volume, "Letters from the Masters of the Wisdom," published in 1919, will be found some graphic statements and indications of the conditions prevailing—statements which shed a flood of light not only on the state of affairs at the time we are discussing, but which are equally illuminating in their application to the course of affairs since and now among the thirsty aspirants for Occult powers and knowledge.

During this period the fourth edition of "The Occult World" was published with its Appendix containing a long letter from the Master "K. H." on the "precipitation" of "Occult letters" by chelas of the Second Section. All these events accompanied the "Kiddle incident"; the attack on H.P.B. by Mr. Arthur Lillie in his pamphlet, "Koot Hoomi Unveiled"; the Coulomb charges and the investigation by the S.P.R.; the lukewarmness or desertions of the Fellows, and the violation of their pledges by lay and accepted probationers of the Second Section.

The first decade passed and its results ascertained and weighed as regarded the Society as a whole, re-organization of the work can be seen in the commencement of *The Path* by Mr. Judge, in April, 1886, and of *Lucifer* in London by H.P.B. in September 1887. Something of the immensity of the change inaugurated in the public work of H.P.B. and Mr. Judge can be seen by merely comparing the character and range of contents of these two magazines with those of the first seven volumes of *The Theosophist* (1879-86); the published books in the period 1885-95 with those of the first decade; the growth in character of work undertaken by the Society in America and England in 1885-95, whether compared with the history of the Society as a whole in its first ten years, or with its work and character in India during the same ten years, or with any of the fruits of the numerous Theosophical Societies now in existence that have sprung up since 1895.

The philosophical and moral lessons and considerations, the *sine qua non* conditions of the Superior Sections, the explanation of the numerous failures, exoteric and esoteric, which beset the work of the first ten years, and which must beset every similar attempt in all times, are nowhere more clearly and authoritatively set forth than in the article entitled "The Theosophical Mahatmas." The general circumstances have already been outlined; the particular occasion was as follows:

Amongst the earliest of the European pledged probationers of the Second Section was Mr. W. T. Brown. He was a young man who had been reared a strict orthodox Christian, was a graduate of the University of Glasgow, and had traveled extensively. In 1883, while in London, he made the acquaintance of Mr. Sinnett and others of the London Lodge, as well as of some leading Spiritualists, some Continental followers of Eliphas Lévi, and students of medieval Rosicrucianism. He was a member of the Central Association of British Spiritualists, joined the London Lodge, and became so deeply interested in what he read and heard of Theosophical teachings that he determined to go to India and devote his life to the "esoteric doctrine." He was witness of some of the phenomena constantly occurring at headquarters, received "Occult" messages from one of the Masters, and besought Col. Olcott, then absent from Adyar on a tour, for permission to share in his work. He received a long, friendly, but very straightforward reply warning him of the immense difficulties to be confronted. Undeterred, he set out to accompany Col. Olcott, and on this trip received further communications from the Master "K. H.," was visited by the Master in "astral body," and finally met the Adept in his physical body, recognizing the Master both from the portrait which he had previously seen, from his "astral" appearance, and from the subject matters discussed. All this occurred during the latter half of 1883. Mr. Brown was so aroused by his experiences and studies that he determined to become a probationary chela, and was accepted on probation in January, 1884. "On that occasion," he says, "I was warned as to the difficulties of the road which I desired to tread, but was assured that by a close adherence to truth, and trust in 'My Master,' all must turn out well."

Mr. Brown was at headquarters during the time of

the Coulomb accusations, returning to England *via* the United States. Next he went to Germany and identified himself with the "Rosicrucians" there. He had written a pamphlet reciting his experiences in India, which was published "under the authority of the London Lodge." Next he published a brief autobiography devoted to his experiences in Rosicrucianism, and finally, early in 1886, came once more to the United States to associate himself with Mrs. Josephine W. Cables.

Mrs. Cables was a Christian Spiritualist and herself afflicted with psychic tendencies. Learning of the Theosophical teachings, she had been largely instrumental in forming the Rochester T.S. in 1882, with Mr. W. B. Shelley as President and herself as Secretary. This was the first Theosophical Society established in America after the formation of the parent T.S. In April, 1884, she established *The Occult Word,* a monthly "journal devoted to the interests of the Theosophical Society, and for the dissemination of Oriental Knowledge." The issues appeared irregularly and the contents show a curious mixture of Christianity, Spiritualism, Mysticism, personal vagaries on diet, "Asceticism," and "Occultism." Mrs. Cables gave frequent talks before the Rochester T.S., held séances, and endeavored by every means in her power to "open up communication" with the Mahatmas. Finally she procured the assistance of Mr. Brown. In the summer of 1886 Prof. Elliott Coues, President of the then American Board of Control of the T.S. endeavored to make of *The Occult Word* the official organ of the T.S. in the United States. Meantime Mr. Judge had started *The Path,* and the character of its contents showed a sure knowledge and the signs of direct contact with the very Powers Mrs. Cables had been seeking to reach in many ways. Very evidently it appeared to Mrs. Cables and Mr. Brown that the unknown Masters had not accorded them that recognition which they felt that they had earned. In *The Occult Word* for October-November, 1886, they published a leading editorial article over their joint signatures. The article is entitled "The Theosophical Mahatmas," and in it the authors say:

> There is a great desire among many of our brothers to be put into communication with the Theosophical Mahatmas, and as we have given much thought to the subject, and evinced great desire to receive even slight tokens from the Masters, it will be useful to our brothers to have some of our reflections. *We have come to the conclusion that it is useless to strain the psychical eyes toward the Himalayas. . . . The Masters have given out nothing new in the literature of our Theosophical Society.* There have been students of mysticism in all ages . . . and all of these have found a world of literature opening to their gaze as they directed their attention to the spheres of the occult. . . . *We need not think, therefore, that we are having a special revelation by means of our Society. . . . Therefore, we need not run after Oriental mystics who deny their ability to help us. . . .*
>
> A great many of us have come to think that we have been running vainly after Eastern mystics and ecstatics, when, within the New Testament itself, we find the Way, the Truth, and the Life. . . . *We are now prepared to stand by our Essenian Master and to "test the spirits" in his name. We have been hunting after strange gods,* and have "denied Him thrice," but with bleeding feet and prostrate spirit we pray that He may take us once more under His wing. . . . We have wandered far and suffered for our wanderings. *We have been living on husks,* while the gospel of love and soul invigoration has been always at our hands. . . . *The "dwellers on the threshold are within."*

To this manifesto H.P.B. herself replied in an article with the same title, which was published in *The Path* for December, 1886. After stating that the feeling expressed by Mrs. Cables and Mr. Brown, "is undeniably shared by many Theosophists" H.P.B. goes on:

> *Whether the complaints are justified, and also whether it is the "Mahatmas" or Theosophists themselves who are to blame for it is a question that remains to be settled.*

We can here give only the briefest extracts from H.P. B.'s article, which constitutes the view of the Superior Sections on the essentials of the path of probation and the causes of the wrecks that line the road. The article itself should be read and pondered by every aspirant to esoteric knowledge until it is ineradicably engraved in his inner nature, for it relates, not to an isolated instance, but to the inviolable law of the higher life. She says:

> To the plain statement of our brothers and sisters that they have been "living on husks," "hunting after strange gods" without receiving admittance, I would ask in my turn, as plainly: "Are you sure of having knocked at the right door? Do you feel certain that you have not lost your way by *stopping so often on your journey at strange doors, behind which lie in wait the fiercest enemies of those you were searching for?*" . . . Our MASTERS are not a "jealous god"; they are simply holy mortals, nevertheless, however, higher than any in this world, morally, intellectually and spiritually, . . . members of a Brotherhood, who are the first in it to show themselves subservient to its time-honored laws and rules. And one of its first rules demands that those who start . . . as candidates . . . should proceed by the straight road, without stopping on every sideway and path, seeking to join other "Masters" and professors often of the Left-Hand Science, that they should have confidence and show trust and patience, besides several other conditions to fulfill. Failing in all of this from first to last, what right has any man or woman to com-

plain of the inability of the Masters to help them? . . .

Once that a Theosophist would become a candidate for either chelaship or favours, he must be aware of the *mutual* pledge, tacitly, if not formally offered and accepted between the two parties, and, *that such a pledge is sacred.* It is a bond of *seven* years of probation. If during that time, notwithstanding the many human shortcomings and mistakes of the candidate (save two which it is needless to specify in print), he remains throughout every temptation *true to the chosen Master,* or Masters (in the case of *lay* condidates), and as faithful to the Society founded at their wish and under their orders, then the theosophist will be initiated . . . thenceforward allowed to communicate with his *guru* unreservedly, all his failings save this one, as specified, may be overlooked; they belong to his future *Karma.* . . .

Thus the chief and only indispensable condition required in the candidate or chela on probation is simply unswerving fidelity to the chosen Master and his purposes. This is a condition *sine qua non,* not . . . on account of any jealous feeling, but simply because *the magnetic rapport between the two once broken, it becomes at each time doubly difficult to re-establish it again.* . . .

Both the writers may have and very likely they did—"hunt after *strange* gods"; but these *were not our* MASTERS. . . .

Yet, to those theosophists, who are displeased with the Society in general, no one has ever made you any rash promises; least of all, has either the Society or its founders ever offered their "Masters" as a *chromo-premium* to the best behaved. For years every new member has been told that *he was promised nothing,* but had everything to expect only from his own personal merit. The theosophist is left free and untrammeled in his actions . . . unless, indeed, one has offered himself and is decided to win the Master's favors. To such especially, I now address myself and ask: Have you fulfilled *your* obligations and pledges? Have you . . . *led the life* requisite? . . . Let him who feels in his heart and conscience that he has— . . let him rise and *protest*. . . . I am afraid my invitation will remain unanswered. During the eleven years of the existence of the Theosophical Society I have known, out of the seventy-two regularly accepted chelas on probation and the hundreds of *lay* candidates—only *three* who have not hitherto failed, and *one only* who had a full success. No one forces anyone into chelaship; no promises are uttered, none except the mutual pledge between Master and the would-be-chela. Verily, verily, many are the called but few are chosen—or rather few who have the patience of going to the bitter end, if bitter we call simple perseverance and singleness of purpose. And what about the Society, in general? . . . Who among the thousands of members does *lead the life?* Shall anyone say because he is a strict vegetarian—*elephants and cows are that*—or happens to lead a celibate life, after a stormy youth in the opposite direction; or because he studies the *Bhagavad-Gita* or the "Yoga philosophy" *upside down*, that he is a theosophist *according to the Masters' hearts?* As it is not the cowl that makes the monk, so, no long hair with a poetical vacancy on the brow are sufficient to make of one a faithful follower of *divine* Wisdom. Look around you and behold our UNIVERSAL Brotherhood so-called! The Society founded to remedy the glaring evils of Christianity, to shun bigotry and intolerance, *cant* and superstition and to cultivate real universal love extending even to the dumb brute, what has it become in Europe and America in these eleven years of trial? . . .

I have never ceased repeating to others as soon as one steps on the Path leading to . . . the blessed Masters . . . his Karma, instead of having to be distributed throughout his long life, falls upon him in a block and crushes him with its whole weight. He who believes in what he professes and in his Master, will stand it and come out of the trial victorious; he *who doubts*, the coward who fears to receive his just dues and tries to avoid justice being done—FAILS. He will not escape Karma just the same, but he will only lose that for which he has risked its untimely visits. . . .

And now repeating after the *Paraguru*—my Master's MASTER—the words He had sent as a message to those who wanted to make of the Society a "miracle club" instead of a Brotherhood of Peace, Love and mutual assistance—"Perish rather, the Theosophical Society and its hapless Founders," I say perish their twelve years' labour and their very lives rather than that I should see what I do to-day: theosophists, outvying political "rings" in their search for personal power and authority; theosophists slandering and criticizing each other as two rival Christian sects might do; finally theosophists refusing to *lead the life* and then criticizing and throwing slurs on the grandest and noblest of men, because . . . those Masters refuse to interfere with Karma and to play second fiddle to every theosophist who calls upon Them and whether he deserves it or not."

The history of the Theosophical Society is the history of the failure of Theosophists in high and low position to *lead the life* inculcated in their own Objects and their own professions; is the record of the failure of the lay and pledged probationers of the Second Section to *keep their pledges* in "simple perseverance and singleness of purpose."

The case of Mrs. Cables and Mr. Brown has been selected because it is public and typical of the hundreds of cases before and since of those who started with fair prospects, in all the glory of a fresh enthusiasm, with all the general and particular advantages, help, and guidance that past Karma and personal contact with the Teachings and the Teachers could give them, and who nevertheless failed miserably because they *would* not, and not because they *could* not, *adhere to the lines laid down* by those very Masters whom they longed to come in contact with as accepted chelas.

Mr. Brown returned to England, later went to India and there married an Eurasian lady; he returned to the fold of orthodox Christianity, and has never since been heard of in connection with chelaship. Mrs. Cables speedily turned the Rochester T. S. into the Rochester Brotherhood, and her magazine into the exponency of the various phases of "Mysticism" and "Occultism" that attracted her fancy from time to time. Neither Mrs. Cables nor Mr. Brown appears ever to have questioned their own instability of purpose, their own inconsistency of action, their own utter failure to abide by the conditions they had themselves invoked. Was this course of conduct unique on their part or was it but a manifestation of those very defects and weaknesses of human nature which must be fought and conquered by the candidate for chelaship?

CHAPTER IX

H.P.B., OLCOTT, AND JUDGE

History is more than the narration of events; even the most personal and short-sighted recognize that actions do not perform themselves. There is no action without a being to make it and to feel its effects. No one's minutest action stands alone and without relation. History is the story of the persons and personages who performed the actions, as well as of the events themselves; but even more, if its chronicle is to be of any value to the student, he must be concerned in the meaning of the incidents which crowd the stage; in the parts played by the various actors in the drama; in the lessons to be learned in relation to the larger drama of life itself in which he and all other sentient beings are concerned.

Behind the arras of the visible lies the real and enduring world of *causation,* the world of immortal Souls engaged in the battle of Life—the pilgrimage of spiritual and mental evolution, in which all are involved. Thus the history of the Theosophical Movement becomes a *study of the operation of the Law of Karma,* in which every living Soul is equally concerned.

The moment anyone takes this position he is on the plane of consciousness of the Superior Sections of the Theosophical Society; he is studying particular persons and their actions in the light of *Universal Principles*—in the light of the teachings of Theosophy, exoteric and esoteric.

From the beginning it was the Theosophical *Society* which attracted the attention of friends and foes alike. As it was the visible body, the heredity and pre-conceptions of the race made the thing visible, the reality. Its declared platform of Objects was universally attractive, so long as those Objects remained in the region of ideals; an abstraction which one could profess without disturbance, external or internal.

But when it was ascertained that the Society was in fact but a vehicle for the dissemination and serious study of Theosophy; when it was seen that the careful study and comparison of the various religions and theories, philosophical and scientific, led straight to the unavoidable inference that the only value in any or all of them lay in what they had in *common,* not in their mutual exclusions; that the various *differences* were mutually contradictory and destructive; that in Theosophy alone was an inclusive Wisdom, self-convincing and self-explanatory of all and everything—then the Theosophical Society became and continued to be the target for every species of assault and attack that the adherents of sectarianism, whether in religion or science, could devise. And when it was perceived by the Fellows that the Objects of the Society were not merely formal and academic; that the serious study of Theosophy produced wholly unlooked-for results in themselves, compelling them to choose between their predilections and their professed principles, by far the greater part either left the Society altogether, or lapsed into the hypocrisy which pretends one course of action while following another. The active and *earnest* Theosophists have always been but a scant fragment of even that handful of humanity which from time to time has called itself Theosophical.

The actual active and visible Head of the Theosophical Society was at all times Col. H. S. Olcott. To his zeal was due its foundation, to his ardent devotion its spread, to his abilities and sacrifices its successes. The Society itself more and more became to him the one Object of his existence; to it and for it he gave his all.

The case was quite otherwise both with H.P.B. and William Q. Judge. To neither of them was the Society ever anything but a body, an instrument, an imperfect and faulty machine for conserving energy and putting it to use. Both of them were Co-Founders with Col. Olcott of the Society, both of them gave without stint to its support and defense, but only and always as a mere means to an end.

As President-Founder of the visible Society, Col. Olcott was prominent before the members and before the public. H.P.B. had as little to do as possible with the conduct of the Society; Mr. Judge was scarcely known at all in connection with it during its first decade. At all times until and unless the exigencies of the *Movement* compelled such appearances and interferences both H.P.B. and Mr. Judge supported and worked through Col. Olcott in the affairs of the Society, making themselves in every public way subordinate to him. His work was the exoteric phase of the Movement; theirs the esoteric.

H.P.B. was the *Teacher;* for purposes of the Movement she was the *direct Agent* of the Lodge of Masters of the Wisdom-Religion. These Masters were and remain, securely veiled from the prying and selfish approach of humanity, Their existence a matter of inference only to all but Their chelas and "those with whom They voluntarily communicate." They are known in the world only through the evidences amassed by H.P.B. in her writings, through the few communications from Them to others who were, in every case, brought into relation with Them by and through H.P.B., and through those longings and aspirations of the human heart which still preserve the faith in Divine Beings, Elder Brothers to suffering and sinful man. So far as the whole West is concerned all that anyone knows or infers of the Masters or Their Wisdom-Religion, or Their chelas, comes, directly or indirectly, from the mission of H. P. Blavatsky. She therefore stood, and stands, in a position of supreme importance to the whole world; for *she stands in the place of the Masters* as Their Messenger until 1975, when she stated that Their next Messenger would come. All others, their statements and their actions, must be viewed in the light of her mission, her teachings, her statements, and her example; for she and none other represented the First Section.

Next to her in importance in the Theosophical Movement was, and is, William Q. Judge, as we shall see in due season. The placing of any persons, however talented or supposedly proficient in Occultism, on the same plane of knowledge and action in the world as these two; the acceptance of any teachings or "messages" as *Theosophy* in contravention of the recorded statements of these two, is to deny in fact the very Source of the Message of Theosophy, is to attribute to the Masters Themselves the fallibility of human nature. To take such a position is to imagine that They chose an untrustworthy direct Agent to deliver Their Message to humanity; that they permitted Their Message to be faultily and imperfectly recorded; that They left the world and the sincere student alike at the mercy of claimants of every kind, and without any sure guide or landmark of philosophy and example.

H.P.B. represented the First Section of the Theosophical Movement; W. Q. Judge represented the Second Section, and Col. H. S. Olcott the Third Section —or Theosophical Society proper. The evidences are abundant and overwhelming, as we shall see. Colonel Olcott was never, from the standpoint of the Superior Sections, other than a probationary chela. It is thus important to consider his dual position: on the one hand, the President-Founder of the Society, its guiding genius and chief figure before the world; on the other hand, a struggling probationer, fighting and failing over and over again in his efforts at self-discipline and self-mastery. In the esoteric study of the Theosophical Movement, the actions of Col. Olcott the President, in all their contradictions and confusions, have to be studied in the light of Col. Olcott, the aspirant for accepted chelaship of the Second Section. Pathetic and disillusioning as is the task, it should be tempered in writer and reader alike by the reflection that the story of Col. Olcott is the story in advance of what confronts every aspirant to the same up-hill Path; the extent to which we learn the lesson of his failures is the measure of our debt to him.

In the article "Chelas and Lay Chelas" before referred to, H.P.B., in discussing the requisites and difficulties of probationary chelaship of the Second Section, illustrates some of her points by incidental reference to Col. Olcott. She says:

> All were refused at first, Col. Olcott, the President himself, to begin with; and as to the latter gentleman there is now [July, 1883] no harm in saying that he was not formally accepted as a Chela until he had proved by more than a year's devoted labors and by a determination which *brooked no denial*, that he might safely be *tested*.

On this subject Col. Olcott himself says in a letter written in 1881 and published in "Hints on Esoteric Theosophy, Number I," that he was "provoked and exasperated" by the "selfish and cruel indifference of H.P.B." to his "yearnings after the truth," as well as by "the failure of the Brothers to come and instruct" him. He himself gives the reasons both for the delay and his own misunderstandings:

> I got that proof in due time [of the existence of Masters]: but for months I was being gradually led out of my spiritualistic Fool's Paradise, and forced to abandon my delusions one by one. My mind was not prepared to give up ideas that had been the growth of 22 years' experiences, with mediums and circles. . . . But now it was all made clear. I had got just as much as I deserved. . . . So . . . I adopted those habits and encouraged those thoughts that were conducive to the attainment of my ends.
>
> After that I had all the proofs I needed, alike of the existence of the Brothers, their wisdom, their psychical powers, and their unselfish devotion to humanity. For six years I have been blessed with this experience . . . and yet after all these years not only not made an adept, but hardly having achieved one step towards adeptship.

Colonel Olcott was in his forty-fourth year at the time; an age, when, owing to the physical and psychical limitations of the human instrument, the constitutional changes necessary to successful chelaship present the extreme of difficulty, even granting that all other conditions are of the most favorable. What his actual condition was is further indicated in the same letter:

> If you will only reflect what it is to transform a worldly man, such as I was in 1874—a man of clubs, drinking parties, mistresses, a man absorbed in all sorts of worldly public and private undertakings and speculations—into that purest, wisest, noblest and most spiritual of human beings—a BROTHER, you will cease to wonder or rather you will wonder, how I could ever have struggled out of the swamp at all, and how I could have ever succeeded in gaining the firm straight road.
>
> No one knows until he really tries it, how awful a task it is to subdue *all* his evil passions and animal instincts, and develop his higher nature. . . .
>
> From time to time one or another Brother who had been on friendly terms with me . . . has become disgusted with me and left me to others, who kindly took their places. Most of all, I regret a certain Magyar philosopher, who had begun to give me a course of instruction in occult dynamics, but was repelled by an outbreak of my old earthly nature.
>
> But I shall win him back and others also, for I have so determined; and *whatever a man really* WILLS, *that he has*. . . .
>
> If my experience is worth anything, I should say . . . that however great a man may be at this side of the Himalayas, he begins his relations with the Brothers on exactly the same terms as the humblest Chela who ever tried to scale their Parnassus; he must "win his way."

Every probationer of the Second Section will be prepared to agree with Col. Olcott's statement of the difficulties of the effort to conquer "these vices of the ordinary personal man"; to sympathize with him in his struggles, failures, and renewed determination to continue on the path of probation. Few as yet have had the experience of the fiery furnace requisite to have a just appreciation of the far more difficult and onerous task of facing and conquering the universal vices inherent in human nature—the very crucible that his position as President-Founder and his "determination which brooked no denial" as an aspirant for chelaship, compelled Col. Olcott to enter. And it is this prolonged ordeal that we must now study in its effects. We have already touched on the failure of the probationers, Col. Olcott among them, "to defend the honour of a brother Theosophist even at the risk of their own lives," when H.P.B. was assailed by the Coulombs, the missionaries, and the Psychical Research Society. We have entered more largely into the primary obligations of chelaship in discussing the failures of Mrs. Cables and Mr. Brown. We must now trace Col. Olcott more particularly in his relation to H.P.B. as chela to Guru, in the incidents preluding the formation of the Esoteric Section of the Theosophical Society.

The pledge taken by Col. Olcott was not different in spirit from that taken by every neophyte of the Second Section. Its essential features, so far as it relates to the matters under review, are contained in the following clauses:

> I pledge myself to support, before the world, the Theosophical Movement, its leaders and its members; and in particular to obey, without cavil or delay, the orders of the Head of the Section in all that concerns my relation with the Theosophical Movement.

The student will do well to note, (1) that the taking of the pledge is voluntary on the part of the applicant;

(2) that it pledges entire obedience to the Head of the Section, who was and is H.P.B., in all that relates to the Theosophical Movement; (3) that her public teachings, the Objects of the Society formed at her instigation, no less than her private teachings and individual instructions, constitute and comprise her orders, which every neophyte of the Second Section pledges himself to obey. Not until the candidate was making strenuous and measurably successful efforts to embody in his own life all Three Objects of the Society was he even eligible for consideration as an applicant for the probationary degree of the Second Section. Not until he fulfilled all the conditions of the pledges of the probationer was he in any way eligible to the higher degrees of the Second Section. Meantime he had constantly to bear in mind that no one would enforce or compel his keeping of his pledge; from start to finish his course must be self-induced and self-devised. In the words of Col. Olcott's letter before quoted from, each applicant would get just as much as he deserved; he need look for no extraneous help "to achieve that which no man ever did achieve except by his own self-development." Or, as expressed in "Chelas and Lay Chelas":

> THE MAHATMAS ARE THE SERVANTS, NOT THE ARBITERS OF THE LAW OF KARMA. LAY-CHELASHIP CONFERS NO PRIVILEGE UPON ANYONE EXCEPT THAT OF WORKING FOR MERIT UNDER THE OBSERVATION OF A MASTER. And whether that Master be or be not seen by the Chela makes no difference whatever as to the result; his good thoughts, words, and deeds will bear their fruits, his evil ones theirs.

Col. Olcott's course may first be discerned by an examination of the contents of *The Theosophist*, which he directed after the departure from India of H.P.B. early in 1885. His prompt efforts to disclaim any reliance upon H.P.B., and his indirect assertion of his own paramount importance have been noted in an earlier chapter.[1] When the American Board of Control was suggested by Mr. Judge to Col. Olcott for the preliminary direction of the rising tide foreseen by Mr. Judge in America, Col. Olcott appointed Prof. Elliott Coues of Washington, D. C., whom he met in London and Germany in the summer of 1884, to be its Chairman and leading figure. From the first moment of his connection with the Theosophical Society Prof. Coues began to cause difficulties. This requires separate treatment; it is sufficient here to mention the fact. Finally, Mr. Judge had recourse to Madame Blavatsky, and through her insistence Col. Olcott dissolved the American Board of Control and assented to the formation of the American Section of the Theosophical Society. The actual facts, so far as they could be stated without exposing the internal discords, were placed on record in the first printed Report of the American Section—that of the second Convention. The "Supplement" to *The Theosophist* for November, 1886, remarks:

> The movement in the United States is gaining strength, but not without friction always to be expected from the contact of strong personalities. . . . The reconstructive plan sent over by the Adyar Council, which supersedes the Board of Control by the organization of an American Section of the General Council, is to be acted upon in December, and it is hoped that all may be pleasantly settled.

There is here no apparent perception that anything was involved beyond the "friction of strong personalities"; no recognition of the fact that the plan came from Mr. Judge and was accepted only because of the insistence of H.P.B.; no comment upon the fact that the new Section was to be purely democratic, entirely independent, and in nominal affiliation only with the Indian autocracy set

[1] See Chapter VII.

up by Col. Olcott under the thin mask of the "Adyar Council."

The Path was noted in a friendly way at its foundation in April, 1886, and occasional brief mention made of its contents. But no notice was taken of the affair of Mrs. Cables and Mr. Brown, nor of "The Theosophical Mahatmas," in which, as we have seen,[2] H.P.B., from her sick bed at Ostend, wrote with the vigor and clarity that the importance of the issues required.

Another matter at the same time received her attention, and this was even more important, from the exoteric standpoint. Ever since Mr. C. C. Massey had raised the question that "Isis Unveiled" denied re-incarnation [3] and had claimed that her later teachings were at variance in other points from her earliest expositions, H.P.B. had merely denied the allegation and declared that there were and could be no contradictions in any of her teachings, since all alike came from the Masters. Beyond that she had held her peace. But after the S.P.R. Report and especially after the divergent activities and teachings promulgated in the London Lodge under Mr. Sinnett's auspices, these old charges began once more to circulate. There was a persistent, private, word-of-mouth effort going on in various quarters to belittle the Occult knowledge and status of H.P.B., and make her out a medium and a student, as fallible as any of the others. The time being ripe, Mr. Judge published a long and leading article by H.P.B., in *The Path* for November, 1886, entitled "Theories About Re-incarnation and Spirits," in which she gave the actual facts once and for all.

No notice was taken of this article by *The Theosophist* for the very good reason that Col. Olcott shared Mr. Massey's opinions and those of Mr. Sinnett and others with regard to H.P.B., and her teachings and status, as long afterwards, he himself admitted.[4]

The publication of *Lucifer* was begun in London in

[2] See Chapter VIII.
[3] See Chapter IV.
[4] Postscript, *The Theosophist*, "Supplement," April, 1895.

September, 1887, with H.P.B., as its guiding genius. For more than a year the only notice taken by Col. Olcott of the magazine, its contents, or its editor, is confined to the following official "Editorial Notice," appearing in *The Theosophist* for November, 1887:

> At the particular request of Madame Blavatsky, the undersigned assumes temporarily legal responsibility for the editorship of the *Theosophist;* she having undertaken special editorial duty, in connection with the members of our London Lodge T. S., involving the public use of her name. Adyar, October, 1887.
>
> H. S. Olcott.

At the Indian Convention, held at the close of December, 1886, the famous T. Subba Row delivered a series of extemporaneous discourses on the "Bhagavad-Gita" to the assembled delegates and visitors. These lectures were published in *The Theosophist* during the year 1887. In the course of his dissertations Subba Row spoke somewhat slightingly of the "Theosophical sevenfold classification of Principles" in Nature and in Man. No defensive notice was taken of the rather invidious tendency of his statements, then or thereafter, by Col. Olcott or those most closely associated with him. In the April, 1887, number, therefore, H.P.B. replied in friendly fashion to Subba Row's criticisms, assuming that they were incidental and oral and their bearing, as affording a basis for cleavage among Theosophists, overlooked. To this Subba Row replied at length, repeating, extending, and fortifying his previous statements, and indulging in some sharp remarks concerning H.P.B. herself. H.P.B. made answer in the August number, clearing up the matter of the "original expounder" of the "sevenfold classification," as Subba Row charged her with being. She simply stated that the classification attacked by Subba Row was not her own, but that originally given out by Mr. Sinnett in his "Esoteric Buddhism." On this she says—what most Theosophical students have overlooked—that "Esoteric Buddhism" was written "absolutely without my knowledge, and as the author understood those teachings from letters he had received."

As Subba Row was a chela, and the issues raised by him largely concerned the Second Section and its work, H.P.B. confined herself strictly to what could be publicly discussed. The controversy caused a considerable breach, as H.P.B. had foreseen, and thereafter Subba Row maintained a coolness towards H.P.B. till the time of his death. Her subsequent correction, in the "Secret Doctrine," of Mr. Sinnett's erroneous teachings, made complete the distrust which had been growing in him since 1883. In the one case and in the other Col. Olcott's sympathies were with his fellow students and not with his Teacher and Guru, H.P.B. In the Subba Row controversy Col. Olcott kept silent. So did Mr. Sinnett, whose erroneous interpretations were the real basis of Subba Row's criticisms directed against H.P.B. But Mr. Judge from far-away America was a diligent watcher of all that took place and in the August, 1887, number of *The Theosophist* with exquisite tact, skill, and perception he reconciled and cleared up the situation, giving the facts, but giving them with all gentleness and discretion. But he paid the price of his loyalty and devotion, no less than of his knowledge and intuition. For this article necessarily had to lay bare the inconsistencies and "authority" of "Esoteric Buddhism." And, no more than Subba Row or Col. Olcott, could Mr. Sinnett endure correction, even at the hands of H.P.B., let alone a young man as obscure as Mr. Judge. Of all this in due sequence. Meantime, to follow the thread of Col. Olcott's ordeal of chelaship.

Immediately after the formation of the American Section in April, 1887, Mr. Judge wrote H.P.B. under date of May 18:

> . . . So many people are beginning to ask me to be Chelas that I must do something. . . . I know a good many good ones who will do well and who will form a rock on which the enemy will founder.

H.P.B. replied, telling Mr. Judge to go ahead in America and she would soon do something herself. In the autumn following she began *Lucifer,* which from its first number contained articles by her or written under her inspiration, all relating to the Second Section, although not so named, and all in preparation for the forthcoming change in the direction of the Movement. The first volume contained the "Comments on Light on the Path," detailing the difficulties and requirements of the disciple striving for chelaship. The number for April, 1888, contained the article "Practical Occultism," by H.P.B., giving publicly for the first time the "private rules" of the Eastern School, notating what would-be chelas had to do for their own safety as well as their progress, and for the first time clearly stating the enormous responsibilities assumed by the Guru or Teacher. This was immediately followed in the May number by "Occultism Versus the Occult Arts," stressing the dangers of impure chelaship and the appalling consequences of falling into the "Left-Hand Path." Coincidently *The Path* was publishing articles of similar import.

To the April, 1888, Convention of the American Section H.P.B. sent a long and formal Letter, which she instructed Mr. Judge to read to the assembled delegates. In this she placed on record publicly and authoritatively her recognition of the status of Mr. Judge in the Movement, saying that it was to him chiefly, if not entirely, that the Society owed its life. The remainder of the Letter was devoted to a recital of the purpose and meaning of the Society and the obstacles that must be overcome by its members. This was the first of a series of annual Letters, four in all, which she addressed to the American Conventions, the last one being written but a few weeks before her death.

If the student will carefully compare the issues of *Lucifer, The Path,* and *The Theosophist* during the years 1887-9 he will be amazed to observe, first, the entire unity and accord in the two first named in all that concerned Theosophy and the Movement; secondly, the marked cleavage shown in the contents of *The Theosophist* during the same period; the utter ignoring in the latter of the cyclic changes under way in the Movement as manifested in the writings of H.P.B. and Mr. Judge.

Mr. Judge went to London and there, at the request of H.P.B., drew up the plans and wrote the rules for the guidance of the forthcoming Esoteric Section of the Theosophical Society. Nothing in relation to the Esoteric Section by name appeared in public print until October, 1888. All that we have been discussing on that subject came to light only after many years. The same is true of the active correspondence which went on during the interval, between H.P.B. and Col. Olcott, and, to a lesser extent, between Mr. Judge and Col. Olcott. True as steel, alike to the purposes which inspired them and to Col. Olcott in his place and share in the Movement, nothing was omitted from their efforts to inform him of the great issues at stake, to strengthen his weak spots, to keep him in line with the real Objects of the Society as well as the Movement.

What Col. Olcott's real sentiments were, what his mingled feelings, what his alternations and violent oscillations during all this period, constitute one of the most vivid examples and illustrations of what may be called the "pledge fever" of probationary chelas. Of all this, also, nothing appeared in public print, save as it was noticeable by such acts of omission and commission as we have been referring to. Long afterwards, in his "Old Diary Leaves," Col. Olcott writes of the events narrated, and it is to that source that we may turn for the private and missing links of evidence which show that the ruffling of the surface of events was but the symptomatic sign of the inner struggle of probation. In spite of the manifold and manifest disloyalty, ingratitude, and other violations of their pledges by students and chelas of one degree of probation or another, of more or less prominence in the Society, neither H.P.B. nor Mr. Judge ever washed any of the Theosophical "dirty linen" in public; ever uttered any reproaches, ever in any way exposed the weaknesses and failings of their students or associates. Only when the Society, the School or the Movement was imperiled by the follies of those whom they were trying in every way to shield and help, did they take the necessary steps to clear the situation. They never either defended themselves or attacked others. Their work was to lay down the lines of teaching and direction, to keep those lines energized, and only when the Cause which they represented was endangered by external pressures or internal ruptures did they intervene.

"Old Diary Leaves" is the personal story of Col. Olcott and has at least the merit of faithfully picturing, albeit unconsciously to himself, "the true history"—not of the Theosophical Society, but of Henry S. Olcott, aspirant for chelaship on "the hard and thorny path." Studied as the diary of a chela on probation, no more important lessons are anywhere recorded for the study and instruction of the student of the esoteric side of the Theosophical Movement, and the causes of the failure of the Theosophical Society, than in "Old Diary Leaves."

The four published volumes of "Old Diary Leaves" bear upon their covers the legend: THE TRUE HISTORY OF THE THEOSOPHICAL SOCIETY.

No doubt this is what Col. Olcott intended and believed them to be. Equally it is beyond question that in the eyes of the world and of Theosophical students generally he has been assumed to be that one who had the greatest knowledge of the facts, the best opportunity for accurate judgments, and the strongest incentive for recording both. These views have been supported by the transparent sincerity that shines from every page of his reminiscences, by the wealth of details given by him, by the fact that he was throughout its life the official Head of the Theosophical Society, that he survived for many years both his colleagues in the pioneer work of the Movement.

Neither of his colleagues ever wrote for publication anything that savored of the autobiographical or were at pains to attract attention to themselves; on the contrary, they "sedulously kept closed," to the utmost extent that the nature of their mission and the indiscretions of their associates permitted, "every possible door of approach by which the inquisitive could spy upon them. The prime condition of their success was that they should never be supervised or obstructed. . . . All that those outside their circle could perceive was results, the causes of which were masked from view." It is passing strange that these statements of the Mahatma "K. H." in his letter to Mr. Hume, and the other statements of the same Adept in his letters reproduced in "The Occult World," have never been applied by Theosophical students to the events and actors in the drama of the Theosophical Movement. What more necessary and important than that the *direct Agent of the Masters in the world* should be shielded and guarded in her Occult nature and functions from all but those who have "earned the right to *know* Them?"

At the outset, then, it should be understood that widely as H.P.B. has been discussed and extensive as have been the controversies which have raged about her mission and her personality the fact remains that only the scantiest and most fragmentary details exist relating to her, after the elimination of all the mass of hearsay and opinion, of claims and counter-claims made by friends and foes as to her Occult status, powers, and relations. She is to be known, if known at all, only through her writings and by those who faithfully "follow the Path she showed, the Masters who are behind."

Her writings are devoted entirely: (1) to placing on record her message of Theosophy and the citation of the evidences and arguments establishing its unbroken existence down the ages; (2) to articles in explanation and application of the Principles of that Message; (3) to instruction, advice, and suggestion to the students, individually and collectively, who to any extent become interested in Theosophy; (4) to the direct and pointed statements made by her in her letters to and in relation to those persons who voluntarily associated themselves in her work and who as voluntarily pledged themselves to her guidance and tuition; (5) to the defense of her mission, its instruments and her associates.

She was interested in and devoted to a CAUSE: nothing else mattered to her, nothing else was of moment to her, save and except as it might hasten or retard that Cause. Her writings, as her works, are wholly impersonal; consequently she never touched upon persons or events save as the exigencies of the Movement, of the Society, or of her pupils made such attention compulsory on her part. And the same state of fact applies in its integrity to William Q. Judge, his writings and his works.

On the other hand, "Old Diary Leaves," including the miscellaneous articles and letters written by Col. Olcott in connection with his Theosophical work, are wholly autobiographical and personal—in their point of view, in their treatment of men and events, in their judgment and conclusions. From the basis of the Superior Sections he was a struggling probationer, wrestling with the foes entrenched in his own inner nature. In his own eyes, and those of so many others, he was the President-Founder of the Theosophical Society, wrestling valiantly with its enemies, without and within. The period from 1881-8 is that of the second septennate of the probationary chelaship both of Henry S. Olcott and of the Theosophical Society as a body, and the struggles of the one are the mirror and the reflex of the struggles of the other. The "wandering from the discipline" of the one is depicted in the stresses which beset the other; their joint departures from their professed Pledges and Objects the compelling reason for the public formation of the Esoteric Section of the T.S.

CHAPTER X

THE FORMATION OF THE ESOTERIC SECTION

THE critical period preceding the formation of the Esoteric Section has been discussed, and its various factors and actors commented on from their several points of view, by the only ones competent to do so at first hand: by H.P.B., by Col. Olcott, by Mr. Judge, and by the Master "K. H." We may examine at this point some of the statements of all of them, in the order named, omitting Mr. Judge for the time being, for the sake of logical, no less than of chronological, continuity.

In April, 1886, H.P.B. wrote a long and important letter to Dr. Franz Hartmann in reply to questions and problems raised by him. Dr. Hartmann, it will be remembered, was at Adyar before, during, and subsequent to the Coulomb charges, the Indian Convention's practical desertion of H.P.B., Mr. Hodgson's investigations for the S.P.R., the resignation and departure of H.P.B. He was familiar with much of the unwritten history of that eventful period. He learned enough, and his intuitions were sufficiently awake, to make him the faithful and loyal friend of both H.P.B., and W.Q.J., through all the troubled voyage of the Theosophical ship. H.P.B.'s letter to him was forced into publicity by the necessities of a decade later. It will be found in full in *The Path*, for March, 1896.

After acknowledging his letter she says:

> What you say in it seems to me like an echo of my own thoughts in many a way; only knowing the truth and the real state of things in the

> "Occult world" better than you do, I am perhaps able to see better also where the real mischief was and lies.

What the truth and the real state of things was in connection with the facts and factors underlying the course of events we are considering is discussed at length:

> As to . . . that portion of your letter where you speak of the "army" of the deluded—and the "imaginary" Mahatmas of Olcott—you are absolutely and sadly right. Have I not seen the thing for nearly eight years? Have I not struggled and fought against Olcott's ardent and gushing imagination, and tried to stop him every day of my life? Was he not told by me . . . that if he did not see the Masters in their true light, and did not cease speaking and enflaming people's imaginations, that he would be held responsible for all the evil the Society might come to? . . .
>
> Ah, if by some psychological process you could be made to see the whole truth! . . . I was sent to America on purpose and sent to the Eddys. There I found Olcott in love with spirits, as he became in love with the Masters later on. I was ordered to let him know that spiritual phenomena without the philosophy of Occultism were dangerous and misleading. I proved to him that all that mediums could do through spirits others could do at will without any spirits at all. . . . Well, I told him the whole truth. I said to him that I had known Adepts, . . . That . . . Adepts were everywhere Adepts —silent, secret, retiring, and who would never divulge themselves entirely to anyone, unless one did as I did—passed seven and ten years' probation and given proofs of absolute devotion, and that he, or she, would keep silent even before a prospect and a threat of death. I fulfilled

the requirements and am what I am; and this no Hodgson, no Coulombs, no Sellin,[1] can take away from me. . . .

When we arrived [in India] and Master coming to Bombay bodily, paid a visit to us . . . Olcott became crazy. He was like Balaam's she-ass when she saw the angel! Then came . . . other fanatics who began calling them "Mahatmas"; and, little by little, the Adepts were transformed into Gods on earth. They began to be appealed to, and made *puja* to, and were becoming with every day more legendary and miraculous. . . . Well between this idea of Mahatmas and Olcott's rhapsodies, what could I do? I saw with terror and anger the false track they were all pursuing. The "Masters," as all thought, must be omniscient, omnipresent, omnipotent. . . . The Masters knew all; why did they not help the devotee? If a mistake or a flapdoodle was committed in the Society—"How could the Masters allow you or Olcott to do so?" we were asked in amazement. The idea that the Masters were mortal men, limited even in their great powers, never crossed anyone's mind. . . .

Is it Olcott's fault? perhaps, to a degree. Is it mine? I absolutely deny it, and protest aganist the accusation. It is no one's fault. Human nature alone, and the failure of modern society and religions to furnish people with something higher and nobler than craving after money and honors—is at the bottom of it. Place this failure on one side, and the mischief and havoc produced in people's brains by modern spiritualism, and you have the enigma solved. Olcott to this day is sincere, true and devoted to the cause. He does and acts the best he knows how, and the mistakes and absurdities he has

[1] A German professor and Spiritualist to whom Dr. Hubbe-Schleiden turned for "messages," after *his* breach with H.P.B., and who, like Mr. Sinnett's "psychics," charged her with bogus communications.

> committed and commits to this day are due to something he lacks in the psychological portion of his brain, and he is not responsible for it. Loaded and heavy is his Karma, poor man, but much must be forgiven to him, for he has always erred through lack of right judgment, not from any vicious propensity.

This letter, it will be noted, was written a year after H.P.B.'s departure from India, a little over a year before the foundation of *Lucifer*, and forms part of the chain of time and action leading to the formation of the Esoteric Section. Both H.P.B. and Mr. Judge from then on made the most strenuous efforts, publicly and privately, in preparations for the restoration of the Society, in Europe and America at least, to a semblance of its original lines, through the Esoteric Section. The obstacles, internally, lay in misconceptions of the philosophy, in the erroneous ideas in regard to the nature of the Masters, in the deeply rooted preconceived opinions of Col. Olcott and many others as to the purposes of the Society. From their point of view the Society had achieved a magnificent success and, under their guidance and direction, was on the highroad to still greater conquests; its drawbacks and limitations chiefly due to the "mistakes" and the "interferences" of H.P.B. How intensely these opinions affected Mr. Sinnett we shall find in due course.[2] How entirely they governed the outlook and controlled the attitude of Col. Olcott we have now to witness. Turning to "Old Diary Leaves," we may join him in India in the summer of 1887, shortly after H.P.B. had removed to London. Beginning with the last chapter of his Third Series he says:

> At Chupra, among my foreign letters I received one from H.P.B. which distressed me much. She had consented to start a new magazine with capital subscribed by London friends

[2] See also in this connection Mr. Sinnett's posthumous book, "The Early Days of Theosophy in Europe."

of hers, while she was still editor and half proprietor of the *Theosophist*—a most unusual and unbusinesslike proceeding. Besides other causes, among them the persuasion of English friends, a reason which strongly moved her to this was that Mr. Cooper-Oakley, her own appointee as Managing Editor, had more or less sided with T. Subba Row in a dispute which had sprung up between him and H.P.B. on the question whether the "principles" which go to the make-up of a human being were seven or five in number. Subba Row had replied in our pages to an article of hers on the subject, and her letters to me about it were most bitter and denunciatory of Cooper-Oakley, whom she, without reasonable cause, charged with treachery. It was one of those resistless impulses which carried her away sometimes into extreme measures. She wanted me to take away his editorial authority, and even sent me a foolish document, like a power-of-attorney, empowering me to send him to Coventry, so to say, and not allow any galley-proof to pass to the printer until initialed by myself. Of course, I remonstrated strongly against her thus, without precedent, setting up a rival competing magazine to hurt as much as possible the circulation and influence of our old-established organ, on the title-page of which her name still appeared. But it was useless to protest; she said she was determined to have a magazine in which she could say what she pleased, and in due time *Lucifer* appeared as her personal organ, and I got on as well as I could without her. Meanwhile, a lively interchange of letters went on between us. She was at strife then, more or less, with Mr. Sinnett, and before this was settled, a number of seceders from his London Lodge organized as the Blavatsky Lodge, and met at her house in Lansdowne Road, where her sparkling personality and vast knowledge of Occult things always ensured full meetings.

In the second chapter of the Fourth Series, which Col. Olcott heads, "The Fears of H.P.B.," he says, by way of preface:

> When I look back through my papers of those days of stress and storm, and read the letters written me from exile by Mme. Blavatsky, the solemn feeling comes over me that the binding mortar of its blocks was stiffened by the blood of her heart, and in her anguish were they laid. She was the Teacher, I the pupil; she the misunderstood and insulted messenger of the Great Ones, I the practical brain to plan, the right hand to work out the practical details.

After a desultory sentence or two the "pupil" continues in regard to his Teacher, the "misunderstood messenger of the Great Ones":

> It is painful beyond words to read her correspondence from Europe, and see how she suffered from various causes, fretting and worrying too often over mares' nests. Out of the sorest grievances I select the defection of T. Subba Rao [Row]; the admission into the *Theosophist* by the Sub-Editor (whom she had herself appointed) of articles which she considered antagonistic to the Trans-Himalayan teachings; the refusal of Subba Rao to edit the *Secret Doctrine* MSS., contrary to his original promise, . . . his wholesale condemnation of it; the personal quarrels of various European colleagues; the war between Mr. Judge and Dr. Coues in America; the threatened renewal of persecution against her if she returned to India, as we begged her to do; . . .

On p. 41 he continues:

> Things were growing more and more unpleasant at Adyar on account of the friction between H.P.B. and T. Subba Rao and certain of his Anglo-Indian backers. They even went so far as to threaten withdrawal from the Society and the publication of a rival magazine if H.P.B. did not treat them better.

On p. 47 he says:

> Portents of a coming storm in our European groups, stirred up or intensified by H.P.B., begin to show themselves, and Judge complains of our neglecting him. Just then Dr. Coues was working hard for the notoriety he craved, and Judge was opposing him.

Finally, on p. 51, referring to the same year (1888) Col. Olcott relates:

> The last week in June brought me a vexatious letter from H.P.B., indicative of a storm of trouble that was raging in and about her.

Chapter IV of the Fourth Series is entitled "Formation of the Esoteric Section," and continues Col. Olcott's reminiscences of this momentous epoch. He first pays tribute to H.P.B. and then proceeds to soliloquize—always to the issue that he was the saviour of the Society against the weaknesses and mistakes of H.P.B. Thus:

> It was remarked at the end of the last chapter that we were now about to review some disagreeable incidents of the year in which H.P.B. was a conspicuous factor. If she had been just an ordinary person hidden behind the screen of domesticity, this history of the development of

> the Theosophical movement might have been written without bringing her on the stage; or if the truth had been told about her by friend and and foe I might have left her to be dealt with by her karma, showing, of course, what great part she had played in it, and to how great a credit she was entitled. But she has shared the fate of all public characters of mark in human affairs, having been absurdly flattered and worshipped by one party, and mercilessly wronged by the other. Unless, then, her most intimate friend and colleague, the surviving builder-up of the movement, had cast aside the reserve he had all along maintained, and would have preferred to preserve, the real personage would never have been understood by her contemporaries, nor justice done to her really grand character. That she was great in the sense of the thorough altruism of her public work is unquestionable: in her times of exaltation self was drowned in the yearning to spread knowledge and do her Master's bidding. She never sold her rich store of occult knowledge for money, nor bartered instruction for personal advantage. She valued her life as nothing as balanced against service, and would have given it as joyfully as any religious martyr if the occasion had seemed to demand the sacrifice. These tendencies and characteristic traits she had brought over with her from a long line of incarnations in which she (and in some, we) had been engaged in like service; they were the aspects of her in-individuality, high, noble, ideally loyal, worthy, not of being worshipped—for no human being ought to be made the cause of slavish adoration —but of aspiration to be like it.

Then the wise pupil, sure of his own discrimination and judgment, proceeds to point out the weaknesses and failings with which his Teacher is afflicted:

Her personality is quite another affair, and afforded a strong background to throw out her interior brightness into stronger relief. In the matter under present discussion, for instance, the front she presents to me in her letters is unlovely to a degree: language violent, passion raging, scorn and satire poorly covered by a skin of soft talk; a disposition to break through the "red tape" of the Society's mild constitution, and to rule or ruin as I might decide to ratify or disavow her arbitrary and utterly unconstitutional acts; a sniffing at the Council and Councillors, whom she did not choose to have stand in her way, a sharp and slashing criticism of certain of her European co-workers, especially of the one most prominent in that part of the movement, whose initials she parenthesized after the word "Satan," and an appeal that I should not let our many years of associated work be lost in the breaking up of the T.S. into two unrelated bodies, the Eastern and Western Theosophical Societies. In short, she writes like a mad person and in the tone of a hyper-excited hysterical woman, . . . Yet, ill in body and upset in mind as she may have been, she was still a mighty factor for me to deal with, and forced me to choose which line of policy I should pursue. The first count in her indictment against me (for, of course, *more suo*, it was all my fault) was that I had decided against her favourite in an arbitration I had held at Paris, that year, between two opposing parties among the French Theosophists; it was, she writes me, "no mistake, but a crime perpetrated by you against Theosophy (doubly underscored), in full knowledge of what X is and fear of Y. Olcott, my friend you are—, but I do not want to hurt your feelings, and will not say to you what you are. If you do not *feel* and *realize it yourself*, then all I can say will be useless. As for P.

> [a Frenchman, subsequently expelled from the Society], you have put yourself entirely in his hands, and you have sacrificed Theosophy, and even the honour of the T.S. in France, out of fear of that wretched little——.

Although on page 23 he specifically declares that "she refused point-blank to lead any Society that did not recognize Adyar as its central head,"—a sheer assertion of his own stated in a manner to indicate it as an indirect citation from one of her letters—on p. 55 he contradicts himself *de but en blanc* by quoting directly from her correspondence:

> She had hatched out a new section, with herself elected as "President," taken a commodious house, and had a sign-board ready to have painted on it either "European Headquarters of the T.S." or "Western Theosophical Society." Seeming to suspect that I might not like it *very* much to have the whole machinery of the Society upset to gratify her whim, and remembering of old that the more she threatened the more stubborn it made me, she writes:
>
> > Now look here, Olcott. It is very painful, most painful, for me to have to put you what the French call *marche en main*, and to have you choose. You will say again that you "hate threats," and these will only make you more stubborn. But this is no threat at all, but a *fait accompli.* It remains with you to either ratify it or to go against it, and declare war on me and my Esotericists. If, recognizing the utmost necessity of the step, you submit to the inexorable evolution of things, nothing will be changed. Adyar and Europe will remain allies, and *to all appearance*, the latter will seem to be subject to the former. If you do not ratify it—well, then there will be two

> Theosophical Societies, the old Indian and the new European, *entirely independent of each other.*

Colonel Olcott says that "This stand-and-deliver ultimatum naturally frightened the 'mild Hindu' members of our Executive Council to fits," and that—"The Paris arbitration above referred to occurred during my European visit of 1888, which kept me there from 26th August to 22nd October, and was made at the entreaty of the Executive Council, as the tone of H.P.B.'s letters had alarmed them for the stability of the movement in the West. The tour should, by rights, have been mentioned before the incidents of the threatened split above alluded to, but H.P.B.'s letters lying nearest to hand, and the trouble being continuous through the two successive years [1888-9], I took it up first."

He then gives the "true history" of the "Paris imbroglio," raging in the "Isis" branch of the T.S. over its conduct by M. F. K. Gaboriau, the editor of *Le Lotus.* Colonel Olcott says:

> In doing this he had become involved in disputes, in which H.P.B. had taken his side, and made a bad mess for me by giving him, in her real character of Co-Founder and her assumed one of my representative, with *full discretionary powers,* a charter of a sweeping and unprecedented character, which practically let him do as he pleased. This was, of course, protested against by some of his soberer colleagues, recriminations arose, and an appeal was made to me.

Colonel Olcott characterizes M. Gaboriau as a "hypersensitive young man . . . who showed an excessive enthusiasm for Theosophy, but small executive faculty."

Colonel Olcott proceeded to Paris and on the 17th September read his formal "decision" to the assembled members. The account in "Old Diary Leaves" recites:

> My action in this affair was taken according to my best judgment, after hearing all that was to be said and seeing everybody concerned; I believe it to have been the best under existing circumstances, though it threw M. Gaboriau out of the active running, caused him and some of his few followers to denounce me unqualifiedly, and led to a pitched battle, as one might say, between H.P.B. and myself on my return to London. The sequel is above shown in her revolutionary action with respect to the reorganization at London. . . . Nearly all the persons engaged in the Paris quarrel were to blame, they having given way to personal jealousies, obliterated the landmarks of the Society, fallen into a strife for supremacy, with mutual abuse, oral and printed. . . .

Judging from the account in "Old Diary Leaves" Olcott was the savior of the T.S. and the Movement, against the "language violent," the "passion raging," the "arbitrary and utterly unconstitutional acts," the "disposition to rule or ruin," the "breaking-up of the T.S. into two unrelated bodies," the "stand-and-deliver ultimatum," the "bad mess" created by H.P.B.—the "mad person," the "conspicuous factor" in the "disagreeable incidents," the "hyperexcited hysterical woman."

In the case in point, the student may turn to the actual "official decision" of Col. Olcott, in contrast to his story as given in "Old Diary Leaves," and there learn whether H.P.B. exceeded her "constitutional powers" in the "Isis Branch" imbroglio. In his own words, as recorded in that "decision":

> It has been objected that Mme. Blavatsky had not the right to act in this matter; that her interference was illegal according to the Rules of the Theosophical Society. . . . But, in point of fact, Mme. Blavatsky is . . . with me Co-

> Founder of the Society, Corresponding Secretary and, *ex officio*, member of the General Council, of the Executive Council and of the Annual Convention, a sort of Parliament held at Adyar by delegates from all countries. . . .
>
> She was, then, perfectly authorized (*compétente*) to issue the order in question as a temporary measure, an order which must be finally submitted for approbation to the President in Council. The Executive Council, in its session of 14th July, formally ratified the measure taken by Mme. Blavatsky, a measure which was urgent, and which I declare to have been legal. . . .

The absolute contradiction between the facts and the story given in "Old Diary Leaves" with its inferences and derogatory statements in regard to H.P.B., shows the utter unreliability of Col. Olcott when his feelings were involved, or when the full facts place him in an unenviable light. Only in the light of a "probationary chela" in the fiery furnace of "pledge fever" can his contradictions be understood and so reconciled with the real honesty of his nature and the genuine devotion which he manifested for the Theosophical Society, of which he was President-Founder and which was the be-all and end-all of existence to him. So identified was it with himself in his consciousness, that more and more he came to view and treat any differences with himself, any correction by his Teacher, as an assault and a menace on the Society.

Colonel Olcott's comments, strictures, and judgments on H.P.B., of which those herein given are but samples of many, stand in melancholy contrast to the Master's own statements in a letter to Col. Olcott at this very time. It is a characteristic anachronism that leads Col. Olcott, in "Old Diary Leaves," Third Series, Chapter VIII, to relate this letter to the joint visit of H.P.B. and himself to Europe in 1884 and the troubles *then* prevalent in the London Lodge; instead of, as was the fact, to the very matters we are considering, in 1888. This letter, which, says Col. Olcott at p. 91, "I received phenomenally in my cabin on board the *Shannon*, the day before we reached Brindisi," is but barely referred to by the Colonel. No one could by any possibility infer the transcendent importance of its contents from the brief quotation given by him. Its textual omission from "Old Diary Leaves" is amply accounted for, (1) by the contents of the letter itself; (2) by the failing faculties of Col. Olcott when "Old Diary Leaves" was written. The brief quotation he gives, however, is sufficient to identify the letter itself, as is also the fact stated that it was received on board the *Shannon*, which was the vessel in which he voyaged in 1888, not in 1884; and, no less, the citations in *Lucifer* for October 15, 1888, where it is stated by H.P.B. that the letter was received by Col. Olcott "only a few weeks ago." The same number of *Lucifer* gives extracts from the letter, the extracts being certified by Col. Olcott himself. Fuller extracts were contained in a pamphlet sent out at the time, entitled "To All Theosophists." The complete text of the letter came to the light of general publicity only after many years. It will be found in the volume, "Letters from the Masters of the Wisdom."

Several momentous facts should be borne in mind in connection with this letter: It was "phenomenally" delivered to Col. Olcott who was voyaging alone, and was at sea, a day from Brindisi, when it was received. Its contents show that it was "precipitated," but a very short time before it was received by the Colonel—a matter of hours or minutes; it refers prophetically as well as historically to other subjects, to which we shall refer later on.[3] At this point it is enough to introduce those extracts which directly relate to Col. Olcott and H.P.B. and shed a clear and authoritative light on their respective natures, status, and functions, no less than on the hidden aspects of the events under consideration. The Master addresses Col. Olcott without preamble or circumlocution:

[3] See Chapters XV and XXIII.

Again, as you approach London, I have a word or two to say to you. Your impressibility is so changeful that I must not wholly depend upon it at this critical time. Of course you know that things were so brought to a focus as to necessitate the present journey. . . . Put all needed restraint upon your feelings, so that you may do the right thing in this Western imbroglio. Watch your first impressions. The mistakes you make spring from failure to do this. Let neither your personal predilections, affections, suspicions nor antipathies affect your action. . . .

Your revolt, good friend, against her "infallibility"—as you once thought it—has gone too far, and you have been unjust to her, for which I am sorry to say, you will have to suffer hereafter, along with others. Just now—on deck, your thoughts about her were dark and sinful, and so I find the moment a fitting one to put you on your guard. . . .

Make *all* these men feel that we have no favourites, nor affections for persons, but only for their good acts and humanity as a whole. But we employ agents—the best available. Of these for the past thirty years, the chief has been the personality known as H.P.B. to the world (but otherwise to us). Imperfect and very "troublesome," no doubt, she proves to some; nevertheless, there is no likelihood of our finding a better one for years to come, and your theosophists should be made to understand it. . . . Her fidelity to our work being constant, and her sufferings having come upon her through it, neither I nor either of my brother associates will desert or supplant her. As I once before remarked, *ingratitude* is not among our vices. With yourself our relations are direct, and have been, with the rare exceptions you know of, like the present, on the psychical plane, and so will continue through force of circumstances. That they are so rare—is your own fault as I told you in my last. To help you in your present perplexity; H.P.B. has next to no concern with administrative details, and should be kept clear of them, so far as her strong nature can be controlled, but this *you must tell to all:—with Occult matters she has everything to do.* We have *not* "abandoned" her. She is *not* "given over to chelas." She is *our direct agent.* I warn you against permitting your suspicions and resentment against "her many follies" to bias your intuitive loyalty to her. In the adjustment of this European business, you will have two things to consider—the external and administrative, and the internal and psychical. Keep the former under your control and that of your most prudent associates jointly; *leave the latter to her.* You are left to devise the practical details with your usual ingenuity. Only be careful, I say, to discriminate when some emergent interference of hers in practical affairs is referred to you on appeal, between that which is merely exoteric in origin and effects, and that which beginning on the practical tends to beget consequences on the spiritual plane. As to the former you are the best judge, as to the latter, she. . . .

There have been sore trials in the past, others await you in the future. May the faith and courage which have supported you hitherto endure to the end. . . .

This letter . . . is merely given you as a warning and a guide. . . .

This letter from the Master, and the influence of H.P.B., prevailed for the time to restore the poise of Col. Olcott, to put him in his proper place, and to prevent any open breach in the Theosophical ranks. As in the spring of 1885, H.P.B. made every effort to shield Olcott himself, no less than the Society at large, from the bad consequences of his ill-advised actions. A "Joint

Note" was published in *Lucifer* along with the extracts from the Master's letter, from the official "decision" of Col. Olcott, and the notice of the Esoteric Section of the Theosophical Society. The form, both of the "Joint Note" and of the "Notice" was made, as with the notices in *The Theosophist* in the spring of 1885, to shield Col. Olcott in his position of President-Founder of the T. S., and to uphold as far as possible his standing before the membership. The "Joint Note" is as follows:

> To dispel a misconception that has been engendered by mischief-makers, we, the undersigned, Founders of the Theosophical Society, declare that there is no enmity, rivalry, strife, or even coldness, between us, nor ever was; nor any weakening of our joint devotion to the Masters, or to our work, with the execution of which they have honoured us. Widely dissimilar in temperament and mental characteristics, and differing sometimes in views as to methods of propagandism, we are yet absolutely of one mind as to that work. As we have been from the first, so are we now united in purpose and zeal, and ready to sacrifice all, even life, for the promotion of theosophical knowledge, to the saving of mankind from the miseries which spring from ignorance.
>
> H. P. BLAVATSKY.
> H. S. OLCOTT.

The public Notice of the Esoteric Section reads:

> THE ESOTERIC SECTION OF THE THEOSOPHICAL SOCIETY
>
> Owing to the fact that a large number of Fellows of the Society have felt the necessity for the formation of a body of Esoteric Students, to be organized on the ORIGINAL LINES devised by the real founders of the T.S., the

> following order has been issued by the President-Founder:
>
> I. To promote the esoteric interests of the Theosophical Society by the deeper study of esoteric philosophy, there is hereby organized a body, to be known as the "Esoteric Section of the Theosophical Society."
>
> II. The constitution and sole direction of the same is vested in Madame H. P. Blavatsky, as its Head; she is solely responsible to the Members for results; and the section has no official or corporate connection with the Exoteric Society save in the person of the President-Founder.
>
> III. Persons wishing to join the Section and willing to abide by its rules, should communicate directly with MME. H. P. BLAVATSKY, 17 Lansdowne Road, Holland Park, London, W.
>
> (Signed) H. S. OLCOTT,
> President in Council.
>
> Attest: H. P. BLAVATSKY.

The astonishing admixture of complacency and *naïveté* exhibited in "Old Diary Leaves" is well illustrated by the following extracts, summing up, from Col. Olcott's point of view, the "title role" played by himself:

> I called two Conventions at London of the British Branches, organized and chartered a British Section of the T.S., and issued an order in Council forming an Esoteric Section, with Madame Blavatsky as its responsible head. . . . This was the beginning of the E.S.T. movement. . . . The reason for my throwing the whole responsibility for results upon H.P.B. was that she had already made one failure in this direction at Adyar in 1884 . . . and I did not care to be responsible for the fulfilment of any special engagements she might make with the new set of students she was now gathering about her, in

her disturbed state of mind. I helped her write some of her instructions, and did all I could to make the way easy for her, but that was all. . . .

My tour realized the objects in view, H.P.B. being pacified, our affairs in Great Britain put in order, and the E. S. started; but . . . the calm was not destined to last and a second visit to Europe had to be made in 1889, after my return from Japan.

CHAPTER XI

THE WORK OF THE ESOTERIC SECTION

After the events narrated in the last chapter, Col. Olcott returned to India, and, at the end of December, held the usual "convention" or "parliament" at Adyar. The full report of the sessions is contained in the "Supplement" to *The Theosophist* for January, 1889.

After the admission that "the Annual Convention of the General Council has ceased to be, save in name, the true parliament or congress of the Branches," the report nevertheless goes on to affirm that the "fair thing" was "evidently to extend the sectional scheme to all countries," while yet "keeping the Headquarters as the hub and the President-Founder as the axle of this wheel of many spokes under the car of Progress . . . with the central point where the President-Founder represents and wields the executive authority of the entire undivided body known as the Theosophical Society."

"The President-Founder's Address" to the Convention opens with an argument to show that he "should be left with the widest discretion" in the management of the Society. Col. Olcott sums up:

> The time has come when I should say, most distinctly and unequivocally, that since I am to stay and be responsible for the progress of the work, I shall not consent to any plan or scheme which hinders me in the performance of my official duty.
>
> . . . I have never interfered with the esoteric or metaphysical part, nor set myself up as a competent teacher. That is Madame Blavatsky's specialty; and the better to enunciate that

> idea I have just issued an Order in Council in London creating an Esoteric Section under her sole direction, as a body, or group, entirely separate and distinct from the Society proper and involving the latter in no responsibilities toward those who might choose to enrol themselves in her list of adherents.
>
> . . . This is my determination: To be . . . loyal and staunch to the colleague you and I, and all of us know and a few of us appreciate at her true worth. This is my last word on that subject; but in saying it I do not mean to imply that I shall not freely use my own judgment, independently of Madame Blavatsky's, in every case calling for my personal action, nor that I shall not ever be most willing and anxious to receive and profit by the counsel of every true person who has at heart the interests of the Society. I cannot please all: it is folly to try; the wise man does his duty as he can see it before him.

The Address gives in brief the story of the troubles in Paris and London. Though these events were then all fresh in his mind; though the Master's words were still ringing in his ears; though the generous protection of H.P.B. still enveloped him and enabled him to "save his face" before the rank and file of the membership—the attitude taken and view expressed testify the same invincible self-complacency that at last wholly absorbed the probationary chela in the President-Founder. Thus:

> It was by the Executive Council found expedient that I should proceed to Europe and attempt to bring our affairs into order. We saw the Continental Branches languishing for lack of superintendence and reciprocal work, although there was reason to hope that the movement might be greatly strengthened and ex-

> panded under the proper organization. . . . I formed new Branches . . .; dischartered the old "Isis" Branch at Paris and chartered a new one . . .; called two Conventions in London . . .; organized and chartered a British Section of the Theosophical Society; and issued an order in Council forming an Esoteric Section of the Society, with Madame Blavatsky as its responsible head. The trouble in the Paris Branch was solely due—as we have almost invariably found to be the case—to personal jealousies and disagreements. The landmarks of the Society had been obliterated and forgotten; there had arisen a strife for supremacy, and, instead of setting the public an example of zealous fraternal union for the propagation of our ideas, the members had fallen to mutual abuse, oral and printed. Both parties were to blame, as I found after patient examination of the documents . . .

In no part of Col. Olcott's published statements is there a hint that might be construed that he at any time found himself in any way at fault; on the contrary, there is everywhere the continuous holding out of himself as the all-important factor in bringing order out of chaos, in holding the Society true to its purposes. Nowhere appears the faintest glimmer of perception that he himself might be the weakest joint in the Society's armor; that it was his failures as a probationer which were constantly upsetting his work as Executive.

It is intensely interesting and instructive to turn from the Adyar parliament to the proceedings of the Convention of the American Section in the April following. Delegates and proxies, democratically elected, were in attendance from all of the twenty-five active Lodges in the United States. The only one not represented was the Gnostic of Washington, D. C., controlled by Dr. Elliott Coues, whose case we shall shortly consider.

The spirit and energizing direction of the American Section, the devotion to a Cause rather than to its instrument, the Society, as contrasted with the work in India under Col. Olcott's autocratic control, are well typified in Madame Blavatsky's Letter to the Convention, presented by Mr. Judge in these words: "I have received from our revered founder, Madame H. P. Blavatsky, a letter for this Convention . . . and beg to lay it before you."

The four Letters of H.P.B. to the Conventions of the American Section are unique. They are the only addresses of H.P.B. to any Theosophical bodies, for she never thus honored either the Indian, the British, or the European Sections. These Letters are the public authoritative statements by the Agent of the Masters in enunciation of the real basis of the Theosophical Society and of all Theosophical endeavor, esoteric and exoteric. This second Letter was written soon after the issuance of the *Preliminary Memorandum* and *First Instruction* to the members of the Esoteric Section. The Letter shows the real spirit of the Movement in the West, the ever-existent dangers to be confronted, her insistent endeavor to keep the line energized in the true direction, and illustrates her exoteric handling of the situation. Thus:

> But you in America. Your Karma as a nation has brought Theosophy home to you. The life of the Soul, the psychic side of nature, is open to many of you. The life of altruism is not so much a high ideal as a matter of practice. Naturally, then, Theosophy finds a home in many hearts and minds, and strikes a resounding harmony as soon as it reaches the ears of those who are ready to listen. There, then, is part of your work: to lift high the torch of the liberty of the Soul of Truth that all may see it and benefit by its light.
>
> Therefore it is that the Ethics of Theosophy are even more necessary to mankind than the scientific aspects of the psychic facts of nature and man . . .

> . . . Once before was growth checked in connection with the psychic phenomena, and there may yet come a time when the moral and ethical foundations of the Society may be wrecked in a similar way. What can be done to prevent such a thing is for each Fellow of the Society to make Theosophy a vital factor in their lives—to make it real, to weld its principles firmly into their lives—in short, to make it their own and treat the Theosophical Society as if it were themselves. Following closely on this is the necessity for Solidarity among the Fellows of the Society; the acquisition of such a feeling of identity with each and all of our Brothers that an attack upon one is an attack upon all. . . .

These statements were at once the recital of history, a warning, an admonition, and, as events have all too plainly proved, a prophecy. Where the danger ever lies, and how to meet it, are considered:

> We have external enemies to fight in the shape of materialism, prejudice, and obstinacy; the enemies in the shape of custom and religious forms; enemies too numerous to mention, but nearly as thick as the sand-clouds which are raised by the blasting Sirocco of the desert. Do we not need our strength against these foes? Yet, again, there are more insidious foes, who "take our name in vain," and who make Theosophy a by-word in the mouths of men and the Theosophical Society a mark at which to throw mud. They slander Theosophists and Theosophy, and convert the moral Ethics into a cloak to conceal their own selfish objects. And as if this were not sufficient, there are the worst foes of all—those of a man's own household—Theosophists who are unfaithful both to the Society and to themselves. . . .
>
> Let us, for a moment, glance backwards at

the ground we have passed over. We have had . . . to hold our own against the Spiritists, in the name of Truth and Spiritual Science. Not against the students of the true psychic knowledge, nor against the enlightened Spiritualists; but against the lower order of phenomenalists—the blind worshippers of the illusionary phantoms of the Dead. These we have fought for the sake of Truth, and also for that of the world which they were misleading. . . . Unless prepared carefully by a long and special course of study, the experimentalist risks not only the medium's soul but his own. The experiments made in Hypnotism and Mesmerism at the present time are experiments of unconscious, when not of conscious, Black Magic. The road is wide and broad which leads to such destruction; and it is but too easy to find; and only too many go ignorantly along it to their own destruction. But the practical cure of it lies in one thing. That is the course of study which I mentioned before. It sounds very simple, but it is eminently difficult; for that cure is "ALTRUISM." And this is the key-note of Theosophy and the cure for all ills; this it is which the real founders of the Theosophical Society promote as its first object—UNIVERSAL BROTHERHOOD.

Thus even if only in name a body of Altruists, the Theosophical Society has to fight all who under its cover seek to obtain magical powers to use for their own selfish ends and to the hurt of others. Many are those who joined our Society for no other purpose than curiosity. Psychological phenomena were what they sought, and they were unwilling to yield one iota of their own pleasure and habits to obtain them. These very quickly went away empty-handed. The Theosophical Society has never been and never will be a school of promiscuous Theurgic rites. But there are dozens of small occult Societies which talk very glibly of Magic, Occultism, Rosicrucians, Adepts, etc. These profess much, even to giving the key to the Universe, but end by leading men to a blank wall instead of the "Door of the Mysteries." These are some of our most insidious foes. Under cover of the philosophy of the Wisdom-Religion they manage to get up a mystical jargon which for the time is effective and enables them, by the aid of a very small amount of clairvoyance, to fleece the mystically inclined but ignorant aspirants to the occult, and lead them like sheep in almost any direction. . . But woe to those who try to convert a noble philosophy into a den of disgusting immorality, greediness for selfish power, and money-making under the cloak of Theosophy. Karma reaches them when least expected. But is it possible for our Society to stand by and remain respected, unless its members are prepared, at least in future, to stand like one man, and deal with such slanders upon themselves as true Theosophists, and such vile caricatures of their highest ideals . . .?

But in order that we may be able to effect this working on behalf of our common cause, we have to sink all private differences. Many are the energetic members . . . who wish to work and to work hard. But the price of their assistance is that all the work must be done in their way and not in anyone else's way. And if this is not carried out they sink back into apathy or leave the Society entirely, loudly declaring that they are the only true Theosophists. Or, if they remain, they endeavor to exalt their own method of working at the expense of all other earnest workers. This is fact, but it is not Theosophy. There can be no other end to it than that the growth of the Society will soon be split up into various sects, as many as there are leaders. . . . Is this prospect one to look forward to . . . ? Is

> this "Separateness" consonant with the united Altruism of Universal Brotherhood? Is this the teaching of our noble MASTERS?

The Letter contained a public reference to the Esoteric Section in these words:

> As many of you are aware, we have formed the "Esoteric Section." Its members are pledged, among other things, to work for Theosophy under my direction. By it, for one thing, we have endeavored to secure some solidarity in our common work; to form a strong body of resistance against attempts to injure us on the part of the outside world, against prejudice against the Theosophical Society and against me personally. By its means much may be done to nullify the damage to the work of the Society in the past and to vastly further its work in the future.

The Letter closes:

> And now a last and parting word. My words may and will pass and be forgotten, but certain sentences from letters written by the Masters will never pass, because they are the embodiment of the highest practical Theosophy. I must translate them for you:—
>
> ". . . Let not the fruit of good Karma be your motive; for your Karma, good or bad, being one and the common property of all mankind, nothing good or bad can happen to you that is not shared by many others. Hence your motive, being selfish, can only generate a double effect, good and bad, and will either nullify your good action, or turn it to another man's profit. . . . There is no happiness for one who is ever thinking of Self and forgetting all other Selves.

> "The Universe groans under the weight of such action (Karma), and none other than self-sacrificial Karma relieves it. . . . How many of you have helped humanity to carry its smallest burden, that you should all regard yourselves as Theosophists? Oh, men of the West, who would play at being the Saviors of mankind before they even spare the life of a mosquito whose sting threatens them! would you be partakers of Divine Wisdom or true Theosophists? Then do as the gods when incarnated do. Feel yourselves the vehicles of the whole humanity, mankind as part of yourselves, and act accordingly. . . ."

> These are golden words; may you assimilate them! This is the hope of one who signs herself most sincerely the devoted sister *and servant* of every true follower of the Masters of Theosophy.

To any sincere student of today the thirty years of history intervening since the date of this Letter furnish their own confirmation and commentary on the prevision, the spiritual insight, the practical common sense and the never-dying courage of H.P.B. They show, as nothing else does or can do, the overwhelming need for a *return to the Source* of all true Theosophical inspiration and endeavor. This from the exoteric standpoint alone. Permissible extracts from the *Preliminary Memorandum* to the E.S. applicants show her esoteric treatment of the same problems:

Immediately following upon the publication in *Lucifer* of the Notice of the formation of the Esoteric Section, H.P.B. sent out to all applicants a formal communication, marked as were all subsequent papers of the Section, *strictly private and confidential.* It contained an introductory statement, a summary entitled "Rules of the Esoteric Section (Probationary) of the Theosophical Society," the "Pledge of Probationers in the Esoteric Section," and some preliminary questions and requirements to be responded to by the applicant. The introductory paragraphs read as follows:

> I forward you herewith a copy of the Rules and Pledge for Probationers of the Esoteric Section of the T.S.
>
> Should you be unable to accept them, I request that you will return this to me without delay.

The Rules referred to recite, amongst others, that no one will be admitted who is not a Fellow of the T.S.; that applications for membership in the Esoteric Section must be accompanied by a copy of the Pledge "*written out* and signed by the Candidate, who thereupon enters upon a special period of probation, which commences from the date of his signature"; that "all members shall be approved by the Head of the Section"—H.P.B.

Some hundreds of the most active and earnest Fellows of the T.S. complied with all the formal requirements above outlined, sent in their Pledges, and entered upon their special period of probation. H.P.B. forwarded to all these the *First Preliminary Memorandum* of the Section. This remarkable document has either been suppressed, altered or ignored, like the Pledge and Rules of the original School, by its unworthy "successors"; while its plain statements of facts, its prescient presentments of principles and their applications to the then present and future, now the past, the present, and the future, have been deliberatly disregarded and corrupted.

The *Preliminary Memorandum* tells the probationers the impelling occasion for the step taken:

> . . . At this stage it is perhaps better that the applicants should learn the reason for the formation of this Section, and what it is expected to achieve.

The Theosophical Society had just entered upon the fourteenth year of its existence; and if it had accomplished great, one may almost say stupendous, results on the exoteric and utilitarian plane, it had proved a dead failure on all those points which rank foremost among the objects of its original establishment. Thus, as a "Universal Brotherhood," or even as a fraternity, one among many, it had descended to the level of all those societies whose pretensions are great, but whose names are simply masks—nay, even SHAMS. Nor can the excuse be pleaded that it was led into such an undignified course owing to its having been impeded in its natural development, and almost extinguished, by reason of the conspiracies of its enemies *openly* begun in 1884. Because even before that date there never was that solidarity in the ranks of our Society which would not only enable it to resist all external attacks, but also make it possible for greater, wider and more tangible help to be given to all its members by Those who are always ready to give help when we are fit to receive it. When trouble arose, too many were quick to doubt and despair, and few indeed were they who had worked for the Cause and not for themselves. The attacks of the enemy have given the Society some discretion in the conduct of its external progress but its real internal condition has not improved, and the members, in their efforts toward spiritual culture still require that help which solidarity in the ranks can alone give them the right to ask. The Masters can give but little assistance to a Body not thoroughly united in purpose and feeling, and which breaks its first fundamental rule —universal brotherly love, without distinction of race, creed, colour or caste, *i. e.*, the social distinctions made in the world; nor to a Society, many members of which pass their lives in judging, condemning, and often reviling other members in a most untheosophical, not to say disgraceful, manner.

For this reason it was decided to gather the "elect" of the T.S., and to call them to action. It is only by a select group of brave souls, a handful of determined men and women hungry for genuine spiritual development and the acquirement of soul-wisdom, that the Theosophical Society at large can be brought back to its original lines. It is through an Esoteric Section alone—*i.e.*, a group in which all the members, even if unacquainted with one another, work for each other, and by working for all work for themselves—that the great Exoteric Society may be redeemed and made to realize that in union and harmony alone lie its strength and power. The object of this Section, then, is to help the future growth of the Theosophical Society as a whole in the true direction, by promoting brotherly union at least among a choice minority.

All know that this end was in view when the Society was established, and even in its mere unpledged ranks there was a possibility of development and knowledge, until it began to show want of real union; and now it must be saved from future dangers by the united aim, brotherly feeling, and constant exertions of the members of this Esoteric Section. Once offered the grand example of practical altruism, of the noble lives of those who learn to master the great knowledge but to help others, and who strive to acquire powers but to place them at the service of their fellow-men, and the whole Theosophical community may yet be steered into action, and led to follow the example set before them.

The Esoteric Section is thus "set apart" for the salvation of the whole Society, and its course from its first step is an arduous and

> uphill work for its members, though a great reward lies behind the many obstacles once they are overcome.

To allay any misapprehensions due to widespread erroneous ideas regarding chelaship and asceticism while at the same time placing before the Candidates the seriousness of the steps contemplated and the absolutely essential prerequisites to any real solidarity or individual evolution, several paragraphs are devoted to direct plain speaking on these subjects. Thus the Candidates are told that one object of the *Memorandum*—

> . . . is to give timely warning to any applicant, should he feel unable or unwilling to accept fully and without reserve, the instructions which may be given, or the consequences that may result, and to do the duties whose performance shall be asked. It is but fair to state at once that such duties will never interfere with, nor encroach upon, the probationer's family duties; on the other hand, it is certain that every member of the Esoteric Section will have to give up more than one personal habit, such as practised in social life, and adopt some few ascetic rules.

Those who may be seeking "powers" and "Occult preferment" are advised:

> This degree of the Esoteric Section is probationary, and its general purpose is to prepare and fit the student for the study of practical Occultism or Raja Yoga. Therefore, in this degree the student—save in exceptional cases—will not be taught how to produce physical phenomena, nor will any magical powers be allowed to develop in him; nor, if possessing such powers naturally, will he be permitted to exercise them before he has mastered the knowledge of SELF, of the psycho-physiological processes . . .

in the human body generally, and until he has in abeyance all his lower passions and his PERSONAL SELF. . . .

Each person will receive in the way of enlightenment and assistance, just as much as he or she deserves, and no more; and it is to be distinctly understood that in this Section and these relations no such thing is known as favour—all depends upon the person's merits—and no member has the power or knowledge to decide what either he or she is entitled to. This must be left to those who know—alone. The apparent favour shown to some, and their consequent apparent advancement, will be due to the work they do, to the best of their power, in the cause of Universal Brotherhood and the elevation of the Race.

No man or woman is asked or expected to do any more than is his or her best; but each is expected to work to the extent of his ability and powers.

The value of the work of this Section to the individual member will depend upon:

1st. The person's power to assimilate the teachings and make them a part of his being; and

2nd. Upon the unselfishness of the motives with which he seeks for his knowledge; that is to say, upon whether he has entered this Section determined to work for humanity, or with only the desire to benefit or gain something for himself.

The *Book of Rules* supplied to each Candidate with the *Preliminary Memorandum* provided specifically amongst other things, that the various Groups into which those accepted were to be formed were *not* for *practical Occultism,* but for mutual study of the Instructions and help in the Theosophic life; gossip, derogatory statements, and the repetition of slanderous and hearsay statements were strictly forbidden; the dangers and evils of cant, hypocrisy, and injustice to others were enforced; claims of Occult powers, boasting or speaking of Occult experiences, whether falsely or truly, discountenanced under penalty; the widest charity, tolerance, and mutual consideration and helpfulness laid down as the *sine qua non* of all true progress. "The first test of true apprenticeship," said the *Rule* on that subject, "is devotion to the interest of another," and continued:

> For these doctrines to practically re-act on the life through the so-called moral code or the ideas of truthfulness, purity, self-denial, charity, etc., we have to preach and popularize a knowledge of Theosophy. It is not the individual or determined purpose of attaining oneself Nirvana, which is, after all, only an exalted and glorious *selfishness*, but the self-sacrificing pursuit of the best means to lead our neighbour on the right path, and cause as many of our fellow creatures as we possibly can to benefit by it, which constitutes the true Theosophist.

CHAPTER XII

MABEL COLLINS AND PROFESSOR COUES

By 1889, despite all obstacles and all limitations, despite all the guerilla warfare of antagnostic elements and all the heavy artillery of the numerous "exposures" of H.P.B., the Theosophical Movement had gained such headway that the word "Theosophy" was part of the vocabulary of every intelligent person. The Theosophical Society was established in every civilized country and in every large city; the public announcement of the Esoteric Section had drawn the attention of the mystically inclined to the fact of the existence of a definite school of Occult instruction. The student will have poorly gauged the force of the powerful metaphysical current at work if he is not prepared for a more striking example of the real Theosophical phenomena than any so far produced. The great storm of 1889-90 does not vary in essentials from those which preceded it. The drama is the same.

Originally a newspaper writer and novelist, Miss Mabel Collins, then a young woman, had joined the London Lodge in 1884. Imaginative and sensitive in temperament she became intensely interested, not in Theosophy, but in the "psychical activities" pursued by many of the members of that Lodge. During that year she produced "The Idyll of the White Lotus." This was followed, early in 1885, by "Light on the Path, a Treatise written for the personal use of those who are ignorant of the Eastern Wisdom, and who desire to enter within its influence. Written down by M. C., Fellow of the Theosophical Society." As this was the first and up to that time the only, apparently simple and direct statement of the Rules of practical Occultism, and as it was plainly hinted that the book was "inspired" it attracted immediate attention. Moreover, its inherent merit, the sustained beauty of its diction, the noble simplicity of its expression of the loftiest ethics, the moral grandeur of the ideals submitted as within the reach of human attainment, at once gave it rank as a Theosophical classic. "Through the Gates of Gold," from the same pen, appeared in 1887. In the autumn of the same year, when Madame Blavatsky began the publication of *Lucifer,* the name of Mabel Collins appeared with her own as Editor. In view of the circumstances it was but natural that Theosophists everywhere should hold Miss Collins in the highest respect and regard.

When, therefore, with the issue of February 15, 1889, the name of Mabel Collins disappeared from *Lucifer,* it was inevitable that a furor of curiosity and interest should set in. This was accentuated by the fact that Miss Collins retired to privacy and gave no hint as to the cause of the breach; *Lucifer* gave no explanations and made no comments; Mr. Judge's *Path* and Col. Olcott's *Theosophist* remained equally silent. There the matter rested, so far as concerned public knowledge of events "behind the scenes," until the month of May.

On May 11, 1889, there appeared in the *Religio-Philosophical Journal* a letter from Dr. Elliott Coues, embodying a letter to him from Miss Mabel Collins. The *Religio-Philosophical Journal* was an old established and leading Spiritualist publication printed at Chicago and edited by Col. Bundy, a life-long Spiritualist and a friend of Prof. Coues. Colonel Bundy had been admitted to membership in the Theosophical Society in 1885, on the recommendation of Prof. Coues and was a member of the Gnostic Branch of the T.S., at Washington, D. C., a Branch founded by Prof. Coues who was and had been its President from the beginning. The *Religio-Philosophical Journal* had previously given publicity to attacks upon H.P.B., by W. Emmette Coleman, whose life was for many years chiefly devoted to that purpose.

The Coues-Collins letters, and other communications from the same source in later issues of the *Religio-Phil-*

osophical Journal, made grave charges against H.P.B., —grave in themselves, and doubly so from the reputation of those who made them.

Of Catholic family and education, Prof. Coues was a university graduate and originally by profession an American Army surgeon attached to various posts and expeditions. Highly educated, exceedingly versatile, of independent means, he became interested in various branches of science and pursued his studies and investigations to such good purpose that he soon ranked as an authority on many subjects. He published various books and was invited to edit that portion of the "Century Dictionary" dealing with his specialties. Early in the 80's of the last century, while still in the prime of life, he awakened to an interest in psychical research, and conducted many experiments of his own with chosen "subjects." He early became a member of the London Society for Psychical Research and was in London in the summer of 1884, at the time the S.P.R. Committee was making its preliminary investigation and report on the Theosophical phenomena. He sought out Col. Olcott who was naturally rejoiced to make his acquaintance, and finding his interest, to induct him into membership in the Theosophical Society. In company with Col. Olcott, Prof. Coues and his wife journeyed to Elberfeld, Germany to meet H.P.B., who was at the time with the trusted and trusting Gebhards. A great and spontaneous affection sprang up between Mrs. Coues and H.P.B.—an affection which never lapsed, on the one side or on the other.

Professor Coues met Col. Olcott again at London and was appointed a member of the newly constituted American Board of Control of the Theosophical Society. On his return to the United States he established the Gnostic Branch of the T. S. In 1885 he was active in the formation of the American Society for Psychical Research along the same lines of inquiry as pursued by its British predecessor. He was elected Chairman of the American Board of Control of the T.S., and in the midst of his multifarious activities in other directions busied himself in correspondence with members of the Society. Of engaging manners and distinguished appearance, as excellent a speaker as he was brilliant a writer, he was a very popular lecturer and gave many addresses before scientific bodies, clubs, and other associations. Although he never made any distinctly Theosophical addresses there runs through all his lectures of the period a definite note of inquiry and suggestion of broader fields of investigation than those passing current under the name of "science." Although he was not a contributor to the Theosophical literature of the times, as editor of the "Biogen Series" he brought out an American edition of Col. Olcott's "Buddhist Catechism," republished the monograph, "Can Matter Think?" and published with an introduction and notes by himself Robert Dodsley's "True and Complete Œconomy of Human Life," originally issued at London in 1750. To this reprint he added the subtitle, "Based on the System of Theosophical Ethics." This phrase, his use of the name "Kuthumi" —a variant spelling of *Koot Hoomi,* the *Mahatma* to whom Mr. Sinnett's "Occult World" is dedicated—some questionable expressions in his introduction and notes, and his personal prominence and known affiliation with the Theosophical Society, gave Mr. Judge occasion to insert in *The Path* for July, 1886, two references, one a review complimentary to the "Biogen Series" and to Prof. Coues personally, and the other a correction of possible misconceptions in the following words:

> The association of the name Kuthumi with the book, so perplexing to understand, is not a biographical fact, as Prof. Coues explains in his "foreword" (p. 10). It only remains to state clearly what is implied in the foreword that the Theosophical Society has no special code of morals, ready made and rigorously defined, for the acceptance of its members on admission.

By the summer of 1886, it became evident that the Board of Control, originally promulgated by Col. Olcott at Mr. Judge's request in order to avoid delay in the conduct of the official routine of the American Branches, was, in the hands of Prof. Coues, a mere exchange of the paternal autocracy of Col. Olcott for the arbitrary autocracy of Prof. Coues. Mr. Judge had recourse to H.P.B. and Col. Olcott, and at a meeting of the Board of Control, held at Rochester, N. Y., at the house of Mrs. Cables on July 4, 1886, additional "orders" from Col. Olcott and his Indian General Council were presented by Mr. Judge, calling for a revised plan whereby an American Section of the General Council was to be formed. In this American Council was to be merged the Board of Control, the members of which, as also the Presidents of Branches, were to become *ex officio* members of the American Council. Provision was also to be made for the election of additional members of the American Council by the votes of the members of the Society.

Notwithstanding this promulgation, Prof. Coues, immediately after his return to his home, issued of his own motion the following:

AMERICAN BOARD OF CONTROL—OFFICE OF THE PRESIDENT.

WASHINGTON, D. C., July 12, 1886.

It is desired that *The Occult Word* become the official organ of the American Board of Control of the Theosophical Society.

Correspondents having notes and news respecting the Society in America are requested to send them to *The Occult Word.* Members and others having the interests of the Society at heart will do well to extend the circulation of *The Occult Word.*

Contributors of articles upon speculative, doctrinal, or operative Theosophy will be individually responsible therefor, as heretofore.

ELLIOTT COUES, President.

It was already an open secret that Mrs. Cables, Editor of *The Occult Word,* another member of the Board of Control, and her associate, Mr. Brown, were disaffected with the "Theosophical Mahatmas," a disaffection which burst into flame a few months later, as has been narrated in an earlier chapter.[1]

In *The Path,* for August, 1886, Mr. Judge, knowing well the tangential activities of Prof. Coues, Mrs. Cables, and others, published in the section, "Reviews and Notes," an article, "Theosophy in the Press," in which, after noting the sudden appearance within a few months of many articles in the daily papers "full of misstatements mixed with ignorance of . . . Theosophy," he goes on to say:

> But some Theosophists have been guilty of ventilating in the papers the statement that Theosophy is astralism, that is to say, that the object of the Society is to induce people to go into the study and practice of spirit raising, cultivating the abnormal faculties, of clairvoyance and the like, ignoring entirely the prime object, real end, aim and *raison d'être* of the movement—universal brotherhood and ethical teaching. In fact, we make bold to assert, from our own knowledge and from written documents, that the Mahatmas, who started the Society, and who stand behind it now, are distinctly opposed to making prominent these phenomenal leanings, this hunting after clairvoyance and astral bodies, and they have so declared most unmistakably, stating their wish and advice to be, that *"the Society should prosper on its ethical, philosophical and moral worth alone."*
>
> Theosophists should haste to see that this false impression created at large, that it is a dangerous study, or that it is any way dangerous, or that we conceal our reasons for doing what we are doing, is done away with. . . . If one or two persons in the Society imagine that the pursuit of psychical phenomena is its real end and aim and so declare, that weighs nothing

[1] See Chapter VIII.

> against the immense body of the membership or against its widespread literature; it is merely their individual bias.
>
> But at the same time, this imagination and misstatement are dangerous, and insidiously so. It is just the impression which the Jesuit college desires to be spread abroad concerning us, so that in one place ridicule may follow, and in another superstitious dread of the thing; which ever of these may happen to obtain, they would be equally well pleased.
>
> Let Theosophists attend to this, and let them not forget, that the only authoritative statements of what are the ends and objects of the Society are contained in those printed in its by-laws. No amount of assertion to the contrary by any officer or member can change that declaration.

In the September, 1886, number of *The Path* was printed the notice of the receipt of the "formal orders" to form the American Council. On this Mr. Judge comments:

> This action is eminently wise, as the term *Board of Control* was misleading, inasmuch as the very foundation of the Society is democratic in its nature, and *control* savored too much of form, ceremonies, discipline, officers, secret reports and all the paraphernalia of an established church.

The expression "Board of Control" was Col. Olcott's coinage. The various stages recounted were accepted by Mr. Judge as necessary intermediate steps in the effort to arrive at real democracy among the American Theosophists. Colonel Olcott was at all times loath to surrender his "paternal government" of the Society as a whole, and he acceded to the gradual democratization of the Society in America only under the steady pressure of Mr. Judge, reinforced by the insistence of H.P.B. He at last consented to issue his "official order" for the formation of the American Section of the Theosophical Society, and at a meeting of the Board of Control, held at Cincinnati in October, 1886, and attended also by delegates and members from numerous Branches, the arrangements were perfected for the first Convention at New York City in April, 1887, at which elected delegates from all the Branches were present, adopted a constitution, and elected officers and a Council. The first formal Convention was held the next year, April, 1888, at Chicago.

Meantime a "lively interchange of letters," as "Old Diary Leaves" phrases it, had been going on, not only between H.P.B. and Col. Olcott over the threatening breach between them on matters of policy and the forthcoming Esoteric Section, but as well among Prof. Coues, Mr. Judge, Col. Olcott, and H.P.B. over affairs in America—as may readily be inferred from what has been stated.[2]

There can be no doubt that Col. Olcott, impressed by the prominence and ability of Prof. Coues, sympathized with that gentleman, whose views were entirely congenial to him. Nor can it, we think, be doubted that Prof. Coues, fully informed as to Col. Olcott's feelings, those of Mr. Sinnett and others, may well have concluded that he had but to lead in the coming battle, and all the disaffected would openly as well as secretly support him. Able, audacious, and subtle, he was writing in one strain to Col. Olcott, in another to H.P.B., and in a third to Mr. Judge. Like so many others he was entirely unaware that H.P.B. and Mr. Judge, working as one in the Cause dear to them, made no moves, the one without the other, nor ever wrote letters or other communications on moot Theosophical matters without supplying each other with copies. Nor was it conceivable to him or to many others prominent in the Society that the Occultism of H.P.B. and Mr. Judge was genuine and not spurious or mediumistic.

[2] See Chapters IX and X.

Colonel Olcott, honest to the core, loyal in his better moments to both his colleagues, was yet, by reason of his personal weaknesses and past life, almost wholly susceptible to the arts of those who knew how to play and prey upon his vanity, his fears and doubts concerning the welfare of his beloved Society, of which he had long since constituted himself the tutelary deity. Much may be read and inferred of the unwritten history of this period from the following extract from one of the President-Founder's letters to Prof. Coues:

> Another warning: Beware how you encourage H.P.B. to act outside her special province of mystical research and esoteric teaching. The Council will stand no nonsense, nor shall I ratify a single order or promise of hers made independently of me and my full antecedent possession of the facts. She telegraphed to abolish the Board of Control and had just issued a revolutionary commission to Arthur Gebhard with an idiotic disregard of the proprieties and her own position. She seems a Bourbon as to memory and receptivity and fancies the old halcyon days are not gone. I shall neither ratify what she has done, nor anything of the sort she may in future do. Within her domain she is queen; outside that—well, fill in the blank yourself. Several attempts have been made to get her to set up a rival society. . . . She has not yet been fool enough to fall into the trap, nor do I think her brain will soften to the point of doing it. She would thereby take a life-contract for a fight; . . . and find herself with enfeebled health, advanced years and a tainted reputation recommencing our work of 1875, without, pardon me, an Olcott to stick to her, as I have, through thick and thin and bear shame and disgrace with mute endurance.[3]

[3] *The Sun,* New York, July 20, 1890. The authenticity of this letter, published by Prof. Coues, was never disputed by Col. Olcott.

At the Chicago Convention at the end of April, 1888, Prof. Coues was present as a delegate and President of the Gnostic Branch of the T.S. He was elected Chairman of the Convention and presided over its sessions. The newspapers of the city gave a good deal of space to the proceedings and reporters were present at all of the open meetings. Following the Convention the *Chicago Tribune* published, without disclosing the source from which it had received them, a letter and *facsimile* of an alleged "message from a Mahatma" to Dr. Coues. Naturally this aroused considerable passing curiosity among the general public, and a very decided interest among American Theosophists. No public notice was taken of the matter either by H.P.B. or Mr. Judge, but the latter wrote privately to Dr. Coues, who responded as follows, under date of May 21, 1888:

> My dear Judge:—I think that on reflection you will find yourself a little hasty in pitching into me about that *Tribune* matter.
>
> . . . Now I saw that letter of which you complain fall down from the air over a person's head, precisely in the same manner as you have seen a like letter fall—one, of which we have since heard a good deal. The writing on one side was in that peculiar hand which I have learned to recognize in several expressions of the will of the Blessed Masters which you have been good enough to send me. . . . The writing on the other side must have been subsequently precipitated and the seal affixed. . . . If K. H. had not wished about 75,000 persons to be advised of the mode in which he brought about the Convention in Chicago he could easily have dematerialized that document. . . . It was clearly the will of the Brotherhood that the T.S. should be thus broadly advertised—and no doubt it would also be by the will of the same august personages, if the "Religio"[4] for example

[4] "Religio" means the *Religio-Philosophical Journal.*

> should contain some day a column or two explaining the delicate and mysterious manner in which rice-paper communications are "precipitated" out of the Akasa.

This is clearly a tacit admission on Coues' part that he furnished the "message" to the *Tribune,* that he "saw" it precipitated, and an insinuation that he had received from Mr. Judge similar "messages." To Dr. Coues' letter Mr. Judge replied intimating that the whole tale, "messages" and all, originated in Dr. Coues' own brain. Under date of June 11, 1888, Prof. Coues replied to Mr. Judge's warnings:

> Dear Judge:—But now comes another trouble. It appears, and not from "Coues' brain," but from a much more material and very likely much stupider source, that you have been opposing my long standing candidacy for the esoteric presidency, in order to keep the ostensible control of T.S. in your own hand and make yourself the real or actual head of the concern in America, leaving me only as a figure-head; and I am referred to all and any newspaper reports which emanate from the Aryan [5] or yourself, as carefully suppressing or at least not putting forward my name, etc.

It had become very well known amongst members of the T.S. in the United States that Dr. Coues, in the course of his personal propaganda had broadly hinted at his own Occult relations with the Mahatmas, and as neither Mr. Judge nor H.P.B. in any way confirmed his claims, more or less questioning and suspicion arose in regard to him and his ulterior purposes. Thus "hoist with his own petard," Dr. Coues endeavored to turn his tactics to better advantage in the attempt to gain for

[5] "Aryan" means the Aryan Theosophical Society of New York City, the re-organization of the parent T.S. Mr. Judge was President of the Aryan Society.

himself the powerful support of H.P.B. in his ambition to be the public head of the Society in America, and as part of his campaign to enfold Mr. Judge in the soiled robes of his own pretended "messages." H.P.B. replied guardedly to his communications; agreeing where she could with Coues' strictures and criticisms on Col. Olcott, Mr. Judge, and the "management" of the Society; encouraging him to live up to his own protestations of loyalty, influence, and devotion to the Society; ignoring his egotism and blandishments; correcting him only where the issue raised was point-blank. On Christmas Day, 1888, he wrote her a bombastic and fulsome letter. Mr. Judge was at the time in England with H.P.B.; Col. Olcott, furious with her action in the Paris T.S. and her plain speaking with him, had just departed after his "pitched battle" with her, and his reconciliation due chiefly to the Master's Letter, as has already been told.[6] Col. Olcott had been in communication with Prof. Coues and had poured out his feelings as we have seen. Prof. Coues' Christmas letter to H.P.B. was intended to avail himself of the supposed strained relations all around. We quote his closing phrases:

> Is your "first-born," the meek Hibernian Judge,[7] still with your majesty? Give my love to him and say, I don't get up very early, but I stay up very late. I am glad you made it all right with your psychologized baby Olcott when he was with you. . . .
>
> And after all, dear H.P.B., I am really very fond and very proud of you, and admire your genius as only a man of genius can. So here's my blessing, and all good wishes, for the greatest woman of this age, *who is born to redeem her times,* and go down to everlasting historical fame.
>
> Ever yours, still in the psychic maelstrom,
>
> DARIUS HYSTASPES II.

[6] See Chapter X.
[7] Mr. Judge was of Irish parentage and birth.

In one of her letters to Dr. Coues, H.P.B. had called Mr. Judge her first-born; Col. Olcott she had spoken of as a psychologized baby when referring to the effects upon him of his twenty years' dabbling with mediums and his never-ending thirst for phenomena. Darius Hystaspes II was a favorite signature of Dr. Coues in writing to H.P.B., as Dr. Faustus was in his letters to Mr. Judge.

On April 16, 1889, just prior to the Convention of the American Section for that year, Dr. Coues wrote H.P.B. a long letter detailing his own greatness and influence, the strength of his Gnostic Branch (it had some thirty members all told, at the time, none of them active Theosophically), and with half-veiled threats tried to induce her to ask the American Theosophists to place him at their head. Thus:

> You appear to have been misinformed or uninformed respecting the Gnostic and its Branches, as well as my own work in your behalf. Both in numbers and in quality of its membership, the Gnostic is unquestionably the leading Branch of the T.S. in the country. Its members are for the most part of a high, refined, educated, and influential class in society, in science and before the world, and most of them are indefatigable in working for the cause to which your own great and noble life is devoted. I am satisfied that if you would do *your* part to give my Gnostics their just dues and recognition, they and I can lift Theosophy clear of the mud which has been thrown upon it and set your own self in a proper light before the world. We all feel keenly the abuse and persecution to which you have been subjected, and anxious to do you full justice and honor. But they are unanimously dissatisfied with the way the society is run at present, and they wonder

where your INTUITION can be, that you fail to see where your obvious advantage lies, in not strengthening and holding up the hands of their representative man [Prof. Coues] . . . Be wise now and be warned in time; you are a very great woman, who should be quick to see that this is no ordinary occasion. I tell you frankly, it is possible that all this prestige, social and personal and professional influence, scientific attainment and public interest, can be thrown on the side of the T.S., as at present constituted, or can be switched off on a new track aside from the old lines. If you cannot SEE this, and understand it, and act accordingly, there is nothing more for me to say, and I must presume that you do not care for my people. Judge and I came to a fair understanding once, and I was carrying out our agreement in good faith, and all was smooth, when something or other, affecting the question of the *Presidency*, interfered, and since then there has been nothing but friction and misunderstanding in the "Esoteric" T.S.—which you know consisted of yourself, myself, and Judge: and your issue of a new and different "esoteric" manifesto did not mend matters. Now be *wise* and POLITIC. . . . The T.S. in America is at present a HEADLESS monstrosity: it must have a visible, official head to represent its real, invisible source. You know whom the majority of the F.T.S. have desired to put forward as their representative theosophist in America. It is only necessary for you to cable the Chicago Convention, to elect him president. Weigh these words well; pause, consider, reflect, and ACT. "If 'twere well done, 'twere well done quickly."

The next day, April 17, 1889, he wrote her further on the same subject and, with incomparable effrontery, included the following choice gems of his egotism and mendacity:

> . . . do you know you are getting great discredit in this country and for what do you suppose? for being *jealous of me!* Can you imagine such flapdoodle? You are not moved by abuse, but you want to know how people think and what they say, and a great many are talking loudly and wildly, that your silence respecting my books in the "Secret Doctrine," and the absence of my name from *Lucifer* (as well as from *The Path*) means that you are afraid of my growing power, and will brook no rival so dangerously near the papal throne of theosophy. . . . There is another queer thing. You have somehow got it stuck in your mind, that I put in the *Chicago Tribune* last year a caricature of the Master K. H. I had nothing whatever to do with the article, which was merely a newspaper skit, and the lithographed effusion was no more a Mahatmic document than this letter. It was simply a piece of newspaper wit.
>
> Judge is a good fellow and means well, and I like him for many things, especially his devotion to you and the masters and their Cause; but dabbling in occultism, especially on a Mahatmic altitude is dangerous except to an Adept!! I am the humble servant of *my* Mahatma.

The American Convention met at the end of the same month. Professor Coues was not present. He was not elected President or any other officer of the American Section. H.P.B. did not cable the Convention as requested. On the contrary, her formal Letter to that Convention had distinct reference to the class of "Theosophists" of which Prof. Coues was such a shining example, as may be observed from the extracts given in the last chapter. And under date of April 30, 1889, she wrote Prof. Coues from London, saying:

Dear Doctor Coues: I have received your two letters and read them as they stand and also between the lines and therefore I mean to be as frank with you as you are frank with me. I will take your two letters point by point.

Point by point she goes over the various matters in Prof. Coues' letters, in friendly, considerate, but severely plain language, and on the subject of the "message from the Mahatma" she says:

3. If you had nothing to do with the *Chicago Tribune* article (tho' you must have influence with your own nephew) then why did you not contradict it, then and there?

4. I know nothing about the number of messages you may have received from Masters through Judge, whom I would never believe capable of it, or any one else. . . . You speak of my seals on those letters. . . . Where did they get this? From Judge, from me or from you? It could hardly have been any except one of us three. . . . Your wise advice that such Mahatma messages should be confined to one channel, "the only genuine and original H.P.B. your friend," was anticipated by Mahatma K. H. in so many words. Then why do you kick against that? You speak of *your* Mahatma, then why don't you send letters in his name instead of those of my Master and Mahatma K. H. That would settle all the difficulties and there would be no quarrel. . . . What you have learned through me, I know, and do not want to know beyond. You may obey or disobey your Master as much as you like, if you know him to exist outside of your psychic visions. As to mine, every man devoid of all psychic powers can see him, since he is a living man. I wish he could be yours, for then, my dearest Dr., you would be spiritually a better man and a less sceptical one than you are.

You speak of your eagerness "to defend and help a woman who has been sadly persecuted, because misunderstood." Permit me to say to you for the last time that no bitterest enemy of mine has ever misunderstood me as you do. . . .

CHAPTER XIII

THE COUES-COLLINS CHARGES AND THEIR AFTERMATH

HAVING failed, alike in his attempts to ingratiate himself with the American Theosophists, to deceive H.P.B. in regard to his own treacherous course, or to disturb her complete confidence and trust in Mr. Judge, and his material being all prepared and ready for the execution of his thinly veiled threats, Prof. Coues made the first assault in his campaign to ruin if he could not rule.

On May 11, 1889, appeared the first Coues-Collins letters in the *Religio-Philosophical Journal;* followed up in the issue of the same journal for June 1, with two more letters from the same source. Succeeding issues followed with additional guns from the Editor, Col. Bundy, from Mr. W. Emmette Coleman, and others, in addition to Prof. Coues. Other Spiritualist and sectarian publications and the secular press followed suit. A manifestly inspired attack on everything Theosophical, including of course H.P.B. and Mr. Judge, raged in many quarters. In England the ground had been equally well prepared, and in *Light* of the issues for May, June, and succeeding months the charges first published in America were repeated, with additions and variations. There, as in the United States, many other publications entered the fray, and there was a revival of the familiar tactics employed five years previously during the Coulomb and S.P.R. attack. The *Religio-Philosophical Journal* did not open its columns to counter evidence, but *Light*, with a display of fairness as commendable as it was unique, gave space as freely to defenders as to assailants. During the summer and autumn another strategem was employed in a manner worthy of the best traditions of the followers of Ignatius Loyola. This jesuitical device was ably carried out through Michael Angelo Lane. Mr. Lane was a newspaper reporter of St. Louis. Becoming interested in Theosophy as early as 1885, he joined the Society and corresponded with the headquarters at Adyar. Later on he became acquainted with Mr. Judge and volunteered his services in New York. After the formation of the Esoteric Section, Mr. Lane made his application for admission thereto as a probationer. He professed the utmost devotion to the Cause and wrote H.P.B. his desire to go to London to be near her and to aid in the work there. He took the pledge of the Esoteric Section, went to London, and was at the London headquarters for several weeks. He mysteriously disappeared on several occasions and very shortly returned to the United States. Thereafter he went from Lodge to Lodge, ostensibly as a Theosophist and member of the Esoteric Section and spread stories among the members to the discredit of H.P.B., of the Section and of the Society. Mr. Lane was promptly exposed as soon as circumstantial statements of his activities were forwarded to London, whereupon he ranged himself openly with Prof. Coues and other enemies of H.P.B., and her work. Professor Coues also had early applied to H.P.B. for the pledge and preliminary papers of the Esoteric Section, and these had been transmitted to him in confidence, the same as to all other applicants. He violated the confidence reposed in him, for these papers and the pledge were printed in the *Religio-Philosophical Journal* during the course of the warfare, and their contents discussed with, and a portion of them given by Prof. Coues directly to the *New York Sun* in an interview.

In his first letter to the *Religio-Philosophical Journal* Prof. Coues stated specifically that "about four years ago," (*i.e.*, in 1885) being interested in "Light on the Path," he "wrote Mrs. Collins a letter, praising it and asking her about its real source." This was because "Light on the Path," said Prof. Coues, "was supposed to have been dictated to Mrs. Collins by 'Koot Hoomi,' or some other Hindu adept who held the Theosophical Society in the hollow of his masterly hand." To this letter of his Miss Collins "promptly replied, in her own handwriting, to the effect that 'Light on the Path' was inspired or dictated from the source above indicated." Dr. Coues goes on to say that *since that time "nothing passed between Mrs.* Collins and myself until yesterday [May 2, 1889], when I *unexpectedly* received the following letter." Miss Collins' letter is dated April 18, 1889, and runs:

> Dear Sir: I feel I have a duty to write you on a difficult and (to me) painful subject. and that I must not delay it any longer.
>
> You will remember writing to ask me who was the inspirer of "Light on the Path." If you had not yourself been acquainted with Madame Blavatsky I should despair of making you ever understand my conduct. Of course I ought to have answered the letter without showing it to any one else; but at that time I was both studying Madame Blavatsky and studying under her. I knew nothing then of the mysteries of the Theosophical Society, and I was puzzled why you should write me in such a way. I took the letter to her; the result was that I wrote the answer at her dictation. I did not do this by her orders; I have never been under her orders. But I have done one or two things because she begged and implored me to; and this I did for that reason. So far as I can remember I wrote you that I had received "Light on the Path" from one of the Masters who guide Madame Blavatsky. I wish to ease my conscience now by saying that I wrote this letter from no knowledge of my own and merely to please her; and that I now see that I was very wrong in doing so. I ought further to state that "Light on the Path" was not to my knowledge inspired by any one; but that I saw it written on the walls of a place I visit spiritually, (which is described in the "Blossom and the Fruit")—there I read

it and I wrote it down. I have myself never received proof of the existence of any Master; though I believe (as always) that the mahatmic force must exist.

Yours faithfully,
MABEL COLLINS.

Professor Coues says of Mabel Collins' letter to him as above:

> I was not surprised at the new light it threw on the pathway of the Theosophical Society, for late developments respecting that singular result of Madame Blavatsky's now famous hoax left me nothing to wonder at.

Next, in the *Religio-Philosophical Journal* of June 1, 1889, Prof. Coues appears with another letter in which he says that in his first communication he did not give the original letter from Miss Collins because—"I could not conveniently lay my hands on it." He says he now gives it "word for word. It is in Mrs. Cooke's handwriting, undated and unsigned." This *undated* and *unsigned* note is as follows:

> The writer of "The Gates of Gold" is Mabel Collins, who had it as well as "Light on the Path" and the "Idyll of the White Lotus" dictated to her by one of the adepts of the group which through Madame Blavatsky first communicated with the Western world. The name of this inspirer cannot be given, as the personal names of the Masters have already been sufficiently desecrated.

Professor Coues adds:

> This is exactly, word for word, what Mrs. Cooke now says she wrongly wrote to me because Madame Blavatsky "begged and im-

plored" her to do so, and which she also wrote at her dictation. It certainly has the genuine Blavatskian ring about it.

In a subsequent communication to the *Religio-Philosophical Journal* Dr. Coues has the hardihood to subscribe himself "F. T. S." (Fellow of the Theosophical Society), but the contents of the letter identify him as its author. Addressing himself to the Editor, Dr. Coues says:

> If your mail resembles mine in quantity and quality of theosophical correspondence since "Mabel Collins' " disavowal of inspiration from Madame Blavatsky's Hindu "controls" it must be curious reading. . . . At this revelation through the *Journal* some people are pleased; other sorry, others angry; some applaud; some condemn; many are curious, and most of them want to argue about it. My mail has a sort of shivery, gooseflesh quality, as if a panic in mahatmic stock were imminent and there is a tendency of the hair of the faithful to stand on end. . . .
>
> First, a good many persons are surprised that I seem to have only now found out that "Light on the Path" was not dictated by our friend Koot Hoomi or any other Eastern adept. Such have always known all about its source and my discovery is discounted as a theosophical chestnut. Let me say to all such that I do not always tell all I know, and that I might have continued silent on the authorship of "Light on the Path," had I not had reasons for publishing Mrs. Cooke's letter just then and there—reasons I reserve for the present.

Examining Prof. Coues' "evidence" as supplied by himself the reader will note that he says he first wrote Miss Collins in 1885 (the year in which "Light on the Path" was first published), asking her about its "real source," and that he was moved to do this both because of the inscription that it was "written down" by her, and because "it was supposed to have been dictated to Mrs. Collins by 'Koot Hoomi' or some other adept who held the Theosophical Society in the hollow of his masterly hand." He says her reply confirmed the supposition.

At the time he wrote Miss Collins he was already himself a member of the Society and of the American Board of Control, was well acquainted with H.P.B., and Mr. Judge, and in communciation with them then and thereafter, up to and including April, 1889, professing the warmest admiration and friendship for both, and the utmost devotion to the Cause they served. It does not appear that at any time during those four years he ever wrote either H.P.B. or Mr. Judge for confirmation of Miss Mabel Collins' affirmation that "Light on the Path" was inspired or dictated by one of the Theosophical Adepts. Yet, either on the assumption that he wanted to verify the source as claimed by Miss Collins or that he all along believed H.P.B. to be the inventor of a "hoax," as his first communication affirms and his last intimates, it is clear that he made no effort to verify Miss Collins' statement. This is the more peculiar, as it is plainly evident he neither knew Miss Collins personally, kept up his intercourse with her, nor had at the time he received her letter of April 18, 1889, any but the scantiest knowledge about her. For he says that in the intervening four years "nothing passed between Mrs. Collins and myself until yesterday" (May 2, 1889); and in his first letter he four times calls her "*Mrs.* Collins," whereas her married name was Cook; while in his later communications he repeatedly speaks of her as Mrs. Cook*e*.

Notable as was his omission in the circumstances, to verify in any way Miss Collins' first statement as to the authorship of "Light on the Path," his course of procedure, when her second letter came, is still more significant. For in that letter she plainly said to him that her own first statement was false, that in fact "Light on the

Path" was not to her knowledge inspired by anyone; that she had never received proof of the existence of any Master; that she knew nothing at the time of the "mysteries of the Theosophical Society."

Quite apart from anything else, these two contradictory statements must have shown Prof. Coues that Miss Mabel Collins' testimony was untrustworthy and valueless without corroboration. Here, from every angle, was something that required and demanded clearing up in mere justice to himself as an honest inquirer interested in getting at the facts. But much more than his own interests were concerned in doing his utmost to ascertain the truth: his fellow Theosophists by thousands were as much concerned as himself, if Mabel Collins' second "explanation" should be true, as much concerned as himself should it be false; finally, remained H. P. Blavatsky, his friend, revered by many, hated by many, accused of an abominable offense by a woman who had already once given him false testimony, and who, he must have known, had recently been dismissed from *Lucifer* and from all association with H.P.B. Certainly every motive of fairness, of common decency, even, would require him to take steps to ascertain the truth or the falsity of Mabel Collins' "explanation" and accusation before making any charges. Yet what did he do? Immediately on receipt of Miss Collins' letter of April 18, he says, "I cabled Mrs. Collins for permission to use her letter at my discretion." "Mrs." Collins obediently replied, "Use my letter as you please." And the same day Prof. Coues enclosed her letter and one of his own to the *Religio-Philosophical Journal*—an ardent Spiritualist publication, vehicle of Mr. W. Emmette Coleman's prolonged and malicious attacks on H.P.B. Thus, in view of the facts, what credence can be attached to the character or veracity of Dr. Elliott Coues' testimony where his motives are so absolutely impeached?

But there is more. In his second communication to the *Religio-Philosophical Journal* Prof. Coues gives, he says, "word for word" the *first* letter sent him by Mabel Collins. "It is in Mrs. Cooke's handwriting" and in it she says, in reply to his original inquiry, "The writer of 'The Gates of Gold' is Mabel Collins who had *it* as well as 'Light on the Path' and 'Idyll of the White Lotus' dictated to her by one of the adepts." In his first communication (dated May 3, 1889) Prof. Coues had already stated that his original inquiry and her reply had occurred "about four years ago"—that is, sometime in 1885—"*since which time nothing passed between Mrs. Collins and myself.*" Now the actual and indisputable fact is that "The Gates of Gold" was not published until 1887—two years after the alleged correspondence had taken place! Thus the "evidence" produced by Prof. Coues against the honor of H. P. Blavatsky not only falls of its own weight so far as she is concerned, but convicts Prof. Coues out of his own mouth of shameless duplicity and an equally shameless mendacity.

Turning now to Mabel Collins' share in the attempted stroke, the reader will note upon examining her two letters that she confesses her own falsehood. In her first letter she says her books were dictated by one of the Adepts; in her second letter she says her falsehood was dictated by H.P.B. If her *first* statement is accepted it was the Adept who dictated her books. But in her second letter she declares (1) "I have myself never received proof of the existence of any Master"; (2) "I knew nothing then of the mysteries of the Theosophical Society."

In her second letter Mabel Collins admits the falsehood in her first but says she told it because Madame Blavatsky "begged and implored me to."

Let us contrast these statements with known and *undisputed* facts.

H.P.B. was in London from the end of July, 1884, till November 11 of the same year, when she sailed for India, less the interval when she was in Germany with the Gebhards. She was in India till April of 1885, during which time she was in the midst of the storm of the Coulomb case and most of the time lying between life and death. From April, 1885, on, she was in Naples, in Germany, in Belgium, returning to England *only* in

May, 1887. During the entire period from November, 1884, until after May, 1887, she neither saw nor had any communications with Mabel Collins. Even while H.P.B. was in England during the fall of 1884 she never even saw Mabel Collins more than two or three times and *at no time did she see her except in the presence of others.* The "Idyll of the White Lotus" was written by Mabel Collins *before she ever met* H.P.B. That work was shown by her in manuscript to Mr. Ewen and Mr. Finch, both well-known and reputable men, to both of whom she stated that the work had been "inspired" by "some one" whose appearance she described. Mr. Ewen showed the manuscript to Col. Olcott, with whom Mabel Collins talked and made the same claim of "inspiration." She told Col. Olcott that the work had been written by her either in trance or under dictation, and described to him the appearance of the "inspirer." All this was *before* H.P.B. *ever set eyes on Mabel Collins.* Furthermore the first edition of the "Idyll," published when H.P.B. was thousands of miles away, and without any intervening communication with Mabel Collins, bore this inscription: "to the *True Author,* the *Inspirer* of this work; It Is Dedicated."

Next, with regard to "Light on the Path": The undisputed facts are that Mabel Collins did not begin that work until November, 1884, just prior to the departure of H.P.B. for India. On November 8 of that year Miss Collins showed H.P.B. a page or two of manuscript of what afterwards became "Light on the Path." H.P.B. was in India when that work was completed and published, yet the inscription and Mabel Collins' various statements at the time and on down to the present date, claim that work, not as her own composition, but "written down" by her. Her last claim in that respect was as recently made as the year 1919.[1] H.P.B. never even *saw* the text of "Light on the Path" until the summer of 1886, when a copy of it was given to her in Germany by Arthur Gebhard.

[1] In an autograph letter, now in the possession of the Editors of the magazine *Theosophy* (Los Angeles, California).

Further, Mrs. C. A. Passingham, a reputable and well-known English woman, wrote to *Light* while the Coues-Collins charges were pending, to the effect that early in 1885 Mabel Collins spent an afternoon and part of the evening at her house. This, Mrs. Passingham thinks, was in February. She continues:

> She expressed a wish to leave early, as she had an "appointment" with "Hilarion" . . . I may add that Mrs. Collins told me herself that the influence under which she wrote the book in question was that of a person whom she had long known, but had only lately identified as being that of an "adept."

On the 12th of June, 1889, Mabel Collins' sister, Ellen Hopkins, wrote a letter to *Light* which is published in that journal for June 15, 1889. The letter follows:

> . . . Will you allow me to state that my sister, Mabel Collins, is too ill at the moment to be able to speak for herself, but I trust that she will be well enough in a few days to furnish you with a reply which will put a very different aspect on the whole affair?

The "few days" spoken of by Ellen Hopkins went by and rolled into months with no statement from Mabel Collins. Meantime pamphlets had been gotten out by "F.T.S.," by Mr. Judge, and by H.P.B. Statements had been made by Archibald and Bertram Keightley, both of whom had known H.P.B. since the summer of 1884, both of whom had been intimate indeed with Mabel Collins, and both of whom had resided almost continuously in the headquarters house with H.P.B., after her return to England in 1887. The several statements, the documentary and other proofs, the establishment of dates, the production of letters of Prof. Coues to H.P.B., all showed conclusively the utter falsity of the charges made by the Coues-Collins alliance.

Professor Coues had overreached himself. He had been thoroughly exposed. The charter of the Gnostic Branch was revoked and Coues himself expelled from the Society. Months later, while preparing a further attack, he endeavored to retrieve his earlier blunder by writing a letter to *Light* which is referred to in the leading editorial of that publication for November 2, 1889. From this it appears that he concocted an *ex post facto* correction by saying that he had been mistaken in fixing the date of his first letter to Miss Mabel Collins as 1885, when it should have been 1887. As proof he told the editor of *Light* that on June 1st, 1889, Miss Collins had cabled him of his mistake and as further proof he sent *a* card of Mabel Collins, *undated,* and *without* the envelope—a card, whether the original or otherwise does not matter, but claimed to be the original,—which *Light* accepted as an "explanation" because "The Gates of Gold" was not published until 1887! The animus of this laggard explanation of Prof. Coues' *impasse* is, we think, entirely clear, and worthy of the same degree of credibility as his other facile statements. It is to be noted that although Mabel Collins was "too ill" to make a concrete statement to *Light* at the time—and before the publication of the pamphlets which proved by dates alone the impossibility of her statements or Coues' being true—she was not too ill to send a cablegram to her co-conspirator warning him of the discrepancy into which his too great facility and too zealous haste had led him. But to return to Miss Mabel Collins' books.

The third of the trio was "The Gates of Gold" which her unsigned note to Prof. Coues attributed to "one of the adepts" and which—her retraction, whether four years later or two does not matter—by implication at least is included in the falsehood which Madame Blavatsky "begged and implored" her to circulate. Let us see as to that.

"The Gates of Gold" was written in 1886. Madame Blavatsky was living at the time in Germany. The book was published in England and in America very early in

1887, while H.P.B. lay on a sick-bed in Belgium. The first edition of the work contained this inscription:

> *Once, as I sat alone writing, a mysterious Visitor entered my study unannounced, and stood beside me. I forgot to ask who he was, or why he entered so unceremoniously, for he began to tell me of the Gates of Gold. He spoke from knowledge, and from the fire of his speech I caught faith. I have written down his words; but alas, I cannot hope that the fire shall burn as brightly in my writing as in his speech.*

All these are *undisputed* facts. As in the case of the "Idyll" and "Light on the Path," this book was written and published when H.P.B. was not in England, when she was not in any communication with Mabel Collins, when she was physically in the gravest condition. Yet all three books bear inscriptions written by Mabel Collins which can be interpreted only as a disclaimer of her own authorship of them and a claim that they were inspired—no matter how or by whom.

Finally, as in the Coulomb case, H.P.B. had everything to risk and nothing to gain by such chicanery as was attributed to her. No one of her enemies ever imagined it plausible for a moment to call her a fool, but a fool as well as a "fraud" she must have been to put herself at the mercy of Madame Coulomb, Mabel Collins, or any one else, for such paltry ends as such rascality, even if successful, would have achieved. For quite without risk or occasion for either the Coulombs' or the Collins' help, she had the recorded testimony of Col. Olcott, of Mr. Judge, of Damodar, of Maj.-Gen. Morgan, of Mr. Sinnett, of Mr. A. O. Hume, of Countess Wachtmeister, of Mr. Hubbe-Schleiden, Dr. Hartmann, Miss Arundale, a hundred others of reputation and character, both as to Adept inspiration, and her own phenomenal powers. What had she to gain, what motive could inspire her, whether in 1885, while a storm was already raging about the Coulomb charges, or in 1887, when her own position as regards Theosophists needed no bolstering—what had *she* to gain, one may ask, by fraudulently procuring what, if believed, would add neither to her own repute nor to that of her Masters, but would only enhance the importance and prestige of *Mabel Collins?*

It thus becomes clear with regard to all three books, first that Miss Collins on her own account both before and since, claimed them to be inspired; secondly, that with regard to any and all of them H.P.B. was physically absent, physically not in communication, physically not in a position to beg and implore Mabel Collins to do or say anything in regard to them. If, then, she "influenced" Miss Collins in any way, it was from a distance and by the use of phenomenal powers indeed. But if she actually possessed such *Occult* powers—and desired to misuse them—why in the name of the commonest of common sense should she betray herself by using cheap physical frauds, when by employing her Occult powers she could procure the wished for result without risk?

Miss Mabel Collins also wrote: "At the time—whether 1885 or 1887 does not matter—I was both studying Madame Blavatsky and studying under her." As Miss Collins was not in communication with H.P.B. nor in her presence from their first meeting in the fall of 1884 till just prior to the commencement of the publication of *Lucifer* in September, 1887, it is certain that during that interval this statement is as inaccurate as her others. Mabel Collins *was* closely associated with H.P.B. in the publication of *Lucifer* from September, 1887, until January, 1889. The contents of the magazine show that whatever Miss Collins wrote was published over her own signature, the same as with H.P.B. and other contributors—and on her own responsibility. Part of her contribution was "The Blossom and the Fruit," a novel for which she made the same claim of an inspirer as with the three works already discussed. At no time and in no place has anyone produced a line written or signed by H.P.B. supporting Miss Mabel Collins' claims to studying under her. On the contrary, H.P.B. *refused to accept Mabel Collins* even as a probationer of the

Esoteric Section until the latter "begged and implored" indeed. She was then placed on probation after warning, and within four days, in the words of H.P.B., "broke her vows, becoming guilty of the blackest treachery and disloyalty to her HIGHER SELF. And when I could no longer keep in the E.S. either herself or her friend, the two convulsed the whole Society with their calumnies and falsehoods." Mabel Collins brought suit in England against H.P.B. for libel. When the case came for trial in July, 1890, a certain letter written by Miss Mabel Collins was shown by H.P.B.'s attorney to the counsel for Miss Collins, who thereupon asked the Court to take the case off the docket, which was done.

Viewing the enormous difference between the three books named and the prior and subsequent writings of Mabel Collins, and the many stories told by Miss Collins and others as to the real source of "Light on the Path" and its companion volumes, and how they were obtained, the student may be interested in the only comment made directly by H.P.B. in those respects. In her letter to *Light* of June 8, 1889, she says, *inter alia,* "When I met her [Mabel Collins] she had just completed the *Idyll of the White Lotus,* which as she stated to Colonel Olcott, had been dictated to her by some 'mysterious person.' Guided by her description, we both recognized an old friend of ours, a Greek, and no Mahatma, though an Adept; further developments proving we were right. This fact, acknowledged by Mrs. Cooke in her dedication of the *Idyll,* sets aside the idea that the work was either inspired or dictated by Koot Hoomi or any other Mahatma." In the pamphlet issued by H.P.B. at the same time, this statement is repeated, together with the following most interesting paragraph:

> Was the dedication *invented,* and a Master and "inspirer" suggested by Mme. [Blavatsky] before the latter had ever seen his *amanuensis* [Mabel Collins]? For that only she proclaims herself in her dedication, by speaking of the "*true author,*" who thus must be regarded *as*

some kind of Master, at all events. Moreover, heaps of letters may be produced all written between 1872 and 1884, and signed Δ^{2}: the well-known seal of one who became an *adept* only in 1886. Did Mme. Blavatsky send to "Miss Mabel Collins" this signature, when neither knew of the other's existence?

The same pamphlet of H.P.B.'s contains also a letter, signed "A Student of *Light on the Path,*" reprinted from *Light* of June 8, 1889, in which the following suggestive ideas are put forth:

Referring to Miss Collins' explanation, it is at once evident that another intelligence besides her own must also have visited the place, "spiritually" or otherwise, where she saw "Light on the Path" written upon its walls, for *someone* must have placed the words there; moreover, that intelligence had command over good modern English as well as being the possessor of high practical wisdom.

We judge, therefore, that Miss Collins was simply the favoured vehicle for the communication of those particular rules of the "Hall of Learning" to the many mortals now needing and hungering for them, and while it is impossible that they could have been written up where she was permitted to observe them, otherwise than by an intelligent Being who had also visited that place, it does not at all follow that he should, or ought to, have made himself or his nature known to her. That would have been creating a basis for personal intimacy which was not necessary and perhaps not advisable.

As regards the manner in which one mind may instruct or inform another, on what may be termed the occult plane, we know at present very

[2] This symbol was used as a signature in the original edition of "Light on the Path," following the numbered "rules."

> little, but the phenomena of psychometry and thought-transference may some day, if scientifically studied, be the means of our understanding those things better.

To whatever conclusions the student may come on the mooted real authorship of "Light on the Path" and its related volumes, what has been adduced will, we believe, serve to make two points, general and particular, very clear. The general point is that expressed in the words of H.P.B. in the "Introductory" to the "Secret Doctrine":

> *It is above everything important to keep in mind that no theosophical book acquires the least additional value from pretended authority.*

Had Theosophical students kept this admonition in mind, whether as regards H.P.B. herself, Miss Mabel Collins, or all the host of those before and since, who have claimed, truly or falsely, to "speak with authority," whether "in the name of the Lord" or "in the name of the Master"—had they been content to study the "message" on the basis of its own inherent merit instead of under the glamour of belief in some authority, real or imaginary, they would quickly have become able to "*test the spirits*" to some purpose.

The particular point is that it is evident alike from Miss Mabel Collins' own statements as to her inspirer and from the quality of the other writings emanating from her pen, that she had not then and has not now, the *remotest knowledge of her own,* either as to the actual source of her three gem products, as to the means by which their substance and form reached her, or as to their substance. She was, in no invidious sense, purely and simply the *medium* of their transmission.

CHAPTER XIV

"THE NEW YORK SUN" LIBEL CASE

WHEN the American Sectional Convention met at Chicago at the end of April, 1890, Mr. Judge's Report as General Secretary contained the following reference to Prof. Coues:

> During the past year there has been no appeal to the Executive Committee from any Branch or individual, and but one case of discipline. On June 11th [1889] formal charges of untheosophic conduct were preferred by Mr. Arthur B. Griggs of Boston against Dr. Elliott Coues, of Washington. These charges were in part based on public imputations by Dr. Coues of fraud and falsehood to Madame Blavatsky, and in part upon unpublished letters in which the Theosophical Society, its teachings, aims, and officers, were treated as shams and deceits. I officially sent a copy of these charges to Dr. Coues in a registered letter, notifying him of the date when the Executive Committee would be prepared to hear his defense. During the intervening time no reply was received, and the Committee, having considered the charges, adjudged them sustained, by a unanimous vote, and on June 22d expelled Dr. Coues from the Theosophical Society. Later events have conclusively shown that it is better for its enemies to be placed without its pale than permitted to remain within it. From this decision there has been no appeal to Col. Olcott, and therefore it is final.

The Theosophical community having thus disembarrassed itself of the traitor within the household, and placed on record its action, Dr. Coues prepared his final thunderbolt. In the *New York Sun* for Sunday, June 1, 1890, the leading editorial article was entitled, "The Humbug of Theosophy." It says:

> The exposure of the imposture of Mme. BLAVATSKY does not seem to lessen at all the prosperity of her humbug religion. . . .
>
> The number of new members admitted during the year was 373, and there was one expulsion, Dr. ELLIOTT COUES of Washington. He is a man of scientific reputation, who showed up the lying and trickery of the BLAVATSKY woman after having been one of her dupes for several years. With her closer intimates she seems to make little attempt to conceal her real character as a charlatan, and her hearty contempt for their folly in taking her seriously. Her long success in keeping up the humbug is, therefore, all the more astonishing. Whether her principal disciple, Col. OLCOTT, is also playing a fraudulent part, it is hard to say. He seems to be very much in earnest, and as she seems to despise him thoroughly and undisguisedly, laughing at his antics, it is perhaps presumable that he is honest and sincere in his credulity. He treats the snuffy old woman as a veritable seeress, and reads her mystical writings with apparent and probably real veneration, though she has described him to her old confederate, Mme. COULOMB, as a muff of the first water. Dr. COUES is of very different stuff, and he did not hesitate to banter her on the success of her trickery. He seems to have seen through her at an early day, and the wonder is that a man of his standing remained in her crowd so long. . . .
>
> Mme. BLAVATSKY has the assurance to write to her American dupes that her charlatanism is

> prospering more than ever, financially and otherwise. She addresses them from a sick chamber, to which she is confined by a mortal disease, and yet she persists in her determination to keep the imposture going until the end. She is an old woman of wonderful will power and of unquestionable intellectual ability. What the motive of her course is, we cannot imagine, unless it be mere love of fun and mischief. It evidently pleases her to make fools of people, and she is likely to go down to history as one of the chief impostors of our day. Whether theosophy will die with her is very doubtful. It has a fascination for a certain class of minds fond of mysticism; and its Buddhistic element is getting to be fashionable at this period. . . .
>
> The men in the business strike us as being made up of arrant humbugs and superficial fellows whom anything like abstract thought drives substantially crazy. But they have succeeded in inducing thousands to take them seriously as profound philosophers.

This ignoble consideration of Madame Blavatsky, her teachings, and her students, was followed, on Sunday, July 20, 1890, by a full-page special article from its Washington correspondent in the form of an interview with Prof. Coues. The editorial page of the *Sun* of the same date contained as its leading article a still more undignified and disreputable treatment of the subject under the caption, "The History of a Humbug." It is, in full, as follows:

> We publish to-day a wonderfully interesting history of the invention of the humbug of Theosophy. It is related by Prof. ELLIOTT COUES of the Smithsonian Institution at Washington, an ornithologist of distinction, who at one time was deceived by Mme. BLAVATSKY's pretensions, but

since has discovered her to be the impostor she is.

This woman is by birth a Russian subject, and is now about 60 years of age, though she looks and pretends to be much older. She is fat, gross, of abominable habits, an intolerable temper, swearing like a pirate and smoking like a chimney, of restless energy and endless craft. Very little is known of her early days, when she was Mlle. Hahn, except that she was married to the Russian whose name she still bears, though she soon left him and entered upon her career of adventure without preserving any prejudices so far as matrimony is concerned.

In other words, her morals may be theosophic, but they are bad. Since she lost her youth she has been living by her wits, sharpened by much experience of travel and the friction of many years of vagabondage. Her profession, so far as she has had any stated employment, has been as a Russian spy. As such, Prof. Coues tells us, she came to New York in 1873, and in that capacity she subsequently went to India with Col. Olcott as her faithful attendant. The device of theosophy was simply contrived by her as a cover for her real designs.

This confirms the theory of her imposture which was advanced after she had been exposed by an investigating committee of the London Society for Psychical Research. That exposure was complete. It was proved beyond a doubt that, with Mme. Coulomb, a French woman, as a confederate, and with the assistance of the mechanical ingenuity of M. Coulomb, she kept up a pretended correspondence with a supernatural Koot Hoomi, deceiving her dupes by the baldest jugglery. The old witch, according to Prof. Coues, was doing it all for no other purpose than to kick up a dust to hide her political intrigues. But she was not so sharp as she thought; the

> Russian Government stopped her pay, and she was driven to using her theosophical imposture itself as a means of making a living. As to OLCOTT, who began his career in the secret service of our own War Department, Prof. COUES seems to think that he is not the wholly guileless and gullible fool he appears, at least not now. Poor fellow, he is in BLAVATSKY's clutches and he can not escape, though he has found her out as a harridan and a humbug. Accordingly he is perforce a humbug himself.
>
> It is a wonderful story how this crafty Tartar entrapped this shrewd Yankee, so that for fifteen years they have together played their game of humbugging people into believing that they are the prophets of a new religion founded on Asiatic wisdom, of which they are both together totally ignorant. Their trickery has been exposed with scientific completeness and exactitude, and yet their impudence is in no wise lessened. They keep straight faces and go on with their humbug, cheered and encouraged, of course, by the folly of men and women who take them seriously.
>
> Prof. COUES' narrative in form and substance makes capital reading.

The Coues interview fills seven closely printed columns of small type. The charges made and the alleged evidence procured by Prof. Coues ostensibly exposed the facts of H.P.B.'s career from 1857 onwards. It is worth while for the student to observe these putative facts in the *Sun* articles, for they include the multitude of attacks before and since upon H.P.B. and Theosophy. The sequel shows their untruthfulness and the basic ignorance or dishonesty of those who make and repeat those charges.

On the statements of Mr. Daniel Dunglas Home, the medium, and Mr. W. Emmette Coleman, Dr. Coues charged H.P.B. with having been a member of the *demi-*

monde of Paris in 1857-8 and mistress of the Prince Emile de Wittgenstein, "by whom she had a deformed son, who died at Kieff in 1868."

On the strength of the report of Mr. Richard Hodgson of S.P.R. fame, she is charged with "having shared the fortunes" of one Metrovitch in Cairo in 1871. This is said to be provable by Madame Coulomb and to be "the key to the power Coulomb had over Blavatsky." This charge is further supported by a letter from Madame Coulomb to Col. Bundy of the *Religio-Philosophical Journal,* and is the charge hinted at by Madame Coulomb, at the close of the preface to her pamphlet against H.P.B. in 1884, but which she feared to make publicly in India.

The next charge definitely makes H.P.B. out a Russian spy from 1873 on. Then she is charged to have been "exploiting as a spiritualist medium" during her five years at New York, and before that at Cairo. Hudson Tuttle, a Spiritualist, is quoted as sponsor for an attack on Mr. Judge. In gambler's terms Prof. Coues characterizes Theosophy, H.P.B., Col. Olcott, and Mr. Judge as "three-card monte with king, queen, and knave. Blavatsky dealt, Olcott steered, Judge played capper."

Madame Blavatsky's authorship of "Isis Unveiled" is declared to be a fiction and on the authority of "a friend of mine" the real author is claimed to be the Baron de Palm, who was a member of the Society in its earliest days and the cremation of whose body was the first in the United States. The de Palm story is told at length in Col. Olcott's "Old Diary Leaves." Prof. Coues goes on to declare, "similar, yet different frauds are the root, stock and branch of other theosophical books."

The Report of the Society for Psychical Research is then taken up, and Dr. Coues affirms:

> The London Society for Psychical Research determined to send one of their number to Madras. Dr. Hodgson went to India in November, 1884, and stayed until April, 1885. The re-

> sult of his investigation was the total collapse of the theosophic fake, and there has not yet been found leather enough in the lungs of all the fakirs combined to reinflate the bubble. Dr. Hodgson's report is elaborate, circumstantial and conclusive. Its force has never been and never will be broken. It is a volume of several hundred pages, with diagrams of the trap-doors on the Blavatsky stage, and facsimiles of Blavatsky's handwriting proved to be identical with that of the mythical Koot Hoomi. It shows that the Coulombs, whatever their own characters, and whatever their animus or purpose, had told the plain, simple truth as far as their disclosures went. Their evidence had already damned the woman; Hodgson's report sealed, certified and executed that sentence.

H.P.B., Col. Olcott, and Mr. Judge are repeatedly charged with being in the Society for money and that it is run for revenue only. Mr. Michael Angelo Lane's exploits are then referred to and he is made sponsor for stories of bogus Mahatmic messages "in very good imitation of the things Mr. Judge has been in the habit of distributing to favorite dupes—these themselves being in imitation of the rice paper missives of Blavatsky's original hoax."

> "How about these 'Mahatmic letters' we heard so much about a while ago, such a one, for example, as the *Chicago Tribune* published in facsimile?" asked the reporter.
>
> "Oh, you mean those Aids to Faith in Blavatsky which went the rounds? Here are a couple. They are at your service if you wish to print them. . . . The subject of the communication is simply bosh, as you perceive; the handwriting is almost unquestionably that of Mr. Judge, who is an expert penman."

Professor Coues then renews the "Kiddle incident" charges as to the source of the Mahatma letters in "The Occult World," and concludes:

> Such is the unspeakably puerile nonsense upon which the Mahatmic myth is erected. Papers prepared for no more cause or consequence than these flimsy forgeries I have obtained from Mr. Judge, and by Blavatsky or some other blatherskite, have made much theosophic history. . . . I could say more but I trust you appreciate the blessing of having two such authentic and impressive missives from beyond the Himalayas in your vest pocket—from as far beyond those heights as Mr. Judge's office in New York—precisely.

Following the *Sun* articles, Mr. Judge in *The Path* for August, 1890, advised all whom it might concern that he had brought suit for libel. Manifestly he had done this only for the protection of the Society and the good name of H.P.B., and to head off similar attacks in other publications, for he himself had been mentioned only incidentally and as rather dupe and tool than arch deceiver, and the same as to Col. Olcott. In his notice Mr. Judge made the significant statement:

> The animus of the writer is so plainly disclosed that it might well serve as an ample answer to the attack. Inasmuch, however, as certain moral charges cannot be permitted utterance with impunity, I have brought suit for libel . . . and am awaiting instructions from Madame Blavatsky as to her own course.

In *The Path* for September, 1890, is printed a letter from Madame Blavatsky whose tone and spirit is in shining contrast with the course and animus of her calumniators. The letter reads:

While I fully agree to the proposition that we should forgive our enemies, yet I do not thereby lose my "appeal unto Caesar," and in that appeal, which is now made to the Law and not to the Emperor, I may keep the command to forgive, while for the protection of the name of a dead friend and the security in the future of Theosophists, I hale into the Courts of the land those who, having no sense of what is right or just, see fit to publish broadcast wicked and unfounded slanders.

For some fifteen years I have calmly stood by and seen my good name assailed by newspaper gossips who delight to dwell upon the personal peculiarities of those who are well known, and have worked on for the spread of our Theosophical ideas, feeling confident that, though I might be assailed by small minds who try their best to bring me into reproach, the Society which I helped to found would withstand the attacks, and, indeed, grow under them. This latter has been the case. It may be asked by some members why I have never replied to those attacks which were directed against Occultism and phenomena. For two reasons: Occultism will remain forever, no matter how assailed, and Occult phenomena can never be proved in a Court of Law during this century. Besides, I have never given public currency to any of the latter, but have always objected to the giving out of things the profane cannot understand.

But now a great metropolitan daily in New York, with no knowledge of the facts in the case, throws broadcast before the public many charges against me, the most of which meet their refutation in my life over a decade. But as one of them reflects strongly upon my moral character and brings into disrepute the honorable name of a dead man, an old family friend, it is impossible for me to remain silent, and so I have directed my lawyers in New York to bring an action against the *New York Sun* for libel.

This paper accuses me of being a member of the *demi-monde* in '58 and '68 and of having improper relations with Prince Emile Wittgenstein, by whom the paper says I had an illegitimate son.

The first part of the charge is so ridiculous as to arouse laughter, but the second and third hold others up to reprobation. Prince Wittgenstein, now dead, was an old friend of my family, whom I saw for the last time when I was eighteen years old, *i.e.*, in 1849, and he and his wife remained until his death in close correspondence with me. He was a cousin of the late Empress of Russia, and little thought that upon his grave would be thrown the filth of a modern New York newspaper. This insult to him and to me I am bound by all dictates of my duty to repel, and am also obliged to protect the honor of all Theosophists who guide their lives by the teachings of Theosophy; hence my appeal to the Law and to a jury of my fellow Americans. I gave up my allegiance to the Czar of Russia in the hope that America would protect her citizens; may that hope not prove vain.—H. P. B.

At the time, the *Sun* was perhaps the most widely circulated and influential of American newspapers. It had at its command every resource of ability, influence, and money, and it is not to be supposed that it was unfamiliar with the technicalities of the New York State laws relating to libel or the difficulties in the way of any one who might try to obtain a verdict against it in such a suit. It had but to establish in court its own good faith and prove or show reasonable cause for belief in and circulation of a single one of its major charges, and the whole history of American jurisprudence in similar cases showed that it would be acquitted. But one thing favored the suit of H.P.B.: the fact that this time, quite the contrary of the Coulomb charges, the S.P.R. report, and the numerous prior attacks upon her and her mission—*this time the charges were direct, made as statements of fact, not of opinion, hearsay, conclusion, inference, or innuendo.* If H.P.B. was actually *guilty* of a single one of the offenses charged against her, she was ruined, ineradicably branded with the stigma of a convicted rogue—her enemies triumphant, her Society exploded, her followers buried in ignominy, her mission and her "Theosophy" a thing of contempt and of derision.

The issue was squarely joined, with no possibility of evasion by either party to the suit. This time it was not a friendless and slandered woman forced into the position where she must suffer in silence or essay the *hopeless task of proving herself innocent* of the fabrications of irresponsible evil- and malicious-minded assassins of her good name. It was a great and powerful newspaper faced with the simple task of *proving her guilty* of a single one of its numerous charges by the simple process of bringing into Court in its behalf the Coues, the Bundys, the Hodgsons, the Coulombs, the Colemans, the Sidgwicks, the Myers, the Masseys, the Lillies, the Collinses, and all the other still living "witnesses" who had fathered or circulated the "evidence" which for so many years had been industriously spread before the public to "prove" H.P.B. a fraud, her phenomena bogus, her teachings a theft or a plagiarism. Certainly, on the assumption that at some time in her life H.P.B. had been indiscreet in her relations with men, at some time participant in questionable transactions, at some time engaged in anything disreputable, at some time party to fraudulent phenomena, at some time profiting by her "hoax," the task before the *Sun* was an easy one.

The case was pressed with the utmost vigor by H.P.B.'s attorneys, but the usual "law's delays" were invoked and taken advantage of in the defense. In *The Path* for March, 1891, a statement of the then status of the suit was published under the caption, "The Libel

Suits Against *New York Sun* and Elliott Coues." The article reads:

> Several letters inquiring about these suits having been received, and various rumors about them having arisen, facts are given.
>
> It is not possible to bring any suit to trial in New York very quickly, as all the calendars are crowded and suitors have to await their turn.
>
> It is not possible in New York to have newspapers notice the progress of suits for libel against other newspapers, as an agreement exists between the various editors that no such publication will be made. Hence the silence about the above-mentioned actions.
>
> The actions were begun in earnest and are awaiting trial. They will be continued until a verdict is reached or a retraction given.
>
> One victory has been gained in this way. The *New York Sun* put in a long answer to Mme. Blavatsky's complaint and her lawyers demurred to its sufficiency as a defence. That question of law was argued before Judge Beach in the Supreme Court, and on the argument *the lawyers for the Sun confessed in open court their inability to prove the charge of immorality on which the suit lies*, and asked to be allowed to retain the mass of irrelevant matter in the answer. These matters could only have been meant to prejudice a jury. But Judge Beach sustained Mme. Blavatsky's objection and ordered that the objectionable matter be stricken out. The case now looks merely like one in which the only question will be the amount of damages, and everything must now stand until the case is reached in the Trial Term. This decision on the demurrer was a substantial victory. The suit against Dr. Elliott Coues is in exactly the same condition.

Madame Blavatsky died in May of the same year—1891—and, under the Laws of New York, her death automatically terminated the suit brought by her against the *Sun*. Mr. Judge, however, continued to press his own suit, although the allegations originally made against himself were rather ridicule than slander. Finally, on September 26, 1892, the *Sun*, which by this time had become convinced of the great wrong perpetrated through it, voluntarily published, in partial amends, an editorial article repudiating the Coues interview, and a long article by Mr. Judge devoted to a tribute to the life-work and character of H. P. Blavatsky. The editorial retraction reads:

> We print on another page an article in which WILLIAM Q. JUDGE deals with the romantic and extraordinary career of the late Madame HELENA P. BLAVATSKY. We take occasion to observe that on July 20, 1890, we were misled into admitting into the *Sun's* columns an article by Dr. E. F. COUES of Washington, in which allegations were made against Madame BLAVATSKY's character, and also against her followers, which appear to have been without solid foundation. Mr. JUDGE's article disposes of all questions relating to Madame BLAVATSKY as presented by Dr. COUES, and we desire to say that his allegations respecting the Theosophical Society and Mr. JUDGE personally are not sustained by evidence, and should not have been printed.

It is probable that few Theosophical students of the present day have ever seen the article written by Mr. Judge on H.P.B. at the invitation of the *Sun*, and included as part of its editorial retraction by the words "Mr. Judge's article disposes of all questions relating to Madame Blavatsky as presented by Dr. Coues." The article itself, and the accompanying editorial endorsement and retraction, should be contrasted with the two editorials from the *Sun* first quoted in the present chapter and with the Coues charges, in order fully to realize the complete reversal of its position by the *Sun*. This can be accounted for only on two grounds: (1) that the *Sun* after vigorous and prolonged efforts to find evidence to support even one of the charges found that they were mere calumnies, and (2) that its publishers were men honorable enough voluntarily to make amends for the wrong done by publishing a retraction, even after the death of H.P.B. had freed them from all risk of damages.

Theosophists, out of loyalty and gratitude to H.P.B. who brought them—at what cost to herself we have partly seen—the message of Theosophy, would do well to inform themselves fully on the Coues-Collins and *Sun* case, for they cover every accusation ever hurled at H.P.B.'s good name and fame; they constitute the only case where the charges were made directly, and by a responsible channel. The outcome of the case constitutes an absolute vindication of H.P.B. and an equally emphatic exposure of the bad faith or the ignorance of those who have since repeated those slanders. Yet years later one and another of the Coues-Collins-*Sun* charges have been repeated and have gained very wide publicity because of the supposed high character of the parties making them, for example, by "Margot Tennant" (wife of Herbert Asquith, ex-Prime Minister of Great Britain, in her "Intimate Diary"), and by the late Count Witte, for many years one of the leading Ministers of the Russian Empire under the *régime* of the late Czar. Count Witte was a cousin of H.P.B., but as he was many years her junior, he knew her only as a boy and saw her but a few times. In his published "Memoirs" the old charges of immorality first directly made by Coues and the *Sun* are circumstantially repeated. He does not profess to speak from knowledge, but for the same inscrutable reasons that have prompted so many others, does not hesitate to repeat these abominable calumnies at second-hand. The outcome of the *Sun* case gives the lie to the Witte slanders upon the dead. Students may be interested to know that Count Witte's own mother, a devoted member of the orthodox Greek Catholic Church, remained to her dying day the warm friend and champion of H.P.B. Vile as must be considered the characters of those who originate or circulate unverified base charges against the living, they are respectable in comparison with those who continue to revile the defenseless dead.

After the battle in the *Sun* and its sequence, Dr. Coues fled ingloriously from the field; his Gnostic society melted away like a shadow, his prestige waned, and he died in obscurity in 1899. His Esoteric Theosophical Society exists only as a forgotten echo of his own bombast and pretense. After the *Sun* retraction he never again ventured to thrust himself on public attention as an "Occultist."

CHAPTER XV

OLCOTT VERSUS H.P.B.

ATTENTION must now be turned from the external aspects of the struggle of contending forces accompanying the progress of the Theosophical Movement, as exemplified in the Coues-Collins' storm, and the arena regarded from another point of view altogether—the issues as personified in H.P.B., Mr. Judge, and Col. Olcott, who, as said, represented in their own persons the three Sections of that Movement, exoteric and esoteric.[1]

In the first decade of the Movement, as manifested in the exoteric Theosophical Society, the work of the three Founders was concordant and coherent. The Society grew rapidly in numbers and influence and became firmly established in America, Europe, and India. Minor opposition attended its course from external antagonistic factors and numerous internal disturbances arose, but none of these was of serious moment, because no dissensions existed among the Founders. Enemies without and trouble makers within could find nothing "whereon to stand" as a fulcrum. The first breach in the solidarity of the Founders was effected in the year 1881. It did not become a matter of public knowledge until 1895, and consideration of it must be deferred until the events of that period, but the fact should be noted in seeking to understand the origins of the successive phases of the Movement.[2]

Public reference was made to the existence of the inner Sections of the Movement at the close of the first seven years. From then on more and more frequent allusions to the Second Section, its superior importance,

[1] See Chapter IX.
[2] See Chapters XXIV and XXXIV.

its rules and discipline, its guardianship of the exoteric work, its provisions for the more earnest and worthy members of the Third Section or Theosophical Society proper, may be found in public print. Finally, in 1888, a definite, formal, public announcement was made of the formation of the Esoteric Section of the T.S., as a probationary degree of the Second Section of the Theosophical Movement. And, under the protection of the "pledge" and the seal of confidence, information was given to all applicants of the real purpose of the Movement, the real status of the Society, the real Objects of the invisible *Founders*—the Masters of Wisdom.

The first ten years was marked, exoterically, by the Coulomb charges and the *Report* of the Society for Psychical Research. Esoterically, both these were made possible and enabled to achieve an immense damage to the Movement, through the hidden rupture between the three Sections of the Movement, the First and Second Sections on the one hand, the Third Section on the other; between the esoteric side of the Movement as personified in H. P.B., Mr. Judge and Damodar, and the exoteric, as personified by Col. Olcott, Mr. Sinnett, and the Indian Council. At the time, the only public signs of this breach were the failure to defend H.P.B. as strenuously as she was attacked; her resignation and departure from India and from active connection with the Society; the public and private disclaimers of Col. Olcott and others of any reliance of their own or of the Society on the assumed Occult status or powers of H.P.B.; their assertion of the ability of the Society to stand on its own merits apart from H. P. Blavatsky as the direct Agent of the Masters; apart from her paramount status as the connecting link between those Masters and the Society; apart from her teachings of Theosophy as the authoritative exposition of the Wisdom-Religion.

Although they had abundant warnings, both from the teachings of Theosophy and from messages received by them directly from the Masters, that their views of H.P.B. were erroneous in fact and illogical in principle, and although not one of them himself had, or professed to have, any Occult powers of his own, nevertheless their fundamentally false view of the nature of H.P.B. compelled them, little by little, to take a divergent path. In the beginning, doubts; next, private dissent and dissimulation; then a middle ground, public temporizing, and secret plotting; finally, open repudiation of her Occult status and standing in the Society, in the Movement, in Theosophy.

The stage of dissent and dissimulation was reached and practiced in 1884 and the following years. Compelled by their involvement with her in the affairs of the Society and their joint sponsorship for the numerous miraculous events attributed to the course of its history, a lukewarm support was publicly given to H.P.B., while in private a determined effort was made to suppress and "control" her in the common interest. During these years W. Stainton Moses ("M.A. Oxon"), C. C. Massey, A. O. Hume, V. V. Solovyoff, W. T. Brown, Mrs. Josephine Cables, Mohini M. Chatterji, Mr. Cooper-Oakley, and numerous others, both members of the Society and probationers of the Second Section, succumbed to inner and outer influences and left the Society, but Col. Olcott, Mr. Sinnett, and many others continued with the Society and its work, because, however much they doubted H.P.B., they were none the less convinced of the existence of the Masters and the value of the Society in the work of the Movement, provided only that they could themselves direct and control its destinies. Followed Col. Olcott's private but violent opposition to the formation of the Esoteric Section, and to the lines of direction that H.P.B. and Mr. Judge were attempting to lay and energize within the Society by the establishment of the Esoteric Section and by their magazines, *The Path* and *Lucifer*.[3]

The cleavage at this time went almost to the verge of the establishment by H.P.B. and Mr. Judge of a new Society composed of those Western Theosophists who would remain true to the original impetus and its lines, and would have so resulted had not Col. Olcott and those

[3] See Chapters IX and X.

associated with his views modified their conduct. Concerned not at all with or over Col. Olcott's or any one's opinions in regard to themselves, but intent only on the Cause itself, H.P.B. and W.Q.J. used every effort to encourage, to sustain, to uphold him and others in their devotion and their place in the Society, so long as work was done and a possibility remained to keep the three lines of the Movement intact, coherent, and in proper relation. Nothing was omitted that might assuage the several vanities, jealousies, ambitions, and fears of Col. Olcott and his co-workers; everything possible was done to convince them that place, power, authority and dominion were not sought by H.P.B.

Then came the Coues-Collins-*Sun* attack. There can be no doubt, we think, that Dr. Coues counted that if he led the assault he would be supported openly by Col. Olcott and others prominent within the Society, and for this he had what to him were sound reasons, as has been indicated.[4] Backed by his own prestige with the general public and that of Olcott and others with the Society's membership, knowing the general discredit heaped upon H.P.B. by the S.P.R. *Report,* knowing well the private opinions of Col. Olcott, Mr. Sinnett, and others in regard to her—what more natural than that he should consider his forces more than ample to so utterly crush the reputation of H.P.B. that she would be permanently eliminated as a factor in the Society, which could then be re-organized and re-built on lines agreeable to himself and his own ambitions, with himself as its bright particular star in the West? Able and astute, his plans succeeded perfectly with Miss Mabel Collins, but his master-stroke failed with Col. Olcott. This he could not know in advance, but his knowledge of conditions and the progress of his correspondence with the President-Founder gave him every reason to believe that the disaffection so artfully fanned would burst to flame in open treason when the battle should be joined. He reckoned without his host in the final issue, but how nearly he succeeded is indicated by the letter to him from Col. Olcott

[4] See Chapters XII and XIV.

which we have given, and by the course pursued by the President-Founder during all that stormy period—a course which we have now to trace.

That course was one which could but aid the battle being waged to destroy the moral reputation and Occult status of H.P.B. and her chief defender, Mr. Judge, so far as that could be achieved without imperiling the Society and his own importance in it to the point of irretrievable disaster. Colonel Olcott was willing to go thus far in order to upset the paramount unofficial influence of H.P.B. and her colleague; reduce them to what he considered their proper place and subordination in the ranks; and at the same time enhance and render secure his own position and power as the recognized Official Head of the Society. In all this Col. Olcott was honest and sincere. It was but the logical development of his own basic misconception and misunderstanding of Masters, Their Movement, and Their Society—all alike menaced by the "irresponsible" and "unconstitutional" procedure of H.P.B. However mistaken or misguided his views, he *was* absolutely honest and devoted to what he conceived to be the best interests of the Society. It was precisely this honesty and devotion to the Society, however inconsistent and illogical his mind might be, that H.P.B. recognized, and that Dr. Coues failed utterly to reckon with.

Negatively, Col. Olcott's state of mind is attested by his total failure to align himself with his colleagues while they were being sorely beset by traitors within and by enemies without. As in 1884-5 and again in 1886-7, his sole thought was for the Society and himself—for the Society as personified in himself. Its troubles and his troubles were, in his opinion, not due to any falling away from its Objects, any mistakes or misunderstandings of his own, but to the wrong and perverse actions of H.P.B. and Mr. Judge. They had gotten the Society, themselves and himself into serious difficulties in spite of his best efforts to prevent. Very well; it was for them to extricate and clear themselves if they could, and in so doing learn a needed lesson. That was their affair, not his.

His duty was to protect the Society and himself as its responsible Head and Guardian, at all hazards and from all hazards; and the chief of these hazards was the "friction of strong personalities," due to the "unauthorized" and "irregular" actions of H.P.B. and W.Q.J., as opposed to his own "official" procedure.

Affirmatively, Col. Olcott's predominating attitude is evidenced (1) by the record made by himself and his intimates at the time; (2) by his own disclosures made many years afterward; (3) by the record made by H.P.B. and Mr. Judge. From all these the student can piece together the pattern which shows the workings of consciousness of the three Founders during the storm of 1889-90.

"Old Diary Leaves," Fourth Series, to which we shall have to refer, was published in book form after the death of Col. Olcott. There are many omissions of the text as originally printed in *The Theosophist*, Volumes 21 and 22, ten years after the events discussed therein. Quotations here given, therefore, should be verified by reference to the original text in *The Theosophist.*

Volume 21, p. 199, Col. Olcott describes the situation just prior to his visit to Europe in 1888. He puts it thus:

> Portents of a coming storm in our European groups, stirred up or intensified by H.P.B., begin to show themselves, and Judge complains of our neglecting him. Just then Dr. Coues was working hard for the notoriety he craved and Judge was opposing him.

Then "Old Diary Leaves" gives extracts from private letters written by Mr. Judge to Col. Olcott, as follows:

> May 21, 1888: I am always striving to keep your name at the top, for until your death you must be at the head.
>
> June 8, 1888: Certain matters are occurring here which need attention and action. . . . His

> (Coues') policy is to place himself at the head of some wonderful unknown thing through which (save the mark!) communications are alleged to come from Masters. He also in a large sense wishes to pull the T.S. away from your jurisdiction and make himself the Grand Mogul of it in this country. . . . *I know that. . . . policy is to retain complete control in you, and my desire is to keep the American Section as a dependency of the General Council in India;* hence you are the President. *It was never my intention to dissever, but to bind,* and the form of our Constitution clearly shows that. That's why no President is elected or permitted here. . . . So I would recommend that you call the Council and consider our Constitution, which ought long ago to have been done—and decide that we are in affiliation and subordination to India and that we are recognized as part of the General Council, with power to have a Secretary as an (official) channel, but not to have a yearly President but only a Chairman at each Convention. . . . I cannot work this thing here properly without your co-operation.
>
> June 15, 1888: Until you two die it is folly for others to whistle against the wind. Masters and Federation!

Colonel Olcott's comments on Mr. Judge's letters show that in January, 1900, when he was writing, he as totally misconceived them, as at the time of their reception in 1888; that he saw in them nothing but "the building up of a new structure of falsehood, fraud and treachery in which to house new idols."

Then followed Col. Olcott's visit to England and his "pitched battle with H.P.B." over the various matters at issue—the trouble in the Paris Branch, the Charter of the Blavatsky Lodge, the formation of the British Section of the T.S., on the model of the previously formed American Section, and the formation of the Esoteric Section.[5] In all these matters at stake, as well as Cooper-Oakley's severance from the editorial staff of *The Theosophist,* Col. Olcott yielded, partly under the influence of his renewed association with H.P.B., partly because he saw that he had come to the parting of the ways. Mr. Judge came over to England and the three Founders became once more, for the time being, apparently of one aim, purpose, and feeling. To strengthen and maintain this bond after their separation and return, each to his own field of labor, H.P.B. and Mr. Judge arranged that delegates from the American and British Section should go with Col. Olcott to Adyar and represent those Sections at the forthcoming "parliament" or Convention of the Society in India, at the end of December, 1888.

Richard Harte, a former New York newspaper man, an old-time personal friend of Col. Olcott, who had been a member of the Society since 1878, was then in London and had acquired considerable reputation among Theosophists as the alleged writer of the famous editorial in *Lucifer* for December, 1887, entitled "Lucifer to the Archbishop of Canterbury, Greeting!" Him, Col. Olcott selected for his editorial associate on *The Theosophist.* Thereupon Mr. Judge arranged with the Executive Committee of the American Council to have Mr. Harte act as delegate for the American Section and to give Mr. Harte instructions to represent to the Indian Convention that the American Section favored the restoration to Col. Olcott of the powers and authority vested in the Indian Council early in 1885,[6] as noted in a former chapter. Mr. Charles Johnston, long a resident of India, was similarly chosen as delegate of the British Section.

Colonel Olcott returned to India later in the fall of 1888. Volume 21, pp. 322-3, gives his reminiscences of the month preceding the Convention. He says:

[5] See Chapter X.
[6] See Chapters VII and XI.

> The Executive Council met as usual, on the following Sunday [after his return], and passed resolutions thoroughly approving of my doings in Europe. . . .
>
> At a Council meeting [in December], a resolution was unanimously passed to convert itself into an Advisory body and restore to me the full executive powers which, in 1885, I had consented to have curtailed, to satisfy some who thought it would be better to have several bosses instead of one. The thing did not work well enough to continue it, and all my colleagues were but too glad to re-shift the responsibility to my shoulders rather than keep it themselves. It was all the same to me, for even during the intervals I virtually had to do all the work, and the Council meetings grew more and more perfunctory—as Council meetings usually do, when there is some leader who may be counted on to pull the stroke-oar and get the boat on the straight course when cross winds blow.

The same pages contain Col. Olcott's comments on two other matters which were to come before the Convention. Of the first of these he says:

> Tranquil days of work and pleasant conversation followed, but before long I began to see signs of discontent spreading to some extent among certain few Branches, the result of underhand schemings by one or two malcontents, who were unfriendly to H.P.B. This passed off in time, although a desperate attempt was made at that year's Convention to make trouble for me. The Bombay Branch sent me, on November 30th, a resolution recommending that T. Subba Row, who had resigned, be asked to come back to us, but I have positively refused to lower the Society's dignity in any similar case, however influential might be the seceder.

The other matter mentioned, which also includes the preceding, is described as follows:

> The Convention Delegates began arriving on the 24th of December. On Christmas Day I got a foolish cablegram from H.P.B., threatening the resignation of herself and the entire Blavatsky Lodge should Cooper-Oakley be re-admitted to membership; the act showing the state of nervous excitement into which the Subba Row imbroglio had thrown her. She used the name of the Blavatsky Lodge and of certain of its members so often in her letters, as condemning me utterly and backing her views unreservedly, that it became at last tiresome. Considering our personal relations, the identity of our ages, and our joint relationship to our Guru, it seemed to me ridiculous that the dicta of a group of junior colleagues, however warm partisans of hers, should influence me to act against my own judgment in questions of management. I wrote her at last that if she sent me any more round robins or protests from the same quarter I should neither read nor answer her letters; our affairs must be settled between ourselves without the interference of third parties. Answering me, she admitted the correctness of my argument and the exasperating documents ceased to arrive.

Theosophical students generally have never gone to the labor necessary in checking Col. Olcott's very numerous misstatements of fact and his very frequent contradictions, but have accepted his testimony and his conclusions alike as accurate and just. The matters just quoted are a case in point. The fact is very plain from his other statements earlier referred to [7] that he himself was the chief "malcontent," for it was *The Theosophist* that precipitated the "Subba Row imbroglio" by publishing the criticisms on the "seven-fold classification

[7] See Chapter X.

of principles." It was himself who supported Mr. Cooper-Oakley, its Editor, to the very point of a rupture with H.P.B. It was himself, in absolute control both of the Council and the Indian Convention, who favored the invitation not to Subba Row only, but to Mr. Cooper-Oakley and others, "to come back to us." It was himself who had the affair all staged to become a *fait accompli* before H.P.B. should hear of it, and only her prompt and decisive cablegram to him two days before the Convention convened, upset the cut-and-dried program. The matter had already gone so far it could not be kept out of the proceedings of the Convention, but her cablegram once more convinced Olcott that he had over-shot his mark. The Convention Report, carefully prepared and edited by Richard Harte to conform to the exigencies of Col. Olcott's course in this and the other actions taken by the Convention, reads as follows:

> Second Day, Friday, December 28, 1888.
>
> The President called on the Secretary to read a resolution of the Bombay Branch, to the effect that the President should urge upon certain ex-Fellows to resume their connection with the Society, and which he, the President, had been particularly requested to lay before the Convention. A debate ensued, in which the unanimous opinion was expressed that such a step would be incompatible with the dignity of the Society. Thereupon Mr. Harte moved, . . . that the document and the whole subject should be laid upon the table, which was carried unanimously.

This was the "desperate attempt at that year's Convention to make trouble for me" over the Subba Row imbroglio that Col. Olcott's reminiscences so graphically and so inaccurately portray and comment upon.

Mr. Harte and Mr. Johnston duly expressed to the Convention the authorized wish of their respective Sections that the executive powers of the President should be restored to him by formal action of the Convention. According to the Report, Mr. Johnston went further and stated on behalf of the British Section: "It was further their opinion that Fees and Dues should be abolished, and the Society be placed upon a basis of voluntary support. As the President had intimated that he intended to place him (Mr. Johnston) on the Committee for the amendment of the Rules, he would not make any further remarks at present." As the Report follows immediately with a copy of the Rules of the British Section and those Rules provided explicitly both for fees for the support of the Section and for contributions to the Society, it is evident (1) that Mr. Johnston either was not correctly reported in his remarks, or (2) that he exceeded his instructions and authority from the newly organized British Section. Page 42 of the Report contains the statement as the conclusion of the "Report of the Executive Council":

> Resolutions were also adopted to submit for favorable consideration suggestions made by the American and British Sections for the abolition of Entrance Fees and Annual Dues, and for the reorganization of the whole Society upon a basis of Sectional Divisions with an autonomous character, but dependent and subject to the supervision and executive control of the President in Council, as representative of the collective autonomy of the whole Society. The Council is of opinion that radical changes in the Rules are needed, and recommend that the whole subject be referred to a Committee on Rules with instructions to report an amended Code to the present Convention, for its approval.

No one, after reading the extracts just given from "Old Diary Leaves" can doubt that the Executive Council was merely Col. Olcott under a convenient cloak. A long set of "Revised Rules" was immediately presented to the Convention and the Report says:

> The Rules, as read out one by one by the Secretary, were debated by Sections, amended, and voted upon. The President was empowered, on motion of Mr. S. Ramaswamier . . . to edit the text, and make necessary corrections therein before sending it to the printer.

The nine pages of the Report immediately following the official proceedings are devoted to elaborate "Introductory Explanations" of the "Revised Rules," which, upon examination, will be found to be in fact an entirely new Constitution.

Turning now to the official Report of the democratic American Section held at Chicago in April, 1889, following, and to the report of Mr. Judge as General Secretary to that Convention on the matters just considered, Mr. Judge there says:

> My Report for this year has to deal with the progress of the Society's work since our last Convention, and certain changes which have been made by the Convention in India in last December. I propose to consider the last first.
>
> The Secretary in charge in India has already sent to most of the Branches a copy of the "Revised Rules." By reading those, together with the Report of the Convention held there, it will be seen that apparently the purpose to revise the rules and abolish fees and dues was proposed by the American and English Sections, acting through their Delegates, Mr. Richard Harte and Mr. Charles Johnston. Mr. Harte was delegated by the Executive Committee, at the time he left London for India, to represent the American Section at that Convention, but, at the same time, written instructions were given him, very definitely stating that all that the American Section required him to do was to endeavor to restore to Col. Olcott the powers which he had voluntarily given up at a previous date, and those

were stated to be the only changes which he should say we were in favor of. It was not then thought that any proposal to abolish fees and dues would be made, and, as Mr. Harte was himself present in New York when our Constitution governing the American Section was passed, and knew our policy in carrying on the work here, it never for a moment occurred to the Executive Committee that it was necessary to say any more than we had said, and as our Constitution declared our autonomy which had been granted prior to the passage of the Constitution, and which has since been affirmed in the Convention in India, even if we had been told in advance what was proposed to be done, we should have thought it to be impossible, as well as injudicious.

The "Revised Rules" also amend the "objects" of the Society by altering them and adding to them, and, in a paper published in the succeeding issue of the "Theosophist" signed "F. T. S." an attempt is made to show that the "objects have never been definitely formulated." This article is full of misconceptions, and, therefore, of wrong conclusions, because the gentleman who wrote it was not acquainted with the facts nor in possession of the records. He refers to the printed "Rules" of each year, and says that in 1882 for the first time they appeared as they were printed last year, but on looking over my records I find, not only that they have always been the same—except in minor elaborations not affecting the substance,—but that they were originally formulated in the shape they appeared before the last Convention in India, at the time that this Society was organized in 1875.

. . . These alterations seem to be injudicious. I therefore suggest to the Convention that a Resolution be passed dissenting from the ad-

> visability of these alterations and requesting a restoration, if possible, to the old form.
>
> In the second place, all dues and fees are attempted to be abolished, and the source of revenue for expenses made to depend on voluntary contributions.
>
> You will note that these "Revised Rules" reaffirm the autonomy we claimed in 1886 which was subsequently ratified. There is no inconsistency in our declaring autonomy in respect to the internal affairs of the Section and, at the same time, our allegiance to the cause and to the Society as a whole.
>
> I am authorized by Mme. Blavatsky to say that she is not in favor of the change, and the majority of the British Section also disagree with it, and have stated that their delegate was not authorized to consent to it.

Mr. Judge goes on to say that, aware of the sentiment of the American and British Sections, he had written to Adyar protesting against the proposed change in the matter of dues, and had received a reply from "Bro. Harte, the Secretary, enclosing a copy of a Resolution passed by the Commissioners in charge during Col. Olcott's absence." That Resolution "suspended until further order" that portion of the "Revised Rules" relating to fees and dues. This was subsequently "ratified" by the Indian "Council" and confirmed by a change in the "Rules" at the next succeeding Adyar Convention, which was not held until 1890, owing to the absence of Col. Olcott in Europe in December, 1889—of which in due course.[8]

By referring to "Old Diary Leaves," Volume 21 of *The Theosophist*, at pages 324-5, comparison of Col. Olcott's comments with those of Mr. Judge can be made. Thus:

[8] See Chapter XVII.

Consistently with my policy to give every chance to my colleagues to try experiments which seemed to them to promise well for the Society's interest, I acceded to their wish that we should try what effect the complete abolition of entrance fees and annual dues, and the trusting for the Society's support to voluntary contributions, would have. Personally, I did not believe in the scheme, though I officially supported it. . . . But the Convention voted for the change, upon the motion of the representatives of the British and American Sections present; I concurred, and issued the necessary Executive Notices, to clear the way.

The first effect was that angry protests broke out in both the Western Sections; H.P.B. wrote me a violent letter, denouncing me as a vacillator and liberally reporting what so and so, her friends and colleagues, said about my inconsistency, after having just effected the organization of a British Section and giving it the right to levy the customary entrance fees and annual dues; while Judge and his party openly revolted and refused to comply with the new order of things. Secretly I was rather amused to see how much of a mess was being made by marplots eager to have a finger in the pie, and was disposed to give them rope to hang themselves with. It was not long before the experiment failed and we returned to the old method. . . .

The other important thing done by the Convention of 1888 was the adoption of the policy of re-organizing the Society's work on the line of autonomous Sections: this having been the motive prompting me originally to grant, in 1886, a Charter to the American Section and, later, one to the new Section in London. The plan had proved an entire success in America, and after two years of testing it in practice it seemed but fair to extend it to all our fields of activity. It

> was an admirable plan in every respect . . . and the Society changed from a quasi-autocracy to a constitutional Fedéralion, each part independent as to its internal affairs, but responsible to every other part for its loyal support of the movement and its ideals and of the Federal Centre, which bound the whole together, like the *fasces* of the lictor, into an unbreakable bundle.

The elaborate "Introductory Explanations" to the "Revised Rules" published in the "Supplement" to *The Theosophist* for January, 1889, was followed in the February number by an article on "The Theosophical Society," and signed in both cases with the initials "F. T. S." Both articles were undoubtedly written by Mr. Harte. It was these articles which were referred to by Mr. Judge in his report to the American Section. Both articles should be examined with great care as they mark the public features of a sustained campaign on the part of Col. Olcott and his associates to subordinate the esoteric aspect of the Theosophical Movement to the exoteric Society, to center the attention of the membership on the Society, and to make of the Indian headquarters and Col. Olcott the prime object of allegiance and devotion, as the visible head and front of the Movement. This campaign was coincident with the Coues-Collins' developments and can be taken only as co-ordinate with them.

"The Theosophical Society" first attempts to show that in the beginning the Society had no determinate purpose, no definite lines of direction, but was an "evolution" from unintended, unforeseen, unexpected stages.

"The Theosophical Society" then takes up the Objects of the Society and speaks of them also as a "development."

Curiously enough, "F. T. S.," goes on to say, later in his article:

> This variation in the declared objects of the Society [those just promulgated in the "Re-

> vised Rules"] must not be taken as indicating any real change in the intentions of the Founders. *There is abundant evidence in their writings and speeches that from the first their purposes were to stimulate the spiritual development of the individual and, to awaken in the race the sentiment of Brotherhood.*

"The Theosophical Society" was followed in the June, 1889, *Theosophist* by two more articles.

CHAPTER XVI

OLCOTT'S ATTEMPT TO CENTRALIZE ALL AUTHORITY

When the January, 1889, *Theosophist* with its Report of the Adyar Convention, and the February number with the articles noted, reached America, Mr. Judge considered them in his report as General Secretary of the Convention of the American Section. How the issues raised were met has been shown in the citations given both from Mr. Judge's report [1] and from the Letter of H.P.B. to the same Convention. *Lucifer* for March, 1889, contained an editorial "On Pseudo-Theosophy," in which, taking advantage of an article in the *London Daily News* which amused itself by some comments on Dr. Franz Hartmann's novel, "The Talking Image of Urur," then running in *Lucifer,* H.P.B. without naming any names discussed the counter-currents in the Society. In *Lucifer* for June she published the article, "It's the Cat," which was "Dedicated to those Members of the T.S. whom the Cap may fit." Again without naming persons, she pays attention to those who would make of her "the cat," *i.e.*, the scapegoat for all the sins of omission and commission of the Society and its members.

It was the habit with the three leading Theosophical publications to send to each other advance proofs of all forthcoming important articles. All the above cited articles should therefore be read, both in connection with the then existing internal and external situation of the Society, and as a prelude to the June, 1889, *Theosophist.*

"Applied Theosophy," its leading editorial, is an article of nearly ten pages. The writer asks:

> The first question that naturally arises is, whether the action of the Theosophical Society

[1] See preceding chapter.

in every respect should be limited to its declared Objects. . . . Of the three Objects two are distinctly separated from everything else. . . . The first Object is altogether different. To "form the nucleus of Universal Brotherhood," is so far from conducing to retirement and concentration, is a purpose so high, so deep, so broad, so universally sympathetic, so distant of realization, that it becomes vague and confused when the attention is directed to it, and to most Fellows this Object is about equivalent in practice to the formation of a nucleus for the recurrence of the Golden Age, or for the reestablishment of the garden of Eden . . .

Here and there a Fellow of the Society outside of India may be found who is willing to accept the Eastern Initiates, whether ancient or modern, as teachers; but the majority prefer to think and theorize for themselves, which is, after all, the best way for anyone to learn who can think and theorize logically.

We have, then, a Society without opinions but with certain "Objects," certain principles, and certain methods, and we have as a result a tendency to certain modes of thought and certain theories of the Universe, to which theories the name of Theosophy has been given. . . . The fact that "The Secret Doctrine" has been so generally understood and so highly appreciated by Theosophists, shows that their own thoughts were not so very much behind the ideas *given out* in that marvellous work.

All this, however, is only what may be called the intellectual or philosophical side of Theosophy; and it is the fruit of the Theosophical Society's influence in only one direction. . . .

The whole tendency of this argument appears clearly, first, to discredit the real and primary Object of the Society, and to make a division in its Three Objects;

secondly, to emphasize that the teachings of the "Secret Doctrine" are neither new to the membership nor in any way an impartation from a higher plane of perception, as the "thoughts" of the membership "were not so very much behind the ideas 'given out' in that work"; thirdly, that H.P.B.'s "theories of the Universe" are merely "the *fruit of the Theosophical Society's influence.*" The Society is not an outcome of H.P.B.'s mission and teaching; on the contrary these are a development of and from the *Society!*

After discoursing on the implications derivable from these premises, Mr. Harte proceeds a step further:

> . . . Since the Theosophical Society has professedly, as a body, no opinions on any subject, it is equally a transgression of its basic principles for it to sustain or promulgate any special system of philosophy, as in practice it decidedly does, under the name of "Theosophy" . . .

Then Mr. Harte, his ground ready, asks:

> Can any means be devised whereby the Fellows of the Society can apply their knowledge and their energies to the practical affairs of life? *Practical Theosophy* is an affair of the future. *Applied Theosophy* is a more modest ambition, and is, or ought to be, a possibility.

Mr. Harte has his answer ready:

> If the Fellows of the Theosophical Society are to apply their Theosophy to the affairs of life, it must be through the Society, and as individual units of the whole,—not as isolated individuals. . . . It is this mystic individuality, "the sum total," that gives strength to all societies and congregations of men, and becomes the real dominating power, to which all contribute some of their force, and which stands behind every unit

> and lends its whole strength to it. Without it a Fellow of the Theosophical Society would be as powerless as any other isolated man or woman in the community. With it behind him an F. T. S. is a power in proportion to the unity and singleness of purpose of the Society to which he belongs.

It is from the *Society* that radiates the "dominating power"; from the *Society* that the members are to draw their sustenance and support, not from any Teacher or Teaching, not from any "self-induced and self-devised exertions" of the individual aspirants. The model to follow, the example to emulate, is pictured by Mr. Harte:

> Who speaks when a priest of the Roman Catholic Church utters a command? *The united power of the Church of Rome.* Who speaks when a disfrocked priest says something? A *non-entity.* Who speaks when the Judge, the General, the Statesman open their mouths? "The State,"—the tremendous and often tyrannical personality that comes into life and action when the units that compose it [are] bound together, through organization, by a common will and a common purpose.

This idea that it is only "through organization," through making the *Society* the prime object of devotion, its "authority" through the voice of its officials supreme over the individual conscience and action, that "Applied Theosophy," can be made a success is argued at length, leading up to the culmination of making the Adyar Headquarters a second Rome, and, by necessary inference, of the President-Founder a Theosophical Pope:

> The Theosophical Society is an ideal power for good diffused over the whole world, but it

requires material conditions, and the most important of these is a material centre, from which and to which the efferent and afferent forces shall circulate. This is a condition of the life of all organizations, and of all organisms, and the Theosophical Society is both; it is an organization on the material plane, an organism on the spiritual. A common centre, therefore, is as necessary for spiritual as for physical reasons. "ADYAR" is not a place only, it is a principle. It is a name that ought to carry with it a power far greater than that conveyed by the name "Rome." ADYAR is the centre of the Theosophical Movement—not "7 Duke Street, Adelphi" [the publication office of *Lucifer*] or "Post Office Box 2659, New York" [the address of *The Path*].

ADYAR is a principle and a symbol, as well as a locality. ADYAR is the name which means on the material plane the Headquarters of an international, or, more properly speaking, worldwide Society. . . . It means on the supra-physical plane a centre of life and energy, the point to and from which the currents run between the ideal and the material. Every loyal Fellow has in his heart a little ADYAR, for he has in him a spark of the spiritual fire which the name typifies. ADYAR is the symbol of our unity as a Society, and so long as it exists in the hearts of its Fellows, the powers of the enemy can never prevail against the Theosophical Society. . . .

What then, to recapitulate, must be our answer to the questions with which we started:—Is such a thing as "Applied Theosophy" possible? If so, of what does it consist?

. . . the Fellows must perceive that the Theosophical Society is a living entity, "ideal" if one chooses to call it so, but an entity *one and indivisible* alike upon the material and on the super-physical plane. We have also seen that

> the visible centre of the Society, ADYAR, is symbolical of the principle of unity, as well as of the material life of the Society, and that in every sense loyalty to ADYAR means loyalty to the objects of the Society and to the principles of Theosophy. . . .

The same—June—number of *The Theosophist* contained a related article by Mr. Harte, signed "F. T. S." and bearing the title, "The Situation." Some extracts follow:

> We have not yet got our proper bearings after the radical change in the Society made by an Order of the President last autumn, and adopted into the Constitution and Rules of the Theosophical Society, by the General Council in the Annual Convention of 1888. This change was the formation of an Esoteric Division of the Society; and this separation of the esoteric element from the exoteric, is not only a disentangling of two things that have different methods and aims, and the mixing up of which in the life and work of the Society has given rise to considerable confusion, but it is, moreover, a weaning of the Society from sources that have previously nourished it. . . . It is pretty generally felt that if the Theosophical Society is to be a moral and spiritual power in the world, it must be in touch with the world and live in the world; using such methods in its dealings with that world as the latter can appreciate and understand, or which, at all events, will not excite its prejudices, and put it into a fury of opposition at the very first go off.

There is here put forward the misstatement that the formation of the Esoteric Section was *due to* and *dependent upon* "an Order of the President"; that the real object of its formation was to *separate* the "esoteric element from the exoteric"; that the "mixing up" of the esoteric with the exoteric aspects of the Movement had given rise to "considerable confusion," and that it was necessary to "wean" the Society "from the sources that have hitherto nourished it." The view is presented that if the Society is to influence the world it must have a worldly incentive to offer, a *worldly* basis and authority in order to "be a moral and spiritual power in the world"; that because its actual Objects, its actual basis, its actual methods have hitherto been *un*worldly, *therefore* it has excited the prejudices of the world, *therefore* it has put the world "into a fury of opposition." What is needed, in this view, is not the basis and methods of H.P.B., which have been the disturbing factor, but the basis and methods of Col. Olcott, Mr. Sinnett, *et al*, who have been using and will continue to use such methods in dealing with the world "as the latter can appreciate and understand." This suggestion implanted, the logical corollary is that H.P.B.'s methods have been a blunder which must be corrected. What her methods have been and how sadly she has misrepresented the Masters, are next implied:

> If there is any reliance to be placed upon what has come to us as the wishes and instructions of those mysterious Personages behind the scenes, by whose orders the Society was founded, then the weaning of the Society from any further professed and ostensible connection with phenomena and invisible wire-pullers (using the term with the greatest respect) has been determined and decreed some time ago. If we are to have faith in anything we have been told as coming from the Masters, we are constrained to believe that it is their wish that the Theosophical Society shall now stand before all men for what it is worth in itself, and that Theosophy shall from henceforth be put before the world as a system of philosophical and ethical truth which stands on its own merits without any adventitious aids.

> props or abutments. This implies at the outset that from henceforth Occultism and Theosophy, which are in reality two very different things, shall be separate in the minds of the Fellows, and in the life of the Society.

The Master's letter to Col. Olcott[2] is referred to to show that H.P.B. should "mind her own business!" Mr. Harte comments:

> That letter refers to the settlement of a dispute among the Fellows in France, but the principle so definitely stated with regard to the division of functions . . . and the formation of an Esoteric Division of the Theosophical Society under the exclusive management and control of Madame Blavatsky was the result of its wider application—it being understood that the President was in no way to interfere with that division, Madame Blavatsky, in return, abstaining in future from any *direct* interference with the worldly or exoteric management of the Society. . . . It may be further stated here, for the benefit of those whom it may concern, that the formation of the Esoteric Section, was in accordance with the instructions received from the Masters.
>
> On both sides this new departure was felt to be a relief. Occultism is above all "rule" or "bye-law" emanating from the will of the governed, which is the only possible basis of a popular government such as that of the Theosophical Society. The result of trying to make two such different things work harmoniously was like that which might be expected from harnessing together a "sacred bull" and a draft horse—the waggon was continually running into the fence, and always in danger of being upset; a danger in no way diminished by the fact that two coach-

[2] See Chapter X.

> men sat on the box seat, each of whom held one of the reins, and pulled it vigorously every now and then without much reference to the ideas of the other, or to "things as a whole." Now, happily, there has been a division of labour, each driver has got his own animal to himself.

Having thus driven home the idea that H.P.B. and Col. Olcott were originally on a plane of entire equality both with regard to the Masters and to the T.S.; that the "interference" of H.P.B. was as displeasing to Masters as it was to Col. Olcott, so that Masters gave Col. Olcott "instructions" to "order" the formation of an Esoteric Section to limit the capacity for harmfulness of H.P.B.; that the "bargain" was that H.P.B. should be let alone in the esoteric "Division" and Col. Olcott no longer interfered with in the Society as a whole—having thus arrived at his explanation of facts and factors, Mr. Harte then pays attention to the "Esoteric Division," its members, and H.P.B. in these terms:

> The head of the Esoteric Division is at liberty to impose pledges, institute degrees, and ordain exercises, and without let or hindrance to issue instructions and orders to those who place themselves under her guidance; . . .
>
> With the affairs of the Esoteric Division this article has nothing to do. That division seems to be a kind of Annex to the Theosophical Society proper, having two doors of exit—one leading up to higher levels, the other leading down and out. Not only do advanced students seek entrance to it, but it appears to have especial attractions for many who are spiritually somewhat crippled. The halt, the maimed and the blind, blissfully unaware of their infirmities, and oblivious of their utter want of preparation, knock incontinently at the door, and the Head of the Division cannot always refuse them a

> chance. At the first little "trial" these weak brothers lose their heads and their holds, fall flat on their noses, and go off howling.
>
> The President and General Council are free to legislate for the Theosophical Society to the best of their knowledge and ability, in conformity with the wishes of the majority of the Fellows. . . .
>
> It is a matter of fact . . . that the Rules of the Theosophical Society have been all along so weak, confused and contradictory, that no other society or persons who wished to receive credit for common sense would probably have put up with them for a day. So long as the esoteric and exoteric elements were mixed up in the Society this state of affairs did not matter. It was inevitable; . . .
>
> The consequences of the former state of affairs is telling on the Society now. . . . No one suspected the want of loyalty to the Society on the part of a portion of the Branches and Sections, until the attempt was made by the late Convention to put a little seriousness and energy into the Society. It looks as if certain of the Sections and Branches have got somewhat too high an opinion of their own importance.

The only Sections which existed prior to the Convention were the American, the British, and the Esoteric, whose Branches, Groups, and Members were primarily interested in Theosophy, not the Society, and who therefore looked to Theosophy and to the example and guidance of H.P.B. and Mr. Judge, not to Col. Olcott and the "Rules and Bye-laws" of the Indian Convention's facile adoption at Col. Olcott's behests. Plain notice is therefore served on these recalcitrants—as they seemed to the President and his associates—that they have no authority, rights, or existence, save by virtue of Col. Olcott's "orders" and that the Power that created them can as easily dissolve them; and it is intimated that that Power will be exercised if former conduct is not superseded by better behavior:

> They [the Sections and Branches] exist only by virtue of Charters issued by the President of the Theosophical Society. It is the fact of the possession of these Charters that makes them different from other little collections of students of Theosophy in the countries where they exist, and gives them what credit they enjoy. . . . Suppose it became necessary to withdraw the Charters of certain Sections, does any one believe for a moment that the Theosophical Society would eventually suffer? At present a large and increasing proportion of the Fellows are "Fellows at large"—that is, unattached to any branch; Fellows in Branches would perceive that their status remained unchanged; and thousands who now sympathize with the objects and work of the Society, but are deterred from joining it by the idea that they are expected to join a branch, would prick up their ears and become interested. These do not care to join the Society now for a variety of reasons:—because they look upon the branches as mutual admiration clubs; because they regard them as the private friends and followers of some one man; because they don't want to be bothered in attending their meetings and listening to things they either know already or do not understand; because they are disgusted with the jealousies and rivalries of Fellows who are prominent in branches; because they do not approve of the branch system at all, which brings the Fellows who belong to branches into unnecessary publicity. If every existing Charter of Section and branch of the Theosophical Society were withdrawn tomorrow, the Society would, in all probability, be a stronger body in a short time than it is now, and

> certainly it would not be a weaker one. Every active Fellow would become a natural recruiting agent, not for a little local branch as at present, but *for the Theosophical Society.*

All this leads up to the summation which is laid before the members, as the cure for the "Situation":

> The Theosophical Society would then exist as a homogeneous whole, composed of loyal Fellows animated by a common spirit, and Adyar would be what it ought to be—the centre of a system for the circulation of Theosophical ideas and literature, and for the organization of Theosophical activities all over the globe. And the Fellows would soon spontaneously form into groups with connections with each other and with Adyar, which would enable them to carry out the work.
>
> These are very obvious considerations. Still, there are people who do not always remember them, and to whom the above remarks may not be without utility.

These articles in the June, 1889, *Theosophist* were immediately followed in the "Supplement" to the July issue by an article entitled "A Disclaimer," the insinuations in which were still more direct and pronounced. It is, in full, as follows:

> The Editor of *The Theosophist* has much pleasure in publishing the following extracts from a letter from Mr. Bertram Keightley, Secretary of the "Esoteric Section" of the Theosophical Society, to one of the Commissioners, which have been handed to him for publication. [Mr. Keightley's letter was in fact a private one to Mr. Harte himself, in reply to a letter from Mr. Harte.] It should be explained that the denial therein contained refers to certain surmises

and reports afloat in the Society, and which were seemingly corroborated by apparently arbitrary and underhand proceedings by certain Fellows known to be members of the Esoteric Section.

Mr. Keightley tells this Commissioner that he must not believe "*that the Esoteric Section has any, even the slightest, pretension to 'boss' the Theosophical Society or anything of the kind.*" Again he says: "*We are all,* H.P.B. *first and foremost, just as loyal to the Theosophical Society and to Adyar as the Colonel can possibly be.*" And yet again he says: "I *have nothing more to say, except to repeat in the most formal and positive manner my assurance that there is not a word of truth in the statement that the Esoteric Section has any desire or pretension to 'boss' any other part or Section of the T.S.*"

It is to be hoped that after this very distinct and authoritative disclaimer no further "private circulars" will be issued by any members of the Esoteric Section, calling upon the Fellows to oppose the action of the General Council, because "Madame Blavatsky does not approve of it"; and also that silly editorials, declaring that Theosophy is degenerating into obedience to the dictates of Madame Blavatsky, like that in a recent issue of the *Religio-Philosophical Journal,* will cease to appear.

The private circulars referred to are the *First Preliminary Memorandum* [3] to applicants to the E.S., issued by H.P.B., and the Report of Mr. Judge as General Secretary to the American Convention, from both of which documents we have already given the germane extracts. The "silly editorial" was an article by Col.

[3] See Chapter XI. The *Preliminary Memorandum* of the Esoteric Section was issued by H.P.B. late in 1888. Its strictures on the failure of the T.S. were the undoubted occasion of Mr. Harte's series of articles in *The Theosophist.*

Bundy in his paper, the *Religio-Philosophical Journal*, in support of the Coues-Collins attack.

To appreciate fully the force and bearing of the various citations given, the student should remember that *The Theosophist* was the official organ of the Society; *The Path* and *Lucifer* being Theosophical, not organizational, publications; further, that *The Theosophist* was the only one of the three with any circulation in India, and was, in addition, sent officially to every Branch throughout the world and had a wide circulation among the Fellows in England, France, and the United States. For a large portion of the membership it was the only means of information concerning the Society, and, in India, the only channel both for Theosophy and the Society. Indian members, therefore, were entirely dependent on it for the accuracy, completeness, and authenticity of its statements.

Immediately following the Convention of 1888, Col. Olcott had departed on a tour in Japan from which he did not return until the latter half of 1889. During his absence Mr. Harte was in entire charge of *The Theosophist*, and was one of the three "Commissioners" to whom he had delegated his powers as President; the other two being Hindu members of his "General Council." It cannot be doubted, both that Mr. Harte was following out a prearranged program in the matter quoted from, and that he was in constant communication with Col. Olcott during the latter's absence on his Japanese Buddhist mission. That his course was fully approved by Col. Olcott is shown by the immediate sequel, as follows:

As soon as the proofs of the two articles quoted from reached America Mr. Judge prepared a long communication taking issue with the facts, the implications, the spirit, and the tendencies thus expressed with every appearance of authority and Presidential sanction in the official organ of the Society. This—and the fact should be noted as an example of the method used by both Mr. Judge and H.P.B. in dealing with Col. Olcott's periodical outbreaks of "pledge fever"—was sent privately by

Mr. Judge direct to Col. Olcott with request for its insertion in *The Theosophist,* on the assumed ground that the articles complained of were written without Col. Olcott's knowledge and that he, no less than Mr. Judge, would hasten to correct the misstatements and false suggestions conveyed by the articles in question.

In the September, 1889, *Theosophist,* Col. Olcott published as the leading editorial and over his own signature an article entitled "Centres of The Theosophical Movement." He refused to print Mr. Judge's article in full, declaring that it—

> Contains passages of a far too personal character for me to admit them. . . . I have taken no part, nor shall I, in the various unseemly quarrels, public and private, which the friction of "strong personalities" among us has and probably always will engender. They are mostly unimportant, involving no great principles or vital issue, and therefore beneath the interest of those who have the high purposes and aims of the Society at heart.

He calls Mr. Judge's criticisms "mayavic delusion." He then quotes Mr. Judge that the "Centre" is wherever H.P.B. may be; that it was originally in New York, then in Bombay, then "a short time at Adyar" (while she was there)—

> . . . for where she is burns the flame that draws its force from the plane of ideas! The mere location of the President in Adyar, and the existence of a library there, do not make that spot our Rome." . . . What would become of this new Rome—Adyar—if an order were received for Col. Olcott and H. P. Blavatsky to betake themselves to America once more and there set up the Theosophical Society Headquarters? Such a thing might happen. It happened before, and the channel for the order was H. P. Blavatsky. Does any one suppose that either Col.

Olcott or H. P. Blavatsky would be obstructed in their actions by the "Revised Rules?"

This query rouses Col. Olcott over what he calls his "irascible colleague's questions and conundrums." He proceeds to argue at length from the record of the various minutes and changes of by-laws and rules that the President-Founder is the real fountain of authority in the Society and the real "Rome" is wherever the President-Founder may be domiciled. He does not claim "spiritual authority," he says, but he does claim he has been "granted absolute and unlimited discretion as to the practical management of our affairs." He has never interfered with H.P.B.:

> . . . who taught and introduced me to my Initiators, but it was I who gave officially to her last year a charter to form her Esoteric Section. Between her and myself there was never any dispute upon these points, she sustaining my exoteric authority as loyally as I have ever recognized her superior connection with the "Founders." . . . Col. Olcott did *not* move the Headquarters to India by any one's order: his "orders" came from the depths of his own heart. . . . If in the course of the Society's development the transfer of Headquarters should ever be advisable—which neither I nor Mr. Judge can now forecast—doubtless I shall receive direct notice with ample time to make all the necessary arrangements in a businesslike and constitutional manner.
>
> . . . But when it is a question of papal infallibilities and Romes, it is just as well to say it was I who proposed the formation of the Society, who had all the early burden of guiding its infant steps, and who, after the collapse of the original legislative scheme of Rules and Bye-Laws, had—as above remarked—all the executive responsibility. . . .

> What the heart is to the body the Headquarters is to the Society, the working centre of its vital action. Its existence is what makes Theosophy a "going concern." . . . While the French and Germans mutually resent interference by each other in their official concerns and both would rebel against interference with them by the British or American Sections and *vice versa,* all unhesitatingly submit their unsettled disputes to the Executive for decision. And again, when there was trouble between personal factions in English Branches and between the American Theosophical leaders, it was to me and to no one else that the disputants looked for equitable composition of their troubles. These are facts beyond dispute, facts going to prove the indispensability of a general centre which shall be the official residence of the central arbitrator and judge, officially placed above the plane of partisanship and of local interests and influences.

These numerous and lengthy extracts will, we believe, serve fairly and fully to place before the reader the views entertained by Col. Olcott and actuating his conduct, his estimate of his own importance, and his attitude towards his colleagues and their status in the Society and in the Movement. Mr. Judge's views may be readily inferred from what has been given. It remains to compare and contrast all with the definite statement of H.P.B. in the *Preliminary Memorandum* already quoted from,[4] and with her equally definite public expression of her own views and attitude as drawn forth and compelled by the several articles mentioned. In *Lucifer* for August, 1889, under the caption, "A Puzzle from Adyar," H.P.B., like Mr. Judge, assumes that *The Theosophist* articles have been written without the concurrence of Col. Olcott and without intention to aid and abet the enemy. "Now what," she asks,—

[4] See Chapter XI.

may be the meaning of this extraordinary and *most tactless "sortie"* of the esteemed *acting* editor of our *Theosophist?* Is he . . . like our (and his) editor-enemies across the Atlantic, also dreaming uncanny dreams and seeing lying visions—or what? And let me remind him at once that he must not feel offended by these remarks, as he has imperatively called them forth himself. *Lucifer*, the *Path* and the *Theosophist* are the only organs of communication with the Fellows of our Society, each in its respective country. Since the acting editor of the *Theosophist* has chosen to give a wide publicity in his organ to abnormal fancies, he has no right to expect a reply through any other channel than *Lucifer*. Moreover, if he fails to understand all the seriousness of his implied charges *against me* and several honorable men, he may realise them better, when he reads the present.

. . . what does he try to insinuate by the following . . .

She then reprints the "Disclaimer" from the "Supplement" to the July *Theosophist,* and analyzes the several insinuations in regard to members of the E.S., who, she says, "stand accused by Mr. Harte . . . of *'arbitrary and underhand proceedings.'* " She asks, "Is not such a sentence a gross insult thrown into the face of honorable men—far better Theosophists than any of their accusers—and of myself?" Of the plain intimation that the American or British Sections or the Blavatsky Lodge or the E.S. wanted to "boss Adyar," she says:

> That the E.S. had never any pretensions to *"boss"* the T.S., stands to reason: with the exception of Col. Olcott, the President, the Esoteric Section has nothing whatever to do with the Theosophical Society, its Council or officers. It is a Section entirely apart from the exoteric body and independent of it, H.P.

> B. *alone being responsible for its members,* as shown in the official announcement over the signature of the President-Founder himself. It follows, therefore, that the E.S., as a body owes no allegiance whatever to the Theosophical Society, as a *Society,* least of all to Adyar.

Next she takes up another statement in the "Disclaimer."

> It is pure nonsense to say that "H.P.B. . . . is loyal to the Theosophical Society and *to Adyar*" (?). H.P.B. *is loyal to death to the Theosophical* CAUSE, *and those great Teachers whose philosophy alone can bind the whole of Humanity into one Brotherhood.* Together with Col. Olcott, she is the chief Founder and Builder of the Society which *was* and *is* meant to represent that CAUSE; and if she is so loyal to H. S. Olcott, it is not at all because of his being its "President," but, firstly, because there is no man living who has worked harder for that Society, or been more devoted to it than the Colonel, and, secondly, because she regards him as a loyal friend and co-worker. Therefore the degree of her sympathies with the "Theosophical Society and Adyar" depends upon the degree of the loyalty of that Society to the CAUSE. Let it break away from the original lines and show disloyalty in its policy to the CAUSE and the original programme of the Society, and H.P.B. calling the T. S. *disloyal,* will shake it off like dust from her feet.
>
> And what does "loyalty to Adyar" mean, in the name of all wonders? What *is* Adyar apart from that CAUSE and the *two* (not *one* Founder, if you please) who represent it? Adyar is the present Headquarters of the Society, because these "Headquarters are wherever the President is," as stated in the rules. To be logical the

> Fellows of the T.S. had to be loyal to Japan while Col. Olcott was there, and to London during his presence here.

She then makes the memorable declaration of the actual existing status of affairs:

> There is no longer a "Parent Society"; it is abolished and replaced by an aggregate body of Theosophical Societies, *all autonomous*, as are the States of America, and all under one head President, who, together with H. P. Blavatsky, will champion the CAUSE against the whole world. Such is the real state of things.

The theory of government of the Society held, practiced and preached by Col. Olcott and his pliant supporters is next covered by her declaration made in that regard also:

> Whenever "Madame Blavatsky does not approve" of "an action of the General Council" (or "Commissioners," of whom Mr. R. Harte is one), she will say so openly and to their faces. Because (*a*) Madame Blavatsky does not owe the slightest allegiance to a Council which is liable at any moment to issue silly and *untheosophical ukases;* and (*b*) for the simple reason that she recognizes but one person in the T. S. beside herself, namely Colonel Olcott, as having the right of effecting fundamental re-organizations in a Society which owes its life to them, and for which they are both *karmically* responsible. If the acting editor makes slight account *of a sacred pledge,* neither Col. Olcott nor H. P. Blavatsky are likely to do so. H. P. Blavatsky will always bow before the decision of the majority of a Section or even a simple Branch; but she will ever protest against the decision of the General Council, were it composed of Archangels and Dhyan Chohans themselves, if their

> decision seems to her unjust, or untheosophical, or fails to meet with the approval of the majority of the Fellows. No more than H. P. Blavatsky has the President-Founder the right of exercising autocracy or *papal* powers, and Col. Olcott would be the last man in the world to attempt to do so. It is the two Founders and especially the President, who have virtually sworn allegiance to the Fellows, whom they have to protect, and teach those who want to be taught, and not to tyrannize and rule over them.

Here, as always, where the weaknesses, the foibles, and the derelictions of her associates and students are involved, H.P.B. writes only under the gravest compulsion, with the extreme of reluctance, and in such terms as to hold wide the door of return to right action with the least possible humiliation to the pride and vanity of human nature. She sums up, and conveys at the same time her appeal to the best in her colleagues, in these terms:

> And now I have said over my own signature what I had to say and that which ought to have been said in so many plain words long ago. The public is all agog with the silliest stories about our doings, and the supposed and real dissensions in the Society. Let every one know the truth at last, in which there is nothing to make any one ashamed and which alone can put an end to a most painful and strained feeling. This truth is as simple as can be.
>
> The acting editor of the *Theosophist* has taken it into his head that the Esoteric Section together with the British and American Sections, were either conspiring or preparing to conspire against what he most curiously calls "Adyar" and its authority. Now being a most devoted Fellow of the T.S. and attached to the President, his zeal in hunting up this mare's

> nest has led him to become more Catholic than the Pope. That is all, and I hope that such misunderstandings and hallucinations will come to an end with the return of the President to India. Had he been at home, he, at any rate, would have objected to all those dark hints and cloaked sayings that have of late incessantly appeared in the *Theosophist* to the great delight of our enemies. . . .
>
> But it is time for me to close. If Mr. Harte persists still in acting in such a strange and untheosophical way, then the sooner the President settles these matters the better for all concerned.
>
> Owing to such undignified quibbles, Adyar and especially the *Theosophist* are fast becoming the laughing stock of Theosophists themselves as well as of their enemies.

And, lest her unfailing clemency should again be misconstrued and abused to their own injury and that of the Cause to which they, no less than herself, are pledged, she concludes with this note of mingled appeal and warning to those at fault:

> I end by assuring him [Mr. Harte] that there is no need for him to pose as Colonel Olcott's protecting angel. Neither he nor I need a third party to screen us from each other. We have worked and toiled and suffered together for fifteen long years, and if after all these years of mutual friendship the President-Founder were capable of lending ear to insane accusations and turning against me, well—the world is wide enough for us both. Let the new Exoteric Theosophical Society headed by Mr. Harte, play at red tape if the President lets them and let the General Council expel me for "disloyalty," if, again, Colonel Olcott should be so blind as to fail to see where the "true friend" and his duty

lie. Only unless they hasten to do so, at the first sign of *their* disloyalty to the CAUSE—it is I who will have resigned my office of Corresponding Secretary for life and left the Society. This will not prevent me from remaining at the head of those who will follow me.

H. P. BLAVATSKY.

CHAPTER XVII

H.P.B. TAKES CHARGE OF THE T.S. IN EUROPE

IT would serve no useful purpose to set out in detail the internecine troubles of the Theosophical Society during the three years which followed. Our aim has been to present only so much of the sequence of events during that melancholy period of stress and strain as might make clear the two horns of the dilemma unavoidably produced by the clash between human nature and the purposes of the Theosophical Movement. That is to say: (1) to indicate clearly the failure of the Society and its responsible officials and leaders to live up to its and their professed Objects; (2) the corresponding necessity under which H. P. Blavatsky and W. Q. Judge labored—either to stand by and permit the Society to become a worldly success but an Occult failure, or to restore the Movement by the formation of the Esoteric Section within the shell of the Society.

The Society tended continually to follow those lines which were attractive to the members and the inquiring public—that is, to run into channels of mere study of comparative religion and philosophy or to experiments and investigations in psychical research. The inflexible devotion to the assimilation of the philosophy of Theosophy, the rigid self-discipline required for the application of Theosophy to their own daily conduct in all the affairs of life—these essential conditions precedent to any realization of the great First Object, possessed no charms for any but the very few. *Theoretical* brotherhood was one thing; the practical application and exemplification of the principles professedly held was quite another thing, then as now.

On the other hand, one has but to read any one of the statements emanating from the Masters of Wisdom from

1877-96, to recognize the great gulf between *Their* view of life and action and that prevailing in the world and in the Society. Philosophy and ethics, *ethics and philosophy* —through the study and application of these alone could the Society and its members hope to benefit the world and themselves. Little by little the opposed fundamental ideas and applications produced those frictions and fractures which at last led to the opening up of broad lines of cleavage. And since actions do not perform themselves, it was inevitable that these fundamental differences should at last become personified in the leading persons and personages whose relations embody the history of the Theosophical Movement.

After the receipt of the advance proofs of *Lucifer* for August 15, 1889, containing "A Puzzle from Adyar," Col. Olcott recognized that the various issues evoked by the Convention proceedings of December preceding and the subsequent promulgations in *The Theosophist,* had been squarely met by H.P.B. and Mr. Judge. Either he would have to proceed in open defiance of them and of their policies, execute a complete "about face," and bring himself once more into line with the principles and procedure they had proclaimed, or take a compromise course. He chose, as usual, the middle course: he determined to go to England and "fight it out" once more with H.P.B., rather than raise the standard of rebellion and thus perforce align himself with Prof. Coues, whose assault threatened not only the ruin of the prestige of H.P.B., but the destruction of the Society as well. He therefore hastened to insert in the "Supplement" to *The Theosophist* for August a formal notice addressed "To the Indian Section," in which he announced his departure for the United Kingdom in these words:

> A promise made last year obliges me to proceed without delay to England for a Society lecturing tour through parts of the United Kingdom.

He arrived in England when the public press, no less than the Theosophical ranks, was agog over the charges and counter-charges incident to the Coues-Collins explosion. He found H.P.B. undaunted, undismayed, undisturbed. Although she lay upon that rack of physical as well as moral pain that was all too soon to destroy her body, never had the lion's heart and the lion's courage that inspired her been more true. She received him with that loyalty and forgetfulness of all but the good in him that had so many times before restored his concert pitch of faith and feeling. Accord was soon reached. He was received by all the English Theosophists with that consideration so dear to his nature. His fears that his importance to the work of the Society and the Movement would be ignored or minimized, evaporated for the time being, and this was facilitated by his discovery that H.P.B. was surrounded by eager and ardent students whose worldly standing and repute far more than compensated for any possible losses due to the defection of Dr. Coues and Miss Collins. To mention only two of the recent recruits, he met Mr. Herbert Burrows, the well-known Socialist in England, man of education and character so great as to command the respect even of those whose class interests were endangered by him, now devoted to Theosophy and to H.P.B. He met Mrs. Annie Besant, champion of the oppressed, fearless follower of her convictions, lead her where they might, now aflame with the glory of a fresh enthusiasm, already the right hand of H.P.B. Under such auspices as these, Col. Olcott departed on his lecturing tour and everywhere found new evidences of a rising tide. On his return to London in December he readily acceded to the expressed wish of the Council of the British Section and issued an "Order" naming H.P.B., with an advisory Committee of three, to exercise his "Presidential powers" in the United Kingdom. Still further to strengthen him against reactionary tendencies on his return to India, H.P.B. put into his hands before his departure a document appointing him her sole representative for the Esoteric Section in Asiatic countries.

During Col. Olcott's absence no Convention had been held at Adyar, but a Bombay Conference was arranged which met at the usual time, adopted stirring resolutions of confidence in H.P.B., and voiced its condemnation of attacks made upon her and its disapproval of the dissentient frictions with the Society. Thus for a time—a brief time, as always—there was concord and some semblance of fraternity throughout the whole vast area of the Society.

But early in the summer of 1890 the Paris Branch once again became the focal point of disturbance which threatened the disruption of the Society. While H.P.B. was doing her utmost to reconcile the warring factions Col. Olcott again intervened and almost an identical situation to that in the fall of 1888 again arose. The various European Lodges, the English Branches, and the numerous "unattached" Fellows in Britain and on the Continent rose in arms and bombarded H.P.B. with letters, resolutions and petitions to clear the situation once and for all from any further "Executive Orders" from Adyar.

Thus confronted, H.P.B. once more acted with characteristic decision, frankness, and loyalty. A brief delineation can but outline in relief the sagacity and the kindness with which she performed the seemingly impossible task thrust upon her.

On July 2, 1890, the Council of the British Section held an extraordinary session with Mrs. Besant in the chair. Letters and resolutions from the various Lodges and unattached Fellows were read, and after full discussion "it was proposed by Dr. [Archibald] Keightley that a requisition, embodying the following views, be drawn up and addressed to the President of the Society":

> The Continental Lodges and unattached members having made an appeal to H.P.B. that they may place themselves directly under her authority, the British Section joins in their demand that the constitutional powers at present exercised by Colonel H. S. Olcott in Europe, shall be transferred to H.P.B. and her Advisory

Council, already appointed to exercise part of such function in the United Kingdom.

H.P.B. cabled Col. Olcott of the action taken by the Council, of her own proposed steps in consequence, and, for his own sake no less than that of the Society, urged him to issue such formal notice as would accept the *status quo* and preserve the appearance of harmony. The "Supplement" of *The Theosophist* for August, 1890, contains two eminently characteristic documents, both signed "H. S. Olcott, P.T.S." The first of these reads in part as follows:

> To secure a better management of the Society's affairs throughout Europe, than I can give from this distance, I do hereby depute to my co-Founder, H. P. Blavatsky, full authority to come to an agreement with the Branches of the United Kingdom, Greece, France, Austria, and Holland, and the non-official groups in Spain, Russia, and other Continental countries, for the consolidation of the whole into one Section, to be designated as the European Section of the Theosophical Society; and to take the general supervision over and have as full management of the same as I could myself.

This was dated "Adyar, 9th July, 1890," seven days *after* the meeting of the Council of the British Section, and the heading, "Headquarters Official Orders," has a delightfully Pickwickian tone in thus "ordering" what was already a *fait accompli.* This order was, of course, written when Col. Olcott had only brief telegraphic advices. So soon as the mails reached India with full details of the transactions of the Council of the British Section, including the resolution above given, the Colonel felt himself compelled to sustain the Presidential dignity by a second Pickwickian "Headquarters Official Order," dated July 29th, and reprinted in the "Supplement" immediately following the first. It runs:

The . . . resolution of the Council of the British Section of July 2, 1890, is hereby cancelled, as contrary to the constitution and by-laws of the Theosophical Society, a usurpation of the Presidential prerogative, and beyond the competence of any Section or other fragment of the Society to enact.

Lucifer for August, 1890, contains the notice sent out by H.P.B.:

THE THEOSOPHICAL SOCIETY IN EUROPE

In consequence of the receipt of letters from all the active Lodges in Europe, and from a large majority of the Unattached Fellows of the Theosophical Society, H. P. Blavatsky is reluctantly compelled to abandon the position which she originally took up at the foundation of the Society.

NOTICE

IN OBEDIENCE TO THE ALMOST UNANIMOUS VOICE OF THE FELLOWS OF THE THEOSOPHICAL SOCIETY IN EUROPE, I, H. P. BLAVATSKY, THE ORIGINATOR AND CO-FOUNDER OF THE THEOSOPHICAL SOCIETY, ACCEPT THE DUTY OF EXERCISING THE PRESIDENTIAL AUTHORITY FOR THE WHOLE OF EUROPE; AND IN VIRTUE OF THIS AUTHORITY I DECLARE THAT THE HEADQUARTERS OF THE THEOSOPHICAL SOCIETY IN LONDON, WHERE I RESIDE, WILL IN FUTURE BE THE HEADQUARTERS FOR THE TRANSACTION OF ALL OFFICIAL BUSINESS OF THE THEOSOPHICAL SOCIETY IN EUROPE.

H. P. BLAVATSKY.

Let no one imagine that this reform in any sense suggests a separation from, or even the loosening in any way of the authority of, my colleague at Adyar. Colonel H. S. Olcott remains, as heretofore, the President-Founder of the Theosophical Society *the world over.* But it has been found impossible for him at such a great distance to exercise accurate discrimination in current matters of guidance of the Theosophical Society. His functions including the official issue of Charters and Diplomas in Europe, errors in the selection of members to whom such Charters and Diplomas are issued (besides the minor evil of delay) have rendered it impossible that the system of government of the Theosophical Society in Europe should be continued as heretofore. In the issue of *Lucifer* for August, 1889, I made use of the following sentences:

> H. P. Blavatsky will always bow before the decision of the majority of a Section or even a simple Branch. . . . No more . . . has the President-Founder the right of exercising autocracy or *papal* powers, and Colonel Olcott would be the last man in the world to attempt to do so. *It is the two Founders, and especially the President, who have virtually sworn allegiance to the Fellows, whom they have to protect . . . and not to tyrannize and rule over them.*

Therefore, owing to the issue of a Charter in ignorance of the actual facts, and the immediate protest made by all the active members of the Lodges, and their unanimous desire that I should exercise the Presidential authority over the Theosophical Society in Europe, bowing to the decision of the majority I have issued the above *official* "NOTICE." To avoid even the appearance of *autocracy* I select as an advisory Council to assist me in the exercise of these functions, in addition to my three colleagues appointed by the President, viz.: Annie Besant, and Messrs. W. Kingsland and Herbert Burrows, Mr. A. P. Sinnett, President of the London Lodge who has cordially joined in this reform, Dr. H. A. W.

Coryn, President of the Brixton Lodge, Theosophical Society, Mr. E. T. Sturdy, and Mr. G. R. S. Mead.

H. P. Blavatsky.

Thereafter peace and peaceful activities attended the work of the Theosophical Society in the West till after the death of H.P.B. The reader who may have been misled as to the facts attendant upon the events just recited, because of the sorry account in the pages of "Old Diary Leaves," Fourth Series, should remember that the Col. Olcott there writing was a broken old man, that he was telling his tale ten years after the events discussed and after the fatal follies of 1894-6, and felt under the overwhelming compulsion to put himself in the best light possible before posterity. His case is not unlike that of de Lesseps, the glory of whose achievement at Suez was, to so many minds, put in total eclipse by the folly, the fraud and the failure at Panama. Only those who, like H.P.B., know human nature and the Karma of the individual through and through—only such have the wisdom neither to ignore the good services, nor to be disturbed by the mistakes or frailties of their associates and helpers—only such have the right to throw the first stone at "poor old Olcott"—and they have none to throw!

CHAPTER XVIII

DEATH OF H.P.B.—HER LAST MESSAGES

H. P. Blavatsky died May 8, 1891, in the sixtieth year of her age. The generation which knew her personally is no more, but the fierce controversies which raged around her living still survive, and not a year passes but her name and nature become the target for renewed discussion. It is not overstating the fact to say that of no character in history is both so much and so little known. We say "known," but the fact is that today, as when she moved among men, she is as much as ever a confronting mystery.

During sixteen years she lived on three continents amid the most alien surroundings, in the light of the most watchful as well as the most hostile publicity. For those who called themselves her friends and followers were not less critical and observant of her every mood, her every word and action, than those who saw in her a charlatan, an emissary of immorality and irreligion. Not one who sought to gain access to her was ever denied the opportunity to question and cross-examine her. Her doors were open to friends and foes alike. Yet today as while she lived she remains an enigma, not because of the mystery with which she cloaked herself, but because she presents to the mind of the race an unsolved problem—an insoluble problem from any but one approach: that of the Wisdom-Religion which she inculcated and exemplified. She was herself the very testimony and witness of that which she taught, but none thought to solve the riddle of the Sphinx of the nineteenth century by an application to her of the philosophy she brought.

In closing the Introductory to the "Secret Doctrine" Madame Blavatsky writes that she has constantly to bear in mind that "every reader will inevitably judge the statements made from the standpoint of his own knowledge, experience, and consciousness, based on what he has already learnt" of life, its phenomena and significance. None that we know of have ever taken home the universal applications of this truism. Those who approached H.P.B. did so, each with his own pre-conceptions. Each was willing to admit the shortcomings of his own knowledge, experience, and consciousness; each was desirous of adding to his knowledge; each was "willing to learn" what he could from H.P.B., but when the opportunity and the test came, *who studied himself in the light of H.P.B.'s knowledge, experience, and consciousness?* Yet if she was, perchance, a Being of another order from mankind, some Buddha in disguise, how could she be truly availed of by any aspirant for Wisdom, unless by a reversal of our accustomed mode of inquiry? It is one thing to study the great doctrine, say, of Karma and Reincarnation, from the standpoint of our own present personal predilections and antipathies, and quite another thing to study our own present selves and natures in the light of these twin truths. Yet, if Karma and Reincarnation be, perchance, the very key to the riddle of existence with all its included contradictions, what other mode can possibly bring that enlightenment and illumination which all seek and which confessedly neither human religion nor human science, any more than our own knowledge, experience, and consciousness have been able to give us?

And again, in the Preface to the "Secret Doctrine" she says that "the publication of many of the facts herein stated has been rendered necessary by the wild and fanciful speculations in which many Theosophists and students of Mysticism have indulged, during the last few years, in their endeavour to, as they imagined, work out a complete system of thought from the few facts previously communicated to them." Although she specifically states that the "Secret Doctrine" is written for the *instruction* of *students* of Occultism, how many of those who call themselves "Occultists" have ever really studied her life or her writings, let alone derived any applications from them? On the contrary, the multitude of books and other writings emanating from self-styled "initiates," "outer heads," and "teachers" who pose as "successors" and "revealers," do they not one and all merely betray themselves as those very "wild and fanciful speculations" of which H.P.B. wrote warningly? If her own students and professed followers and disciples have made such sorry use, and betray such sorry understanding, of the very genius, principles, and practices of the philosophy she taught, how could they or can they but grossly and grievously err in their understanding of H.P.B. herself—the living embodiment of what she taught?

And, finally, in closing the Preface, she used this ancient maxim of jurisprudence:

"*De minimis non curat lex*"—The Law takes no account of trifles. Her followers and disciples have taken account of little else! The *Society* engrossed them—not its *Objects*. Comparative religion and philosophy engrossed them—not the attempt to detect the vital principles which underlie them all. Phenomena engrossed them—not the effort to investigate the unexplained *laws* of their occurrence. "Progress" engrossed them—not *Brotherhood*. "Doctrines" engrossed them—not the universal applications of *Theosophy*. Speculations engrossed them—not the serious *study* of what was given them for their guidance and instruction. If this is true as regards the Society she founded and the message she delivered, how could it be other than true in the case of the attitude of the students toward herself? Scarce one but put on record his experiences and opinions in relation to H.P.B. Trifles—trifles—what she ate and what she wore. How she looked and how she "behaved." How she stood and how she sat. What this one thought and what that one had to say of her: Speculations, fancies, inferences, world without end. All trifles, trifles, illuminant only of the narrow radius of the "knowledge, experience, and consciousness" of the beholders of this greatest phenomenon of the centuries.

Every lawyer knows that the best evidence of anything

is the thing itself; the best evidence in regard to anyone the acts and words of that one himself. Too many concern themselves with reputation—too few with *character*. Those who are ardent to learn the *truth* in regard to anyone or anything must soon come to distinguish between reputation and character. The one depends upon hearsay and opinion, upon the thousand forces influencing the testimony and inferences of the witnesses; the other depends upon nothing and no one but the subject himself. And particularly is this watchfulness necessary in the study of anyone who has made or sought to make his mark upon the times. The opportunism of immediate self-interest colors us all far more than any of us realize. History is for the most part a record of reversals of judgment. Who of those that shine with ever-increasing luster through the night of time ever enjoyed in his lifetime, or for generations after, that *reputation* which his *character* justified?

And the same state of facts applies in its integrity to what one might at first glance conceive to be the impersonal world of ideas. For, with newer weapons and changed alignments the war of ideas is still the same today as in all the past. Men still wrestle and war over opposing ideas as to God, as to Nature, as to Man. The problems of Good and Evil, of Justice and Injustice, of Life and Death, are as far off from solution, as apparently insoluble, as ever. If men cannot yet come to a stable conclusion in regard to the very fundamentals of existence and action, how fatuous he who looks for uniformity or unanimity in their applications. Neither human science, human religion, nor human philosophy offers, or ever has offered, any but fallible and tentative, but mutable and partial, explanations or applications concerning those things which are the *universal* experience of mankind. Yet each presumes today, as always, to sit in the judgment seat, and pronounce anathema or approval in the light of its own "knowledge, experience, and consciousness" on those very subjects on which each will abstractly admit its own utter incompetency! Could logical absurdity go farther?

H.P.B. showed the unbroken prevalence in time and space of a knowledge that includes *all* life and action, and demonstrated to a Q. E. D. that such knowledge and its Adept-custodians exist today as always; that They are the Source from which has sprung everything that the world has that is permanent in every field of human inquiry. What makes men incompetent to weigh that testimony, to proceed to its verification by actual experience of their own? Nothing in the world but human prejudice and conceit, human superstition and materialism, masquerading as religion and science.

Whatever the testimony and opinion of her critics, friendly or hostile, one thing stands out like a flame in the night with regard to the character of H. P. Blavatsky —she was consistent throughout in all that she said and did. Few there be of her critics who can endure the same test of sincerity and good faith. Her profession of faith, her declaration of principles, may be found in the Preface of "Isis Unveiled" in 1877. All the rest that issued from her life and pen in the prolific years that followed flowed with as mathematical consistency as the theorems of geometry issue from its fundamental axioms and apothegms.

There is never anything but two things to consider —the credibility and the competency of the witness. Search as they did with might and main to find some faintest thread whereon to hitch the imputation of base motives, and thus to destroy her credibility—not one of all the assassins of her reputation ever was able to produce aught that might savor of self-interest in anything she ever said or did. Incredible follies are ascribed to her—follies so egregiously stupid as to fall of their own weight when attributed even to a child or a dolt; impossible immoralities are charged against her—impossible even physically, for her body was that of an androgyne, an hermaphrodite. Slanders and calumnies without number have been perpetrated against her, but every imputation against her motives—and we have assiduously examined the charges of her detractors by hundreds—rests upon no other basis than suspicion, accusation, repetition. In no solitary instance is one solitary *fact* adduced that would stand a moment's impartial examination. To the contrary, not one of the hundreds of original and repeated charges leveled against her but betrays the animus, the interested motives of the *accusers*—not of their victim.

If we turn to the question of her competency, two things become more convincingly sure the more her career is examined: (1) No single fact adduced by her has ever been upset by counter-evidence; (2) no postulation laid down by her has ever been rendered untenable philosophically, logically, or evidentially. Her testimony as to facts, her conclusions and theories in regard to the facts, remain as invincible as ever. No one of all her enemies and opponents ever evinced any appetite to assail her philosophy, none ever tried conclusions with her logic and boasted afterwards of his success; none ever showed in his own life the sincerity, the tolerance, the generosity of spirit, the ardor for Truth, lead where it might, that burned with a quenchless light throughout her whole career. One has but to compare the record of H. P. Blavatsky for sincerity and consistency with that of any of her detractors, any of her followers, or *with his own as known to himself,* to gain some glimmer of recognition that here in our own times in the personage known as H. P. Blavatsky is one who, in the luminous zone of the eternal great, shines with an undimmed light, needing no borrowed radiance; a Messenger from other Spheres indeed.

To the Theosophical student who has gained from her and from her mission some flying spark of grateful perception of the Immortal and the Immortals, nothing can call for deeper reflection or more profound consideration than what may best be called her dying declarations. The accretions of human experience, as concentrated in our jurisprudence, have led all men everywhere to attach a momentous significance to the last words, whether of saint or sinner. The equitable authority of a dying declaration is everywhere held to equal the sanction of the most solemn oath or other attestation.

April 15, 1891, three weeks before the cord broke, she signed her last Message to the American Theosophists in Convention assembled:

> Suffering in body as I am continually, the only consolation that remains to me is to hear of the progress of the Holy Cause to which my health and strength have been given; but to which, now that these are going, I can only offer my passionate devotion and never-weakening good wishes for its success and welfare. . . . Fellow Theosophists, I am proud of your noble work in the New World; Sisters and Brothers of America, I thank and I bless you for your unremitting labours for the common cause so dear to us all.
>
> Let me remind you all once more that such work is now more than ever needed. The period which we have now reached . . . is, and will continue to be, one of great conflict and continued strain. If the T.S. can hold through it, good; if not, while Theosophy will remain unscathed, the Society will perish—perchance most ingloriously—and the World will suffer. I fervently hope that I may not see such a disaster in my present body. The critical nature of the stage on which we have entered is as well known to the forces that fight against us as to those that fight on our side. No opportunity will be lost of sowing dissension, of taking advantage of mistaken and false moves, of instilling doubt, of augmenting difficulties, of breathing suspicions, so that by any and every means the unity of the Society may be broken and the ranks of our Fellows thinned and thrown into disarray. Never has it been more necessary for the members of the T.S. to lay to heart the old parable of the bundle of sticks than it is at the present time; divided, they will inevitably be broken, one by one; united, there is no force on earth able to destroy our Brotherhood. Now I have

marked with pain a tendency among you, as among the Theosophists in Europe and India, to quarrel over trifles, and to allow your very devotion to the cause of Theosophy to lead you into disunion. Believe me, that apart from such natural tendency, owing to the inherent imperfections of Human Nature, advantage is often taken by our ever-watchful enemies of your noblest qualities to betray and to mislead you. Sceptics will laugh at this statement, and even some of you may put small faith in the actual existence of the terrible forces of these mental, hence subjective and invisible, yet withal living and potent, influences around all of us. But there they are, and I know of more than one among you who have felt them, and have actually been forced to acknowledge these extraneous mental pressures. On those of you who are unselfishly and sincerely devoted to the Cause, they will produce little, if any, impression. On some others, those who place their personal pride higher than their duty to the T.S., higher even than their pledge to their divine SELF, the effect is generally disastrous. Self-watchfulness is never more necessary than when a personal wish to lead, and wounded vanity, dress themselves in the peacock's feathers of devotion and altruistic work; but at the present crisis of the Society a lack of self-control and watchfulness may become fatal in every case. But these diabolical attempts of our powerful enemies—the irreconcilable foes of the truths now being given out and practically asserted—may be frustrated. If every Fellow in the Society were content to be an impersonal force for good, careless of praise or blame so long as he subserved the purposes of the Brotherhood, the progress made would astonish the World and place the Ark of the T.S. out of danger. . . .

Your position as the fore-runners of the sixth sub-race of the fifth root-race has its own special perils as well as its special advantages. Psychism, with all its allurements and all its dangers, is necessarily developing among you, and you must beware lest the Psychic outruns the Manasic and Spiritual development. Psychic capacities held perfectly under control, checked and directed by the Manasic principle, are valuable aids in development. But these capacities running riot, controlling instead of controlled, using instead of being used, lead the Student into the most dangerous delusions and the certainty of moral destruction. Watch therefore carefully this development, inevitable in your race and evolution-period, so that it may finally work for good and not for evil; and receive, in advance, the sincere and potent blessings of Those whose good-will will never fail you, if you do not fail yourselves. . . .

And now I have said all. I am not sufficiently strong to write a more lengthy message, and there is the less need for me to do so as my friend and trusted messenger, Annie Besant, she who is my right arm here, will be able to explain to you my wishes more fully and better than I can write them. After all, every wish and thought I can utter are summed up in this one sentence, the never-dormant wish of my heart, "Be Theosophists, work for Theosophy!" Theosophy first, and Theosophy last; for its *practical* realization alone can save the Western world from that selfish and unbrotherly feeling that now divides race from race; one nation from the other; and from that hatred of class and social considerations that are the curse and disgrace of so-called Christian peoples. Theosophy alone can keep it from sinking into that mere luxurious materialism in which it will decay and putrefy as civilizations have done. In your hands, brothers, is placed in trust the welfare of the coming century; and great as is the trust, so great is also the responsibility. My own span of life may not be long, and if any of you have learned aught from my teachings or have gained by my help a glimpse of the True Light, I ask you, in return, to strengthen the Cause by the triumph of which that True Light, made still brighter and more glorious through your individual and collective efforts, will lighten the World, and thus to let me see, before I part with this worn-out body, the stability of the Society secured.

May the blessings of the past and present great Teachers rest upon you. From myself accept collectively the assurance of my true, never-wavering fraternal feelings, and the sincere, heartfelt thanks for the work done by all the workers.

From their servant to the last,

H. P. Blavatsky.

This moving valedictory to the American Theosophists was read to the Convention by Mrs. Besant, whom H.P.B. had sent to America for the purpose and to meet Mr. Judge.

Again, but ten days before her departure, H.P.B. affixed her signature and the date, as to a Testament, to the article "My Books," which was published in *Lucifer* for May 15, 1891, immediately following her death. It is the last article written by H.P.B. She says:

Isis was full of misprints and misquotations; it contained useless repetitions, most irritating digressions, and to the casual reader unfamiliar with the various aspects of metaphysical ideas and symbols, as many apparent contradictions; much of the matter in it ought not to be there at all, and also it had some very gross mistakes due to the many alterations in proofreading in general, and word corrections in particular. Finally, the work, for reasons that will now be explained, has no system in it. . . .

The full consciousness of this sad truth dawned upon me when, for the first time after its publication in 1877, I read the work through from the first to the last page, in India in 1881. And from that date to the present, I have never ceased to say what I thought of it, and to give my honest opinion of *Isis* whenever I had an opportunity for so doing. This was done to the great disgust of some, who warned me that I was spoiling its sale; but as my chief object in writing it was neither personal fame nor gain, but something far higher, I cared little for such warnings. For more than ten years this unfortunate "masterpiece," this "monumental work," as some reviews have called it, with its hideous metamorphoses of one word into another, thereby entirely transforming the meaning, with its misprints and wrong quotation marks, has given me more anxiety and trouble during a long lifetime which has ever been more full of thorns than of roses.

But in spite of these perhaps too great admissions, I maintain that *Isis Unveiled* contains a mass of original and never hitherto divulged information on occult subjects. . . . Prepared to take upon myself—*vicariously* as I will show—the sins of all the external, purely literary defects of the work, I defend the ideas and teachings in it, with no fear of being charged with conceit, since *neither ideas nor teachings are mine,* as I have always declared; and I maintain that both are of the greatest value to mystics and students of Theosophy. . . .

The first enemies that my work brought to the front were Spiritualists, whose fundamental theories as to the spirits of the dead communicating in *propria persona* I upset. For the last fifteen years—ever since this first publication—an incessant shower of ugly accusations have been poured upon me. Every libellous charge, from immorality and the "Russian spy" theory down to my acting on false pretences, of being a chronic fraud and a *living lie*, an habitual drunkard, an emissary of the Pope, paid to break down Spiritualism, and Satan incarnate, every slander that can be thought of, has been brought to bear upon my private and public life. The fact *that not a single one of these charges has ever been substantiated;* that from the first day of January to the last of December, year after year, I have lived surrounded by friends and foes as in a glass-house,—nothing could stop these wicked, venomous, and thoroughly unscrupulous tongues. It has been said at various times by my ever-active opponents that (1) *Isis Unveiled* was simply a rehash of Eliphas Lévi and a few old alchemists; (2) that it was written by me under the dictation of Evil Powers and the *departed spirits* of Jesuits (*sic*); and finally (3) that my two volumes had been compiled from MSS. (never before heard of), which Baron de Palm—he of the cremation and double-burial fame—had left behind him, and which I had found in his trunk! On the other hand, friends, as unwise as they were kind, spread abroad that which was really the truth, a little too enthusiastically, about the connection of my Eastern Teacher and other Occultists with the work, and this was seized upon by the enemy and exaggerated out of all limits of truth. It was said that the whole of *Isis* has been dictated to me *from cover to cover* and *verbatim* by these invisible Adepts. And, as the imperfections of my work were only too glaring, the consequence of all this idle and malicious talk was that my enemies and critics inferred—as well they might

—that either these invisible inspirers had no existence, and were part of my "fraud," or that they lacked the cleverness of even an average good writer.

Now, no one has any right to hold me responsible for what any one may say, but only for that which I myself state orally, or in public print over my signature. And what I say and maintain is this: Save the direct quotations and the many afore specified and mentioned misprints, errors and misquotations, and the general make-up of *Isis Unveiled,* for which I am in no way responsible, (*a*) every word of information found in this work or in my later writings, comes from the teachings of our Eastern Masters; and (*b*) that many a passage in these works has been written by me *under their dictation.* In saying this no *supernatural* claim is urged, for no *miracle* is performed by such a dictation. Any moderately intelligent person, convinced by this time of the many possibilities of hypnotism . . . and of the phenomena of *thought-transference,* will easily concede that if even a hypnotized subject, a mere irresponsible medium, *hears the unexpressed thought* of his hypnotizer, who can thus transfer his thought to him—*even to repeating the words read by the hypnotizer mentally from a book*—then my claim has nothing impossible in it. Space and distance do not exist for thought; and if two persons are in perfect mutual psycho-magnetic *rapport,* and of these two, one is a great Adept in Occult Sciences, then thought-transference and dictation of whole pages, becomes as easy and as comprehensible at the distance of ten thousand miles as the transference of two words across a room.

Hitherto, I have abstained—except on very rare occasions—from answering any criticism on my works, and have even left direct lies and slanders unrefuted, because in the case of *Isis*

I found almost every kind of criticism justifiable, and in that of "slanders and lies," my contempt for the slanderers was too great to permit me to notice them. . . . But, as *Isis* is now attacked for at least the tenth time, the day has come when my perplexed friends and that portion of the public which may be in sympathy with Theosophy are entitled to the whole truth—*and nothing but the truth.* Not that I seek to excuse myself in anything even before them or to "explain things." It is nothing of the kind. What I am determined to do is to give *facts*, undeniable and not to be gainsaid, simply by stating the peculiar, well-known to many but now almost forgotten, circumstances, under which I wrote my first English work. I give them *seriatim.*

(1) When I came to America in 1873, I had not spoken English—which I had learned in my childhood colloquially—for over thirty years. I could understand when I read it, but could hardly speak the language.

(2) I had never been at any college, and what I knew I had taught myself; I have never pretended to any scholarship in the sense of modern research; I had then hardly read any scientific European works, knew little of Western philosophy and sciences. The little which I had studied and learned of these, disgusted me with its materialism, its limitations, narrow cut-and-dried spirit of dogmatism, and its air of superiority over the philosophies and sciences of antiquity.

(3) Until 1874 I had never written one word in English, nor had I published any work in any language. Therefore—

(4) I had not the least idea of literary rules. The art of writing books, of preparing them for print and publication, reading and correcting proofs, were so many closed secrets to me.

(5) When I started to write that which developed later into *Isis Unveiled,* I had no more

idea than the man in the moon what would come of it. I had no plan; did not know whether it would be an essay, a pamphlet, a book, or an article. I knew that *I had to write it*, that was all. I began the work before I knew Colonel Olcott well, and some months before the formation of the Theosophical Society.

Thus, the conditions for becoming the author of an English theosophical and scientific work were hopeful, as everyone will see. Nevertheless, I had written enough to fill four such volumes as *Isis*, before I submitted my work to Colonel Olcott. Of course he said that everything save the pages dictated—had to be rewritten. Then we started on our literary labours and worked together every evening. Some pages, the English of which he had corrected, I copied: others which would yield to no mortal correction, he used to read aloud from my pages, Englishing them verbally as he went on, dictating to me from my almost undecipherable MSS. It is to him that I am indebted for the English in *Isis*. It is he again who suggested that the work should be divided into chapters, and the first volume devoted to SCIENCE and the second to THEOLOGY. To do this, the matter had to be reshifted, and many of the chapters also; repetitions had to be erased, and the literary connection of subjects attended to. When the work was ready, we submitted it to Professor Alexander Wilder, the well-known scholar and Platonist of New York, who after reading the matter, recommended it to Mr. Bouton for publication. Next to Col. Olcott, it is Professor Wilder who did the most for me. It is he who made the excellent *Index*, who corrected the Greek, Latin and Hebrew words, suggested quotations and wrote the greater part of the *Introduction* "Before the Veil." If this was not acknowledged in the work, the fault is not mine, but because it was Dr. Wilder's express wish that his name should not appear except in footnotes. I have never made a secret of it, and every one of my numerous acquaintances in New York knew it. When ready the work went to press.

From that moment the real difficulty began. I had no idea of correcting galley-proofs; Colonel Olcott had little leisure to do so; and the result was that I made a mess of it from the beginning. Before we were through with the first three chapters, there was a bill for six hundred dollars for corrections and alterations, and I had to give up the proofreading. Pressed by the publisher, Colonel Olcott doing all that he possibly could do, but having no time except in the evenings, and Dr. Wilder far away at Jersey City, the result was that the proofs and pages of *Isis* passed through a number of willing but not very careful hands, and were finally left to the tender mercies of the publisher's proof-reader. Can one wonder after this if "Vaivaswata" (Manu) became transformed in the published volumes into "Viswamitra," that thirty-six pages of the Index were irretrievably lost, and quotation-marks placed where none were needed (as in some of my own sentences!), and left out entirely in many a passage cited from various authors? If asked why these fatal mistakes have not been corrected in a subsequent edition, my answer is simple; the plates were stereotyped; and notwithstanding all my desire to do so, I could not put it into practice, as the plates were the property of the publisher; I had no money to pay for the expenses, and finally the firm was quite satisfied to let things be as they are, since, notwithstanding all its glaring defects, the work—which has now reached its seventh or eighth edition, is still in demand.

And now—and perhaps in consequence of all

this—comes a new accusation: I am charged *with wholesale plagiarism* in the Introductory Chapter "Before the Veil."

Well, had I committed plagiarism, I should not feel the slightest hesitation in admitting the "borrowing." But all "parallel passages" to the contrary, as I have not done so, I do not see why I should confess it . . .

[*Isis*] . . . is an inexhaustible mine of misquotations, errors and blunders, to which it is impossible for me to plead "guilty" in the ordinary sense. . . . I have no author's vanity; and years of unjust persecution and abuse have made me entirely callous to what the public may think of me—personally.

But in view of the facts as given above; and considering that—

(*a*) The language in *Isis* is not mine; but (with the exception of that portion of the work which, as I claim, was *dictated*), may be called only a sort of translation of my facts and ideas into English;

(*b*) It was not written for the public,—the latter having always been only a secondary consideration with me—but for the use of Theosophists and members of the Theosophical Society to which *Isis* is dedicated;

(*c*) Though I have since learned sufficient English to have been enabled to edit two magazines . . . yet, to the present hour I never write an article, an editorial or even a simple paragraph, without submitting its English to close scrutiny and correction.

Considering all this and much more, I ask now every impartial and honest man or woman whether it is just or even fair to criticize my works—*Isis* above all others—as one would the writings of a born American or English author. What I claim in them as my own is only the fruit of my learning and studies in a department, hitherto left uninvestigated by Science, and almost unknown to the European world. I am perfectly willing to leave the honour of the English grammar in them, the glory of the quotations from scientific works brought occasionally to me to be used as passages for comparison with, or refutation by, the old Science, and finally the general make-up of the volumes, to every one of those who have helped me. Even for the *Secret Doctrine* there are about half-a-dozen Theosophists who have been busy in editing it, who have helped me to arrange the matter, correct the imperfect English, and prepare it for print. But that which none of them will ever claim from first to last, is the fundamental doctrine, the philosophical conclusions and teachings. Nothing of that have I invented, but simply given it out as I have been taught; or as quoted by me in the *Secret Doctrine* (Vol. I, p. 46) from Montaigne: "I have here made only a nosegay of culled (Eastern) flowers, and have brought nothing of my own but the string that ties them."

Is any one of my helpers prepared to say that I have not paid the full price for the string?

H. P. Blavatsky.

CHAPTER XIX

THE CRISIS IN THE SOCIETY

At the time of H.P.B.'s death Mr. Judge was in New York, Mrs. Besant in mid-ocean on her homeward voyage from her visit as H.P.B.'s messenger to the Convention of the American Section, Col. Olcott in Australia, whither he had gone partly on business for the Society, and partly on account of his health, which was greatly impaired. On receipt of the news of H.P.B.'s death Mr. Judge cabled to London that he would come on the first boat and to keep her things intact till his arrival. Cables were also exchanged between Mr. Judge and Col. Olcott, and the latter, who was on the point of departing for New Zealand, advised both London and New York that he would go at once to England.

The death of H.P.B. necessarily aroused great uncertainties and speculations as to what might befall the Society, its Esoteric Section, and the solidarity of its unwieldy and poorly amalgamated elements. Her presence being removed, her pervading influence no longer being directly exercised, her commanding voice no longer possible to be heard, what was going to be done by her lieutenants and by the rank and file of her followers? Although she had never held any but a purely nominal official position during the entire life of the Society, H.P.B. had none the less been not only the inspiring genius of its foundation but its guiding star.

It will be remembered that the membership, the proceedings, the meetings, and the instructions of the Esoteric Section were all under the seal of secrecy,[1] every member making the most solemn pledge in that as in other respects. Neither Col. Olcott nor Mr. Sinnett were members of the Esoteric Section; Dr. Coues had

[1] See Chapter IX.

been declined admission; Miss Mabel Collins had been admitted and dismissed for flagrant violation of her pledges, as had Mr. Michael Angelo Lane. There were very few members of the E.S. in India and the Orient generally, few on the Continent of Europe, the larger membership being from the beginning in the United States and, next to that, in England. As no one was received who was not also a member in good standing of the T.S.; as the bulk of the financial and other support of the T.S. came from England and the United States, and nearly all the literature of Theosophy and most of the periodicals devoted to it were printed in the English language, the formation and rise of the Esoteric Section afforded ample occasion for speculations, doubts, and fears on the part of Col. Olcott, Mr. Sinnett, and others who were prominent in the Society and well pleased with its conduct and progress on lines satisfactory to themselves. They saw in the Esoteric Section a standing menace, because it was a secret body pledged, not to the Society but to the Theosophical *Movement;* looking, not to the Organization and its Officers for direction, but to H.P.B. and Mr. Judge; concerned not at all with the "neutrality" of the Society on all matters of philosophy, religion, and science, but pledged to study, promulgate, and practice *Theosophy.*

Mrs. Annie Besant had become a convert to Theosophy early in 1889, very shortly after the defection of Miss Mabel Collins and Dr. Coues. She had ceased her connection with Mr. Charles Bradlaugh and with atheistic and socialistic activities, joined the "household" of H.P.B., been admitted to the Esoteric Section, had become President of the Blavatsky Lodge, was made by H.P.B. Co-Editor of *Lucifer,* and within a few months her reputation, her ardor, and her intellectual abilities made her the right hand of H.P.B. In the eyes of the world and of most members of the Society, she was the foremost light in the Theosophical firmament after H.P.B., and destined after H.P.B.'s death to become the central luminary in the Theosophical heavens. She had been the prime supporter of the movement among

European and English Theosophists to use Alexandrian methods to cut the Gordian knot of Col. Olcott's incessant intermeddling through his Presidential ukases in the active conduct of the work in the West, which resulted in the taking over by H.P.B., at the almost unanimous request of the membership, of the Presidential powers and authority for the whole of Europe—an action which Col. Olcott accepted with what grace he could. As will be remembered, a British Section modeled on the same democratic lines as the original American Section, had been formed near the close of 1888. After H.P.B. had assumed the Presidency of the European Societies and the European "unattached" Fellows, in the summer of 1890, she had planned to organize them, together with the Branches and Lodges in Great Britain, into a single autonomous Section, nominally and in aim an integral portion of the Theosophical Society, recognizing and supporting Col. Olcott as titular President-Founder of all the Societies the world over, but actually and practically entirely independent of any jurisdiction outside of or other than the democratic decisions of its own Branches and Fellows, in delegate Convention assembled.

The situation Mr. Judge had to meet was thus one of great and peculiar difficulty. On the one hand was the jealousy felt by Col. Olcott, Mr. Sinnett, and others, over the influence of the Esoteric Section on the fortunes of the exoteric Society. On the other hand was the problem of Mrs. Besant, as placed before him by H.P.B. in her letter to him of March 27, 1891, shortly before her death. Although of great ability, strong will, and intense devotion, Mrs. Besant was, as stated in that letter, "not psychic or spiritual in the least—all intellect." From being a confirmed materialist for many years, she had been a Probationer of the Esoteric Section but two years, while *accepted chelaship in Masters' Lodge* requires a minimum of seven years' probation under the most favorable circumstances. Her ordeals of chelaship were yet to come; nevertheless she was the most prominent member, both of the Society and the

Esoteric Section, and it was certain the English and European members would follow her course, whatever it might be.

So soon as Mr. Judge reached London he called together as Vice-President a Consultative Emergency Council, consisting of the European Advisory Council, as named by H.P.B., and the members of the General Council of the British Section. A meeting was held on May 23 and it was resolved to summon a convention of the European and British Sections to meet at the London Headquarters on July 9, 1891. Also, as the representative of H.P.B. in the Esoteric Section, he called a conference of its Advisory Council which was held on May 27, 1891. There were present Mr. Judge, Mrs. Besant, Miss Alice Leighton Cleather, Miss Isabel Cooper-Oakley, Miss Laura M. Cooper, Messrs. H. A. W. Coryn, Archibald Keightley, William Kingsland, Miss Emily Kislingbury, Messrs. G. R. S. Mead, W. R. Old, E. T. Sturdy, Constance Wachtmeister, Messrs. W. Wynn Westcott and Claude F. Wright. Aside from Mr. Judge all those named were then residents of England, were actively connected with the Society and its work, were all members of the E.S. formally admitted by H.P.B. under pledge during the preceding two and a half years, and all were Councillors E. S. T.—an advisory body appointed by H.P.B. to assist her in the multitudinous details of the Esoteric Section, whose name had meantime—in 1889—been changed to that of the "Eastern School of Theosophy." A general discussion took place, participated in by all those present. The important matters of the meeting (with one exception[2]), and the decisions reached were embodied in a circular letter dated the day of the meeting, and signed by all those in attendance, Mr. Judge signing "for the entire American Council E. S. T., and individually," and each of the others signing as "Councillor E.S.T." A copy of this circular, which was headed "Strictly private and confidential," was sent to each member of the E.S.T. Although signed by all, the actual wording of the cir-

[2] See Chapter XXVI.

cular was the work of Mrs. Besant, with some changes and corrections suggested by Mr. Judge and concurred in by those present at the meeting. As a portion of the circular there was included an address to the members of the E.S.T., signed by Mrs. Besant and Mr. Judge.

That portion of the circular signed by all who attended the conference recites:

> The American Councillors were represented by Bro. William Q. Judge, with full power, and *Bro. Judge attended as the representative of H.P.B. under a general power as given below.*

This "general power" is the document by H.P.B. dated December 14, 1888, which will be given in full later on.[3]

Additional decisions reached by the full Council at the meeting are set forth in these extracts:

> In virtue of our appointment by H.P.B. we declare:
>
> That in full accord with the known wishes of H.P.B. the visible Head of the School, *we primarily record and declare that the work of the School ought and shall be continued and carried on along the lines laid down by her, and with the matter left in writing or dictated by her before her departure . . .*
>
> That her words to Bro. Judge in a recent letter were read stating that this Section (now School) is the "throbbing heart of the Theosophical Society."
>
> That it was resolved and recorded that the highest officials in the School *for the present* are Annie Besant and William Q. Judge. . . .
>
> That having read the address drawn up by Annie Besant and William Q. Judge, we put on record our full accord with it.
>
> *That this Council records its decision that its appointment was solely for the purpose of as-*

[3] See Chapter XXXI.

> *sisting* H.P.B. *in a consultative way,* and that as she had full power and authority to relieve us from duty at any time, our office and that of each of us ends with the above resolution passed in order as far as possible in our power *to place the future conduct of the School on the basis directed and intended by her;* therefore we collectively and individually declare that our office as Councillors ceases at this date, and that from henceforth with Annie Besant and William Q. Judge rest the full charge and management of this School.

The address to the members of the E.S.T., signed by Mr. Judge and Mrs. Besant, and incorporated in the circular, was in fact partly written by each, though signed by both. Their joint and several remarks are characteristic in more ways than one. In that portion actually written by Mrs. Besant she says:

> . . . it is our duty, as the two selected by H.P.B. as her agents and representatives after her departure, to specially speak to each one of you respecting the duty laid on the School by her retirement from the visible control of its affairs. The future of this body depends on the way in which this test of steadfastness and loyalty is endured by the members collectively and individually. . . . it will ill become her pupils if they desert the great Cause to which her life was given, and invite the terrible Karma that must fall on those who break the solemn pledge that each of us has made. The School is the heart of the Society; if the heart ceases to throb, the Society must die, as a living power, and slowly decay while passing into a mere sect. . . . It is not that the Masters *will* not help the School if we are supine; it is that they *cannot,* for they are bound by law, not by law of man's creation but by the immutable Law of na-

ture which always works through agents appropriate to the end in view.

This is followed without a break by that portion of the address which was written by Mr. Judge:

> Consider the position of the School: we are no longer a band of students taught by a visible Teacher; we are a band of students mutually interdependent, forced to rely on each other for our usefulness and our progress, until our very brotherliness in mutual help shall draw a visible Teacher back among us. H.P.B. remains one of our Heads though H. P. Blavatsky is "dead," and the Heads of the School have not withdrawn Their guidance in withdrawing the presence chosen to represent Them for a time on which we have rejoiced to lean.
>
> Especially important is it that at the present juncture we should bear in mind the words of H.P.B., written at the conclusion of the *Key to Theosophy*. In laying stress on the knowledge and wisdom that will be required by those on whom it falls to carry on the work of the Society after her departure, she explains that those qualities only can save the Theosophical Society from ending in failure. All previous attempts have thus failed (in accomplishing their mission in full) because they have degenerated into sects, and we have her word for it that unless we be freed from bias, "or at least taught to recognize it instantly and so avoid being led away by it, the result can only be that the Society will drift off to some sandbank of thought or another, and there remain a stranded carcase to moulder and decay." . . .
>
> There, then, is our next pressing work, our most mighty responsibility. For if we of this School, Brothers and Sisters, cannot accomplish this task, the Theosophical Society is doomed.

> Not in vain will come to you these tones of her living voice, speaking across "the change that men call death," for we know that she lives and is watching with grave, strong interest how they acquit themselves whose pledge can in no wise be altered by her departure into the invisible. That pledge was not given to the personality, it was given to Masters' Lodge and given also to the Higher Self invoked to witness it. It can therefore never be recalled, however much it may be denied.
>
> We who write to you claim over you no authority save such as she delegated to us. We are your fellow students, chosen by her—the Messenger of the Masters of Wisdom—as Their channels to the measure of our ability, during this period of darkness. . . .
>
> We believe in H.P.B. and in the Masters, and it is enough to us that they say, "Go and carry on our work along the lines on which you have been instructed. . . ."
>
> For the use of all of us, there are written teachings left by H.P.B. in our hands that will give food for study and thought for many a year to come, and though the main duty of the Esotericist is service to others, and not personal advancement in knowledge, it is characteristic of her thought for us that behind her she left intellectual and spiritual food for the earnest student, as well as the charge to complete her unfinished work.

The circular as signed by all the Councillors recorded that H.P.B.'s "last words in reference to the School and its work were: 'KEEP THE LINK UNBROKEN! DO NOT LET MY LAST INCARNATION BE A FAILURE.'" The reference by Mr. Judge in the joint address of Mrs. Besant and himself, to the "Key to Theosophy" was to the concluding section entitled "The Future of the Theosophical Society," and to be found at p. 304 of the original edition of that work.

Thus was the crisis in the School occasioned by the death of H.P.B. met and resolved by the determination that its conduct should henceforth be "on the lines laid down by her, and with the matter left in writing or dictated by her before her departure," and by the decision to leave its future "charge and management" with Mrs. Besant and Mr. Judge.

CHAPTER XX

ATTEMPTS TO SUPERSEDE H.P.B.'S INFLUENCE

Colonel Olcott arrived in England at the end of June, Mr. Judge remaining in London to meet him and to participate in the Convention of the European Section called for July 9, 1891. Colonel Olcott was made acquainted in a general way with what action had been taken in connection with the affairs of the Esoteric Section. The common feeling of loss, the general sense of uncertainty as to the future, the pressing necessity for concord, the hopeful augury provided by the circular of May 27 to the E.S., and the awakened sense of individual responsibility for the success of the Movement, now that its great Messenger was no more among them, all combined to allay frictions, dispel rivalries, and arouse the spirit of real fraternity. There being then present in London the best known and most respected leaders of the Society from Asia, America, and England, the Convention of the European Section, in the circumstances recited, became the first real convocation and assembly of the whole Society since its foundation.

Colonel Olcott, as President-Founder of the whole Society, presided at the sessions, Mr. Judge attended as Vice-President of the Society, as General Secretary of the American Section, and as Chairman of the Executive Committee of the American Section. Mrs. Besant was present as President of the Blavatsky Lodge of London, at the time the largest of the Societies in Great Britain. The various British and Continental Lodges were represented by delegates or proxies. In addition there were numerous visiting Fellows from the United States, from India, and from Australia, all of whom bore the cordial, if unofficial, greetings from the scattered members and Branches.

The London Lodge was not represented in person by its President, Mr. Sinnett, nor by any delegate. From the beginning of his leadership of the London Lodge Mr. Sinnett's influence had held it aloof from the general activities of the Society at large, though nominally a Branch of the Society. When the Blavatsky Lodge was formed at London shortly after H.P.B. had taken up her permanent residence in England, its original membership was entirely composed of former members of the London Lodge. Mr. Sinnett had been equally opposed, both to its formation and to the policy of active public propaganda for membership regardless of class distinctions. The formation of the Blavatsky Lodge, the publication of the "Secret Doctrine," with its corrections of his presentation of the teachings of Theosophy in his book "Esoteric Buddhism," and other matters which he could not approve, had all served to alienate his sympathies. His London Lodge discontinued all but closed meetings for its members only and formed a quasi-exclusive body. The active efforts of Col. Olcott, with whom he had always remained on terms of friendship, the olive branch tendered by Mrs. Besant and others, and the consideration shown him by Mr. Judge, so far prevailed as to ameliorate the somewhat strained situation, and the London Lodge sent a letter to the Convention.

This letter, signed by the Secretary, Mr. C. W. Leadbeater, is distinctly formal, not to say reserved, in its tone. It recites the history of the London Lodge, gives a chronological account of its activities, and concludes with the following paragraph:

> On the formation of the "British Section" in 1889, the London Lodge asserted the principle of complete autonomy as that on which it preferred to proceed; and with the concurrence of the President of the Parent Society, Col. Olcott, it remained an independent Branch of the Society outside that organization. Later on, when Madame Blavatsky formed the European Sec-

> tion under her own Presidentship, on principles which provided merely for a consultative council to assist her in discharging the functions of that office, the London Lodge cordially consented to be included in that arrangement. Clinging with great tenacity, however, to the principle of autonomy, it will now revert to its former status, and while heartily in sympathy with all bodies recognized as parts of the world-wide Theosophical Society, which Madame Blavatsky and Colonel Olcott founded, it will not take any share in the administration or control of any other branches, and will continue responsible alone to the original authority from which it sprang in reference to the conduct of its own affairs.

This letter was read to the Convention by Mr. G. R. S. Mead, General Secretary of the European Section, and was received without comment or objection. The full text of the letter of the London Lodge will be found in the Official Report of the Convention. The Convention itself is denominated on the cover and text page, not as a convention of the European Section, T.S., but as The Theosophical Society in Europe, the name adopted by H.P.B.

The proceedings of the Convention were opened by Mrs. Besant with a brief address of welcome to Col. Olcott.

Mr. Judge warmly seconded Mrs. Besant's remarks, and in taking the chair Col. Olcott spoke with great feeling.

Mr. Judge offered Resolutions for the creation of an H.P.B. Memorial Fund, to be devoted to such publications "as will tend to promote that intimate union between the life and thought of the Orient and the Occident to the bringing about of which her life was devoted." In seconding these resolutions Mrs. Besant said:

> . . . will the Convention permit me to add that it certainly has the approval of all those who

> were closely connected with her during the latter years of her life; that her leaving us is in no manner a change in her position in this Society, nor a change in the lines along which her work will be directed. . . . May I say for those who lived most closely with her that what she was with us in her visible presence she is to us still: friend and guide, teacher and master. We know no change because she has passed from the visible into the invisible, and in asking you to found this memorial we ask you to found it, not to a dead teacher, but to a living energy, an energy as real now as it was real when clothed in the body of H. P. Blavatsky; a memorial indeed of our love to her, but of a love of a living presence whom we recognise amongst us still.

A letter of greeting, signed by Mr. Judge as General Secretary, was read from the American Section:

> It is with great pleasure that I convey to you the brotherly and affectionate greetings of the American Section of our beloved Society, knowing that had I the time to call that Section together it would, without a dissenting voice, thank you for the work you have done, and encourage you to go on to still better work for the future. It would also, I am sure, give you full assurance of the value of organizing yourselves into a single body, for experience has shown us that only thus can good and wide work be done, and in no other way can you carry to a successful issue the task left by our beloved friend and co-worker, H.P.B. Unity is strength; division leads to weakness, decay and final dissolution. Hence the American Section views with pleasure the prospect of all the European Branches being closely massed together with a common object, a single organization. May your deliberations lead not only to greater energy in your own field but also

> to an added interest, sympathy and strength throughout the whole area of International Theosophical work.

When the Convention had concluded its work, the President-Founder made some parting remarks, from which we quote:

> Our task is done. We have met together in this friendly Conference; we have discussed the method of laying the basis for the future work of the Society; we have come to a fraternal agreement to make all parts of the Society work together in harmony; we have linked hands across the Atlantic and across the Southern seas, and pledged ourselves to each other to carry on this mission which was undertaken by H.P.B., and which we have been sharers in. The outside world are looking with curiosity to see what effect the death of H.P.B. will have upon us. The answer is to be obtained in the proceedings of this Convention. . . . In her death H.P.B. speaks more potently to us even than she did in her life. The tattered veil of the personality has been drawn aside, and the individuality which we knew only as a light shining from afar, is now before us to guide us on our way. . . . Whatever strength we have to the outside world depends upon the purity of our principles, the unselfishness of our behaviour, and our loyalty to the eclectic platform of our constitution. . . . No greater shock could possibly have come to us than the death of Mme. Blavatsky, and if the movement has survived it, then take my assurance that nothing whatever can affect us so long as we keep in view the principles upon which our movement is based and go fearlessly on to what lies to our hand to do. . . . Let us determine that at all costs this Society shall be kept impartial, calm, fraternal, benevolent, tol-

> erant, as regards all groups of the family of mankind. If we do this, if we place a guard upon any disposition on our part to be narrow, or prejudiced, or sectarian, we shall have earned the gratitude of our generation, and be remembered by posterity as those who sought to do good to their fellow men; but if, on the contrary, we allow ourselves to be influenced by these petty considerations of social position, or of race, or differences of creed, we will die out and be remembered only as an unworthy Association that lifted a banner which it was not fit to carry. . . .

Lucifer for June, July, and August, 1891, contains a great number of articles on H.P.B. by leading members of the Society. These articles were reprinted in a volume entitled "H.P.B., In Memoriam by Some of Her Pupils." Like the proceedings of the Council of the Esoteric Section and those of the European Convention, these articles breathe the best and purest spirit, for they betoken the renaissance for the time of the gratitude, the loyalty, the reverence felt for H.P.B. Jealousies, ambitions, vanities, misunderstandings of all kinds were for the moment dormant. It was as if, for the time being, her freed spirit enveloped them all, putting all lesser feelings aside and lending to each and all some measure of the inspiration which for so many years had burned in her with an unwavering flame.

The quoted matter will make clear and convincing the fact that in the period immediately following the death of H.P.B., all elements in the Society felt deeply the impulse of that Brotherhood which it was H.P.B.'s mission and the work of the Society to teach and practice. Certainly no one can read the Minutes of the E.S. Conference, the Report of the European Convention, and the memorial articles on H.P.B. without being struck by the unanimous recognition of the mission of H.P.B. and by the solemn declarations and pledges made to carry on the work of the Society on the lines laid down by her, with the material left by her, and with her example ever before them as that of a still living and guiding Teacher.

After the Convention, then, the workers scattered, each to his own field of labor. Mrs. Besant took entire charge of the conduct of *Lucifer*, with Mr. G. R. S. Mead associated with her as Sub-Editor. She herself plunged into incessant activities, writing, lecturing, encouraging and inspiring all those who surrounded her to an energy and devotion second only to her own. This as to the public work of the exoteric Society. Within the ranks of the Esoteric Section she was not less earnest and untiring. As Co-Head of the Section with Mr. Judge, practically the entire interests of the School in Britain, on the Continent, and in the Orient were in her care. Her reputation, gained before her entrance into the Theosophical world, made of her a constant subject of newspaper comment, and her presence at any meeting was enough to attract a large audience. Theosophical activities and growth doubled and tripled in England under her influence and example, and its secondary benefit throughout the world was felt by every worker in every land. Wherever her name was mentioned, Theosophy was equally the subject of discussion. Wherever Theosophy was spoken of, Annie Besant was naturally looked upon as its unequaled exponent and she was hailed by members and outsiders alike as the great and worthy successor of H.P.B.

Mr. Judge returned to America and resumed the active conduct of his magazine, *The Path*. The work of the American Section, of which he was continuously from its organization the General Secretary, made heavy inroads upon his time and energies. The active American membership in the T.S. was at that time larger than in all the rest of the world, and growing rapidly. The American membership in the Esoteric Section comprised two-thirds of the entire body and called for unceasing and difficult attention. Next to H.P.B., Mr. Judge's personal correspondence with members throughout the world was by far the heaviest. His health had been undermined by the drain of recent years and by the relentless and sustained attacks and antagonisms without and within the Society with himself as their object along with H.P.B. The good-will and good feeling reached during the London conferences, the apparent healing of all distempers within the Society, the fresh alliance of all the forces in the common object of carrying on the work on the lines established by H.P.B.—all these gave him new vigor and a strength sufficient for his increased burdens.

Colonel Olcott, now past sixty, patriarchal in appearance, cordial by nature, looked upon with the utmost respect and reverence by the rank and file of the membership as being the President-Founder of the Society, the earliest as the lifelong colleague of H.P.B., and the one chosen by the Masters as Head of the Society, might be said to have had his cup of glory full at this epoch. His journey had restored his physical health; the reception accorded him at London had reassured him as to the solid place he held in the affections of the membership in the Occident as in the Orient; the pledges of devotion by all the Western leaders in the Society to H.P.B., to the Cause, to his beloved Society, and to him personally, had brought out all that was generous, genial, and optimistic in his nature. He could see everywhere the work to which he had given his all through long years of hardship, often of ignominy, now sustained by able and devoted lieutenants, respected where it had once been despised, spoken of in flattering terms where once both it and himself had been received with contumely. Wherever he went he was the Chief. He determined to return to India by America, and his journey was broken from city to city by meetings at which he was the commanding figure. His entire journey during the months of his absence from Adyar was a kind of triumphal progress, strewn with testimonials of the love and gratitude of his colleagues and of the world-wide membership of the Society. Returned to India, his arrival was signalized by the Indian members in a manner not less warmly appreciative of his services.

In December, 1890, while H.P.B. lay between life and

death, Mrs. Besant had published on her own motion, and without the knowledge of H.P.B., a ringing article in *Lucifer* entitled "The Theosophical Society and H.P.B." The occasion for this article was the private propaganda that was diligently being promoted in derogation of H.P.B. by adherents of Col. Olcott and Mr. Sinnett for her action in taking over the Headship of the newly formed Theosophical Society in Europe. In this article Mrs. Besant wrote with great force and conviction in support of the following numbered propositions which she italicized in her article:

> Now touching the position of H.P.B. to and in the Theosophical Society, the following is a brief exposition of it, as it appears to many of us:
>
> (1) *Either she is a messenger from the Masters, or else she is a fraud.*
>
> (2) *In either case the Theosophical Society would have had no existence without her.*
>
> (3) *If she is a fraud, she is a woman of wonderful ability and learning, giving all the credit of these to some persons who do not exist.*
>
> (4) *If* H.P.B. *is a true messenger, opposition to her is opposition to Masters, she being their only channel to the Western World.*
>
> (5) *If there are no Masters, the Theosophical Society is an absurdity, and there is no use in keeping it up. But if there are Masters, and* H.P.B. *is their messenger, and the Theosophical Society their foundation, the Theosophical Society and* H.P.B. *cannot be separated before the world.*

Having thus advanced her theorems and worked them out to a satisfactory Q.E.D., Mrs. Besant's article closed with the inevitable corollary from her demonstration:

> . . . If the members care at all for the future of the Society, if they wish to know that the Twentieth Century will see it standing high

> above the strife of parties, a beacon-light in the darkness for the guiding of men, if they believe in the Teacher who founded it for human service, let them now arouse themselves from slothful indifference, sternly silence all dissensions over petty follies in their ranks, and march shoulder to shoulder for the achievement of the heavy task laid upon their strength and courage. If Theosophy is worth anything, it is worth living for and worth dying for. If it is worth nothing let it go at once and for all. It is not a thing to play with, it is not a thing to trifle with . . . let each Theosophist, and above all, let each Occultist, calmly review his position, carefully make his choice, and if that choice be for Theosophy, let him sternly determine that neither open foe nor treacherous friends shall shake his loyalty for all time to come to his great Cause and Leader, which twain are one.

Such a proclamation as this, coming from one who was, in the eyes of the world, even more than in the Society, the foremost power in the movement next to H.P.B. herself, could but align the ranks and silence, for the time being, all covert as well as open belittling of H.P.B.

After the death of H.P.B., as the no less clear proclamation in the E.S. circular became common knowledge throughout the Society, the determination of the Council, of Mr. Judge and Mrs. Besant, to follow strictly the aims and lines and teachings of H.P.B., produced such a revival of activity, such an exhibition of common Brotherhood and loyalty to the First Object and, no less, to H.P.B. as the Teacher, as had never been witnessed during her lifetime. Followed the Convention of the British and European Sections with their renewed asseverations, and the many articles breathing the most profound respect and devotion to H.P.B. and her mission from the lips of every well-known Theosophist.

On August 30, 1891, Mrs. Besant bade farewell to the

Secularists with whom, in collaboration with Mr. Charles Bradlaugh, she had labored for so many years. Her address was entitled "1875 to 1891: A Fragment of Autobiography." This memorable speech was circulated far and wide. After recounting her fifteen years of battle and achievement, her hard-won steps of progress to her conversion to Theosophy through her reviewing the "Secret Doctrine," her meeting with H.P.B., her examination of the famous S.P.R. *Report* with its charges of fraud against H.P.B., Mrs. Besant astounded the meeting, the world, and the members of the Theosophical Society with this bold and categorical statement:

> You have known me in this hall for sixteen and a half years. You have never known me to lie to you. My worst public enemy, through the whole of my life, never cast a slur upon my integrity. Everything else they have sullied, but my truth never; and I tell you that since Madame Blavatsky left, I have had letters in the same writing and from the same person [as the writer of the disputed "Mahatma" letters alleged in the S.P.R. *Report* to have been written by H.P.B.]. Unless you think that dead persons write—and I do not think so—that is rather a curious fact against the whole challenge of fraud. I do not ask you to believe me, but I tell you this on the faith of a record that has never yet been sullied by a conscious lie. Those who knew her, knew that she could not very well commit fraud, if she tried. She was the frankest of human beings. It may be said, "What evidence have you beside hers?" My own knowledge. For some time, all the evidence I had of the existence of her Teachers and the existence of those so-called "abnormal powers" was second-hand, gained through her. It is not so now; and it has not been so for many months; unless every sense can be at the same time deceived, unless a person can be, at the same moment, sane

> and insane, I have exactly the same certainty for the truth of those statements as I have for the fact that you are here. Of course you may be all delusions invented by myself and manufactured by my own brain. I refuse—merely because ignorant people shout fraud and trickery—to be false to all the knowledge of my intellect, the perceptions of my senses, and my reasoning faculties as well.

Lucifer for October, 1891, contained another unequivocal declaration by Mrs. Besant in its leading article, "Theosophy and Christianity." She says:

> . . . THEOSOPHY is a body of knowledge, clearly and distinctly formulated in part and proclaimed to the world. Members of the Society may or may not be students of this knowledge, but none the less is it the sure foundation on which the MASTERS have built the Society, and on which its central teaching of the Brotherhood of Man is based. Without Theosophy Universal Brotherhood may be proclaimed as an Ideal, but it cannot be demonstrated as a Fact. . . .
>
> Now by Theosophy I mean the "Wisdom Religion," or the "Secret Doctrine," and our only knowledge of the Wisdom Religion at the present time comes to us from the Messenger of its Custodians, H. P. BLAVATSKY. Knowing what she taught, we can recognise fragments of the same teachings in other writings, but her message remains for us the test of Theosophy everywhere. . . . Only, none of us has any right to put forward his own views as "Theosophy" in conflict with hers, for all that we know of Theosophy comes from her. When she says "The Secret Doctrine teaches," none can say her nay; we may disagree with the teaching, but it remains "the Secret Doctrine," or Theosophy;

> she always encouraged independent thought and criticism, and never resented differences of opinion, but she never wavered in the distinct proclamation "The Secret Doctrine *is*" so-and-so. . . .
>
> Theosophists have it in charge not to whittle away the Secret Doctrine. . . . Steadily, calmly, without anger but also without fear, they must stand by the Secret Doctrine as she gave it, who carried unflinchingly through the storms of well-nigh seventeen years the torch of the Eastern Wisdom. The condition of success is perfect loyalty. . . .

It must be evident to any student that these several proclamations referred alike to those within and without the Society, of high and low degree, who found it to their interest to belittle or calumniate H.P.B. In the months following the death of H.P.B. the natural impulse of gratitude on the part of the rank and file of the membership toward H.P.B. received an accession, a countenance, and a support from Mrs. Besant's affirmations of the status of H.P.B. and bold defiance of "treacherous friends" within the Society, that effectually put in prudent silence those who before had belittled publicly and privately the authoritative character of H.P.B. as the Messenger of the Masters.

But after Col. Olcott's tour and return to India it is clear that the testimonials he had received of the respect accorded to him and his position of President-Founder gave him a re-inforced feeling of security and strength. Likewise, from his past conduct, it is evident he had expected that with the death of H.P.B. she would no longer remain a living power in the Society. That part of his nature which so often had risen in rebellion against H.P.B. living, as the dominant factor in the Society of which he felt himself the true and competent Head, once more became restive, alarmed, and decisive of his action. What the inner councils of his thoughts and what the outcome are clearly discernible in his Address to the "Seventeenth Convention and Anniversary of the Theosophical Society, at the Headquarters, Adyar, Madras," India, at the end of December, 1891. The Address is contained in full in the Report of the Convention; also issued as a "Supplement" to *The Theosophist* for January, 1892. We quote the germane remarks:

> As the Co-Founder of the Society, as one who has had constant opportunities for knowing the chosen policy and wishes of the Masters, as one who has, under them and with their assent, borne our flag through sixteen years of battle, I protest against the first giving way to the temptation to elevate either them, their agents, or any other living or dead personage, to the divine status, or their teachings to that of infallible doctrine. . . .
>
> If she had lived, she would have undoubtedly left her protest against her friends making a saint of her or a bible out of her magnificent, though not infallible writings. I helped to compile her "Isis Unveiled" while Mr. Keightley and several others did the same by "The Secret Doctrine." Surely we know how far from infallible are our portions of the books, to say nothing about hers. She did not discover, nor invent Theosophy, nor was she the first or the ablest agent, scribe or messenger of the Hidden Teachers of the Snowy Mountains. The various scriptures of the ancient nations contain every idea now put forth, and in some cases possess far greater beauties and merits than any of her or our books. We need not fall into idolatry to signify our lasting reverence and love for her, the contemporary teacher, nor offend the literary world by pretending that she wrote with the pen of inspiration. Nobody living was a more staunch and loyal friend of hers than I, nobody will cherish her memory more lovingly. I was

> true to her to the end of her life, and now I shall continue to be true to her memory. But I never worshipped her, never blinded my eyes to her faults, never dreamt that she was as perfect a channel for the transmission of occult teaching as some others in history have been, or as the Masters would have been glad to have found. As her tried friend, then, as one who worked most intimately with her, and is most anxious that she may be taken by posterity at her true high value; as her co-worker; as one long ago accepted, though humble, agent of the Masters; and finally, as the official head of the Society and guardian of the personal rights of its Fellows, I place on record my protest against all attempts to create an H.P.B. school, sect or cult, or to take her utterances as in the least degree above criticism. The importance of the subject must be my excuse for thus dwelling upon it at some length. I single out no individuals, mean to hurt nobody's feelings. I am not sure of being alive very many years longer, and what duty demands I must say while I can.

To complete the picture as limned in the preceding extracts and comments, one may turn to the published statements of Mr. Judge during the same period. In *The Path*, for June, 1891, he sounded the following note of mingled confidence, caution, and advice:

> The death of H. P. Blavatsky should have the effect on the Society of making the work go on with increased vigor free from all personalities. The movement was not started for the glory of any person, but for the elevation of Mankind. The organization is not affected as such by her death for her official positions were those of Corresponding Secretary and President of the European Section. The Constitution has long provided that after her death the office of Corre-

> sponding Secretary should not be filled. The vacancy in the European Section will be filled by election in that Section, as that is matter with which only the European Branches have to deal. She held no position in the exoteric American Section, and had no jurisdiction over it in any way. Hence there is no vacancy to fill and no disturbance to be felt in the purely corporate part of the American work. The work here is going on as it always has done, under the efforts of its members who now will draw their inspiration from the books and works of H.P.B. and from the purity of their own motive.
>
> All that the Society needs now to make it the great power it was intended to be is first, *solidarity*, and second, *Theosophical education*. These are wholly in the hands of its members. The first gives that resistless strength which is found only in Union, the second gives that judgment and wisdom needed to properly direct energy and zeal.
>
> Read these words from H. P. Blavatsky's *Key to Theosophy*.

Then follow the quotations before referred to in the circular of the Esoteric Section from which we have quoted. In *The Path* for August, 1891, the leading article begins with this quotation:

> "INGRATITUDE IS NOT ONE OF OUR FAULTS." WE ALWAYS HELP THOSE WHO HELP US. TACT, DISCRETION, AND ZEAL ARE MORE THAN EVER NEEDED. THE HUMBLEST WORKER IS SEEN AND HELPED. . . .

The text immediately following runs thus:

> To a student theosophist, serving whenever and however he could, there came very recently —since the departure from this plane of H. P. Blavatsky—these words of highest cheer from

> that Master of whom H. P. B. was the reverent pupil. Attested by His real signature and seal, they are given here for the encouragement and support of all those who serve the Theosophical Society—and through it, humanity—as best they can; given in the belief that it was not intended that the recipient should sequestrate or absorb them silently, but rather that he should understand them to be his only in the sense that he might share them with his comrades, that his was permitted to be the happy hand to pass them on as the common right, the universal benediction of one and all.

The article is signed "Jasper Niemand." This pen name had by that time become known and loved throughout the Theosophical world as the recipient of the famous "Letters That Have Helped Me" from "Z. L. Z., the Greatest of the Exiles," originally published in *The Path* during the lifetime of H.P.B., and by many Theosophists then supposed to have been written by H.P.B. herself. Not till some years later was it made known that "Z. L. Z." was Mr. Judge, and "Jasper Niemand" Mrs. Archibald Keightley (Julia Campbell-Ver Planck). The article from which we have been quoting was written and published during the absence of Mr. Judge in England following H.P.B.'s death, and without his knowledge, as Mrs. Keightley was in editorial conduct of *The Path* during Mr. Judge's absence. The article, the message from the Masters with which it began, and the claim that the message had been received subsequent to the death of H.P.B., stirred Col. Olcott to the depths. He wrote to Mr. Judge about it in strong terms, as he saw in it nothing but an attempt to attract attention to H.P.B., Masters and Mr. Judge himself. Mr. Judge replied at length to Col. Olcott, and this letter was later published in *Lucifer*. As we shall have occasion later to refer to this correspondence,[1] no comment is necessary at this stage of our study.

[1] See Chapter XXVI.

Succeeding articles and notes in *The Path* gave attention to Col. Olcott's place in the T.S. with respect and loyalty; noted Mrs. Besant's claim to the receipt of messages subsequent to H.P.B.'s death; and in January, 1892, had for its leading article "Dogmatism in Theosophy." This article was written partly to make clear the real position to be assumed by all Theosophists, partly to moderate the intemperate zeal of some enthusiasts who were wont to quote H.P.B. to "put a quietus" on their opponents whose views of H.P.B. or her teachings were not the same as their own; partly as an open declaration of Mr. Judge's own attitude, in response to Col. Olcott's criticisms and public statements. We quote from "Dogmatism in Theosophy":

> The Theosophical Society was founded to destroy dogmatism. This is one of the meanings of its first object—Universal Brotherhood. . . .
>
> In the *Key to Theosophy,* in the "Conclusion," H.P.B. again refers to this subject and expresses the hope that the Society might not, after her death, become dogmatic or crystallize on some phase of thought or philosophy, but that it might remain free and open, with its members wise and unselfish. And in all her writings and remarks, privately or publicly, she constantly reiterated this idea. . . .
>
> If our effort is to succeed, we must avoid dogmatism in theosophy as much as in anything else, for the moment we dogmatise and insist on our construction of theosophy, that moment we lose sight of Universal Brotherhood and sow the seeds of future trouble.
>
> . . . Even though nine-tenths of the members believe in Reincarnation, Karma, the seven-fold constitution, and all the rest, and even though its prominent ones are engaged in promulgating these doctrines as well as others, the ranks of the Society must always be kept open, and no one should be told that he is not orthodox or not

a good Theosophist because he does not believe in these doctrines. . . .

But at the same time it is obvious that to enter the Society and then, under our plea of tolerance, assert that theosophy shall not be studied, . . . shall not be investigated, is untheosophical, unpractical, and absurd, for it were to nullify the very object of our organization. . . .

And as the great body of philosophy, science, and ethics offered by H. P. Blavatsky and her teachers has upon it the seal of research, of reasonableness, of antiquity, and of wisdom, it demands our first and best consideration. . . .

So, then, a member of the Society, no matter how high or how low his or her position in its ranks, has the right to promulgate all the philosophical and ethical ideas found in our literature to the best ability possessed, and no one else has the right to object, provided such promulgation is accompanied by a clear statement that it is not authorized or made orthodox by any declaration from the body corporate of the T.S. . . .

CHAPTER XXI

GROWING DIVERGENCES—OLCOTT RESIGNS AS PRESIDENT

THUS the real issue—the Theosophical Movement *versus* the Theosophical Society—once more became the wager of battle within less than a year after the death of H. P. Blavatsky. Doubtless this view will come as a shock to very many Theosophical students who have been educated to the belief that some particular organization is *the* Theosophical Society and who have therefore taken Theosophy, the Theosophical Movement, and their particular Society to be essentially one and the same thing. They do not see that this is the very pitfall into which the different Christian sects have fallen, and has come about in the same way—through biased and partisan guidance on the part of those whom they have trusted as teachers and leaders, and through their own failure to make diligent, open-minded investigation and comparison of the opposing and contradictory teachings and testimony.

Altruism was the self-imposed standard of action for all Fellows of the Theosophical Society, altruism and spiritual knowledge the self-pledged criterion of every Probationer of the Esoteric Section. Every Fellow of the T.S. must therefore be studied in his conduct, not by the sins of omission or of commission of his fellows, but in the light of his own devotion to the great First Object of the Society. Every Probationer of the Esoteric Section must be weighed in the balance, not of his rank, standing, or reputation in the world or in the Society, but in the light of his solemn declaration: "I pledge myself to endeavour to make Theosophy a living power in my life." The formulation of the Objects of the Society was so definite and inclusive that no man can err as to what those Objects mean.

When *The Theosophist* for January, 1892, with its report of the Adyar Convention just held, reached America Mr. Judge published in his magazine *The Path* for March, 1892, three articles of momentous import. The importance which the world-wide membership must necessarily attach to Col. Olcott's proclamation, because of his position as President of the whole Society; because of his known long-continued and intimate relations with H.P.B., and because of the reverence and respect in which he was held as President-Founder, compelled consideration. The first article is entitled "The Future and the Theosophical Society," and begins abruptly:

> In 1888 H. P. Blavatsky wrote:
>
> Night before last I was shown a bird's-eye view of the theosophical societies. I saw a few earnest reliable theosophists in a death struggle with the world in general and with other—nominal and ambitious—theosophists. The former are greater in number than you may think, and *they prevailed*—as you in America *will prevail,* if you only remain staunch to the Master's programme and true to yourselves. And last night I saw. . . . The defending forces have to be judiciously—so scanty are they—distributed over the globe wherever theosophy is struggling with the powers of darkness.

The article follows this with another quotation from the "Key to Theosophy," the section entitled "The Future of the Theosophical Society," to which we have before referred, and continues:

> Every member of the Society should be, and many are, deeply interested in the above words. The outlook, the difficulties, the dangers, the necessities are the same now as then, and as they were in the beginning in 1875. For, as she has often said, this is not the first nor will it be the last effort to spread the truth and to undertake

the same mission . . . to lead men to look for the one truth that underlies all religions and which alone can guide science in the direction of ideal progress. In every century such attempts are made, and many of them have been actually named "theosophical." Each time they have to be adapted to the era in which they appear. And this is the era . . . of freedom for thought and for investigation.

In the first quotation there is a prophecy that those few reliable theosophists who are engaged in a struggle with the opposition of the world and that coming from weak or ambitious members will prevail, *but it has annexed to it a condition that is of importance. There must be an adherence to the program of the Masters. That can only be ascertained by consulting her and the letters given out by her as from those to whom she refers. It excludes the idea that the Society was founded or is intended as "a School for Occultism!"*[1]

Referring to a letter received (1884) from the same source we find: *"Let the Society flourish on its moral worth, and not by phenomena made so often degrading."* The need of the west for such doctrines as Karma and Reincarnation and the actual Unity of the whole human family is dwelt upon at length in another . . .

This is the great tone running through all the words from these sources. It is a call to work for the race and not for self, a request to bring the west and the east the doctrines that have most effect on human conduct, on the relations of man to man, and hence the greatest possibility of forming at last a true universal brotherhood. *We must follow this program and supply the world with a system of philosophy which gives a sure and logical basis for ethics, and that can only be gotten from those to whom I have ad-*

[1] The italics in this quotation are our own.

> *verted; there is no basis for morals in phenomena, because a man might learn to do the most wonderful things by the aid of occult forces and yet at the same time be the very worst of men.*
>
> A subsidiary condition, but quite as important as the other, is laid down by H.P.B. in her words that we must "remain true to ourselves." This means true to our better selves and the dictates of conscience. *We cannot promulgate the doctrines and the rules of life found in theosophy and at the same time ourselves not live up to them as far as possible. We must practice what we preach, and make as far as we can a small brotherhood within the Theosophical Society.*

Mr. Judge goes on to say that these things must be done, not only as an example to the world, but because as an Occult and scientific fact unity of action gives a ten-fold power. He calls attention to what has already been achieved in modifying the thought of the day, by bringing Theosophy to the front of thought and notice, despite all oppositions without and within, but warns the members against the futility of hoping to enlist the co-operation of the churches in the attempt to destroy priestcraft and dogmatism. The article concludes:

> Our destiny is to continue the wide work of the past in affecting literature and thought throughout the world, while our ranks see many changing quantities but always holding those who remain true to the program and refuse to become dogmatic or to give up commonsense in theosophy. Thus will we wait for the new messenger, striving to keep the organization alive that he may use it and have the great opportunity H.P.B. outlines when she says, "Think how much one to whom such an opportunity is given could accomplish."

The second of the articles referred to is a review of the Proceedings of the Adyar Convention. Kindly consideration is given to Col. Olcott and his labors, and occasion is taken to speak with generous warmth of Mrs. Besant and her potentialities for good in the Society. Attention is paid to the Colonel's remarks on H.P.B. in his Presidential Address. Mr. Judge's comments follow:

> [Col. Olcott] indulges in some remarks as to the grave error he and H.P.B. made, as he thinks, in being intolerant towards Christianity. Those who have carefully read her writings and have known her as well as Col. Olcott know that there has been very little intolerance from our side, but that there has been, as there always will be, a constant irritation on the part of dogmatists who perceive that the pure light of theosophy makes dogmatism see its death-warrant very visibly before its eyes. Neither H.P.B. nor Col. Olcott, nor any one else in the Society who has understood its mission, can suppose there has been any intolerance of true Christianity, as that is confined in any city to a small number of persons.
>
> Col. Olcott also said that he did not believe H.P.B. thought she was going to die, and that in his opinion her death was a surprise to her. With this we cannot agree in the least. He had not been with her for some time and did not know of the many warnings she had been lately giving to all her immediate friends, including the Editor of this magazine, of her approaching demise. In some cases the notice she gave was very detailed, in others it was by question, by symbolical language, and by hint, but for the year or more before her death she let those who were close to her know that she was soon to go, and in one case, when a certain event happened, she said, "That means my death." We have

> great respect for Col. Olcott, but cannot agree with him in this matter. . . .
>
> . . . Further, in speaking of a tendency he saw on the part of some to dogmatise on H.P.B., Col. Olcott paid her a tribute and at the same time said there ought to be no idolatry; but while he was right in that, yet at the same time the very Masters of whom he spoke, and from whom he heard through H.P.B., said in a letter that has long been published that H.P.B. had everything to do with the occult department of the work of the members of the Society. This must not be forgotten.

The third of the articles mentioned came with the shock of a complete surprise to all but a handful. Its consequences were so far-reaching, exoterically and esoterically, that we give it in full herewith, as it is probable that few, if any, Theosophists of the present day know even the bald facts as publicly disclosed. The article is entitled "Resignation of Presidency T.S. by Col. Olcott," and its text is as follows:

> The following correspondence sufficiently explains itself. It is inserted here in order that American members generally may be in possession of the information. It will be remembered that Col. Olcott determined to resign some time ago, but was induced to alter his decision and to take a vacation in order to restore his health, but although the rest did him good we were all sorry to see, even so lately as when he visited America in 1891, that traces of old trouble remained, and at the 16th Annual Convention, [the one just held] he again said that he could not do the work he used to do. So, feeling that the Society is firmly established, he now resigns official position. He will continue to reside in India and do literary work for the Society's benefit, and no doubt will aid his successor very

> much in placing the Adyar Oriental Library on a better footing than ever. At the April Convention [of the American Section] in Chicago resolutions will probably be passed upon the matter, and will include the expression of our high appreciation of his long services. By some it is proposed to suggest at that meeting that the American Section desires him to have at Adyar a free life-residence. This would be fitting.

This is followed by the text of the two letters mentioned—the first from Col. Olcott as President to Mr. Judge as Vice-President, and dated at Adyar, January 21, 1892. In his letter Col. Olcott gives as his reason for the present, as for the two former occasions when he had expressed the wish to retire, the state of his health, and adds that he has now "obtained permission to carry out the wish." The two former occasions were his expressions at the Adyar Convention at the close of 1885 (not 1886, as he gives it in his letter), and again in 1890. While the statements made of his impaired health were true in all three cases, in none of them was it the real underlying reason. The first time was because of the strong reaction in India against the treatment accorded H.P.B. during the Coulomb troubles and afterward. Although all had shared in the timid and disloyal course adopted, the resentment shown against Col. Olcott by those who had before been his advisers and supporters, was unjust in that it was an attempt to make him the scapegoat of atonement for the common sin. It was due to the privately exercised influence of H.P.B. and Mr. Judge and their loyal friends that the Convention refused to accept Col. Olcott's resignation and reiterated its gratitude and loyalty to him in his onerous position of President of the whole Society. And again, in 1890, his desire to resign was due in fact to the rebellion in England and Europe which culminated in a revolution —H.P.B. taking over, at the almost unanimous request and insistence of the various Lodges and unattached Fellows, the Presidency of the Theosophical Society in Europe. Seeing Europe lost to his authority, and America emancipated from his "exercise of Presidential powers," with all the more important and devoted Western Fellows members of the Esoteric Section pledged to follow the instructions of H.P.B. in all Theosophical relations, Col. Olcott had experienced all that bitterness of heart which must come to those who, having exercised plenary powers, now find themselves reduced to the position of a figurehead. Justly feeling that he had given his all to the Society and that during his long years of "paternal authority" he had done his best for the children dear to his heart, Col. Olcott, like all zealous-hearted but proud and sensitive soldiers, was moved to resign rather than to resignation. On this second occasion, as on the first, H.P.B. and Mr. Judge, had shown the kind of loyalty which animated *them.* Loyalty to the *Cause* had compelled them to hold true to the lines laid down from the beginning, at whatever cost of misunderstanding or risk of rupture to external machinery or relations; loyalty to Col. Olcott, the struggling probationer who had earned help in his hour of need by his devoted efforts and sacrifices, whose *heart* was still true, whatever his mental and psychic errancies and personal flux of feelings in regard to themselves—this principle of true Occultism had caused them to make every effort to soothe the President-Founder's ruffled vanity, to sweeten the bitter pill of his acceptance of the changes enforced by the necessities of the occasion. And they had succeeded, for Col. Olcott accepted the new status of affairs with the best grace he could muster and went on with his part of the work—a part which they knew he had performed and could still perform, better than any man living.

But if Col. Olcott had suffered on the two former occasions, the iron which had now entered his heart and driven him once more to "resign" was a thousand times more poignant, it was a veritable crucifixion of his personal nature, coupled with a sense of injustice which was unendurable; hence his "resignation."

The hidden facts behind this resignation have never to this day been disclosed. The only direct public references to the real cause of Col. Olcott's resignation are to be found in a letter addressed by Mr. Herbert Burrows to the editor of *The English Theosophist,* and published in that magazine for November, 1895; in the editorial article in the same magazine for December, 1895, entitled "The Resignation Mystery, 1892," and in the extremely reticent and guarded statement by Mr. Judge in the pamphlet issued in April, 1895. None of these references does more than to indicate that other reasons than ill health lay at the bottom of the President-Founder's sudden determination to "resign."

While Col. Olcott was at London in the summer of 1891, following H.P.B.'s death, he was a guest in the house of Miss F. Henrietta Müller. This lady, well-to-do, well-educated, moving in the best classes of society, was an "eccentric" at a time when things now commonplaces of everyday life were accounted marked if not reprehensible "eccentricities." She advocated the "equality of the sexes"; she was an ardent "suffragist"; she proclaimed her views on any and all subjects with entire freedom of expression; she lived according to her own ideas of propriety and decorum. In other words she was, according to her lights, an independent and honest woman. No breath or taint of scandal attached to her name. She had become a member of the Theosophical Society and was as active and ardent an exponent of her views in this relation as on all others.

Colonel Olcott, of a personal nature not dissimilar to her own, enjoyed her hospitality and her companionship. Moreover, his heart, heavy over the perception of all that was involved in the death of H.P.B., had been lightened by the reception accorded him by his associates, by the new harmony and unity arrived at during the period of the first Convention of the European Section. His physical health rebounded to the changed environment and his mental and moral health no less. He conducted himself toward all with that frankness, that *bonhomie* and *naiveté,* that mixture of child and man of the world, which was his enduring personal charm. He traveled Britain, visited Sweden, and returned to India *via* America, Japan, and Ceylon, receiving everywhere a heartfelt reception and attention. Once in India, his long-time hold upon the affections of the members was manifested by a thousand spontaneous incidents. He must have felt himself, as he had never felt during the lifetime of H.P.B., the chief figure in the Society and in the confidence of its world-wide membership. Then came the Adyar Convention and the reassertion of his old self-confident, self-complacent nature in his condescending and corrective remarks on the "worship" of H.P.B. and his delineation of her nature and place in the work while living.

What, then, was the shock which followed, each student must imagine for himself, but its intensity can be briefly indicated by the recital of the dramatic elements supplied by the fact as follows. Colonel Olcott had visioned in Mrs. Besant a worthy "successor" to H.P.B., a successor with whom he could work in full harmony and mutuality of understanding, as he had never been able to do with H.P.B. herself. He had besought her to come to India, and Mr. Bertram Keightley, then in India and acting as General Secretary of the Indian Section and as Col. Olcott's chief aid, had formally seconded this desire on the part of the Indian Section and opened a subscription to pay the expenses of the hoped-for tour. Yielding to these solicitations Mrs. Besant had agreed to visit India and deliver a number of lectures. Just prior to the time of her expected departure announcement was made that Mrs. Besant was suffering from the exhaustion due to a prolonged period of overwork, was threatened with a collapse, and that her physician had ordered a sea voyage and a brief period of complete relaxation to restore her. This also was all true enough, but in fact Mrs. Besant took her "sea voyage" to New York and return, and delivered a number of lectures in the United States, in place of Adyar and India. No one seems to have questioned the sudden change of plans, or the incongruity between the prescribed relaxation and the strenuous activities of her brief stay in America. What had happened was this: Charges of "grave immorality"—to quote Mr. Herbert Burrows' words—had been made to Mrs. Besant in England against Col. Olcott for his conduct while in London. Mrs. Besant had listened to these accusations, had investigated them according to her own ideas of what constitutes an investigation, until she also became convinced that the charges were true. She had cabled Mr. Judge demanding immediate action on his part as Vice-President of the whole Society for its purification and protection. Mr. Judge replied suggesting it would be well for Mrs. Besant to come to America with the evidence. Accordingly Mrs. Besant sailed for New York, reaching there November 27, 1891, and departing December 9, giving four public lectures, two in New York, one in Philadelphia, and one in Fort Wayne, Indiana, besides an address to the members of the Aryan Society and a talk to a private meeting of members of the E.S. She recounted to Mr. Judge circumstantially and in detail the charge and the evidence to which she and Miss Müller were parties and demanded of Mr. Judge as Vice-President of the Society and her Co-Head in the Esoteric Section that he forthwith require of Col. Olcott his resignation.

Mr. Judge cross-questioned her as to the facts and her knowledge of them. Then he called in Mr. E. August Neresheimer to whom he had Mrs. Besant repeat the charge and her statements of the evidence. He did the same with another friend and associate whose name it is not necessary to mention. To both of these Mrs. Besant repeated in detail and with particularity the facts of which she claimed to be possessed. To both of these Mrs. Besant repeated and reaffirmed her demand for instant action. Mr. Judge thereupon wrote a letter to Col. Olcott, not as Vice-President, but as an old friend, and in this letter advised Col. Olcott of the charge made and the evidence alleged to substantiate it, and suggested to him whether, *if the charge were true*, he had not better resign. This letter Mr. Judge gave to Mrs. Besant, who said that she had already arranged that a "London member, a man of means, would go to India as special messenger so as to avoid all risks from spies at Adyar."

Miss Müller had already gone to India from London. The special messenger went to India, delivered Mr. Judge's letter; Col. Olcott denied the charge, but *put in his resignation of the Presidency,* as we have seen.

Why did Col. Olcott thus resign *if innocent?* Yet resign he did, without explanation and without protest, as without consideration of the effect upon the Society of his resignation, both in the loss of his services and in the infinitely greater loss that would accrue if his resignation "under fire" should in any way become public knowledge. But a rational explanation must exist for every action, however irrational. The ample explanation is to be found in the understanding of the personal characteristics of Col. Olcott and a knowledge of his earlier life. Capable and energetic, very honest and very vain, he had achieved what in the world is called an honorable career; he had been a successful student, soldier, writer, lawyer. Exceedingly credulous he was, and as is the case with all credulous people of ability and honesty, also exceedingly suspicious when his sensitiveness to ridicule was in any way pricked by the fear that he might have been duped. In his middle life he had been a "man of clubs, drinking parties, mistresses," as he had himself publicly stated in his letter to Mr. Hume printed in "Hints on Esoteric Theosophy," published in 1882. He knew that he had many enemies, both as a man and as President of the Theosophical Society, and he had never been able to overcome his jealousy of H.P.B. and Mr. Judge, both of whom he fancied were envious of his superior position in the Society and desirous of supplanting him. He knew that if he refused to retire under fire and demanded an investigation of the charge made against him, the accusation would become public, and he, like many another even less open to calumny than himself, would be made the victim of ceaseless repetitions of the charge. Galling as it was to resign and retire, it was less galling than to endure the stings of the vermin of the press and to see or fancy that he saw, wherever he might go, the whisper and the knowing nod of those whose feast is scandal.

Colonel Olcott's letter of resignation as published in *The Path* was immediately followed by the text of Mr. Judge's letter of acknowledgment, dated February 22, 1892. Mr. Judge's letter formally acknowledged, paragraph by paragraph, the several statements contained in the President-Founder's epistle, and, in closing, contained the following expression of recognition and appreciation:

> . . . the Sections of the Society will, however rejoice when they read that you, in tendering your resignation of your official position, and in declaring continued loyalty to the movement —which indeed none could doubt,—assure us that the Society shall have as long as you live the benefit of your counsel when asked. Of this we shall as a body most surely avail ourselves, for otherwise we would be shown incapable of valuing history, as well as ungrateful to one who so long has carried the banner of Theosophy in the thickest of the fight.
>
> With assurance of universal sympathy from the American Section, I am, my dear colleague, your friend and brother,
>
> WILLIAM Q. JUDGE.

CHAPTER XXII

CONVENTIONS OF 1892—OLCOTT WITHDRAWS HIS RESIGNATION

THE Sixth Annual Convention of the American Section was held at Chicago on April 24 and 25, 1892. It was attended by delegates or proxies from all of the 60 active Lodges in the United States, as well as by many Fellows individually. The great growth of the Movement and of the Society is indicated by the comparative figures of former years. In 1886, eleven years after the formation of the Society, and the year in which *The Path* was founded, the entire number of Branches was 8; in 1887 there were 12; in 1888, 19; in 1889, 26; in 1890, 45; in 1891, 57; and by the end of 1892 the total had risen to 69. This enormous relative and actual increase can be ascribed to no adventitious circumstances, to no lavish outlay of money and the proselyting spirit, nor to the presence and work of persons of international reputation and prestige. It was wholly due to impersonal and consistent presentation of the fundamental ideas and principles of Theosophy, to an undeviating active adherence to the spirit which animated H. P. Blavatsky. Attention to the Second and Third Objects was at all times strictly subordinated to the great First Object.

Although lacking the presence of both H.P.B. and Col. Olcott; although a large portion of its dues and contributions was regularly remitted to India for the support of Col. Olcott's work there as well as of the Headquarters proper (for the Indian Section was never at any time self-sustaining in any sense); and although the American Section had been the very centre of the most violent eruptions within the Society, the work had so prospered within a period of five years that at the time of the Sixth Sectional Convention the active membership, both in the Society and in the Esoteric Section, was, in the United States, greater than in all the rest of the world. Mr. Judge, holding like H.P.B. a merely nominal official position in the Society, but, like her, indefatigable in the propagation of *ideas* and their practical application, wedded to a Cause, not to an administration and an organization, was the living, human focus from which radiated the energy of which that Cause and its Messenger were the inspiration.

Two letters were read from Col. Olcott, the first through pandit S. E. Gopalacharlu, Recording Secretary of the T.S. at Headquarters. It contained the following reference to Col. Olcott's retirement:

> The President Founder requests you to enter the text of his resignation and explanatory letter in the Official Report of your Convention, and to kindly say to his American brothers that the withdrawal from office is merely the relinquishment of an official position which, for reasons public and private, he felt he had no longer the moral right to retain. His love of the Society is so profound as to have taken possession of his whole being, and nothing but the sense of paramount loyalty to its highest interest would have impelled him to retire.

This letter was dated March 16, 1892. The other letter to which reference is made is Col. Olcott's Circular to all the Fellows of the Society. It is dated January 27, 1892. It reiterates the publicly ascribed reason of ill-health as the occasion of his retirement and states that his remarks are "intended to remove from your minds all misconceptions," as to the cause of his resignation. He continues:

> It may seem strange that I should announce this decision so soon after the Convention [at Adyar]; but I feel that this is the most suitable time, as the Conventions of the American and European Sections will be held in three or four months' time, so that any measures which

my retirement renders necessary may be fully discussed at their Sessions. . . .

Thus the three Sections of the Society are in thoroughly good hands, and my personal direction is no longer indispensable. . . .

I have no intention of leaving India nor any desire to live elsewhere. This is my home, and I wish to die among my own heart-brothers, the Asiatics. I shall always be ready to give all needed help to my successor, and to place at the disposal of his Staff my best counsel, based upon an experience of some forty years of public life and seventeen years as President-Founder of the Society. . . .

In bidding you an official farewell, I have but to express my gratitude for a thousand evidences of your loving trust, and to pray you to judge compassionately of my shortcomings.

The Report of Mr. Judge to the Convention, as General Secretary of the American Section, is filled with matter of enduring importance historically and of timeless value to the student of the principles and modulus of action of true Occultism. He begins with a retrospect of the important events and the important lessons of the past year, enforcing them by quotations from the first Letter of H.P.B. to the American Convention of 1888. In his view the two most important events of the past year were the death of H.P.B. and the work undertaken by Mrs. Besant, both of which events he treats from the standpoint of the Second Section:

Duty kept her [H.P.B.] in London until she had finished the *Secret Doctrine,* the book that led Annie Besant into the Society from the negations of materialism, and then all-grasping death claimed the body of H. P. Blavatsky. From my intimate acquaintance with H.P.B. for these many years and from her constant letters, I know that she remained in England

> and this world much longer than her desires would keep her, in order that a telling blow could be struck at the great monster of disbelief. And that blow was delivered in the country which still greatly influences the thought of America, by the conversion of a lifelong champion of those who believe in no religion to theosophy, the most spiritual of all sciences and religions. I do not say this as praise for Annie Besant, nor merely as rejoicing that we acquired another noble heart and eloquent advocate, but to point out that many thousands of minds must have been shaken from their confident assertions of disbelief when they saw that their old-time champion went over to theosophy; and at the same time members of the dogmatic sects perceived by the same event that, even if one gives up the negations of materialism, it does not follow that he must fall back again into the arms of any church or sect. Hence, then, by the acquisition without effort, but naturally, of one who was so long and so publicly known to all English-speaking peoples as the champion of negation in belief and altruism in endeavor, a telling, wide-vibrating blow was given to disbelief. And then H.P.B.—friend and fellow student—left us, on what other high mission bent we know not.

It is interesting to compare the foregoing viewpoint and expression with the attitude and remarks of Col. Olcott on the same subjects as expressed in his Presidential Address in December, 1891,[2] from which we have quoted. Mr. Judge continues:

> The news of our loss in May, so soon after our successful Convention, created comment throughout the world; many members of the Society would have easily joined in a sudden re-

[2] See Chapter XX.

treat from the field; and newspapers, together with croaking enemies of the Society, prophesied its fall, supposing that our movement was built on a personal worship of one woman. But scarce a moment elapsed ere a new resolve sprang up in the hearts of all, and actual correspondence has proved that through the world our members determined to be true to the cause and the objects outlined in that letter of 1888 I quoted to you. The structure of sixteen years' growth did not tremble in the least.

Considering that the circumstances demanded it, and after advising with near friends, I sailed on May 13th, 1891, for London to consult our Fellows there to the end that a general unity of policy and action might be decided on. The event proved the propriety of the journey. As Vice-President of the entire Society, I had the great pleasure of presiding over the preliminary meetings in London to draft the necessary Constitution; and afterwards took part in July in their Convention, the president of which was Col. Olcott and where was adopted a form of constitution the same as that commended by our beloved H.P.B. in the extracts I have read you from her letters. That was the first theosophical convention of the European Branches, and must be regarded as the beginning of a new cycle for that Section as ours of 1888 was for us. It was most interesting and important in every respect.

He speaks of the disposition of H.P.B.'s ashes, one portion of which was sent to India and the other divided between the London and American headquarters. He tells of the acquisition by the Aryan Society of New York of a building designed for the permanent headquarters of the American Section. He then takes up the resignation of Col. Olcott, submits the official letters exchanged, advises as to the course of action necessary in the premises to provide for the succession to the Presidency of the whole Society, urges the adoption of a recommendation from the American Section that Col. Olcott be offered a life-residency at Adyar, and suggests that a subscription be opened to provide for the Colonel's pecuniary needs, "as a testimonial, however inadequate, of the gratitude of this Section for his long and devoted services." During the Convention the following resolutions were introduced and unanimously adopted:

> *Whereas,* Col. Henry S. Olcott, President-Founder of the Theosophical Society, has tendered his resignation of the office of President to take effect May 1st *proximo,* and has requested that a successor be elected to the office of President of the Theosophical Society, and,
>
> *Whereas,* The General Secretary and Vice-President has taken the votes of all the Branches of this Section on the question of who shall be successor to the said office of President of the Theosophical Society, the said votes being unanimously in favor of William Q. Judge, and they being now duly reported to and before this Convention;
>
> *Resolved,* That the American Section in Convention assembled hereby tenders to Col. H. S. Olcott the expression of its profound gratitude and sincere appreciation for his unselfish devotion and long and faithful services for the Society which he helped to found and which is so largely indebted to him for its beneficent work and the recognition it has won in every quarter of the globe.
>
> *Resolved,* That in our estimation the position of Col. Olcott as "President-Founder" of the Society is, and must forever remain, unique. Another may succeed him in the office of President and assume the duties of the office, but can never be "President-Founder."
>
> *Resolved,* That this Convention confirms and

ratifies the votes of said Branches, and as such Convention declares its choice for President to succeed Col. H. S. Olcott to be said William Q. Judge. But it is further

Resolved, That the American Section in Convention hereby requests Col. Olcott to revoke his said resignation and remain President of the Society, deeming that it is not yet time for him to retire from said office, and it being possible for him to remain in said official position although his health may demand that the amount of his work be reduced to a minimum so far as traveling and speaking are concerned; and the General Secretary and Vice-President is hereby directed to at once notify Col. Olcott by telegraph and letter of this request, forwarding copies thereof, to the end that all further proceedings relative to said retirement be suspended until such time as the sense of the European and Indian Sections on this point be obtained: that in the meantime it is the opinion and desire of this Section that the said resignation be not yet accepted but laid over for further consideration; and that, when the sense of the said European and Indian Sections shall have been obtained, the General Secretary and Executive Committee of this Section shall call a special meeting of the Council of the Section to consider the question upon the report to be made thereupon by the General Secretary and Vice-President, and

Resolved, That this Section now declares its vote to be that when said office of President shall become vacant the successor to said Col. Olcott shall be said William Q. Judge, who shall hold said office for life unless removed for cause, and that he have power to nominate his successor as now provided in the General Constitution in respect to Col. Olcott; and that the General

Constitution be amended so as to provide in accordance with the foregoing, and that when the office of Vice-President shall become vacant, the choice of this Section for said office of Vice-President is Brother Bertram Keightley.

Resolved, That this Section requests that Col. Olcott, when he shall have retired, if ever, be offered a life residence at Adyar Headquarters.

Resolved, That the European and Indian Sections of the Society be and they are hereby requested to co-operate with this Section in endeavoring to carry out the letter and the spirit of these resolutions, and that the General Secretary of this Section immediately forward to said Sections an official copy of the same.

Resolved, Therefore, that this Section hereby re-elects to the office of General Secretary of this Section its present Secretary, William Q. Judge.

In accordance with the Convention's instruction to telegraph Col. Olcott of the American Section's request for the withdrawal of his resignation, Mr. Judge cabled the substance of the resolution adopted and, at the final session of the Convention, read the assembled delegates Col. Olcott's telegraphic reply:

> Am willing to do anything that is just and fair; I must stop here [Adyar] until I hear definitely from you [by mail].

During the Convention Mr. Judge introduced the following resolution, which also was unanimously adopted, as an offset to the charges of "dogmatism" in the T.S. and the "worship" of H.P.B.:

> *Whereas,* It is frequently asserted by those ignorant of the facts of the case and of the literature of the Society that the T.S. or its leaders seek to enforce certain beliefs or in-

terpretations upon its members, or to establish a creedal interpretation of any of its philosophical propositions; therefore

Resolved, That the T.S. as such, has no creed, no formulated beliefs that could or should be enforced on any one inside or outside its ranks; that no doctrine can be declared as orthodox, and that no Theosophical Popery can exist without annulling the very basis of ethics and the foundations of truth upon which the whole Theosophical teachings rest; and in support of this resolution appeal is made to the entire literature of the Society, and the oft-repeated statements published wide-spread by H.P.B., Col. Olcott, Mr. Judge, and every other prominent writer and speaker upon the subject since the foundation of the Theosophical Society.

The full proceedings of the Convention were published in the Official Report. Copies of the various resolutions in relation to Col. Olcott's tendered resignation were sent to the General Secretaries of the European and Indian Sections, their substance printed in *The Path* and *Lucifer,* and a large publicity secured in the secular press. Mr. Judge wrote Col. Olcott both officially and privately, and in the latter capacity sent him a message received from one of the Masters. It is this message and a communication received direct by himself that Col. Olcott refers to in his final Official Letter on the subject of his resignation. Meantime, under date of April 27, immediately after receipt of Mr. Judge's cabled news of the action of the American Convention, Col. Olcott issued "Executive Orders" in relation to the difficulties in the way of his immediate retirement, and paves the way for the withdrawal of his resignation in these words:

Notice is therefore given that, without again vainly trying to fix an actual date for my vacating office, I shall do my utmost to hasten the completion of all legal business, so that I may

> hand over everything to Mr. Judge, my old friend, colleague and chosen successor.

The latter part of this statement refers to the provision of the General Constitution adopted by the Indian Council and confirmed by the "Adyar Parliament" some years before, empowering Col. Olcott to *nominate* his successor in office; and, while the American Section had expressed its choice of Mr. Judge as that successor, the European and Indian Sections had not yet had the opportunity to express their wishes, whether on the question of accepting Col. Olcott's resignation or the choice of his successor.

This "Executive Notice" was followed on May 25 by another "rescript" from Col. Olcott, reading:

> To Theosophists
>
> I have just received a digest of the Resolutions passed by the American Convention relative to my retirement and Mr. Judge's re-election as General Secretary of the Section. As my resignation was not thoughtlessly offered nor without sufficient reasons, I shall not cancel it —save as I have been forced to do temporarily in the financial interest of the Society—until a long enough time has been given me to see what effect the invigorating air of these lovely mountains [Col. Olcott's Notice was issued from Ootacamund in the Nilgherry Hills, India] will have upon my health, and I become satisfied that a return to executive work is essential to the welfare of our movement. Besides the meeting of the European Convention in July I am expecting other important events to happen and I shall give no answer until then. Meanwhile, however, my heart is touched by the universal tokens of personal regard and official approval which have reached me from all parts of the world.
>
> H. S. Olcott.

This Note was published in *Lucifer* for July 15, 1892, just prior to the meeting of the European Convention. It was not perceived by the English and Continental Theosophists to be an intimation from Col. Olcott that he was, in fact, waiting to receive from them a request and re-affirmation similar to the action taken by the American Convention under the influence of Mr. Judge's strong stand for the retention of the old "war-horse" of the Society.

Lucifer for May, 1892, refers to the action taken by the American Convention, as reported by Mr. Mead who had attended the Convention as a delegate from the English Theosophists. The substance of the various resolutions adopted is given and Mrs. Besant comments:

> . . . these resolutions, of course, do not bind the Society and no definite arrangement can be come to until the European Section has added its voice to those of the other Sections. With a Society extending all over the world, it takes a long time to reach a decision, but it is pleasant to see the good feeling which is manifested on all sides, and the strong wish to recognize good service in the past as giving claim to the utmost consideration. It is clear that Bro. Judge will be the next President, whether now or at some future date, but whether he will take office at once or not will remain doubtful for some months. Meanwhile, as no practical difficulty is caused by the delay, we can all possess our souls in patience, and rejoice, at the brotherly feeling shown in the American Section, alike in the wish to delay parting with the President-Founder as long as possible, and in the unanimous choice of a successor.

The Convention of the European Section met at London on July 14, 1892. Mr. Judge, who was present, was, on Mrs. Besant's motion, unanimously elected Chairman. Mrs. Besant's report of the Convention in the August

Lucifer, recites that "the Chairman delivered an earnest opening address, recalling the memory of H.P.B., and speaking of the work done by Col. Olcott, the President-Founder, "work that no one else had done" and to be ever held in grateful remembrance in the Society. He also read a telegram from Col. Olcott, wishing success to the Convention, and a letter of greeting from the American Section. . . ."

In this letter of greeting, which was signed by Mr. Judge as General Secretary, for the Executive Committee of the American Section, he speaks on the subject of Col. Olcott's resignation as follows:

> At our Convention in April last we asked you to unite with us in a request to Colonel Olcott to revoke his resignation. This we did in candour and friendship, leaving it to you to decide your course. We recollected what was so often and so truly said by H. P. Blavatsky, that this organization, unique in this century, partook of the life of its parents. One of them was Col. Olcott. It would be disloyal to our ideals to hurry in accepting his resignation, even though we knew that we might get on without his presence at the head. And if he should hold to his determination our loving request would fill his remaining years with pleasing remembrances of his brothers without a trace of bitterness. . . .

The Convention began its regular business—so runs the account in *Lucifer*—"by receiving the votes of the Section as to the election of President, the General Secretary [G. R. S. Mead] moving:

> *Whereas,* the President-Founder T.S., Colonel H. S. Olcott, owing to ill-health, has placed his resignation in the hands of the Vice-President, William Q. Judge; and
>
> *Whereas,* the votes of the European Section T.S., having been duly taken by the General

> Secretary, and the result declared that the choice of the European Section of a President to succeed Col. Olcott is William Q. Judge:
>
> *Resolved:* that this Convention unanimously and enthusiastically confirms this vote, and chooses William Q. Judge as the succeeding President of the T.S.
>
> Brother Jose Xifre [Delegate from Spain] seconded the resolution—continues *Lucifer*—and it was endorsed by a delegate from each country and carried with much applause. And so was taken an important step in the history of the T.S., and there remains only the Indian Section to speak its choice in unison, we may hope, with the American and the European, so that the first choice of a President may be unanimous.

A second resolution offered by Mrs. Besant provided for the opening of a fund as a testimonial to Col. Olcott. The Convention ordered a telegram of greeting to be sent to Col. Olcott. Another resolution was proposed and carried unanimously, as follows:

> *Whereas,* this Convention has taken into due consideration the resolutions of our American brethren at their last Convention touching the resignation of the President-Founder; and
>
> *Whereas,* we have heard the answer of the President-Founder himself to these resolutions.
>
> *Resolved:* that while agreeing most cordially with the fraternal spirit of good-will that has animated the resolutions of our Brethren, and desiring always to co-operate with them in this liberal and commendable spirit, we consider that the answer of the President-Founder renders any further action impossible.

Another resolution unanimously passed declared the neutrality of the T.S. in matters of religious and philosophical opinion, and re-affirmed the freedom of the Society from any creed, dogma, or formulated belief other than its three proclaimed Objects.

The action taken by the European Section with reference to his tendered resignation filled Col. Olcott with disappointment and placed him in a most cruel dilemma. Encouraged by the American Convention in its resolutions, restored to confidence in a way out of the predicament in which he had placed himself, braced by private letters of Mr. Judge and the Message transmitted to him as from the Masters, Col. Olcott, to whom his position and title were as the breath of life and to whose fulfillment he had given that life, evidently had expected no other outcome to the European Convention than the passage by it of resolutions of the same tenor as the American Convention's, urging him to withdraw his proffered resignation. That he took stock of his paramount longing is apparent from the "Supplement" to *The Theosophist* for September, 1892.

EXECUTIVE ORDERS

THEOSOPHICAL SOCIETY

PRESIDENT'S OFFICE,
21st August, 1892.

THE PRESIDENT'S RETIREMENT

In January last, confined to my room by sickness, lame in both feet, unable to move about, save on crutches, and yearning for rest after many years of incessant work, I carried out a purpose long entertained and sent the Vice-President my resignation of the Presidentship. I should have exercised my constitutional right and named him as my successor if I had not been told that the American and European Sections would not consent to having the office filled during my lifetime, this being, they thought, the truest compliment that could be paid me. Immediately I began building the cottage at

Ootacamund on land bought in 1888, as a retreat for H.P.B. and myself in our old age.

On the 11th February, however, the familiar voice of my Guru chided me for attempting to retire before my time, asserted the unbroken relation between Himself, H.P.B. and myself, and bade me to receive further and more specific orders by messenger, but without naming the time or place.

The Indian Section had, as early as February last, unanimously agreed to recommend that, if I were really compelled to retire, the Presidential office should not be filled during my lifetime, but my duties performed by the Vice-President, acting as P.T.S. Nearly all the Indian branches and most influential members, as well as the Branches and chief members in Australasia and Ceylon, and many in Europe and America wrote to express their hope that I might yet see my way to retaining an office in which I had given satisfaction.

Under date of April 20th, Mr. Judge cabled from New York that he was not then able to relinquish the Secretaryship of the American Section and wrote me, enclosing a transcript of a message he had also received for me from a Master that "it is not time, nor right, nor just, nor wise, nor the real wish of the .·. that you should go out, either corporeally or officially."

The Chicago Convention of the American Section, held in the same month, unanimously adopted Resolutions declaring their choice of Mr. Judge as my constitutional successor, but asking me not to retire.

The London Convention of the European Section, held in July, also unanimously declared its choice of Mr. Judge as my successor and adopted complimentary Resolutions about myself, but abstained from passing upon the question of my remaining in office under the misapprehension

—how caused I know not—that I had definitely and finally refused to revoke my January letter of resignation. The fact being that the terms of my May note upon the subject . . . left the question open and dependent upon the contingencies of my health and the proof that my return to office would be for the best interest of the Society.

A long rest in the mountains has restored my health and renewed my mental and physical vigor, and therefore, since further suspense would injure the Society, I hereby give notice that I revoke my letter of resignation and resume active duties and responsibilities of office: and I declare William Q. Judge, Vice-President, my constitutional successor, and eligible for duty as such upon his relinquishment of any other office in the Society which he may hold at the time of my death.

H. S. Olcott, P.T.S.

The Path for October, 1892, contains the following under the title "Col. Olcott's Revocation"—

To the Members and Branches of T.S. in U. S.:

On the 30th of August, 1892, I received the following telegram from Col. H. S. Olcott:

"To Judge, New York: Col. H. S. Olcott remains president" (of the Theosophical Society).

Notice of this revocation of his resignation of the office of President was immediately given by me through the newspaper press of the country. His official letter arrived September 24th and is given hereunder with the accompanying circular. They are now printed for general information, and will go to the Secretaries of Branches as soon as possible.

The election of successor to the presidency

having been held in all the Sections, and the choice having been unanimous, there will be no new election for the office, but the General Council, consisting of the President and General Secretaries, will make the needed Constitutional alterations. The well-working machinery of the Sections will go on with no change of officials, and the President-Founder will remain at the head of the organization till the very last, thus fulfilling the promise given in his resignation of never ceasing to devote himself to the Cause of the Society which he has so long worked for in season and out of season, in every land and in many climates.

William Q. Judge,
Gen. Sec'y Am. Sec.

This was followed by the text of Col. Olcott's official notification and the text of the "Executive Circular" which we have given.

CHAPTER XXIII

H.P.B.'S "SUCCESSORS"—THE PUBLICATION OF "OLD DIARY LEAVES"

THE Adyar parliament following the withdrawal by Col. Olcott of his resignation was held at the close of 1892, and is notable for several matters. The Presidential Address of Col. Olcott illustrates the workings of his mind over recent events. On the subject of his late resignation he reiterates that it was prompted by ill health, and in discussing his resumption of duties as President he calls it a "sacrifice demanded by the best interests of the Society." On the action taken by the various Sections he says:

> The Indian Section expressed its desire that I should hold office for life, even without performing the duties; the American Section begged me to reconsider and cancel my resignation; and the European Section, misled by ignorance of the exact phraseology of an Executive Order which I had published, into supposing that I had absolutely refused to resume the Presidentship, simply elected Mr. Judge as my successor.

The student may compare these statements with the facts as set forth in the two preceding chapters. It is important that this should be done, as this matter of his resignation and the two bogies of "dogmatism in the T.S., and the "worship of H.P.B." continued to haunt the mind of Col. Olcott. The Presidential Address of 1892 also contains the admission by Col. Olcott that the so-called Adyar Conventions were neither official nor unofficially representative of the whole Society; it marks also the recrudescence of the effort made in 1888-9 to focus the attention of the members upon the *Society*, upon *Adyar*, upon the *official* authority of the President-Founder, as detailed in Chapters XV and XVI. Col. Olcott said on these subjects:

> The loose federal organization of the Society in autonomous Sections, provides a very efficient means of local management, but is apt to give rise to a powerful disintegrating tendency, leading individual Sections to lose sight of the unity of the Society, in an all-absorbing interest in their own special work.
>
> Under the present Rules, no General Convention of the whole T.S. is now held; and the federal unity of the whole body finds expression only in my Annual Report, which is sent to every Branch of the Society throughout the world.
>
> My Annual Report, therefore, assumes a special historic value and great importance, as it is the only means by which the members and Branches of the Society have brought before them a complete view of the Society's work as a whole. . . . For it must be remembered that the gathering I am now addressing is a purely personal one, and in no sense a Representative Convention of the whole T.S. . . . it is simply a gathering of Theosophists to whom I am reading my Annual Report before despatching it to all parts of the world. . . .
>
> It is only by viewing our work from the standpoint of the Federal Centre, the real axis of our revolving wheel, that the net loss or gain of the year's activity can be estimated. Thus, for instance, intense action is the feature within the American Section, while a marked lassitude has of late been noted in the Indian work. Europe, manifesting a maximum of activity in London, a lesser yet most creditable degree at Paris, Barcelona, The Hague, in Sweden and

elsewhere, shows seven new Branches to India's eight and America's thirteen. Thus while the outlook is not exhilarating in one part of the world, it is highly encouraging, taking the field as a whole.

An instructive contrast is offered by considering the state of the Society and the Movement in India and the Orient generally. The "marked lassitude" of which Col. Olcott speaks is made very plain by turning to the Report of Bertram Keightley, General Secretary of the Indian Section, included in the Report of the Proceedings of the Adyar Convention at the end of 1892. His report shows 145 Branches on the roll of the Indian Section, and he speaks in detail of their condition. He summarizes as follows:

> It is foolish for us to console ourselves for the many deficiencies of our Indian Section, by pointing to our long list of Branches and gazing with placid satisfaction at the numerous shields on these walls, when we know in our inmost hearts, that there are, as my report shows, *only five Branches that are really doing satisfactory work.*

When the student remembers that the Indian Section and the Orient generally, had been, since 1885, exclusively under the unquestioned control and inspiration of the President-Founder, supported at all times by the loyal co-operation of H.P.B. and W.Q.J., supported also in great part by dues and voluntary contributions from America and England, and by numerous volunteer workers who went in a steady succession from the West to the East, but two conclusions can be drawn: *First,* that Col. Olcott's ideas as to the proper basis for work were erroneous; *second,* that the spirit of the First Object and the teachings of Theosophy made no *practical* appeal either to the Hindus or to himself. They, like himself, were interested primarily in the Second and

Third Objects and in the Society as a forum for their discussion—not in Brotherhood and "the vital principles which underlie the philosophical systems of old."

Turning now from the public phases of events and their discussion in the Sectional Conventions, in the various Reports, and in the three leading magazines, *The Theosophist, Lucifer,* and *The Path,* it is informative to review the trend of the Esoteric Section or School during the same period and in relation to the same issues. The re-organization of the School and the reaffirmation of principles and policies as contained in the Circular of May 27, 1891, have already been described.[1] Under the clear and logical lines thus established the work of the School proceeded apace, free from dissensions or disharmonies. The public writings of H.P.B. and of others recommended by her, the private Instructions issued by H.P.B., and the various papers with "Suggestions and Aids" supplied by Mr. Judge and Mrs. Besant as joint Heads of the School, afforded abundant and consistent material for study and application in daily life. The Rules of the School itself, the incentive provided by its teachings and purposes and the example of Mr. Judge and Mrs. Besant were ample to make the members active and energetic in the public promulgation of Theosophy and in the support of the T.S., while the very freedom from any taint of authority, external supervision or prescribed regulations but caused the members to be voluntarily more self-sacrificing in time, money, and work to make the exoteric Society a real and true success in the line of its proclaimed Objects. It should be clearly borne in mind that the Instructions of H.P.B. to the E.S.T. were in no sense orders, but simply more definite and specific statements of Teaching than are contained in her exoteric writings. The Rules of the School were, in the same way, not regulations to be enforced by any outside pressure of superior authorities, but those statements of discipline and conduct which each member voluntarily gave his "most solemn and sacred word of honor" to enforce

[1] See Chapter XIX.

upon himself in his own thoughts and actions. And it should be remembered that while thousands of members of the T.S. were not members of the E.S., no one could enter or remain in the E.S. who was not also a member of the T.S. In a word: the exoteric Theosophical Society had three defined Objects and was committed to no religion, no philosophy, no science, no system of thought; the Esoteric School had the same Three Objects, but in addition its members were voluntarily pledged to do their utmost to make those Objects effective in their own lives through the study and practice of *Theosophy,* exoteric and esoteric. As, outside of Col. Olcott and Mr. Sinnett, nearly all of those most active in the Society were pledged probationers of the Esoteric School, there was necessarily room for speculation, question, doubt, and suspicion among members of the exoteric Society not members of the E.S. as to that body. As has been noted,[2] these fears possessed Col. Olcott long before the formation of the E.S., and continued till long afterwards. H.P.B. had done her utmost to allay them during her lifetime. It was not long after her death before the stand taken in regard to her and her work by the reorganized E.S. became a matter of more or less common knowledge in the exoteric Society, and it was this which in fact stirred Col. Olcott to renewed apprehension lest there arise an "H.P.B. cult," "worship" of H.P.B., "dogmatism in the T.S." and a "breach of the neutrality of the T.S." in matters of opinion and belief, and led to his public remarks in his Presidential Address at the Adyar Convention at the close of 1891. How these apprehensions and misapprehensions were met publicly by Mrs. Besant and Mr. Judge has already been shown.[3] Within the School itself a circular, "strictly private and only for E.S. members" as usual, was sent out on March 29, 1892. It began with an "IMPORTANT NOTICE" in italics, reading as follows:

> *The E.S.T. has no official connection with the Theosophical Society.*

[2] See Chapters X and XI.
[3] See Chapter XX.

> *When first organized it was known as a section of the T.S. but it being seen that the perfect freedom and public character of the Society might be interfered with, H.P.B., some time before her departure, gave notice that all official connection between the two should end, and then changed the name to the present one.*
>
> *This leaves all T.S. officials who are in the E.S.T. perfectly free in their official capacity, and also permits members if asked to say with truth that the School has no official connection with the T.S. and is not a part of it.*
>
> *Members will please bear this in mind.*
>
> ANNIE BESANT
> WILLIAM Q. JUDGE.

The body of the circular contained an added reference to the subject under the caption, "THE T.S. AND THE SCHOOL":

> Members must carefully remember that the School has no official connection with the Society [T.S.], although none are admitted who are not F.T.S. [Fellows of the T.S.] Hence the T.S. must not be compromised by members of the School. We must all recollect that the T.S. is a free open body. So if one of the Heads is also an official in the T.S., his or her words or requests as such T.S. official must not under any circumstances be colored or construed on the basis of the work of this School.
>
> This caution is necessary because some members have said to the General Secretary of the U. S. Sect. T. S. [Mr. Judge] that they regarded his words as such official to be an order. This is improper and may lead to trouble if members cannot see their plain ethical duty under the pledge. They are, surely, to work for the T.S., but must also use their common-sense *and never let the T.S. become dogmatic.*

Although this circular was signed by both Mrs. Besant and Mr. Judge, it was in fact written by Mr. Judge, and its occasion is an illustration of the difficulties under which he, like H.P.B. before him, labored in trying to secure continuity of policy in line with proclaimed principles on the part of associates. The occasion was as follows: Following the public news of the resignation of Col. Olcott, Mrs. Besant, then full of faith in Mr. Judge and of zeal to influence others to adopt her own particular ideas, had sent out on March 10, 1892, a circular letter to all members of the School urging the election of Mr. Judge to the office of President of the T.S. This circular of Mrs. Besant's was sent out without Mr. Judge's knowledge. So soon as he learned of it he prepared the circular of March 29, from which we have been quoting, to offset as far as possible the mischief it might lead to, and to restate the true position without chagrin for Mrs. Besant.

The aftermath of Mrs. Besant's circular is equally interesting and instructive. As Mr. Judge had anticipated, some members of the E.S. took Mrs. Besant's circular as an "order," and others resented it as an interference; still others saw in it an attempt of the E.S. to control the T.S. and make a breach in the neutrality of the exoteric Society. And when the July, 1892, Convention of the European Section ignored the request of the American Section to join with it in asking Col. Olcott to revoke his resignation, and instead accepted the resignation as a *fait accompli,* its action was ascribed by many to the E.S. influence exerted by Mrs. Besant's circular. And since Mr. Judge seemed in their eyes to have been the beneficiary, as he was chosen President in place of Col. Olcott, it was easy for the jealous and suspicious minded to conclude that the whole proceeding had been, if not actually engineered by him, at least carried through with his tacit approval. And this was actually one of the charges against him in the affairs of 1894-5. It is now time that the actual facts and real actors should be known and the circular to the E.S. of March 29, 1892, three months before the European Convention of that year, shows Mr. Judge's entire innocence and good faith. More, when the suspicions spoken of were voiced, as they were, immediately following the European Section Convention in July, 1892, by partisans and friends of Col. Olcott and by others envious of the sudden rise to prominence and power of Mrs. Besant, Mr. Judge joined with Mrs. Besant in signing the circular sent out by her from London, dated August 1, 1892, explaining and defending her action. This circular, written by Mrs. Besant, and sent to all E.S. members, is really a key to the workings of her consciousness when her actions, good or bad, were questioned by anyone. She says:

> You will see that Annie Besant, as one of the two to whom MASTERS committed the charge of the E.S.T., was discharging an obvious duty when she called on members of the School to show strength, quietness, and absence of prejudice, and to try and infuse similar qualities into the branches of the Society at such an important time as the first Presidential Election. The direction to act as pacificators and to make harmony their object, is in exact accord with the word of our Teacher, H.P.B. . . .
>
> There remains the statement, not made as one of the Outer Heads, that Annie Besant hoped that the choice of the Society would fall upon William Q. Judge, as President, and it was suggested . . . that this would be taken as a direction to Esotericists to vote for him, although they were told, in so many words, that as no direction had come each must use his own best judgment. But had a far stronger form of advice been used, would the liberty of members have been unfairly infringed? Once more a glance at the past may help us. The first form of pledge in the School bound the disciple "to obey, without cavil or delay, the orders of the Head of the E.S. *in all that concerns my relation with the Theosophical Movement.*" On be-

> coming an Esotericist he voluntarily abdicated his liberty as regarded the Exoteric Society, and bound himself to carry out in the Exoteric Society the orders he received from the head of the E.S.
>
> It is true that this simple frank pledge was altered by H.P.B. in consequence of the criticism of some, who feared lest obedience against conscience should be claimed by her; but, as she herself said, the remodeled clause was a farce. She changed it, not because the new form was good, but because Western students were, many of them, not ready to pass under Occult training. They do not understand the privilege of obedience, when rendered to such as are the MASTERS. . . .
>
> Obedience is forced on none: . . . Meanwhile let all feel assured that neither of us two will make any attempt to give orders to the School, except in its societies and ordinary work, and that you are free to accept or reject our advice as you will.

Certain exceptions must be taken to the foregoing as to matters of fact: (1) the original "pledge" was not, in fact, in the wording given in quotation by Mrs. Besant; (2) no member was ever asked, attempted to be influenced, or permitted to "abdicate his liberty" in the exoteric Society, or "bind himself to carry out in the exoteric Society the orders he received from the Head of the E.S.," either by H.P.B. or Mr. Judge or in any messages received through them from the Masters; these are Mrs. Besant's own interpretations and conclusions; (3) "obedience to the Masters," is one thing, obedience to the "Outer Head of the E.S.," quite another thing, whether that "Outer Head" were H.P.B., Mr. Judge, Mrs. Besant, or anyone else; (4) the pledge, Rules, and Instructions of the E.S.T. were for the help and guidance of the members in their relation of *pupils* to a *teacher* in a *School,* not for the regulation and government of an organization by its *authorities*, and were uniformly so stated to be and so construed by both H.P.B. and W.Q.J.

It may be asked, Why did not Mr. Judge himself take exceptions to this circular of Mrs. Besant's which he signed with her? The answer is obvious to any mind which can grasp the spirit of the Movement and the related facts. Mr. Judge *did* take exceptions *in advance*, by stating the true position in the circular of March 29, 1892,—the same position that both H.P.B. and himself had repeatedly taken previously, both in the School and in the public Society.[4] When Mrs. Besant asked him to sign with her this defensive circular of August 1, 1892, he was placed in the same position as H.P.B. so often was in relation with Col. Olcott: Having stated the true position on his own account, he went to the utmost limits to shelter and support a colleague who had erred, and left to the discrimination of the students themselves to make their own application. To have done other than as he did would have been himself to violate the spirit of the School, to infringe on the freedom of the members, to expose the mistakes of a co-worker and to invite a rupture. All the members of the School had the pledge, the various E.S. communications of H.P.B., and her *Preliminary Memoranda and Instructions;* it was for the members to *apply* them to the case in hand, uncoached and uninterfered with. To have interfered, except in a drastic emergency where the course was not clear upon reflection, was to retard or subvert the very purposes of the School as set forth in one of the most important of the Rules:

> It is required of a member that when a question arises it shall be deeply thought over from all its aspects, to the end that he may find the answer himself; and in no case shall questions be asked . . . until the person has exhausted every ordinary means of solving the doubt or of acquiring himself the information sought. *Otherwise*

[4] See Chapter XVI.

his intuition will never be developed; he will not learn self-reliance; and two of the main objects of the School will be defeated.

In other words, the very object of the mission and message of H.P.B., esoteric and exoteric, was to destroy that *authority* which human nature alternately seeks to impose or to lean upon. Another episode, equally illustrative of this human tendency to substitute some authority for self-knowledge, as of its other pole, the ambition to pose "as one having authority" before the ignorant, the credulous, and the self-seeking, is to be found in the question of "successorship" which was raised immediately after the death of H.P.B.

In human jurisprudence succession relates to the transmission of property, rights, privileges, power, authority, obligations, and responsibility. Ecclesiastically, the doctrine generally denominated apostolic succession is as old as popular religion and is integral with the idea of a priesthood. "The King never dies," and "the King can do no wrong," are two ancient phrases which convey the conception of the "divine right of kings" and the transmission of the kingly office from predecessor to successor. In religious history both myth and tradition, as well as accredited records, show that in all times, among all peoples, in all religions, there has been a deeply imbedded corresponding notion that spiritual knowledge and its concomitants can be conveyed by some sort of gift or endowment. This proceeds from the assumption that the Founder can convey His nature to His Disciples, they to their disciples, and so on in an unbroken line of transmission, the same as a physical object can be passed on from hand to hand. Inseparably bound up with this popular dogma are the ideas that some particular tribe, or caste or association, made up of the individuals thus endowed and their followers and believers, are the *chosen* vehicle of this apostolic succession, which is conveyed by birth, by baptism, by laying on of hands, by election, by ordination, by other rites and ceremonies; and that a peculiar and sacred authority attaches by virtue thereof to the particular individuals and associations, who are thus able to bind or loose, to save or damn the common herd of mankind. The whole claim of the Brahmin caste in India, of the Roman Catholic Hierarchy, of the Greek Catholic Church, of the Anglican Communion, to consideration rests upon this popular superstition and upon the vast edifice of theological subtleties erected by endless generations of false prophets and priests. It is the basis of Judaism and Mohammedanism, and the various Protestant Christian sects equally depend on this dogma.

The prime mission of H. P. Blavatsky, as of every other religious Founder and Reformer, was to destroy this monstrous parasite on human faith in the Divine in Nature and in Man, in the only way it can ever be destroyed: By pointing out its fundamental inequity and injustice on the one hand, and, on the other, by spreading far and wide true basic concepts of Deity, of Law, and of Man,—ideas so unassailably just, so logically sequential, so scientifically buttressed, so philosophically sound, so self-evidently manifest in every department of nature, that none but the fool and the false could fail to grasp them. "Isis Unveiled," from beginning to end, was written with this very object in view, as were all her other writings; the Theosophical Society and its Esoteric Section had the same great objective: The *Theosophical Movement* exists for no other purpose than to supplant this monstrous heresy on true religion, pure and undefiled, by giving mankind *Knowledge* in place of belief; Teachers in place of priestly authority. To quote all that H.P.B. has written upon this subject and its cognates is to quote all that she ever wrote. But two citations from "Isis Unveiled" will serve to give her views; for her reasons, arguments, and evidences, the student must study the work itself. Thus, near the close of Volume 2 (p. 544), she says:

> The present volumes have been written to small purpose if they have not shown . . . that . . . apostolic succession is a gross and palpable fraud.

And again, page 635 of the same volume:

> The world needs no sectarian church, whether of Buddha, Jesus, Mahomet, Swedenborg, Calvin, or any other. There being but ONE Truth, man requires but one church—the Temple of God within us, walled in by matter but penetrable by any one who can find the way; *the pure in heart see God.*

When H.P.B. died the first question in the minds of many of the members, as in public curiosity, was, Who will be her successor? At once the newspapers responded to this gullibility and desire for sensation. Within a week from the death of H.P.B. the Paris press announced that Madame Marie Caithness, Duchess of Pomar, had been "chosen" by H.P.B. as her successor. The Duchess had been a long-time friend of H.P.B., who had been her guest during the stay in Paris in 1884; she was "psychic"; she was greatly interested in the "Occult"; she was socially prominent. It was enough! She was promptly accepted by many French "spiritists" with Theosophical leanings as the new wearer of the mantle of the prophet. The fire promptly spread to England; Mrs. Besant was "written up" as the successor. She was brilliant; she was famous; she had been the right hand of H.P.B. for two years; she was an Occultist; she was head and shoulders above any Theosophist before the public; *ergo*, she was the successor. In America the same curiosity and interest existed and Mr. Judge was considered the foreordained successor. But when the versatile reporters sought to interview him, he received them in a body and made to them the succinct statement: "Madame Blavatsky was *sui generis.* She has, and can have, no 'successor.' "

Nevertheless, the appetite existed and public curiosity did not lack for nourishment. A score of mediums and psychics in as many different cities announced for themselves, on the strength of real or pretended messages from their several guides and controls that they were, each of them, the successor of Madame Blavatsky. Not a month passed but a new successor was heralded by some trustful believer in his claims, or claimed for himself by some less modest aspirant. In nearly every large center of the Society there was to be found some Occultist who was not averse to letting it be known that he was "in communication with the Masters," and each of these had his believers and his imitators. Late in 1891, Mr. Henry B. Foulke of Philadelphia, Pa., claimed to be Madame Blavatsky's successor. Mr. Foulke had been a member of the Esoteric Section, and had corresponded with H.P.B. His claim was that H.P.B. had "appointed" him during her life and that since her death he had received communications from her confirming the appointment, bidding him demand recognition and take over the direction of the Society and the guidance of the School. He therefore wrote to Col. Olcott, Mrs. Besant, and Mr. Judge, offering to submit his "proofs," and, upon their refusal to pay any attention to him or his claims of successorship, made his claims public through the newspapers. Mrs. Besant and Mr. Judge promptly suspended him from his membership in the Esoteric Section; whereupon he resigned from the E.S. and from the Society. Mr. Foulke and his claims were taken up by a number of papers, notably the *Wilkes-Barre (Pa.) Times.* Mr. Judge wrote two letters on the subject to the *Times*, and these were reprinted by Mrs. Besant in *Lucifer* for March, 1892. For their present as well as their historical value, we give here the text of the germane portions of these two letters by Mr. Judge, as published in *Lucifer,* accompanied by Mrs. Besant's comment: "As non-theosophists . . . were to some extent misled by the preposterous fiction, W. Q. Judge sent the following letters to the paper in which the statement first appeared":

Editor *Times:*

Will you permit me to correct the statement . . . that Madame Blavatsky appointed as her "successor" Mr. Henry B. Foulke, and "guaranteed" to him the "allegiance" of the "higher spiritual intelligences and forces." As one of Madame Blavatsky's oldest and most intimate friends, connected with her most closely in the foundation and work of the Theosophical Society, and familiar with her teachings, purposes, ideas, forecasts, I am in a position to assure . . . the public that there is not an atom of foundation for the statement quoted.

Madame Blavatsky has no "successor," could have none, never contemplated, selected, or notified one. Her work and status were unique. Whether or not her genuineness as a spiritual teacher be admitted matters not: she *believed* it to be so, and all who enjoyed her confidence will unite with me in the assertion that she never even hinted at "succession," "allegiance," or "guarantee." Even if a successor was possible, Mr. Foulke could not be he. He is not a member of the Theosophical Society, does not accept its and her teachings, had a very slight and brief acquaintance with her, and pretends to no interest in her views, life or mission. Of her actual estimate of him I have ample knowledge.

But anyhow, no "guaranteeing of allegiance of spiritual forces" is practicable by anyone. Knowledge of and control over the higher potencies in Nature comes only by individual attainment through long discipline and conquest. It can no more be transferred than can a knowledge of Greek, of chemistry, psychology, or of medicine. If a person moves on a lofty level, it is because he worked his way there. This is true in spiritual things as in mental. When Mr. Foulke produces a work like *Isis Unveiled* or *The Secret Doctrine,* he may be cited as H.P.B.'s intellectual peer; when he imparts such impulsion as does *The Voice of the Silence,* he may be recognized as her spiritual equal; when he adds to these an utter consecration to the work of the T.S. as his lifelong mission, he may participate in such "succession" as the case admits. But it will not be through alleged precipitated pictures and imagined astral shapes. The effect of these on Theosophy . . . may be stated in one word—nothing.

Yours truly,

William Q. Judge,

Gen. Sec'y American Sec.

Editor *Times:*

Will you allow me a word—my last—respecting the Foulke claim to succeed Mme. Blavatsky.

First. If Mr. Foulke . . . has precipitated pictures of Mme. Blavatsky produced since her demise . . . Precipitations are not uncommon, but are no evidence of anything whatever save the power to precipitate and the fact of precipitation. Spiritualists have always asserted that their mediums could procure these things. Chemists also can precipitate substances out of the air. So this point is wide of the Society and its work.

Second. As I said in my previous letter, when Mr. Foulke, or any one, indeed, proves by his work and attainments that he is as great as Mme. Blavatsky, every one will at once recognize that fact. But irresponsible mediumship, or what we call astral intoxication, will not prove these attainments nor constitute that work.

Third. Mme. Blavatsky was Corresponding Secretary of the Theosophical Society, and its Constitution years ago provided that office, out of compliment to her, should become extinct upon her death. . . . The Society will hardly hurry to revive it for the sake of one who is not a member of the body and who has never thrown any particular glory upon it. Scarcely either because he is a medium—and not even a good one—who prates of receiving messages from beyond the grave assumed to be from Mme. Blavatsky. He may assert that he has baskets full of letters from Mme. Blavatsky written before her death, and we are not interested either to deny the assertion or to desire to see the documents.

Fourth. The Theosophical Society is a body governed by Rules embodied in its Constitution. Its officers are elected by votes, and not by the production of precipitated letters or pictures of any sort. It generally elects those who do its work, and not outsiders who masquerade as recipients of directions from the abode of departed souls. It is not likely to request proposed officers to produce documents . . . brought forth at mediumistic séances before the wondering eyes of untrained witnesses. . . .

Fifth. Mr. Foulke's possession of any number of letters written by Mme. Blavatsky prior to her demise, offering him "leadership" or "succession," might please and interest himself, but can have no other effect on the corporate body of the Society. Let him preserve them or otherwise as he may see fit; they are utterly without bearing or even authority, and if in existence would only serve to show that she in her lifetime may have given him a chance to do earnest sincere work for a Society she had at heart and that he neglected the opportunity, passing his time in idle, fantastic day-dreams.

Yours truly,

WILLIAM Q. JUDGE,
Gen. Sec'y American Sec.

In the "Supplement" to *The Theosophist* for April, 1892, Col. Olcott paid his compliments to the "successorship" idea in the following paragraph, printed under the title, "H.P.B.'s Ghost":

A rubbishing report is circulating to the effect that H.P.B. chose Mr. Foulke of Philadel-

> phia, as her "Successor," and ratified her act by appearing in a spiritualistic circle and painting for him her portrait. As to the picture having been painted I say nothing save that it is no more improbable than other portrait paintings in mediumistic circles: but this does not imply that she painted it. And to offset that theory one has but to refer back to an old volume of *The Theosophist* to find that she and I, anticipating some such nonsense, published our joint declaration that under no circumstances should we visit after death a medium or a circle, and authorizing our friends to declare false any story to the contrary. As for her naming a "Successor," Beethoven or Edison, Magliabecchi or Milton might just as well declare A, B or C the heirs of their genius. *Blavatsky nascitur, non fit.*
>
> H. S. O.

Mrs. Besant in the "Watch-Tower" of *Lucifer*, for May, 1892, follows up this and her reprint a couple of months before of the two letters by Mr. Judge, with the following:

> There is a wonderful amount of masquerading under the name of H. P. Blavatsky in the post-mortem realms, but the various mummers do not agree in their presentations. . . . Each new mumming spook claims to be the real and only one, and the latest of them claims to be the first real appearance, all the others being humbugs. With this spook I heartily agree on all points save one—that I include itself with the rest.

In *The Path* for July, 1892, Mr. Judge has an opening editorial article on the subject for the edification of his readers. The article is entitled, "How She Must Laugh." We quote:

> Since the demise of H. P. Blavatsky's body, a little over a year ago, mediums in various parts

of the world have reported her "spirit" as giving communications . . .

Those who communicate these extraordinary reports from H.P.B. are not accused by us of malice or any improper motive. The first "message" came privately from one who had known her in life but whose views were always quite in line with the message. The others represent the different private opinions of the medium or clairvoyant reporting them. Such is nearly always the case with these "spirit messages." They do, indeed, come from psychic planes, and are not strictly the product of the medium's normal brain. But they are the result of obscure thoughts of the medium which color the astral atmosphere, and thus do no more than copy the living. In one case, and this was the hugest joke of all, the medium made a claim to at once step into H.P.B.'s shoes and be acknowledged the leader of the Society.

How she must laugh! Unless mere death may change a sage into an idiot, she is enjoying these jokes, for she had a keen sense of humor, and as it is perfectly certain that Theosophists are not at all disturbed by these "communications," her enjoyment of the fun is not embittered by the idea that staunch old-time Theosophists are being troubled. But what a fantastical world it is with its Materialists, Spiritualists, Christians, Jews, and other barbarians as well as the obscure Theosophists.

Although H.P.B.'s position in regard to "succession" was made known in the very beginning of her mission, and although Mrs. Besant and Col. Olcott, following Mr. Judge, put their views on record in full accord, as shown by the foregoing quotations, we shall find that the ghost of "apostolic succession" was raised again within less than three years. It, together with the other events we have been recounting, and Col. Olcott's "Old

Diary Leaves," supplied the necessary groundwork and material on and out of which was fabricated the "Judge case." Until all these connected and connecting events are co-ordinated in the mind of the student like the features of a map he will be unable to trace intelligently the divergent courses soon to be taken by the various "pilgrims"; unable to understand the *débâcle* which befell the Society; unable to solve the mystery of the confusions and contradictions in the Theosophical world of today; unable to find and follow the "straight and narrow path" of the true Theosophical Movement; unable to do his part in restoring the work of the Movement to its pristine unity and purity.

"Old Diary Leaves" was begun by Col. Olcott in *The Theosophist* for March, 1892. Its commencement was, therefore, coincident in time and occasion with the issue of the "worship" of H.P.B., with the issue of "dogmatism in the T.S." and "the neutrality of the T.S.," with the issue of the relation of the Esoteric School to the T.S., and with Col. Olcott's resignation as President of the Society. This prolonged series of personal reminiscences was continued from month to month in *The Theosophist*, with occasional brief interruptions, until the death of Col. Olcott in 1907. Thus during fifteen years a steady stream of autobiographical articles flowed through the pages of the oldest and most widely circulated of the Theosophical magazines and the only official organ of the Society; articles written by the man who had from the beginning been the President of the Society and who, after the death of Mr. Judge in 1896, was the sole survivor of the original three Founders. "Old Diary Leaves" is written in an easy, lucid, and interesting style; it abounds in personal recollections of H.P.B.; it overflows with stories of marvelous and mysterious phenomena; it deals graphically with the human and anecdotal side of the various actors in the Society's life—a side purposely ignored in all the writings of H.P.B. and W. Q. Judge. No one who has studied the life and writings of Col. Olcott can doubt his honesty, his frankness, his sincerity—the admirable qualities, in short, which make up the charm of human nature. And certainly no genuine chela, or even Probationer of the Second Section, can ever fail to sympathize with him in his struggles with those elements of human nature which are the real foes of every aspirant in *Occultism.* That he failed in the supreme trials of the neophyte does not dishonor nor militate against his real virtues, nor render less the debt which every Theosophist must gladly acknowledge to him for his great sacrifices and services. The final test of character, however, is not in the strength, but in the weaknesses of the candidate, and history is filled with the record of those whose defects became the axis for the overthrow of all that they labored mightily to achieve.

For nearly twenty-five years "Old Diary Leaves" has been read by Theosophists and others of the present generation. Its statements have been accepted without question by most students, and their views in respect to Madame H. P. Blavatsky, Mr. W. Q. Judge, and many others have been colored and formed by the opinions of Col. Olcott and those whose interest it was to support them. Few indeed have taken thought or trouble to submit the different actors and exponents in Theosophical history to any critical examination. Yet the criteria of correct judgment are not difficult to ascertain or to apply. Most judgments are formed upon hearsay, and that testimony is almost always accepted with least question which is most conformable to the interest or the nature of the would-be judge. Seldom is any witness subjected to the test of the comparison of his different statements on the same subjects, let alone their comparison with the statements of others; still more rarely are the motive and animus of a witness subjected to scrutiny. Yet the whole course of human jurisprudence has shown that unless these and other precautions are rigidly observed the judgment is certain to be misled and a false verdict reached. Just as a biased attitude may, and but too often does, exist in the would-be judge unconsciously to himself, so it may and often does exist in a witness otherwise candid and sincere, and this is pre-eminently the case with Col. Olcott; so pre-eminently that it requires but casual comparison of his various statements to see that Col. Olcott is anything but a dependable witness; the more untrustworthy because his very honesty and frankness tend to lead the reader astray as the Colonel was himself led.

When he began the writing of "Old Diary Leaves," he was more than sixty years of age, broken in health, deeply wounded in his feelings over the charges which caused him to offer his resignation; over the apparent ingratitude with which his lifelong services had been rewarded; over the loss of an official pre-eminence and prerogative dear to his heart; over the seeming unconcern with which his resignation was received by Theosophists at large; and dejected in spirit by the prospect of being speedily forgotten and replaced in the esteem of the members by younger colleagues who had hardly received a wound while he was rejected for the very scars he had suffered in their service. He could but too easily vision H.P.B. placed on a pedestal and himself neglected in his old age, destined to an equally neglected memory. He could but too easily see Mr. Judge elected his successor—Judge who was but a boy while he was bearing the brunt of battle—and receiving the acclaim and honors made possible by his own sacrifices. His memory, never dependable, as he himself often declared, became a quicksand as the years progressed and the storms broke upon his beloved Society. He was in his seventy-fifth year when the last instalment of "Old Diary Leaves" was written—and the last ten years of his life were doubly embittered; embittered by the private contumely and neglect of those who had used him as their tool; embittered by the perception too late of his colossal blunders, which yet he had not the strength and stamina publicly to acknowledge, though he did so in private to the one of the early years most loved by him, and most loyal to him through all his divagations.[5] These

[5] See *The Word* for October, 1915, article "Colonel Olcott: a Reminiscence." The anonymous writer was in fact Mrs. Laura Langford (Mrs. L. C. Holloway) one of the two authors of "Man: Fragment of Forgotten History."

things being recognized, justice can be done to his colleagues and to the "true history of the Theosophical Society" without doing injustice to Henry S. Olcott. Until even justice is done to all, how can the work of the Theosophical Movement be restored? And how can that justice be done except in the spirit of the Preface of "Isis Unveiled"? The investigator must proceed "in all sincerity; he must do even justice, and speak the truth alike without malice or prejudice; he must show neither mercy for enthroned error, nor reverence for usurped authority. He must demand for a spoliated past, that credit for its achievements which has been too long withheld. He must call for a restitution of borrowed robes, and the vindication of glorious but calumniated reputations."

"Old Diary Leaves," after serial publication in *The Theosophist* during three years, were issued in book form in 1895. This first volume contains a "*Foreword*" especially written by Col. Olcott. His real motives in writing his reminiscences are there for the first time publicly acknowledged—motives entirely unknown and unsuspected by Theosophical students during their magazine publication. He says:

> The controlling impulse to prepare these papers was a desire to combat a growing tendency within the Society to deify Mme. Blavatsky, and to give her commonest literary productions a quasi-inspirational character. Her transparent faults were being blindly ignored, and the pinchbeck screen of pretended authority drawn between her actions and legitimate criticism. Those who had least of her actual confidence, and hence knew least of her private character, were the greatest offenders in this direction. It was but too evident that unless I spoke out what I alone knew, the true history of our movement could never be written, nor the actual merit of my wonderful colleague become known. In these pages I have, therefore, told the truth about her

> and about the beginnings of the Society—truth which nobody can gainsay. . . . I have pursued my present task to its completion, despite the fact that some of my most influential colleagues have, from what I consider mistaken loyalty to "H.P.B.," secretly tried to destroy my influence, ruin my reputation, reduce the circulation of my magazine, and prevent the publication of my book. . . .
>
> . . . Karma forbid that I should do her a featherweight of injustice, but if there ever existed a person in history who was a greater conglomeration of good and bad, light and shadow, wisdom and indiscretion, spiritual insight and lack of common sense, I cannot recall the name, the circumstances or the epoch.

For contrast one has but to turn to the Henry S. Olcott of the summer of 1891, immediately after the death of H.P.B. *Lucifer* for August 15 of that year contains a long memorial article by Col. Olcott, entitled "H.P.B.'s Departure." We quote:

> . . . There is no one to replace Helena Petrovna, nor can she ever be forgotten. Others have certain of her gifts, none has them all. . . . Her life, as I have known it these past seventeen years, as friend, colleague and collaborator, has been a tragedy, the tragedy of a martyr-philanthropist. Burning with zeal for the spiritual welfare and intellectual enfranchisement of humanity, moved by no selfish inspiration, giving herself freely and without price to her altruistic work, she has been hounded to her death-day, by the slanderer, the bigot and the Pharisee. . . . In temperament and abilities as dissimilar as any two persons could well be, and often disagreeing radically in details, we have yet been of one mind and heart as regards the work in hand and in our reverent allegiance

> to our Teachers and Masters, its planners and overlookers. We both knew them personally, she a hundred times more intimately than I. . . . She was pre-eminently a double-selfed personality, one of them very antipathetic to me and some others. . . . One seeing us together would have said I had her fullest confidence, yet the fact is that, despite seventeen years of intimacy in daily work, she was an enigma to me to the end. Often I would think I knew her perfectly, and presently discover that there were deeper depths in her selfhood I had not sounded. I could never find out *who she was,* not as Helena Petrovna, . . . but as "H.P.B.," the mysterious individuality which wrote, and worked wonders. . . .
>
> We had each our department of work—hers the mystical, mine the practical. In her line, she infinitely excelled me and every other of her colleagues. I have no claim at all to the title of metaphysician, nor to anything save a block of very humble knowledge. . . .
>
> . . . She knew the bitterness and gloom of physical life well enough, often saying to me that her true existence only began when nightly she had put her body to sleep and went out of it to the Masters. I can believe that, from often sitting and watching her from across the table, when she was away from the body, and then when she returned from her soul-flight and resumed occupancy, as one might call it. When she was away the body was like a darkened house, when she was there it was as though the windows were brilliant with lights within. One who had not seen this change, cannot understand why the mystic calls his physical body, a "shadow."

Here are two violently contradictory opinions of H.P.B.—both of them from the pen of Col. Olcott. It is certain that H.P.B. had not changed from 1891 to 1895; what caused the change in Col. Olcott, and which of his opposed utterances is the more nearly accurate, the more expressive of the highest and best in him? The one view is the view expressed by the Master Himself in the letter written Col. Olcott in the early fall of 1888, the view consistently held by Mr. Judge, and consistently supported by the best evidence of all—the evidence furnished by the life and teachings of H. P. Blavatsky. The other view is the view of the S.P.R., of Mrs. Cables, of Mr. Hume, of Prof. Coues, of Miss Mabel Collins, of Mr. A. P. Sinnett. Colonel Olcott, like many another, had every *opportunity* to know the "real H.P.B.," and the world and the students took it for granted that he *did* know.

It is curious, and at this point of related value, to turn to two quotations from "Old Diary Leaves." They may afford the intuitional student a hint on some of the mysteries and methods of true Occultism, and serve at the same time to show how little able Col. Olcott was to avail himself of the rare opportunities his services brought him. Chapter XVI of the first volume of "Old Diary Leaves" discusses the mystery of H.P.B. and, amidst a mass of Col. Olcott's speculations interspersed with the alleged facts recited, makes certain highly significant statements. But first it should be noted that Chapter XIV propounds *seven distinct hypotheses* to try to "explain" H.P.B., and it and the following chapter are devoted to trying to make the facts fit one or another of these theories of the Colonel's. The mere fact that he submits seven theories should show anyone that however fertile Col. Olcott's imagination in trying to resolve the mystery, it *was* a mystery, and one he was unable to solve. Finally, in Chapter XVI he gives the two incidents spoken of. He says that one summer evening just after dinner in New York days and while it was still early twilight, he was standing by the mantel while H.P.B. sat by one of the front windows. Then:

> I heard her say "Look and learn"; and glancing that way, saw a mist rising from her head and shoulders. Presently it defined itself into the likeness of one of the Mahatmas. . . . Absorbed in watching the phenomenon, I stood silent and motionless. The shadowy shape only formed for itself the upper half of the torso, and then faded away and was gone; whether re-absorbed into H.P.B.'s body or not, I do not know. . . . When I asked her to explain the phenomenon she refused, saying that it was for me to develop my intuition so as to understand the phenomena of the world I lived in. All she could do was to help in showing me things and let me make of them what I could.

This incident is recited by Col. Olcott to suggest "that H.P.B.'s body became, at times, occupied by other entities." It seems not to have occurred to him at all that perhaps he was being afforded a glimpse of the "real H.P.B.," nor was he, who asked her for an explanation, able to relate the experience with which he was favored to the true rationale of its exhibition, given in the twelfth chapter of the second volume of "Isis Unveiled" in one of the numbered paragraphs. All he saw was a very wonderful phenomenon, and all he was able to make of it was a new speculation. So absolutely engrossed was he at all times in gratifying his thirst for phenomena and in speculations on their nature that he never had time or inclination to try to see if *her* explanations of their nature and rationale might not afford the very solution he was so desirous of gaining.

In Chapter XVII, he follows with an incident of a year or two later and sees no connection! He is telling of some of the communications he received from the Masters. He says:

> One quite long letter that I received in 1879 [from one of the Masters], *most strangely alters*

> *her sex, speaks of her in the male gender, and confounds her with the Mahatma "M"* . . . It says—about a first draft of the letter itself which had been written but not sent me: "Owing to certain expressions therein, the letter was stopped on its way by order of our *Brother* H.P.B. As you are not under my direct guidance but *his* (hers), we have naught to say, either of us"; etc. And again: *"Our Brother* H.P.B. rightly remarked . . ." etc.

One may compare the foregoing with the remark of the Master "K. H." in his letter of 1888 to Col. Olcott: "The personality known as H.P.B. to the world (*but otherwise to us*)."

Still another most interesting sidelight on the "mystery of H.P.B." and of Occultism in general, may be found in *Lucifer* for October 15, 1888 (the month of the public announcement of the Esoteric Section). There a correspondent makes some "Pertinent Queries" in regard to statements in Mr. Sinnett's "Esoteric Buddhism." In the "Editor's Answer" to these pertinent queries H.P.B. takes occasion to make some remarks regarding the Masters. She says (italics ours):

> . . . among the group of Initiates to which his [Mr. Sinnett's] own mystical correspondent ["K. H."] is allied, *are two of European race*, and that one who is that Teacher's superior [the Master "M"] *is* also of that origin, being half a Slavonian in his "present incarnation," as he himself wrote to Colonel Olcott in New York.

Just why H.P.B. should put the phrase "present incarnation" in quotes is worth some intuitional effort, as is also the fact that "H. P. B." was herself precisely and exactly *"half a Slavonian"* in *her* then "present incarnation."

One word more: Col. Olcott's "faith" in H.P.B., in Masters, in Theosophy, rested upon exactly the same basis as his "faith" in Spiritualism during the preceding twenty years. That basis was *phenomena*—not philosophy, logic, ethics, altruism. "Old Diary Leaves" shows this on nearly every page. His memorial article above quoted from so states specifically. When this is recognized his vagaries can be understood, his failures overlooked, his misjudgments forgiven, his misconceptions allowed for, and the solid value of his services to the Society and to Buddhism given generous tribute.

CHAPTER XXIV

CONTROVERSY OVER H.P.B.'S STATUS AS AGENT OF THE MASTERS

By the spring of 1893 the internal situation of the Society was fast approaching a climax paralleling that of 1888, and, as in the earlier case, it occurred contemporaneously with a flood-tide of external interest and prosperity. "Old Diary Leaves" was steadily undermining the reverence and respect of the members for H.P.B. as a Teacher, by representing her as a mere thaumaturgist. The theories and speculations to account for her phenomena, the vagaries of character and habits attributed to her, could only lead to the inference that, however gifted in some ways, she was but an irresponsible medium, not a Messenger direct from the great Lodge of Masters. This constant stream of belittlement by the President-Founder of the Society who was generally considered as her most intimate friend and associate was not less injurious to her Occult status than that of the Psychical Research Society in its celebrated *Report*. The Letter of the Master, "K. H.," phenomenally delivered to Col. Olcott on shipboard in the early autumn of 1888, at a time when he was harboring and expressing the same feelings and views, was forgotten or lost sight of, and H.P.B. was more and more coming to be regarded by many members as at best an uncertain channel between the Masters and the world; a channel to be utilized under reserve, if not to be scrutinized with actual doubt and suspicion. Now that she was dead, even that questionable link was severed and the members, left to themselves, were peculiarly open to suggestion and direction. To whom should they look if not to the President-Founder? And when they were offered his views, clothed with official authority, expressed with the utmost candor, sincerity and good faith, what more natural than the deductions that the Society was of far more importance than a Philosophy derived through a questionable source; phenomena more valuable than study; propaganda more necessary than altruism? What more natural than the inference that the living President-Founder was now, and always had been, the real mainstay of the Movement and of the Society?

What was Mr. Judge to do in these circumstances? If he held his peace, the Society and the membership were certain to be irremediably led astray from the prime Objects proclaimed insistently by the MASTERS, by H.P.B. and himself. Should he permit the lines of Teaching, of policy and of practice laid down by H.P.B. to be swept aside and himself join in building up a great organization with purely utilitarian and exoteric aims? Or should he do as she had done in 1888—hold to the "lines laid down" regardless of all else that might befall? For now, even more than in 1888, the whole tendency in the Society was to achieve a great public success, while in the Esoteric School an increasing percentage of the members were avid to convert it into a "hall of Occultism," and were pursuing the "Third Object" to the exclusion of all else. Was H.P.B. to become a mere memory, the MASTERS an empty and far-off inaccessible abstraction, THEOSOPHY secondary to the Theosophical Society, and that Theosophy to be twisted, perverted, corrupted, by the interpretations of students, the "fresh revelations" of the horde of psychics and "occultists" who were already proclaiming their "successorship" to H.P.B. and delivering "messages from the Masters of H.P.B." in contradiction to what she had taught and exemplified?

The great issues at stake must have given him pause, and he must have realized that in entering the lists in defense of the Teachings and Mission of H.P.B. he was inviting a far more unequal combat than any she had ever brought upon her devoted head. For H.P.B. had had the prestige of a pioneer, the philosophy she had recorded was her standing witness; her phenomena, however misrepresented, were none the less irrevocably attested by the very ones who now sought to usurp her robes; and she had had at all times devoted defenders—Judge foremost of all. But Mr. Judge was now alone; he had been purposely kept in obscurity during the first ten-year cycle of the Society's life; he was little known to the membership at large outside the United States; he was without literary or oratorical or official reputation; he had at all times sustained and defended the President-Founder as strongly in his place as he had H.P.B. in hers. He was of necessity a thorn in the side of all those who sought to profit the Society and themselves by ignoring or minimizing the unique status of H.P.B.—who were equally ready to treat her as an asset or a liability, as might best serve their purposes. What was Mr. Judge to do?

Under date of March, 1893, he issued to the American members of the E.S. a circular entitled "We Have Not Been Deserted." He wrote:

> It is very proper to answer the question which has come to many, expressed or unexpressed, whether since the death of H.P.B.'s body the E.S.T. has been in communication with the Masters who ordered her to start the E.S.T.? . . .
>
> We have not been deserted at all, and the Masters have all along been watching and aiding. They have communicated with several of those who by nature are fit; those who have made themselves fit; and with those who are, by peculiar Karma, in the line of such communication. None of these messages go by favor or by the desire of some to have them. . . .
>
> There are in the School certain persons known to me who have been in communication with the Masters for some time, but they do not know each other, and have never by word or sign given out the fact. . . . In America the line of communication is not ruptured. It is true that it is

not as strong as it was when H.P.B. was here, but we cannot expect always to have the same amount of force working, for there is a law, based on cycles, which requires such line of force to be stopped or weakened now and then. The stoppage however is never total, but at certain periods it is confined to the few. We have the misfortune to know that at one time many of the Masters were publicly at work here in our early years and that the opportunity for us was missed by reason of the materialistic and naturalistic tendencies of the day and of our education. Our missing it did not, however, prevent the doing by those personages of the work in hand. A more narrow confinement of these lines of action and communication will come at a later day, strictly in accord with the laws I have referred to. But we have only to do our duty and to work for the future so as to be able to return to the work at a better time in some other life. Within the last nine months some communications have been received from the Masters *bearing on the general work,* for they have ceased (as by rule) to deal much in personal concerns, but They do not fail to help in the real and right way the efforts of all members who sincerely work for others. Those who are at work for their own benefit will meet with the exact result of such a line of action, that is, they will not go far and will lose much at death which is sure to come to us all. But unselfish work makes the effect sink down into each one's own nature and therefore preserves it all.

Furthermore, some years ago the Masters said that in the course of time I should see that certain facts had to come out. Some of these I now give, and shall give them in *The Path* publicly. *First,* the Masters both certified in writing, about 1884, that the *Secret Doctrine* was dictated by them to H. P. B., she only using

> and about the beginnings of the Society—truth which nobody can gainsay. . . . I have pursued my present task to its completion, despite the fact that some of my most influential colleagues have, from what I consider mistaken loyalty to "H.P.B.," secretly tried to destroy my influence, ruin my reputation, reduce the circulation of my magazine, and prevent the publication of my book. . . .
>
> . . . Karma forbid that I should do her a featherweight of injustice, but if there ever existed a person in history who was a greater conglomeration of good and bad, light and shadow, wisdom and indiscretion, spiritual insight and lack of common sense, I cannot recall the name, the circumstances or the epoch.

For contrast one has but to turn to the Henry S. Olcott of the summer of 1891, immediately after the death of H.P.B. *Lucifer* for August 15 of that year contains a long memorial article by Col. Olcott, entitled "H.P.B.'s Departure." We quote:

> . . . There is no one to replace Helena Petrovna, nor can she ever be forgotten. Others have certain of her gifts, none has them all. . . . Her life, as I have known it these past seventeen years, as friend, colleague and collaborator, has been a tragedy, the tragedy of a martyr-philanthropist. Burning with zeal for the spiritual welfare and intellectual enfranchisement of humanity, moved by no selfish inspiration, giving herself freely and without price to her altruistic work, she has been hounded to her death-day, by the slanderer, the bigot and the Pharisee. . . . In temperament and abilities as dissimilar as any two persons could well be, and often disagreeing radically in details, we have yet been of one mind and heart as regards the work in hand and in our reverent allegiance

> to our Teachers and Masters, its planners and overlookers. We both knew them personally, she a hundred times more intimately than I. . . . She was pre-eminently a double-selfed personality, one of them very antipathetic to me and some others. . . . One seeing us together would have said I had her fullest confidence, yet the fact is that, despite seventeen years of intimacy in daily work, she was an enigma to me to the end. Often I would think I knew her perfectly, and presently discover that there were deeper depths in her selfhood I had not sounded. I could never find out *who she was,* not as Helena Petrovna, . . . but as "H.P.B.," the mysterious individuality which wrote, and worked wonders. . . .
>
> We had each our department of work—hers the mystical, mine the practical. In her line, she infinitely excelled me and every other of her colleagues. I have no claim at all to the title of metaphysician, nor to anything save a block of very humble knowledge. . . .
>
> . . . She knew the bitterness and gloom of physical life well enough, often saying to me that her true existence only began when nightly she had put her body to sleep and went out of it to the Masters. I can believe that, from often sitting and watching her from across the table, when she was away from the body, and then when she returned from her soul-flight and resumed occupancy, as one might call it. When she was away the body was like a darkened house, when she was there it was as though the windows were brilliant with lights within. One who had not seen this change, cannot understand why the mystic calls his physical body, a "shadow."

Here are two violently contradictory opinions of H.P.B.—both of them from the pen of Col. Olcott. It

> "If this can be of any help to ———, though I doubt it, I, the humble undersigned Faquir, certify that the *Secret Doctrine* is dictated to (name of H.P.B.), partly by myself and partly by my brother ———."

A year after this certain doubts having arisen in the minds of individuals, another letter from one of the signers of the foregoing was sent and reads as follows. As the prophecy in it has come true, it is now the time to publish it for the benefit of those who know something of how to take and understand such letters. For the outside it will all be so much nonsense.

> "The certificate given last year saying that the *Secret Doctrine* would be when finished the triple production of (H.P.B.'s name), ———, and myself was and is correct, although some have doubted not only the facts given in it but also the authenticity of the message in which it was contained. Copy this and also keep the copy of the aforesaid certificate. You will find them both of use on the day when you shall, as will happen without your asking, receive from the hands of the very person to whom the certificate was given, the original for the purpose of allowing you to copy it; and you can then verify the correctness of this presently forwarded copy . . . All this and more will be found necessary as time goes on, but for which you are well qualified to wait."

The first two certificates reproduced in the above article were originally sent to Dr. Hubbe-Schleiden, a well-known German *savant*, who had been intensely interested in the phenomena and teachings of H.P.B. but who, like so many others, found it difficult to understand or accept her explanations of them and their source;

and who consequently wavered between the theories of mediumship and chicanery to account for them. His own statement in regard to the facts and his expression of opinion in regard to them will be found in a communication over his own signature embodied in the Countess Wachtmeister's "Reminiscences of H. P. Blavatsky and the 'Secret Doctrine,'" the original edition of which was issued at London, late in 1893, six months after the publication in *The Path* from which we have been quoting.

The same number of *The Path* which contained the article on the authorship of the "Secret Doctrine"—April, 1893—also contained the third of a series of articles on the "Earth-Chain of Globes," to which attention was directed in the E.S.T. Circular quoted from. The articles, and others on related subjects, were signed "William Brehon," another of the pen names used by Mr. Judge. These articles were written because of the fact that Mr. Sinnett and others sharing his views were once more actively promulgating the theories of planetary and human evolution originally presented by him in "Esoteric Buddhism"—theories and interpretations to the correction of which H.P.B. had devoted many pages in the "Secret Doctrine." Mr. Sinnett, without recanting or seeking to reconcile his views with those expounded by H.P.B., had, nevertheless, after a somewhat ironical communication to *Lucifer*[1] remained quiescent until after her death. Encouraged, perhaps, by the note struck in "Old Diary Leaves," his London Lodge had resumed its public activities and Mr. Sinnett had been privately expressing the opinion that H.P.B. had, in her later years, been "under other influences than those of the Masters." In particular, a "Transaction of the London Lodge, No. 17," had just been issued, giving a paper by Mr. W. Scott Elliott on "The Evolution of Humanity." This "Transaction" not only continued the grossly materialistic conception of the "planetary

[1] Mr. Sinnett's communication, and H.P.B.'s notes thereon, will be found in *Lucifer* for November, 1888, p. 247 *et seq.*, under the caption, "'Esoteric Buddhism' and the 'Secret Doctrine.'" We know of nothing more illustrative of the contrasted spirit of H.P.B. and her critics.

chains" promulgated by "Esoteric Buddhism," but went still farther in that it announced, in terms which could not be otherwise interpreted than as claiming to be "on the authority of the Masters," the specific "facts" that Mars was the last planet inhabited by our humanity, Mercury is to be the next, and Europe will be destroyed by fire in "about 18,000 years." These "facts" are accompanied by the statement that much of the contents of the "Transaction" are "given out to the world for the first time." The confusions thus inaugurated were added to by the fact that *The Path* for June, 1893, contained an enthusiastic commendation of this "Transaction" in a review signed with the initials "A. F." This was the signature of Alexander Fullerton, formerly an Episcopalian clergyman, who had become greatly interested in Theosophy, had relinquished his clerical profession and had volunteered his services to the American Section. As he was highly educated, an excellent writer and speaker, his services had been gladly availed of. He acted as Secretary for Mr. Judge, edited the *Forum*, a Sectional publication devoted to questions and answers on Theosophy, lectured frequently before the Aryan Lodge in New York City, contributed many signed articles to *The Path*, attended to much of the heavy volume of correspondence coming to *The Path* office and the Sectional headquarters, and was generally regarded throughout the American Section as Mr. Judge's "right hand man." Mr. Fullerton had been in India, was very fond of Col. Olcott, and had conceived an enormous admiration for Mrs. Besant and Mr. Sinnett. He had been the pastor of "Jasper Niemand" through whom he had become interested in Theosophy and through whom he became connected with the work. He retained many of the characteristics of the typical minister, and was very sensitive, not to say jealous, of his own importance. His review of the London Lodge Transaction, then, coming as it did in connection with the other matters mentioned, caused great rejoicing in some quarters, and in others raised the presumption that Mr. Judge had receded from the consistent position hitherto maintained by him in regard to H.P.B.'s teachings. The situation contained, therefore, all the necessary ingredients for a comedy or a tragedy. Mr. Judge met it by publishing over his own signature a leading editorial in *The Path* for July, 1893, to correct all misconceptions. He wrote:

> In the June PATH there was printed a review of a pamphlet issued by the London Lodge T.S., and this magazine may perhaps be construed as committed to an approval of everything contained in the pamphlet, although the private initials of the reviewer were annexed to the remarks. The pamphlet referred to brings up an old dispute which we had thought was settled by what is found in *The Secret Doctrine*. . . . H.P.B., the only person in actual and constant communication with the Masters, corrected the mistake made by Mr. Sinnett. . . . Her correction of the misconception was made upon the written authority of the same Masters who sent through her the letters on which *Esoteric Buddhism* was written.
>
> On the ground of authority in respect to this question, about which none of the Theosophical writers have any information independent of what the Masters have written, we must conclude that the statement in *The Secret Doctrine* is final. If no other point were involved, there would be no necessity for going further with the matter, but as the consistency of the entire philosophy is involved, it is necessary to advert again to this subject.

Mr. Judge then proceeds to take up this question of a consistent philosophy and argues in line with the "Secret Doctrine" that to assume that Mars and Mercury constitute a portion of the "Earth-Chain of Globes" is to destroy the consistency of the philosophy. In the course of his article he uses the significant expression:

> We do not understand that Mr. Sinnett has said that H.P.B. was not reporting the Masters . . . or that the Masters have denied that they hold the above views.

This article by Mr. Judge placed squarely before the members the direct contradiction between the exposition of the sevenfold scheme of the universe as presented by Mr. Sinnett in "Esoteric Buddhism" and as set forth by H. P. Blavatsky in the "Secret Doctrine." As both presentations ostensibly came from the same source—the Masters of Wisdom—it followed that either Mr. Sinnett or H.P.B. was in error. And as the subject was one on which the generality of members could not be assumed to possess any direct knowledge of their own, they either must fall into the logical absurdity of accepting two mutually destructive hypotheses, or must choose between them. He therefore pointed out that on the basis of authenticity and authority, H.P.B. must be the safer guide and reinforced this point by calling attention (1) to the direct messages from the MASTERS to Dr. Hubbe-Schleiden while the "Secret Doctrine" was being written; (2) to the direct message from the Master "K. H." to Col. Olcott *after* the "Secret Doctrine" was completed—in both cases the messages being to recipients who doubted the standing of H.P.B. with the MASTERS. Moreover, in the message to Col. Olcott, under circumstances which have already been set out,[2] the Master took occasion to say:

> *Since 1885, I have not written, nor caused to be written, save through her agency, direct or remote, a letter or a line to anybody in Europe or America, nor communicated orally with, or through, any third party. Theosophists should learn it. You will understand later the significance of this declaration, so keep it in mind.*

This letter of the Master's contained a reference to existing conditions at the time it was sent—August,

[2] See Chapter IX.

1888—; to the precedent situation of which they were the recrudescence—the Fall of 1884—; and, no less, *to the then future.* Let the reader now turn to Letter IV in the book, "Letters from the Masters of the Wisdom." It was sent to Miss Francesca Arundale at the same time and place—Elberfeld, Germany, late in 1884—as the two certificates mentioned, and forms part of the same *mise en scène.* Except for privately circulated copies, the letter to Miss Arundale never became accessible to Theosophical students until May, 1910, when it was published in *The Theosophist,* under the title, "Advice from a Master." It was copied in *The Theosophic Messenger* for July, 1910, and republished in *The Theosophist* for October, 1917, in the "Reminiscences" of the recipient. It was also printed in the *Vahan* for February, 1912, and apparently up to that time Mr. Sinnett did not know of its having become public property. The letter begins abruptly: *"The day of the separation is close at hand,"* and contains the most solemn of warnings to the London Lodge, its officers and members, for their departure from the lines laid down by the Masters. When Mr. Sinnett learned of the publication of the letter he wrote to the *Vahan* a communication which shows how *he* regarded it. He says:

> I regret its reappearance at this period for two reasons. Firstly, it is calculated to give rise to misconceptions on the part of those who may imagine it to have had a more recent origin, and secondly because letters of that kind may excite painful impressions among some of their readers, who may suppose them to be the actual composition throughout of the Masters whose initials may be appended to them. . . . In reference to the letter just published I wish emphatically to declare that I do not regard it as embodying the *ipsissima verba* of the Master, . . . though very likely conveying . . . some message which, in substance, he wished to send. Some of its "advice" would already have been

out of date twenty years ago. It is all the more inapplicable to the present time.

The reader should remember that the letter to Miss Arundale was written to her as an officer of the London Lodge; that it was sent just after the Coulomb explosion and when Messrs. Sinnett, Olcott, Massey, and many others were full of doubts and suspicions in regard to H.P.B.; and, finally at a time when the London Lodge, under Mr. Sinnett's charge, was about to enter upon a prolonged period of exclusiveness as regards the public, and devotion to psychical experimentation as regards its leading members.[3]

From the date of that letter till her death in 1891, H.P.B. *never had anything to do with the London Lodge;* on the contrary, on her return to England in 1887, the Blavatsky Lodge was formed out of members of the London Lodge who had remained true to her teachings, and the formation of the Blavatsky Lodge was bitterly opposed, both by Mr. Sinnett and Col. Olcott. More; from the time of that letter to Miss Arundale, Mr. Sinnett believed H.P.B. to be a deliverer of bogus messages from the Masters—as we shall show over his own signature in its appropriate relation.[4] After the next year—1885—Sinnett and those under his influence tried, through mediums, psychics, and sensitives among their own number, to obtain "communications from the MASTERS of H.P.B.!" They got "communications," as any *séance* will yield up communications; hence the warning to Olcott in the letter of 1888, for the Master knew that Mr. Sinnett's spurious messages would one day be cited in opposition and contradiction to the authoritative statements of H.P.B.[5]

[3] Many additional messages from the Masters, on the same subjects and sent during the same period, are now available to students in "The Mahatma Letters to A. P. Sinnett," compiled by A. Trevor Barker. They fully confirm the teachings of H.P.B. and the position taken by Mr. Judge in regard to them.

[4] See Chapter XXXIII.

[5] All this is made amply clear to present-day students by the posthumous publication of Mr. Sinnett's "Early Days of Theosophy in Europe."

Judge knew in 1893 that this had been going on for years and that the time had come to put the membership on notice; hence the articles quoted. His signed editorial in *The Path* for July, 1893, on "Mars and Mercury," was preceded, in the June issue, by another signed leading article, entitled "Masters, Adepts, Teachers, and Disciples," evidently intended to enforce the logical, as the July article treated of the authoritative, significance of the opposing currents running riot beneath the placid surface of the Society's life. We quote:

> This article is meant for members of the T.S., and chiefly for those who keep H.P.B. much in mind, whether out of respect and love or from fear and envy. Those members who believe that such beings as the Masters may exist must come to one of two conclusions in regard to H.P.B., either that she invented her Masters, who therefore have no real existence, or that she did not invent them, but spoke in the names and by the orders of such beings. If we say that she invented the Mahatmas, then, of course, as so often said by her, all that she has taught and written is the product of her own brain, from which we would be bound to conclude that her position on the roll of great and powerful persons must be higher than people have been willing to place her. But I take it most of us believe in the truth of her statement that she had those teachers whom she called Masters and that they are more perfect beings than ordinary men.
>
> The case I briefly wish to deal with, then, is this: H.P.B. and her relations to the Masters and to us; her books and teachings; the general question of disciples or chelas with their grades, and whether a high chela would appear almost as a Master in comparison to us, including every member from the President down to the most recent applicant.

The last point in the inquiry is extremely important, and has been much overlooked by members in my observation. . . . An idea has become quite general that chelas and disciples are all of one grade, and that therefore one chela is the same as another in knowledge and wisdom. The contrary, however, is the case. Chelas and disciples are of many grades, and some of the Adepts are themselves the chelas of higher Adepts. . . . So much being laid down, we may next ask how we are to look at H.P.B.

In the first place, every one has the right to place her if he pleases for himself on the highest plane, because he may not be able to formulate the qualities and nature of those who are higher than she was. But taking her own sayings, she was a chela or disciple of the Masters, and therefore stood in relation to them as one who might be chided or corrected or reproved. . . . But looking at her powers exhibited to the world, and as to which one of her Masters wrote that they had puzzled and astonished the brightest minds of the age, we see that compared with ourselves she was an Adept. . . .

Now some Theosophists ask if there are other letters extant from her Masters in which she is called to account, is called their chela, and is chided now and then, besides those published. Perhaps yes. And what of it? Let them be published by all means, . . . As she has herself published letters . . . from the Masters to her in which she is called a chela and is chided, it certainly cannot matter if we know of others of the same sort. For over against all such we have common sense, and also the declaration of her Masters that she was the sole instrument possible for the work to be done, that They sent her to do it, and that They approved in general all she did. And she was the first direct channel to and from the Lodge, and the only one up to

> date through which came the objective presence of the Adepts. We cannot ignore the messenger, take the message, and laugh at or give scorn to the one who brought it to us. . . .
>
> There only remains, then, the position taken by some and without a knowledge of the rules governing in these matters, that chelas sometimes write messages claimed to be from the Masters when they are not. This is an artificial position not supportable by law or rule. It is due to ignorance of what is and what is not chelaship, and also to confusion between grades in discipleship. It has been used as to H.P.B. The false conclusion has first been made that an accepted chela of high grade may become accustomed to dictation given by the Master and then may fall into the false pretense of giving something from himself and pretending it is from the Master. It is impossible. The bond in her case was not of such a character as to be dealt with thus. One instance of it would destroy the possibility of any more communications from the teacher. It may be quite true that probationers now and then have imagined themselves as ordered to say so and so, but that is not the case of an accepted and high chela who is irrevocably pledged, nor anything like it. This idea, then, ought to be abandoned; it is absurd, contrary to law, to rule, and to what must be the case when such relations are established as existed between H.P.B. and her Masters.

This, and the articles on Mars and Mercury, in connection with a letter of Mr. Judge's published in *Lucifer* for April, 1893, and to which we shall recur,[6] precipitated what before was concealed, as a catalytic agent produces a chemical reaction. Mr. Sinnett was the first to declare himself openly, which he did in an article entitled "Esoteric Teachings," which he sent to *The Path* where it ap-

[6] See Chapters XX and XXVI.

peared in the number for September, 1893. He also sent copies to *Lucifer*, where it appeared in the issue for August 15, 1893, and to *The Theosophist*, in which it appeared for the month of September, 1893. In each case the article was commented on by the editors of the several publications. Mr. Sinnett says:

> Some recent references in *The Path* to portions of the original esoteric teachings embodied by me in *Esoteric Buddhism* seem to call for remarks on my part in reply. The line of criticism in question has culminated in an article which appears in *The Path* for July, entitled "Mars and Mercury."
>
> . . . The question is one which, on its own merits, will only be of interest within the area of serious Theosophic study; but the controversy that has now arisen really involves some of the deepest questions affecting the future well-being of the Theosophical Society and the progress of the movement. . . .
>
> For a long time after the publication of *Esoteric Buddhism* the statement concerning Mars and Mercury remained unchallenged. It scarcely seemed possible that any one imbued with respect for the Masters' teaching could challenge it . . . In later years when the *Secret Doctrine* was published by Madame Blavatsky, I found to my great surprise that she had asserted a new view of the planetary chain, altogether at variance with that previously given out, . . . On the basis of this declaration some Theosophical students have felt bound by their loyalty to Madame Blavatsky to put aside the earlier teachings of the Masters conveyed through myself, and to argue that I misunderstood my instructions. . . . The really important point developed by the controversy has to do with the question, What was Madame Blavatsky's position really in the occult world,

> and what kind of authority should be attached to the writings she has left behind her?
>
> I hope no one will take the explanation I am now forced to give as implying any abandonment by me of the position respecting Madame Blavatsky I have always maintained. I showed in the fragmentary biography I put together at her own wish . . . that she was truly in close relations with the great Masters of esoteric wisdom. That she was one of their partially initiated disciples was also unquestionable for anyone who has been in independent touch with the realities of the occult world. . . .
>
> It is not my business here to offer hypotheses to account for the strange misapprehensions into which Madame Blavatsky fell when writing the *Secret Doctrine,* not merely as regards these questions of Mars and Mercury, but also in regard to some other points which have not yet attracted attention. That Madame Blavatsky was capable of making mistakes when endeavoring to amplify and expand the occult teaching of the Masters is the all-important conclusion to which I think all unbiassed minds in the Theosophical Society must be brought by a consideration of the matter under discussion.

Mr. Sinnett then enters into details and argues in defense of his interpretations of teachings from the letters of the Masters to himself, his questions and the Masters' replies, and says, "the notion that there could be any ambiguity about my question or the answer, in the circumstances, is an insult to common sense,—not to speak of Adept wisdom." He then adds forthwith the following declaration:

> I am entitled to add that at a very recent date, within the last few months since this subject has been under discussion, the Master himself in communication with me made the following comment on the situation. . . .

> Few persons in touch with the principles of occultism will be surprised to hear me quoting recent words addressed to me by the Master. . . . During Madame Blavatsky's lifetime my privileges of communication with the Master through channels of which she knew nothing were private and personal and I was precluded from speaking of them. That prohibition has since been removed. . . . For many Theosophists, I know, Madame Blavatsky represented the whole movement. . . . For many such persons Madame Blavatsky may have been the only teacher from which they received occult enlightenment. Immense as is my respect for her attainments, for her industry and devotion to the work she undertook, it is, nevertheless, a fact that I myself did not receive my Theosophic teaching directly from her, but in the way described; and long before her death my relations with the Master were carried on through the intermediation of one of his *chelas,* quite outside the range of Madame Blavatsky's connexions. . . .

The student can compare these several statements of Mr. Sinnett with the extracts from the Masters' letters from which we have quoted, as well as with the other citations from Mr. Judge's articles, and with statements of H.P.B. in the first volume of the "Secret Doctrine," and thus see clearly the gross contradiction, both as to facts and relations, between the contrasted positions. One pertinent fact should once more be called to the student's attention in reference to Mr. Sinnett's claim of unbroken connection with the Masters. By referring to the "Occult World," Mr. Sinnett's earliest book, the student can find in a direct quotation from one of the Master's letters at that time (letters sent "through H.P.B.") the plain, categorical statement that They will not give direct instruction or correction to any one not "irrevocably pledged." It is a well-known fact in Theosophical history not only that Mr. Sinnett was never pledged at all to Them, even as a probationary chela, but refused to pledge himself even to the probationary requirements. His position never was other than that of a man of the world who refused to submit himself to any obligation of any kind. But he was intensely interested in phenomena; then, in the idea of Masters, and was able to render enormous service to the Society and the Movement because of his education, literary ability, and standing in India. Hence the letters to him, all "through the agency of H.P.B., direct or remote," up to the year 1885, when, having broken away and taken a tangent of his own, he received no more communications from the *Masters of H.P.B.*,—his messages through psychics and mediums to the contrary notwithstanding.

Mr. Judge, following the example set by H.P.B. in the earlier controversy, published Mr. Sinnett's communication to *The Path* in full and followed it with an article of his own, "How to Square the Teachings." In this article he reviewed Mr. Sinnett's arguments, treated their author with the utmost respect, acknowledged his great service to the work of the Movement, but reinforced his own former statements on the controversy by stating that he had himself seen the Masters' letters to H.P.B. containing the corrections embodied in the "Secret Doctrine." Mr. Judge ignored entirely Mr. Sinnett's claims in reference to unbroken communications with the Masters, but upheld the integrity of H. P.B. as the trustworthy channel, and showed how Mr. Sinnett's misunderstanding of the original teaching came about.

In publishing Mr. Sinnett's article in *Lucifer* Mrs. Besant prefaced it with a comment of her own, in which she deals as kindly with Mr. Sinnett as does Mr. Judge, but states her own position unequivocally:

> With regard to H. P. Blavatsky's position in the movement, some of us are quite satisfied to know that she was a Chela of one of the Mas-

ters, helped and taught by and in constant communication with Him; for the teaching she brought us we are deeply grateful, and we do not care to benefit by the message and constantly cavil at and find fault with the messenger. Because we are not continually "nagging" at and belittling her, we are often accused of setting her on too lofty a pedestal, of idolizing her, and claiming for her infallibility. We do nothing of the kind, though we prefer to leave to her ever active adversaries the task of pulling her to pieces, and we listen in pained silence when those who should be her friends put weapons against her into her enemies' hands. For myself, the fire of loving gratitude to her burns ever in my heart, and while I recognize that she most probably made some errors in her writings, I recognize also that she knew far more than I do, that her teaching is invaluable to me, and that until I stand in knowledge where she stood any criticism by me is likely to be full of blunders.

Touching Mars and Mercury, each must decide for himself, if he feels it necessary to come to a decision. Having no personal knowledge on the subject, I am obliged to judge from general considerations. In any doubtful matter I prefer to follow H. P. Blavatsky's teachings, and in this particular case it is more congruous with the whole evolutionary scheme than that of Mr. Sinnett, and therefore in itself it recommends itself more to my judgment.[7]

Colonel Olcott follows the publication of Mr. Sinnett's article with a comment signed with his initials. His own leanings are indicated by the following quotation:

[7] Three months later Mrs. Besant receded and took an equivocal position (*Lucifer*, November, 1893); two years later she reversed herself completely and sided emphatically with Mr. Sinnett's contentions (*Lucifer*, December, 1895). All this was a sequence to her falling into the same methods of "communication" as Mr. Sinnett. But see succeeding chapters.

> The inestimable services which Mr. Sinnett has rendered our movement in the past, and his unfaltering loyalty to the Masters and to H.P.B. personally . . . would entitle him to occupy the free platform of *The Theosophist*, . . . Like every other contributor to our pages, he is responsible for his facts and opinions, and neither I nor the T.S. is to be held accountable for the same. His assertion that he is, and for many years has been, in frequent epistolary intercourse with Mahatma K. H. is most important and interesting, since, if valid, it goes to prove what has always been affirmed, that the Adepts are the friends and benefactors of the race, not the appanage of single individuals or groups of persons. . . . If Mr. Sinnett's remarks with regard to the human fallibility of H.P.B. should give offense to any, these should still bear in mind that the writer was her devoted friend when friends were few, and learnt from her Teachers direct that loyalty to an idea did not imply wilful blindness as to the merits or deficiencies of its exponents.

If now the student will turn to Chapter IX herein, he will have no difficulty in relating the controversy just described to the discussion arising out of Subba Row's discourses on the "Bhagavad-Gita," delivered before the Indian Convention in December, 1886. H.P.B. *knew then what was to come;* otherwise how account for the exact disclaimers and specific warnings contained in her articles in *The Theosophist* for April and August, 1887, and in her correspondence with Col. Olcott on Mr. Cooper-Oakley's fatuousness in admitting the Subba Row criticisms—disclaimers and warnings that neither Olcott nor any other save W. Q. Judge saw rhyme or reason in at the time? Two additional quotations from H.P.B.'s articles at that time are germane here, besides those given in Chapter IX, though the whole series in *The Theosophist* should be carefully studied. She said, in

April, 1887 (*The Theosophist,* Volume 8, p. 448):

> In a most admirable lecture by Mr. T. Subba Row . . . the lecturer deals, incidentally as I believe, with the question of septenary "principles" in the Kosmos and Man. The division is rather criticized. . . .
>
> This criticism has already given rise to some misunderstanding, and it is argued by some that a slur is thrown on the original teachings. This apparent *disagreement* . . . is certainly a dangerous handle to give to opponents who are ever on the alert to detect and blazon forth contradictions and inconsistencies in our philosophy. . . . Therefore, now, when he calls the division "unscientific and misleading," . . .
>
> A few words of explanation . . . will not be out of place. . . . That it is "misleading" is . . . perfectly true; for the great feature of the day—materialism—has led the minds of our Western Theosophists into the prevalent habit of viewing the seven principles as distinct and self-existing *entities,* instead of what they are —namely, *upadhis* and correlating states—three *upadhis,* basic groups, and four principles. . . .
>
> We have *unfortunately*—for it was premature—opened a chink in the Chinese wall of esotericism, and we cannot now close it again, even if we would. I for one had to pay a heavy price for the indiscretion but I will not shrink from the results. . . .

Subba Row replied with further strictures and personal allegations directed at H.P.B. as the author of the "sevenfold" classification of "Esoteric Buddhism." In the August, 1887, *Theosophist,* H.P.B., forced to definitive and direct reply to Subba Row's charges that she was the "original expounder" of the statements in "Esoteric Buddhism," and "Man: Fragments of Forgotten History," said:

> This is hardly fair. *Esoteric Buddhism* was written absolutely without my knowledge, and as the author understood those teachings from letters he had received, what have *I* to do with them. . . . Finally "Man" was *entirely re-written* by one of the two "chelas" and from the same materials as those used by Mr. Sinnett for *Esoteric Buddhism;* the two having understood the teachings, each in his own way. What had I to do with the "states of consciousness" of the three authors, two of whom wrote in England while I was in India. . . .
>
> This will do, I believe. The *Secret Doctrine* will contain, no doubt, still more *heterodox* statements from the Brahminical view. No one is forced to accept *my* opinions or teaching in the Theosophical Society, one of the rules of which enforces only mutual tolerance for religious views.
>
> Most of us have been playing truants to this golden rule as to all others; more's the pity.

Finally, as we noted in Chapter IX, Mr. Judge contributed to the discussion in the August, 1887, *Theosophist,* from which we quote:

> The greatest schisms often come about through the supporters of one cause disputing over mere terminology. Mr. Subba Row . . . condemned the "sevenfold classification" which has come to be very largely accepted among Theosophists . . . This brought out a reply which was published in *The Path,* and one which H. P. Blavatsky wrote for *The Theosophist.* . . .
>
> As his [Subba Row's] articles appeal to my eyes and mind, the real difficulty seems to be, not with *any* and *all sevenfold* classifications, but with the *particular sevenfold classification* found in *Esoteric Buddhism* and other theosophical works. . . .

> . . . in Mr. Sinnett's book some division had to be adopted that Western minds could grasp until they were able to go higher. But for my part I have never understood that his book was gospel truth. The great basis of our Society would be undermined by any such doctrine, just as much as his own progress would be retarded did he fancy that the views expressed by him were his own invention . . . many decades will pass away, and many false as well as ridiculous systems will arise, grow up and disappear, before the whole truth will be known. . . .

Thus the matter stood in the fall of 1893: an open breach in the Society and among its leaders on the question of one of the most important Theosophical teachings as to Nature and Man; an equally sharp cleavage of opinion as to the status of H. P. Blavatsky in the Occult world. Was she a *Teacher,* the *direct Agent* of the Masters of Wisdom, or was she a mere "medium" and "psychic" used as a tool by Them at times, and at other times, shorn of Their help and guidance, a mere inventor and deliverer of bogus "messages" in Their names?

CHAPTER XXV

ANNIE BESANT IN AMERICA, 1892-1893

It will be recalled[1] that an urgent invitation had been extended to Mrs. Besant to visit India in the fall of 1891, following the death of H.P.B. This visit was canceled, ostensibly because of the ill-health of Mrs. Besant due to prolonged strain and overwork; actually because of the charges made to her against the moral character of Col. Olcott, on account of which she came to the United States to place them before Mr. Judge. This was her second visit to America, her first having been in the spring preceding to attend the Convention of the American Section as the bearer of H.P.B.'s last Message to the American Theosophists.

In the early fall of 1892, the invitation to visit India was again extended to Mrs. Besant. Colonel Olcott, Bertram Keightley and others, Hindu as well as English officials and prominent members of the Indian Section, wrote her on the need for her presence there. The fund to pay her expenses, started in 1891, was largely increased by voluntary contributions. Mrs. Besant consulted Mr. Judge, who advised against her going and, instead, recommended that she visit the United States on a lecturing tour. Mrs. Besant accepted his advice and the Indian members were satisfied, for the time being, by arrangements made to send to Adyar two of the English workers connected with the "household" at Avenue Road. Messrs. Sidney V. Edge and Walter R. Old were accordingly "loaned" to the Indian headquarters where they went late in 1892, the one becoming assistant secretary there and the other taking the place of Mr. Bertram Keightley, who arranged to return to Eng-

[1] See Chapter XXI.

land early in 1893. Both Mr. Edge and Mr. Old entered at once into the work of the Indian Section and the affairs at Headquarters, and were active contributors to the pages of *The Theosophist;* becoming, in short, diligent and satisfactory aides to Col. Olcott in his multifarious duties and activities. Mr. Keightley assigned as his reason for returning to England the advanced age and precarious health of his mother, to whom he was much attached. This was true; but as in many similar cases the announced occasion was not the compelling reason—as we shall see.

Mrs. Besant arrived in New York on November 30, 1892. From then until her departure at the end of February, 1893, she was incessantly engaged in public lectures, in addresses public and private to the various American Branches and the Groups of the Esoteric Section, in receptions, conferences, interviews, and correspondence which brought her the acquaintance and esteem of practically every Theosophist in the United States. The general arrangements for her tour had been carefully planned by Mr. Judge, but in every local centre the resident members looked after the details of her visit with such attention and assiduity that her mission before the public was an overwhelming success, while amongst the Theosophists themselves, her progress was a continuous ovation. She visited, with the exception of the South, every large centre in the United States, east and west. The largest halls and theatres were packed to capacity with attentive and respectful audiences. The press throughout the country was filled with interviews and articles descriptive of her remarkable history, her oratorical ability, her personal characteristics, her pre-eminence in the Theosophical world, her presumed Occult attainments and powers. A great outburst of curiosity and interest in her and her doctrines preceded and followed her wherever she went.

On her return to England she published, under the title "Speeding the Message," an account in *Lucifer* for April of her American trip. In the editorial section—"On the Watch-Tower"—she commented on the lessons gained on her American trip in these words:

> Elsewhere in these pages I have given a brief account of my American tour, but I want to place on record here my testimony to the splendid work done in America by the Vice-President of our Society, the General Secretary of the Section, WILLIAM Q. JUDGE. H.P.B. knew well what she was doing when she chose that strong quiet man to be her second self in America, to inspire all the workers there with the spirit of his intense devotion and unconquerable courage. In him is the rare conjunction of the business qualities of the skilful organizer, and the mystical insight of the Occultist—a combination, I often think, painful enough to its possessor with the shock of the two currents tossing the physical life into turbulence, but priceless in its utility to the movement. For he guides it with the strong hand of the practical leader, thus gaining for it the respect of the outer world; while he is its life and heart in the region where lie hidden the real sources of its energy. For out of the inner belief of members of the T.S. in the reality of spiritual forces springs the activity seen by the outer world, and our Brother's unshakable faith in the MASTERS and in Their care for the movement is a constant encouragement and inspiration to all who work with him.

Immediately following Mrs. Besant's tour the annual Convention of the American Section was held in New York at the end of April, 1893. Fifty-five Branches were represented by delegates or proxies and an unusually large number of visiting members attended the sessions. Mr. Bertram Keightley attended the Convention and read letters of greeting from the Indian and European Sections. Numerous other messages were received from abroad, amongst them an official letter from the President-Founder. This letter is important as showing the position assumed by him and the means taken to express his personal views. We quote the letter in full:

THE THEOSOPHICAL SOCIETY
PRESIDENT'S OFFICE
ADYAR, MADRAS, 23 March, 1893.

The Delegates of the American Section in Convention Assembled:

Brethren:

During the past year you have been giving abundant proofs of the tireless zeal with which you have pursued the work of our Society. The results prove the truth of the oft-repeated statement of our MASTERS that their help is always given to the earnest and unselfish worker. We have but one danger to dread and guard against. This is the subordination of general principles to hero-worship, or admiration of personalities. I shall not excuse myself for frequent recurrence to this theme, for I am convinced that, if the Society should ever disintegrate, this will be the cause. The MASTERS wrote in *Isis* that "men and parties, sects and schools are but the mere ephemera of the World's day"; and, following the precedent of their great recognized exemplar, Buddha Sakyamuni, they taught me to believe *nothing* upon authority, whether of a living or a dead person. I pray you to keep this ever in mind; and when I am dead and gone to recollect that the admission of the microbe of dogmatism into our Society will be the beginning of its last and fatal sickness.

Wishing you for the coming year a continuance of prosperity, and expressing a hope that I may sometime personally attend a Session of your Convention, I am fraternally and affectionately yours,

H. S. OLCOTT,
President Theosophical Society.

This was the second formal pronouncement by the President-Founder with all the authority of his official sanction, ostensibly to warn the members of the Society against dogmatism, authority, and hero-worship; actually, to reduce H.P.B. to the level of a dead person in place of a still potent and vital factor as the Teacher of Theosophy. His first attempt in this direction was the Adyar Presidential Address at the close of 1891, from which we have quoted.[2] This had been followed by his "Old Diary Leaves," and a continuous active propaganda in his official as well as personal correspondence and speech. He had ignored the repeated articles of Mr. Judge and Mrs. Besant in *The Path* and *Lucifer* upholding the entire neutrality of the Society on all matters of opinion, the perfect freedom everywhere accorded in America and Europe for the fullest expression of the most contradictory views. What he could not endure was that anyone should choose to regard H.P.B. as a Teacher *par excellence,* should dare publicly to express such an opinion, should act upon it. His voice was never at any time raised against those who belittled her; he never called attention to the fact that it was H.P.B. herself who had warned first, foremost, and insistently against "popery" in any guise, and herself set the constant example of rejecting homage of any kind. Nor did he ever inform the members that no one was for an instant tolerated at Adyar or in India who did not implicitly obey himself in all things, while both England and America were notable throughout for constant conflicts of opinion amongst workers. It seems never to have occurred to him that he had himself from the very beginning been the very one, and the only one of prominence, who had claimed and exercised arbitrary authority, who had fought consistently against any semblance of genuine democracy in the government of the Society. "Councils" appointed by himself and changeable at his will, "constitutions," "by-laws," "Executive Orders," and so on, all emanating from himself, all expressive of his own ideas and importance, were the continuous and

[2] See Chapter XX.

glaring signs of his own violation of the spirit of the Movement and the Society. Over and over his official utterances no less than his actual practices proclaimed his firm conviction that the Society needed a "ruler," and himself that ruler "chosen" to rule by the Masters. Though he denied the validity of H.P.B.'s writings and rejected their authenticity when they or she came in conflict with his own ideas and desires, he did not hesitate to quote them as Masters' words when they could be bent to his own ends. Thus, in the letter just quoted, he says: "*The Masters wrote* in 'Isis.'" So far as he and the members were concerned, it was *H.P.B. who wrote* in "Isis." Quite true he had H.P.B.'s word (as a matter of fact and not of "authority") that *all* she wrote was Masters' teaching, *all* she did was Masters' will, and equally true that her statements were confirmed to him and to others by direct Messages to them from those very Masters Themselves. But all this was mere testimony; testimony which he was quite as ready to reject when it suited him, as to quote when he could make use of it. But when Judge or any other, convinced that H.P.B. was Masters' "*direct Agent*" and her writings *Their* Teachings and Instructions, *followed* her teaching and example, even against the "executive notices" of the President-Founder and his proclaimed opinions, they were of necessity guilty of the "unpardonable sin" and were injecting dogmatism and hero-worship into the Society. When they declared as their view that the Society existed for the sake of Theosophy and that the Teacher was more important than the "ruler," then, equally of necessity, it could appear to Col. Olcott only as treason against the Society and a violation of its neutrality.

The *Report* of the American Section's Convention contained Col. Olcott's letter as also the letter of the Indian Section read by Mr. Bertram Keightley and signed by him as General Secretary of the Indian Section. It contains a sentence which the reader should compare with quotations from Mr. R. Harte's earlier articles [3] in *The Theosophist,* written prior to the formation of the

[3] See Chapter XVI.

Esoteric Section in 1888, when Col. Olcott was in the throes of his battle with H.P.B. Mr. Keightley says:

> We look hopefully forward to a time when the headquarters of the whole Society will in reality be its living heart and centre, sending out vitalizing spiritual influences, knowledge, and guidance to all its parts, as was the case when our revered teacher, H.P.B., resided there.

The same *Report* contains also some remarks of Mr. Judge as General Secretary of the American Section, which it cannot be doubted were written in view of the letter of Col. Olcott as President and of Mr. Keightley as General Secretary of the Indian Section. They were intended to make clear the perfect freedom and right of *individual* expression of opinion, no matter what or by whom, in distinction from *official* declarations vesting with the sanction of office and authority any personal views of any kind. He says:

> I hold that no officer or committee of the T.S. should appear in print as publisher or approver of any general treatises, doctrinal expositions, or other controversial matter, and that they should confine their official names to diplomas, charters, blanks, general information about T. S., and the like. *Following this policy I have never placed on my private publications my official title nor the office title, as I insist that if we follow any other policy we cannot keep the Society out of dogmatism or out of a reputation for dogmatizing. Every member has perfect freedom to issue over his individual name what books or publications he deems proper, and that I have long exercised, but I have no right in any way, however slight, to attach the T.S. to any publication which gives private views on Theosophy.*

The American Convention was followed by the Convention of the British and European Section in July,

1893. Mr. Judge attended as delegate from the American Section and was chosen as Chairman of the Convention. In his closing address to the assembled delegates and visitors he recurred to the subjects of government and dogmatism. We quote here some of his salient sentences:

> . . . The Society grew, members increased, work spread, the organization embraced the earth. Now was this growth due to a constitution and red tape? No; it was all because of the work of earnest men and women who worked for an ideal. Red tape, and votes, and laws to preserve votes, or to apportion them, are useless for any purpose if they are such as to hamper effort. Bind your soul about with red tape, and like the enwrapped mummy it will be incapable of movement.
>
> If you will regard its history in Europe, you will see that it came to its high point of energy without votes, without rules, supported and sustained by unselfish effort. Was it H.P.B. alone who made it grow here? No, for she alone could do nothing. She had to have around her those who would work unselfishly. . . .
>
> The next point I would like you to consider is that of dogmatism. A great deal has been said about the fear of a dogmatic tendency and of the actual existence among us of dogmatism. This I consider to be all wrong and not sustainable by facts. The best way for you to produce dogmatism is by continually fearing and talking about it, by waving about the charge of dogmatism on every occasion. In that way you will soon create it out of almost nothing.
>
> What is dogmatism? To my mind, it is the assertion of a tenet that others must accept. Is that what we do as a body? I think not. Certainly I do not do it. In my opinion, oft declared, anyone who asserts in our Society that

one must believe this or that theory or philosophy is no Theosophist, but an intolerant bigot.

But those who have spoken of dogmatism have mistaken energy, force, personal conviction and loyalty to personal teachers and ideals for dogmatism. Such are not dogmatism. One has a perfect right to have a settled conviction, to present it forcibly, to sustain it with every argument, without being any the less a good member of the Society. Are we to be flabby because we are members of an unsectarian body, and are we to refuse to have convictions merely because no one in the Society may compel another to agree with him? Surely not. My friends, instead of being afraid of a future dogmatism of which there is no real sign now, we should fear that it may be produced by an unreasonable idea that the assertions of your own convictions may bring it about. I feel quite sure that those who accuse us of dogmatism have no fixed ideal of their own. . . .

Too many have failed to make brotherhood a real thing in their life, leaving it merely as a motto on their shield. Our brotherhood must naturally include men and women of very various characters, each with different views of nature, having personal characteristics which may or may not grate on others, as the case my be. The first step, then, to take is to accept and tolerate personally all your fellows. In no other way can we begin to approach the realization of the great ideal. The absence of this acceptation of others is a moral defect. It leads to suspicion, and suspicion ruptures our union. In our assembly where harmony is absent, and brotherhood is not, the labors of those assembled are made almost nil, for an almost impenetrable cloud rolls out and covers the mental plane of all present. But let harmony return, and then

> the collective mind of all becomes the property of each, sending down into the mind of everyone a benediction which is full of knowledge.

Nor was Mrs. Besant in any way behind in affirming the full freedom of expression in the Society, or the declaration of her own convictions on questions of teaching and of policy. Thus in *Lucifer* for May, 1893, she published a paper by Mr. W. F. Kirby on "French Spiritism." In his paper Mr. Kirby states:

> the doctrines of Reincarnation and Karma, though now justly regarded by all Theosophists as of paramount importance . . . were not openly propounded by the Society until the publication of Mr. Sinnett's *Esoteric Buddhism* in 1883.

To this statement Mrs. Besant appends an editorial note, reading as follows:

> Our friend, Mr. Kirby, has perhaps forgotten that the *Theosophist* was first published in 1879 and *Isis Unveiled* in 1876 [this should be 1877]. We should also remember that the doctrines of Karma and Reincarnation are not propounded by the Theosophical Society, but only by those of its members who believe in the Esoteric Philosophy or some other system of Philosophy or Religion in which these doctrines are taught. The T.S. has three objects, but no doctrines. We may perhaps wisely add that the presentation of Theosophical teachings by any writer is not authoritative. We should certainly take objection to the statement as to Devachan in this article.—Eds.

Again, in the same number, in reviewing Mr. W. Scott-Elliott's paper in the London Lodge Transaction to which we have referred,[4] on the "Evolution of Humanity," *Lucifer* says:

[4] See Chapter XXIV.

> We must take exception to the phrase in its second paragraph that it is to be "regarded as an authoritative statement." Authoritative, it may be, to those who accept the authority on which it is based—what this is, is nowhere stated—but not authoritative so far as the T.S. is concerned. . . . We notice that Mr. Scott-Elliott agrees with Mr. Sinnett . . . Those who follow the teachings of the *Secret Doctrine* will, of course, dissent . . .

In the "Watch-Tower" of the August, 1893, *Lucifer* Mrs. Besant editorially reiterates her own convictions as follows:

> The keynote of the work for each of us is that of devotion to the MASTERS, as the great Servants of Humanity. . . . Here again the influence of H.P.B. makes itself strongly felt; for she trained us to look on this work as theirs . . . And as, since she left us, the signs that some of us had learned to recognize as from Them continued to occur, and we found the communication was not broken, but remained open to us just to the extent that each was able to take advantage of it, our knowledge of Them has been a living and a growing knowledge. . . .
>
> Nor do I fear to thus frankly state the fact of my knowledge of the existence of MASTERS. . . . From observations made in Europe and America of the many societies I have visited, I am able to say that just in so far as the MASTERS are recognized as "Facts and Ideals" by the members, so far also are the societies progressive and influential. While carefully guarding the Theosophical Society as a whole, and each of its branches, from erecting belief in the MASTERS into a dogma which members must tacitly, if not openly, accept, every member who does believe in Them should be ready to say so

> if challenged, and should never shrink from saying that he carries on his work on lines that he thinks They approve.

Next, Mrs. Besant goes on to discuss the proper attitude to hold when issues are raised, whether of teaching or policy, on which different or contradictory views are held. It is of such major importance as setting forth the practice and principles of H.P.B. and Mr. Judge—practice and principles with which Mrs. Besant was then in full sympathy—that we reproduce it in full:

> It may be as well to remind the readers of LUCIFER that one of the lines laid down by H.P.B. for the conduct of this magazine—and she would not have adopted and carried on a policy in antagonism to the wish of her MASTER—was the admission to its pages of articles with which she totally or partially disagreed, where the articles raised questions bearing on Theosophical teachings or interests. Her statement is worth reproducing:
>
> "Free discussion, temperate, candid, undefiled by personalities and animosity, is, we think, the most efficacious means of getting rid of error and bringing out the underlying truth. . . . Keeping strictly in its editorials and in articles by its individual editors, to the spirit and teachings of pure Theosophy, it [LUCIFER] nevertheless frequently gives room to articles and letters which diverge widely from the Esoteric teachings accepted by the editors, as also by the majority of Theosophists. Readers, therefore, who are accustomed to find in magazine and party publications only such opinions and arguments as the editor believes to be unmistakably orthodox—from his peculiar standpoint—must not condemn any article in LUCIFER with which they are not entirely in accord, or in which expres-

sions are used that may be offensive from a sectarian or a prudish point of view, on the ground that such are unfitted for a Theosophical magazine. They should remember that precisely because LUCIFER is a Theosophical magazine, it opens its columns to writers whose views of life and things may not only slightly differ from its own, but even be diametrically opposed to the opinion of the editors."

This is the policy followed still by LUCIFER, and it should be understood that the publication of such articles, say, as those of Mr. Sinnett and of Mr. Sturdy in the present issue, by no means implies any agreement with the views put forward on the part of my colleague G. R. S. Mead or of myself.

The reference to the articles by Mr. Sinnett and Mr. Sturdy were, in the one case, to Mr. Sinnett's communication on "Esoteric Teaching" from which we have already quoted.[5] In the other case Mrs. Besant was referring to an article on "Gurus and Chelas," in which Mr. Sturdy expressed very emphatically his views on the subject. Mr. Sturdy's article was manifestly inspired indirectly by the numerous claims and counter-claims of "chelaship" and "messages from the Masters" made by or on behalf of various members. Directly, it was, we think, undoubtedly occasioned by a brief article with the same title, and bearing the signature, "A Hindu Chela," published in *Lucifer* for May preceding. Whatever the source or origin of the article by the "Hindu Chela," it is strictly true to the principles and conduct of the Second Section, so far as those have ever been disclosed. In publishing Mr. Sturdy's article Mrs. Besant did not state that she had suppressed its three closing paragraphs, in which Mr. Sturdy discloses his real animus in writing. Mr. Sturdy was a close follower of Col. Olcott and a great admirer of Mr. Sinnett and Mrs.

[5] See preceding chapter.

Besant. It was well understood that his suppressed statements actually were aimed at Mr. Judge, and while Mrs. Besant had already begun to listen to hints and innuendoes against the good faith of Mr. Judge, she was still publicly supporting him and his policies as the policies of H.P.B. The student will do well to read, re-read, and relate as closely as possible the stream of matter in the *Theosophist, Lucifer,* and *The Path* during the year 1893, if he is to discern the weaving of the meshes of the web of the fatal plot of 1894. We can but barely indicate some of the most significant of the knots that were being tied. First, then, let us turn to *The Theosophist* for October, 1893, in which Mr. Sturdy's article is reproduced in full, with an editorial note by Col. Olcott as editor of *The Theosophist*. Colonel Olcott's note reads:

> The three paragraphs within brackets having been expurgated by the editors of *Lucifer* for reasons of their own, and Mr. Sturdy regarding them as the pith of his argument, we print the whole article by his request and commend it to the attention of the reader.—Ed. *Theos.*

Mr. Sturdy's expurgated paragraphs read as follows:

> Of concrete things and persons we need concrete proofs. Of concrete letters and messages from living men, we need concrete evidence; not metaphysical or mere argumentative proof. Yet you can never *disprove* these claims. If I choose to send a letter in green, blue, or red or any other coloured ink or pencil and tell you I received it from a Mahatma for you, or merely say nothing and enclose it in a letter to you, you may be very much astonished, but you can prove no lie or forgery against me. If you are wise you will act as if you had never received it; unless indeed you make a mental note or two against me; one of folly for my having done

such a thing and given no proofs, and another of watchfulness as to my character generally.

Nor does it seem probable that the Mahatmas, who, as we know, teach no dogmas, but always act by the amount of understanding an individual has, would encourage a system of mere statement and claim without accompanying proof; for this would be to lay the seeds in men's hearts of a faith in the statements of other men quite outside their experience and quite unsupported, men whose hearts they had not fathomed. This would lead back to all the evils of the past, not forward into light and knowledge.

All such is glamour: there is no false mystery in chelaship; all nonsense about "developing intuition" is merely making excuses for what cannot be proven and is about the same in the end as the Christian "faith." Let a man go on his path acting sternly by what he *knows*, not by what he is asked or persuaded to believe. Let him act by no directions which may be merely the thoughts of others no wiser than himself. How does he know? He does not know. Then let him be quite clear and straightforward in this, that he does not know.

In *Lucifer* for October, 1893, Mrs. Besant wrote over her signature an article in reference to "Gurus and Chelas" and took a strong stand against the spirit and logic of Mr. Sturdy's article. A brief quotation will disclose her position on what she calls the "fundamental difference" between Mr. Sturdy's views and her own:

Is the most sacred and sublime of all human relationships nothing more than an intellectual bond, entered into with questions that appear to make the initial stage one of mutual suspicion, to be slowly removed by prolonged knowledge of each other in physical life? Not so have I been

> taught, little as I know of these high matters, and the process described by Bro. Sturdy is the complete reversal of all that I have heard as to the methods of the school to which I was introduced by H.P.B.

Mr. Sturdy, it will be remembered, was himself not only a member of the Esoteric School but also had been one of the "E.S.T. Council" appointed by H.P.B., and had been present at the meeting at 19 Avenue Road on May 27, 1891, when the E.S. was reorganized immediately after the death of H.P.B.[6] To understand the breach indicated by the "Gurus and Chelas" articles, these must be related not only to the matters we have been discussing, but in particular to an existing situation and a series of events which were due to it, which we have so far but barely hinted at, so that students might more readily grasp the connection when it required consideration. Let us first treat of the events themselves, and then go into the situation which gave rise to them.

We have earlier mentioned that at the meeting of the E.S. Council on May 27, 1891, all that transpired, with one exception,[7] was covered in the circular of the same date sent to all members of the Esoteric School. That omitted matter was a message from one of the Masters received during the deliberations, and by Mrs. Besant read to those present. We shall recur to this subject again, so that it is sufficient here to speak of the fact. This meeting was under the pledge of secrecy, as was the circular sent to the E.S. members. Immediately following this, and while Mr. Judge was still in England, following H.P.B.'s death, *The Path* for August, 1891, edited during Mr. Judge's absence by "Jasper Niemand" (Mrs. Archibald Keightley, or Julia Campbell-Ver Planck, as her name was then), began with a powerful article on "A Theosophical Education." This article was headed with a message from one of the Masters,

[6] See Chapter XIX.
[7] See Chapter XIX.

and was signed by Jasper Niemand. It should be remembered that at that time no one knew who Jasper Niemand was except Mr. Judge and Mrs. Ver Planck herself. The article went on to say that the "message" had been received by a "student theosophist" *since* H.P.B.'s death, that the message was from H.P.B.'s Master and was "attested by His *real* signature and seal." We have italicized the word "real" because we shall later have to return to the subject.[8]

Following this, on August 30, 1891, Mrs. Besant, in St. James' Hall, London, made a farewell address to the Secularists with whom she had worked for so many years prior to her becoming a Theosophist. The great hall was packed with her old co-workers. Her lengthy address was entitled "1875-1891: a Fragment of Autobiography." Near the close of this address she pledged her word, her senses, her sanity, and her honor that "*since* Madame Blavatsky left, *I have had letters in the same writing and from the same person,*" *i.e.,* from the "Mahatma" from whom the "messages" transmitted by H.P.B. during her lifetime had been believed by Theosophists to emanate.

Naturally, these two public proclamations, the anonymous one in *The Path,* the other the solemn personal affirmation of Mrs. Besant, both of them direct, sweeping, and unqualified, aroused a furore in the world and particularly amongst Theosophists. Because of Mrs. Besant's statement it was inevitably inferred that she herself was in "communication with the Masters" and this inference was strengthened by her subsequent statements to various newspaper interviewers, and by other direct statements similar to the one in *Lucifer* for August, 1893, from which we have quoted in the present chapter. No one, reading Mrs. Besant's various statements during the three years following H.P.B.'s death, and granting her sanity and honesty, could do other than infer that she spoke from direct, immediate personal knowledge and experience of her own, and not from hearsay, inference, or dependence on any one else's assumed pow-

[8] See Chapter XXXIV.

ers and knowledge. These affirmations, coupled with her great reputation and towering place in the Theosophical world, caused numbers of Theosophists throughout the world to look to her, her writings, and her example, as the sure guide to follow. In the Esoteric School the members considered her as little, if any, short of H.P.B.'s stature in the Occult world, and this was particularly the case in England, Europe, and Asia. Her influence, therefore, with the membership both of the Society at large and of the Esoteric School grew to be tremendous and surpassed that of any other living person, while in the world she was the propagandist who could command the most attention, the largest audiences, the greatest publicity in the press. Judge, declining the Presidency by securing the revocation of Olcott's resignation, writing in his magazine largely under pseudonyms, confining his official activities to the routine of a "General Secretary" of a Section, at all times avoided publicity to the utmost possible extent. He was unceasing in his devotion to the work of the School, to the promotion of the First Object, and to the dissemination of *Theosophy*. Such publicity as befell him was due rather to the outspoken praise of Mrs. Besant and others, and to the attacks upon him, direct and indirect, for his vigilant efforts to keep the name, the fame, and the writings of H.P.B. alive before the membership as their example and their guide, than to any necessity of his work or official position, which was at all times purely nominal, as had been the case with H.P.B. herself. And the student may be interested to know that from the year following the death of H.P.B. till his own passing in 1896, his was a sick and over-burdened body, as was H.P.B.'s after the fiery furnace of 1884-5. In fact, during the years 1893-5, Mr. Judge was in such condition that he was for the most of the time able to speak but in whispers, and much of his work was done either in bed, or while traveling in search of physical relief.

Mrs. Besant's fame and reputation for "Occultism," her continuous lectures, her vast and unceasing emission of writings, her capacity for continuous work under unending pressures, her confident surety of opinion and conviction in all things, made her every day more and more the "leader" of the Society. She overshadowed Col. Olcott and Mr. Sinnett as she overshadowed Mr. Judge—with this difference: she was convinced that Mr. Judge had been the real colleague of H.P.B., and that the others were not only "lesser lights" in an Occult sense than Mr. Judge, but that they had not been, and were not, true to Masters and H.P.B. as Mr. Judge was. Her support it was, chiefly, her looking to Judge for counsel and advice, that gave him standing with the general membership outside America.

Colonel Olcott and Mr. Sinnett, both exceedingly tenacious of whatever opinions they held, both greatly enjoying the prestige which they had acquired, the one as President-Founder, and the other as the President of the London Lodge and writer of the most popular treatises on Theosophy, could but be affected by the rise of Mrs. Besant into the luminous zone of the Theosophical firmament. Neither of them had been pleased, either with H.P.B. and her "interferences," or with her partiality—as it must have seemed to them—toward the obscure and unpretentious young man upon whom Theosophy and the Society perforce had to depend in America. With the passing of H.P.B. it could but have seemed the natural and the appropriate thing for them to step, with proper expressions of regret and appreciation, into the place made vacant by the death of "the old lion of the Punjab." But when Mr. Judge kept on speaking and writing of H.P.B. as though she were still living and still the surpassing factor of the Movement, her writings the criterion by which to weigh and act, it was too much! Were they never to receive that recognition which was rightly theirs? With Mr. Judge out of the way H.P.B. had been easier to deal with while she was alive; with Judge out of the way, it would be easy to deal with H.P.B. dead. But when Mr. Judge found in Mrs. Besant a supporter and defender, both of H.P.B. and himself, and their brief triumph seemed threatened, without a chance of viability, it was much too much!

Hence the issues of "hero worship," of "dogmatism," of the "neutrality of the T.S."; hence "Old Diary Leaves"; hence the revived activities of the London Lodge with its "Transactions"; hence the swift coming to the surface of disharmony, disunion, charges and counter-charges, claims and counter-claims.

CHAPTER XXVI

BEGINNINGS OF THE "JUDGE CASE"

WHEN the "Message" in the August, 1891, *Path* came to Col. Olcott's attention he wrote Mr. Judge. Then ensued a long private correspondence between the two, Judge doing his best to mollify the President-Founder while yet holding the position of uncompromising loyalty to H.P.B. and her Mission, and to the policies he was pursuing; Col. Olcott, determined to bring matters to an issue once and for all and enforce his own authority and standing as the "Official Head" of the Society. Colonel Olcott's strategy and tactics were grievously interfered with and upset for the time being by Mrs. Besant's charges against his moral character which caused him to "flee from the field of battle" by resigning under fire. When Mr. Judge came to his support and rescue, the better nature of Col. Olcott was once more in the saddle, and his public and official, as well as his private and personal, acts and statements became once more for a brief period those of the earlier years of his probation. But when it was whispered in his ear that it was Mr. Judge himself who had concocted the charges against him, with the purpose to unseat him in the love and veneration of the membership, and that Mr. Judge had come to his aid only through fear of being unmasked, Col. Olcott, old, sick, and disheartened, threw off his faint-heartedness, once more girded on his armor and weapons and re-entered the lists for a *combat a l'outrance*—"for the sake of the Masters and the Society," as he verily believed. It seems never to have occurred to him to write Mr. Judge his fears and suspicions direct and ask the facts; it seems never to have occurred to him to investigate or verify in any way the suspicions breathed to him. His vanity pricked, his jealousies aroused, his own sincerity and devotion mocked, as it must have seemed to him, he took his fears for facts, his suspicions for certainties, and was thenceforth as sure of the "ingratitude" and the "disloyalty" of Mr. Judge as before he had been of H.P.B.'s. His fiery courage, his impetuous nature, all his noble and strong qualities were thenceforth blindly at the service of the masked and hidden enemies of the Theosophical Movement.

While Mrs. Besant was on her third visit to America in the winter of 1892-3, Mr. Judge showed her the correspondence with Col. Olcott. One of the letters of Mr. Judge was on questions raised by Col. Olcott on the "message" in *The Path* of August, 1891.[1] Mrs. Besant asked and obtained from Mr. Judge consent to the publication of this letter in her magazine *Lucifer,* where it appeared in April, 1893, immediately after her return from the United States. This letter was, according to the restriction imposed by Mr. Judge, not published as to Col. Olcott, but as to "An Indian Brother," and was given by Mrs. Besant the caption, "An Interesting Letter."

So soon as *Lucifer* with the "interesting letter" reached India, Col. Olcott took action. In *The Theosophist* for July, 1893, appear two articles in criticism of the views expressed by Mr. Judge in the "interesting letter." The second of these, signed "N. D. K." (the initials of N. D. Khandalavala, a prominent Indian member), is an argument, from a similar point of view to that of Mr. Sturdy in "Gurus and Chelas," against the danger of mere substitution by the unwise of "Masters" for a personal "Savior." "Reliance on Masters as ideals and as facts" seems to N. D. K. mere folly. N. D. K. says:

> Does not the Christian missionary come canting after us with exactly the same words? Substitute the words "Jesus and Saviour" for "Masters" in the sentences of Mr. Judge, and

[1] See Chapter XX.

> they will read like a propaganda of the Evangelist preachers.

N. D. K. objects very strongly to Mr. Judge's saying that he "knows out of his own experience" of the existence of Masters and suggests that Mr. Judge "systematically and exhaustively bring forward his experiences for the benefit of us all. . . . There is no virtue whatsoever in boldly making an assertion, and withholding the evidence upon which the assertion has been based." Most objectionable of all to N. D. K. is Mr. Judge's statement that his means of identifying a "message" is "within himself," and not by means of external evidences such as signatures, seal, etc. This, N. D. K. thinks, is very bad indeed. He quotes from H.P.B. on the great need for "unbiassed and clear judgment" in all matters, but apparently has never read H.P.B.'s article in *Lucifer* for September, 1888, on "Lodges of Magic" in which she discusses this very question of the evidences of messages from the same standpoint as Mr. Judge's statements, in reply to those who were whispering about that some of *her* Messages were fraudulent, others genuine, etc. N. D. K.'s implications would all apply equally to H.P.B. as to Mr. Judge, and, as the student may discern for himself by comparison of statements, all that Mr. Judge wrote in his "interesting letter" had before him been said by H.P.B., to the same annoyance of the "doubting Thomases" who, themselves unable to "communicate," nevertheless wanted "proofs" satisfactory to themselves. N. D. K.'s article has for title and subtitle, "THEOSOPHY IN THE WEST. THE TENDENCY TOWARDS DOGMATISM."

The other article in *The Theosophist* had for title, "Theosophic Freethought" and is signed by Messrs. Walter R. Old and Sidney V. Edge, Col. Olcott's two chief lieutenants at the time. Mr. Old, like Mr. Sturdy, had been a member of the "E.S.T. Council" during H.P.B.'s lifetime and had been present at the Avenue Road meeting of May 27, 1891. "Theosophic Freethought" must have been written and published with the full endorsement of Col. Olcott. The writers profess to regard Mr. Judge's statements as "virtually . . . a dogma" and the publication of his letter as in itself a "leading to dogmatism." They go on to say:

> Hence we cannot conclude otherwise than that a personal declaration of belief coming from Mr. Judge and unsupported by any evidence showing how, in the face of general experience, he has attained that belief, is extremely inimical to the spirit of our Society. . . .
>
> Another dangerous dogma advanced by Mr. Judge is the statement that "a very truism, when uttered by a Mahatma, has a deeper meaning for which the student must seek, but which he will lose if he stops to criticize and weigh the words in mere ordinary scales." . . . if we push it to its ultimate issue, as Mr. Judge seems anxious to do, its thoroughly noxious and unwholesome nature becomes simply overpowering. . . .
>
> Of the same nature as the above, and of equally dangerous tendency, is the statement in regard to messages received from a Master that "The signature is not important. The means of identification are not located in signatures at all. If you have not the means yourself for proving and identifying such a message, then signature, seal, papers, water-mark, what-not, are all useless. As to 'Master's Seal,' about which you put me the question, I do not know. Whether he has a seal or uses one is something on which I am ignorant." . . .
>
> To sum up: it appears from Mr. Judge's letter:
>
> 1. A Theosophist of high standing and authority in the Society has a right to widely affirm the existence of Masters as a matter of personal experience, without adducing proofs of his experience.

2. That others may, unchallenged, assert the same with equal force, upon the authority of his unproved personal statement.

3. That so long as he is prepared to take the Karma of such assertions, it is not a matter of concern to any other member of the same body.

4. That the progress of the T.S. lies in fidelity to the "assertions" of a few of its members.

5. That a truism when uttered by a Mahatma becomes something more than a truism.

6. That letters received from a Mahatma will not permit of the usual tests of identification.

7. That the only test is one's own intuition.

The reader, with the collateral circumstances in mind and the text of Mr. Judge's "interesting letter" before him, can take these criticisms by Messrs. Old and Edge one by one and compare them in spirit and fairness, as well as in logic, with the manner and matter of Mr. Judge's statements. The irony of the situation is enhanced by the simple fact that none of the "messages" which formed the basis of the shafts leveled at Mr. Judge had been received by him, or had been made public by him, and that he had scrupulously avoided any statements direct or indirect that might direct or attract attention to himself as Master's agent. On the other hand the statements made by Mrs. Besant and Mr. Sinnett were in such form and made in such circumstances as directly to challenge acceptance or rejection on their mere *ipse dixit*. And the same was exactly true of Col. Olcott. No "evidence" was ever offered by either of these three, no arguments, no citations of teachings, to support their claims. Each repeatedly claimed "communications from the Masters of H.P.B.," with himself as the sole "authority" for the claims; each, at one time and another, rejected the "authenticity" of messages coming *through H.P.B.*, the "rejected" messages of H.P.B. always those which, if genuine, upset their own teachings and their own claims. In contrast with this, the student can easily ascertain for himself by examination that the "fraudulent" messages attributed to both H.P.B. and Mr. Judge were in every case in strict accord with the whole philosophy of Occultism as recorded by them during twenty years, and with all the "accepted Messages" from the Masters.

Setting aside the possibility that there may be modes of communication and means of verification of Occult communications which are absolute to Masters and "accepted Chelas," and wholly unknown and unsuspected by any others—setting all this aside, what possible "proofs" are there of the genuineness of an alleged communication from "other planes of being"?

The records of all religions are full of communications from God, demons, angels, discarnate "spirits," what-not. Modern Spiritualism and psychical research swarm with the statements of such communications. The proofs, when investigated, always come down to two things: (1) the affirmation of the recipient that he has received the communication and that *he* knows the source of the message; (2) the phenomenal accompaniments—light, a voice, a vision, objects moved without physical contact, words and letters "precipitated," facts related and events described unknown to the recipient, or supposedly known to him alone, prophecies, and so on. These proofs have in all ages been sufficient to satisfy multitudes of recipients and masses of believers, and to excite to fury the incredulity of others. But when the thoughtful man compares the respective "revelations" he always finds them in gross contradiction, one with another; more, he finds the accepted *explanation* of the recipients and their followers inconsistent within itself, and impossible of reconciliation with the everyday demonstrated facts of life, and *their* accepted explanation. One would think, to listen to any of the votaries of these communications, that there remain no *mysteries* in life to explain, whereas, any reflective mind must admit that life holds little else than mysteries, and that the true explanation and understanding of God and Nature and

Man are as far from human solution as ever. The most that can be truly said by the layman is that all these proofs demonstrate is that "there are more things in heaven and earth, Horatio, than are dreamt of in your philosophy."

It remains true, as H.P.B. wrote at the time of the *New York Sun* libel, that "Occult phenomena can never be *proved* in a Court of Law during this century." "Messages," whether from Masters or from other sources, must continue to be for the "uninitiated" a matter of intelligent or unintelligent, of consistent or inconsistent, belief or disbelief. Phenomena at best are but accompaniments, not certificates, and if the Source of any message is metaphysical and transcendental, its verification must be looked for on the plane of its origin, not that of its receipt. Hence the repeated statements of H.P.B. and Mr. Judge, as well as those of the Masters in the generally accepted communications from Them, that "messages" as well as Messengers must be judged on their *philosophical and moral worth,* not on the basis of "authority" or phenomenal accompaniments. But to return to "Theosophic Freethought."

A footnote to the article by Messrs. Old and Edge says, in connection with Mr. Judge's remarks on "Master's Seal":

> In regard to this statement we can only remark that Mr. Judge's memory must be seriously defective. We must therefore remind him that a very important step in connection with the re-organization of the Esoteric Section of the T.S. was taken, after the death of H.P.B., on the authority of a certain message, purporting to come from one of the Mahatmas, and which bore, as Mr. Judge will now remember, a seal-impression, said by him to be that of "the Master." No doubt Mr. Judge will take the opportunity of either rectifying his statement or of showing how his acting upon the author-

ity of "the Master's" seal at one time, and professing ignorance of it at another, may be regarded as consistent.

Advance proofs of *The Theosophist* containing the article on "Theosophic Freethought" were sent to many persons in England and the United States, and the article itself was at once issued from Adyar with a Madras imprint and sent broadcast throughout the Society in pamphlet form. No public attention was paid to it by either Mr. Judge or Mrs. Besant, as, under the proclaimed neutrality of the T.S., any member thereof had full freedom and liberty to hold any opinions that might seem acceptable to him, and to express them. We have before called attention to the fact that no member of the T.S. was bound to any obligation other than *assent* to the First Object, and to the other fact that the Esoteric Section or School admitted only (1) those who *accepted in full* the Three Objects of the T.S.; (2) who professed full belief in and acceptance of *Theosophy* and pledged themselves to "endeavor to make Theosophy a living power" in their life; who pledged themselves to "support before the world the Theosophical *Movement* and its Founders"; (3) who pledged themselves to strict voluntary obedience to the Rules of the School. These rules were clear and unequivocal. Every member of the E.S., before being permitted to enter it, was furnished with a copy of the *Preliminary Memoranda,* the pledge, and the Book of Rules, so that he might inform himself fully of the conditions of his entrance and continuance in the School, as well as of the *sine qua non* conditions precedent to any progress in esotericism. Thus whoever entered the School did so voluntarily with full knowledge in advance of what was required of him, with full warning that his difficulties would lie within himself, and pledged his "most solemn and sacred word of honour" to all the conditions.

Both Mr. Old and Mr. Edge were members of the Esoteric School, the former having entered during the life of H.P.B., the latter after her passing. As the statements, criticisms, and charges in the Old and Edge article, and particularly the footnote just quoted, were in direct violation both of the spirit and the letter of some of the clauses of the pledge and certain of the Rules of the School, prompt and decisive action was taken by Mr. Judge and Mrs. Besant as Co-Heads of the E.S. Both Messrs. Old and Edge were in that geographical section which was under the immediate jurisdiction of Mrs. Besant. She therefore drew up a "strictly private and confidential" circular letter dated "August, 1893," which was signed by Mr. Judge with her and sent from London to all E.S. members throughout the world. At the same time both Messrs. Old and Edge were suspended from membership in the E.S.

This circular, which was headed, "To All Members of E.S.T.," reads, in part, as follows:

> In the July *Theosophist* [1893] an article appeared signed by W. R. Old and S. V. Edge, entitled "Theosophic Freethought," as a criticism on Brother Judge's letter in *Lucifer*. No objection except that of good taste could be made to the article considered as a criticism, since Brother Judge concedes to every one a right to their opinions and to the expression of such in every case except where questions of a pledge or of honor are concerned. So with the article we are not concerned, but we are with the foot-note of it. . . .
>
> The article was given to public printers and sent in advance to many persons in Europe, but it was not sent in time to London, where Brother Judge was in July, to permit our cabling to India, and no previous notice was given Brother Judge, nor was he asked his views.
>
> This foot-note is, *first*, a violation of the pledge of secrecy made by Brother Old . . . and *second*, is a violation of honor and confidence as a member of the Council of the E.S.T. By reason of the above we are compelled to take action.

> Therefore . . . we have for the present suspended them [Messrs. Old and Edge] from their membership in the E.S.T. . . .
>
> But the statement in above foot-note is itself untrue. The reorganization of the School in 1891 was not based on a message from the Master: it was based on several letters and certificates from H.P.B. (see Council Minutes) explicitly making William Q. Judge her representative in America, and on one from her assigning to Annie Besant the position she was to hold after her [H.P.B.'s] death. . . .

The circular also contained a signed statement by Mrs. Besant and other Councillors present at the meeting on May 27, 1891, refuting in positive terms the assertions and implications in the footnote to Messrs. Old and Edge's "Theosophic Freethought." To this we shall refer again in its proper connection.[2]

To complete the picture of the marshaling of the opposing forces the reader should now turn to *The Theosophist* for May, June, July, and August, 1893, and read carefully the successive instalments of Col. Olcott's "Old Diary Leaves" first printed during those months. After the preliminary details of his first thirteen chapters, covering his acquaintance with H.P.B. and the crowding events culminating in the publication of "Isis Unveiled" in 1877, the Colonel pauses to discuss the writing of that work, the "collaboration" of the Masters in its production, the nature of H.P.B., and the possible explanations of the mysteries of which he had caught many glimpses during the preceding three years. In Chapter XIV he lays down the seven hypotheses of which we have earlier spoken,[3] and proceeds to argue and discuss them through the succeeding chapters in the fashion already indicated. In the August number he propounds his central idea, the dominant note to which he has all along

[2] See Chapter XXXI.
[3] See Chapter XXIII.

been leading up. He says that H.P.B. *"appears to have been the subject of a distinct mental evolution."*

What he meant by this is very clearly shown and argued in the body of the chapter and subsequently. He meant that H.P.B. at best was a *student* of the Wisdom-Religion, the same as any and all others; that when she began her mission she was both ignorant and misinformed on many subjects and teachings which afterwards she learned as she "progressed." Her sole and questionable advantage was in the possession of psychic and clairvoyant faculties which enabled the Masters to *use* her for Their purposes in the same way and under the same disadvantages as a control or guide uses a Spiritualist medium or that a mesmerist or hypnotizer uses a sensitive or subject.

He proceeds to illustrate this fundamental idea of his by saying:

> Take, for instance, her teachings on Re-incarnation, the strong foundation-stone of the the ancient occult philosophy, which was affirmed in the *Secret Doctrine* and her other later writings. When we worked on *Isis* it was neither taught us by the Mahatmas, nor supported by her in her literary controversies or private discussions, of those earlier days. She held to, and defended, the theory that human souls, after death, passed on by a course of purificatory evolution to other and more spiritualized planets. . . .
>
> She told Mr. Walker R. Old—who is my informant—that she was not taught the doctrine of Re-incarnation until 1879—when we were in India. . . .
>
> Ultimately, the doctrine of Re-incarnation was fully accepted and expounded, both in its exoteric sense and esoterically.

In the course of his chapter he suggests that he has "notes" of a conversation between one of the Mahatmas and himself in which the Adept affirmed the same theory of "purificatory evolution" on "higher spheres." Naïvely he inquires:

> Is it possible that Re-incarnation was not taught this Adept by *his* Master, and that he, as well as H.P.B., had to learn it subsequently? There are said to be sixty-three stages of Adeptship and it is not impossible.

Colonel Olcott's views of H.P.B. as a "student" had been very succinctly voiced by Mr. Old at the White Lotus Day commemoration at Adyar on May 8, 1893, and printed in *The Theosophist* for June. Mr. Old was introduced by Col. Olcott and made the address of the day. He said:

> It is provided in the Constitution of the Society, that perfect freedom of opinion shall be allowed to all its members; but nothing would be more dangerous to the catholicity of our doctrines than to suppose this to convey with it the right, to any individual member, of forcing his views upon others; or of reading into the writings of H.P.B., or any other person connected with the movement, anything of authority; or yet of enunciating therefrom a dogma or *credo* which shall be considered pre-eminently Theosophical or binding upon Theosophists generally. And the dangers we have to face are undoubtedly of this nature . . .
>
> What we now need to recognize is the merit of that self-devotion to the cause of Truth which characterized the life-work of H.P.B. No impartial student of her writings can fail to recognize the indications of a steady unfoldment of mind, an ever-widening spiritual perception, with the concomitant changes of view-point and modifications of doctrine.

Colonel Olcott, Messrs. Sinnett, Bertram Keightley, Old, Sturdy, Edge, the leading Hindus, and many others of lesser prominence were now all of one mind in regard to the "dangers" besetting the Society and the Movement; their ideas regarding H.P.B. now sown broadcast in America, England, Europe, and India. The machinery of the Society was in their hands, its most widely circulated publication under their control. What else was lacking in the equipment necessary to relegate H.P.B. and her defender, Judge, to the background, to subordinate the teachings of Theosophy given out by these two colleagues to the "more recent teachings" and the "progressive development" of other "students" and "Occultists" more in harmony with the "official authority" of the President-Founder? What was still essential to do away with the policy and example of H.P.B. and Mr. Judge and replace them by a management and guidance from Adyar, without risk of failure for the conspirators behind the scenes, and without breaking up the Society? The storm of 1884-5 had shown that however violent the commotion, attacks from without could not destroy the integrity of the Movement nor the prestige of H.P.B. with the members. The Coues-Collins-Lane-*Sun* conspiracy had come far nearer achieving its object in 1889-90, because it had been hatched within the Society, and had the tacit sympathy and support of Col. Olcott until he saw that its success would ruin the Society. But it, too, had failed, because H.P.B. and Mr. Judge were both alive and had, in the newly formed Esoteric Section, a loyal battalion of members of the Society pledged to Theosophy *first*.

This time the conspiracy had all the elements of victory in hand save one only. Could Mrs. Besant be brought to join hands with Col. Olcott, Mr. Sinnett, and the rest, the combination would be invincible. But for more than two years she had already taken her stand in the most positive manner, for all that H.P.B. and Judge had from the beginning proclaimed and fought for, in principle and in practice. Could she be brought to change sides on the very eve of battle?

Determined to banish the spectre of the "dead" H.P.B. whose memory was still a more potent influence than their living claims to preferment, it was all too clear that this could not be done except by ruining the reputation of Mr. Judge. Could Mrs. Besant be made the fulcrum of their energies, then Mr. Judge could be routed, H.P.B. consigned to the region of eulogiums, and a victorious future assured to the Society and its "leaders." There would be no greater risk than that a few recalcitrants might have to be read out of the Society or forced to resign or secede.

But Mrs. Besant was no ignorant and superstitious "Christian," like Madame Coulomb, and therefore not to be approached with threats and bribes. She was no psychic or medium like Mrs. Cables and Miss Mabel Collins, therefore to be swept off her feet by some astral intoxication or personal experience in psychology. Nor was she an Elliott Coues, brilliant but conscienceless, educated but steeped in ethical savagery, to whom Theosophy was a mere means to personal ends. If she were to be seduced and suborned—made to serve as dupe and tool of "the mighty magic of Prakriti,"—then indeed would need be called in play the fine art of oriental subtlety and sophistication in the mysteries of the governing forces in human life; subtlety and sophistication laughed at by the wisest of Western minds, whose very incredulity and scepticism in regard to their own susceptibility to the sway of "Occult powers" makes them, at occasion, victim to their own virtues. Messrs. Hume, Sinnett, Massey, Olcott, and many another able, sincere and honorable-minded man had been, in turn and in successive links, so influenced, all unknown to themselves, that their course had become the exact opposite to that taught and pursued by Masters and by H.P.B.; the opposite of the very course originally taken by themselves. And the substitution of charts, the change in direction, had been so subtly accomplished that the more the victims went astray, the more profoundly convinced they were of the rectitude and consistency of their conduct!

The welter of fact and opinion covering the years 1893-5 is not easy to assemble, assort, relate, and marshal into something like order and proportion. Yet this is the task that confronts, not merely the historian, but every Theosophical student who would be true to his duty, to the Movement and himself. A firm conclusion must be reached or the student will always be harassed by doubts, bewilderments, uncertainties. Such a firm conclusion will be arrived at either as the result of knowledge acquired at first hand and weighed with impartiality in the light of the principles of Theosophy, or it will rest upon no better basis than hearsay and reliance upon authority—mere blind faith, of which the world has ever held an overplus and from which all mankind suffers continually.

Under the criteria afforded by the Theosophy which all the protagonists professed, the student has to take into consideration not only the physical facts and factors, but he has to ascertain and evaluate factors and phenomena metaphysical—the Psychic, the Manasic, the Spiritual components of actions and events. These various constituents are not disjunctive and sequential, but integral and correlative, their governing importance as prime factors of correct judgment in inverse order to that habitually employed by mankind. Moreover, since it is certain that whatever, either of Truth or error or falsehood there may be in the world, or whatever their ultimate source, they have all reached mankind through the agency of human beings, it follows that the student must, of necessity, weigh actors as well as actions; persons and personages as well as their statements; motives and character as well as opinions and belief. And there is no alternative route, Theosophically or practically, either to accurate knowledge or correct judgment. As so well put in the Preface to H. P. Blavatsky's "Key to Theosophy":

> To the mentally lazy or obtuse, Theosophy must remain a riddle; for in the world mental as in the world spiritual each man must progress by his own efforts. The writer cannot do the reader's thinking for him, nor would the

> latter be any the better off if such vicarious thought were possible.

As with all conspiracies, much of what occurred in 1893 and subsequently is enveloped in the obscurity of secrecy and silence. But there is no maxim, exoteric or esoteric, more profoundly true than the aphorism that "murder will out." Perception, inference, and testimony are all essential components of true knowledge, and when the ascertainable facts, the relevant testimony extant, are fitted together, all the rest becomes a matter of unavoidable inference to the logical mind: the Great Betrayal is exposed in all its hideous blackness, and the subsequent degradation and disintegration of the Theosophical Movement into sects and sectaries seen to be the Karmic consequence of the actions of the students themselves.

CHAPTER XXVII

MRS. BESANT CHANGES SIDES

It is only by observing with utmost care the sequence of events in 1893 and 1894 that the student will be able to perceive the causal and invisible springs from which those events emanated, and thus to relate the exoteric to the esoteric aspects of the record made by the opposing forces on the field of battle. In this respect it is like the study of a game of chess, with its successive alternating moves of the effigies of the different classes by the opposing protagonists: Judge on the one side, the President-Founder on the other; the capture of the "Queen" the essential of the "checkmate."

Mr. Bertram Keightley, whose indiscretions had formed one of the ingredients of the Coues-Collins explosion, had been sent temporarily to the United States by H.P.B. There, under H.P.B.'s instructions, Mr. Judge had put him to work to enable him to recover his stamina. Despite his follies, H.P.B. had written most kindly of him to various American workers, as he well deserved in view of his many services to the Cause.

In a little while Mr. Keightley, finding that the American members looked up to him as one who had been close to H.P.B. for years, began to speak as an "Occultist" upon the many problems treated of in H.P.B.'s Instructions to the Esoteric Section. These interpretations of Mr. Keightley's were taken by many as "authoritative," and Mr. Keightley was considered as the "representative" of H.P.B. This finally compelled H.P.B. to issue the Notice of August 9, 1890. This Notice was, in its essential matters, as follows:

> 3. The only "orders" in Instructions which I issue in the U. S. are through Mr. William Q.

> Judge, or those which I myself sign my name to with my physical hand.
>
> 4. Any report or statement by any one of orders or instructions alleged to be by me in any other form than as stated in the foregoing paragraph are and shall be false; and any member acting on any other sort of order and without first sending the same to Mr. William Q. Judge will be expelled from the Section.
>
> 5. I desire above all that the members of this Section shall exercise as much common-sense as they are capable of and that they shall avoid all dealings with astral messages, reports, spooks and the like until they shall have attained the requisite knowledge and ability.

Mr. Keightley was recalled to London and at the end of the year 1890 transferred to India, whither he went in time to serve as the delegate of the American, British, and European Sections at the Adyar Convention. During the year 1891 Mr. Keightley remained in India as a volunteer helper at the headquarters and at the Adyar Convention at the close of 1891 was elected General Secretary of the Indian Section. His work in India brought him an acquaintance with every prominent member of the Society and a thorough knowledge of the condition of affairs in the Indian Branches. The deplorable state in which he found them is set forth at length in his "Report" to the Indian Convention at the close of 1892—a Report given in detail in the "Supplement" to *The Theosophist* for January, 1893, and to which we have before adverted.[1]

Mr. Bertram Keightley was a man of wealth, of good education and excellent abilities. He had become attached to H.P.B. at the time of her European visit in the summer of 1884. He and his nephew, Dr. Archibald Keightley, had contributed freely in time, money, and work to the activities in England which followed upon H.P.B.'s settlement there in 1887. To them more than

[1] See Chapter XXIII.

to any and all others was due the sustentation of the work in England until the conversion of Mrs. Besant in the early summer of 1889. His relation to the Movement naturally brought him a personal acquaintance which, by 1893, covered the whole area of the Society, in the United States, in England, on the Continent, and in Asia. It was known by all that he had been firmly loyal personally to H.P.B. during all the troubled events of the last seven years of her stormy career, and it was known by some that he had done what few indeed were able to do—he had submitted without resentment to drastic correction and discipline at H.P.B.'s hands. Naturally materialistic he had, like all materialists whose attention is finally awakened, been intensely interested in the psychical aspect of the teachings of Theosophy. Having no capacities—or infirmities—of his own in a psychical way, he was the more impressed by those who had, or claimed to have, such "gifts." It was this tendency which had involved him with Miss Mabel Collins. In India, a land which teems with "Gurus" and their "disciples" whose whole life-effort is the development of abnormal faculties, he soon came in contact with devotees of the various sorts of Yoga, and amongst these was G. N. Chakravarti, whose destiny it was to become the first of the evil geniuses of Mrs. Besant.

Gyanendra Nath Chakravarti was born a Brahmin of the Sandilya Gotra. In his twentieth year he became, through the influence of his uncle, a member of the Cawnpore Branch of the T.S. Young as he was, he was selected as a member of the Committee which, at the Convention in December, 1884, unanimously recommended that no defense be made on behalf of H.P.B. against the Coulomb charges. In the intervening years he had contributed occasional articles to *The Theosophist* and was, in 1893, President of the Students Theosophical Association at Allahabad. He had been educated in Western ideas, first at a missionary school at Benares, then at Calcutta University, and at Muir College, Allahabad. Subsequently, he had filled the chair of physical science at a college in Bareilly, and, at the time of meeting Mr. Bertram Keightley, he was Professor of mathematics at Muir College. He had also studied law and had been admitted to practice in the English courts in India. Nor had his breeding been in any wise neglected from the oriental standpoint. He had been strictly reared in all the observances of his caste, was thoroughly versed in the scriptures and traditions of Brahminism, and was highly esteemed by his co-religionists as well as among the English. He was well known to Col. Olcott and on friendly terms with both native and English members of the T.S. in India.

Although Prof. Chakravarti had not been active Theosophically and was not a member of the Esoteric Section but was, on the contrary, a chela of one of the numerous Yoga systems in India, Mr. Bertram Keightley soon came to believe him to be, if not a Mahatma, at least an Occultist of high rank and in direct connection with the Masters of H.P.B. Moreover, in the congenial atmosphere of Col. Olcott and the other workers at headquarters, Mr. Keightley found tendencies and predilections in the line of the Third Object fully in flower. In the circumstances it was inevitable that these influences should divorce him more and more from the lines followed by H.P.B. and those wedded to her view of the true mission of the Theosophical Society.

By the spring of 1893, "Old Diary Leaves" and the direct personal exertion of Col. Olcott's influence had largely accomplished their intended purpose in India and to a considerable degree in the West. The time was ripe to carry the war of ideas into the enemy's country. This was the real occasion for Mr. Bertram Keightley's going from India, first to the United States and then to England, and no better ally or agent could have been selected for the work in hand. Accordingly, Mr. Keightley attended the Convention of the American Section in April, 1893, as delegate from the Indian Section and as bearer of Col. Olcott's Presidential communication, as has been recited.[2]

As will more and more appear, Mr. Judge knew well

[2] See Chapter XXV.

the real purpose behind all of Col. Olcott's moves, and saw those moves clearly long in advance. Concurrently with the questions ostensibly raised over dogmatism and neutrality, with the unsolved problem of the status of H.P.B. and her teachings, with the corollary difficulties evoked by the dust of side issues raised to obscure the real cause of conflict and thus confuse the membership, Mr. Judge knew he had to face the hidden source of all these dangers. This was the secret Brahminical hostility to the great First Object of the Society, which had been slowly festering since 1881, which had perverted the Movement in India, and which, if not checked, must result in the corruption or destruction of the Society in the West. Mr. Judge had, therefore, for a long time been steadily at work to allay Brahminical suspicions that the Society was a Buddhist propaganda in disguise, and to bring the Society in India to a more close adhesion to the line of the First Object. Just prior to Mr. Bertram Keightley's return to the West he had begun an active public campaign along the same lines. He contributed to *Lucifer* for April, 1893, a striking article, "India, A Trumpet Call at a Crisis," to which the student is referred, in connection with the "Interesting Letter," published in the same number of *Lucifer*. At the same time he drew up an eloquently worded and moving appeal which he addressed "To the Brahmins of India," and this he sent to as many Hindu members as could be reached. This circular he also published in *The Path* for May, 1893, with a prefatory note, reading as follows:

> The subjoined circular has been sent by me to as many Brahmins as I could reach. I have purposely used the words "Brahmins of India" in the title because I hold to the view of the *Vedas* and the ancient laws that the Brahmin is not merely he who is born of a Brahmin father. In America lack of accurate knowledge respecting Indian religions causes a good deal of misapprehension about Brahmanism and Buddhism,

> as very many think Buddhism to be India's religion, whereas in fact it is not, but, on the contrary, the prevailing form of belief in India is Brahmanism. This necessary distinction should be remembered and false notions upon the subject dissipated as much as possible. Buddhism does not prevail in India, but in countries outside it, such as Burmah, Japan, Ceylon, and others. The misconception by so many Americans about the true home of Buddhism if not corrected may tend to cause the Brahmins to suppose that the T.S. here spreads abroad the wrong notion; and no form of religion should be preferred in the T.S. above another.

Still earlier than the above articles, Mr. Judge had written privately to Mr. George E. Wright, a leading member of the Chicago Branch, suggesting that an effort be made to secure representation for the T.S. at the World's Parliament of Religions to be held at the Chicago Fair in 1893. This was in the Fall of 1892. Mr. Wright set to work and after some difficulty the necessary recognition was achieved and dates arranged for the Theosophists. The idea of Theosophical representation was received with acclaim in Europe and India as well as among the American members. When Mr. Bertram Keightley arrived in America Mr. Judge at once broached to him the advisability of Brahminical as well as Buddhistic representation at the Parliament and, without disclosing more than the apparent advantages, suggested that such representation should be under the auspices of the T.S., and requested Mr. Keightley's advice and aid in procuring representation the most distinguished possible. Mr. Bertram Keightley urged the selection of Chakravarti as representing the Brahmins and H. Dharmapala, a distinguished Ceylonese, for the Buddhists. He undertook to secure the consent of Chakravarti. Accordingly, subscriptions were opened in the United States and in England to defray the traveling expenses of the two delegates.

Serious difficulties at once supervened, for while Chakravarti was very agreeable to the proposed plan, grave objections were raised among the Brahmins. Such a mingling with "Mlechhas" (foreigners) was offensive to their teachings and traditions, and it was a violation of caste for a Brahmin to cross the seas. Thus, if he attended at all, Chakravarti would be "out-caste" for the time being and would be compelled upon his return either to renounce his caste or to submit to purificatory rites which, to Western minds, would be superstitious and degrading, and to an orthodox Brahmin extremely humiliating.

Nevertheless, the difficulties were resolved and all objections overcome. Chakravarti formally accepted the invitation to attend the Parliament as the guest of the Society. Three Brahminical associations were induced to countenance his mission by appointing him to represent them. They were: the *Hari Bhakti Prodayini* of Cawnpore; *Varnashrama Dharma Sabbha* of Delhi, and the *Sanatan Dharma Rakshani Sabbha* of Meerut. All this, as may be inferred, occupied several months in its accomplishment.

Meanwhile Mr. Judge had followed up the articles mentioned by publishing an editorial in *The Path* for July, 1893, with the significant title, "A Plot Against the Theosophical Society." Ostensibly this was drawn up as a warning concerning a renewed series of attacks on H.P.B. by certain enemies outside the Society (Messrs. W. Emmette Coleman and Vv. Solovyoff, although not mentioned by name), but the real caution is contained in the concluding paragraph, reading as follows:

> There is some likelihood that slight assistance will be rendered by one or two disaffected persons in India, who in the past have aided in spreading similar attacks which have been published in spiritualistic journals. From time to time we may be able to present further plans and purposes of this brigade of plotters for the

> information of theosophists in advance. The plotters expect this to hurt the Society, but theosophists should know that nothing can hurt it if they remain loyal to their convictions, if they endeavor to understand the theosophic philosophy, if they avoid personalities and confine themselves, as was suggested by one of the Adepts long ago, to philosophical and ethical propaganda designed to benefit the moral nature of the community in which a Theosophist may live. No plot can avail against this. But we have thought it well, on behalf of the conspirators, to publish this notice as a preliminary to further details when the time is ready.

Other articles in *The Path* all written and published in view of the disastrous undertow already pulling the members from their allegiance to the First Object of the Society and their reverence for H.P.B., have already been noted. All these articles had an application to events immediately at hand and forthcoming, and not merely an informative and teaching value on Theosophical doctrines. The same is true of Mr. Judge's rendition of the "Bhagavad-Gita" and his "Ocean of Theosophy." The one gave to the students a faithful version of the greatest of the Brahminical philosophical disquisitions; the other put into clear English a correct presentation of Theosophical teachings, free from the crudities of Mr. Sinnett's "Esoteric Buddhism," and without the materialistic bias and speculations of that book. The "Ocean" remains to this day the one authentic treatment in small compass of the whole of the vast subjects dealt with in the "Secret Doctrine," and is, in fact, a simplified and brief version of Madame Blavatsky's great work. It was first issued early in 1893.

As before indicated in the case of H.P.B. in analogous conditions, we believe that the various references and quotations covering Mr. Judge's activities show clearly his prescience. They show too the successive steps he took to allay and counteract the currents running beneath the smooth and prosperous surface of affairs.

Later in the year 1893 Mr. Judge published in the September *Path* the article "Our Convictions; Shall We Assert Them?" This was in reply to an inquiry as to whether the neutrality of the Society precluded the expression by a member of convictions sincerely held by him "for fear of a vague future dogmatism." The article re-affirmed the view that every member, being free to hold such opinions as he might choose, he had necessarily the same freedom of expression, so long as such expression was not made in the name of the Society or as an official, nor to coerce others who might hold and express contrary opinions. In the November *Path* Mr. Judge printed "Impolitic Reference—'H.P.B.,'" followed in the December *Lucifer* by "Blavatskianism in and out of Season." These articles struck the same note of freedom of *individual* opinion and expression, and at the same time accentuated the danger of their abuse by enthusiasts, as well as voicing a strong caution against mere reliance on and following of any one, however highly esteemed, as an "authority." Mrs. Besant wrote a very clear essay on the same subjects. Her article was entitled "Conviction and Dogmatism," and was published in *The Path* for October, *Lucifer* for November, and *The Theosophist* for December.

As in the similar cases during the lifetime of H.P.B., the students for the most part read the various articles published, talked of them, wondered in some cases who and what might be hinted at, but when the very test came to which these articles related, were unable to make any application. Of these, the most instructive example is that of Mrs. Besant. She had had the benefit of nearly two years of close relations with H.P.B. Of all the defenders of H.P.B.'s good faith and mission she had been the most outspoken. The student will recall her article "The Theosophical Society and H.P.B.," written without H.P.B.'s knowledge, though published before her death, as well as the article "Theosophy and Christianity," published some months after the passing of H.P.B. Likewise her part of the proceedings of the Council of the E.S. immediately after H.P.B.'s passing, and her repeated remarks during the European Convention in July, 1891, evinced the same rigid, uncompromising view of the unique status and importance of H.P.B. as Messenger and Teacher.[3] She had adhered with intense conviction to these views during the two following years, and had supported Mr. Judge with fervor as the one man in the Society who was true to the lines laid by H.P.B. and fully cognizant of them. Her quoted articles and others equally significant showed the depths of her convictions. She suspended Mr. Walter R. Old from his membership in the Esoteric School for his veiled attack in the article on "Theosophic Freethought." This was in August, 1893, and the suspension was declared by her to be because, "*first*, a violation of the pledge of secrecy made by Brother Old, and *second*, is a violation of honor and confidence as a member of the Council of the E.S.T." Furthermore she declared in the same circular that Mr. Old's "statement is itself untrue," and proceeded to give forthwith a formal declaration of the facts in rebuttal of Old's claim—a declaration signed by herself and others present at the Council meeting of May 27, 1891. In the same month—August, 1893—in her "Answers to Correspondence" in the E.S. she had given the letter of H.P.B. written in 1889 in which H.P.B. had declared Judge to be the Link between the American Esotericists and the Masters. This statement by H.P.B. was as follows:

> London, Oct. 23, 1889.
>
> . . . The Esoteric Section and its life in the U.S.A. depend upon W.Q.J. remaining its agent and what he is now. The day W.Q.J. resigns, H.P.B. will be virtually dead for the Americans. W.Q.J. is the *Antaskarana* (the "Link") between the two *Manas* (es), the American

[3] See Chapters XIX and XX.

thought and the Indian—or rather the trans-Himalayan esoteric knowledge. *Dixi.*

H.P.B. .·.

While she was in the United States to attend the Parliament of religions Mrs. Besant joined with Mr. Judge in signing a prefatory note which was published in *The Path* for October, 1893, and entitled, "A Word on the 'Secret Doctrine,' An Old Letter Republished." The letter in question was a long extract from the famous letter from the Master "K. H." phenomenally delivered to Col. Olcott on shipboard in August, 1888, at the time Olcott was on his way to London to "fight it out with H.P.B." over the question of the formation of the E.S.[4] The prefatory note ran:

> There is so much discussion going on just now in the Theosophical movement as to the value of the *Secret Doctrine,* as to the amount of aid given to H. P. Blavatsky in the compilation of it, and as to her position as a Teacher in Occult matters, that it appears to us that the republication of an old letter—published in 1888—which bears on these questions, is peculiarly timely, and may be of service to many who did not have the opportunity of reading it on its first issue. The letter is, of course, of no authority for those members of the T.S. who do not share our sentiments of reverence for the Masters, but for those who do, the interest of it will be great. It was received in mid-ocean by Col. Olcott, P.T.S., and was originally published with his consent in a small pamphlet entitled "An Explanation important to all Theosophists," issued by H.P.B.
>
> ANNIE BESANT.
> WILLIAM Q. JUDGE.

In the same month—that is, October, 1893—Mrs. Besant had had published in her magazine, *Lucifer,* her

[4] See Chapter X.

article on "Gurus and Chelas," before referred to.[5] At the same time Mrs. Besant prepared the article on "Conviction and Dogmatism," mentioned. Thereafter she was silent on the great issues waging publicly and privately in the Society and the E.S. until after her arrival in India. The occasion of this silence and the great change it betokened must now be considered.

All arrangements having been perfected, G. N. Chakravarti left India in June and journeyed to England where he remained two months, chiefly as the guest of Mr. Bertram Keightley. He met all the leading Theosophists in Britain and was intensely active among them during his entire stay. His coming had been anticipated with the utmost interest, as may be imagined, and his suavity, his versatility and great knowledge, added to the lure of oriental mystery with which he was surrounded, gave him a vogue that rose to veneration on the part of the "household" at Avenue Road. Toward the end of August he sailed for America in company with Mrs. Besant, Miss Müller, and others. In the United States the party was received by Mr. Judge and leading American Theosophists as distinguished visitors. Chakravarti soon rose to the position of an unique presence, almost an ambassador from the East. His share in the proceedings of the Parliament became a mission more than a function, so that he was invited to participate in the dedicatory ceremonies at the opening of the Congress of Religions. The Theosophical program during the Congress was by all odds the most notable and noteworthy success of the proceedings, and in this success Prof. Chakravarti and Mrs. Besant held the leading place. The effect of all this upon the general public and the membership was immediate and marked. An immense interest in everything Theosophical sprang up. The whole Theosophical world was elated. To be called a "Theosophist" was equivalent to "honorable mention"; to enjoy the personal acquaintance of Chakravarti and Mrs. Besant a coveted distinction.

[5] See preceding chapter.

Mrs. Besant had already acquired fame as an Occultist and ascetic. She had become a strict vegetarian in diet; she carried her own table utensils with her on her travels; she followed rigidly the various "practices" laid down in oriental schools for "development." The *savoir faire,* the gravity of decorum, the great ability of Chakravarti, the extreme respect he manifested towards her, the deference of Mr. Bertram Keightley toward this friend who was almost if not quite a Master, all weighed heavily and cumulatively with Mrs. Besant. She had discovered that Chakravarti possessed and practised "psychic powers," and as, in spite of all her proclamations and all her practices she was woefully deficient in these "gifts," it was inevitable that she should view him with more than admiration. "Not psychic or spiritual in the least—all intellect," as H.P.B. had written of her to Mr. Judge in the letter of March 27, 1891—it is all too clear that it was borne in on Mrs. Besant that here was her coveted opportunity to acquire those powers and faculties of which she knew only at second hand. She suffered herself to be "magnetized" by Chakravarti, and came more and more under the spell of his charm. On his part, Chakravarti received her devotions with elaborate punctilio. On their common journeying he watched over her with protective care to shield her from too close contact with the unworthy. He slept outside her door that she might be fitly sheltered from all disturbance, and advised with her as to her occult "progress."

All this, it need scarcely be said, was in direct violation of her pledge in the Esoteric Section, as well as in spirit and in letter a breach of the Rules of the E.S. Quite naturally these conspicuous mutual attentions did not altogether escape notice from unfriendly as well as friendly sources. Mr. Judge took occasion, therefore, to call to Mrs. Besant's attention the adverse interpretation that might easily be placed upon her conduct, as well as to caution her in regard to the Rules of the School governing the relations of Probationers with teachers and teachings outside the strict lines established in the *Preliminary Memoranda* and in the *Instructions*.

It will be recalled that when Mrs. Besant had first been invited to visit India, immediately following the European Convention of 1891, her trip had been given up on the ostensible grounds of her health—in reality because of the charges she went to New York to place before Mr. Judge.[6] When again urged to visit India in 1892 she had consulted Mr. Judge and had, on his advice, visited the United States on a lecturing tour, as recounted.[7] When Mr. Bertram Keightley returned to England in the spring of 1893, he laid before Mrs. Besant a renewed request from the Hindus for a visit from her the following winter, and this was supplemented by urgent entreaties of Col. Olcott's. Immediately after her return from her American trip she yielded to these insistencies and herself published the news in the "Watch-Tower" of *Lucifer* for June, 1893.

Mrs. Besant and Prof. Chakravarti arrived at London on their return from America, early in October, 1893. After a short stay in England, Chakravarti sailed for home, followed a week later by Mrs. Besant and the Countess Wachtmeister. Mrs. Besant arrived at Colombo early in November, where she was met by Col. Olcott and a party of headquarters aides. Six weeks were spent in Ceylon and in reaching Adyar, where the party arrived on Christmas Day, 1893, just preceding the Convention. At the Convention Mrs. Besant delivered five lectures and, after a short rest, proceeded on a tour of India, accompanied by Col. Olcott and others. This tour engaged her until March, 1894, when she set sail once more on her return voyage to England. In all the annals of the Theosophical Society there is nothing comparable to this Indian visit of Mrs. Besant's. From the first moment of her landing hers was a vice-regal progress and a triumph. Natives and Europeans, members and non-members of the Society, crowded her with

[6] See Chapter XXI.
[7] See Chapter XXVI.

attentions. The pages of *The Theosophist* during the months of her presence in India were burdened with descriptions and laudations devoted to the *avatara* "Anna-bai," as she was christened by the enthusiastic Hindus. During her trip she visited the sacred places of India, held conferences with leading priests, proclaimed herself an Indian in heart and feeling, and took the Brahminical thread. An article contributed by her over her signature to the native publication, the daily *Amrita Bazar Patrika,* expresses in her own words some of her views at the time—views which explain in part the frenzy of adulation she excited among the Hindus; views of extreme interest when contrasted with Mrs. Besant's activities in India for the past eight or ten years. We quote from the reprint in *The Theosophist,* "Supplement" for March, 1894:

> My work in the sphere of politics is over, and I shall never resume it . . .
>
> I say this in answer to your suggestion that I should be aroused to take interest in Indian "affairs." To be able to lay at the feet of India any service is to me full reward for the many sufferings of a stormy life through which the power of service has been won. But the India that I love and reverence, and would fain see living among the nations, is not an India westernized, rent with the struggles of political parties, heated with the fires of political passions, with a people ignorant and degraded, while those who might have raised them are fighting for the loaves and fishes of political triumph. I have seen too much of this among the "progressed and civilized nations" of the West to have any desire to see such a civilization over-spreading what was Aryavarta. The India to which I belong in faith and heart is . . . a civilization in which spiritual knowledge was accounted highest title to honour, and in which the whole people reverenced and sought after spiritual

truth. To help in turning India into another Great Britain or another Germany is an ambition that does not allure me; the India I would give my life to help in building is an India learned in the ancient philosophy, pulsing with the ancient religion,—an India to which all other lands should look for spiritual light,—where the life of all should be materially simple, but intellectually noble and spiritually sublime.

The whole of my life and of my energies are given to the Theosophical Society, because the Society is intended to work in all nations for the realisation of this spiritual ideal; for the sake of this it deliberately eschews all politics, embraces men of all parties, welcomes men of all faiths, declines to ostracise any man, any party or any faith. I may not mingle in a political fray which would make one temporary party regard me with enmity; for the message of spiritual life belongs equally to both and may not be rendered unacceptable by its bearer wearing a political garment which is a defiance of those clad in other political robes. The politician must ever be at war; my mission is one of peace. Therefore I enter not the political field; and in the religious field I seek to show men of every faith that they share a common spiritual heritage and should look through the forms that divide them to the spirit that makes them one. It is the recognition of this which makes Hinduism ever a non-proselyting religion. . . .

I write this lengthy explanation of my absolute refusal to have anything to do with politics because any expression of love and confidence from Indians goes straight to my heart, . . . because I honestly believe that the future of India, the greatness of India and the happiness of her people, can never be secured by political methods, but only by the revival of her philosophy and religion. To this, therefore, I must give all my energies, and I must refuse to spread them over other fields.

ANNIE BESANT.

Now, having traced the successive moves of Mr. Judge, and having followed Mrs. Besant's successive positions on the chessboard, it is necessary to review Col. Olcott's share in the strategy and tactics of the rapidly culminating manoeuvres. We have shown him in his "Old Diary Leaves," in his Presidential Addresses, in his letter to the American Section Convention of 1893, in his part in the "White Lotus Day" celebration at Adyar on May 8, 1893, in his use of Mr. Sturdy as a pawn, and of Mr. Walter R. Old as a more important piece through which to make his moves. We have partly indicated the glamour of deference, devotion, and extravagant attentions with which Mrs. Besant was enveloped by Col. Olcott and his followers in sequence to the mission of Mr. Bertram Keightley and the Occult lure held out by Prof. Chakravarti. This should be contrasted with the attentions paid at the same time by the President-Founder to Mr. Judge and H.P.B. Thus:

When the first copies of Mr. Judge's "Ocean of Theosophy" arrived at Adyar, Col. Olcott took time to write a review of the book. It will be found in *The Theosophist* for September, 1893. Colonel Olcott calls it an "interesting little volume" which is "another proof of Mr. Judge's tireless activity and commercial enterprise." He says that in print, paper, and binding it is "faultless" and "far and away beyond anything we can do at Madras." He goes on: "I wish I could unqualifiedly praise his present work; but I cannot. It contains some errors that are flagrant." The errors are then detailed; some typographical; some, errors of derivation of words; others, words said to be Sanskrit which are not; Mr. Sinnett was not "an official in the Government of India," but the Editor of the *Pioneer* newspaper. And, as it seems to the President-Founder, "Mr. Judge makes a sad mistake in saying 'in place of the

"Absolute" we can use the word space,' and making it one of the divisions of the sevenfold universe." As Mr. Judge's brief sentences thus quoted from do but repeat in skeleton H.P.B.'s statement of the "First Fundamental Proposition" of the "Secret Doctrine," Col. Olcott's strictures in reality apply to those numbered statements in the "Secret Doctrine" concerning which H.P.B. said, in presenting them, "on their clear apprehension depends the understanding of all that follows" in her great work. Colonel Olcott closes this first of the two paragraphs of his review by saying: "Other errors might be pointed out; but I need not enlarge, since the task is ungrateful, and they will be quickly recognized by Indian readers."

But the real animus of the review is contained in the concluding paragraph. It is as follows:

> What I regard as most unfortunate is the habit which my old friend, in common with other of H.P.B.'s pupils whom I have known, but who long ago deserted her, has fallen into, of hinting that he could, and he would, disclose ultimate mysteries properly veiled from the common people. Examples occur in this book, and moreover he unhesitatingly declares (Preface) that his "bold statements" (*i.e.*, the whole presentation of the subjects treated) are "made . . . upon the *knowledge* of the writer," and that he "has simply written that which I (sic) have been taught and which has been proved to me (sic)." When we consider the stupendous declarations of cosmic and human evolution and order that are made upon our friend's bare authority, it strikes one how much more nobly we would stand before the thinking and aspiring world, if Mr. Judge would make good this statement by adducing proofs that he has written that only which he "knows" and which "has been proven" as true. Or, at least, he might have taken a bit more pains and avoided downright errors in fact

> and metaphysic. Does he, for example, wish us to believe that it has been *proven* to him that the Absolute is a septenary principle, and that Charlemagne reincarnated as Napoleon I, and Clovis of France as the Emperor Frederic III—proven? I trow not. This is a very loose fashion of asserting instead of proving which is spreading and which is very detrimental to a cause possessing enough solid merit in itself to make its way if discreetly engineered. —H. S. O.

Any reader can turn to the Preface and the text of the "Ocean" and determine for himself whether Col. Olcott's blows are struck fairly or foully, and whether Mr. Judge throughout the book, faithfully epitomizes the teachings of the "Secret Doctrine."

The President-Founder's criticism of the "Ocean" which included its author, Mr. Judge, and H.P.B. the Teacher, and her Teachings, in its invidious implications, was followed in the October, 1893, *Theosophist* by an Editorial Note, signed with Col. Olcott's initials, to an article by "N. D. K." taking mild exceptions to the statements in the August installment of "Old Diary Leaves" on H.P.B.'s ignorance of "reincarnation" at the time of the writing of "Isis Unveiled." Colonel Olcott goes still further than in "Old Diary Leaves." He says that not only did H.P.B. not teach reincarnation but that "she really taught the opposite." He goes on to claim credit *for himself* for the "discovery" in 1881 of the "idea of Individuality and Personality." "*After that*" (italics Col. Olcott's), it was taught by H.P.B., . . . and, generally, made current as our belief."

The Adyar Convention at the close of December, 1893, was opened by the President-Founder in person with his Annual Address delivered in the presence of Mrs. Besant. Beginning with his second sentence he sounds public official paeans to Mrs. Besant and himself. We quote from the Report in the "Supplement" to *The Theosophist* for January, 1894:

> The night's blackness is rolling away, the dawn of a happier day is breaking. Thanks—as I believe—to the kind help of those whom I call my Masters . . . our patient and loyal persistence is about being rewarded by help of the most valuable kind, for they have sent me "Annabai" [Mrs. Besant] to share my burden, relieve our mental distress, and win the respect and sympathy of good people. While she is not yet able to quite fill the void left by the departure of my co-founder, H.P.B., she will be in time, and meanwhile is able to render service that her Teacher could not, by her peerless oratory and her scientific training. This meeting will be historical, as marking her first appearance at our Annual Conventions:—her first, but not her last, for I have some reason to hope that she will devote a certain part of her future years to Indian work. [Great applause.]
>
> Mrs. Besant's and my close association in the Indian tour now in progress, and the consequent mutual insight into our respective characters and motives of action, has brought us to a perfect understanding which, I believe, nothing can henceforth shake. She and I are now at one as regards the proper scope and function of the E.S.T. as one of the activities carried on by our members. . . . Whatever misunderstandings have occurred hitherto with respect to the exact relationship between the Society, as a body, and the Esoteric Section which I chartered in 1888—now known as the Eastern School of Theosophy—and of which she is the sweet spirit and the guiding star, have passed away—I hope, forever.

The reader should bear in mind the specific declaration of H.P.B. that "the E.S.T. has *no relation whatever* with the Theosophical Society *as a body,*" and the historical fact that its formation was opposed and its conduct under H.P.B. disapproved of by Col Olcott.

The President-Founder's Address goes on to refer to the recent Congress of Religions at the Chicago Fair, and says:

> In common with every other working member in the Society, I am encouraged by this demonstration to unflagging persistence in the work, and very recent assurances from sources I most respect [he means the Masters], give me the conviction of speedy and complete success. At the same time I am warned to expect fresh disagreeable surprises; but for these, long experience has fortified me, and the Society, as heretofore, will emerge purer and stronger than ever. The Society is gradually learning that personalities are but broken reeds to lean upon; and that the best of us are but mortals, fallible and weak.

Repeated further laudatory references to Mrs. Besant appear throughout the remainder of the Presidential Address. Miss Müller and Prof. Chakravarti are spoken of with commendation. Considerable time is spent in arguing once more the advisability and necessity of Adyar as a central focus of the movement. That the President-Founder is the real inspiration and authority of the Society is affirmed in the following sentences:

> The Chief Executive has already become in great part, and must ultimately be entirely the mere official pivot of the wheel, the central unit of its life, the representative of its federative character, the umpire in all intersectional disputes, the wielder of the Council's authority.

Then the President goes on to say, without a break:

> I abhor the very semblance of autocratic interference, but I equally detest that spirit of nullification which drives people to try to subvert constitutions under which they have prospered and which has proved in practice well

> fitted to promote the general well being. This feeling has made me resent at times what seemed attempts to make the Society responsible for special authorities, ideas and dogmas which, however good in themselves, were foreign to the views of some of our members, and hence an invasion of their personal rights of conscience under our constitution. As the official guardian of that instrument, my duty requires this of me, and I hope never to fail in it.

Finally, at the close of his Address, the President-Founder returns once more to the epiphany of Mrs. Besant and says:

> With the formation of my present close acquaintance with Mrs. Besant, my course has become very clearly marked out in my mind. Unless something unexpected and of a very revolutionary character should happen, I mean to abandon the last lingering thought of retirement and stop at my post until removed by the hand of death. "Annabai" will in time become to me what H.P.B. was, and I shall try to prove as staunch and loyal a colleague to her as I think you will concede I have been to my lamented co-Founder of this Society. In her bright integrity, her passionate love of truth, her grand trained intellect and her unquestioning altruism, I feel a strength and support which acts upon me as the elbow-touch of the comrade to the soldier in battle. Disciples of the same Master, devoted to the same cause, and now friends who know and trust each other, we may, I hope and pray, henceforth resemble in this movement the Aryan god, who is dual when looked at from two aspects, but when properly understood is but one and indivisible. [Great applause.]

When these remarks of Col. Olcott's are weighed in the light of preceding events and measured in their relation to the framework of circumstances by which they were surrounded, there can be no question of their gravity or that they were deliberately calculated. They were spoken at the most important convocation yet held in India after the one at the end of 1884. There the planned purpose was negative—to leave the most important personage connected with the Society unsupported and undefended against an assault leveled, not against her as an individual, but as the Head and forefront of the Theosophical Movement. It was the first great test of the professed devotion to Brotherhood—the First Object of the Society. It ended in *desertion*, rather than in active *disloyalty.* Injurious as its effects were, it would have been ruinous had H.P.B. had to depend on the Hindus and Col. Olcott; as it was, its reactionary effects were felt chiefly in India, so far as the Society was concerned.

But in 1893, the disloyalty was positive; it was a planned assault, by the chief officer of the Society, aided and abetted by its leading members. It was *that very plot against the Theosophical Society,* of which Mr. Judge had written months before—against *brotherhood as that word had been used in the declaration of the First and Second Sections in 1881,* as it had been exemplified by Masters and H.P.B., as it had been taught in Theosophy, and in the Rules, the *Preliminary Memoranda* and the Instructions of the Esoteric School.

Colonel Olcott intended his statements to be received as his authoritative and official proclamation to all who might look to him for direction. It is therefore well worth while for the student to examine them closely in relation to the tissues of the web spun to the occasion of his designed pattern. Stripped of redundancies and tergiversations the extracts given come to this: the President-Founder of the Society, speaking as its Official Head, declares:

(1) That the Masters have rewarded his "patient and loyal persistence" by sending him Mrs. Besant "to fill the void left by the de-

> parture of H.P.B.," and who is "able to render service that her Teacher could not";
>
> (2) That he has come "to a perfect understanding with her that nothing can henceforth shake," so that he and Mrs. Besant "are now at one as regards the proper scope and function of the E.S.T.," of which "she is the sweet spirit and the guiding star";
>
> (3) That he himself has "already become in great part, and must ultimately be entirely" the "central unit" in the "life" of the Society, the "representative," the "umpire," the "wielder of the Council's authority";
>
> (4) And, finally, that "very recent assurances" from the Masters warn him "to expect fresh disagreeable surprises," from which, however, he is assured that the Society "will emerge purer and stronger than ever."

These statements of his are put forth *officially*, although he "abhors the very semblance of autocratic interference" and "resents attempts to make the Society responsible for special authorities, ideas and dogmas" which "are foreign to the views of some of our members, and hence an invasion of their personal rights of conscience under our constitution," and although "personalities are but broken reeds to lean upon, and the best of us are but mortals fallible and weak."

Indicative as these contrasted declarations are of that "loss of moral balance unconsciously to himself"—as H.P.B. had written must be the fate of those who "wander from the discipline"—indicative as they are when weighed only in the light of what preceded and accompanied the Presidential Address, they become ever more profoundly significant when viewed in unbroken continuity with the succeeding events.

The facts, unknown then, are knowable now. Through Messrs. A. P. Sinnett and Bertram Keightley first, Chakravarti next and Col. Olcott finally, Mrs. Besant was infected with doubts and suspicions of H.P.B., then of

Mr. Judge, as Col. Olcott had himself succumbed to the same influences in 1881. The potion, in increasing doses, mixed with subtle flatteries, by degrees led Mrs. Besant to the point where, "in the name of the Masters" she was induced to break her "most solemn and sacred word of honor" and "for the honor of the Society" to violate her pledges in the E.S.

At Adyar Mrs. Besant counseled with Mr. Walter R. Old, who, smarting under his "wrongs," told his psychic tale of inference and hearsay. At Adyar Mrs. Besant attended a dark cabinet at which were present besides herself, Mr. Old, Col. Olcott, Messrs. Edge and Sturdy, and Countess Wachtmeister. Here their mutual doubts were well confirmed, each by the others, their mutual burdens of circumstantial evidence adjusted to fit their several interpretations. William Q. Judge was weighed in the balance, tried, convicted, condemned of Theosophical infamies, and plans made to carry the sentence into execution. From November, 1893, until March, 1894, the conspirators day by day wrote and spoke of *brotherhood*, and night after night plotted fruitfully its negation.

Early in January Mrs. Besant, Col. Olcott, and their party resumed the tour of India temporarily suspended during the Convention. Allahabad—home of Prof. Chakravarti—was reached early in February. There, as was most fit and proper, the final step was taken, and in accordance with the plan agreed upon, Mrs. Besant handed to Col. Olcott the following:

> ALLAHABAD, Feb. 6th, 1894.
>
> To the President-Founder of the Theosophical Society.
>
> Dear Sir and Brother,—
>
> Some little time ago an appeal was made to me by members of the T.S. belonging to different Branches, to set their minds at rest as to the accusations made against the Vice-President of the Society, Bro. W. Q. Judge, with reference to certain letters and sentences in the alleged

writings of the Mahatmas. As it is to the detriment of the whole Society that such accusations —believed to be true by reputable members of the Society—should be circulated against a prominent official without rebuttal and without investigation, I ask you, as the President of the Society, to direct that the charges made shall be formulated and laid before a Committee, as provided by Art. VI, Secs. 2, 3 and 4.

Fraternally yours,

ANNIE BESANT.

On the next day Colonel Olcott wrote the following official communication to Mr. Judge:

THEOSOPHICAL SOCIETY,
PRESIDENT'S OFFICE

AGRA, Feb. 7th, 1894.

To William Q. Judge, Vice-President T.S.
Dear Sir and Brother,—

I enclose herewith a certified copy of Annie Besant's formal letter to me, dated Allahabad, Feb. 6th inst. In it she demands an official enquiry, by means of a Committee, into the matter of your alleged misuse of the Mahatmas' names and handwriting.

By virtue of the discretionary power given me in Art. VI of the Revised Rules, I place before you the following options:

(1) To retire from all offices held by you in the Theosophical Society and leave me to make a merely general public explanation, or—

(2) To have a Judicial Committee convened, as provided for in Art. VI, Sec. 3, of the Revised Rules, and make public the whole of the proceedings in detail.

In either alternative, you will observe, a public explanation is found necessary: in the one case to be limited as far as possible and made general; in the other to be full and covering all the details.

I suggest that if you decide for a Committee you fix London as the place of meeting, as by far the most central and convenient to all concerned. But whether you choose New York, London, or elsewhere, I shall in all probability be represented by proxy, unless something now unforeseen should arise to make it imperative that I shall personally attend.

As it will be much better that I should know your decision before Annie Besant leaves India (March 20th), I would ask you to kindly cable me the word "first" if you choose to resign; or "second" if you demand the Committee.

Fraternally yours,

H. S. OLCOTT,

President Theosophical Society.

CHAPTER XXVIII

THE AMERICAN SECTION SUPPORTS JUDGE

THE reader should remember—what was unknown to the membership at the time and, in most cases, unknown to Theosophical students since—that the plot against Judge had been in process for nearly two years, had been gradually perfected in all its details, and merely came openly to a head with the letters of Mrs. Besant and Col. Olcott last mentioned. Mr. Judge was simply the target in 1894-5 as H.P.B. and Mr. Judge had been the target in 1889-90, and as H.P.B. alone had been the target in 1884-5. The real plot was against *what they represented.* H.P.B. and Mr. Judge strove to nourish and strengthen the Theosophical Society—the Third Section—as an *instrument* for the purposes of the First and Second Sections, and their Three Objects.

Colonel Olcott's Inaugural Address on November 17, 1875, showed clearly how *he* viewed the Objects of the Society—a view that any Spiritualist, any devotee of psychic research, any materialistic scientist, Ishmael or pariah of orthodoxy or sectarianism, any curiosity seeker, might take, and that multitudes *did* take. From that view Col. Olcott never wholly departed, whether as President-Founder, or as Probationer of the Second Section. He held in abeyance, he suppressed, he yielded his views from time to time, as occasion might seem to warrant, or necessity compel, but that was all. The Third Object—as he understood and applied it—was *first* with him and with by far the great majority, whether officers, leaders, writers, or the mere *polloi* of Fellows and Esotericists. In other words, nine-tenths of those who joined the Society or the E.S.T. viewed the Objects in inverse order and proportion.

H.P.B. knew this. Mr. Judge knew this. So did

Damodar. What were they to do? They had to take the mind of the race as they found it, and do what they could in the mental environment of the race. Hence the two volumes of "Isis," devoted the one to "Science," *i.e.,* the Third Object; the other to "Theology," *i.e.,* the Second Object—as *Masters* view those great subjects and Objects. The opposing views, whether of principles or applications, never could and never can be reconciled; one or the other has in the end to prevail, whether in the individual or in any body of individuals such as the Theosophical Society. Hence the Esoteric Section when the Society at large threatened to break away and become an instrument, however great, of the inverted view of its purposes. Hence the steady stream of deserters from the Society; hence, too, the constant stream of attacks, never directly against *Theosophy,* the *Society,* or its *Objects,* but against H.P.B.; against her and Mr. Judge; finally, as we have seen, against Mr. Judge alone.

Against these guerilla tactics H.P.B. consistently employed one and the same "grand strategy": in reply to all shafts leveled, without or within the Society, against her teachings, her messages, her phenomena, and herself as their sponsor, she devoted herself to the promotion of *solidarity* and a *Theosophical education;* to strenuous efforts to *educate* the membership to some apprehension of Theosophical *principles,* and some *application* of those principles to the ever varying course of events. She constantly preached and practised Unity, Study, and Work.

We have been at pains to give extracts and abundant references, so that the inquiring student might be able to verify for himself:

(1) The opposing *ideas* embodied in H.P.B. on the one side and Col. Olcott on the other, and the gradual alignment of leaders and followers into opposing armies fighting, consciously and unconsciously, for the supremacy in this "war of ideas."

(2) The clear recognition and teaching by H.P.B. of the gigantic nature of the impending struggle, whether between the "Higher and lower self" of the in-

dividual combatant, or between the opposing forces in this modern *Mahabharata;* and her consequent avoidance to the last degree of *forcing* the issue with anyone, friend or foe, faithful or unfaithful.

(3) Her unvarying practice, when the issue was about to be forced upon her, of writing some article or series of articles which presented *in advance* the real points involved, the real issues at stake, the real principles to be applied. Only when the battle was joined, and at its crucial moment did she, like *Krishna,* take her *Arjunas* into conference in the midst of the flying arrows and name the generals of the opposing army; it was her method of stripping bare both issues and advocates.

We have been at pains to do the same thing in the case of Mr. Judge, and for the same reasons. We have shown him, while the plot was brewing in secrecy and darkness, confining himself to the promotion of harmony and good-will, regardless of the dissensions and differences of opinions amongst officers, leaders, and members. We have shown him giving clear expression of his own views as an individual on the varying questions raised. We have shown him from time to time publishing articles on principles, policies, and applications in advance of events, but which, when related to those events, show unmistakably his prescience on the plane of Causes. One more example of his identity with the path pursued by H.P.B. is germane to the events of the first half of 1894.

The leading articles in *The Path* for the months of October, November, and December, 1893, and January, 1894, were devoted to the subject of the "Occult Arts," and in subtitles treatment was successively accorded to "Precipitation," to "Disintegration and Reintegration," and to "Some Propositions by H. P. Blavatsky." The latter contained, with some comments, a reprint of the first ten of the numbered propositions in chapter twelve of Volume 2, "Isis Unveiled." The other articles discussed the Occult rationale of phenomenal "messages," and the phenomena of "appearance and disappearance of objects."

These teachings of Occultism in their philosophical,

logical, moral, and scientific bearings, had been before the students for seventeen years. Why should Mr. Judge re-discuss at all, let alone at that particular time, what was a mere repetition of what should long since have been common knowledge on the part of every Theosophist? What other answer is there, in view of all that preceded and all that followed, than that he *knew* what was coming; *knew* that it would find the students as unready as ever *intelligently* to discern between divided counsels, warring claims, rival pretensions, contradictory "messages from the Masters of H.P.B."? He knew that the students had really *learned* little or nothing, either from fact or philosophy, and hence were ripe to be swept away, not by knowledge or evidence, but by claims and the *prestige of the accusers.* He knew that the hour was come for a new wager of the same old gage. He therefore could but repeat the teachings and the admonitions of Occultism to the *Arjunas* about to enter on the "field of battle," and await the issue.

Equally, the extracts and references abundantly given will serve to show, on the opposing side, both the policies pursued and the ideas relied upon. Throughout the long interval of preparations, of the "marshaling and the survey of armies" up to the last moment, the friendliest intercourse was kept up with Mr. Judge. All direct public references to him, as to H.P.B., were clothed by the chief conspirators in terms of apparent respect and confidence. Where allusions were made that were questionable they were always Janus-like, and for these two-faced utterances men like Mr. Sturdy and Mr. Old were used as tools. Where direct issues were broached it was always on some subject on which the membership had and could have no actual knowledge—as the discussion on "Mars and Mercury" and the "Sevenfold system"—or it was on some topic clearly meritorious in itself, as those on the neutrality of the Society, on dogmatism, on authority, on hero-worship, on the degree of authenticity to be attached to the writings of H.P.B.; on her status as the Agent of the Masters and so on. But under cover of all these apparently innocent and worthy objects of discussion, there went on a distinctly cumulative campaign the effect of which was to leave an adverse impression of H.P.B. as Messenger, as Teacher, as Example, and to force upon Mr. Judge either to remain silent or to defend the *bona fides,* the knowledge, the *dependability* of H.P.B.

Following her path in all things, Mr. Judge crossed no bridges till he came to them. Not till the protagonists came into the open and made their hostile attack in force could he, any more than she, meet the issue face to face, and he well knew what form that attack would take.

At that time from four to six weeks were required for the transit of the mails from interior India to New York City. In consequence, the President-Founder's Official letter of February 7 [1] did not reach Mr. Judge until March 10, 1894. He at once took two steps, one privately in the E.S.T., as one of its Heads; the other publicly, as an individual member of the Theosophical Society. Both these actions are, in our view, of profound teaching value to every real student, alike in their manner and their matter, for what was said and for what was left unsaid.

The circular to the E.S.T. was headed, "Recall of the Instructions." Its opening paragraph reads:

> The members in the U. S. should know the facts about the divulgement of the Instructions [The various papers issued in the School by H.P.B. during her lifetime are what is meant by the "Instructions"]. Some time ago a former member in India retired and refused to give up his papers. Later it became evident that they were given out to persons not members. This was clearly shown by the fact that a person in California published the contents of the notice sent from London on the suspension of Messrs. Old and Edge coupled with the statement that the same person had the other papers. It was also evident that some spy was left some-

[1] See preceding chapter.

where in the E.S. who continued to help the retired member. All of these things were published from time to time in papers in India and England and it became apparent that it was absolutely necessary to call in the Instructions to the end that means might be devised for greater security for all members. This recall was no reflection on members who are faithful. Hence the notice.

The remainder of the circular is devoted to admonitions to charity towards any who might violate his pledges; to injunctions to self-watchfulness, mutual loyalty, and study. And for something to study in lieu of the recalled Instructions the last chapter in the second volume of "Isis Unveiled" is referred to as "something which if rightly understood contains the secrets of Occultism." Neither Col. Olcott, Mrs. Besant, nor any of the others involved were referred to.

His public step is clearly shown by the heading and opening paragraph which follow:

From
William Q. Judge,
144 Madison Ave.,
New York.

March 15th, 1894.

Charges against William Q. Judge.

To all Members of the Theosophical Society:

It is disagreeable to talk much of oneself, but sometimes it is necessary, and in this case it has been made a necessity by the action of others, as also by the existence of many vague and suppressed rumors which have been flying about in quarters not public but sufficiently alive to compel action on my part. Hence I now make known in advance that which has been spoken obscurely for some time, and which is now before me officially from the President, Col. H. S. Olcott, to

> the end that all members of the Society and friends of my own in all parts of the world shall be in possession of facts so that surprise and perhaps confusion may be prevented.

Mr. Judge then goes on to say that "the assertion is made in India that I have been guilty of '*misuse of the names and handwriting of the Mahatmas,*'" and that this has been "officially communicated to the President." He does not mention Mrs. Besant's name at all in connection with the proceedings taken by the President-Founder, but merely that "an investigation is demanded through an official inquiry," and therefore Col. Olcott "conceiving himself required and authorized to take action" has written the official letter which we have given in the preceding chapter. He gives the "options" placed before him in the President-Founder's letter and says:

> On March 10th I cabled him as follows: Charges absolutely false. You can take what proceedings you see fit; going to London in July.

Mr. Judge next makes clear the reason for this cablegram and the form of his reply. He says:

> The charge is made against me as Vice-President: I have replied as an individual and shall so continue; inasmuch as in my capacity of Vice-President my duties are nominal. . . . The only charges that could be made against the Vice-President would be those of failing to perform his duties, or misusing the office when there were any duties attached to it. On the face of this very vague charge, then, it is evident that there is nothing in it relating to the official Vice-President.

The charge as related to official malfeasance being thus disposed of for the time being, Mr. Judge next considers it as related to himself as one of the leading members of the Society:

> Inasmuch as I was the first presiding officer of the Theosophical Society at its preliminary meeting in September, 1875, and its first Secretary at such meeting; that I was not only H. P. Blavatsky's intimate friend and direct pupil but that I have been conspicuous as an upholder of Theosophical doctrines, as also an upholder, with many other friends in every part of the globe, of H. P. Blavatsky's good name, high motive, and great powers against the ridicule of the world and much opposition from certain members of the Society she founded; that I have been elected to succeed Col. Olcott as President of the Society and have been officially declared his successor by him; it is important and imperative that I should make this matter public, and I now do so, and state my unqualified, explicit, exhaustive denial of the said charge, asserting most unreservedly that it has no foundation.

The reasons and the necessities compelling this public facing of the charges and their public unequivocal denial, thus given, Mr. Judge's circular then considers the constitutional procedure and gives it in detail. He concludes this part of his circular by saying: "Perhaps when the Committee is convened I shall, for the first time, have particulars as to persons, dates, and the like of the charges made, none of which up to this time I have had except in the form of rumor." He then considers the possible effects of these charges on others than himself:

> More acutely than any personal grievance, do I feel the probability of a deplorable influence being at first exercised on the Theosophical movement by the making of these charges. I do not think it will have a lasting effect for injury. The rumors to which I have referred have been used by the enemies of the Society to show, if possible, dissension among us and to found a charge of rottenness; they have printed the mat-

> ter in a scandalous form both in Europe and America, pretending that in my official and private capacities I am in the habit of sending alleged "Mahatma messages," and then added ribald jokes of their own. This I have not hitherto noticed, because all members know that the correspondence and work of the Society are open to all and entirely devoid of the elements alleged to exist by these opponents; we are all perfectly aware that our strength lies in our devotion and constant work. The present situation will therefore result in clearing the air and consolidating our ranks in all directions.

Next, Mr. Judge refers to the second of the two "options" placed before him by the President-Founder, and says that he refused to cable the word "second," as requested by Col. Olcott's letter, for the reason that thus to do would be to mean "I *demand* a Committee." He continues:

> The reason is not that an investigation is avoided. Such an investigation will not be avoided. But on constitutional and executive principle I shall object from beginning to end to any committee of the Theosophical Society considering any charge against any person which involves an inquiry and decision as to the existence, names, powers, functions, or methods of the "Mahatmas or Masters." I shall do this for the protection of the Theosophical Society now and hereafter, regardless of the result to myself. The Society has no dogma as to the existence of such Masters; but the deliberations of an official committee of the Society on such a question, and that is the first inquiry and decision necessarily beginning such a deliberation, would mean that the Theosophical Society after over nineteen years of unsectarian work is determined to settle this dogma and affix it to the

Constitution of the Society. To this I will never consent, but shall object and shall charge the Committee itself with a violation of the Constitution if it decides the question of the existence of "Masters" or Mahatmas; if it should affirm the "Masters" existence it will violate the law; if it should deny Their existence a like violation will result; both decisions would affirm a dogma, and the negative decision would in addition violate that provision of our law, in Art. XIII, Revised Rules, which makes it an offense to "wilfully offend the religious feelings of any Fellow" of the Society, inasmuch as the belief so negatived is religiously held by many hundreds of the Fellows of the Society. I intend to try once for all to definitely have settled this important question, and to procure an official decision affirming now and forever the freedom of our Society.

Hence the President's alternatives . . . are mistakes, and are the initial steps to the promulgation of the dogma of belief in the "Masters." The first alternative is furthermore a judgment in advance, ridiculous in itself yet serious as emanating from our highest official. It precludes him from sitting on the Committee, and that point also I shall raise before the Committee. The whole proposal he makes brings up serious and complicated questions of Occultism touching upon the matter of the existence, powers, functions, and methods of those "Masters" in whom many Theosophists believe but as to whom the Theosophical Society is perfectly agnostic and neutral as an organized body. For that reason no one in official position ever thought of making a public matter of the many assertions made here and there by members of the Society, that they individually communicated with beings whom they called "Masters," "Mahatmas," nor of the assertions publicly

> made by prominent members that certain philosophical statements recently published in our literature were directly from the very "Masters" referred to by Col. Olcott, although those statements contradicted others made by H. P. Blavatsky on the declared authority of the same "Masters."
>
> On all these grounds, then, I shall object to a Theosophical Society Committee, while of course there will never be any objection from me to a proper investigation by a body of persons who know enough of Occultism as well as of Theosophy to understandingly inquire into these matters.

From the matter already before him in the course of this History, the reader can easily determine for himself the accuracy as to statements of fact, the consistency of adherence to the proclaimed Constitution and Rules of the Society, the sincere devotion throughout to the Objects of the Society, and the principles of Occultism shown by Mr. Judge; the candor and unevasiveness of his reply to the letter and "options" of the President-Founder.

The closing paragraphs of Mr. Judge's circular meet the remainder of the queries bound to arise from the President-Founder's letter and the reply as quoted in the foregoing extracts. On these natural queries thus forced to the front against his will, Mr. Judge speaks as directly, as simply and impersonally as H.P.B. herself had done when silence was no longer possible. He says:

> But some of you may wonder if all this leaves in doubt the question whether I believe in the "Masters." I believe the Masters exist, that They actually help the T.S. Cause, that They energise and make fruitful the work of all sincere members; all this I can say to myself that I know, but to prove objectively to another that such beings exist is impossible now so far

as my intelligence can perceive. "Letters from Mahatmas" prove nothing at all except to the recipient, and then only when in his inner nature is the standard of proof and the power of judgment. Precipitation does not prove Mahatmas, for the reason that mere mediums and non-mahatmas can make precipitations. This I have always asserted. By one's soul alone can this matter be judged, and only by his work and acts can one judge at first as to whether any other person is an agent of the Masters; by following the course prescribed in all ages the inner faculties may be awakened so as to furnish the true confirmatory evidence. I have not lost any of my belief in these beings, but more than ever believe in Their existence and in Their help and care to and over our Society's work.

Finally I may say that my personal belief in Mahatmas is based on even stronger evidence than Theosophical arguments or the experience of others. As is known to some Theosophists, I have not been entirely without help and guidance from these exalted friends of the T.S. The form which the whole matter has taken now compels me to say what I have never before said publicly, namely, that not only have I received direct communications from Masters during and since the life of H. P. Blavatsky, but that I have on certain occasions repeated such to certain persons for their own guidance, and also that I have guided some of my own work under suggestions from the same sources, though without mentioning the fact.—William Q. Judge.

Copies of this circular of Mr. Judge's were at once mailed to as many members of the Society as possible. The mask of concealment being thus stripped away and the whole Society made conversant with what had hitherto been whispered from one to another in the form of innuendo, the first effect was distinctly disastrous to the plans of the chief conspirators in India. Copies reached London and were seen by Mr. Geo. R. S. Mead, then Editor of *Lucifer* under Mrs. Besant, and General Secretary of the European Section. Mr. Bertram Keightley, still General Secretary of the Indian Section, was at the time in London and he also read Mr. Judge's circular. Both were honorable and well-meaning men and whatever countenance they had hitherto lent to the hints and suspicions against Mr. Judge, their sense of fair play and common decency was outraged by the arrogant unbrotherliness and offhand assumption of Mrs. Besant and the President-Founder. Even if Mr. Judge was guilty, he was entitled to the preliminary assumption of his innocence until that guilt was conclusively established, and this by the commonest application of the principles of ordinary human practice. Moreover by what process of reasoning could Mrs. Besant and Col. Olcott take upon themselves the duty of holding star-chamber proceedings to condemn any member or tender him "options" to "resign" or be "tried" by a Committee, when the very proceedings already so unwarrantably taken were in fact a violation of the Rules of the Society, no less than those of Occultism? Perhaps the plain, manly, straightforward statements in Mr. Judge's circular gave them for the moment some realizing sense of the enormous inequity committed. At all events they saw at once that it was Mrs. Besant and the President-Founder who had grossly violated the principles all professed as well as the plain provisions of the Constitution of the Society. Under the date of March 27, 1894, therefore, they issued over their joint official signatures as the General Secretaries of the two sections, the European and the Indian, a circular entitled: *"For the information of the Members of the European and Indian Sections of the Theosophical Society."*

This circular begins by reciting that Messrs. Mead and Keightley had seen an unofficial copy of the letter of Mrs. Besant of February 6 and of Col. Olcott's of February 7, as given, and repeats the text of the two letters. The circular of Messrs. Mead and Keightley is addressed to Col. Olcott as President-Founder of the T.S., and proceeds to insist that any further proceedings taken must be "strictly constitutional and impartial," and continues:—

> It is therefore our plain duty as the General Secretaries of two out of the three Sections of the T.S. and members of its General Council, to call your attention officially to the following points with a view to safeguarding (1) the Constitution, (2) the non-sectarian character, and (3) the impartiality of the Theosophical Society.
>
> *First:* By Art. VI, Sections 2 and 3, of the "Constitution and Rules of the Theosophical Society" as officially ratified and promulgated by yourself on Dec. 31st, 1893, it is enacted that, in the event of charges being preferred against the President, or Vice-President; (*a*) the said charges shall be in writing, and (*b*) copies thereof shall "at once" be forwarded to the accused and "to each member of the General Council."
>
> We now desire to point out that you have *not* followed the procedure laid down in either of these respects, for:
>
> 1. Your official letter to Mr. W. Q. Judge above referred to, contains no copy in writing of any charges, does not give the names of the persons who bring such, and even contains no *specific* statement of what are the exact charges brought.
>
> 2. No official copy either of "charges in writing" or even of your above-mentioned letter to Mr. Judge has reached either of us; although sufficient time has elapsed since your letter reached Mr. Judge in America for an unofficial copy thereof to be received in England.
>
> Therefore, as members of the General Council of the T.S. we emphatically protest against this departure from the rules of procedure by

> yourself of your official duty as President toward your colleagues on the General Council of the Society.

In endeavoring to digest the conflicting mass of matter covering the "Judge case" and get at the actual facts, the inquirer will need to relate closely the multitude of statements made by the various principals in the tragedy. One instance, as example and guide, may be noted in the above. The reading of the successive Reports of the Adyar parliaments and quotations already given from "Old Diary Leaves," will conclusively establish that the "Constitution and Rules" were tinkered with each year by the President-Founder, acting through his pliant "General Council" in the first instance and then "officially ratified and promulgated" by himself. It will be noted that the "Constitution and Rules" were "revised" and "ratified" and "promulgated" anew at the Adyar Convention at the end of 1893. Now, let the reader compare Col. Olcott's Presidential Address at that Convention, the laudations of Mrs. Besant, the "recent assurances of fresh disagreeable surprises," the secret conclave of Col. Olcott, Mrs. Besant, Messrs. Old and Sturdy and Countess Wachtmeister during the Convention, Mrs. Besant's letter to Col. Olcott demanding a Committee to "enquire" into the "charges" made by "reputable members" against Mr. Judge, and Col. Olcott's letter with its "options" to Mr. Judge to resign under fire or be "investigated" by a Committee framed by Col. Olcott under "revised" rules planned in advance—and the whole scheme is exposed.

The circular of Messrs. Mead and Keightley goes on:

> *Second:* We recognize that, acting under the general discretionary power conferred upon the President by Art. VI, Sec. 1, it was competent for you as President to take action in the matter. But we feel strongly that, in order to protect and maintain that very Constitution whose guardian you are, it was your duty in your *official* letter to Mr. Judge to have insisted upon

and resolutely maintained the following points:

1. That the free platform of the Society precludes *any official* declaration by the T.S. or any Committee representing it, upon the question whether "Mahatmas" do or do not exist (see Art. XIII, Secs. 2 and 3 ("Offenses");

2. That, therefore, no enquiry into the conduct of any officer of the Society *in his official capacity,* which would involve as its basis a declaration of Yea or Nay upon the above question, can be carried out by any *official* committee of the T.S.;

3. That, accordingly, Sections 2, 3 and 4 of Art. VI are not applicable to the charges indicated by your letter to Mr. Judge;

Third: We desire further to point out that in *officially* giving Mr. Judge the alternatives of resigning all his offices in the T.S. or submitting to the enquiry proposed, you have again departed from the procedure laid down by the Constitution.

Moreover by so doing you place yourself *officially* in the position of having prejudged the case and virtually announce before any enquiry has taken place or even any *specific* charges have been formulated, that you believe Mr. Judge guilty.

It appears to us that such an attitude is inconsistent with that strict impartiality and justice which ought to characterize at least the official actions of the President of the T.S., and that it is calculated to bring discredit upon the Society by laying its chief executive officer open to the charge of condemning a colleague without even giving him a hearing.

In conclusion we hereby place on record our most emphatic protest against the above-cited departures from constitutional procedure; and we officially request a formal reply and declaration thereupon from yourself as President-

Founder of the T.S. and official guardian of its free Constitution.

This we call for as General Secretaries for Europe and India respectively, and as members of that General Council of the Theosophical Society from which, as recited in Art. VI, Sec. 1, you "derive your authority" as President of the T.S., and to which, as therein provided, you "are responsible for its exercise."

Finally we beg to inform you that we shall forthwith notify our respective Sections of the present correspondence, and shall also communicate to them your reply when received, as the members are already unofficially informed of the matter.

We are, dear Sir and Brother,

Fraternally yours,

BERTRAM KEIGHTLEY,
Gen. Sec. Indian Sec. T. S.

G. R. S. MEAD,
Gen. Sec. European Sec. T. S.

Meantime, so sure had Col. Olcott been of the efficacy of his plans of battle that he had committed himself still further and still more irretrievably. Mr. Judge had received his letter of February 7 on March 10, 1894, as mentioned, and on the same day had cabled Col. Olcott an absolute denial of the charges, a point-blank challenge to him to do his worst.

Immediately on receipt of this cablegram Col. Olcott took counsel with himself and his allies. Mrs. Besant was still in India; Chakravarti's subtle mind still available. Mr. Judge had refused to resign; he had defied the options extended him; he had declared his innocence. "For the honor of the Society" another weighty move could be made. Accordingly, Col. Olcott forwarded forthwith two fresh "official" letters. The first of these was formally addressed to Mr. Judge as General Secretary of the American Section. It runs:

THEOSOPHICAL SOCIETY,
PRESIDENT'S OFFICE,
20 March, 1894.

To the General Secretary,
American Section T. S.

Dear Sir and Brother:

In compliance with Section 3 of Article VI of the Revised Rules, I enclose herewith a copy of certain charges preferred against Mr. William Q. Judge, Vice-President T.S. and General Secretary of the American Section, by Mrs. Annie Besant, F.T.S.; which charges will be laid before a Judicial Committee, to be convened at our London Headquarters on the 27th June next, for the consideration and disposal of the same, as provided for in the Section of the Article above specified.

Upon receipt of this you will kindly take the orders of your Executive Committee for the nomination of two members of the said Judicial Committee, to sit as representatives of the American Section, and consider and dispose of the charges.

Fraternally yours,
H. S. OLCOTT,
President Theosophical Society.

The second letter was addressed to Mr. Judge as "Vice-President, T.S." and its text is as follows:

THEOSOPHICAL SOCIETY,
PRESIDENT'S OFFICE,
20 March, 1894.

To William Q. Judge, Esq.,
Vice-President, T. S.

Dear Sir and Brother:

As required by the provisions of Article VI of our Revised Rules, I herewith enclose for your information and action a copy of certain charges preferred against you by Mrs. Annie Besant, F.T.S., and notify you that for their consideration and disposal a Judicial Committee will be convened at our London Headquarters on the 27th June next. I have to request that you will nominate to me the two additional members of the Committee whom you wish to sit and adjudge the case as your personal representatives.

As the accused party you will, of course, be debarred from sitting and voting in the Committee either as Vice-President T.S. or General Secretary of the American Section; but you are entitled to enjoy the full opportunity to disprove the charges brought against you.

Pending the decision of the Judicial Committee, I hereby suspend you from the office of Vice-President T.S. as required by our Revised Rules.

I am, Sir, fraternally yours,

H. S. Olcott,
President Theosophical Society.

The first of these letters would compel Mr. Judge as its General Secretary to himself place the charges and the correspondence before the forthcoming Convention of the American Section due to be held at San Francisco, April 22, 1894, and thus put him on the defensive before his own Section against charges sanctioned by the President-Founder and Mrs. Besant, the two most important and influential members of the Society—the two who had posed hitherto as his dear friends and colleagues in the Society and the Movement.

The second of these letters would force Judge as Vice-President to inform the members that he had been suspended by the President-Founder and thus himself be made the medium of conveying to them the information that the President of the whole Society felt himself compelled by the gravity of the case to suspend the Vice-President in advance of the Judicial Committee. It requires but little imagination to enable any one to picture to himself the consummate ingenuity of these stratagems, whereby the Convention, the American members, the press and the public would be influenced to draw inferences wholly adverse to Mr. Judge, wholly favorable to Mrs. Besant and the venerable President-Founder, thus reluctantly, but gravely and sternly, doing their duty "for the honor of the Society" even where the guilty party was a high official and their dearest friend.

It is more than interesting, it is one of the most telltale signs of the animus behind the whole of the "Judge case," to observe how, in the second of the above letters, Col. Olcott betrays himself in spite of all his prepared "revised" Rules with its "Sections" and "Articles" devised to lend a legal coloring to the planned attack. He tells Mr. Judge: "You are entitled to enjoy the full opportunity to *disprove* the charges brought against you." There never was any "opportunity" to *prove* the charges, which rested wholly upon hearsays, suspicions, circumstances innocent in themselves, and *"messages from the Masters" received by Mrs. Besant and Col. Olcott via Chakravarti and Mr. Walter R. Old.*

One has but to recall the well-known legal maxims that it is for the accusers to prove their charges, not for the accused to prove his innocence, and that any accused person must be assumed to be innocent until the charges are proven—one has but to bear these commonest of all safeguards for the unjustly accused in mind, to perceive over and over again in the progress of the "Judge case" how his accusers acted at every step in defiance of every canon of ordinary human fairness and decency. The procedure of the Society for Psychical Research and its famous (or infamous) Committee in 1884-5 so violated, as we have earlier shown, every instinct of common justice in its "investigation" of H.P.B. and her phenomena, as to earn for it the pity or the contempt of every fair and intelligent mind. The Coues-Collins-Lane-*New York Sun* "exposure" was the same thing repeated with greater ability and with conscious venom. But the

"Judge case" is infinitely worse in its travesty of justice, and has been, therefore, infinitely worse in its consequences to Humanity.

To the honor of Mr. Judge be it spoken that at the Convention of the American Section his Report as General Secretary breathes the same unwaveringly calm, fraternal tone as always—toward the workers, toward the President-Founder, toward Mrs. Besant. No man, we think, can read the Convention Report and contrast it with the Report of the Adyar Convention preceding, and not be cognisant of the difference between professional and genuine altruism.

A formal letter from Mr. Mead as General Secretary of the European Section, dated March 31, and addressed "To the General Secretary of the American Section," was read. This was a request that the recent correspondence be placed before the American Section. Accordingly, Mr. Judge laid before the Convention the letter of Mrs. Besant of February 6 to Col. Olcott; the latter's official letter of February 7; a copy of the Keightley-Mead circular letter; the two letters of Col. Olcott of March 20; and other correspondence *ad interim.* All were referred to appropriate Committees.

At this Convention of the American Section April 22-3, 1894, there were present delegates and proxies from all of the sixty-one active Branches.

Resolutions were unanimously adopted:

1. That the expense to which Mr. Judge has been put in printing and circulating his statement should be borne by the American Section;

2. That "this Convention, after careful deliberation, finds that such suspension of the Vice-President is without the slightest warrant in the Constitution and altogether transcends the discretionary power given the President by the Constitution, and is therefore null and void";

3. That "this Section, in Convention assembled, hereby expresses its unqualified protest against the said illegal action by the President of the Society, and can see no necessity for such action, and that even did the Con-

stitution contain any provision for a suspension such action would be wholly needless and unbrotherly, inasmuch as, by the Constitution, the Vice-President has no duties or power save in case of death, resignation, or accusation of the President."

The existing situation on the whole subject of Mahatmas and Messages from Mahatmas or Masters, and the actual status of the whole problem, under the Objects and Constitution of the Theosophical Society, were declared in two Resolutions introduced by Dr. Jerome A. Anderson. Both of these Resolutions were unanimously adopted. They are of such value and importance in giving a matter-of-fact formulation of the issues that we reproduce them in full:

> *Whereas,* many members of the Theosophical Society, including the late Madame Blavatsky, Col. Olcott, W. Q. Judge, Mrs. Annie Besant, A. P. Sinnett, and others, have at various times and places expressed their belief in the existence of certain Mahatmas or Masters, and have claimed to be in communication with the same; and
>
> *Whereas,* the President, Col. Olcott, at the request of one of the members, Mrs. Annie Besant, has recently demanded an official investigation by means of a Judicial Committee of the Theosophical Society, to decide whether or not Wm. Q. Judge is in communication with the said Mahatmas, and whether or not the said Wm. Q. Judge has "misused the names and handwriting of the said Mahatmas"; and
>
> *Whereas,* Under the Constitution and Rules of the Theosophical Society it is declared that the Society, as such, is not responsible for the personal opinions of its Fellows, nor for any expression thereof, and that no Fellow, Officer, or Council, of the Theosophical Society, or of any Section or Branch thereof, shall promulgate or maintain any doctrine, dogma, or belief as be-

ing that advanced or advocated by the Society (Art. XIII); and the President having officially and constitutionally in his executive order of May 27th, 1893, relative to the World's Religious Parliament, declared this neutrality, especially in these words:

> "Of course it is to be distinctly understood that nothing shall be said or done by any Delegate or *Committee of the Society* to identify it as a Body with any special form of religion, creed, sect, or any *religious or ethical teacher or leader;* our duty being to affirm and defend its perfect corporate neutrality in these matters."

Therefore,

Resolved: That, in the opinion of this Convention, the action of the President, Col. Olcott, in calling such Judicial Committee to consider said charge was uncalled for, unconstitutional, illegal, and improper.

Resolved: That this Convention hereby cordially endorses the interpretation of the Rules and Constitution of the T.S. recently expressed in a circular to members, signed by the General Secretaries of the European and Indian Sections, and in the private circular of March 15th, 1894, issued by William Q. Judge.

Resolved: That this Convention hereby reaffirms the entire freedom of the platform of the T.S. and the religious and other opinions of its members, which entitles all and any of them to claim to be in communication with, to receive letters from, or to act as agents for, those above referred to as Mahatmas or Masters; or, on the other hand, to express disbelief in the proper title of any member to make such claim or claims, or disbelief in the existence of said Mahatmas.

Resolved: That this Convention declares its unswerving belief in the integrity and uprightness of the Vice-President of the T.S., Wm. Q. Judge, and expresses to him the most cordial thanks of the Section for his unrecompensed and self-sacrificing years of labor on behalf of the T.S. as a whole.

Whereas: This Section regards official investigation into the existence and methods of Mahatmas, and a dogmatic verdict rendered upon such investigation, as not only illegal under the Constitution but impossible in the absence of more profound knowledge of the science of Occultism, and, therefore, absurd in the present instance, although such inquiry and investigation are always proper privileges of individual members as such, therefore

Resolved: That, if in the face of this protest and opinion of this Section, there is to be an investigation to decide whether or not William Q. Judge is or was in communication with said Mahatmas, and whether or not he has "misused the names and handwriting of said Mahatmas," or whether or not pretended or real communications or orders from said alleged Mahatmas have been issued or given out by him, then, in the opinion of this Section, an investigation should also be had to decide whether or not Col. Olcott, A. P. Sinnett, Annie Besant, and others have had, given, or promulgated such or any communication from the Mahatmas, whether real or pretended; and that they be required to show evidence of the possession of a commission from said Mahatmas, and of the truthfulness of their claims as heretofore frequently made and announced by them in public.

Resolved: That, in the opinion of this Section, only a Body of Mahatmas appearing at the sessions of the Committee could decide whether or not any communication was or is a genuine or fraudulent Mahatmic message.

Advices of the action taken by the Convention of the American Section were cabled to Col. Olcott at once. We may now follow them to Adyar and observe the moves made on that side of the great checker board of Theosophical events.

CHAPTER XXIX

THE "JUDICIAL ENQUIRY" IN LONDON

COLONEL Olcott's two letters of March 20, 1894, to Mr. Judge—the one to him as General Secretary of the American Section and the other addressed to him as Vice-President of the T.S.—as detailed in the last chapter, were drawn up immediately following the receipt of Mr. Judge's cabled denial of the "charges," and just prior to Mrs. Besant's departure from India. They were the President-Founder's only communication to the Convenvention of the American Section—the largest, the most active, the most influential of all the three Sections of the Society. When one contrasts the length and character of his Annual Address at the preceding Adyar Convention with the nature of these two letters, but one inference can be drawn: The President-Founder had determined to "fight it out" once more, and this time to the hilt; he had burned his bridges behind him; it was to be a fight without quarter that should leave the victor in undisputed possession of the field. The spectacle of a living H.P.B. continually upsetting his most cherished plans to make of the Theosophical Society a world force with himself as its world-wide Head, had been well-nigh intolerable. Her continual insistence on Brotherhood as she understood it; her continual interference "in the name of the Masters" with his "practical" guidance of the Society; her Esoteric School pledged to *Theosophy* and the Theosophical Movement instead of the Society, pledged to follow her Instructions instead of his revised Rules—all this had been a continual thorn in his side. But each time that the "moment of choice" had been precipitated he had avoided the final wager of battle; the odds were too great, the liens established too strong.

But now—*now* was no longer dependent on H.P.B. for "messages from the Masters"; Mrs. Besant, the "sweet spirit and the guiding star" of the Esoteric School, the strongest factor in the Society as well as in the School, the most potent influence on the world at large as well as in the Society—Mrs. Besant was now his firm ally. Opposed to his ideas, his plans and policies, stood out only Mr. Judge. Two years had shown that Mr. Judge could not be moved from his firm allegiance to H.P.B. and all that H.P.B. had represented. Messrs. Sinnett, Bertram Keightley, Old, Sturdy, and Edge, the Countess Wachtmeister, the Hindus *en masse,* the great bulk of the English and European Theosophists—all these he could count on as imbued with the same ideas as himself. The time was come to banish the spectre of H.P.B. by driving Mr. Judge into exile—to make of the Theosophical Society what it should have been and ought to be.

His letters to Mr. Judge were well calculated to create confusion, bewilderment, uncertainty, among the American Theosophists—to throw Judge on the defensive, a helpless defensive, far more a helpless defensive than had paralyzed H.P.B.'s activities following the Coulomb-S.P.R. bombshell in 1884-5. So much for the American field. Remained England, Europe, and India to be aroused to the offensive. Mrs. Besant was returning to England, whence she could not only direct the battle there, but could reasonably be expected to muster succors and strong levies in the United States in spite of all that Mr. Judge or his friends could avail. And Mr. Walter R. Old was no mean understudy; he, too, was returning to England at the same time as Mrs. Besant.

The "Supplement" to *The Theosophist* for February, 1894, had contained a printed slip pasted to its pages and headed "To Members and Friends." It was dated January 29, 1894, and signed by "Walter R. Old, Rec. Sec. T.S." Mr. Old's notice informed the members that, "acting under medical advice received during a recent illness," he was going to England for the summer and would leave India at the end of March. The familiar "explanation" of his departure merely cloaked the fact that as his part of the tactics planned he was to return to England to aid in spreading among the English Theosophists the slanders dignified as "charges" against Mr. Judge. Mr. Old was well known in England, where he had many friends and much influence as a "psychic," as an "astrologer," as a former member of the E.S.T. Council, as a friend of H.P.B.'s and as in high favor with the President-Founder as well as with Mrs. Besant. For it must be remembered that the suspension of Mr. Old from the E.S.T. was unknown at that time except by rumor among the general membership of the Society, while his intimacy with Col. Olcott and Mrs. Besant was a matter of common knowledge.

The two letters to Mr. Judge were immediately followed up by Col. Olcott in the April, 1894, *Theosophist*, with an eight-page article devoted to "Annie Besant's Indian Tour." It is given over to the most fulsome laudations. We say "fulsome" because, like his similar remarks in his preceding Presidential Address, these reiterated encomiums on Mrs. Besant must necessarily be construed, not merely as extraordinary tributes of personal regard and esteem, but, in the light of collateral circumstances, as carefully planned, deliberately carried out steps of a predetermined march. Step by step with the belittlements of H.P.B. and the accusations published and circulated about Judge, marched the public cumulation of official and personal tributes to Mrs. Besant.

The investigator of today will naturally compare and contrast the declarations of Col. Olcott in the mentioned article and in his Presidential Address, with the numerous statements made by him in regard to H.P.B., both those hitherto quoted and those with which the whole series of "Old Diary Leaves" is larded. He will offset the President-Founder's strictures on H.P.B. and Mr. Judge with his laudations of Mrs. Besant and his scarcely less veiled extolments of himself. He will consider scrupulously the attendant circumstances and the "controlling impulse" governing Col. Olcott in his "Old

Diary Leaves" as recounted by himself in his *Foreword* to the first published volume. He will compare them with the various statements and acts of H.P.B. and Mr. Judge and all with the common objects and principles professed, to determine the consistency or inconsistency of each.

The extraordinary article on Mrs. Besant was followed in the "Supplement" to the May *Theosophist* by something more extraordinary still. In it will be found the text of an Executive Notice, the real significance of which has never yet been grasped by Theosophists at large, any more than it was at the time. We give it in full:

> Adyar, 27th April, 1894.
>
> The undersigned avails of Mrs. Annie Besant's forthcoming visit to the Australasian Colonies, to invest her with the functions of President's Commissioner, with authority to represent him in all current Society business during her tour, and act for him and in his name in disposing of the same, as perfectly as though it were his individual act. Mrs. Besant is empowered to organize a Section or Sections; to authorize the formation of Branches; to admit persons to the Fellowship; to regulate disagreements and disputes within the Society; to remit at her discretion in cases of great poverty the whole or any part of any fee or other pecuniary contribution chargeable as a condition of membership; and, generally, to exercise the same powers as are constitutionally enjoyed by the undersigned in his Presidential capacity.
>
> Mrs. Besant will, of course, make or cause to be made to the undersigned a full report of her official actions under the above special commission and according to the revised rules of the Society.
>
> H. S. Olcott, P.T.S.

The Presidential "discretionary powers" are officially stretched to give Mrs. Besant sanction in advance to a range of arbitrary and unchecked authority that becomes the more astounding the more closely it is examined. She can organize at will, and upon terms named by herself, "a Section or Sections," under "revised Rules" that will give such Section or Sections the same voice and standing in the General Council as the existing democratic Sections. She can "authorize the formation of Branches" to an extent and upon terms that will control the Section or Sections she is to organize. She can "admit persons to fellowship"—or deny them, inevitably—upon terms that will control the Branches. She can remit dues in whole or in part. Finally, she can "regulate disagreements and disputes within the Society." What does this mean, if it does not mean that she can exercise absolute and unappealable authority, root, stalk, and branch, to any extent necessary to organize and control a Section or Sections wholly pliant to her own will and purposes? What becomes of democracy, of neutrality, of individual liberty of conscience, under such canons of organizations and government? That at any time, in any event, under any circumstances, such powers should be claimed, such authority desired, by any one soever, Master or man, is a categorical negation of every Object for which the Theosophical Society was supposed to stand. That they should have been exercised in the then existent circumstances, tells to what lengths the conspirators were prepared to go. The student has but to examine into the original Preamble and By-Laws of 1875, the Rules adopted in December, 1879, the Constitutions of the American and British Sections of 1887 and 1888, and compare them with the "revised Rules" adopted by Col. Olcott's obedient General Council in December, 1893, to discern how, in the interim, the Society had been engineered into an absolute autocracy wherein, under the forms adopted, the members had no rights whatever, "constitutionally," save such as the General Council might choose to allot them, no voice and no appeal save as the "discretionary powers" of the President might be "exercised" as an "act of grace."

So much for the general significance that must be attached to this Executive Notice; it is integral with the battle openly begun at the Adyar Convention at the end of 1888, the "Revised Rules" of 1893 but the full bloom of the "revised rules" of 1888. But what of its special import? That also must be inquired into.

The answer is simple. Mr. Judge's circular and that of Messrs. Mead and Keightley had reached Adyar; the news of the action taken by the Convention of the American Section had been received. The plans of the accusers were completely upset; the tables were turned; what was to be done? To appreciate Col. Olcott's dilemma, to understand his consternation, the student should marshal the opposing situations as before him at the end of April, 1894. Thus:

I. Backed by the revised Rules, confident that the prestige of Mrs. Besant and himself with the membership and the world would make their charges carry the assumption of guilt, the unavoidable inference was that Mr. Judge would avail himself of the option to resign. On the contrary, Mr. Judge had denied absolutely any wrongdoing and, instead of retiring to the shelter of silence, had himself made public the full facts, and had announced his determination to meet the issues: (1) that the whole proceeding was utterly unconstitutional; (2) that he would not oppose but would submit himself to any competent investigation that did not involve the neutrality of the Society or set up a dogma; in other words, try out the facts of who was and who was not "in communication with the Mahatmas."

II. Messrs. Mead and Keightley, counted on as allies and aids in the fight on Mr. Judge, had half risen in rebellion; had declared that it was the President-Founder himself who was guilty of gross violation of the Constitution and the neutrality of the Society; had appealed to their respective Sections—the European and Indian—with a statement of the facts, and had announced their opposition to any attempt to set up a dogma on the subject of Mahatmas, and had demanded of the President-Founder a categorical official reply to the points raised by them.

III. The Convention of the American Section, with all the correspondence before it, had, as a democratic body, unanimously voted its protest against the spirit and the substance of Col. Olcott's actions; had re-elected Mr. Judge its General Secretary; had declared its entire confidence in him as a man, as a Theosophist, as an officer in the Society; had taken a firm stand against any official interference with the freedom of speech and conscience of any member, high or low; had declared, if any "Judicial Committee" were to sit upon the question of Mahatmas and communications from them, that such investigation must be complete and must include Col. Olcott, Mrs. Besant, Mr. Sinnett, and all others as well as Mr. Judge who had claimed to be in receipt of "messages from the Masters."

Colonel Olcott had counted with the confidence based on fifteen years' experience that the Indian Section would obey any lead he might choose to give. He had counted that since the members and the other Sections had not hitherto *actively* opposed his repeated tampering with the Rules and his repeated executive ukases, no *organized* resistance would be offered to his plans to force Mr. Judge into exile by charges that in their very nature would paralyze any defense. Mrs. Besant had counted that her influence was strong enough with the British-European Section to make the members accept as proven any charges she might make, merely because she made them. Both she and Col. Olcott had counted that Mrs. Besant's prestige was so great in America that no concerted defense could be made of Mr. Judge in the American Convention by those who might still believe in him. Sure of India, sure of Britain, sure at worst of a split in America, they had nothing to fear even when Mr. Judge cabled on March 10 his denial of the charges and his refusal of their options. If the matter came to a trial before a Judicial Committee, they held that Committee in the hollow of their hands. If the matter should go before the Sections they had expected to control two out of the three absolutely, with the assurance that at best Mr. Judge could count on nothing better than a split in the American Section. Mrs. Besant and Mr. Old, therefore, had sailed confidently for England toward the end of March to complete their preparations at home for the forthcoming "trial." Colonel Olcott, on his part, went forward as confidently in India.

Now, in a little month, the whole situation was reversed. Desperation took the place of confidence. The conspirators were divided by distance; deserted by two of their strongest allies; America unanimous in support of Judge; counter-issues raised that they could not meet. What was to be done?

This was the situation in which Col. Olcott found himself toward the close of April, 1894. Yet he could not retreat; the battle was joined; he must go forward. What hurried interchanges took place between the conspirators any thoughtful reader can infer for himself from merely visualizing the status of affairs and studying the President-Founder's consequent steps. The first of these was the Executive Notice given. Its purpose is clear; if the warfare should be carried before the Sections, as it was certain now that it must at last, *two* Sections were absolutely requisite even to assure a "drawn battle." India was safe for the conspirators; America had already declared for Mr. Judge; Britain was still a hopeful prospect, but no more. Mr. Judge had friends there; who could say what might happen? But if Australia were organized into a Section—organized by Mrs. Besant robed with the Presidential "discretionary powers" to accept or reject whom she would—then the new Australasian Section could be made as safely and entirely a "pocket borough" as India was already. Hence the Notice dated April 27, 1894.

Chakravarti was a lawyer along with his other accomplishments; N. D. Khandalavala was a judge in one of the Indian courts. Them and others the President-Founder consulted and the result was still another Executive Notice, published in the "Supplement" to the May *Theosophist* immediately following on the Notice transferring to Mrs. Besant his extraordinary, emergency-planned "discretionary powers" to organize an

Australasian Section. Because of its telltale significance, both in connection with the preceding events narrated and with what followed, we give it in full for the careful study of all students. It is dated on the same day as the Special Commission to Mrs. Besant—April 27, 1894—and reads:

> The following facts are published for the information of members of the Society:
>
> On February 6th last, while at Allahabad, Mrs. Annie Besant handed the undersigned a written demand that certain accusations "with reference to certain letters and in the alleged writings of the Mahatmas," injurious to the public character of Mr. W. Q. Judge, Vice-President of the Society, should be dealt with by a Committee as provided by Art. VI, Secs. 2, 3 and 4.
>
> On the following day, from Agra, a copy of this letter was forwarded by the undersigned to Mr. Judge without the expression of any opinion as to the validity or otherwise of the accusations in question. No specific charges having then been filed, this was merely a preliminary measure.
>
> From a motive of delicacy no question was asked the accused as to his guilt or innocence, but the undersigned, in the exercise of his discretion, gave Mr. Judge the option of resigning his office or submitting the case to investigation. The implication being, of course, that *if guilty*, he would wish to retire quietly, or if *innocent*, to be brought before the Committee, and thus set at rest, once and for all, the injurious rumors afloat, in different parts of the world.
>
> The alternative offered carried with it, as will be clearly seen, no intimation that the rumors were true, nor that the undersigned believed them so, or the contrary.
>
> Mr. Judge having cabled a denial of his guilt,

the first step prescribed by the Constitution for such cases was then taken, *viz.*, the ordering of a "Judicial Committee" as provided for under Art. VI; the official notification of the same to the accused and the members of the General Council; and the serving upon each of a copy of the detailed charges and specifications, then drafted by Mrs. Besant as Accuser. The provisions of our Constitution were thus strictly followed out, and there has been no deviation whatever.

It was hoped by the undersigned that the whole matter would have been kept private until the Committee had met, disposed of the charges and rendered its verdict, which would then have been officially promulgated by him.

But the opposite policy having been adopted by the accused and the General Secretaries of the European and Indian Sections, and printed circulars having been distributed by them throughout the whole world, secrecy is no longer possible, and hence the present Executive Notice is issued, with the deepest regret for its necessity.

The undersigned deplores that his colleagues, Mr. Mead and Mr. Keightley, should have acted in such haste as to have committed the indiscretion of censuring him for breaches in procedure and a violation of the Constitution of which he was not guilty. He regrets also that the fact of Mrs. Besant's being the accuser should not have been mentioned, if the public was to be taken into confidence at all at this preliminary stage.

A detailed reply to Messrs. Mead and Keightley's letter is in preparation and will be circulated to all Branches.

To correct misapprehensions, the undersigned has to state that in the opinion of eminent counsel (Members of the Society) the trial of the charges against Mr. Judge does not involve the question of the existence or non-existence of the Mahatmas or their connection with the Society.

The Judicial Committee is notified to meet in London on June 27th, and the undersigned finds himself compelled to attend, contrary to his wishes and expectations. He will leave Adyar about the middle of May for London, via Marseilles.

H. S. Olcott, P.T.S.

Taking this Notice of the President-Founder *seriatim*, careful examination and comparison will disclose:

That it is published officially as a statement of the "facts" and for "the information of the members";

That its second paragraph conveys that Mrs. Besant made a "demand" for the Committee. The fact being, as we shall soon see over Col. Olcott's own signature, that the alleged "demand" was made *at his own request*;[1]

That his own letter to Mr. Judge, conveying the same "demand" was forwarded "without expressing any opinion as to the validity or otherwise of the accusations in question." The fact being, as we shall abundantly verify over Col. Olcott's own signature, that he was at the time and for nearly two years had been, firmly of the opinion that Mr. Judge was guilty of transmitting bogus messages.[2] The third paragraph discloses that such was the prejudgment of Col. Olcott and Mrs. Besant that both the "demand" was made and Col. Olcott's letter of February 7 was written *when no specific charges had been filed, even.* Yet Col. Olcott did not hesitate to require of Mr. Judge that he should either resign or be tried for charges not yet even formulated. By referring to Col. Olcott's two letters to Mr. Judge dated March 20, 1894, and reproduced in full in the last chapter, the student will note that in the intervening period the

[1] See succeeding chapter—Col. Olcott's Note to Mrs. Besant's statement before the British Convention.

[2] See Chapter XXXIII *post*—Col. Olcott's statement in "The Case against William Q. Judge" is dated January 28, 1893.

charges had been formulated and the two letters drawn up on the eve of Mrs. Besant's departure from India. On the strength of these "formulated" charges Col. Olcott arbitrarily "suspended" Mr. Judge from the Vice-Presidency, in advance of any *trial.* These items all show unmistakably both bias and conspiracy, to conceal which and give the impression of impartiality and legality to the steps taken is the manifest purpose of the Notice of April 27, put out for the "information" of the members.

Its purpose is, plainly, so to twist the facts as to cause the members to believe, not only that he had acted impartially and only as compelled by the constitutional provisions, on Mrs. Besant's demand, but that Mr. Judge and Messrs. Mead and Keightley had behaved in a manner to be "deplored" by making known the actual facts and conditions to the whole Theosophical world; furthermore, he evades and denies his own primary responsibility in the phrase that he "regrets that the fact of Mrs. Besant being the accuser should not have been mentioned." The fact being that as Mrs. Besant was merely a private member of the Society and President of the Blavatsky Lodge, a London Branch, she had neither duty, right, nor privilege, under the Constitution and Rules of the Society, to bring any charges against any officer of the Society, or against any member, save of her own Branch, and that she acted directly at his instigation and request.

The "detailed reply to Messrs. Mead and Keightley's letter," that the Notice states is "in preparation and will be circulated to all Branches," was never, so far as we know, either "prepared" or "circulated." All that he ever issued was a "plea in extenuation," similar to the above quoted Notice.

It will be noted that the "eminent counsel (Members of the Society)," in whose "opinion" the trial of the charges "does not involve the question of the Mahatmas or their connection with the Society," are not named. They were, in point of fact, Chakravarti and the others, as stated, and although Col. Olcott lugs in this "opinion" to "correct misapprehensions" the fact is, as again we shall soon see, that he completely reversed himself and the said "eminent counsel" at the meeting of the Judicial Committee.

Finally, the reader should compare and contrast the concluding paragraph of the Notice, in which Col. Olcott announces that he "finds himself compelled to attend" the meeting of the Judicial Committee, "contrary to his wishes and expectations," with the statement in his letter to Mr. Judge of February 7: "I shall in all probability be represented by proxy, unless something now unforeseen should arise to make it imperative that I shall personally attend." The whole procedure had been so carefully planned, and looked so entirely certain to the conspirators in the beginning, that there had been no thought other than, if Judge should have the hardihood to refuse to resign and, instead, stand trial, the controlled Committee would find him "guilty" out of hand, on the mere presentation of the "charges" sponsored by Mrs. Besant, backed by the President-Founder from Adyar, who could then, "after the Committee had met, disposed of the charges and rendered its verdict," have "officially promulgated" the pre-arranged "decision." Now, in view of all that had happened to set awry their well-laid plans, it was not enough to make Mrs. Besant the Presidential Special Commissioner; it was not enough to publish another Executive Notice for the "information of the members"; it was become "imperative" indeed that Col. Olcott should "personally attend" the meeting of the Judicial Committee, lest worse befall than had already occurred; lest the Committee not only find Mr. Judge "not guilty," but proceed to investigate on its own behalf the actions of the President of the Society in his usurpation of powers, in the claims of himself and his fellow accusers to "messages from the Masters."

Skipping the intervening period of public silence and private wagging of heads, of external decorum and secret diligent planning of ways and means to avoid a defeat or a fiasco, we may attend the meeting of the Judicial Committee and then the immediately following Convention of the British-European Section, and observe what took place. The proceedings are officially reported in a record published in full in *The Path*, in *Lucifer*, in *The Theosophist*, immediately following the Convention, and also in a pamphlet officially issued under the title "THE NEUTRALITY OF THE THEOSOPHICAL SOCIETY. AN ENQUIRY INTO CERTAIN CHARGES AGAINST THE VICE-PRESIDENT, HELD IN LONDON, JULY, 1894. WITH AN APPENDIX. PUBLISHED BY THE GENERAL COUNCIL OF THE THEOSOPHICAL SOCIETY, FOR THE INFORMATION OF MEMBERS. JULY, 1894." So runs the title-page. Let us first examine the "Enquiry" and then the "Appendix."

The President-Founder arrived promptly in London, but the Enquiry was not held on the date set, June 27. The time until July 7 was occupied in various abortive attempts to reach a compromise that would obviate official disposition, but Mr. Judge insisted that since the whole procedure up to date had been taken officially by the President-Founder, with himself as defendant against charges of dishonorable conduct, and with issues raised prejudicial to the Society as well as himself, it could only properly be disposed of by formal official action. Accordingly, Col. Olcott summoned a meeting of the General Council on July 7. There were present Col. Olcott, who presided, Mr. Bertram Keightley, who was chosen as Secretary of the Council meeting, Mr. G. R. S. Mead; and Mr. Judge who took no part in the proceedings. Col. Olcott read to the meeting a formal letter by Mr. Judge, stating (1) that he had never been *elected* Vice-President of the Society, and was not, therefore, *legally* the Vice-President of the Society; (2) that even if adjudged *de facto* Vice-President of the Society, he was not thereby amenable to charges of "misuse of Mahatmas' names and handwriting," since, even if guilty, such offenses would be those of a private individual and not as an officer of the Society; hence not subject, under the Constitution, to trial by a Judicial Committee of the Society as an official malfeasance. A legal opinion from a New York lawyer, Mr. M. H. Phelps, a member of the Society, was then read in support of Mr. Judge's contentions.

The matter was then debated, Mr. Judge remaining silent. Colonel Olcott informed the meeting that at the Adyar Convention of 1888 he had himself "appointed" Mr. Judge Vice-President by virtue of his own "prerogative" to make such an appointment and had published such title in the official list of Officers of the Society, and that this appointment was unanimously "confirmed" by vote at the Indian General Convention of 1890, although the "official report" of that Convention "did not record the fact." Hence, he declared, Mr. Judge "was and is Vice-President *de facto* and *de jure*."

Having heard what Col. Olcott had to say as to the first point raised by Mr. Judge, the Council meeting made no decision, but passed to the second question. On this point renewed discussion took place, Mr. Judge remaining silent as before. The minutes read:

> The matter was then debated. Bertram Keightley moved and G. R. S. Mead seconded:
>
> "That the Council, having heard the arguments on the point raised by William Q. Judge, it declares that the point is well taken; that the acts alleged concern him as an individual; and that consequently the Judicial Committee has no jurisdiction in the premises to try him as Vice-President upon the charges as alleged.
>
> "*The President Concurred.* Mr. Judge did not vote. The motion was declared carried.
>
> "On Mr. Mead's motion, it was then voted that above record shall be laid before the Judicial Committee. Mr. Judge did not vote."

This proceeding having been had, Col. Olcott then laid before the Council meeting a further point raised by Mr. Judge, to wit: that Mr. Judge's election by the American, the British, and Indian Sections, as successor to the President in 1892 (at the time of Col. Olcott's resignation), "became *ipso facto* annulled upon the President's resumption of his office as President." "On motion," reads the official minutes, "the Council declared the point well taken, and ordered the decision to be entered upon the minutes. Mr. Judge did not vote."

Colonel Olcott then called the meeting's attention to the resolution of the American Section Convention which declared in effect that the suspension of Mr. Judge was without warrant in the Constitution and transcended the President's discretionary powers. On this it was moved, seconded, and passed, Mr. Judge not voting, that "the President's action was warranted under the then existing circumstances" and that the American Section's "resolutions of protest are without force."

Next, by motion (Mr. Judge not voting), "the council then requested the President to convene the Judicial Committee at the London Headquarters, on Tuesday, July 10, 1894, at 10 a. m. The Council then adjourned at call of the President."

The Judicial Committee met on July 10, as required. There were present all the members of the Committee, as follows: Col. Olcott as President-Founder, in the chair; Messrs. G. R. S. Mead and Bertram Keightley as General Secretaries of the European and Indian Sections; Messrs. A. P. Sinnett and E. T. Sturdy as delegates of the Indian Section; Messrs. Herbert Burrows and W. Kingsland as delegates of the European Section; Dr. J. D. Buck and Dr. Archibald Keightley as delegates of the American Section; Messrs. Oliver Firth and E. T. Hargrove as special delegates representing the accused—all as provided for under the "revised Rules" adopted at the Adyar Convention in December preceding. Mr. Judge was present as the accused, but not voting as General Secretary of the American Section. Mrs. Besant was present as the accuser. It should be noted that of the eleven members of the Judicial Committee, the Chairman, Col. Olcott, and Messrs. E. T. Sturdy and A. P. Sinnett were already fully convinced in advance of the guilt of Mr. Judge; Messrs. Bertram Keightley and G. R. S. Mead convinced of Judge's guilt, but equally convinced that he could not be "tried" for his offenses; Messrs. Herbert Burrows, W. Kingsland, and Oliver Firth, strong friends of both Mrs. Besant and Col. Olcott, but still in doubt as to Mr. Judge's guilt and the legality of the whole proceedings. Of the remaining members of the Judicial Committee Dr. Buck and Dr. Archibald Keightley were fast friends of both the accused and the accuser, as well as of Col. Olcott; Mr. E. T. Hargrove was a young barrister of excellent family just then coming into prominence among the London members of the Society, friendly to all parties, but, as the after events showed, well assured in his own mind, like Dr. Buck and Dr. Archibald Keightley, both that Mr. Judge was innocent of any wrong-doing and that the whole affair was a colossal blunder as well as legally defective.

The meeting of the Judicial Committee being opened by the President-Founder, he read to the assembled Committee a formal letter from Mr. Judge as General Secretary of the American Section, stating that in the opinion of the Executive Committee of the American Section that Section was entitled to an extra vote in the Judicial Committee by reason of the fact that its General Secretary, being the accused, would not vote in the proceedings. On motion James M. Pryse, well known both in New York and London, was added to the Judicial Committee as a substitute for the General Secretary of the American Section.

Colonel Olcott, as Chairman, then declared the Judicial Committee to be duly constituted, and at once proceeded to read the following remarkable address as President-Founder of the Society. We give it in full, omitting only those parts already covered in the various documents quoted from:

Gentlemen and Brothers,

We have met together today as a Judicial Committee . . . to consider and dispose of certain charges of misconduct, preferred by Mrs. Besant against the Vice-President of the So-

> ciety, and dated March 24th, 1894 [it should be noted that the two letters to Mr. Judge, purporting to give the "charges" as an enclosure, and "suspending" the Vice-President in consequence, were both dated March *20th*, 1894, four days *before* the date here given] . . .
>
> In compliance with the Revised Rules, copies of the charges brought by the accuser have been duly supplied to the accused and the members of the General Council. . . .
>
> Upon receipt of a preliminary letter from myself, of date February 7th, 1894, from Agra, India, Mr. Judge, erroneously taking it to be the first step in the *official enquiry* into the charges, from my omission to mark the letter "Private," naturally misconceived it to be a breach of the Constitution, and vehemently protested in a public circular addressed to "the members of the Theosophical Society," and of which 5,000 copies were distributed to them, to all parts of the world. The name of the accuser not being mentioned, the wrong impression prevailed that I was the author of the charges, and at the same time intended to sit as Chairman of the tribunal that was to investigate them.[3] I regret this circumstance as having caused bad feeling throughout the Society against its Chief Executive, who has been the personal friend of the accused for many years, has ever appreciated as they deserved his eminent services and unflagging devotion to the Society and the whole movement, and whose constant motive has been to be brotherly and act justly to all his colleagues, of every race, religion, and sex.

Having thus followed up the line adopted in the Notice of April 27 which we have given, Col. Olcott proceeds in his Address to the Judicial Committee to argue

[3] See *post*, Col. Olcott's Note to Mrs. Besant's statement before the Convention on July 12, 1894, for his direct admission of his own responsibility for the charges.

and give his own opinions and conclusions on the various questions raised by Mr. Judge at the meeting of the General Council three days preceding, as recited, and concludes this portion of his Address by stating:

> From the above facts it is evident that W. Q. Judge is, and since December, 1888, has continuously been, *de jure* as well as *de facto*, Vice-President of the Theosophical Society. The facts having been laid before the General Council in its session of the 7th inst., my ruling has been ratified; and is now also concurred in by Mr. Judge. He is, therefore, triable by this tribunal for "cause shown."

The President-Founder then passes to the second point raised by Mr. Judge. It is interesting to note that in this passage he enlarges the original charge as contained in his letter of February 7. He says:

> The second point raised by the accused is more important. If the acts alleged were done by him at all—which remains as yet *sub judice*—and he did them as a private person, *he cannot be tried by any other tribunal than the Aryan Lodge, T.S., of which he is a Fellow and the President. Nothing can possibly be clearer than that.* Now, what are the alleged offenses?
>
> That he practiced deception in sending false messages, orders and letters, as if sent and written by "Masters"; and in statements to me about a certain Rosicrucian jewel of H.P.B.'s.
>
> That he was untruthful in various other instances enumerated.
>
> Are these solely acts done in his private capacity; or may they or either of them be laid against him as wrong-doing by the Vice-President? This is a grave question, both in its present bearings and as establishing a precedent for future contingencies. We must not make a mistake in coming to a decision.

In summoning Mr. Judge before this tribunal, I was moved by the thought that the alleged evil acts might be separated into (*a*) strictly private acts, *viz.*, the alleged untruthfulness and deception, and (*b*) the alleged circulation of deceptive imitations of what are supposed to be Mahatmic writings, with intent to deceive; which communications, owing to his high official rank among us, carried a weight they would not have had if given out by a simple member. This seemed to me a far more heinous offense than simple falsehood, or any other act of an individual, and to amount to a debasement of his office, if proven, . . . The issue is now open to your consideration, and you must decide as to your judicial competency.

Although the original charge was "misuse"—*i.e.*, imitating—"the handwriting of the Mahatmas," yet Col. Olcott proceeds to give it as his opinion that——

The present issue is not at all whether Mahatmas exist or the contrary, or whether they have or have not recognizable handwritings, and have or have not authorized Mr. Judge to put forth documents in their names. I believed, when issuing the call, that the question might be discussed without entering into investigations that would compromise our corporate neutrality. The charges as formulated and laid before me by Mrs. Besant could, in my opinion, have been tried without doing this.

After this extraordinary admission and affirmation Col. Olcott proceeds to hasten to his own defense for having brought matters thus far and for what he now finds himself compelled to do—that is, to reverse himself completely:

. . . I must refer to my official record to prove that I would have been the last to help in violating a Constitution of which I am, it may be

> said, the father, and which I have continually defended at all times and in all circumstances. On now meeting Mr. Judge in London, however, and being made acquainted with his intended line of defense, I find that by beginning the enquiry we should be placed in this dilemma, *viz.*, we should either have to deny him the common justice of listening to his statements and examining his proofs (which would be monstrous in even a common court of law, much more in a Brotherhood like ours, based on lines of ideal justice), or be plunged into the very abyss we wish to escape from. Mr. Judge's defense is that he is not guilty of the acts charged; that Mahatmas exist, are related to our Society, and in personal connection with himself; and he avers his readiness to bring many witnesses and documentary proofs to support his statements.

The reader should engrave the foregoing upon his memory. It is Col. Olcott's and therefore Mrs. Besant's own admission, (1) that the constitutional questions raised by Mr. Judge were raised for the sake of the Society and not to evade "trial"; (2) that his "line of defense" which makes the real "dilemma" for his accusers, is simply that Mr. Judge "avers," as Col. Olcott states, not only that he is not guilty, but that he is prepared to *prove* his connection with the Mahatmas. And although these very constitutional questions and Mr. Judge's very avowal of innocence and readiness to meet an investigation were stated in Mr. Judge's circular of March 15, and although Col. Olcott six weeks later (in the Notice of April 27) declares that in the opinion of "eminent counsel" as well as himself the trial can properly take place as summoned, the President-Founder at London finds himself in a dilemma indeed. What if the trial should proceed and Mr. Judge *actually prove* his messages? Not to listen to Mr. Judge's defense would be so monstrous indeed that not even the dullest or most prejudiced would fail to see its inequity, however they may have been blinded to the monstrous inequity of bringing these hearsay "charges" in the first place. How Col. Olcott evaded the real issue and at the same time did in fact what he had just characterized as "monstrous even in a common court of law, much more in a Brotherhood like" the Theosophical Society, may be seen in his next words:

> The moment we entered into these questions we should violate the most vital spirit of our federal compact, its neutrality in matters of belief. . . . For the above reason, then, I declare as my opinion that this enquiry must go no further; we may not break our own laws for any consideration whatsoever. It is furthermore my opinion that such an enquiry, begun by whatsoever official body within our membership cannot proceed if a similar line of defense be declared. If, perchance, a guilty person should at any time go scot-free in consequence of this ruling, we cannot help it; the Constitution is our palladium, and we must make it the symbol of justice or expect our Society to disintegrate.

Thus, in this one paragraph, is the admission in Col. Olcott's own words and decision, of the impropriety and illegality of the original bringing of the "charges"; the admission that every constitutional contention raised by Mr. Judge was correct; the admission that Mr. Judge was ready and willing to produce his proofs of Mahatmic intercourse; the admission that such a "line of defense" upset the whole procedure, and that the Enquiry "must go no farther"—thus debarring Mr. Judge, foully accused of dishonorable conduct, even from being "entitled to enjoy the full opportunity to *disprove* the charges brought against you," as Col. Olcott had written him March 20, when suspending him from the Vice-Presidency pending the meeting of the Judicial Committee. In thus himself ignobly retreating from the field of battle the President-Founder in the bitterness and humiliation of his enforced reverse, cannot forbear a

Parthian shot at his still untouched target as a prelude to his final admission:

> Candor compels me to add that, despite what I thought some preliminary quibbling and unfair tactics, Mr. Judge has traveled hither from America to meet his accusers before this Committee, and announced his readiness to have the charges investigated and decided on their merits by any competent tribunal.

The reader should impress these remarkable statements on his memory for the reason that when he comes to the final *debacle* he will find both Col. Olcott and Mrs. Besant solemnly affirming over and over again that Mr. Judge was "guilty," as if that "guilt" had been *proven;* that he *evaded* a trial; that he *escaped* a trial through pleading what the lawyers call a demurrer. Still more, because in the quarter century since these lamentable episodes, not once but a hundred times have Mrs. Besant and Col. Olcott repeated the same statements to those who believed in all good faith their utterly untrustworthy testimony in any matter where the whole truth would show them grossly at fault or grievously in error. The reader should remember that their impeachment is out of their own mouths, not from other witnesses—Col. Olcott's as just given, Mrs. Besant's as shall follow in the extracts to be given from the Appendix to the "Neutrality" pamphlet.

After the foregoing remarks Col. Olcott argues in extenuation of himself against the resolutions adopted by the Convention of the American Section, then reverses his action complained of therein.

> It having been made evident to me that Mr. Judge cannot be tried on the present accusations without breaking through the lines of our Constitution, I have no right to keep him further suspended, and so I hereby cancel my notice of suspension, dated February 7th, 1894 [here again is a significant admission, albeit unintentional;

> for the date of the letter of suspension, as *officially* forwarded, was March 20], and restore him to the rank of Vice-President.

The remainder of the President-Founder's Address to the Judicial Committee is a half-apology for the "inconvenience" caused the members and others by the convocation of the Committee, and a plea for "brotherhood."

Mr. Mead then submitted to the Judicial Committee the minutes of the General Council meeting of July 7, as given. The Judicial Committee then adopted the following resolutions:

> *Resolved:* That the President be requested to lay before the committee the charges against Mr. Judge referred to in his address.
>
> The charges were laid before the Committee accordingly.
>
> After deliberation, it was:
>
> *Resolved:* that although it was ascertained that the member bringing the charges [Mrs. Besant] and Mr. Judge are both ready to go on with the enquiry, the Committee considers, nevertheless, that the charges are not such as relate to the conduct of the Vice-President in his official capacity, and therefore are not subject to its jurisdiction.

It will be observed from the foregoing that the report merely states that the resolutions were "adopted" by the Committee without giving the votes, pro and contra. The reader should understand that the delegates favorable to Mr. Judge left it to the others to decide whether to proceed or not.

Another resolution affirmed that a trial of the kind under enquiry would violate the neutrality of the Society in matters of religious opinion. On this "four members abstained from voting," according to the report. Their names are not given. Another resolution adopted the President's Address, and still another resolution was adopted asking the General Council to print and circulate a report of the proceedings. The question was then raised whether the charges against Mr. Judge should be included in the printed report. On this Mr. Burrows moved and Mr. Sturdy seconded a resolution that "if the Proceedings were printed at all the charges should be included." We think, in view of all the circumstances connected, and more particularly the step subsequently taken by them, that this resolution was introduced with the full knowledge and acquiescence of both Mrs. Besant and Col. Olcott. But when the assembled delegates came to see the full iniquity of officially spreading broadcast a series of charges after having denied the accused the opportunity of meeting and rebutting them, this motion was too much for even the most prejudiced to stomach and be responsible for. The report says: "On being put to the vote the resolution was not carried." Once more, the report carefully abstains from mentioning who voted for and who against this infamous resolution. After this, the report states, "The Minutes having been read and confirmed the Committee dissolved."

It will be noted that every resolution adopted by the General Council in its session of July 7, and all the proceedings of the session of the Judicial Committee on the 10th were taken in exact accord with the remarks of the President-Founder in his Addresses to the two bodies. This shows two things, (1) that the sessions were the mere carrying out of a "cut-and-dried" program arranged by Col. Olcott and Mrs. Besant; (2) that they controlled the majority action of both bodies. A third matter is still more worthy of note: that in the entire proceedings, both of the General Council meeting and those of the Judicial Committee, Mr. Judge and those representing him took an entirely passive part. Having in his formal letters addressed to the two bodies, raised the necessary legal questions, and avowed his readiness to meet directly any trial of the real issues at stake, Mr. Judge remained silent throughout, leaving it to his persecutors to take what steps they would. He made no attack on any of his enemies; he demanded no enquiry into the gross malfeasance shown by the President-Founder; he brought no charges against those present whom he knew to be manipulating the proceedings; he did not ask that those who had themselves claimed to be "in communication with Masters" be put upon their *voir dire* and submitted to the same ordeal that had been thrust upon him; he made no comments, raised no objections, demanded no retractions, no apology. He had simply met squarely all that had been rumored, circulated, charged against him; that done, he had taken no advantage of the dilemma and the wrong-doing of his opponents. He had fulfilled to the uttermost scruple the rules of Occultism, its requirements of Brotherhood, and uttered no word of complaint or reproach at their violation by those sworn, like himself, to the First Object of the T.S., the pledge and Rules of the School of the Masters. His enemies he did not look upon as his personal foes, nor as intentionally dishonorable, but as probationers in the fiery furnace of "pledge fever," knowing not what they did. As they had broken away from the lines, he could not help them, but he could, and did abstain from pushing them further afield. He knew that now all the facts were of record, so that no student need be misled by partisan or corrupted testimony. The whole Theosophical world could know that those high in the counsels of the Society had brought charges, had racked the world for evidences to sustain them, had had the entire proceedings in their own hands, and had themselves been forced by the hollowness and inequity of their own conduct to reverse themselves completely, in order to save, not the Society, but *themselves*.

CHAPTER XXX

BRITISH CONVENTION DISMISSES CASE AGAINST JUDGE

The proceedings of the Judicial Committee occupied the greater part of July 10, 1894. Its sole essential decision was that it had no jurisdiction under the Constitution and Rules of the Society to enquire into the charges made against Mr. Judge. After recording this decision and requesting the General Council to publish the entire proceedings, the Judicial Committee adjourned *sine die.*

Purely negative as was the decision of the Judicial Committee, it produced momentous and immediate consequences—consequences evidently wholly unanticipated by either Col. Olcott or Mrs. Besant. For, no sooner were the details of the proceedings noised about among the Theosophists then assembled in London for the Convention of the European Section, than a sharp reaction set in against the two accusers who had played the leading part in the great scandal which had been convulsing the Society for the preceding five months. The very course that Col. Olcott and Mrs. Besant had felt constrained to adopt to save themselves was a direct, though tacit, admission that they had been wholly in the wrong, legally as well as morally, in bringing the charges at all, and this unavoidable inference contained within itself a terrible backlash.

In bringing the charges in the first place, Mrs. Besant had declared that they were believed in by reputable members of the Society and should be investigated; Col. Olcott, that it had been his *duty* under the Constitution to summon Mr. Judge for trial and to suspend him from his office of Vice-President in the interval. Both had affirmed repeatedly that they were personal friends of Mr. Judge and were moved by the desire to free him from the taint of calumny and afford him the opportunity to meet the accusations directly and disprove them if he could. Judge had raised three direct issues: (1) that his offense, if any, was not as Vice-President but as an individual, and therefore not triable under the Constitution and Rules of the Society, but by the Branch to which he belonged—the Aryan Society of New York; (2) that any trial by the Society of alleged "imitating the handwriting of *Mahatmas*" was necessarily to involve the question of the existence of such Beings and Their connection with the Society and individuals in it, thus affixing a dogma to the Society; (3) that if, notwithstanding, his accusers were determined to proceed, he stood ready to produce witnesses and documents to *prove* his own direct connection with these Mahatmas.

The members could but remember that Mr. Judge had instantly raised all three questions in his circular of March 15, the moment the charges were sponsored by Col. Olcott and Mrs. Besant. They could but remember that Col. Olcott, in suspending him from office, had grandiloquently informed him that he should be afforded an opportunity to *disprove* the charges. They could but remember that Col. Olcott in his Executive Notice of April 27 had affirmed that in his own opinion and that of "eminent counsel, members of the Society," Mr. Judge could be tried "without involving the neutrality of the Society." The President-Founder's Address to the Judicial Committee could be looked upon, therefore, only as a square backdown from the position originally assumed and maintained down to the very date of the "trial," and, since Mrs. Besant was bound up with him in the course taken throughout, it was equally a complete reversal on her part.

It was perfectly well known to all that the "Constitution and Rules" had been arranged year after year by Col. Olcott to suit his own ideas, and it was an open secret to many that the present Rules had been "revised" to clear the way to the "trial." And it was well understood by all that the majority of the General Council and of the Judicial Committee was entirely plastic to the President-Founder's wishes—so much so that many "neutrals" and friends of Mr. Judge as well as the followers of Col. Olcott and Mrs. Besant were surprised beyond measure at the turn of events. What had occurred to upset an apparently ready-made program which had kept the Society in a ferment for five months with a scandal most hurtful to all and most injurious to the reputation of its Vice-President? The facts were still undetermined, the mischief unrepaired, by this apparently arbitrary and final decision of the Judicial Committee under the influence of Col. Olcott's Address. Were Col. Olcott and Mrs. Besant sincerely repentant of the wrong done? Or was it to be inferred as the true explanation of this mysterious change of front in the face of Mr. Judge's defense that the accusers did not want the facts known; that they feared he could *prove* his claim of communications from the Mahatmas; feared that that done, a clamor would go up for Mrs. Besant, Col. Olcott, Mr. Sinnett, and all others who had claimed communications, also to prove *their* claims; feared the consequences if *all the facts* should become public?

It can, then, well be imagined what commotion ensued when all the inferences deducible from Col. Olcott's Address and the decision of the Judicial Committee were freely aired. On the 11th, therefore, Mrs. Besant and Col. Olcott found themselves in a most unenviable position. Restive under the fire of criticism, as is ever the case with those most ready to lay down the law for others, it behove them to do something—anything—to escape the threatened engulfment. Mrs. Besant proposed to Dr. J. D. Buck that, in view of the situation, a "Jury of Honor" be impaneled to pass upon the "charges," and suggested the names of Messrs. Sinnett, Bertram Keightley, Sturdy, Burrows, and Firth for membership on such a jury. This was declined on the grounds that Mr. Judge had not yet been supplied with certified copies of the documents proposed to be used as "evidence" against him; that it would require time for him to produce witnesses and documents in rebuttal; finally, that the majority of the names submitted were those of men known to be already prejudiced against him, and that a jury, if chosen, should be composed of members qualified to weigh and pass upon principles, processes, and evidences necessarily connected with "precipitations" and other "Occult" phenomena. As there were few indeed of the well-known Theosophists then in London who had not already expressed opinions for or against the questions involved, and fewer still who were ready to "qualify" as competent judges of the facts of Occult phenomena, it was speedily seen that the expedient of a Jury of Honor would leave the situation worse than ever.

Yet to leave matters as they were was intolerable, whether from the standpoint of the predicament of the accusers or the more noble one of the well-being of the Society. Mrs. Besant next proposed that she herself prepare a statement of the case, that Mr. Judge do the same, and that the two statements be read before the Convention of the European Section which then, with the statements before it, should serve as a jury and take such action as to it might seem proper. Dr. Buck accepted this proposition on behalf of Mr. Judge and the statements were accordingly read at the third session of the Convention on the evening of July 12th. Both statements are here given in full from the text of the "Neutrality" pamphlet.

Statement by Annie Besant

Read for the Information of Members at the Third Session of the European Convention of the T.S., July 12th, 1894.

I speak to you tonight as the representative of the T.S. in Europe, and as the matter I have to lay before you concerns the deepest interests of the Society, I pray you to lay aside all prejudice and feeling, to judge by Theosophical standards and not by the lower standards of the world, and to give your help now in one of the gravest crises in which our movement has found itself.

There has been much talk of Committees and Juries of Honour. We come to you, our brothers, to tell you what is in our hearts.

I am going to put before you the exact position of affairs on the matter which has been filling our hearts all day. Mr. Judge and I have agreed to lay two statements before you, and to ask your counsel upon them.

For some years past persons inspired largely by personal hatred for Mr. Judge, and persons inspired by hatred for the Theosophical Society and for all that it represents, have circulated a mass of accusations against him, ranging from simple untruthfulness to deliberate and systematic forgery of the handwriting of Those Who to some of us are most sacred. The charges were not in a form that it was possible to meet, a general denial could not stop them, and explanation to irresponsible accusers was at once futile and undignified.

Mr. Judge's election as the future President of the Society increased the difficulties of the situation and the charges themselves were repeated with growing definiteness and insistence, until they found expression in an article in *The Theosophist* signed by Messrs. Old and Edge. At last, the situation became so strained that it was declared by many of the most earnest members of the Indian Section that, if Mr. Judge became President with these charges hanging over him unexplained, the Indian Section would secede from the T.S. Representation to this effect was made to me, and I was asked, as well-known in the world and the T.S. and as a close friend and colleague of Mr. Judge, to intervene in the matter.

I hold strongly that, whatever may be the faults of a private member, they are no concern of mine, and it is no part of my duty as a humble servant of the Lords of Compassion, to drag my brother's faults into public view, nor to arraign him before any tribunal. His faults and mine will find their inevitable harvest of suffering, and I am content to leave them to the Great Law, which judges unerringly and knits to every wrong its necessary sequence of pain.

But where the honor of the Society was concerned in the person of its now second official and (as he was then thought to be) its President-Elect, it was right to do what I could to put an end to the growing friction and suspicion, both for the sake of the Society and for that of Mr. Judge; and I agreed to intervene privately believing that many of the charges were false, dictated and circulated malevolently, that others were much exaggerated and were largely susceptible of explanation, and that what might remain of valid complaint might be put an end to without public controversy. Under the promise that nothing should be done further in the matter until my intervention had failed, I wrote to Mr. Judge. The promise of silence was broken by persons who knew some of the things complained of, and before any answer could be received by me from Mr. Judge, distorted versions of what had occurred were circulated far and wide. This placed Mr. Judge in a most unfair position, and he found my name used against him in connection with charges which he knew to be grossly exaggerated where not entirely untrue.

Not only so, but I found that a public Committee of Enquiry was to be insisted on, and I saw that the proceedings would be directed in a spirit of animosity, and that the aim was to inflict punishment for wrongs believed to have been done, rather than to prevent future harm to the Society. I did my utmost to prevent a public Committee of Enquiry of an official character. I failed and the Committee was decided on. And then I made what many of Mr. Judge's friends think was a mistake. I offered to take on myself the onus of formulating the charges against him. I am not concerned to defend myself on this, nor to trouble you with my reasons for taking so painful a decision; in this decision, for which I alone am responsible, I meant to act for the best, but it is very possible I made a mistake—for I have made many mistakes in judgment in my life, and my vision is not always clear in these matters of strife and controversy which are abhorrent to me.

In due course I formulated the charges, and drew up the written statement of evidence in support of them. They came in due course before the Judicial Committee, as you heard this morning. That Committee decided that they alleged private, not official, wrong-doing, and therefore could not be tried by a Committee that could deal only with a President or Vice-President as such. I was admitted to the General Council of the T.S. when this point was argued, and I was convinced by that argument that the point was rightly taken. I so stated when asked by the General Council, and again when asked by the Judicial Committee. And this put an end to the charges so far as that Committee was concerned.

As this left the main issue undecided, and left Mr. Judge under the stigma of unproved and unrebutted charges, it was suggested by Mr. Herbert Burrows that the charges should be laid before a Committee of Honour. At the moment this was rejected by Mr. Judge, but he wrote to me on the following day, asking me to agree with him in nominating such a Committee. I have agreed to this, but with very great reluctance, for the reason mentioned above; that I feel it no part of my duty to attack any private member of the T.S., and I think such an attack would prove a most unfortunate precedent. But as the proceedings which were commenced against Mr. Judge, as an official have proved abortive, it does not seem fair that I—responsible for those proceedings by taking part in them—should refuse him the Committee he asks for.

But there is another way, which I now take, and which, if you approve it, will put an end to this matter; and as no Theosophist should desire to inflict penalty for the past—even if he thinks wrong has been done—but only to help forward right in the future, it may, I venture to hope, be accepted.

And now I must reduce these charges to their proper proportions, as they have been enormously exaggerated, and it is due to Mr. Judge that I should say publicly what from the beginning I have said privately. The President stated them very accurately in his address to the Judicial Committee: the vital charge is that Mr. Judge has issued letters and messages in the script recognizable as that adopted by a Master with whom H.P.B. was closely connected, and that these letters and messages were neither written nor precipitated directly by the Master in whose writing they appear; as leading up to this there are subsidiary charges of deception, but these would certainly never have been made the basis of any action save for their connection with the main point.

Further, I wish it to be distinctly understood that I do not charge and have not charged Mr. Judge with forgery in the ordinary sense of the term, but with giving a misleading material form to messages received psychically from the Masters in various ways, without acquainting the recipients with this fact.

I regard Mr. Judge as an Occultist, possessed of considerable knowledge, and animated by a deep and unswerving devotion to the Theosophical Society. I believe that he has often received direct messages from the Masters and from Their chelas, guiding and helping him in his work. I believe that he has sometimes received messages for other people in one or other of the ways that I will mention in a moment, but not by direct writing by the Master nor by His direct precipitation; and that Mr. Judge has then believed himself to be justified in writing down in the script adopted by H.P.B. for communications from the Master, the message psychically received, and in giving it to the person for whom it was intended, leaving that person to wrongly assume that it was a direct precipitation or writing by the Master Himself—that is, that it was done *through* Mr. Judge, but done *by* the Master.

Now personally I hold that this method is illegitimate and that no one should simulate a recognized writing which is regarded as authoritative when it is authentic. And by authentic I mean directly written or precipitated by the Master Himself. If a message is consciously written it should be so stated: if automatically written, it should be so stated. At least so it seems to me. It is important that the very small part generally played by the Masters in these phenomena should be understood, so that people may not receive messages as authoritative merely on the ground of their being in a particular script. Except in the very rarest instances, the Masters do not personally write letters or directly precipitate communications. Messages may be sent by Them to those with whom They can communicate by external voice, or astral vision, or psychic word, or mental impression, or in other ways. If a person gets a message which he believes to be from the Master, for communication to anyone else, he is bound in honour not to add to that message any extraneous circumstances which will add weight to it in the recipient's eyes. I believe that Mr. Judge wrote with his own hand, consciously or automatically I do not know, in the script adopted as that of the Master, messages which he received from the Master or from chelas; and I know that, in my own case, I believed that the messages he gave me in the well-known script were messages directly precipitated or directly written by the Master. When I publicly said that I had received after H.P.B.'s death letters in the writing H. P. Blavatsky had been accused of forging, I referred to letters given to me by Mr. Judge, and as they were in the well-known script I never dreamt of challenging their source. I know now that they were not written or precipitated by the Master, and that they were done by Mr. Judge, but I also believe that the gist of these messages was psychically received, and that Mr. Judge's error lay in giving them to me in a script written by himself and not saying that he had done so. I feel bound to refer to these letters thus explicitly, because having been myself mistaken, I in turn misled the public.

It should be generally understood inside and outside the Theosophical Society, that letters and messages may be written or may be precipitated in any script, without thereby gaining any valid authority. Scripts may be produced by automatic or deliberate writing with the hand, or by precipitation, by many agencies from the White and Black Adepts down to semi-conscious Elementals, and those who afford the necessary conditions can be thus used. The source of messages can only be decided by direct spiritual knowledge or, intellectually, by the nature of their contents, and each person must use his own powers and act on his own responsibility, in accepting or rejecting them. Thus I rejected a number of letters, real precipitations, brought me by an American, not an F.T.S., as substantiating his claim to be H.P.B.'s successor.[1] Any good medium may be used for precipitating messages by any of the varied entities in the Occult world; and the outcome of these proceedings will be, I hope, to put an end to the craze for receiving letters and messages, which are more likely to be subhuman or human in their origin than superhuman, and to throw people back on the evolution of their own spiritual nature, by which alone they can be safely guided through the mazes of the super-physical world.

If you, representatives of the T.S., consider that the publication of this statement followed by that which Mr. Judge will make, would put an end to this distressing business, and by making a clear understanding, get rid at least of the mass of seething suspicions in which we have been living, and if you can accept it, I propose that this should take the place of the Committee of Honour, putting you, our brothers, in the place of the Committee. I have made the frankest explanation I can; I know how enwrapped in difficulty are these phenomena which are connected with forces obscure in their workings to most; therefore, how few are able to judge of them accurately, while those through whom they play are not always able to control them. And I trust that these explanations may put an end to some at least of the troubles of the last two years, and leave us to go on with our work for the world, each in his own way. For any pain that I have given my brother, in trying to do a most repellant task, I ask his pardon, as also for any mistakes that I may have made.

ANNIE BESANT.

[1] Mrs. Besant here refers to Mr. Henry B. Foulke of Philadelphia, whose claims were recited and discussed in Chapter XXIII.

(The above statements as to precipitated, written, and other communications have been made long ago by both H. P. Blavatsky and Mr. Judge, in *Lucifer, The Path,* and elsewhere, both publicly and privately.—A. B.)

(Note by Col. Olcott.—I cannot allow Mrs. Besant to take upon herself the entire responsibility for formulating the charges against Mr. Judge, since I myself requested her to do it. The tacit endorsement of the charges by persistence in a policy of silence was an injustice to the Vice-President, since it gave him no chance to make his defence; while, at the same time, the widely-current suspicions were thereby augmented, to the injury of the Society. So to bring the whole matter to light, I with others, asked Mrs. Besant to assume the task of drafting and signing the charges.—H. S. O.)

Statement by Mr. Judge

Since March 1st, charges have been going round the world against me, to which the name of Annie Besant has been attached, without her consent as she now says, that I have been guilty of forging the names and handwritings of the Mahatmas and of misusing the said names and handwritings. The charge has also arisen that I suppressed the name of Annie Besant as mover in the matter from fear of the same. All this has been causing great trouble and working injury to all concerned, that is, to all our members. It is now time that this should be put an end to once for all if possible.

I now state as follows:

1. I left the name of Annie Besant out of my published circular by request of my friends in the T.S. then near me so as to save her and leave it to others to put her name to the charge.

It now appears that if I had so put her name it would have run counter to her present statement.

2. I repeat my denial of the said rumoured charges of forging the said names and handwritings of the Mahatmas or of misusing the same.

3. I admit that I have received and delivered messages from the Mahatmas and assert their genuineness.

4. I say that I have heard and do hear from the Mahatmas, and that I am an agent of the Mahatmas; but I deny that I have ever sought to induce that belief in others and this is the first time to my knowledge that I have ever made the claim now made. I am pressed into the place where I must make it. My desire and effort have been to distract attention from such an idea as related to me. But I have no desire to make the claim, which I repudiate, that I am the only channel for communication with Masters; and it is my opinion that such communication is open to any human being who, by endeavoring to serve mankind, affords the necessary conditions.

5. Whatever messages from the Mahatmas have been delivered by me as such—and they are extremely few—I now declare were and are genuine messages from the Mahatmas so far as my knowledge extends; they were obtained through me, but as to how they were obtained or produced I cannot state. But I can now again say, as I have said publicly before, and as was said by H. P. Blavatsky so often that I have always thought it common knowledge among studious Theosophists, that precipitation of words or messages is of no consequence and constitutes no proof of connection with Mahatmas; it is only phenomenal and not of the slightest value.

6. So far as methods are concerned for the reception and delivery of messages from the Masters, they are many. My own methods may disagree from the views of others and I acknowledge their right to criticise them if they choose; but I deny the right of anyone to say that they know or can prove the non-genuineness of such messages to or through me unless they are able to see on that plane. I can only say that I have done my best to report—in the few instances when I have done it at all—correctly and truthfully such messages as I think I have received for transmission, and never to my knowledge have I tried therewith to deceive any person or persons whatever.

7. And I say that in 1893 the Master sent me a message in which he thanked me for all my work and exertions in the Theosophical field, and expressed satisfaction therewith, ending with sage advice to guard me against the failings and follies of my lower nature: that message Mrs. Besant unreservedly admits.

8. Lastly, and only because of absurd statements made and circulated, I willingly say that which I never denied, that I am a human being, full of error, liable to mistake, not infallible, but just the same as any other human being like to myself, or of the class of human beings to which I belong. And I freely, fully and sincerely forgive anyone who may be thought to have injured or tried to injure me.

WILLIAM Q. JUDGE.

Taking Mr. Judge's statement first, the student will note its terseness and its impersonality. Not once does he strike a defensive or an offensive chord. The tone is historical and dispassionate, as if he were discussing abstractions in which neither he nor anyone present could have the slightest personal concern. Although but a third the length of Mrs. Besant's statement, Mr. Judge gives in clearest terms all the items around which the original charges arose. He tells what the original accusations were, the coupling of Mrs. Besant's name with them, why he made no mention of her in his circular, and gives in explicit words what he has done, why he did it, and why he makes his statement. The real issue stands out clear: Did he or did he not receive and transmit "messages from the Mahatmas"? He says he did so receive and so transmit messages from Them, but declines pointblank to say how or in what manner they were transmitted to or through him. He refers to what should have been common knowledge to all Theosophists—that the phenomenal accompaniments are neither proof nor disproof of the source of a message; that no one can be sure of the genuineness of a message unless he is able to see on the plane of its origin, that is to say, on the plane of causation. The whole statement might have been written by H.P.B. or by one of the Masters, for it does but repeat her and Their replies when the same questions were raised in regard to her messages and her other phenomena. In the whole statement there can be found no word of recrimination, of recantation, or evasion. He neither argues, disputes, nor extenuates. What he can tell, he tells simply, but he maintains the reticence of the genuine initiate concerning the *modus operandi* of Occult Science: "I did not so receive it; I cannot so impart it."

Careful comparison of Mrs. Besant's statement with that of Mr. Judge will disclose the points of agreement and of contrast, both in matters of fact and in tone. On the real issue involved—whether or not Mr. Judge was in communication with the Masters and received messages from them—she makes two significant and direct admissions:

> I believe that he has often received direct messages from the Masters and from Their chelas.
>
> I believe that he has sometimes received messages for other people.

What, then, was the assumed offense that had led her to bring the charges against Mr. Judge? Mrs. Besant states it several times:

> The vital charge is that Mr. Judge has issued letters and messages in the script recognizable as that adopted by a Master with whom H.P.B. was closely connected, and that these letters and messages were neither written nor precipitated directly by the Master in whose writing they appear.
>
> I believe that he has . . . received messages . . . in one or other of the ways that I will mention in a moment, but not by direct writing by the Master nor by His direct precipitation.
>
> I believe that Mr. Judge wrote with his own hand, consciously or automatically I do not know, in the script adopted as that of the Master, messages which he received from the Master or from chelas.
>
> I know now that they were not written or precipitated by the Master, and that they were done by Mr. Judge, but I also believe that the gist of these messages was psychically received.

Mrs. Besant expresses her views on the subject very succinctly:

> *Now personally I hold that this method is illegitimate and that no one should simulate a recognized writing which is regarded as authoritative when it is authentic. And by authentic I mean directly written or precipitated by the Master Himself. If a message is consciously written it should be so stated; if automatically written, it should be so stated. At least so it seems to me.*

We have italicized the foregoing, because to our mind it is the key to the whole difficulty which beset Mrs. Besant and so many others. In the first place, it shows that despite all her subsequent claims and affirmations, Mrs. Besant had no real knowledge of *Occultism,* but depended first, last, and all the time on externalities. Had she been an *accepted* chela, even, she would have known for herself how such messages are produced, and would have been under no necessity to speculate, guess, "believe" this, that, or the other, nor would she have attached any importance whatever to script, signature, seal, what-not. Moreover, this statement of hers shows that she had labored under gross ignorance even of what had been given out years before both by H.P.B. and Masters. For, in the Appendix to the fourth and *post* editions of "The Occult World" Mr. Sinnett had given a long letter direct from the Master "K. H." on the very subject of "precipitations" in connection with the Kiddle incident, which showed the *Master Himself* "guilty" on his own confession of the very "method" which Mrs. Besant holds to be "illegitimate." And in the extremely important article, "Lodges of Magic," H.P.B. in *Lucifer* for October, 1888—at the time of the public formation of the E.S.T.—goes at length into this very question. And with good reason: Mr. Sinnett and others had been whispering about the identical "charges" against her of "forgery" and "false messages." Like Mrs. Besant, these students had received "messages" through H.P.B. which comported with their ideas, and other "messages" which upset their preconceptions. The one they had pronounced "genuine"; the other "false." H.P.B. set out to show the absurdity of this position, and her remarks should have been a standing lesson both to all thirsty aspirants for "precipitated messages" and to all neophytes in Occultism. H.P.B. wrote:

> We have been asked by a correspondent why he should not "be free to suspect some of the so-called 'precipitated' letters as being forgeries," giving as his reason for it that while some of them bear the stamp of (to him) undeniable genuineness, others seem from their contents and style, to be imitations. This is equivalent

to saying that he has such an unerring spiritual insight as to be able to detect the false from the true, though he has never met a Master, *nor been given any key by which to test his alleged communications.* The inevitable consequence of applying his untrained judgment in such cases would be to make him as likely as not to declare false what was genuine, and genuine what was false. Thus what *criterion* has anyone to decide between one "precipitated" letter, or another such letter? Who except their authors, or those whom they employ as their *amanuenses* (the *chelas* and disciples), can tell? For it is hardly one out of a hundred "occult" letters that is ever written by the hand of the Master, in whose name and on whose behalf they are sent, as the Masters have neither need nor leisure to write them; and that when a Master says, "*I* wrote that letter," it means only that every word in it was dictated by him and impressed under his direct supervision. Generally they make their chela, whether near or far away, write (or precipitate) them, by impressing upon his mind the ideas they wish expressed and if necessary aiding him in the picture-printing process of precipitation. It depends entirely upon the *chelas's* state of development, how accurately the ideas may be transmitted and *the writing model imitated.* Thus the *non-adept* recipient is left in the dilemma of uncertainty, whether, if one letter is false, all may not be; for, *as far as intrinsic evidence goes, all come from the same source,* and all are brought by the same mysterious means. But there is another, and a far worse condition implied. For all that the recipient of "occult" letters can possibly know, and on the simple grounds of probability and common honesty, *the unseen correspondent who would tolerate one single fraudulent line in his name would wink at an unlimited repetition of the deception.*

More and more as the student studies, connotes, compares, he will be struck by the unconscious inconsistencies in Mrs. Besant's statement. Here was a professedly devoted student of H.P.B.'s, a self-styled Occultist, pledged member of the E.S.T., who apparently, from her own statements, had no doubt that Mr. Judge was in "direct communication with the Masters," yet who believed at the same time that he was "giving a misleading material form" to Their messages, a method which she held to be "illegitimate," so illegitimate that she felt impelled to charge him with "forgery of the handwriting of the Mahatmas"—and at the same time H.P.B., whom she called her "teacher," had taught that this was the very practice of the Masters Themselves, and her own messages had been produced in identically the same way!

Moreover, Mrs. Besant proceeds to argue as if it were something hitherto unknown, that "it should be generally understood . . . that letters and messages may be written or may be precipitated in any script, without thereby gaining any valid authority." In thus arguing she was but repeating what H.P.B. and Mr. Judge had been teaching for years; but if she knew this to be the fact, why should she have attached such importance to "Mahatmas' handwritings" precipitated "in a material form" through Mr. Judge or any one else? If "the source of messages can be decided only by direct spiritual knowledge," *and if she had that knowledge* so that she knew, as she claimed, that Mr. Judge's messages themselves were genuine, why did she not *affirm their genuineness* to the doubters instead of charging Mr. Judge with "forgery"? Or if the source can be decided only "intellectually by the nature of their contents," why did she not discuss the *contents* instead of the *form* of the disputed messages? And if "each person must use his own powers and act on his own responsibility in accepting or rejecting them," what occasion or right at any time on the part of any one to charge any other with "fraud" in connection with any "messages" soever? One wonders what miraculous ideas of Masters and Their powers over "time, space and matter" possessed Mrs. Besant and others. Did they think that Masters could work *miracles* and produce or precipitate messages at great distances and through intervening matter *without an instrument* of some kind at the receiving end? Without an *amanuensis* at the far pole, to use H.P.B.'s telltale hint in the extract just given?

The lack of logical perspective, the loss of discrimination, the havoc of "pledge fever" possessing the accusers is still further shown in Mrs. Besant's statement of how she was led to bring the charges in the first place. For, she says, they came to her from "persons inspired largely by personal hatred for Mr. Judge," and from "persons inspired by hatred for the Theosophical Society and all that it represents." If this was so—and it was indubitably true—what was the natural, the logical, above all the ethical and moral course for Mrs. Besant to take—Mrs. Besant "well known in the world and the T.S. and a close friend and colleague of Mr. Judge"? Was it not to have taken up the cudgels *in defense* of her friend and brother whom she knew to be in direct communication with Masters; to have shown to all and sundry that such messages were to be judged by their "intellectual and spiritual contents" not by "handwriting," seals, and other phenomenal incidents? *To have brought charges against his slanderers instead of against their innocent victim?*

But what did she do, by her own confession—for it is no less? She "agreed to intervene privately." That intervention consisted in her writing to Mr. Judge January 11, 1894, following the Christmas, 1893, secret conference at Adyar. In this letter she told him she had the proof of his "guilt," and demanded, as the price of her silence, that he should resign from the T.S. and the E.S., giving up his offices in both, "or the evidence which goes to prove the wrong done must be laid before a committee of the T.S." Yet her statement says: "I agreed to intervene, privately, believing that many of the charges were false, dictated and circulated malevolently, that others were much exaggerated and were largely susceptible of explanation, and that what might remain of valid complaint might be put an end to without public controversy." Before this letter could possibly reach Mr. Judge, his defamers, she says, broke their promise of silence. Then what does Mrs. Besant do? After consultation with Chakravarti, Olcott, and Mr. Old, she wrote on February 6 her formal demand to Col. Olcott for the "investigation by a Committee." She says that all this "placed Mr. Judge in a most unfair position, and he found my name used against him in connection with charges which he knew to be grossly exaggerated where not entirely untrue." Undoubtedly; but by whose consent and voluntary action was this use of her name and broadcasting of scandal and calumny made possible?

As if this were not enough, Mrs. Besant, according to her own statement, although she "saw that the proceedings would be directed in a spirit of animosity, and that the aim was to inflict punishment," nevertheless, in her own words: "I offered to take on myself the onus of formulating the charges against him."

Once Mrs. Besant's statement and related actions are understood and weighed, the well-nigh unanswerable query arises: the facts being as they were, how could she do as she did?

Weighing the situation from the merely human standpoint, the evidence justifies and compels the inference that Mrs. Besant lacked the sense of ethical perception and was, by consequence, constitutionally incapable of recognizing the moral obliquity of her own conduct as portrayed by herself in her statements. Despite the countless admonitions of H.P.B., and the abundant examples with which the years were strewn, of the pitfalls and dangers which beset the path of those who "wander from the discipline enjoined," Mrs. Besant had taken no part of the lessons home to herself. Her case was that of countless others, only a more illustrious example, of those failures in Occultism of which the records are over full. What was their snare? Again it is profitable to recur to the statements of H.P.B. In the article "Lodges of Magic" quoted from above, H.P.B. gives it concisely:

> Hence, not a step in advance would be made by a group of students . . . without any guide *from the occult side* to open their eyes to the esoteric pitfalls. And where are such guides, so far, in our society? "They be blind leaders of the blind" both falling into the ditch of vanity and self-sufficiency. The whole difficulty springs from the common tendency to draw conclusions from insufficient premises, and play the oracle before ridding oneself of that most stupefying of all psychic anaesthetics—IGNORANCE."

A Probationer of but two years' standing at the death of H.P.B., Mrs. Besant began at once to "play the oracle," to "fall into the ditch of vanity and self-sufficiency," to "draw conclusions from insufficient premises." H.P.B. *dead* (to her) she first looked to Mr. Judge as "guide from the Occult side," and his strong help lifted her out of more than one esoteric pitfall. Came the day when the plaudits of the multitude acclaimed her as an "authority." Why should she have to look to Mr. Judge for inspiration, for messages, for direction and correction? Why could she not force the doors to the unseen world on her own account? Was there not Mr. Sinnett with his "sensitives" in "communication with the Masters"? Was there not Chakravarti with his new and wonderful "method of meditation" by which the results she craved could be procured?

That Mrs. Besant never inspected her own conduct, never applied to herself the precepts she was constantly proclaiming to others, is, again, sharply shown in the opening paragraph of her statement to the Convention. She says to the delegates: "I pray *you* to lay aside all prejudice and feeling, to judge by Theosophical standards and not by the lower standards of the world." Suppose Mrs. Besant had taken that admonition home to herself, as the Rules of the E.S. enjoined, would there have been any "Judge case"? Would there have been the ruin of the Theosophical Society?

These things were missed by Mrs. Besant; they were missed by the students of the first generation of the Movement. Will they be missed by the students of today?

Certain it is, that the delegates and members assembled at the third session of the European Section on the evening of July 12, 1894, saw none of the inconsistencies, none of the lessons contained in what they were witness of. One and all rejoiced that concord, as they thought, was once more restored, harmony once more triumphant, fraternity once more regnant, and that naught remained but to go on victoriously to still greater heights. For, as the "Neutrality" pamphlet recites:

> Having heard the above statements, the following resolution was moved by Mr. Bertram Keightley, seconded by Dr. Buck, and carried *nem. con.*
>
> *Resolved:* that this meeting accepts with pleasure the adjustment arrived at by Annie Besant and William Q. Judge as a final settlement of matters pending hitherto between them as prosecutor and defendant, with the hope that it may be thus buried and forgotten, and—
>
> *Resolved:* that we will join hands with them to further the cause of genuine Brotherhood in which we all believe.

At the conclusion of the official proceedings of the third session of the European Sectional Convention which terminated with the adoption of the foregoing *Resolutions,* a spontaneous outburst of fraternal feeling animated all the delegates and visiting members of the Theosophical Society. On all sides those who had been rent by partisan emotions, those who had endeavored to remain neutral and impartial, leaders and followers alike, joined in mutual congratulations and felicitations over what seemed to be a complete restoration of unity and harmony.

As the members separated and left the hall, they were handed copies of a leaflet being distributed just outside the door. When this leaflet was read, and the names attached to it noted, more or less of uncertainty arose as to its possible import. Although its statements were such as to meet the approval of any one, the peculiar circumstances in which it was drawn up and circulated raised at once the question of its necessity and application. Not till long afterward did Mrs. Besant and Col. Olcott admit and affirm that it was intended to apply to Mr. Judge and to leave still open the charges which all had thought to be disposed of once and for all by the London proceedings. These proceedings were, as stated, officially reported in the "Neutrality" pamphlet. In printing the proceedings in the August, 1894, number of *Lucifer,* Mrs. Besant preceded them in her editorial notes, "On the Watch-Tower," with some comments introductory of the text of the leaflet spoken of, as follows:

> This number of *Lucifer* contains the text of the Enquiry into the charges made against Mr. W. Q. Judge. The statement appended to it, read by myself at the evening meeting of the Convention on July 12th, gives succinctly my own position in the matter, and contains all that I need say on the past. The future lies before us, and the Society will go forward unbroken; it has surmounted imminent danger of disruption, which threatened it. Had Mr. Judge succeeded to the Presidency, according to the election of 1892, with these charges hanging over him, India would have rejected him and the Society would have been rent in twain; but in the course of these proceedings, that election has been declared null and void, and the choice of the Society of its future President remains unfettered. A further gain is the putting an end to the exaggerated attacks made on Mr. Judge, and their

> reduction to a definite form. Yet another is the clear reminder that the precipitation of a letter does not give it any authoritative character, and that no particular script should be accepted as evidence of the Mahatmic origin of a message. The Society will be in a healthier state for this clearing of the air, and will be in less danger from credulity and superstition, two of the deadliest foes of a true spiritual movement.

The unconscious evasion by Mrs. Besant of her direct responsibility for the questionable consequences of her own actions, as already shown in connection with her Statement before the Convention, is again illustrated in the above-quoted editorial, by simply adding the undeniable but omitted facts to her quoted words. Thus:

> the charges made against W. Q. Judge [by myself as their responsible sponsor];
>
> The Society has surmounted imminent danger of disruption which threatened it [because of those charges, made by me and inspired by Col. Olcott and Messrs. W. R. Old and G. N. Chakravarti];
>
> Had Mr. Judge succeeded to the Presidency with these charges hanging over him, India would have rejected him and the Society would have been rent in twain [because that was the alternative offered me by Olcott, Old, and Edge, and Countess Wachtmeister, if I would not join them in the campaign against the good repute of Judge];
>
> A further gain is the putting an end to the exaggerated attacks made on Mr. Judge [attacks whose only validity was given them by my assuming responsibility for them];
>
> Yet a further gain is the clear reminder that the precipitation of a letter does not give it any authoritative character, and that no particular script should be accepted as evidence of the

> Mahatmic origin of a letter [a reminder which both H.P.B. and Mr. Judge had been repeating publicly and privately for years, but which Col. Olcott, Mr. Sinnett, myself, and many others had forgotten or ignored, so that, in making these charges against Mr. Judge because of doubt whether they were "precipitated" messages and whether the script was "authentic," we had been relying on "precipitation" and "script" as "evidence," by their "authoritative character" of their "Mahatmic origin"];
>
> The Society will be in a healthier state from the clearing of the air [which Col. Olcott, I, and others, befouled by bringing these charges], and will be in less danger from credulity and superstition [into which Col. Olcott and I, no less than many humbler members, fell in attaching "authority" and "evidence" to "precipitations" and "scripts"].

When the suppressed facts are added to Mrs. Besant's editorial statement above given, they shed a penetrating and clarifying light on the second editorial immediately following, and on the leaflet mentioned, and show that once again, as so often before and since those fateful days, to no one do Mrs. Besant's homilies apply so aptly and so fatally as to herself. She proceeds:

> TRUTH BEFORE AND IN ALL THINGS
>
> The following declaration is aimed at an opinion too often finding expression among would-be Occultists of an untrained type, that what is falsehood on the material plane may in some "Occult" way be truth on a higher plane, and that the plea of "Occultism" excuses conduct inconsistent with a high standard of righteous living. The spread of such views would demoralize the Society, and would tend to degrade the lofty ideal of Truth and Purity which it has been the effort of every great re-

> ligious teacher to uphold and enforce by example. Some of us, feeling this strongly, drew up the circular printed below, and the seven signatories represent a large body of opinion in different sections of the Theosophical Society.

If students of today, as then, instead of merely being content to approve these ethical formularies and to take it for granted that those who express noble sentiments are themselves inspired thereby, would rigidly examine and *apply* them, first and foremost, to themselves and those who utter them, none but the pharisees would have cause for complaint. Mrs. Besant and three of her co-signatories—Col. Olcott, Mr. Sinnett, and Mr. Bertram Keightley—were mainly responsible for the rupture of 1895, as they were for the events now being discussed. Four of those signers—Mrs. Besant, Col. Olcott, Mr. Sinnett, and Mr. Leadbeater—continued with the Theosophical Society for many years—the Society of which Mrs. Besant and Mr. Leadbeater are today the recognized and responsible heads and guides, exoterically and esoterically. With the intervening twenty-five years of history made by them, the humblest student of Theosophical philosophy and events should have no difficulty in determining beyond peradventure for himself who were and are "would-be Occultists of an untrained type," and who throughout the long course of Theosophical history have in *practice* taken the perverted path that "falsehood on the material plane may in some 'Occult' way be truth on a higher plane, and that the plea of 'Occultism' excuses conduct inconsistent with a high standard of righteous living." The existing ferment throughout the entire world-area of Mrs. Besant's Society proves who, now as then, then as now, have spread views which have demoralized the Society and degraded the lofty ideal of Truth and Purity.

Mrs. Besant's second editorial, as given, was immediately followed by the text of the leaflet which we give in full for its value to all those capable of making the application in the right quarters.

To Students of Occultism.

Occultism and Truth

"There is no Religion higher than Truth."
(Motto of the Theosophical Society)

The inevitable mystery which surrounds Occultism and the Occultist has given rise in the minds of many to a strange confusion between the duty of silence and the error of untruthfulness. There are many things that the Occultist may not divulge; but equally binding is the law that he may never speak untruth. And this obligation to Truth is not confined to speech; he may never think untruth, nor act untruth. A spurious Occultism dallies with truth and falsehood, and argues that deception on the illusory physical plane is consistent with purity on the loftier planes on which the Occultist has his true life; it speaks contemptuously of "mere worldly morality"—a contempt that might be justified if it raised a higher standard, but which is out of place when the phrase is used to condone acts which the "mere worldly morality" would disdain to practice. The doctrine that the end justifies the means has proved in the past fruitful of all evil; no means that are impure can bring about an end that is good, else were the Good Law a dream and Karma a mere delusion. From these errors flows an influence mischievous to the whole Theosophical Society, undermining the stern and rigid morality necessary as a foundation for Occultism of the Right Hand Path.

Finding that this false view of Occultism is spreading in the Theosophical Society, we desire to place on record our profound aversion to it, and our conviction that morality of the loftiest type must be striven after by everyone who would tread in safety the difficult ways of the

Occult World. Only by rigid truthfulness in thought, speech and act on the planes on which works our waking consciousness can the student hope to evolve the intuition which unerringly discerns between the true and the false in the super-sensuous worlds, which recognizes truth at sight and so preserves him from fatal risks in those at first confusing regions. To cloud the delicate sense of truth here, is to keep it blind there; hence every Teacher of Occultism has laid stress on truthfulness as the most necessary equipment of the would-be Disciple. To quote a weighty utterance of a wise Indian Disciple:

> "Next in importance, or perhaps equal in value, to Devotion IS TRUTH. It is simply impossible to over-estimate the efficacy of Truth in all its phases and bearings in helping the onward evolution of the human soul. We must love truth, seek truth, and live truth; and thus alone can the Divine Light which is Truth Sublime be seen by the student of Occultism. When there is the slightest leaning towards falsehood in any shape, there is shadow and ignorance and their child, pain. This leaning towards falsehood belongs to the lower personality without doubt. It is here that our interests clash, it is here the struggle for existence is in full swing, and it is therefore here that cowardice and dishonesty and fraud find any scope. The 'signs and symptoms' of the operations of this lower self can never remain concealed from one who sincerely loves truth and seeks truth."

To understand oneself, and so escape self-deception, Truth must be practiced; thus only can be avoided the dangers of the "conscious and unconscious deception" against which a MASTER warned His pupils in 1885.

Virtue is the foundation of White Occultism; the Paramitas, six and ten, the transcendental virtues, must be mastered, and each of the Seven Portals on the Path is a virtue, which the Disciple must make his own. Out of the soil of pure morality alone can grow the sacred flower which blossoms at length into Arhatship, and those who aspire to the blooming of the flower must begin by preparing the soil.

H. S. Olcott,
A. P. Sinnett,
Annie Besant,
Bertram Keightley,
W. Wynn Westcott,
E. T. Sturdy,
C. W. Leadbeater."

This circular was conspicuous for the names signed to it; still more so for those not attached to it. Neither Mr. Judge nor any other of the many prominent Theosophists from America and Europe then present in London was asked to join in the circular. In the circumstances, the names actually signed can be construed only as being those of the principals in the cabal formed against Mr. Judge. Mr. Old's name was omitted out of prudential considerations; he was still under suspension in the E.S.T., but he was present in England during the time, was still on terms of intimate friendship with the leaders, and was in daily intercourse with them. Chakravarti was in India, but it requires no especial exercise of "Occult powers" to discern that the "wise Indian Disciple" whose "weighty utterance" was included in the text of the circular was none other than he, and his share in the strategy cannot be doubted. His "messages from the Master," which inspired and sustained the tactics of the whole course of "the case against W. Q. Judge," continued the preponderant influence over Mrs. Besant until she succumbed to the allurements of still another "Initiate" and his "messages" from the same "Masters"—Mr. C. W. Leadbeater—when she quietly dropped Chakravarti as being "under the influence of the dark Powers."

This Mr. Leadbeater was originally a curate in a rural parish of the Church of England. He had been interested in Spiritualism for many years when he read Mr. Sinnett's two earliest books. Thereafter he held *séances* with Mr. W. Eglinton, a famous medium of the time who had been at Adyar while H.P.B. was there. Eglinton, like Mr. W. Stainton Moses (M.A. Oxon) had been helped by H.P.B. and had received various evidences through her of the existence of Masters, and joined the London Lodge in 1884. In a *séance* with Mr. Eglinton early in 1884, Mr. Leadbeater endeavored through the latter's "control," "Ernest," to get in "communication with the Masters." This is referred to in Letter VII of "Letters from the Masters of the Wisdom," a Letter received by Leadbeater through H.P.B. many months later, after he had avowed his desire to return with her to India.

Accordingly Mr. Leadbeater went to India with H.P.B. late in 1884 and was at Adyar during the time of Mr. Hodgson's investigations there, and became acquainted with the various Hindus at headquarters, notably with Subba Row. From Adyar Mr. Leadbeater was sent to Ceylon by Col. Olcott and while there began his career of infatuation with boys, his first relation of that kind being with C. Jinarajadasa, now Vice-President of Mrs. Besant's theosophical society.

Mr. Leadbeater returned to England in 1889, taking the boy with him. From then on he was intimate with Mr. Sinnett for whose son he served as tutor, and for Mr. Sinnett himself as the "psychic" through whom Mr. Sinnett kept up his supposed communications with the "Masters of H.P.B."

Mr. Leadbeater was never at any time a member of the E.S.T.S., nor in any way connected with H.P.B., after his return to England. Mr. Sinnett made him Secretary of the London Lodge after his return to England in 1889. The course and practices, public and private, of the London Lodge were wholly at variance with the Occult discipline taught by H.P.B.—were, in fact, identical with mediumism, psychical research, and Hatha Yoga.

No public rupture occurred during the life of H.P.B., but the relations between the London Lodge and those of the Blavatsky Lodge were of the slightest, and purely formal.

The first breach in the accord between Mrs. Besant and Mr. Judge was due, not only to the influence of Chakravarti but, as well, to that of Mr. Sinnett. While a member of the E.S. and one of its Co-Heads, Mrs. Besant joined the London Lodge, and took part in the experiments of Messrs. Sinnett, Leadbeater, and the rest of the inner *coterie,* thus violating her pledges, and pursuing two absolutely antithetical systems of "Occult development." When Chakravarti came to London, the ground for Mrs. Besant's subornation had, therefore, already been well prepared. It is one of the ironies of the situation, as thus prepared, that ultimately, in 1907, Mr. Sinnett rejected the "Adyar manifestations" for which Mrs. Besant stood sponsor, and was forced to join in the "white-wash" of Mr. Leadbeater, whose practices with boys were exposed in the fall of 1906—and that Mrs. Besant was forced by the exigencies of her own situation to turn against Messrs. Sinnett, Chakravarti, and Leadbeater in order to defend herself against the taint of the latter, the doubts thrown on the "Adyar manifestations," and secure the coveted position of President of the society after the death of Col. Olcott.

Later on her further necessities caused Mrs. Besant to adjust the breach with Mr. Sinnett by making him Vice-President, and with Mr. Leadbeater by procuring his return to the Society, from which he had resigned during the investigation in 1906. Forced to choose between two competing augurs, she chose Mr. Leadbeater rather than Chakravarti, whose usefulness to her was outlived, and since that period Mr. Leadbeater has been the "power behind the throne" of Mrs. Besant's exoteric and esoteric autocracy.

There is an enduring moral in all this for every sincere pilgrim on the probationary Path, no less than for the thoughtful enquirer into the mysteries of the workings of human consciousness. Unless the Theosophical student deliberately adopts and applies the philosophical and historical attitude in his consideration of such a complicated network of actions and actors as is presented in the three-fold evolution of the Theosophical Movement, he will, in his turn, fall victim to his own preconceptions and lack of discrimination, even though he be one who "sincerely loves truth and seeks truth"—to quote from the very circular under discussion. And thus only, in very truth, can be avoided the dangers of the "conscious and *unconscious* deception,"—to repeat the words of the real Master, whom Mrs. Besant quoted as if they applied to others only and not to herself as well.

To illustrate what is here endeavored to be considered, we may turn to the very message [2] itself from which Mrs. Besant quotes. It was "precipitated" in a letter from Tookaram Tatya in 1885 to Col. Olcott, and was addressed *to the President-Founder himself* and *all* his associates. Taking Damodar's indiscretions as a text from which to point a lesson as well as draw a moral, the MASTER said:

> *This ought to be a warning to you all. You have believed "not wisely but too well." To unlock the gates of the mystery you must not only lead a life of the strictest probity, but learn to discriminate truth from falsehood. You have talked a great deal about Karma but have hardly realised the true significance of that doctrine. The time is come when you must lay the foundation of that strict conduct—in the individual as well as in the collective body—which, ever wakeful, guards against conscious as well as unconscious deception.*

[2] For the complete text of this message, see "Letters from the Masters of the Wisdom," Adyar, Madras, India, 1919. Damodar is not mentioned by name in the message itself but in a note by the editor of the book, Mr. Jinarajadasa.

Philosophically, here is a "message from the Master," which any one might approve or disapprove *on its merits,* according to his judgment of its moral worth, quite irrespective of its writer, the method of its transmission, or the attendant circumstances. Historically, Mrs. Besant and Col. Olcott both approved this message, believed in Masters and Their Wisdom, accepted and promulgated Their greater "message" of Theosophy, were both "probationary Chelas" of these Masters. In weighing their conduct, therefore, they have to be measured by their consistency or inconsistency with the *Theosophy* and the *discipline of the School* they had made their own. Did they or did they not act in accord with the principles and rules by which they had bound themselves? The testimony of circumstance in connection with this "warning" which the leaflet quotes is of value. The message was sent following the Coulomb "exposure," the desertion, by Col. Olcott and the rest, of H.P.B. As repeatedly indicated by the course of events and their recital in this history, Col. Olcott and the others believed H.P.B. had been guilty, *at times,* of fraud, and that Damodar was a weakling imitator and blind worshiper of H.P.B. The anguish, the sense of the insult to the soul, the shame and humiliation of all this to a sensitive boy like Damodar, can be all too easily imagined by the most indurated. It well-nigh broke Damodar's heart; it was his "fall," indeed, and justified the Master's saying in the same message that the "poor boy . . . had to undergo the severest trials that a neophyte ever passed through, to atone for the many questionable doings in which he had over-zealously taken part, bringing disgrace upon the sacred science and its adepts."

The point is that *that message was not addressed to Damodar* (who was speedily called by the very Masters to Their Company) but to *Col. Olcott and his associates, individually and collectively, and its moral was for them,* not Damodar, who had succeeded despite his "many questionable doings" in achieving full accepted chelaship. How did *Col. Olcott and his associates take the warning?* As before they had believed H.P.B. and

Damodar "guilty" on accusations "inspired by hatred for the Theosophical Society and for all that it represents," so, in 1894, they formed the same belief in regard to Mr. Judge, and on the same "evidence" from the same sources. It seemed never to occur to Col. Olcott that here was a sharp, a very sharp reproof and lesson, for *him* to accept and *apply to himself*. For, during the ensuing three years he was engaged in a constant struggle with H.P.B. and with Mr. Judge who supported her, in opposition to the formation of the E.S.T., as he himself exposes in his "Old Diary Leaves." What his feelings were is there plainly given by himself. Another, and still sharper, warning was given him and others, therefore, in the "message" in August, 1888. Next, during the ensuing two years, he tacitly encouraged Prof. Coues in *his* attacks on H.P.B. and Mr. Judge, and abstained from any defense of his colleagues; finally, H.P.B. was compelled to *take away from him and his interference* the Theosophical Society in Europe. After the death of H.P.B., he began again to succumb to the old tendencies and temptations, despite all former experiences and warnings, and despite all that Judge could do to aid him, as H.P.B. had done before; finally, he passed under the cumulative sway of his own past actions and failures to heed the warnings given, to the place where he became the *active* tool, with Mrs. Besant and others of lesser repute, of "persons inspired by personal hatred of Mr. Judge and of the Theosophical Society and all that it represents."

Do we charge Mrs. Besant, Col. Olcott, or any of the lesser agents, with conscious, deliberate, premeditated, malicious intent and effort to assassinate the good name of Mr. Judge?

Far, far from it. We charge them with nothing. We recite the facts on record, a record made by themselves, and argue from the facts such conclusions as sound logic may make inevitable. We weigh those facts in the light of the teachings of Theosophy, the Rules and Instructions of the E.S.T. We have endeavored to pursue with them the identical course followed with regard to

H.P.B. and Mr. Judge. That the conclusions reached are at polar antitheses in the one case and the other is due, not to differences in *teachings,* for they all professed the same teachings and the same regard for the rules of Occultism. The inevitable conclusions logically following from the facts and the philosophy show in the one case a steadily widening breach between profession and practice; in the other a steadfast adherence in every vicissitude and strain to the self-imposed standard of conduct. But this being assumed for the moment by the reader, and it being granted that Col. Olcott, Mrs. Besant, and their coadjutors in 1894-5 were *sincere* throughout, the unavoidable question confronts writer and reader alike: What *is* the explanation of the conduct and actions of Mrs. Besant, Col. Olcott, and the rest? We answer: In the "warning addressed to all Esotericists" in the *Preliminary Memorandum* of the E.S.T. They were the victims of "pledge fever"; they were not "awake and on guard" against *unconscious self-deception; they believed they could depart from the discipline of the School of the Masters, violate the Rules of the School,* and yet "avoid the esoteric pitfalls." In the words of the *Second Preliminary Memorandum,* they "lost their moral balance unconsciously to themselves." Mere neophytes, mere probationers of the Second Section, they posed as *Teachers of Occultism.* They "spit back in the face of their Teacher"—in the graphic words of the Master they professed to revere and obey. Instead of "wiping away the filth with which the Teacher had been defiled by the enemy," they first remained supine when the Teacher was attacked, and ended by defiling that Teacher themselves. H.P.B. knew what had been, what was, and what was to be. At the time of the Coues-Collins-Lane-*New York Sun* assaults, when her sole vigilant defender was Mr. Judge, who was also assailed as infamously and venomously as herself, she wrote warmly of Mr. Judge, as she did so many times before and after, and called "on all those who will remain true to their pledges to do their duty . . . *when the time comes,* and especially by their American brother," who is "hated by certain persons as unjustly as I am by some unprincipled enemies who would still call themselves Theosophists."

Ecclesiastical history is filled, East and West, with the records of those *sincere* persons, prelates and laity alike, who *not having "learned to discriminate truth from falsehood"* in men, things, and methods, however facilely they intellectually grasped "the empty virtue of an abstract truth," were led, step by step, by their own *Karma* to the point where they *in all sincerity* made a mockery of the Teaching and the Teacher they professed to revere and obey—*where they saw and did evil, because that evil appeared to them good.* How else have all the religious persecutions of all time come about? How else all the false religions and the countless sects?

To continue our narrative. After his return to the United States Mr. Judge reprinted the "Occultism and Truth" circular, with this appended note, initialed by himself:

> The general propositions found in the above as to morality and the higher type of Occultism are so old and have been so widely spread, so often dwelt on in the work of the Theosophical Society, that one would hardly suppose any member was unacquainted with them; but a good thing cannot be too often repeated, and hence all must instantly concur. The circular was issued in London for distribution, and a copy having been sent to New York it is published according to the desire of the signers.
>
> W. Q. J.

Mr. Judge made no comments, raised no questions, voiced no complaints, ignored the inspiring motive behind the circular. He did the same with the article "T.S. Solidarity and Ideals," written by Col. Olcott as President of the Society as his contribution to the epilogue of the London Enquiry, and sent, "with fine Italian hand" to *The Path.* Mr. Judge published it in full as the leading article in the October number, and let it stand upon its merits as one of the "exhibits" in the case. Colonel Olcott sent copies also to *Lucifer* and *The Theosophist.* It was partially reprinted in *Lucifer* in the September number with a bracketed editorial addendum: "*This is an extract from an article which will appear in full in* The Path." *The Theosophist* printed it in its November number with a footnote, "From *The Path.*" The circumstances require a brief extract from the article for comparison with former pronunciamentos of the President-Founder, no less than to complete the setting of the stage following the London Enquiry. The President-Founder says:

> The time seems to have come for me to say a word or two about the constitution and ideals of the Theosophical Society, so that they may be made perfectly plain to the thousands of new colleagues who have entered our membership within the past five years. . . .
>
> After the lapse of nineteen years, the small group . . . who casually met in . . . New York City, has expanded into a Society with nearly four hundred chartered Branches in the four quarters of the globe. . . .
>
> What is the secret of this immense development, this self-sowing of Branches in all lands?

The President-Founder gives the answer as it appears to him: It is the Constitution and proclaimed ideals of the Society." He speaks of the Society's aim (Objects) as calculated "to attract all good, broadminded, philanthropic people alike." He discusses Theosophy and says:

> One reason for our too general confusion of ideas, is that we are prone to regard Theosophy as a sort of far-away sunrise that we must try to clutch, instead of seeing that it is a lamp to light our feet about the house and in our daily walks. It is worth nothing if it is but word-spinning, it is priceless if it is the best rule and ideal of life. . . . I know, what many

> others only suspect, that Theosophy is the informing life of all religions throughout the world. The one thing absolutely necessary, then, is to cast out as a loathsome thing every idea, every teaching which tends to sectarianize the Theosophical Society. We want no new sect, no new church, no infallible leader, no attack upon the private intellectual rights of our members. . . .
>
> Hypocrisy is another thing for us to purge ourselves of; there is too much of it, far too much among us. The sooner we are honest to ourselves the sooner we will be so to our neighbors. We *must* realize that the theosophical ideal of the perfect man is practically unattainable in one life. . . . Once realizing this, we become modest in self-estimate and therefore less inflated and didactic in our speech and writings. *Nothing is more disagreeable than to see a colleague, who probably has not advanced ten steps on the way up the Himalayan slope towards the level of perfection where the great adepts stand and wait, going about with an air of mystery, Burleighan nods and polysyllable words implying that he is our pilotbird and we should follow him. This is humbug, and, if not the result of auto-suggestion, rank hypocrisy. We have had enough of it, and more than enough. . . .*

After paying his respects in the sentences we have italicized to his hypothetical "colleague," whom every one understood to mean Mr. Judge, the President-Founder, after a further paragraph in the same vein, calls on all members to join in "forgetting ourselves in building up the Society." This leads him naturally from the Society to his favorite theme:

> From the office windows of Madison Avenue or Avenue Road, Adyar seems very far away, and the fact of its being the actual centre of the

> whole movement is sometimes apt to be forgotten. . . .
>
> The heart, or evolutionary centre, is Adyar, or whatever other place may have the Executive Staff in residence; just as Washington is the heart of the American Union. . . . The boast of all Americans is that the Federal Government lies like eider-down upon the States in times of tranquillity, yet proves as strong as tempered steel at a great national crisis. So in the lesser degree is the federal constitution of the Theosophical Society, and in that sense have I ever tried to administer its business. We have passed through the recent crisis with ease and safety because of our Constitution, and it is due to that that we are today stronger and more united than ever before. . . .

Thus passed, or seemed to pass, the great storm in the exoteric body, the Theosophical Society. The crisis in the Esoteric Section must now be considered.

CHAPTER XXXI

THE "EASTERN DIVISION" AND "WESTERN DIVISION"

APPARENT calm having been restored to the exoteric body of the Theosophical Society by the proceedings and results of the London Enquiry, as narrated, remained the far more difficult problem of a corresponding readjustment in the affairs of the Esoteric School of which Mrs. Besant and Mr. Judge had been, since the death of H.P.B., the Co-Heads.

The London proceedings had demonstrated for the moment to the satisfaction of all one thing, at least, and that was that "Occult" phenomena, genuine or spurious, mediumistic or adept, formed no part of the business of the Theosophical Society, either under its proclaimed Objects or under its Constitution, Rules, and by-laws. This had been the one point insisted on by H. P. Blavatsky throughout her lifetime, and no less insistently pressed by Mr. Judge after her death. The great wrong and evils inflicted by the bringing of the charges had thus been, to that extent, turned to good, and the attention of all members, high and low, once more directed to the consideration and practice of the ethical, philosophical and scientific basis and objects of the Society. A corollary resultant benefit was the practical realization for the time being that Occult phenomena cannot, in the present state of human evolution, be *proved,* from the evidences available to the reasoning mind; proved, we mean, in the same sense and to the same extent that physical phenomena can be proved to the satisfaction of an impartial judge and jury in a court of law. In legal affairs the trial of a disputed issue, actual or moot, presupposes an accepted code of principles, laws, and processes, for the determination of the facts, their causation, bearings, and the resultant decree of judgment—accepted by and acceptable to all parties to the issue, regardless of whether the ensuing decision be for the plaintiff or the defendant. Manifestly no such code exists in the world for the determination of metaphysical cases at issue, and no more did nor does it exist, among *believers* in the "Occult."

The "Judge case," and all similar cases, before and since, including the very status of H. P. Blavatsky, and the existence and status of her *Mahatmas* Themselves, has, before the bar of public and learned opinion, no locus whatever, using that word in its exact, mathematical sense. And certainly among Theosophists, however assured their *faith* in the reality of "the Occult world and its inhabitants," the whole question of Occult phenomena has been from the beginning, and still remains, *sub judice,* whether as to their principles, laws, and processes, or their actuality. They pertain, in their causal and effectual aspects, exclusively to the domain of the unknown First and Second Sections of the Theosophical Movement—that is to say, to the Masters, Adepts, and chelas of Occultism.[1] As shown by the repeated statements of the *Mahatmas* Themselves, no less than by the repeated statements of H.P.B. and Mr. Judge, *mediumistic* phenomena are one thing, the phenomena of *Occultism* quite another matter altogether, and it was never intended to perform or produce any Occult phenomena at any time of a character and accompaniment to *prove* their verisimilitude to the recipient and other witnesses. To have done that would have been, as often stated by the Mahatmas, to have overwhelmed the mind of the race and to have induced and precipitated an irreparable catastrophe. The time has not yet come to teach and *demonstrate* the realities of the Occult world. Every "phenomenon" in connection with the career of Mr. Judge, no less than in connection with the mission of H.P.B. herself, was therefore left,

[1] See, for example, the letters of the *Mahatma* "K. H." to Messrs. Sinnett and Hume in "The Occult World," the first edition of which was issued in 1881.

and purposely left, partially enshrouded in mystery for the recipients and witnesses. Their mission was *preparatory* to the great task of the twentieth century—the work of the Messenger of 1975. It was to arouse and provoke thought and inquiry, at all events among a choice minority, by the injection into the mind of the race of the *ideas* and *ethics* of the Wisdom-Religion, and such phenomena as were performed can be distributed into two main classes: (1) those which were incidental, because unavoidable, concomitants of their nature and work, and this class was little perceived or pondered by even the most intelligent of the students; (2) those phenomena which were produced *intentionally* in specific cases for or before given individuals. These were extremely limited in number and variety, when all is said, no two of them were identical in circumstance and environment, and no publicity was ever given any of them, *in the first instance,* either by H.P.B. or Mr. Judge. The Karma of their publicity, as the Karma of their performance, was that of the recipients and witnesses, who had earned what they received, and having received such tokens, broadcasted them—against the admonition and the warning of H.P.B. and Mr. Judge in every case, be it noted.

The "Esoteric Section" was not formed until, in the words of H.P.B., the *Society* had "proved a failure" and "become a sham," because it had departed both from the original impulse and the original program. And in this "failure" and this "sham" must, of necessity, be included all those officers and leaders of the Society, however highly placed or esteemed, who had brought about that departure. The Karma of the first fourteen years was the Karma of the Society, including its officers and members; the Karma of the ensuing seven years was the Karma of the "Esoteric Section." The Society had been weighed in the balance and found wanting, though it still lived on and was vicariously sustained by the "Esoteric Section" as a utilitarian instrument. The events of 1894-5 were the testing-out of the "Esoteric Section" itself as a worthy or unworthy vessel.

No more than the Theosophical Society was the "Esoteric Section" intended to be or become a "Hall of Occultism," "a factory for the manufacture of adepts." This is shown by all the esoteric as well as exoteric writings and "messages" of Masters as well as H.P.B. and Mr. Judge. It is succinctly but unmistakably shown on the very first page of the *First Preliminary Memorandum* where it is specifically stated (the italics being our own):

> This degree of the Esoteric Section is *probationary,* and its general purpose is to *prepare and fit* the student for the *study* of Practical Occultism or Raja Yoga. Therefore, in this degree the student—save in exceptional cases—will *not be taught how to produce physical phenomena,* nor will *any* magical powers be *allowed* to develop in him; nor, if possessing such powers naturally, will he be *permitted to exercise them* before he has *mastered* the *knowledge* of SELF, of the psycho-physiological processes (taking place on the occult plane) in the human body generally, and until he has in *abeyance all his lower passions* and his PERSONAL SELF.

All those who entered the E.S. did so voluntarily and were in honor bound either to abide by its conditions, or leave it altogether. As before shown, great pains were taken with each applicant that he should be fully informed of the nature of the School, its pledge, its Rules, its purposes and requirements, *before he entered.* Each and all were warned of the *occult* consequences—consequences which no one could avoid for them—of persistent violation of the School conditions *sine qua non;* while each one was notified before entrance that grave violation of the School Discipline would entail his suspension or expulsion for the sake of those who might remain loyal.

The conduct of Col. Olcott throughout the "Judge case" was a violation of the Constitution and Rules of the exoteric Theosophical Society and a departure from its Objects—the self-imposed criterions which he had not only accepted as a member but was in honor bound, as President-Founder, to be first and foremost, not only in enforcing upon the membership, but in himself rendering obedience to them. But the case of Mrs. Besant was far more serious. Her entire part in the "Judge case" was a gross breach of her pledge and an equally gross infraction of the Rules and Discipline of the Esoteric Section which, for her, was the self-assumed canon of conduct. All this quite apart from any consideration of the guilt or innocence of Mr. Judge of the offenses charged against him. In the one case the Constitution and Rules of the Society had provided from the first that charges against a member must be brought and could be tried only before the Branch to which the accused belong. It may be remarked here, for the sake of the record, that the charges made against Mr. Judge *were* brought before his Branch, the Aryan Theosophical Society of New York City, and, by the *unanimous* vote of the Council and members of that Branch, rejected. In the other case the Rules and Discipline of the School provided that *no charge of any description should be made by any member against another,* except *within the School.* How grave was Mrs. Besant's conduct, from the standpoint of the School, can be seen from the following extracts from the *Rules:*

> Groundless condemnation, on hearsay, of others, Theosophists or not, must be refrained from, and charity to each other's faults widely practiced among those within, as well as for others without, the Theosophical area.
>
> Repetition of statements derogatory to others must be avoided.
>
> A derogatory or slanderous statement made against a fellow-Theosophist, in the presence of a member [of the School], shall not be permitted by him to pass without protest, unless he knows it is true, in which case he should remain silent.

> No member shall, in any circumstances, bring any charge of whatever nature against another member except [under the School procedure].
>
> Suspicions as to the character of the members of the School are prejudicial to advancement. In short, any malevolent feeling, especially malice, envy or revenge toward any person, high or low, creates peculiarly obstructive conditions in the student's path, and will absolutely prevent progress of every sort.
>
> No member of this School shall belong to any other body, association, or organization for the purpose of mystic study or occult training.

We are not here arguing that these Rules from the "Book of Discipline" of the School are true statements either of theory or practice; we are submitting them as the Code of conduct voluntarily accepted and affirmed by Mrs. Besant on her "solemn and sacred word of honor" as the true standard of ethics by which she would abide. Mrs. Besant was not only a member of the School, but of its Second Degree or so-called Inner Group, and one of its Heads, and therefore the more bound in honor to the most strict adherence to its time-honored practice. In considering the Theosophical life and conduct of all those connected with the Society or the Esoteric School therefore, they are not to be weighed, either by what they themselves claimed, or by what others said of them, or by worldly standards of action, but by their loyalty to, or departure from, the self-declared Objects of the Society, the self-assumed Obligations of the School. Only from this basis can their conduct be intelligently considered, fairly measured.

The Objects, Constitution, and Rules of the Society were just as binding upon H. P. Blavatsky and William Q. Judge as upon any one else, and their conduct in that respect is the criterion of judgment on their actions within the Society. And, with respect to the School of the Esoteric Section, they were, like Mrs. Besant or any other member, bound to act according to its precepts or leave it. A due understanding of these considerations will make the Theosophical record of H.P.B. and W.Q.J. stand out in solitary grandeur against the broken ground of total and partial failures of their colleagues and co-workers in the Theosophical Cause. It was their very allegiance to the declared Objects and *democratic* organization of the T.S., that brought them into almost constant conflict with others, nominal but ambitious Theosophists. And in the Esoteric School itself it was their rigid and undeviating adherence to the letter as well as the spirit of the "Book of Discipline" which made H.P.B. unpalatable and Mr. Judge obnoxious to those whose self-confidence was such that they "took the law into their own hands" when the pledge and Rules interfered with their own ideas and desires. It was this obedience to the Constitution, the Rules, the Objects of the Society, which required Mr. Judge to raise the Constitutional questions involved in the attempted "trial" by the Judicial Committee, and which equally debarred him from proffering just charges against the President-Founder for the latter's flagrant breach of the Theosophical conventions, moral and legal. In the same way he was debarred from making charges against Mrs. Besant before the Society, while in the School itself, the "Book of Discipline" requires that two warnings shall be given before the suspension or expulsion of "the Disciple who shows himself whether willingly or inadvertently disloyal to the letter and spirit of any law."

The first of these warnings had been given to Mrs. Besant by Mr. Judge as the "representative of H.P.B.," and as Co-Head of the School in September, 1893 (at the time of her visit to the Parliament of Religions at Chicago), because of her relations with Chakravarti, whose "Occult" pupil she had become, and with whom she discussed her School relations, duties, and conduct, in addition to taking him as her Guru. The first of the "Occult consequences" which befell Mrs. Besant was her yielding to the cajoleries of the enemies of Mr. Judge and sponsoring and "prosecuting" the charges against him. Immediately following the close of the Judicial Committee meeting and the proceedings of the European Convention which was supposed to have terminated the "Judge case" so far as the Society was concerned, a meeting became necessary between Mrs. Besant and Mr. Judge to adjust the status of the Esoteric School, and at this time Mrs. Besant received her second warning, as the "Book of Discipline" made imperative.

With regard to the School itself a joint circular letter, *"strictly private and only for E.S.T. Members,"* was sent out to all members over the signatures of the two Heads. The London copy is dated July 18, and the American copy August 1, 1894. It contains the recital of the conditions prevailing in the School, the respective accredited positions of the two Heads at the reorganization of the School immediately following the death of H.P.B., and the agreement reached for the future conduct of the E.S.T. We quote so much as is necessary to make clear the summary just given:

> *To the members of the E.S.T.:*
>
> You all know that during the last few months the activity of the E.S.T. has been to a great extent suspended in consequence of events which are matters of public notoriety. The issue of these is now before the T.S., and each must form his own judgment upon them. . . . So far as the T.S. is concerned, it has passed through a grave crisis; but it goes forward unbroken in its great work in the world. The E.S.T. should do the same.
>
> In the E.S.T. time is needed for the full restoration to a state devoid of friction, as well as for the revival of as perfect mutual trust and confidence as human nature will permit. Without this full restoration and revival no two persons can act as a single channel for spiritual influences.
>
> But we have our fundamental unity and channel in the Masters and in their mouthpiece

—Our Teacher in this School—our recognized Head, H.P.B. .·. On this the School was founded and rests today. We will proceed under the arrangements made and left by her at the time of her passing away. She declared that William Q. Judge was the Antaskarana, or channel for the Americans, and made him under herself the sole authority in America by the following Documents.

Then follow the copies of the Document of December 14, 1888, and the Document of October 23, 1889, as originally contained in the circulars of May 27, 1891 and August, 1893. They are as follows:

ESOTERIC T. S. SECTION

As Head of the Esoteric Section of the Theosophical Society, I hereby declare that William Q. Judge of New York, U. S. A., in virtue of his character of a chela of thirteen years' standing and of the trust and confidence reposed in him, is my only representative for said Section in America, and he is the sole channel through whom will be sent and received all communications between the members of said Section and myself, and to him full faith, confidence, and credit in that regard are to be given. Done at London, this fourteenth day of December, 1888, and in the fourteenth year of the Theosophical Society.

(Seal) H. P. BLAVATSKY. .·.

LONDON, *October* 23d, 1889.

. . . The Esoteric Section and its life in the U.S.A. depend upon W.Q.J. remaining its agent anad what he now is. The day W.Q.J. resigns, H.P.B. will be virtually dead for the Americans. W.Q.J. is the Antaskarana between the two *Manas* (*es*), the American thought and the

Indian,—or rather the trans-Himalayan esoteric knowledge. *Dixi.*

H.P.B. .·.

P. S. W.Q.J. had better show and impress *this* on the mind of *all those it may concern.*

The circular continues:

She [H.P.B.] made the then Inner Group the Council, under herself, for the remaining part of the School, and shortly before her departure made Annie Besant its chief officer, as Chief Secretary of the I[nner] G[roup] and Recorder of the Teachings, by the following:

E.S.

ORDER

I hereby appoint in the name of the Master, Annie Besant Chief Secretary of the Inner Group of the Esoteric Section and Recorder of the Teachings.

April 1, 1891. H.P.B. .·.

The circular then goes on:

Thus it was when she departed.

Out of these two appointments was constituted (see Council Minutes, 1891) the Dual Headship in 1891 for the management of the School, an arrangement that has not on the whole at any time worked well in practice. At the present time the only way to preserve the E.S.T. unbroken and give time for the restoration of the mutual trust referred to and to smooth out friction is by returning to the above arrangements. We remain throughout the world the one School —"the throbbing heart of the T.S."—founded by H.P.B., recognizing her as our Teacher and the Masters as our foundation, having in common her Headship, the Instructions she left, and the Rules of the School. . . .

It is to be noted (1) that the above written documents of H.P.B.'s were the ones upon which was effected the reorganization of the School after the death of H.P.B.; (2) that these same documents were referred to in the joint circular to the E.S. in August, 1893, at the time of the suspension of Messrs. Old and Edge; (3) that as just shown they are again reiterated as the basis of the agreement reached in London in July, 1894, following the "Judicial Committee" Enquiry. All these circulars were signed by Mrs. Besant, and for the most part written by her, including the one of July 18, from which we have been quoting. There are thus three solemn asseverations by her to all members of the School as to what were, on the authority of H.P.B., the respective positions and relations of herself and Mr. Judge—the last of these asseverations the most important of all, from the standpoint of the light they shed on Mrs. Besant's character, for it shows, like her Statement before the European Convention, a complete about face on the subject of the charges against Mr. Judge. It shows out of her own mouth as well, and for the third time, that the position accorded her by H.P.B. was in fact that of "Secretary and Recorder," not "Successor of H.P.B.," as she claimed less than a year later, and has since maintained, as we shall see.

How Mrs. Besant fulfilled her duties as *Recorder of the Teachings* is shown in many ways, but most glaringly by two standing witnesses: the "Third and Revised Edition" of the "Secret Doctrine," and the spurious "Third Volume" of the "Secret Doctrine" issued by her in 1897. Any reader can compare the Original Edition of the "Secret Doctrine" with the Third and Revised Edition, edited by Mrs. Besant and Mr. Mead. Despite the assurances contained in their *Preface*, the comparison will show *more than forty thousand changes* from the text of the Original Edition, ranging all the way from mere trivialities, through important alterations, to *deliberate suppression of all those paragraphs of the Original Edition* of two volumes which showed unmistakably what the genuine Third Volume (already, with the Fourth Volume, completed by H.P.B. before her death) consisted of. The utter disappearance without a trace left behind, of the *genuine* Third and Fourth Volumes of the "Secret Doctrine" remains to this day an unrevealed mystery. And as to Mrs. Besant's spurious "Third Volume," her own Preface alone is ample to convince any careful student, able to sift statements, that it is nothing more than a hodgepodge of rejected manuscripts, "literary remains," private papers originally issued to the E.S.T. during the lifetime of H.P.B., and largely *rejected manuscript of the first volume of the Original Edition.* For it is, or should be, well known to every Theosophical *student* that, as repeatedly announced in the earlier volumes of *The Theosophist,* H.P.B.'s original intention was that the "Secret Doctrine," should be a revised edition of "Isis Unveiled," and in pursuance of that intention she wrote one entire volume, prior to 1886, when returning confidence and trust in her by the mass of members of the T.S. enabled her to enlarge her plan and write an entirely new work. A copy of that early first volume was sent by H.P.B. to *Subba Row* for criticism and comment. Followed his breach with H.P.B. as already narrated. He refused to do anything with it. It is matter from that rejected manuscript which is incorporated in Mrs. Besant's "Third Volume." And—notable phenomenon—the fact is admitted by Mrs. Besant herself in *The Theosophist* for March, 1922—twenty-five years after the event. Why did she concoct this spurious "Third Volume" in the first instance? And why did she in 1922 let slip the truth which in 1897 she not only suppressed, but replaced by an untruth? The answer to the first query can be seen by reading her article "East and West" in *Lucifer* for May, 1895, written during the throes of the recrudescent "Judge case." She there states in discussing the celebrated "Prayag Letter" or "Message to Some Brahmins," to the consideration of which we shall soon come,[2] that the message, which Mr.

[2] See Chapter XXXIII.

Judge had declared to be genuine, is in her opinion spurious. She says, after giving her reasons:

> These facts seemed to me *to necessitate the rejection of the letter as being in flagrant contradiction with H.P.B.'s teachings, and it is certainly no more supported by the third volume* of the "Secret Doctrine," which was placed in my hands by H.P.B., than by the other two. *Why so wild an assertion, which will be proved false by the forthcoming publication of the third volume, should be made, I do not know.*

Neither the "facts" (reasons) alleged by Mrs. Besant for rejecting the "Message to Some Brahmins," nor its "contradiction with the teachings of H.P.B.," are remotely suggested, even by inference, by anything contained in Mrs. Besant's "Third Volume" nor is the "wild assertion" of Mr. Judge that the message is true in substance in any way impugned by any of the writings of H.P.B., the matter of the "Third Volume" included—as any one can verify for himself by reference to the contents of the "Third Volume" itself. But Mrs. Besant's article "East and West," and her following article, "The Prayag Letter,"[3] were written in self-defense and self-extenuation. "East and West" contains, *inter alia,* another astounding illustration of Mrs. Besant's lack of trustworthiness, for she says:

> *Instead of denouncing "faith in the gods" as a superstition,* [the substance of the "Prayag Message"] H.P.B. *professed it.* . . .

We ask any student of Theosophy to consider whether misrepresentation could reach to greater audacity than is shown in this single sentence?

In Mrs. Besant's "Third Volume" are incorporated the private papers originally issued by H.P.B. to the E.S., and in reprinting these Mrs. Besant not only falsely

[3] See *Lucifer,* for July 15, 1895, Volume 16, pp. 375-9, for "The Prayag Letter," and pp. 185-94, May, 1895, for "East and West."

declared them to be a part of the "third volume of the *Secret Doctrine* which was placed in my hands by H.P.B.," not only broke the seventh clause of her solemn pledge as a member of the Esoteric School, but corrupted them by more than *twelve hundred* alterations, perversions, suppressions, and substitutions of text.

Why did she let the truth escape her lips twenty-five years later, unless it be that *she had forgotten her original statements in a fresh exigency in her career?* Her remarks in *The Theosophist* for March, 1922, bear no other rational construction when read in connection with those in the April number immediately following. She did the same thing in regard to this very "Prayag Message," as we shall see very soon. It will have long since been noted by the careful reader of this History, that the unavoidable impeachments of Col. Olcott's, Mr. Sinnett's, and Mrs. Besant's testimony on controversial questions of teaching and of fact, have been in every case out of their own mouths and those of their own witnesses. An exhaustive study and comparison of their own writings and actions has forced us, as we believe it will force any student, to the conviction that their evidence is utterly untrustworthy on any subject in which their self-interest was aroused. Not even Eusebius and Constantine in their successful efforts to bend the teachings and the influence of Christianity to their personal, theological and political purposes showed such ethical blindness coupled with intellectual ability to mislead those who trusted them.

Returning to the circular of date at London July 18, and New York August 1, signed by Mrs. Besant and Mr. Judge as Co-Heads of the E.S.T.: it possesses great interest and value, not merely to the historian but to all students of Theosophy seeking to unravel the baffling mysteries of the present and the past. First, this circular confirms and reaffirms the accuracy of the original Minutes of May 27, 1891, the reorganization of the School then effected, the status of Mrs. Besant and Mr. Judge, and the basis and evidence on which that status was established. Second, this confirmation and reaffirmation was made *after* the "Enquiry into the charges against W. Q. Judge" by the Judicial Committee; *after* Mrs. Besant had read her Statement to the European Convention, and *after* it had, at her request, acted as a "Jury" to "dispose of the whole matter," and had so disposed of it. Certainly if the Statement of Mrs. Besant and this Circular signed by her are to be construed as the sincere testimony and good faith declarations of an honest witness under conditions the most solemn possible, then they give the lie, direct and irrefutable, to her subsequent asseverations on the same subject matters during the heat and fury of her second onset on the name and fame of Mr. Judge. On the other hand, if her subsequent affirmations are to be taken as true, they show Mrs. Besant in the role of a bearer of false witness in July, 1894. Either point of view shows Mrs. Besant to have been deaf, dumb, and blind to all moral sense, for her two sets of statements covering the same matters at issue are beyond any possibility of reconciliation. The second attack on Mr. Judge must now be traced.

CHAPTER XXXII

"WESTMINSTER GAZETTE" ATTACKS THE SOCIETY

Mr. Judge left London July 18, 1894, to return to New York; Col. Olcott, after a brief tour of England, Scotland and Ireland, departed for India. Mr. Bertram Keightley also returned to India to resume his duties as General Secretary of the Indian Section, and to be near Chakravarti, whose pupil he had become—and has since remained to this date. Mrs. Besant at once set sail for Australia to form Branches and establish an Australasian Section of the T.S. under the *carte blanche* authority given her by the President-Founder in his "Executive Notice" of April preceding, the text of which was given in a former chapter.[1] She also bore with her from the European Section Convention just held, its authority for her to represent the European Section as its delegate to the "Adyar Parliament" to be held in December following.

Mr. Walter R. Old remained in England, while his associate in the article "Theosophic Free Thought," Mr. Sydney V. Edge, continued to serve as Sub-Editor of *The Theosophist*. Mr. Old had judiciously retired from London to a near-by town during the "Enquiry," but kept in close touch with the progress of events at the hearing before the Judicial Committee and the subsequent session of the European Convention devoted to the "Judge case." Displeased by Mrs. Besant's too close coupling of his name and Mr. Edge's with her statement before the Convention that "for some years past persons inspired largely by hatred for Mr. Judge, and persons inspired by hatred for the Theosophical Society and for all that it represents, have circulated a mass of

[1] See Chapter XXIX.

accusations against him,'' Mr. Old, who knew that Col. Olcott, Chakravarti, Countess Wachtmeister, and Mrs. Besant were equally in the mire with himself, was not only aggrieved, but in a quandary as well. To break with these intimate friends and associates by exposing the whole truth was to bring ruin to them and himself instead of to Mr. Judge. To remain silent was to assume the whole burden of the joint iniquity himself. He therefore took the matter up with Col. Olcott. The result was a formal letter addressed by him to Col. Olcott as ''President-Founder.'' This was published by Mrs. Besant in the August, 1894, *Lucifer*, the same number which contained the ''Truth and Occultism'' circular and the text of the ''Neutrality'' report on the ''Judge case.'' Mrs. Besant published Mr. Old's letter with this prefatory statement in brackets:

> Colonel Olcott asks us to publish the following. We do so, *omitting a passage to which we cannot give* publicity.

The text of Mr. Old's letter will be found in *Lucifer*, Vol. 14, pp. 463-4. We give a few of its unconsciously telltale sentences. He says to Col. Olcott (italics preceding and following being ours):

> As you were associated with me in your capacity of *Editor* of *The Theosophist* at the time of the publication of the joint article by Mr. Edge and myself, *you will be able to speak from personal knowledge* as to our attitude in this connection. . . . Annie Besant would, I think, *admit that the text of her statement is open to misinterpretation* in this particular instance. The association of the two paragraphs referred to would certainly lead to a conclusion which, I think, *she would be the last to desire.*

There the matter rested until October following, all the recent protagonists and their followers of every degree being apparently busy in renewed Theosophical activities and in healing the sores caused by the late "Judge case." Under cover of these activities, however, the campaign against Mr. Judge was kept up by word of mouth and through private correspondence, by Mrs. Besant, by Col. Olcott, by Countess Wachtmeister, and by Mr. Sinnett, as shown by subsequent events and admissions of the several parties.

In October, 1894, the London *Westminster Gazette* began the publication of a series of articles by Edmund Garrett, entitled "Isis Very Much Unveiled; the Story of the Great Mahatma Hoax." This series, the editorial articles which accompanied it and the printed correspondence, ran on for two months without cessation. All former Theosophical storms rolled into one were but as a barometric fall to the monsoon which it presages, in comparison with the havoc wrought in the Theosophical Society's ranks by this publication. It was immediately gotten out in book form by the *Westminster Gazette*, and the book had a tremendous circulation. Some one paid for sending copies to all Lodges of the Theosophical Society.

Mr. Garrett was an exceedingly clever and brilliant writer. No "trial by newspaper" ever had an abler advocate for the plaintiff. Moreover, Mr. Garrett was plainly honest. He concealed neither the sources of his information, his own detestation of Theosophy and its Society, nor that his object was to destroy what he detested.

Mr. Garrett was a personal friend of Mr. Walter R. Old, and it was Mr. Old who inspired him to write his series of articles and who supplied most of the documentary matter employed by Mr. Garrett with rare skill in making his case. Mr. Old was the only one of the numerous *dramatis personae* whom Mr. Garrett's serio-comedy treated with respect. All the others were targets for his keen wit, Mrs. Besant most of all. Colonel Olcott was mercilessly lampooned, H.P.B. and Mr. Judge held forth as a couple of able tricksters and charlatans who had made dupes and fools of Mrs. Besant, Col. Olcott, and the rest, with bogus phenomena and bogus messages from equally bogus Mahatmas.

It was clearly evident from the documents used by Mr. Garrett that Mr. Old had been aided by both Col. Olcott and Mrs. Besant, for some of the papers cited could not have been otherwise obtained. This is practically admitted by Mr. Old in a letter to *Lucifer*, which will be found in its issue for December 15, 1894, Volume 15, pp. 337-8—and this despite his denial of the fact in the same letter. We quote, italics ours:

> The published facts are just those which came into the evidence of Col. Olcott and Bertram Keightley, and upon which the charges were based and action taken; *and they are, moreover, part of a body* of evidence, which, *from the outset,* it was *decided to publish.* I take the whole Karma of my own action, and I affirm that it is wholly independent of connivance or instigation on the part of anyone.

At the same time Mr. Old addressed a letter to the *Westminster Gazette*, which was published, and which was also included in the matter of Mr. Garrett's book. We quote so much as is necessary to establish or confirm the links already given, italicized portions being, as before, our own emphasis of Mr. Old's words:

> The writer of those articles has named me, quite correctly, as having taken the first step in forcing an inquiry into the case against Mr. Judge. For this act of mine, I was suspended from my membership in the Esoteric Section, under the authority of the joint signatures of William Q. Judge and Annie Besant, Outer Heads of the E.S.T., and my name was dishonourably mentioned before the members of the E.S. among whom I numbered many an old friend and colleague. . . . *After* her official action in suspending me from membership Mrs.

> Besant was, of course, bound to hear my justification. This happened at Adyar in the winter of 1893. Mrs. Besant's first remark to me after reading the case and examining the documents was, *"You were perfectly justified by the facts before you."*
>
> *In the presence* of the president-founder Col. Olcott, Mrs. Besant, Countess Wachtmeister, Mr. E. T. Sturdy, together with Mr. Edge and myself, *it was decided that the task of officially bringing the charges should devolve upon Mrs. Besant,* and that the whole of the evidence should be *published.* . . .

Mr. Old goes on to tell of Mrs. Besant's formal demand to Col. Olcott for the investigation, Col. Olcott's official letters to Mr. Judge, and the Judicial Committee meeting, *"with the abortive and disingenuous result already known."* He then continues:

> But what of the "full publication of all the details?" What of us Theosophists who had brought these charges against Mr. Judge? Were we not left in the position of persons who had brought charges without proving them? The position was one I felt to be intolerable.

It never occurred to Mr. Old, any more than to Mrs. Besant and the others, that there was anything "intolerable" in spreading privately and publicly calumnies dignified as "charges" and "evidences," even in the ordinary human sense of decency, let alone as Fellows in a Society whose First Object was brotherhood, and as members of an Esoteric School pledged "never to listen without protest to any evil thing said of a Brother Theosophist and to abstain from condemning others." But when publicity played the spotlight upon the authors of the "mass of accusations," then, indeed, the position became "intolerable"—first to Mr. Old, and then to Mrs. Besant and Col. Olcott.

After arguing that it was his "duty" to supply ammunition to Mr. Garrett, whom he calls a "Philistine," in order that "a system of truth" should not be "raised from a fabric of fraud," Mr. Old says:

> It will, therefore, be clear to all members of the T.S. and the public generally that I am responsible for the facts occurring in Mr. Garrett's articles *only so far as they apply to the charges against Mr. Judge*. . . . I do not lose sight of the fact that, however mistaken or misled many of the Theosophical Society may be, as regards the traditional "Mahatmas" and their supposed "communications," they are nevertheless as sincere in their beliefs as many of their more orthodox fellows, and have as much right to respectful consideration. *I particularly regret that Mrs..Besant should have been placed in this awkward public position by the present exposure.*
>
> Of Madame Blavatsky I speak as I knew her. At the time I made her acquaintance she had forsworn all "phenomenalism," so that I never saw any occult phenomena at any time. I believe that *for her* [these italics are Mr. Old's] the Mahatmas existed, and I believe she *thought them* to be embodied personalities. *Colonel Olcott has another theory,* and others have their own. . . . Finally I have been through the Theosophical Society with my eyes open, and for more than five years have been, officially and unofficially, as fully "in the Theosophical Society" as one can well be; and while I am certain that many are fully convinced of the truth of their own beliefs in these matters, I am also fully assured that a large number are in the position of *persons self-deceived, who have unfortunately committed themselves too far to review their position without almost disastrous consequences to themselves and others.*

Applying this last italicized clause of Mr. Old's, the question arises, Was it H.P.B. and Mr. Judge who had thus committed themselves, or Mr. Old and his associates in the campaign against Mr. Judge, which speedily became of necessity a campaign against H.P.B.? The further question arises, What was Mr. Old doing in the Theosophical Society and particularly in its Esoteric School, for five years, with the views, expressed and implied, just given? Or did these views arise in him after being suspended from the E.S. for violation of his pledge and the Rules? Mr. Old follows with this statement:

> I have the fullest conviction . . . that no such thing as evidence of the existence (in an ordinary sense) of the Mahatmas, or of their connexion with the T.S. as a body or with its members individually, is obtainable by a person pursuing ordinary methods of investigation.

The fact itself is a truism to any man of the most casual information and common sense, and was repeatedly affirmed by H.P.B. and Mr. Judge; but if Mr. Old himself had this conviction, how could he know that H.P.B. or Mr. Judge, or anyone else, *was*, or *was not*, in communication with these Mahatmas, and what becomes of his "mass of accusations"?

We think the inference is irresistible that Mr. Old, Mrs. Besant, Col. Olcott, and the rest, suffering the stings of wounded pride and vanity, pricked at being "hoist with their own petard" by the outcome of the "Judge case," and convinced by his conduct during the preceding months that he would make no counter-attacks upon them, whatever they might do, proceeded, the one publicly, the others at first privately, to defend and extenuate themselves in the reaction that followed the London Enquiry, by intimating that they "could an' they would" produce evidence that would damn, and doubly damn, Mr. Judge. It seems never to have occurred to any of them that *ex parte* accusations, private or public, or "trial by the newspapers" was in any way disreputable, or that an accused person, even one "guilty" of suspected "messages from the Masters," was entitled to the presumption of innocence, and freedom from the circulation of "accusations" by all honorable persons, until *proven* guilty. Nowhere, in any of the immense mass of printed matter poured out by his defamers, is there one solitary hint that any of his accusers ever took the straightforward course of going direct to Mr. Judge with their alleged "evidences" and asking him to explain and rebut what seemed to them questionable.

What did Mr. Judge do? He did what he had to do—nothing in so far as the Theosophical Society was concerned; in the Esoteric School, that which the "Book of Discipline" made obligatory upon him, and which, according to his own declaration, was also directly "By Master's Order." In the circular letter with that heading, issued by him to all members of the Esoteric School under date of November 3, 1894, he deposed Mrs. Besant from her Co-Headship in the School.

In this circular Mr. Judge says that he has "put off writing it since March, 1894," although "it then seemed to me as necessary as it is now," but that he was "directed to wait for the conclusion of the matter of the charges made against" him. He says he has since seen the wisdom of the directions to "wait," because had he written it while the "charges" were still undisposed of the Theosophical Society would have been "mixed up" with the troubles in the Esoteric Section which had no official relation to the Society. "We have now," he proceeds, "to deal with the E.S.T. and with our duty to it and to each other; and among those others, to Mrs. Besant."

He then briefly rehearses the story of the foundation of the E.S.T., its history, the Inner Group, the reorganization of the School following the death of H.P.B.—all of which has already been told in detail in the course of this History. He makes public to the members the fact that the actual formation of the School originated with himself, in a letter to H.P.B. in May, 1887, a year and a half before the public announcement, and that the foundation followed the lines suggested by him. He also advised the members that he himself had never taken the School or Inner Group pledges, having made his own vows in 1874 direct to the Masters—all of which is borne out by recorded public and private statements by H.P.B. He then speaks of Mrs. Besant as follows:

> Mrs. Annie Besant has been but five years in this work, and not all of that time engaged in occult study and practice. Her abilities as a writer and speaker are rare and high for either man or woman, her devotion and sincerity of purpose cannot be doubted. She gave many years of her life to the cause of the oppressed as she understood it: against the dread blight of materialistic belief in herself, she worked thus without hope in a future life and in every way proved her altruistic purpose and aim. Since 1889 she has done great service to the T.S. and devoted herself to it. But all this does not prevent a sincere person from making errors in Occultism, especially when he, as Mrs. Besant did, tries to force himself along the path of practical work in that field. Sincerity does not of itself confer knowledge, much less wisdom. H.P.B. ∴ and all the history of occultism says that seven years of training and trial at the very least are needed. Mrs. Besant has had but five. Mistakes made by such a disciple will ultimately be turned to the advantage of the movement, and their immediate results will be mitigated to the person making them, provided they are not inspired by an evil intention on the person's part. And I wish it to be clearly understood that Mrs. Besant has had herself no conscious evil intention; she has simply gone for awhile outside the line of her Guru H.P.B. ∴, begun work with others, and fallen under their influence. We

should not push her farther down, but neither will the true sympathy we have blind our eyes so as to let her go on, to the detriment of the whole movement.

Mr. Judge discusses *in extenso* the recent charges and troubles in the Society and the School, from the standpoint of the Second Section, treating their real origin, their strategy and tactics, as having their source in the everlasting struggle of human evolution—the contending forces of the Light and Dark sides of Nature and Being. He concludes this part of his narrative by saying that the difficulty focalized anew "when in January or February [1894] Annie Besant finally lent herself unconsciously to the plot which I detail herein; but prior to that (from August, 1893), those managing that plot had begun to work upon her." He places the root of the plot in India and says that the opposing forces to the Theosophical Movement,—

> . . . have succeeded in influencing certain Brahmins in India through race-pride and ambition, so that these, for their own advantage, desire to control and manage the T.S. through some agent and also through the E.S.T. They of course have sought, if possible, to use one of our body, and have picked out Mrs. Besant as a possible vehicle. One object of the plot is to stop the current of information and influence started by H.P.B. .·. by deflecting thought back to modern India. To accomplish this it is absolutely necessary to tear down the tradition clustering around the work of H.P.B. .·. ; her powers and knowledge have to be derogated from; her right to speak for the Masters has to be impugned; those Masters have to be made a cold abstraction; her staunch friends who wish to see the real work and objects carried on have to be put in such a position as to be tied hand and foot so as not to be able to interfere with the plans

> of the plotters; it has to be shown that H.P.B. . . . was a fraud and a forger also. These men are not the Chelas of our Masters.
>
> The name of the person who was worked upon so as to, if possible, use him as a minor agent . . . for the influencing of Mrs. Besant is Gyanendra N. Chakravarti, a Brahmin of Allahabad, India, who came to America on our invitation to the Religious Parliament in 1893. At the first sincerely desirous of helping the race by bringing to the American people the old truths of his forefathers, he nevertheless, like so many before him, permitted ambition to take subtle root in his heart. Fired with the ambition of taking position in the world as a Guru, though doubtless believing himself still a follower of the White Brotherhood, he is no longer in our lines; on the contrary his mediumship and weakness leave him a vehicle for other influences also.

Mr. Judge then goes on to tell of a message in regard to himself received by Chakravarti, in which the Master commended Mr. Judge and his work, and says: "I informed Mrs. Besant in September, 1893, of the message." This message was the one referred to by Mr. Judge in his statement before the European Convention in July, 1894, as being undisputed by Mrs. Besant. The circular continues:

> But afterwards, when Mr. Chakravarti's work under me was finished, and when ambition aroused through that visit, had grown strong, he tried to destroy the effect of that message on Mrs. Besant's mind by cunningly construing it to mean that, although I was thus in all things commended, the last part of it contradicted the first and supported the charge of forgery and lying. This is madness when not deliberate. . . . She accepted the cunning construction, permitted herself to think that the Master could commend me for all the work I had

done, of which the pretended acts of forgery would be a part, and at the same time send me a delusive message, part of which was to be immediately used as condemnation if brought forward by me. If I was guilty of what I was accused, then Master would be shown as conniving at forgery and lying—a most impossible thing. The only other possibility is that Mr. Chakravarti and I "got up" the message. But he and Mrs. Besant have admitted its genuineness, although she is perfectly unable herself to decide on its genuineness or falsity. But further, Mrs. Besant admitted to several that she had seen the Master himself come and speak through my body while I was perfectly conscious. And still further, H.P.B. .·. gave me in 1889 the Master's picture, on which he put this message: "To my dear and loyal colleague, W. Q. Judge."

Now, then, either I am bringing you a true message from the Master, or the whole T.S. and E.S.T. is a lie, in the ruins of which must be buried the names of H.P.B. .·. and the Masters. All these stand together or they fall together. Let it be proved that H.P.B. .·. is a liar and a fraud, and I will abandon the T.S. and all its belongings; but until so proved I will remain where I was put. Lastly, as final proof of the delusions worked through this man and his friends I will mention this: Many years ago (in 1881) the Masters sent to the Allahabad Brahmins (the Prayag T.S.) a letter which was delivered by H.P.B. .·. to Mr. A. P. Sinnett, who handed a copy over to them, keeping the original. It dealt very plainly with the Brahmans. This letter the Brahmans do not like, and Mr. Chakravarti tried to make me think it was a pious fraud by H.P.B. .·. He succeeded with Mrs. Besant in this, so that since she met him she has on various occasions said she thought it was a fraud by H.P.B. .·., made up entirely, and not

> from the Master. . . . Only delusion would make Mrs. Besant take this position; deliberate intention makes the others do it. It is an issue that may not be evaded, for if that letter be a fraud then all the rest sent through our old teacher, . . . are the same. I shall rest on that issue; we all rest on it.
>
> Mrs. Besant was then made to agree with these people under the delusion that it was approved by the Masters. She regarded herself as their servant. It was against the E.S.T. rules. When the rule is broken it is one's duty to leave the E.S.T. . . . Mrs. Besant was put in such a frightful position that while she was writing me most kindly and working with me she was all the time thinking that I was a forger and that I had blasphemed the Master. She was made to conceal from me, when here, her thoughts about the intended charges. . . . Not until the time was ripe did she tell me, in her letter in January [1894] from India, asking me to resign from the E.S.T. and the T.S. offices, saying that if I did and would confess guilt all would be forgiven and everyone would work with me as usual. . . . She was induced to believe that the Master was endorsing the persecution, that he was ordering her to do what she did. . . .
>
> In all this Chakravarti was her guide, with others. . . .[2]
>
> We are all therefore face to face with the question whether we will abide by Masters and their Messenger on the one hand, or by the disrupting forces that stand on the other, willing to destroy our great mission if we will but give them the opportunity.

It seems to us that in all the foregoing Mr. Judge was endeavoring to do by the E.S.T. what, in his circular

[2] During this same period—1893-5—Mrs. Besant had joined Mr. Sinnett's *coterie* and was also receiving "messages" through Mr. Leadbeater, at the time Mr. Sinnett's "psychic."

of March 15, 1894, he endeavored to do by the members of the T.S.: To strip the difficulties to their abstract root and show the real issues at stake. Two views prevailed in the Society at large and in the E.S.T. with regard to Theosophy, to Masters, and to their Messenger. The view held out by H.P.B. and consistently maintained by her and by Mr. Judge was that *Theosophy* is a body of Knowledge, "ancient, constant and eternal," as the "Bhagavad-Gita" has it, not subject to change, not an "evolving system of thought"; Masters the Custodians of that Knowledge, and H.P.B. their direct Agent in the world, the Society, and the E.S.T. On this basis and the simple proposition of *falsus in uno, falsus in omnibus,* Theosophy, H.P.B. and Masters, together with all those who accept that view, stand or fall together. This is the view argued at length by H.P.B. in the extract given in the last chapter, culminating in the proposition that if a single one of her "messages" were found false, if Masters were found winking at a single fraud perpetrated by her in their name, she and they were capable of unlimited repetitions of the same fraud. Her formal documents in regard to Mr. Judge—in the Coues case, in the *Second Preliminary Memorandum,* in that of December 14, 1888, of October 23, 1889, in her *Notice* of August 9, 1890, in her first and last Letters to the Conventions of the American Section for 1888 and 1891—not to speak of numerous private letters to "doubting Thomases" and loyal students, all establish one and the same fact: that she held out Mr. Judge to the students in the same light that the Masters held her out, her authorized Agent and "direct representative," as she was that of the Masters. And that this was originally the view of Mrs. Besant, both in respect to H.P.B. and Mr. Judge, has been abundantly shown; the first by her article in *Lucifer* for December, 1890, "H.P.B. and the Theosophical Society" and her article in *Lucifer* for October, 1891, "Theosophy and Christianity"; the second in her signature to the Minutes of the E.S. Meeting of May 27, 1891, and, *after* the "Judge case," by her signature to the circular of July

18, and August 1, 1894, not to speak of her repeated statements publicly in *Lucifer*.

Those who espoused the opposing view believed in Masters, in many shades of belief and understanding; in the Theosophical Society as the vehicle of Their work; in H.P.B. as a human instrument of Their teaching, medium, psychic, chela of some degree or another, sometimes speaking on Their account and sometimes on her own, her writings therefore to be dissected and divided by each according to his judgment, as hers or her Masters; therefore in her Theosophy as being no different or other than their own—her understanding and interpretation to be accepted or rejected, improved and extended, as each might esteem himself capable and persuade others to the like opinion. They saw no incongruity in consulting other mediums, or in developing mediumship and psychism in themselves along any lines that seemed profitable; in according the messages thus received the same treatment of acceptance or rejection, in whole or in part, as they accorded to H.P.B. and to each other. Thus Col. Olcott, Mr. Sinnett, Mr. Bertram Keightley, Mabel Collins, Mr. Walter R. Old, and many others, and finally Mrs. Besant, accepted some of the messages and writings of H.P.B. as genuine, others as fraudulent; the same with the messages of Mr. Judge; ultimately the same with each other,—for in 1907 Mr. Sinnett, Mr. Mead, Mr. Bertram Keightley, and others who were her firm allies in 1894-5, broke with Mrs. Besant over the famous "Adyar manifestations" at the period of the death of Col. Olcott. Mr. Sinnett who regarded highly the "clairvoyance" of Mr. Leadbeater in 1895, ceased to have any respect for Mr. Leadbeater's "occult" powers when the latter took a tangent of "revelations" which opposed and obscured Mr. Sinnett's own coruscations. Colonel Olcott, who took Mrs. Besant to be the promised substitute for H.P.B., came to disbelieve in her spiritual powers, almost to disbelieve in her ordinary integrity, as was well known to many in the years before his death. Mr. Leadbeater, whom Col. Olcott thought to be the most brilliant star in the Occult hierarchy, broke the Colonel's heart by his frank admission before the London Committee of 1906 of teaching nameless practices to young boys as a cure for "evil thought-forms." Mrs. Besant, who from 1893 till 1906, was a firm believer in the powers of Chakravarti and his connection with the Masters, and to whom she looked for the "messages" that should guide her conduct, came at last to believe that Chakravarti was under "dark influences," and substituted Mr. Leadbeater as her "occult" mentor.[3] All these persons, joined together under a common influence, were determined in 1894-5 to "purify the Society" by the destruction of the reputation and influence of Mr. Judge. But in their subsequent careers they took tangential paths. Of all the coterie of 1894-5, only one, Mr. Bertram Keightley, still follows the faded Theosophical star of Chakravarti. In private, and to various persons, both Col. Olcott and Mrs. Besant repeatedly admitted that they had wronged Mr. Judge, that their course in 1894-5 was a mistaken course, but —such are the karmic consequences of infidelity to the pledges of Occultism—they were never able to regain the stamina and sense of honor to publicly admit their folly, and thus undo as best they could the evil they had unconsciously made themselves the tools and instruments of. For the one, there must be much of extenuation as well as charity; for the other—there can be only charity. But it is owing today, as it was in 1893-5, that the truth should be made known without fear or favor, as without malice, that those whose only demerit is ignorance and whose only fault reliance upon authority, may choose their path in knowledge of the opposing issues and the parts played by the respective proponents of the two mutually irreconcilable views of the Theosophical Movement, which includes all, the false as the true, the foolish as the wise, in its mighty stream.

[3] See the various articles in *The Theosophist*, March-September, 1907, immediately following the death of Col. Olcott. The unnamed competitor of Mrs. Besant for Col. Olcott's nomination for President after his death was Bertram Keightley, Chakravarti's staunch supporter.

Mr. Judge closed his circular of November 3, 1894, with the following:

> E.S.T. Order
>
> I now proceed a step further than the E.S.T. decisions of 1894,[4] and solely for the good of the E.S.T., I resume in the E.S.T. in full all the functions and powers given to me by H.P.B. .·. and that came to me by orderly succession after her passing from this life, and declare myself the sole head of the E.S.T. ∴. Hence, under the authority given me by the Master and H.P.B. .·., and under the Master's direction, I declare Mrs. Annie Besant's headship in the E.S.T. at an end.

A notice of this E.S.T. Order was at once cabled to Mrs. Besant in Australia, where she then was; and a copy of the entire circular was forwarded to her at Colombo, Ceylon, where she arrived on December 18, 1894, *en route* to attend the Adyar Convention scheduled for the holidays as usual. Immediately Mrs. Besant drew up a counter-circular which, dated Colombo, December 19, was as quickly as possible sent out under a London imprint, to all members of the E.S.T. After a preliminary paragraph devoted to explanations of her delay in sending out her statement, she makes the following comments:

> I do not know if the statements as to Mr. Judge's part in the foundation of the E.S.T. are or are not true. H.P.B. never mentioned to me the alleged facts, except the one that Mr. Judge had not taken the ordinary pledge, he being already pledged.

This statement can scarcely be taken as other than a convenient hiatus of memory on Mrs. Besant's part,

[4] This was a typographical error in the original circular. The date should be 1891, as the reference is to the Avenue Road meeting on May 27 of that year, following the death of H.P.B.

seeing that it was herself who read at the Council Meeting of May 27, 1891, the bundle of documents establishing the veracity of Mr. Judge's statements. Mrs. Besant goes on to discuss her own status at the time of the departure of H.P.B., the status of the Inner Group, and Mr. Judge's participation in the meeting of May 27, 1891. Thus:

> . . . H.P.B. did, when I left her [to go to America to attend the Convention at the end of April, 1891], give me a sealed statement, constituting me Chief Secretary of the I. G. and Recorder of the teachings. She also wrote to Mr. Judge stating that I was her "Successor," when she had to leave us, and Mr. Judge read that extract to our little group at Avenue Road when he came over after her death, as constituting—with her statements to himself—the basis for the future arrangements. . . . Ere leaving for America I asked her if I might discuss the I. G. Instructions with Mr. Judge; she answered: No, not unless he took the pledge. When he came to London after her death I told him this, and the first of the spurious "messages" was the assent to his question if he might enter the I. G. without taking the pledge. It seemed to all of us natural and right that he should come in, and we joyfully welcomed him.

If the reader will turn to the extracts, given in Chapter XIX of this History, from the Official Minutes of the Avenue Road meeting of May 27, 1891, to which Mrs. Besant refers above, he will find that it was not a meeting of the Inner Group, but of the Advisory Council, English and American, although the members of the Inner Group were all members of that Council. The opening words of those Minutes recited:

> A full meeting of the Council, as appointed by H.P.B., was held at the Headquarters of the Theosophical Society in Europe, 19, Avenue

> Road, London, England, on May 27, 1891. The American Councillors were represented by Bro. William Q. Judge, with full power, and *Bro. Judge attended as the representative of H.P.B. under a general power given as below.*

The "general power" mentioned was the document of December 14, 1888, which is reproduced in full in the Minutes.

Further, referring both to the various documents mentioned as well as to H.P.B.'s letter to Mr. Judge about Mrs. Besant, of which she speaks, as "stating that I [Mrs. Besant] was her 'Successor,' " the Minutes say "which *we now here* have read,"—not, as Mrs. Besant puts it, "*Mr. Judge* read that extract *to our little group* at Avenue Road." It was *after every Councillor* had read those documents and that letter that the Minutes were drawn up, giving to *Mr. Judge, not Mrs. Besant,* the status of "*the representative of H.P.B.*" The status accorded Mrs. Besant, on the documents and letter, was Chief *Secretary* and *Recorder* of the teachings of H.P.B. to the Inner Group. Those Minutes were signed by every Councillor without exception, Mrs. Besant included.

This circular of Mrs. Besant's, written *after* Mr. Judge's action in terminating her Co-Headship of the E.S.T., is the origin of her claim to be the "Successor" appointed by H.P.B. She had either to accept the action of Mr. Judge or reject it; she chose the latter course and the Successor claim was her foundation. If the letter of H.P.B. to Judge, dated March 27, 1891, meant what Mrs. Besant claimed it meant, it stands to reason that she would have broadcasted the text of that letter, *of which she had a copy.* She never did so, and the presumption must stand heavily against her on that account alone, quite apart from H.P.B.'s known position on the subject of "apostolic succession" and the position taken by herself at the time of the Foulkes' claim to be H.P.B.'s Successor. Moreover, as often happens in cases of concerted action on an insecure basis, one of the "partners" in the "case against W. Q. Judge" went too far for safety in her zeal. Early in 1895 Countess Wachtmeister put out a pamphlet in support of Mrs. Besant, entitled "H.P.B. and the Present Crisis in the Theosophical Society." On p. 4 of that pamphlet she gives—correctly—the particular extract from H.P.B.'s letter to Mr. Judge covering the "Successor" myth, as follows:

> Judge, *she is a most wonderful woman,* my right hand, my successor, when I will be forced to leave you, my sole hope in England, as you are my sole hope in America.

With all of this, every one familiar with Mrs. Besant's career and the situation in the Theosophical world in 1891, must entirely agree, as did Judge. Did H.P.B. mean Successor in the sense which Mrs. Besant claimed and claims—*apostolic* succession?

It so happens that H.P.B. refers to the same subject, to the same conditions, and uses the very same terms, in closing section of "The Key to Theosophy"—to mention a specific instance—and she there says regarding "the future of the Theosophical Society," in reply to a postulated question:

> I spoke rather of the great need which our successors in the guidance of the Society will have of unbiassed and clear judgment.

It will be noted that both in Countess Wachtmeister's textual copy from the letter, and in the above quotation from the "Key," H.P.B. spelled the word with a small letter, not with a capital "S" as Mrs. Besant puts it in her circular—a telltale change indeed.

We have gone thus fully into Mrs. Besant's claim of being the "Successor" of H.P.B., because her Theosophical prestige before the world, now as then, rests exoterically on the fact of her being the "most wonderful woman" that H.P.B. called her, and esoterically on her claim to be the Successor of the Messenger of the nineteenth century. To any *student* of the teachings of H.P.B., the mere fact that any one should claim to be her "Successor" is evidence merely of the delusion, the ignorance, or the guile of the one making such a claim.

Mrs. Besant, in the paragraph last quoted from her circular of December 19, 1894, presents another of those curious idiosyncrasies of character and inconsistencies of conduct with which her career abounds. She says: "Ere leaving for America I asked her (H.P.B.) if I might discuss the I. G. Instructions with Mr. Judge; she answered: 'No, not unless he took the I. G. pledge.'" Yet in literally the next breath she says: "When he came to London after her death *I told him this,* and the first of the spurious 'messages' was the *assent* to his question if he might enter the I. G. *without* taking the pledge. *It seemed to all of us natural and right that he should come in, and we joyfully welcomed him.*" Now, if she had *instructions* from H.P.B. *not* to admit Mr. Judge without his taking the pledge, what kind of a Successor was she to admit him pledge-free? Or, if she was a genuine Successor how came it that she violated her "Instructions" and admitted him on the strength of a *spurious* "message"? What is the "Occult" nature of that Successor who by her own confession is unable to tell a "spurious" from a genuine message from the Masters? Or violates the Instructions received?

Mrs. Besant's circular goes on to say:

> The "plot," *so far as I know,* is the purest delusion. What is said of Mr. Chakravarti I *know* to be false, and I can but feel the profoundest pity and sorrow for him who uses the holy name of the Master to cover such a charge.

We have inserted italics above, because we do not doubt that Mrs. Besant spoke truly in saying "so far as I know." And although she claimed to "know" that what was said of Chakravarti was "false," she has many times, since 1906, said the same thing of Chakravarti herself that Judge wrote in 1894. Was Mrs. Besant right then and wrong since 1906, or vice versa, on the nature of the "influences" exerted through Mr. Chakravarti?

Mrs. Besant states, with reference to Mr. Judge's E.S.T. Order":

> The "E.S.T. Order" . . . I reject. I shall pursue my work quietly, with such of the Council left by H.P.B. as think it right to work with me. Mr. Judge thinks it right to rend the School in twain, and I can only go on steadily as I have learned. We have come to the parting of the ways. I recognize no authority in Mr. Judge. Not from his hands did I receive my work; not into his hands may I surrender it.
>
> And now, brothers and sisters, you must choose your road, grievous as the choice must be to you. Mr. Judge casts me aside, breaks the last tie between us that remained.

It seems not even remotely to have suggested itself to Mrs. Besant that it was her own actions, not those of Judge, that had "rent the School in twain"; that it was herself who had "broken the last tie which remained." How she "pursued her work," is now to be witnessed.

CHAPTER XXXIII

MRS. BESANT TRIES TO DRIVE JUDGE OUT OF THE SOCIETY

> I SHALL pursue my work quietly, with such as think it right to work with me—I can only go on steadily as I have learned—to you who will stand where H.P.B. left us together and work with me, I have also a word to say: Remember the ancient rule: "Hatred ceaseth not by hatred; hatred ceaseth by love." Follow peace and charity; attack none; blame none; impute no evil motives; cast not back reproaches.

Thus wrote Mrs. Besant on December 19, 1894, at the conclusion of her circular announcing her rejection of the Order of Mr. Judge dated November 3, in the E.S.T., and her pronouncement: "I recognize no authority in Mr. Judge." This was her declaration of policy, her adjuration to all those who might believe in her protestations. We have but to follow in epitome her conduct for the ensuing six months under this self-proclaimed standard of action for herself and those who might trust to her guidance, to learn by the test of her actions, the measure of her good faith.

Immediately she took ship for India to attend the two Conventions—the customary "Anniversary Meeting" and the regular annual session of the Indian Section, to both of which she was a delegate from the European Section. *En route* she prepared a fresh Statement of more than five newspaper columns, which she entitled "The Theosophical Society and *The Westminster Gazette.*" This she dated December 23, 1894, and, immediately on arriving at Adyar, gave it to the *Madras Mail* for publication, sending, at the same time, a copy to London for publication in the *Daily Chronicle*. This article is filled with self-extenuations and self-defense against the gibes and jeers leveled at her in the *Westminster Gazette* series; with invective and charges against Mr. Judge, supported by the most astonishing misstatements of facts as formerly solemnly attested by herself—misstatements resting entirely upon her *ipse dixit,* and unaccompanied by a single verifiable reference as to their truth.

Quite naturally the propaganda which had been steadily carried on in India by Col. Olcott, Mr. Bertram Keightley, Countess Wachtmeister, and Miss Müller, all under cover and all unopposed, had aroused the certainty that extraordinary happenings were scheduled for the Conventions. This drew a very large attendance of visitors as well as delegates. The publication in the *Madras Mail* could but accentuate the excitement and serve to pave the way for what was to follow.

Colonel Olcott's Presidential Address, aside from its usual statistics and the necessary accompanying explanatory matter, was almost entirely devoted to the recrudescent "Judge case." It shows plainly that the President-Founder, in full accord with Mrs. Besant and the rest, had determined to force Judge out of office and out of the Society even at hazards which had been counted and discounted—the withdrawal from the Society of a great portion of its membership. As his own words expressed it:

> I have had it intimated that if Mr. Judge should be forced to resign, the American Section will secede in a body, form an American Theosophical Society independently, and elect him President. And I should not be surprised if a large number of excellent people in the European Section should unite with the Americans in the event of a split.

The recent London Enquiry was called an "unavoidable failure," even while admitting that "both the General Council and Judicial Committee voted to quash the proceedings against the accused on a point which, although technical was nevertheless irrefutable."

The President-Founder went on to say:

> As we cannot legally try Mr. Judge, Vice-President, for alleged misdemeanors committed by W. Q. Judge, individual; and as the individual cannot be tried for his private opinions, we have to fall back upon the moral aspect of the case.

There being no "case against Judge" either as officer or individual under the Constitution and Rules of the Society, some other scheme had to be conjured up in order to oust him, and the "moral aspect of the case" as interpreted by Col. Olcott, was of necessity the device adopted to force the issue. That moral aspect, Col. Olcott argues, requires Mr. Judge to resign because he has been accused, and he proceeds to cite as "precedents" among others, the resignation by Madame Blavatsky in 1885, and his own resignation in 1892. He does not remind his audience that H.P.B.'s resignation, as she herself wrote Col. Olcott on April 11, 1885, was due to the cowardly desertion of her by Col. Olcott and his Council and Convention at the time of the Coulomb-*Christian College Magazine* accusations against her, and not at all because of the accusations. Nor does it occur to him now, any more than when he tendered his own resignation in 1892, that for an official to resign under the fire of charges by his associates is uniformly properly construed as either a confession of guilt or a lamentable exhibition of moral cowardice.

The President-Founder takes it for granted that Mr. Judge is guilty of the offenses charged but, as faced him in the case of H.P.B. herself, is under the necessity of finding some way to reconcile his view with the known and lifelong devotion and work of Mr. Judge in the Theosophical cause. How could Mr. Judge both be "guilty" and yet be free from "guilty knowledge and intent," from "moral responsibility"? His answer is, "mediumship or psychism"; a medium or psychic "is often irresistibly impelled by an extraneous force to do acts of turpitude of which he is incapable in his normal state of consciousness." This perfectly true and well-known fact, it is argued, will account for Mr. Judge's "wrongdoing," and either permit or compel his resignation without the imputation of actual criminality. He proceeds:

> At this moment, I have knowledge of at least seven different psychics in our Society who believe themselves to be in communication with the same Mahatmas and doing their work, who have each a knot of disciples or adherents about them, and whose supposed teachers give orders which conflict with each others'!

What Col. Olcott does not state is that among these "seven psychics" were Chakravarti, Countess Wachtmeister, Mr. Old, Mr. Sinnett's "sensitive" Mr. Leadbeater, all leagued in the cabal against Mr. Judge, nor that the "messages" that Mrs. Besant, Mr. Sinnett, and himself had been receiving from the "Masters," coming "through" these various "psychics," were the real foundation of the whole attack—not any mundane "proof." Nor does he trouble to explain why, all being "mediums and psychics" alike, it was Mr. Judge alone who must be driven into outer darkness.

Near the close of his Address Col. Olcott makes a remarkable admission, the possible bearings of which seem never to have occurred to him. He says:

> My objective intercourse with the Great Teachers ceased almost entirely on the death of H.P.B., while any subjective relations I may have with them is evidence only to myself and would carry no weight with third parties.

If his "objective intercourse with the Great Teachers" had "ceased almost entirely with the death of H.P.B.," *why was this the case?* Mere death or mere physical distance forms no barrier whatever to "objective intercourse" between an *accepted* chela and those in the same or a higher class than himself, nor is *any* intermediary necessary. These words of Col. Olcott's are an unconscious confession of a number of tremendous facts: that he was never himself an *accepted* chela; that he had to depend on H.P.B. or *some one else* for "objective intercourse"; that not being even an accepted chela himself, he had no means of *knowing* such a chela even if encountered, and no means of *knowing* whether any "communication," objective or subjective, was genuinely from its professed source; that he had to depend on "third parties" and mere externalities both for his "messages" and his means of verification. Certainly it never occurred to him that he *might* have "guessed wrong" once more, that Mr. Judge *might* be what H.P.B. said he was in 1888, "a chela of thirteen years' standing," and what the Master himself called Mr. Judge, "my dear Colleague"; never occurred to him that it *might* be his own attitude that cut him off from H.P.B. dead, from Mr. Judge and the Masters living, and thus compelled him to have recourse, as Mr. Sinnett and Mrs. Besant had, to more facile and pliant "psychics."

If these things never occurred to Col. Olcott, Mrs. Besant, Mr. Sinnett, Mr. Bertram Keightley, Chakravarti, Mr. Old, the Countess Wachtmeister, and other leaders and respected Heads in the Society, how should they have occurred to the great mass of sincere and trusting members who looked up to them as disciples who had been near to H.P.B. and who had been favored with "messages from the Masters"?

As soon as Col. Olcott had concluded his Address and the other formal matters were out of the way, Mrs. Besant rose and presented a long Preamble and Resolution, which was seconded by Mr. Bertram Keightley, as follows:

> Seeing that a series of articles has appeared in the *Westminster Gazette*, London, containing charges of deception and fraud against Mr. W. Q. Judge, now Vice-President of the Theosophical Society; and

> Seeing that a strong body of evidence has been brought forward against the accused, and seeing that the attempt by the Society to bring the matter to an issue last July was defeated by Mr. W. Q. Judge on a purely technical objection to the jurisdiction of the committee; and
>
> Seeing that Mr. Judge, being Vice-President of the whole Society, has issued a quasi-privately-circulated attack against one Section thereof, thus stirring up ill-feeling within the Society, and endeavouring to set the West against the East, contrary to the first object of the Society generally, and to the second object specifically; and
>
> Seeing that this is the first occasion since July on which a representative body of Theosophists has been gathered together; and
>
> Seeing that immemorial custom requires of every honourable man holding a representative office in any Society to at once tender his resignation under such circumstances as are stated above;
>
> Therefore the anniversary meeting of the Theosophical Society
>
> Resolves; That the President-Founder be and is hereby requested to at once call upon Mr. W. Q. Judge, Vice-President, Theosophical Society, to resign the office of Vice-President; it being of course open to Mr. Judge if he so wishes, to submit himself for re-election, so that the Society may pass its judgment on his positions.

It would, we think, be difficult to measure the shameless effrontery of these Preambles and Resolutions, the subterfuges employed in their declarations and wording. What were the recorded facts thus dressed to play their several parts in the grim travesty of justice for which the stage had been so sedulously prepared?

As shown by the "Neutrality" pamphlet officially issued under Col. Olcott's direction, the facts were:

(I) That both the General Council and the Judicial Committee, a majority of each in sympathy with the *accusers,* had none the less felt constrained to vote that neither the Society as such, its Council or its Judicial Committee, had any occasion to "investigate" the charges made against Mr. Judge either as Vice-President or as individual member of the Society—and they had done this at Col. Olcott's express plea; Mr. Judge had merely pointed out to them their own Rules and Constitution. Caught in their own toils, they had to avowedly break their own loudly proclaimed devotion to the "Constitution and Rules" in order to "get at" Mr. Judge, or else beat a retreat to "save their own face." They chose the latter and to mask their discomfiture essayed the scheme of a "Jury of Honour," packed as the Committee had been. Detected and put to the shame of another defeat, they had proposed the Convention of the European Section as the jury, which Mr. Judge had at once accepted.

(II) The "strong body of evidence" published by the *Westminster Gazette* was none other than an exact duplicate of the "evidence" prepared by Mrs. Besant for the London Enquiry, plus Mr. Garrett's hostile and biting interpretations and applications from it against all concerned. Every member of the General Council and of the Judicial Committee saw and read that "evidence" before voting, Mr. Judge alone being refused more than an oral inspection during the Enquiry. The Council and Committee both voted not to include the "evidence" in the "Neutrality" Report, the iniquitous nature of such a proceeding being too much for the moral stomachs even of some of the most partisan.

(III) Mr. Judge was never at any time *elected* Vice-President of the Society; he was "appointed" by Col. Olcott in the arbitrary exercise of his "discretionary powers," and simply accepted the situation *status quo* as there were no functions to fulfill so long as Col. Olcott remained President, and when the latter "resigned" in 1892, Mr. Judge was *elected President by the unanimous vote of all the Sections;* this office he not only never claimed, but actually was the active agent in procuring the withdrawal by the Colonel of the tendered resignation. The "Neutrality" Report shows that Mr. Judge pointed out that he was never anything but *de facto* Vice-President, and this point was admittedly correct, if *de jure* meant *elected* Vice-President. Furthermore, it was Mr. Judge who pointed out the anomalous situation arising from the fact that he was himself the *duly elected* President and that this should be formally rescinded by the General Council in order to make *de jure* as well as *de facto* the *Presidency of Col. Olcott,* which was done. What the "Neutrality" Report did *not* take occasion to show was the fact, interesting and valuable at this point, that the only *elective* offices held by Mr. Judge in the Society were those of President of the Aryan Lodge at New York City, and General Secretary of the American Section from its organization, to both of which offices he was *unanimously re-elected after* the charges were made by Mrs. Besant, *after* the "suspension" of his office of Vice-President by Col. Olcott. Colonel Olcott knew that he had at any moment the same identical power to "remove" Mr. Judge from the Vice-Presidency that he had to "appoint" him in the first place, or to "suspend" him. What other inference can be drawn from these facts alone but that his persecutors were determined to ruin the reputation of Mr. Judge, destroy his influence, and drive him into an exile of disgrace?

(IV) Mr. Judge's circular to the E.S.T. of November 3, 1894, referred to in the "Preambles" as a "quasi-privately-circulated attack against one Section thereof, thus stirring up ill-feeling within the Society, and endeavoring to set the West against the East,"—this circular was issued neither as an Officer of the T. S. nor as a Fellow of the Society, but as Head of the E.S.T. to its members,—a body having "no connection whatever with the T.S." One has but to read the extracts given from Judge's circular to see in any event, how grossly his remarks have been twisted to arouse the Hindus to the pitch needed. The lugging in of fresh charges—the violation of "the first object of the T.S. generally, and the second object specifically,"—is manifestly mere Jesuitry: *For, if true, it constituted an offense actually triable before a Judicial Committee under the Constitution and Rules then in force, a crime by Mr. Judge both as Officer and as Fellow, and it was the plain duty of the President-Founder to proceed without delay to the necessary legal and official steps.* But the Resolution offered, the debate that ensued, the Resolution the next day of the Indian Section, and all the rest of the relentless course followed, alike showed that these fresh charges were made only for effect and to throw dust in the eyes of the membership.

In arguing her motion to adopt these Preambles and Resolutions, Mrs. Besant made a speech that fills over ten pages of fine type in the Report of the Convention's proceedings. There was the same covering of fine phrases about "duty," "charity," "forgiveness," etc., as in the quotations from her Colombo circular with which this chapter begins; the same assertions as in the *Madras Mail* article, without an iota of verifiable references to establish her statements. She characterizes Judge's action as "dishonourable," but in kindness admits that Mr. Judge, being a "medium" may have been guilty of merely "unconscious fraud." "Mediumship," urges Mrs. Besant, "is an excuse for the individual against moral judgment. It is no excuse for an official who under mediumship commits acts of moral turpitude." The speech is a classic example of special pleading.

Following Mrs. Besant, Mr. Bertram Keightley, Captain Banon, Miss Müller, S. Subramanier, Dr. Hubbe-Schleiden, E. M. Sasseville, a pseudo-representative of the American Section, C. V. Naidu, the Countess Wachtmeister, V. C. Seshacharry, and Col. Olcott made speeches, all strongly laudatory of Mrs. Besant and condemnatory of Mr. Judge. Some were for "expelling" Mr. Judge forthwith by Resolutions requesting the President-Founder to take that action without delay; which gave excellent opportunity for remarks on "fairness," "tolerance," "justice," etc.

Of all the remarkable speeches of that remarkable day

none excelled the statement of Miss Müller. As both Col. Olcott and Mrs. Besant sat silent during and after her remarks, and as no protest was raised by anyone, it must be inferred that all shared in the responsibility for them and were accessories to the stupendous moral iniquity of Miss Müller's declarations. For it will be remembered that Miss Müller was party—and very much party—to the charges of "grave immorality" against Col. Olcott in the autumn of 1891; charges which were brought *by* Mrs. Besant *to* Mr. Judge, as has been narrated.[1] The spirit of the meeting may be well instanced by quoting some of Miss Müller's remarks. She said:

> Were I to expend the utmost eloquence that I can command, and bring before you the details of the most damning facts which can be brought against Mr. Judge, I could not bring against him a more final and conclusive charge than has been brought by Mrs. Besant in the speech that she has made. I am not concerned to give you further information about him, for you have the fullest information. But I am concerned to say that it is for us members now to take a stand which we have never before taken in the Society. We are tired and we will no more have the policy of condoning what is wrong. We are tired and we will have no more of the policy of compromising with liars, and with those who are publicly accused and almost proved to be forgers and swindlers and vulgar impostors. We shall not have these men as leaders of the Society; rather we shall have the Society come to an end. . . . Mrs. Besant has brought the charges against her colleague and friend, for whom I know she feels so great a tenderness, that she cannot press home against him that justice which time demands that we shall press home. . . . So it is not for her, but it is for us to do all that is required. . . . We have got to do our

[1] See Chapters XXI and XXII.

duty before the world, however disagreeable it may seem to the Theosophical Society. This is the first opportunity we have had of expressing an opinion upon Mr. Judge. . . . Mrs. Besant brought charges against Mr. Judge in regard to his conduct, during the time of the Convention in July last year. These articles in the *Westminster Gazette* prove to the hilt to anybody that he is a fraud and a deceiver and a common impostor; and finally there is this beautiful specimen of his cleverness and villainies, this breaking of his most solemn pledge to those very Masters whose names he so shamefully attacks. We have had once before a specimen of this of Mr. Judge. Do we not remember that at the time of my first visit, in 1891 or 1892, Mr. Judge brought some very serious charges against Col. Olcott? Practically, he said to him "You are President. You turn out: we won't have you any more." Why? "Because I want to step into your shoes." He did not succeed in that. Still, like a bad man and a foolish man, to-day he comes with a repetition of the same things. He tells Mrs. Besant "You turn out." Why? "Because I want to step into your shoes." If he is determined, if he is clever and strong enough to defeat us, it will only be at the cost of breaking up the Society. Why do we want him to be expelled? Not because we are antagonistic to him and against him, but because his stay any more in office means, not only the future fall of the Society from being what it might become—a centre of light, a means of radiating truth, a means of leading the members to spiritual life. If he is kept any more the Society will become exactly the opposite. The various societies will become badges of black magic. For averting a terrible danger to the Society, it is for us to speak strongly on this occasion, with no uncertain voice.

By such appeals the delegates were prepared for the vote. During the entire session, it will be noted, there was no voice raised in question of the un-Theosophical and inhuman methods employed; no demand for the production of proof, no opposition to the utter unconstitutionality of the whole trumped-up procedure, no call for an orderly and equitable hearing. The numerous letters, protests, memorials, and resolutions in defense or support of fair treatment of Mr. Judge, which both Col. Olcott's Address and Mrs. Besant's speech indicated had been received, were suppressed and not one word of their contents placed before the Convention. All took it for granted that the accused,—with such accusers,—must be guilty, and when the President-Founder put the resolutions to vote, they were adopted without a dissenting voice. On the next day the Convention of the Indian Section was held and there a further set of resolutions, moved by Tookaram Tatya and seconded by A. Nilakata Shastri, were unanimously adopted. These provided (1) that the President-Founder be requested to call upon Mr. Judge to resign; (2) that the President-Founder be requested to call on Mr. Judge "to make a full and satisfactory reply to the charges against him within six months from January 1, 1895"; and (3) "failing such answer, to take such steps as may be necessary for his expulsion from the Theosophical Society."

The hue and cry was on. The Report of the Convention was sent out as a "Supplement" to *The Theosophist* and to all Branches and Lodges throughout the world. It contained the full text of the various speeches. The speeches of Mrs. Besant and Mr. Bertram Keightley, and Mrs. Besant's article in the *Madras Mail* were at once issued in pamphlet form and copies of each pamphlet sent out to all members of the Theosophical Society.

Immediately after the adjournment of the Conventions Mrs. Besant started on a tour of India and the scenes of the former year were largely repeated. The trustful Hindus, looking to Col. Olcott and her as the guardian and savior of the Society, knowing nothing of the Movement in the West save as its reflections reached them *via* the double refraction afforded by the Eastern heredity in general and the distorted versions given them, showed the utmost loyalty and devotion to what they conceived to be the true course. The Australasian Section was in very much the same state. Newly organized by Mrs. Besant under the Presidential *carte blanche* already detailed, knowing of the Society and the Movement only by way of London and India, impressed with the ability, energy, and fervor of Mrs. Besant, it was wholly natural that this Section should, as she had implied in her speech to the late Convention at Adyar, be influenced to follow her course, whatever it might be. Mr. J. C. Staples of England, friend both of Mrs. Besant and Col. Olcott, had, under her suggestion, been appointed General Secretary of the newly forming Section. Mr. Staples had come out to the Orient and had been present at the Adyar Conventions. From there he had gone direct to Sydney to undertake his new duties. Thus out of the four Sections of the Society it was certain that two of them were dependable in the effort to ostracize Mr. Judge. The only battle-ground was the American and the European Section, and the alliance had been by no means idle there, merely because Col. Olcott and Mrs. Besant had been away ever since the London Enquiry.

Mrs. Besant's speech indicated some of the steps already taken during her absence but under her generalship. Mr. Mead had sent out, as General Secretary of the European Section, a circular to Lodge Officers and other influential members, asking them to signify if they "approved of Mr. Judge being called upon to make explanation. Out of the 80 circulars sent out, 65 answers have been returned. These 65 unanimously demand that explanation should be made."

After the formal declaration of "war to the knife and the knife to the hilt" at the Adyar Conventions, the two chief allies were busy with the Indian tour and the preparation and forwarding of plans to bring the fray to a conclusion in England at the July, 1895, Convention of the European Section. The first public intimation of the plan of final battle is contained in the "Supplement" to *The Theosophist* for March, 1895, in a "Special Editorial Notice" signed with Col. Olcott's initials. He says:

> The presence of the undersigned in his official capacity being again indispensable in London, for the final settlement of the Judge case and the intersectional frictions which have grown out of it, his intention is to sail early in May.

The explanation for this declaration does not become public until a month later when, in the "Supplement" to *The Theosophist* for April, 1895, Col. Olcott publishes after long delay the text of two letters, the one formally addressed to him as President-Founder by Mrs. Besant and dated January 20; the other his reply, equally formal, dated a month later, February 21. In her letter Mrs. Besant requests Col. Olcott to again place in her hands "the documents on which were based the charges preferred by me last July against Mr. W. Q. Judge." Mrs. Besant's letter discloses that:

> A proposal has been made to call a Special Convention of the European Section T.S. on my return to Europe, for the purpose of discussing the attitude to be taken by the Section towards this case, and there is a general demand for the production of these papers for the information and guidance of Members.

In his reply, he says that he has kept the papers "under lock and key" since "the abortive meeting" of the Judicial Committee, as he "considered it improper to give them publicity unless new and imperative contingencies should arise." The new and imperative contingencies having been satisfactorily produced through the joint efforts of Mr. Old, Mrs. Besant, and himself, Col. Olcott proceeds to advise Mrs. Besant:

> Such is now the fact; and as it is evident that the case can never be equitably settled without the circulation of these papers, . . . before

> you sail, I shall confide the documents to your custody once more. . . .

A very significant admission of Col. Olcott's in his letter to Mrs. Besant is found in his statement: "Mr. Judge complains that he was not permitted to see them." He therefore imposes on Mrs. Besant the conditions that she shall, in addition to placing copies of the papers in the hands of the General Secretary of the European Section (Mr. G. R. S. Mead) "for distribution to Branches and Members," see that he also supplies "a certified copy of the evidence to Mr. Judge for his information and use."

In the course of the long controversy Mrs. Besant repeatedly stated, the last time in April, 1895, that she had *in the beginning* furnished Mr. Judge with the "documents" in the case, so that he might know what the exact charges against him were, and their supporting documentary evidence, and might have an opportunity both to verify the one and know what he was to defend himself against in the other. Mr. Judge had repeatedly stated that he did not have this necessary information, and there was, therefore, a point-blank contradiction. Colonel Olcott's letter to Mrs. Besant, above referred to, shows clearly and conclusively that from Christmas, 1893, until after February 21, 1895, a horde of charges, slanders and calumnies, had been circulated privately, publicly, and officially by the leading member and the leading officer of the Society, against Mr. Judge, while never once had he been given a chance to know definitely and accurately the text of the charges nor the letters and other documentary evidence proposed to be used against him.

In merely human jurisprudence in every civilized country in the world the established and settled legal procedure is the right of the accused to know what he is charged with and to have copies and inspection of the complete original letters or other documents proposed to be used against him. Not only was this denied Mr. Judge from first to last, but the *complete* text of the letters, etc., employed by the accusers, *never was made public.* Only extracts were ever given, and the only protection against *garbled extracts,* against *matter taken entirely out of its context,* was the assurance of the accusers that the extracts were genuine, the context in harmony with the extracts given!

Turning now to England, we may follow the successive developments there, after the *Westminster Gazette* firebrand had been cast into the Theosophical camp. In *Lucifer* for November, 1894, the editor during Mrs. Besant's absence, her assistant, Mr. Mead, the General Secretary of the European Section, wrote in the "Watch-Tower" under the caption: "Mine Own Familiar Friend in Whom I Trusted," as follows:

> Just as we go to press a series of articles, making a most indiscriminate and vicious onslaught on several of our friends and colleagues, is being published in *The Westminster Gazette.* We are deeply sorry to have to inform our readers that the inspirer of this attack is Mr. W. R. Old, who witnessed the passing away of H. P. Blavatsky. Virulence and misrepresentation can, however, only defeat their own ends.

Closely associated as he was, in friendship, in sympathy, and in interest with Mrs. Besant, Mr. Mead found himself in hard case what course to pursue. It would appear from his note, "A Difficult Position," in the next —the December—number of *Lucifer,* that he tried at first to take a position of impossible "neutrality." He writes:

> . . . I find my present position in the Theosophical Society an excessively difficult and trying one, . . .
>
> I am not only a private individual with my own feelings, opinions, beliefs, convictions, struggles and trials, but also the editor of LUCIFER with my colleague Annie Besant, the editor of the *Vahan* [the sectional magazine in Europe] with my colleague James M. Pryse, and the

> General Secretary of the European Section of the Theosophical Society. . . .
>
> I am between the fires of contradictory opinions, and bow my head so that fire may accomplish its purpose, or miss its aim, as karma wills it.

Mr. Mead therefore opened his columns to "The Clash of Opinion," under which caption he published resolutions, letters, and other communications pro and con that month to the extent of six pages of text; in January seven pages. By that time the results of the campaign had begun to tell; the February, 1895, *Lucifer* begins with a twenty-seven page article forwarded by Mrs. Besant from India and entitled "The Theosophical Society and the Present Troubles." Mrs. Beasant opens in practiced vein:

> There are times when silence becomes a betrayal of trust, and when a great cause may be ruined by the weakness of its friends; times when the truest charity is the clearest speech, and when love for the many who are bewildered and pleading for light must overbear the love for an individual. To speak a truth needed for the helping of thousands is obedience to the Law of compassion and not a breach thereof.

Mrs. Besant proceeds to "speak the needed truth" for the "bewildered pleaders for light": "The messages . . . to which I referred publicly in August, 1891, were not genuine. . . ." This refers to her Hall of Science speech in August, 1891, already quoted from in a former chapter.[2] How does she explain her present affirmation in view of her former oaths and avowals? Simply that she was "mistaken," her "first-hand knowledge," her "Successorship," etc., to the contrary notwithstanding. Three pages of this are followed by the complete text of the *Madras Mail* article and of her speech before the

[2] See Chapter XX.

Adyar Convention. How does she explain her Statement before the European Convention sitting as a "Jury of Honour" in July preceding? She says:

> I must now, in this crisis, add some further words. . . .
>
> There were other "messages" in the recognised script that did not come under what I said in July . . . that I thought the gist of them had been psychically received. Rightly or wrongly—I am inclined to think wrongly—I did not feel justified in saying that I regarded some of these other messages as deliberately written by Mr. Judge in the pursuance of objects he regarded as desirable . . . without a shadow of authority from any higher source.

The "evidence" before her in July, 1894, was identically the same as the "evidence" when she wrote the above words. What proofs does she give to support this change of front now? Why did she not, in July, say what she now says, that some of the messages were "deliberately written by Mr. Judge, without a shadow of authority from any higher source"?

> Debarred from producing the evidence which would have substantiated the assertion, I shrank from making in public on my unsupported word a statement so damaging to the reputation of another; that which I was prepared to prove before the Committee, I was not prepared to state in public without the right to substantiate by evidence an assertion so grave. As much of the evidence has now been published, I feel at liberty to mention the opinion I formed from it at the time.

Because she was "debarred" from "making in public" a statement that Mr. Judge had *deliberately forged messages from the Masters,* she therefore *did* make publicly to the Convention the statement:

> . . . I wish it to be distinctly understood that I do not charge and have not charged Mr. Judge with forgery in the ordinary sense of the term. . . .
>
> I regard Mr. Judge as an Occultist . . . animated by a deep and unswerving devotion to the Theosophical Society. I believe that he has often received direct messages from the Masters and from Their chelas, guiding and helping him in his work.

Mrs. Besant's long article is accompanied by fifteen pages of "Clash of Opinion" in the same—February, 1895—number of *Lucifer*. Although it is entitled the clash of opinion, the published matter consists, first of a letter of more than five printed pages by Mr. Mead addressed to the European Section, in which he aligns himself very strongly against Mr. Judge. Its tone is expressed in this extract:

> Ever since the charges were brought Mr. Judge has kept on persistently adding to his claims, and his friends have now arrived at placing him on so high a pedestal that H. P. Blavatsky is left sitting on a very low stool in comparison.

Mr. Bertram Keightley follows Mr. Mead with more than two pages, concluding:

> . . . I fully and entirely endorse all that Mrs. Besant has written and I shall always consider it a great honour to thus find myself associated with her.

Alas for the mutability of mundane oaths. Since 1906, when Mrs. Besant herself discovered that Chakravarti was under the influence of the "dark powers," Mr. Keightley has sedulously avoided the "great honour" of finding himself associated with Mrs. Besant, and maintained his liens with Chakravarti.

Alexander Fullerton, of whom we have earlier spoken,[3] follows Mr. Keightley with two pages. Mr. Fullerton says that "from the first I have held the unqualified conviction that a thorough investigation was imperatively due," but that he has received a "message" himself "in two parts," direct from the Master, the first part warning him "against judging from surface facts"; the second advised Mr. Fullerton that "Mr. Judge had, in all respects, both as to silence and as to speech, followed the Master's order," and that Mr. Fullerton's own duty in the premises "was clear." Mr. Fullerton states, in explanation:

> Had the channel of this information been Mr. Judge or connected with him, the questions raised by the charges and still unsettled would have prevented my acceptance of it. It was, in fact, a channel altogether independent, previously known to and verified by me, one affirmed through important and conclusive experience as an actual disciple of the Master, and at times used for communications.
>
> The communication went counter to all my convictions, judgments and inferences. It opposed the investigation I deemed obligatory, and the suspicions I regarded inevitable. It directly denied what I thought my own duty, and affirmed the policy I considered disastrous. Only one consideration could reconcile me to vacating the position I believed true—*the certainty that the message enjoining this was genuine.* This certainty I possessed.

Undoubtedly many sincere students at that time, and many sincere students of today, as in the intervening years, have asked themselves and others when perplexities have arisen, the question, Why do not the Masters interfere and clear up the situation? They had forgotten then, as they forget today, what H.P.B. wrote in the

[3] See Chapter XXIV.

First Preliminary Memorandum in 1888, on this very subject:

> . . . the fact that a member has concluded that a crisis of some kind or other is at hand, when according to his wise opinion the Master or Masters ought to speak or interfere personally, is no sound reason for such personal interference. . . .
>
> The additional help, instruction, and enlightenment will always come from the inner planes of being, and will . . . always be given *when deserved.*
>
> *To achieve this,* the attitude of mind . . . is that which shall tend to *develop the faculty of intuition.* . . .
>
> It is required of a member that when a question arises it shall be deeply thought over from all its aspects, to the end that he may find the answer himself . . . *Otherwise his intuition will never be developed; he will not learn self-reliance; and two of the main objects of the School will be defeated.*

If these wise words had been taken to heart in the various "crises" and "clashes of opinion" throughout Theosophical history, individual and collective, all the struggles of the Society, the School, and the units thereof would have been successfully overpassed.

The utter impossibility of Occult help to those who *will not* follow the instructions given, whose hearts and minds are filled with doubt, questionings, suspicions, of the very channels through which alone the needed and longed-for aid can come, is well shown by Mr. Fullerton's own case. For, in spite of the "certainty of the genuineness of the message" which he declared he possessed, and which made him declare: "I now support Mr. Judge's policy . . . avowedly on the ground of this message"—in spite of all this, Mr. Fullerton kept up his communications with Mrs. Besant, Col. Olcott, and Mr. Sinnett, for each of whom he had a very high regard, personally and Theosophically, but all of whom were engaged in acting directly the opposite of the course enjoined in the "message." Influenced by what he heard from them, by his own inner state of mind, and in particular by a letter from Mr. Sinnett (to which we shall recur) [4] Mr. Fullerton finally, early in April, 1895, concluded that Judge was a very guilty man indeed, deserted him, went over to the "enemy," and, immediately after the Convention of the American Section in the same month, issued a circular announcing his affiliation with the enemies of Mr. Judge. He did this, while still remarking in the circular, "I am still utterly unable to explain or account for the message referred to. . . ."

Subsequently, in 1906-7, Mr. Fullerton had still another change of heart, and broke with Mrs. Besant over the "Adyar manifestations" at the time of the death of Col. Olcott and the original "Leadbeater trouble." He never recovered from the shock incident to the fall of these idols from the pedestal on which he had placed them, and died, a broken man, a few years later. But to return.

The remaining space in "The Clash of Opinion" in the February *Lucifer* is taken up with resolutions of Lodges, etc., adverse to Mr. Judge. *Lucifer* for March contains in all over twenty-five pages devoted to the "Judge case," including a letter from Mr. Judge himself, dated at New York, January 25, 1895. In this Mr. Judge says:

> A long and sustained attack has been made on me . . . which it is thought I should reply to more fully than I have as yet. A very good and decisive reason exists for my not making that full reply and explanation, and it is time Theosophists should know it. It is as follows:
>
> I have not been furnished with copies of the documentary evidence by which the charges are said to be supported . . . open enemies of mine have been allowed to make copies of them, and

[4] See Chapter XXXIII.

> also to take facsimiles, but they have been kept from me although I have demanded and should have them. It must be obvious to all fair-minded persons that it is impossible for me to make a full and definite reply to the charges without having certified copies of them.
>
> I arrived in London, July 4, 1894, and constantly, each day, asked for the copies and for an inspection of the papers. Mrs. Besant promised both, but never performed her promise. . . . These facts the members should know, as they ought, at last, to understand the animus under the prosecution. I shall not reply until I have full, certified copies. It would seem that I am in this matter entitled to as much opportunity and consideration as my open enemies have had.

Mrs. Besant was not yet returned home from India, so Mr. Mead inserted Mr. Judge's letter, immediately followed by one from Mr. *Old* in reply to Mr. Judge's contentions. Mr. Old says:

> I beg to show, briefly, that these statements of Mr. Judge's are utterly false, and that Mr. Judge is the first person who has ever imputed to Mrs. Besant "the lie direct."

Mr. Old then quotes from Mrs. Besant's speech before the Adyar Convention, as reprinted in *Lucifer* for February preceding as his "proof' that Mr. Judge was "utterly false"! What Mrs. Besant had said was:

> I sent a complete copy of the whole statement that I proposed to make, to Mr. Judge . . . that he might know everything I was going to say, every document I was going to use, and every argument I was going to employ.

We have already shown, from Col. Olcott's letter to Mrs. Besant of February 21, news of which had, of course, not yet reached England, the admission that copies had *not* been furnished Mr. Judge. This very letter of Mr. Old's, its publication in *Lucifer,* its defense of Mrs. Besant's falsehood by attempting to give the "lie direct" to Mr. Judge, and Mr. Mead's adopting it as his own reply as editor of *Lucifer* to Mr. Judge's letter, all show the collusion steadily existing between Mr. Old and "his own familiar friends."

In April, 1895, Mrs. Besant, once more on English soil, issued her pamphlet, "The Case Against W. Q. Judge," a booklet of eighty-eight pages. The first twenty-two pages of this pamphlet are given over to defense of herself, to her usual exhibition of adeptship in special pleading, and to invective against Mr. Judge. The remainder of the pamphlet consists, according to her statement, of the charges and evidence as originally prepared for the London Enquiry, plus a half dozen pages of additional matter. The pamphlet closed with the following:

NOTICE

> If some definite action with regard to Mr. Judge shall not have been taken by the European Section before the meeting of its Annual Convention in July, we, the undersigned, shall —failing any full and satisfactory explanation having been made by Mr. Judge before that date, or his voluntary secession from the Society—propose and second at that Convention the following resolution:
>
> *Whereas* Mr. W. Q. Judge has been called on to resign the office of Vice-President of the Theosophical Society by the Indian, Australasian, and European Sections, but has not complied with their request; and
>
> *Whereas* he has evaded the jurisdiction of the Judicial Committee of July, 1894, refused a Jury of Honour, and has since given no full and satisfactory explanation to the Society in answer to the charges brought against him;
>
> *Resolved:* That this Convention of the European Section of the Theosophical Society unites

with the Indian and Australasian Sections in demanding his expulsion from the Society, and requests the President-Founder to immediately take action to carry out the demands of these three Sections of the T.S.

ANNIE BESANT, F.T.S.
G. R. S. MEAD, F.T.S.

Coincident with the publication of this pamphlet, copy was prepared for the May *Lucifer* in consort therewith. This included a letter from Mr. Fullerton dated April 19, announcing his recantation of the position taken in his circular and letter printed in *Lucifer* for February, as noted. In his new communication Mr. Fullerton says, speaking of the "message" first mentioned by him:

> Of the integrity and moral character of the pupil through whom the message came to me I have and can have no question. *Collusion or falsehood is inconceivable. Nevertheless, utterly unable as I am to understand the case, . . . I am obliged to recall any endorsement of the proceedings or policy of Mr. Judge.*

This was a powerful weapon in Mrs. Besant's hands. She comments:

> Mr. Fullerton has been the steady centre in Mr. Judge's office, . . . universally respected for his probity and devotion. . . . *It is of the first importance to show that honest men cannot continue to work with Mr. Judge, unless they are prepared to be betrayed behind their backs in the work of the Society,* and that Mr. Judge's own conduct, and his continued deceptions, force us, however reluctantly, to say: *"Mr. Judge must be expelled from the Society, for his methods are dishonest and he corrupts his fellow-workers."* Unless America saves us from the necessity of demanding his expulsion, by seceding from the parent Society, Europe must

endorse the demand for expulsion coming from India and Australasia.

All this is interesting and instructive as showing the animus behind the whole "Judge case" from the beginning, however carefully concealed until public avowal served to aid the success of the plot. But it is more—it is an instructive lesson in how Mrs. Besant writes history and dresses the facts for those who trust her. For, years afterwards, at Chicago, during the Sectional Convention of 1907, in replying to questions addressed to her, newly elected President to succeed Col. Olcott, she "explained" her stand in the "Leadbeater case" by telling her audience:

> No, I have never been in favor of expulsion. In the trouble that arose round a great Theosophist, Mr. Judge, many years ago, when a motion was brought forward in India for his expulsion, I opposed it.[5]

In addition to the matter to which attention has been called, numerous other pamphlets were issued and circulated among all members in Europe, India and Australasia, the most notable being the one by Countess Wachtmeister; a great mass of newspaper interviews, letters and comments fed the fury and excitement, and private correspondence, as with Mr. Fullerton, was kept up wherever there was opportunity to arouse doubt, suspicion or fear in the minds of members. The march of the assaulting columns having been followed as faithfully as possible, it now remains to observe the measures taken by the defense.

[5] "Theosophical Lectures," Chicago, 1907, The Rajput Press.

CHAPTER XXXIV

THE AMERICAN SECTION DECLARES ITS AUTONOMY AND ELECTS JUDGE ITS LIFE-PRESIDENT

When the *Westminster Gazette* articles had reached their climax and their charges, evidence and conclusions had been spread abroad, Mr. Judge wrote a letter to the *Gazette,* dated at New York, November 26, 1894. This was published in the *New York Sun* on December 3, and in the *Gazette* in its issues of December 8 and 10. Judge was, of course, well aware that anything he might say would serve the *Gazette* only as so much added advertising and be used by it only to animadvert; but he had also to consider his duty as Theosophist and Occultist not only toward his fellow students who might be friendly disposed or temperately minded, but his duty as well to those who, however they might be opposed to him or engaged in conspiracy against his good name, were none the less Souls, and not to be fought with their own unfair weapons. He therefore, as before, and as H.P.B. before him, limited himself strictly and solely to the issues involved. As stated by himself in his note to the *Sun* accompanying the copy of his letter to the *Gazette*:

> These three questions have been raised: (1) Have I been hoaxing the Society by "bogus messages from the Mahatmas"? (2) Are there such beings, and what are they? (3) Do the prominent Theosophists live by or make money out of the Theosophical Society?

Except that he goes to some extent into the details of the various allegations of the *Gazette*, Mr. Judge does not vary from his Statement before the London Convention of July, 1894. The letter, together with additional matter, was printed and circulated in pamphlet form, both from London and from New York, under the title "Isis and the Mahatmas." Other pamphlets in defense of Mr. Judge were issued by Dr. Archibald Keightley, and others. Documentary and other facts were given and attention called to the numerous discrepancies and contradictions in the various statements issued by Mrs. Besant and Col. Olcott. References were made to similar charges against H.P.B. and various citations given from her writings, to support both the Theosophical and Occult arguments advanced. No bitterness was shown and no counter-attacks made, the general position taken being simply that the accusers were either suffering from "pledge fever," or were misled by appearances. Attention was repeatedly called to the fact that every charge now made against Mr. Judge had been made, not only against him during the life of H.P.B., by Prof. Coues and others, but the identical charges also made against H.P.B. herself by the Society of Psychical Research and Prof. Coues; that the teachings and actions of Mr. Judge were in strict accord and consonance with the Instructions and other writings of H.P.B., and the "messages" through him accompanied by the same circumstances as those through H.P.B. and Damodar. In most of the defensive writings issued by the various students stress was laid on all these facts and on the other fact that H.P.B.'s highest tributes to Mr. Judge had been written during the very period when Col. Olcott was most bitter against her and Mr. Judge (preceding the formation of the E.S.T.), and during the height of the Coues case, after the *New York Sun* charges.

Aside, then, from the E.S.T. Circular of November 3, 1894, and the "Isis and the Mahatmas" letter, Judge gave scant notice to the hail of missiles discharged by his attackers within and without the Society, but went calmly on with his work. This is shown (1) by the contents of *The Path* during those fateful months, in contrast with the other magazines; (2) by the papers and letters sent out by him to the E.S.T.; (3) by his private, personal letters to his warm friends and adherents. Many of these latter will be found in the second volume of the "Letters That Have Helped Me." Nothing is more wonderful than the serenity, the good-will, the wisdom and faith exemplified in these letters, written from the heart to those who trusted him, who would have followed any course set by him. If bitterness, if coldness, if uncharity, if evil-mindedness of any kind had been in him—any self-pity, any resentment at his accusers—surely it would have come out in these intimate letters, written in such circumstances, without a thought of their ever being seen by any but the recipients. They were not published for years after his death.

Mr. Judge knew as none other the fiery strains and pains of the "path of probation," successful or unsuccessful though the candidate might be, and had no stones to fling. He knew what the real poison was which had corrupted the original faith of Mr. Sinnett and Col. Olcott, and was to corrupt the faith of Mrs. Besant. Thus knowing, he regarded himself as merely the indirect target for the real enemies of the Movement, invisible, unbelieved in, even by those who were being made the tools and therefore the victims of the opposing forces. In order, therefore, as much as possible to get the real issues before the students at large, he followed up the reference in his E.S.T. Circular of November 3, 1894, to the "plot against the Movement," and to the message to the Allahabad Brahmins in the Prayag T.S. in 1881, by publishing in *The Path* for March, 1895, the full text of that famous "message," after all the charges against himself had been published and republished the world around, and all possible changes rung on them. But first a word on the circumstances.

The "Prayag Psychic T.S." of Allahabad, India, was one of the earliest of the Branches to be formed in India after the arrival there of H.P.B. and Col. Olcott in 1879. Gyanendra N. Chakravarti and his uncle were two of its early members; Mr. Sinnett and Mr. Hume were prominent in its affairs in its early years. Its membership consisted largely of high caste Brahmins and it was one of the most influential Branches in India for years. It was, so far as we are aware, the only Lodge of the Theosophical Society which did not, professedly at least, adopt the "First Object." Its avowed object was "psychical research." During the early days in India "messages from the Mahatmas" phenomenally received, were numerous and large numbers of interested persons were thus favored. Complaints were made by the Brahmin members of the Prayag T.S. that, whereas "low caste" men and "mlechhas" (foreigners) such as Mr. Hume, Mr. Sinnett, and other "beef-eating, wine-drinking Englishmen" received messages, *they* had been neglected. In time a "message" came, dealing with these very complaints and telling *why* the Brahmins and others like them had received no "messages." There is no dispute anywhere as to the above facts, nor the further fact that the "message" was delivered by H.P.B., to Mr. Sinnett to give to the Prayag Brahmin members. Damodar (or whoever the "receiving wire" may have been) was manifestly no English scholar at that time, and of the Mahatmas Themselves only one was named as having any knowledge of English. Thus the "message" was, in form, in distinctly *babu* English. Neither the "sending" Mahatma nor the "receiving" chela was known to anyone except H.P.B., on whom, therefore, all the responsibility of the "message" rests: this by all accounts. We give the "message" in full as published in *The Path* from a copy sent by one of those very Brahmins to Mr. Judge in 1893. The original "message" was retained by Mr. Sinnett.[1]

> Message which Mr. Sinnett is directed by one of the Brothers, writing through Madame B(lavatsky), to convey to the native members of the Prayag Branch of the Theosophical Society.
>
> The Brothers desire me to inform one and all of you *natives* that unless a man is prepared to

[1] The original text of the "Prayag Letter" has now been made accessible to students in No. CLXXXIV of "The Mahatma Letters to A. P. Sinnett."

become a thorough Theosophist, *i.e.*, to do what D(amodar) Mavalankar did—give up entirely caste, his old superstitions, and show himself a true reformer (especially in the case of child marriage), he will remain simply a member of the Society, with no hope whatever of ever hearing from us. The Society, acting in this directly in accord with our orders, *forces no one to become a Theosophist of the Second Section.* It is left with himself at his choice. It is useless for a member to argue "I am one of a pure life, I am a teetotaller and an abstainer from meat and vice, all my aspirations are for good, etc.," and he at the same time building by his acts and deeds an impassable barrier on the road between himself and us. What have we, the disciples of the Arhats of Esoteric Buddhism and of Sang-gyas, to do with the Shasters and orthodox Brahmanism? There are 100 of thousands of Fakirs, Sannyasis, or Sadhus leading the most pure lives and yet being, as they are, on the path of *error* never having had an opportunity to meet, see, or even hear of us. Their forefathers have driven the followers of the only true philosophy upon earth away from India, and now it is not for the latter to come to them, but for them to come to us, if they want us. Which of them is ready to become a Buddhist, a *Nastika*, as they call us? Those who have believed and followed us have had their reward. Mr. Sinnett and Mr. Hume are exceptions. Their beliefs are no barrier to us, for they have none. They may have bad influences around them, bad magnetic emanations, the result of drink, society, and promiscuous physical associations (resulting even from shaking hands with impure men), but all this is physical and material impediments which with a little effort we could counteract, and even clear away, without much detriment to ourselves. Not so with the mag-

> netic and invisible results proceeding from erroneous and sincere beliefs. Faith in the gods or god and other superstition attracts millions of foreign influences, living entities and powerful Agents round them, with which we would have to use more than ordinary exercise of power to drive them away. We do not choose to do so. We do not find it either necessary or profitable to lose our time waging war on the unprogressed *planetaries* who delight in personating gods and sometimes well-known characters who have lived on earth. There are Dhyan Chohans and Chohans of darkness. Not what they term *devils*, but imperfect intelligences who have never been born on this or any other earth or sphere no more than the Dhyan Chohans have, and who will never belong to the "Children of the Universe," the pure planetary intelligences who preside at every Manvantara, while the Dark Chohans preside at the Pralaya.

Mr. Judge declares: "this is a genuine message from the Master, allowing, of course, for any minor errors in copying." He goes on—what he very well knew but which then had not been publicly avowed by her—that "Mrs. Besant has several times privately stated that in her opinion" the message "was a 'forgery or humbug' gotten up by H.P.B." He adds:

> If it be shown to be a fraud, then all of H.P.B.'s claims of connection with and teaching from the Master must fall to the ground. It is now time that this important point be cleared up.

Mrs. Besant, Col. Olcott, Mr. Sinnett, and all the rest, had sedulously, *before the public*, kept up the mask of devotion to H.P.B. in all the campaign against Mr. Judge, and had charged him over and over again with being false to H.P.B. as to the Masters and the Society. He knew what their real opinion of H.P.B. was—the same as their opinion in regard to himself—but knew also that very many students quite innocently and sincerely believed the public protestations of loyalty to H.P.B. to be genuine. So, to place the matter squarely before all, and to "bring to light the hidden things of darkness," he published the "Prayag message" and sent, as usual, advance proof sheets to *Lucifer* and to *The Theosophist*. The answer was prompt and characteristic in all three cases—Mr. Sinnett, Mrs. Besant, and Col. Olcott.

Mr. Sinnett kept still; not a word publicly from him, but a private letter to Mr. Fullerton which the latter, unknown to Mr. Sinnett, gave to the *Boston Herald* for publication on April 27, 1895.

Mrs. Besant, in addition to the extracts quoted earlier,[2] said: "I do not regard the letter [message] as genuine, but *I have never attributed it to H.P.B.*"

As the only responsible person connected with the "message" was H.P.B., this statement of Mrs. Besant's was more ingenious than ingenuous. Furthermore, she proceeded to *charge Mr. Judge himself with doubting the genuineness of the message!* (*Lucifer,* Volume 16, pp. 185-94, 375-9.)

The advance proofs of *The Path* reached Adyar just as *The Theosophist* was going to press with the April number, the "Supplement" of which, as noted, contained the interchange of the letters of January 20 and February 21 between Mrs. Besant and Col. Olcott. This is what he wrote:

"Postscript"

> We stop the press to make room for some needed comments on an article by Mr. Judge in the March number of *The Path,* of which advance proofs have been kindly sent us from New York. . . . The message is one of the most transparently unconvincing in the history of Mahatmic literature. It bears upon its face the seal of its condemnation. It is an ill-tempered

[2] See Chapter XXXI.

attack . . . Mr. Judge asserts that "this is a genuine message from the Masters, allowing, of course, *for minor errors in copying*"; and concludes his comments on the document by saying: " . . . if it be shown to be a fraud, then all of H.P.B.'s claims of connection with and teaching from the Master must fall to the ground. It is now time that this important point be cleared up."

It certainly *is* time; and . . . the undersigned . . . will help towards the clearing up so far as he can. He picks up the gauntlet for the honor of the Masters and the benefit of the Society.

In so many words, then, he pronounces the message a false one, and if this is likely to shatter H.P.B.'s oft-declared infallibility, as the transmitter of only genuine messages from the Masters, so let it be; the sooner the monstrous pretense is upset the better for her memory and a noble cause. . . . it does not follow that H.P.B. consciously falsified; the simple theory of mediumship has explained many equally deceptive and even more exasperating messages from the invisible world: and she herself has written and said to the spy Solovyoff, that at times she was possessed by evil influences. We know all the weight that such a suggestion carries, and yet repeat it in the full conviction that the discoveries of hypnotic science have already furnished proof of its entire reasonableness.

The putative "message," moreover, grossly violates that basic principle of neutrality and eclecticism on which the Theosophical Society has built itself up from the beginning; and which the self-sacrificing action of the Judicial Committee, at London last summer, vindicated, to the satisfaction of all the Sections. . . . The moment that the dogma is established that the genuineness of H.P.B.'s series of Mahatmas letters depends upon the acceptance of such a fraud as the above, the Society will have to find another President, for it would soon become the game-preserve of rogues.

H. S. Olcott.

Adyar, March 27, 1895.

What Mr. Sinnett wrote privately was, as stated, published in the *Boston Herald* on April 27, 1895, the day before the meeting in Boston of the Convention of the American Section. He wrote as follows:

> . . . I have known for a great many years that many letters in the Mahatmas' handwriting, coming through Madame Blavatsky herself were anything but what they seemed.
>
> The trouble in this respect began about the year 1887, when Madame Blavatsky was in this country [England] and desirous of carrying out many arrangements with the society in London of which I personally disapproved. To my surprise I received through her letters in the familiar handwriting of the Mahatma K. H. which endorsed her views and desired my compliance. These gave me great distress at the time, though I did not at first suspect the *bona fides* of the origin.
>
> The flavour of their style was unlike that to which I had been used during the long course of my previous correspondence with the Mahatma, and gradually my mind was forced to the conviction that they could not be really authentic. A year or so later, when the Coulomb scandal had for the moment almost overwhelmed Madame Blavatsky's influence here, I visited her in her retirement at Würzburg, and in the intimate conversation that ensued she frankly avowed to me that the letters to which I have above referred had not proceeded from the Mahatma at all.
>
> She had in fact procured their production in order to subserve what she conceived to be the

right policy of the society at the time—falling into the fatal error of doing evil that good might come. There is no room for supposing that I am mistaken in my recollections of what passed. These are clear and definite, and were the subject of much conversation between myself and theosophical friends at the time.

Moreover, at a somewhat later date, when Madame Blavatsky was staying at Ostende, I again referred to the matter, and said that I considered myself to have been hardly used, in so far as my deepest sentiments of loyalty to the Mahatma had been practiced upon for purposes with which he had nothing to do. Madame Blavatsky, I remember, replied: "Well, you were not much hurt, because, after all, you never believed the letters were genuine. . . ."

The last article written by Mr. Judge before his death in March, 1896, was entitled "H.P.B. was not Deserted by Masters." This was a dying declaration of the good faith, the genuineness, the nature, and the mission of H.P.B. In it Mr. Judge wrote that Mr. Sinnett had taxed H.P.B. with fraud in London during her lifetime. This was published in *The Path* (under its new name of *Theosophy*) in April, 1896, immediately after Mr. Judge's death. When the copies reached England Mr. Sinnett wrote a letter to the magazine, dated at London May 6, 1896, in which he said in reference to Mr. Judge's statement:

> *I never said anything of the kind, and I never in my life* called Mme. Blavatsky a fraud.
>
> The accusation is doubly absurd because for many years past and since before the period referred to I have had means of my own for knowing that Mme. Blavatsky had not been deserted by the Masters, and I know that she was in their care up to the last day of her life. . . .
>
> I merely write now to dissipate the delusion on which Mr. Judge's article is founded, and to

> express at the same time my regret that his latest utterances concerning myself should have been colored by stories as to my sayings and mental attitude that were entirely untrue.

We may add that in course of the preparation and authentication of the materials for this History, the present writers wrote to Mr. Sinnett at London in 1915, sending him a certified copy of the letter published in the *Boston Herald*, and asking him to verify the accuracy of the printed text. In reply Mr. Sinnett sent an autograph letter to the writers, admitting the correctness of the publication—and adding that he regretted the bringing up of these "old matters," saying, "*I have long since forgiven Madame Blavatsky and Mr. Judge for the wrongs they did me.*" Mr. Sinnett's posthumous book, "The Early Days of Theosophy in Europe," published in 1922, at last publicly avows his actual feelings from 1881 onwards and readers are referred to that work to learn the amazing lengths to which Mr. Sinnett's "messages" through his "sensitives" led him.

To return. The Convention of the American Section was held at Boston, April 28 and 29, 1895. That which was hidden had been brought to light; that which had been obscurely circulated for many years against the good faith of H.P.B. by those who posed before the public and the Society as her true students and loyal supporters, had been forced to be said publicly. Every student, every member of the Society and of the E.S.T. knew, or could easily learn, the *facts*—naked, unmasked, at last: that the charges against Judge were the same charges, resting upon the same "evidence," made and sponsored by the same persons, as the charges against H.P.B. The issues were clear, the war of ideas squarely before the Society and its members. They could choose H.P.B. and Mr. Judge; they could choose Mr. Sinnett, Mrs. Besant, Col. Olcott—one party or the other as "representing the Masters"; they could not choose both.

The eighty-nine active Lodges composing the Section

were all represented in full by delegates in person or by proxy. In addition there was a great gathering of visiting Fellows from all over the United States and some from abroad. Dr. J. D. Buck was elected permanent Chairman. Dr. Archibald Keightley was present from London as the delegate of a number of English Branches. A letter from a number of Fellows in Australia was read, as also an official letter from Mr. G. R. S. Mead, as General Secretary of the European Section. Mr. Mead wrote to say:

> It is with deep regret that I have to inform you that the European Section of the Society is unable to be represented at your Convention by a Delegate, owing to divided opinions with regard to the present crisis through which the Society is passing. . . .

There was no letter or other communication received either from the Indian Section or from the President-Founder.

Mr. Judge's report as General Secretary contained the usual information on the work of the preceding year. It contained a brief rehearsal of the charges made against him, the meeting of the Judicial Committee the preceding July, the *Westminster Gazette* articles, the subsequent proceedings at the Adyar Conventions, and the various resolutions adopted demanding his "resignation" and an "explanation." On all this his report says:

> . . . I have replied, refusing to resign the Vice-Presidency. And to the newspaper attack I have made a provisional and partial reply, as much as such a lying and sensational paper deserved. . . . But I have an explanation, and I renew my declaration of innocence of the offenses charged. As I have said in London and since, the messages I delivered, privately, are genuine messages from the Master, procured through me as a channel, and the basis of the attack on me is unbelief in my being a channel.

The usual work of the Convention proceeded and when all routine matters were concluded, Mr. C. A. Griscom, Jr., read a series of resolutions, with a preamble reciting the difficulties and obstacles of the continued work of the Movement. The essential resolutions were:

> First, that the American Section, consisting of Branches of the Theosophical Society in America, in convention assembled, hereby assumes and declares its entire autonomy and that it shall be called from and after this date "The Theosophical Society in America";
>
> Second, that the administration of its affairs shall be provided for, defined, and be under a Constitution and By-Laws, which shall in any case provide for the following:
>
> (*a*) A Federation of Branches. . . .
>
> (*b*) That William Q. Judge shall be President for life. . . .
>
> RESOLVED, that the Theosophical Society in America hereby recognizes the long and efficient services rendered to the Theosophical Movement by Col. H. S. Olcott and that to him belongs the unique and honorary title of President-Founder of the Theosophical Society, and that, as in the case of H.P.B. as Corresponding Secretary, he can have no successor in that office.

The First Session of the Convention then adjourned. At the Second Session debate was had upon the resolution as indicated. A historical sketch of the Society was submitted, showing its *de facto* and nominal nature as a single Society since 1879. Speeches were made by Mr. Fullerton, and by Dr. J. W. B. LaPierre, President of the Minneapolis Lodge—both strongly opposing the adoption of the resolutions. The speeches in opposition were listened to with close attention and entire respect for the speakers. Dr. LaPierre's speech included a written Protest. In fact, the bulk of the time was occupied by the speakers in opposition to the resolutions, and their remarks are given in full in the Convention official Report. At the conclusion the list of Branches and Councillors was called and a formal vote taken. The totals showed 191 votes in favor of the resolutions and 10 against.

Thus did the "American Section of the T.S.," cease to exist, to reorganize as "The Theosophical Society in America."

After the close of this Second Session of April 28, Dr. Keightley read a detailed Reply by Mr. Judge to the charges of misusing the names and handwritings of the Mahatmas. This Reply was afterwards printed in pamphlet form.

Two sessions were held on April 29 as the T.S. in A.; a Constitution and By-Laws were adopted; officers and an Executive Committee elected. The following letter from the Executive Committee of the newly organized Theosophical Society in America, and signed by Mr. Judge as its President, was sent to the Convention of the European Section:

> *From the Theosophical Society in America to the European Theosophists, in Convention assembled as, "The European Section of the Theosophical Society."*
>
> Brothers and Sisters: We send you our fraternal greeting, and fullest sympathy in all works sincerely sought to be performed for the good of Humanity. Separated though we are from you by very great distance we are none the less certain that you and we, as well as all other congregations of people who love Brotherhood, are parts of that great whole denominated The Theosophical Movement, which began far back in the night of Time and has since been moving through many and various peoples, places and environments. That grand work does not depend upon forms, ceremonies, particular persons or set organizations,—"Its unity throughout the world does not consist in the existence

and action of any single organization, but depends upon the similarity of work and aspiration of those in the world who are working for it." Hence organizations of theosophists must vary and change in accordance with place, time, exigency and people. To hold that in and by a sole organization for the whole world is the only way to work would be boyish in conception and not in accord with experience or nature's laws.

Recognizing the foregoing, we, who were once the body called The American Section of the T.S., resolved to make our organization, or merely outer form for government and administration, entirely free and independent of all others; but retained our theosophical ideals, aspirations, aims and objects, continuing to be a part of the theosophical movement. This change was an inevitable one, and perhaps will ere long be made also by you as well as by others. It has been and will be forced, as it were, by nature itself under the sway of the irresistible law of human development and progress.

But while the change would have been made before many years by us as an inevitable and logical development, we have to admit that it was hastened by reason of what we considered to be strife, bitterness and anger existing in other Sections of the Theosophical world which were preventing us from doing our best work in the field assigned us by Karma. In order to more quickly free ourself from these obstructions we made the change in this, instead of in some later, year. It is, then, a mere matter of government and has nothing to do with theosophical propaganda and ethics, except that it will enable us to do more and better work.

Therefore we come to you as fellow-students and workers in the field of theosophical effort, and holding out the hand of fellowship we again declare the complete unity of all theosophical workers in every part of the world. This you surely cannot and will not reject from heated, rashly conceived counsels, or from personalities indulged in by anyone, or from any cause whatever. To reject the proffer would mean that you reject and nullify the principle of Universal Brotherhood upon which alone all true theosophical work is based. And we could not indulge in those reflections nor put forward that reason but for the knowledge that certain persons of weight and prominence in your ranks have given utterance hastily to expressions of pleasure that our change of government above referred to has freed them from nearly every one of the thousands of earnest, studious and enthusiastic workers in our American group of Theosophical Societies. This injudicious and untheosophical attitude we cannot attribute to the whole or to any majority of your workers.

Let us then press forward together in the great work of the real Theosophical Movement which is aided by working organizations, but is above them all. Together we can devise more and better ways for spreading the light of truth through all the earth. Mutually assisting and encouraging one another we may learn how to put Theosophy into practice so as to be able to teach and enforce it by example before others. We will then each and all be members of that Universal Lodge of Free and Independent Theosophists which embraces every friend of the human race. And to all this we beg your corporate official answer for our more definite and certain information, and to the end that this and your favorable reply may remain as evidence and monuments between us.

Fraternally yours,

William Q. Judge,

President.

Upon the simple principle that the integrity of the Theosophical Movement was paramount to the organizational unity of the Theosophical Society when its component elements were a house irreconcilably divided against itself, the action of the Boston Convention was a logical as well as an inevitable necessity. Regardless of the merits of the contending forces all but the most bigoted could see that two or more organizations at one upon ideals and at peace upon externalities were infinitely nearer to the practical possibility of fraternity, the prime proclaimed object of all. The Letter thus drawn up was a concrete expression of these ideas, and for that reason was addressed to the "European *Theosophists* in Convention assembled," not to the "Convention." For the hopes and good wishes therein expressed, there was, in addition, ample ground both in the matter of precedent and in the statements of H.P.B. and Col. Olcott himself. For the T.S. had very early been in cordial affiliation and alliance with the Arya Somaj, an entirely separate organization; the London Lodge under Mr. Sinnett's guidance had in 1891 definitely and officially declared its own organizational independence of the T.S., had refused to have anything whatever to do with its official proceedings or procedure, while expressing a similar attitude toward both the T.S. and the President-Founder, and this action of the London Lodge had been received and accepted without protest by the European Convention in July, immediately following the death of H.P.B., and with the President-Founder in the chair; Col. Olcott had accepted the self-declared official independence of the "Theosophical Society in Europe," with H.P.B., as its President in the summer of 1890, under circumstances so nearly parallel as to be practically identical; and he had formally and officially "authorized" the so-called "Esoteric Section" or "Esoteric School,"—an independent body within the T.S., a body, moreover, over which he had absolutely no control and which had been formed by H.P.B. expressly and declaredly because the T.S. was, in her opinion, "a dead failure" and a "sham." In her famous "Puzzle From

Adyar" article she had publicly declared: "There is no longer a 'Parent Society'; it is abolished and replaced by an aggregate body of Theosophical Societies, *all autonomous.*" Colonel Olcott had directly stated, on the occasion of that struggle: "If you want separate Societies, have them by all means"; and during the very course of the "Judge case" itself, his Presidential Address at the Adyar Convention in December, 1894, had clearly shown that he anticipated the very action taken by the Boston Convention, while his letters to Judge and others during the months succeeding that Address plainly indicated that he would officially recognize any action the Boston Convention might take, and continue in amity and harmony in the work of the Theosophical Movement with his former associates in the new Society.

The President-Founder touched at Zumarraga, Spain, on his way to attend the Convention of the European Sectión at London. There he received the various documents apprising him of the proceedings of the Boston Convention, as well as the news of the various activities of his associates in the "case against W. Q. Judge." He at once issued an "Executive Notice," formally admitting that "the American Section, *exercising its indisputable right, in lawful Convention assembled,*" had declared itself completely autonomous and "has thus as effectually broken its relation with the Theosophical Society as the United States of America did their colonial relations with Great Britain on July 4, 1776." After arguing the question of the *de jure* or *de facto* existence of the T.S., the Executive Notice concludes as follows:

> While it would have been better if the work in hand could have been continued as heretofore in a spirit of unity and mutual reliance, yet the undersigned considers that a separation like the present one was far more prudent than the perpetuation of ill-feeling and disunity within our ranks by causes too well known to need special reference. The undersigned offers to his late

> American colleagues his best private and official wishes for the prosperity, usefulness and honourable management of their new Society.
>
> H. S. OLCOTT,
>
> President-Founder of the Theosophical Society.

Apart from the manifest fact that there was in the mind of Col. Olcott no consciousness that the disunity and the separation had been caused and forced by himself and Mrs. Besant, the closing sentences of his Executive Notice expressed in words the same ideas as were embodied in the Letter from the T.S.A. to the "European Theosophists in Convention assembled." How far his words were representative of his actual intentions and determination is shown by the course taken at the Convention of the British-European Section.

That Convention met at London on July 4, 1895—notable date—with the President-Founder in the chair. Colonel Olcott formally advised the Convention of the receipt of the Letter from the T.S.A., but refused to place it before the Convention, saying: "I declare the thing out of order and not admissible."

A sharp discussion ensued, various delegates opposing both the spirit and the decision of the President-Founder. Mrs. Besant then made a characteristic speech, concluding:

> I would ask you (if the President-Founder would be good enough to waive his perfectly just and legal ruling) to allow the letter to be read, and then let it lie on the table, passing it over in absolute silence so to speak.

A motion to that effect was made by Mrs. Besant, seconded, and carried. Colonel Olcott then read the Letter to the Convention. Mr. Fred J. Dick of the Dublin Lodge at once moved: "That this Convention do receive the communication with pleasure and do draft a reply thereto."

This was seconded, but at once a hot debate ensued, for to have adopted it would have been to accept the olive branch tendered from the new society. Mrs. Besant therefore moved as an amendment: "That the letter do lie upon the table."

Oliver Firth seconded Mrs. Besant's amendment. The amendment was carried—39 to 13—and accordingly the letter was "laid on the table" and the American overtures rejected.

Thereupon Mr. E. T. Hargrove, one of the delegates, rose to a "question of privilege" and said that the treatment given by the Convention to the Letter from the T.S.A. was not only an ignominious refusal of proffered amity but the official abandonment by the large majority of the European Section of the fundamental principle of all Theosophical work—brotherhood. He called upon all who took this view to leave the hall. Accordingly a third of the delegates and visiting Fellows retired and proceeded to take steps to organize a "Theosophical Society in England" in affiliation with the T.S.A.

The Convention of the European Section continued its session and before adjourning adopted the following Resolution:

> *Resolved:* That this Convention regrets that the Theosophical Society in America should have addressed to it a letter of greeting containing much contentious matter, and in a form which makes it impossible to accept it officially, yet the delegates wish to assure their late colleagues in America of their hearty sympathy in all matters pertaining to the true principles of Theosophy and Universal Brotherhood.

During the session of the Convention the President-Founder, in the chair, welcomed to its sessions Dr. Mary Weeks Burnett who had come over from the United States on behalf of Mr. Fullerton, Dr. LaPierre, herself, and other dissenters from the action taken by the Boston Convention. At the request of Col. Olcott, Dr. Weeks read a formal letter from these, declaring allegiance to the President-Founder, to the T.S., and repudiating the T.S.A.

The President-Founder appointed Mr. Fullerton General Secretary of an "American Section" of the Theosophical Society to be formed; announced that all former F.T.S. and all former Lodges and Branches must choose between the T.S. and the T.S. in A., and that all accepting the action of the Boston Convention would, *ipso facto,* forfeit all connection with the T.S.—all Charters revoked and all Diplomas of Fellowship canceled. He appointed Mr. Sinnett Vice-President of the T.S. in lieu of Mr. Judge, declaring that Mr. Judge had "by his own act lost his membership in the Society."

Thereafter Col. Olcott, Mrs. Besant, Mr. Sinnett, and all those under their influence continually spoke and wrote of the "secession" of the American Section, and of their former associates as "seceders." Mr. Judge was continuously referred to as a former devoted Theosophist who had "gone wrong," and as a "forger"; those who believed in him as deceived and deluded.

Thus perished all hopes that the two societies might proceed in emulation, not rivalry; in peace, not controversies and antagonisms.

We promised to show, over their own signatures, that the "case against Judge" began to take on the aspects of an organized secret conspiracy as far back as the beginning of 1893, while yet all the participants were maintaining publicly toward Mr. Judge an attitude of the most cordial co-operation and confidence, and while privately maintaining all the appearances of intimate friendship and trust. This has already been abundantly done in respect of Mrs. Besant and others. In Col. Olcott's case it is certified by one of the documents included in Mrs. Besant's "Case Against W. Q. Judge"—the document relating to the "Panjab Seal." Though the "Case Against W. Q. Judge" was not published until April, 1895, the document in question was given by Col. Olcott to Mrs. Besant at the midnight conference at Adyar on Christmas, 1893. The document bore the signature of Col. Olcott, and the date, *January 28, 1893.*

This leads to a consideration of the two things on which the whole "Judge case" rests for its "evidence" of bogus messages, which seemed so convincing to Col. Olcott, Mrs. Besant, and others, *after* Chakravarti and other Brahmins had played on the prospective tools (or victims, as one wills). First let it be understood that it is the clear and undisputed fact that the "Judge messages" were unique in two respects as compared with all the wide range of "messages" received through numerous "psychics" after H.P.B.'s death: (1) some of them bore a "seal"; (2) they were *all* in the handwritings attributed from *1870* to *1891* to the "precipitations" of the Masters "M" and "K. H." It was the messages received *through* H.P.B. that Mr. Hodgson, the Committee of the Society for Psychical Research, their two handwriting experts, Mr. Sims and Mr. Netherclift, and numerous others, attributed to the "forgery" of H.P.B. herself and Damodar.

Had it not been for the "seal" and the "handwritings" there would have been no "Judge case"; for, although six "Charges and Specifications" were drawn up, Mrs. Besant herself in her Statement before the London Convention, July 12, 1894, said plainly that the chief and only real ground for the "charges" was the "misleading form" of the Judge messages, and herself affirmed her belief that the "messages" were, *as to fact and substance,* genuine.

I. It is known that a "seal" appeared on messages very early; Dr. Franz Hartmann speaks of it in his "Report of Observations," at Adyar—a pamphlet issued in September, 1884; the testimony in "The Case Against W. Q. Judge," recites the "seal" on various messages received during the lifetime of H.P.B., notably one received by Mr. Bertram Keightley at New York in 1890; and, finally, as we shall quickly show, was testified to by Mrs. Besant, Countess Wachtmeister, and others, as having been seen by them on messages received through *H.P.B.*

II. As to the "Panjab Seal" itself, around which the "Judge case" hinged in connection with the handwriting problem. According to Col. Olcott's "Statement" in "The Case Against W. Q. Judge," he bought, in 1883, a "seal" in imitation of the Master "M's" "cryptograph," and this imitation "seal" he gave to H.P.B. According to Mr. Bertram Keightley's "Statement" he first saw this "seal" in 1888; H.P.B., being ill, asked him to get out for her "a small box containing some of her 'occult possessions' "—the phrase "occult possessions" being used by Mr. Keightley in quotes in such manner as to give the impression that the words were H.P.B.'s, not his own. He opened the box at her request, and among other things saw this "seal." On his asking her what it was, she replied, as he gives her words: "Oh, it is only a flapdoodle of Olcott's." Keightley says that the resemblance of this "seal" to Mahatma "M's" "cryptograph" caused him, in connection with H.P.B.'s remark, to examine it closely and "to photograph it very strongly on my memory." So strongly, according to him, that when he received the message in New York in 1890 (during H.P.B.'s lifetime), he noted a "seal impression like the one I had seen with H.P.B." The message was received in Mr. Judge's office on a cablegram sent to Mr. Judge and therefore opened by Judge,—as Mr. Keightley had given Judge's name and address for the receipt of cables to himself. Mr. Keightley goes on: "I thereupon asked Judge if he had put the seal there; to this he replied that he knew nothing about it." Mr. Keightley seems *never to have asked H.P.B. about this "seal impression"*—or if he did he says nothing of it. Nor does he mention that *the cablegram itself*—on which the "precipitated seal" and message occurred—*was from H.P.B.,* and it is the statement of Mr. Claude Falls Wright, another of the original "Inner Group," who was present at the time, that on the night of Mr. Bertram Keightley's return to London from America in the summer of 1890, H.P.B. questioned Mr. Keightley about her telegram to him, and when he said he had lost it, she produced *the identical telegram, seal, message and all, before his eyes,*—and then chided him "for losing things"!

After the date *1888, note well,* there is no evidence of anyone ever having seen the "seal" itself; no evidence of what became of it; but it was *not* among H.P.B.'s possessions *after her death* when those were searched and examined. There was not then, and there never was, *anything whatever to connect Mr. Judge with the possession of this "Panjab seal."*

In August, 1891, *The Path,* as narrated, published an article by "Jasper Niemand," then unknown as an identity, beginning with a "message from the Master," alleged by the writer to have been received *after* the death of H.P.B., and "attested by His *real* seal."[3] We have earlier called attention to this word "real" in connection with the "seal." Colonel Olcott wrote Mr. Judge, as told, and Mr. Judge replied with the "Interesting letter" published later on by Mrs. Besant in *Lucifer* for April, 1893. In that letter Mr. Judge tells Col. Olcott he "knows nothing about" the "seal"—meaning thereby the "Panjab Seal." That, to Col. Olcott's suspicious mind, was proof positive that Mr. Judge had in some way gotten hold of the imitation seal and was using it to bolster bogus messages being produced by Mr. Judge to attract attention to himself as "Master's agent." No other explanation ever occurred to Col. Olcott or to any of the others. When Mr. Judge denied that he had anything to do with the "Jasper Niemand" message, Col. Olcott could only think Mr. Judge was lying to escape an *impasse.* He exchanged confidences with Mr. Walter R. Old, who had been a member of the E.S.T. Council and present at the Avenue Road Meeting of May 27, 1891, when the "W. Q. Judge's plan is right" message had been received—with *a* "seal" on it. Mr. Old wrote that the E.S.T. had been reorganized on the basis of that message—a plain, unornamented falsehod, as we have seen, and shall further show. This was in the article "Theosophic Freethought," for which Messrs. Old and Edge were suspended from the E.S.T., as narrated. Now let us take Mrs. Besant's own series of statements in regard to that message and its "seal," etc.

[3] See Chapters XX, XXV, and XXVI.

(1) On July 6, 1891, less than six weeks after the Meeting itself, Mrs. Besant drew up a statement which she sent to Mrs. Julia Campbell-Ver Planck at New York City—Mrs. Ver Planck then well known Theosophically and who afterwards married Dr. Archibald Keightley, but who was then entirely unknown to Mrs. Besant or anyone else except Mr. Judge as being identical with "Jasper Niemand." Mrs. Besant's statement reads:

> London, July 6th, 1891.
>
> I took from William Q. Judge, on the *afternoon* of May 27th, 1891 [the meeting was held that *night*] certain papers selected from a number of letters in his possession. These I took one by one, read them, folded them up, *tied them into a packet,* and said I would read them myself to the Council, as they concerned Bro. Judge. I opened this packet myself in the Council meeting, in my place as chairman. I took up the papers one by one and read them (or parts of them) aloud, and on raising one of them saw a piece of paper lying between it and the next *that was not there when I tied them together.* After reading those remaining I took it up, and found it was a slip bearing some words written in red and signed with .·.'s initials and *seal.* The words were: "W. Q. Judge's plan is right."
>
> The paper is attached hereto.
>
> ANNIE BESANT.

(2) In December, 1891, Mrs. Besant attended an E.S.T. meeting at the Astor House in New York City, with Messrs. Robert Crosbie, Henry Turner Patterson, Thaddeus P. Hyatt, and William Main. There, the discussion turned, *inter alia,* on the "phenomena" occurring since H.P.B.'s death, the "message" in *The Path* for August preceding, and Mrs. Besant's remarkable public statements in her "Hall of Science" speech on

August 30, 1891, and, naturally, on the "Judge's plan is right" message of May 27, 1891, to which, among others, she referred in that speech. *All four* of these gentlemen, all well-known Theosophists of unblemished repute, afterwards testified that Mrs. Besant "stated in the most positive and unqualified manner that the message from the Master which she found at a meeting of the Council of the E. S. in London amongst other papers, *could not have been placed there by Mr. Judge or anyone else.*"

(3) At Taplow, England, on the evening of June 15, 1893, Mrs. Besant met and talked with Dr. and Mrs. Keightley on the subject of this Council meeting, the incident being brought up by reason of the advance proofs from *The Theosophist* of "Theosophic Freethought." Dr. and Mrs. Keightley were both members of the E.S. T., and personal friends at the time with Mrs. Besant as well as Mr. Judge. No action had as yet been taken in the E.S.T. on Mr. Old's and Mr. Edge's actions. In the discussion they asked Mrs. Besant "*what she had done with the parcel of letters between the time when she read and tied them together* [in the afternoon] *and the moment of taking them into the Council with her* [in the evening]. She replied that "*she had locked them in a drawer in her room, where no one could have access to them, and took them from there into the Council Meeting, and that they were not out of her possession for a moment.*"

(4) Very shortly after the above meeting Mrs. Besant drew up the E.S.T. circular dated "August, 1893," which, signed by her and Mr. Judge, was sent to all members of the E.S.T. Very full extracts have already been given in this History from that circular but a portion was reserved for its appropriate setting. We give that portion now. Mrs. Besant first gives the historical background:

> In *Lucifer* for the month of April, a letter by Brother Judge to an unnamed Indian member [Col. Olcott] was published. The letter was

> in reply to many others sent by the Indian member to him, and while dealing with particular questions was deemed by the editor of *Lucifer* [Mrs. Besant] to contain matters of general T.S. interest. In that letter Bro. Judge referred to *a* seal about which his correspondent had asked, and said in effect that he did not know if the Master was in the *habit* of using *the seal referred to*, but Bro. Judge did not state to the Indian [Col. Olcott] the fact that he (Judge) knew of an impression of the seal having appeared upon one or two occasions on letters from the Master to other persons; Bro. Judge not wishing to debate that question and also because—as he now again states to you—such a seal having appeared on letters from Masters to him in his own previous and personal experience was extraneous so far as *he* was concerned, though it did not invalidate any message.

As we have earlier quoted, Mrs. Besant goes on to discuss the Old-Edge article in the July *Theosophist*, gives their "foot note" in reference to the "message" of May 27, 1891—that the E.S.T. was reorganized on the strength of that message with its "seal"—and to suspend Messrs. Old and Edge for their breach of the School Rules and discipline. She then says:

> *But the statement in the above foot-note is itself untrue. The reorganization of the School in 1891 was not based on a message from the Master;* it was based on several letters and certificates from H.P.B. (see Council Minutes) explicitly making William Q. Judge her representative in America, and on one from her assigning to Annie Besant the position she was to hold after her (H.P.B.'s) death. These were in Brother Judge's possession and *were exhibited to the Council.* Brother J. D. Buck, one of the American Council, was also then in London. He, *among others,* suggested *prior to the*

> *meeting a similar plan of reorganization to that proposed by Brother Judge,* and Dr. Buck personally drew up just prior to the Council meeting the new form of the pledge. At the meeting of the Council the plan was submitted *by Annie Besant with some of the passages from H.P.B.'s letters.*

Mrs. Besant then goes on to give the text of a statement drawn up by herself and signed by herself and "such of the Councillors present [at the Meeting of May 27, 1891] whom we can reach at this moment." This statement is dated "London, July 14, 1893," and reads as follows:

> The plan for the reorganization of the E.S.T. rendered necessary by the passing away of H. P. Blavatsky, was laid before the English division of the General Council *by Annie Besant, who had in her possession a bundle of letters from which she read extracts.* These constituted William Q. Judge *H. P. Blavatsky's representative with full powers* in America, and appointed Annie Besant as *Chief Secretary* of the Inner Group (the highest grade *in the E.S.T.*), and *Recorder* of the Teachings. These were the documents upon which the reorganization of the School was based, and the recognition of William Q. Judge and Annie Besant as Outer Heads was made. *The arrangement was rendered inevitable by these letters of H. P. Blavatsky, its Head,* and nothing beyond her *expressed directions* was necessary to insure its acceptance by the Council. Towards the *close* of the proceedings a message was received from Master, "Judge's plan is right." This was written on a small piece of paper *found among the papers in the sight of all by Annie Besant.* The message *bore the impression of a seal, and the impression was recognized by Countess Wachtmeister*

> *and others as that of the Master, being identical with impressions on letters received during the life-time with us of H. P. Blavatsky.*
>
> The message was received as a *most satisfactory sign of approval* of the arrangement proposed, but that arrangement *was in no sense arrived at in consequence of it,* being, as stated, based on H. P. Blavatsky's own letters and accepted as *her directions.*

This statement is signed with the following names: Constance Wachtmeister, G. R. S. Mead, Annie Besant, Laura M. Cooper, W. Wynn Westcott, and Alice Cleather. Immediately following the statement Mrs. Besant appends a memorandum signed by herself alone, as follows:

> I myself selected from among *many letters of H.P.B.'s* those referred to above, and tied them together. *There was no paper with Master's writing bearing above words among them before the meeting.*

(5) It was concerning this "message" in particular, and others merely incidentally, that Mrs. Besant later made so many contradictory and bewildering statements during the dark days from the early fall of 1893 till the conclusion of the "Judge case." Chakravarti was in London when this very circular of August, 1893, was sent out, but had not then gotten Mrs. Besant into his Occult toils. Up till then Mrs. Besant was true to Mr. Judge, all Mr. Sinnett's, Mr. Bert Keightley's and Col. Olcott's insinuations failing to do more than make her "a little uneasy," as she wrote herself in "The Case against W. Q. Judge." That pamphlet tells a pitiful and sorry tale to one who reads it in the light of the ordered facts out of her own mouth, as given in the foregoing numbered paragraphs, and in the light of the *pledge, Rules,* and *Book of Discipline* of the School. It is the proof of the corruption of Annie Besant, not of "forgery" by W. Q. Judge. She herself says (pp. 12-13) that up to September, 1893, when she went to America

in company with Chakravarti and Miss Müller "the idea was to me incredible that a man who had worked so devotedly . . . could deliberately imitate the scripts of the Masters. . . . Of evidence at that time I had none, only vague accusations, and so far was I from crediting these that *I remember saying that before I could believe Mr. Judge guilty, I should need the word of the Master, given to me face to face.*" To whom did she say that? Chakravarti?

At all events Chakravarti had gotten very close to her, as narrated, and had "magnetized" her many times so that she might be able to "see and hear the Master." Mrs. Besant goes on:

> . . . *The result was that I made a direct appeal to the Master,* when alone, stating that *I did feel some doubt* as to Mr. Judge's use of His name, and *praying* Him to *endorse or disavow* the messages I had received.
>
> . . . *He appeared to me as I had so often before seen Him, clearly, unmistakably,* and I then *learned from Him directly that the messages were not done by Him, and that they were done by Mr. Judge.* . . . The order to take action was *repeated to me at Adyar* [Christmas, 1893] . . . and *I was bidden to wash away the stains on the T.S.* "Take up the heavy Karma of the Society. Your strength was given you for this." *How could I, who believed in Him, disobey?*

These alleged "appearances" must have taken place in the *Fall of 1893.* How then, in the face of them if genuine, could she make the statement she did before the European Convention in *July, 1894? Who was it she saw and heard; by what means and under what influences?* But if it were, as she thought, *the Master of H.P.B.,* one must wonder why that Master let her go on being deceived by "bogus" messages for more than two years after the death of H.P.B.; one wonders, too, why she should not have taken her first, her earliest doubts, to Him, and why, if she could reach Him, "clearly, unmistakably,'' she was under any necessity to get ''messages'' at second hand, be it from H.P.B., from Judge, from Chakravarti, from Mr. Leadbeater, or any one else; and why her ''messages'' all supposedly from the same Master, should give each other the lie, and lead her from one labyrinthine passage to another.

CHAPTER XXXV

JUDGE'S DEATH AND THE TINGLEY "SUCCESSORSHIP"

After the British Convention in July, 1895, all hopes necessarily vanished, whether of official affiliation or of fraternal emulation between the two societies. Colonel Olcott, Mrs. Besant, Mr. Sinnett, and their supporters entered on an active campaign in England, Europe, India, and Australia, and the membership in their society was largely augmented during the years immediately following the split in the parent Society. Their followers in America, few in number, rallied around the efforts of Mr. Fullerton to revive the "American Section," but those efforts were futile for the most part until subsequent to the dissensions in the T.S. in A., a year and a half after the death of Mr. Judge.

The newly organized "Theosophical Society in America," free from dissentient elements, continued to follow the same lines of propaganda as had characterized its activities from its original inception in 1887 as the democratic "American Section." In affiliation with the T.S. in A. was the "Theosophical Society in England," comprising about a third of the British Theosophists who had "bolted" from the British Convention in July, 1895. Besides these, a considerable number of individual members on the Continent, and a few members in Australia adhered to the same program of teaching and of practice.

The "Esoteric Section" of the T.S. in A. continued with the original Instructions, pledge, and conduct as maintained by H.P.B. The "Esoteric Section" inaugurated by Mrs. Besant was required to sign a new "pledge"; additional "instructions" were sent out, among them Mrs. Besant's version of the troubles in the

"School"; and, for the first time in the history of the E.S., members were given for study the writings of Mrs. Besant and of Mr. Leadbeater as of equal authenticity and value with the writings of H.P.B. In 1897 the spurious "Third Volume" of the "Secret Doctrine" was issued, containing the garbled reprint of the original *Preliminary Memorandum* and Instructions of H.P.B. to the E.S.T. May 14, 1899, Mrs. Besant withdrew all the original papers and pledges of the School. Since that time the E.S.T. in the Besant fragment of the original T.S. and E.S. has gradually departed from the lines originally laid down by H.P.B., until only the forms remain. The writings and examples of the "Successor" and her satellites have been studied and emulated to the gradual extinction of the original message of Theosophy recorded by H.P.B. This successful and unnoticed substitution was facilitated by the misfortunes which befell the T.S. in A. within less than one year after the separation.

From the autumn of 1893, when the attacks upon him became virulent, Mr. Judge's health slowly gave way. At the time of the Boston Convention in April, 1895, his condition was such that he was able to take but little active part in the proceedings. By October of that year his condition had grown so alarming that at the insistence of friends and physicians he went to Carolina in a vain endeavor to recuperate. This proving of no avail and it becoming increasingly evident that his life could not be prolonged, he returned North by slow stages, spending a fortnight at Cincinnati with Dr. J. D. Buck and other well-known Theosophists. He reached New York City early in February and from then on rapidly declined. Mr. Judge died on Saturday, March 21, 1896, a little less than a year after the separation.

Nothing in Theosophical history has been more obscured and therefore more misunderstood than the series of events immediately following the death of Mr. Judge. In the same way that Mrs. Besant has been accepted and followed in the largest of the existing Theosophical Societies as the "Successor" of H.P.B., so in the other of the two fragments of the parent association was Mrs. Tingley accepted and followed as the "Successor" of Mr. Judge and, through him, of H.P.B. as well. For more than a quarter of a century these two rivals to the mantle and the prestige of the Messenger and her Colleague have filled the world with their claims and assertions. From each of the original fragments numerous defections have inevitably occurred, in each case consisting of some new claimant to "messages from the Masters" with his devoted adherents. All trace back to one and the same basic idea—that of "apostolic succession"—the fecund source of all the sects and sectarianism into which has split up and degenerated every great religion, although each of them was originally, like the message and the mission of H.P.B. herself, a periodic public manifestation of the undying Theosophical *Movement*.

It is not to be presumed that the great bulk of the membership had at any time any knowledge of their own, whether of the Occult nature and status of H.P.B. and Mr. Judge, or of any of the numerous others, Mrs. Besant and Mrs. Tingley among them, who at one time and another have claimed "apostolic succession" and to deliver "messages." Yet the members of the T.S. in A. accepted, as greedily and as readily, the Tingley claim of successorship as had been done before them by those who accepted Mrs. Besant in the same rôle.

Mr. Judge dead, all was confusion and uncertainty among the rank and file of the membership of the Society and of its E.S.T. Some sort of announcement was eagerly looked forward to that should clear the way to the unbroken continuance of the School, the Society, and their common activities. On Friday, March 27, a brief notice announced a "General Meeting of the E. S.T." at the Headquarters, 144 Madison Avenue, New York City, for the following Sunday, March 29, at noon. As many near-by members as possible attended this meeting and were passive participants in what took place. A prepared one-page announcement was read by Mr. E. T. Hargrove as part of the proceedings and this, stamped with the same date as the meeting, was immediately afterwards mailed to all members of the E.S.T. in the United States and throughout the world. This announcement, headed "strictly private and confidential," reads in full:

> Brothers and Sisters: We have been earnestly considering the future of the E.S.T. and its government, during the examination of our elder brother W. Q. Judge's private papers. These papers already show that the future of the School was not left to chance, nor to our mere judgment. They contain astonishing revelations concerning our late Outer Head and definitely prove that he was far greater than superficially appeared. We think it right to inform you at once of this fact, and that his position in the Lodge was higher and his connection with Masters far more intimate and constant than was generally supposed by most members of the School. His papers further show that he did not stand alone in the work, but that, unseen and unknown to all but the very few, he had assistance right at hand, and that he left this assistance behind him, not withdrawn by his death. In regard to this matter we must ask you for the present to remember that even as he trusted us, so you must trust us. But we shall issue a further communication as soon as possible, proving from his own papers the correctness of all that is written above.
>
> Fraternally and faithfully yours,

This announcement was signed, in order, by E. T. Hargrove, Jas. M. Pryse, Joseph H. Fussell, H. T. Patterson, Claude Falls Wright, Genevieve Ludlow Griscom, C. A. Griscom, Jr., and E. Aug. Neresheimer—all well-known members then residing in and near New York City, all active in the Aryan Lodge, the T.S. in A., the E.S.T., the conduct of *The Path,* and the other work centering at the headquarters.

There is no record that any of the members receiving this announcement examined it rigidly for its concordance with or application of the writings and example of H. P.B. and Mr. Judge. No one seems to have inquired how any "private papers" could "definitely prove" that Judge was an "elder brother," his "position in the Lodge" and his "connection with Masters far more intimate and constant," so that "he was far greater than superficially appeared." No one seems to have asked himself or others whether the public work and writings of Mr. Judge for twenty years were not the real evidence of his true nature, rather than any *post mortem* claims made by others, ostensibly on his behalf, regardless of any or all "private papers" alleged to bolster them. Nor did any one question the further assertion that "unseen and unknown to all but the very few" Mr. Judge had left "assistance behind him, not withdrawn by his death." No one inquired how, if this "assistance" had been "unseen and unknown to all but the very few" *before* his death, it was to be "definitely proved" *after* his decease. On the contrary, the membership awaited eagerly and with the "trust" called for, the "further communication proving from his own papers the correctness of all" the astounding claims made in the communication of March 29.

That communication was followed within the week by a nineteen-page pamphlet, also "strictly private and confidential," which was mailed to all members. It is dated April 3, 1896, and contains an address to the members, signed by the same names as the announcement of March 29, together with what is declared to be "a verbatim report of a general E.S.T. meeting held in New York at Headquarters on Sunday, March 29, at 12:30 P. M." The address proceeds:

> This is done according to the directions of the late Outer Head, William Q. Judge. The papers left by him provided for the future management of the School by the present Outer Head, a Council, and an Advisory Council in Europe. The Outer Head is known to and is in

> communication with the Council, but, according to direction and for reasons in part explained in the report of the above mentioned E.S.T. meeting, the name and identity of W. Q. Judge's occult heir and successor is to remain unknown to the members in general for one year. Speculations as to who this Outer Head may be are useless and will prove injurious if indulged in. Both the name and person are practically unknown in the Theosophical Society, having been confided by Mr. Judge to but a very few chosen and trusted friends. Needless to say, the Outer Head is not among those named as being on the Council.
>
> The Council consists of the undersigned and other members to be added as soon as they have been communicated with.
>
> The Advisory Council in Europe remains the same as heretofore.

Although it is declared that all this is done "according to the directions of the late Outer Head, William Q. Judge," neither then nor thereafter were those "directions" reproduced or made accessible for examination. Although it is declared that "the papers left by him provided for the present Outer Head, a Council, and an Advisory Council in Europe" to manage the School, those "papers" were never exhibited for their authenticity to be inspected. These "instructions" and these "private papers" alleged to have been "left" by Mr. Judge, by virtue of which the membership accepted Mrs. Tingley as "the occult heir and successor" appointed by Mr. Judge, are directly and irreconcilably in contradiction, not only to the whole teaching of Theosophy and to H.P.B.'s specific statement in "Isis Unveiled" (Volume 2, p. 544), that "apostolic succession is a gross and palpable fraud," but, as well, in complete antithesis to Mr. Judge's own statements and arguments in the Foulke's case, as quoted in full in Chapter XXIII herein.

After this saddling upon Mr. Judge of responsibility for the claims thus asserted, the address proceeds:

> We are further directed to say to you that:
>
> *"By raising themselves to the point of Trust and Intuition, expected by the Master, which enables them to take the present pledge, members are actually advancing towards real Initiation; they are once more 'reborn,' their past is left behind and they begin to receive* THE NEW LIGHT THAT HAS GONE OUT FROM THE LODGE."

There can be no doubt that the foregoing was intended to be construed, and was construed by the members as a "message from the Master"—presumably received through the "occult heir and successor." A still more significant index of the pressure brought to bear on the members and of the real basis of the whole affair is contained in the next succeeding paragraph, which runs:

> We have only to add to the statements made by us at the E.S.T. meeting, minutes of which are enclosed, that individually and unitedly we have continued to receive unmistakable proof that the Outer Head appointed by W. Q. Judge is in direct communication with Masters, with H.P.B. and with the "luminous youth" or "Rajah," as that Adept has been variously named. This latter fact depends solely upon our most solemn testimony, but those who knew and trusted W. Q. Judge should take his decision as final and sufficient in itself.

The only way these "Council" members whose signatures attest this notable address could have *unmistakable proof* of superphysical "messages" would be, according to the teachings of Theosophy, by their being themselves either *accepted chelas* or *Adepts*. But since their "solemn testimony" relates exclusively to "direct communication with Masters, H.P.B., and Judge" on the part of the new "Outer Head," it must follow that their "unmistakable proof" rested on "messages" received *through* Mrs. Tingley. Their "solemn testimony" is mere hearsay and possesses the same degree of validity as the "testimony" to any other "communicating spirit" through any medium or psychic. But the expression used, "we have *continued* to receive unmistakable proof," is vitally telltale when weighed with the rest of the pretended "evidence" of Mr. Judge's "instructions" and "private papers." The phrase shows that the "unmistakable proofs" trace back in their origin, *not to anything left in writing by W. Q. Judge,* but to bogus "messages from the Master" received through the same source or sources as the "messages" read to the general E.S.T. meeting of March 29. To those "messages" we shall soon come.

The address which prefaces the pamphlet of April 3, 1896, is immediately followed by the printed text of the "Minutes" of the E.S.T. meeting. The minutes begin with a statement by Mr. E. T. Hargrove. After calling for the assent of all present to absolute privacy regarding the proceedings, Mr. Hargrove read the text of the one-page announcement which we have already given. As "evidence" of the "correctness of the statements made" in that announcement, Mr. Hargrove then read what he declared to be "passages from the Chief's diary and from other papers that he has left behind which were not written for the benefit of others, but for his own use, and have all the more significance on that account."

These "extracts" are all, allegedly, from the "Master," and dated November and December, 1894. The "messages" given are all trivial in the extreme and appear to relate entirely to the bitter controversy raging at that time over the charges made by Mrs. Besant against Mr. Judge. There is in them nothing of philosophy or ethics, nothing of reference to events then pending, not well known to hundreds of others besides the "Master" and Mr. Judge; nothing not already public at the time of their date and on record for years before. This set of "extracts" covers slightly less than two printed pages and is referred to by Mr. Hargrove as "*proving* our Chief's constant intercourse with Masters." In themselves they contain no intimation of "Mr. Judge's occult heir and successor." That they were inserted merely to set up the "constant intercourse with Masters" as a background for what was coming, is clearly indicated by Mr. Hargrove's next remarks:

> Now in regard to the assistance which he received—assistance from a living person, I am going to speak of this person, but not by name. I will call that person "Promise." That is not the real name; it is simply invented by myself, and whether it is a man, woman, or child, or merely a voice in the air, matters not in the least: therefore I will speak of that person as "he."

After this preface there follow nearly six pages of further "extracts," accompanied with running comments by Mr. Hargrove. The first is an alleged "message" from H.P.B., dated January 3, 1895. This "message," Mr. Hargrove declared, was part of one from which "extracts" had been read at the time to an E.S. meeting and also sent to London to the "Advisory Council." Mr. Hargrove in presenting his extracts from this message, said: "they contain important references" to "Promise." A quotation will serve to illustrate the "importance" of this and the other messages alleged to be from Mr. Judge's "occult diary." Thus:

> Our dear chela, you have at last found your fellow chela, who was one of ours years ago, consecrated to the work then, and now by the Master's will brought face to face with you. . . . As your light shines into "Promise's" soul, fears will disappear as the dew before the sun.
>
> The forces are out and annihilation is the only thing that can interfere. "Promise" should have been in place with us at the beginning, but for

your folly and his lack of trust in the Master. Let me tell you some of the things I have learned since I absented myself from the outer world. Many of the problems of life that should have been solved if we had been more together have come up before me and I have learned much. I am, next to the America work, interested in Spain. Ireland can take care of itself. In the pine woods I have found a Lodge which I knew something of before I went away. There seven chelas and the light they show that some day will be better known, I will describe to you at our next meeting. There is much connected with it that can be used for irradiating forces in this country, for there is a subtle connection. Be sure that at our next meeting this is not forgotten. Slowly the light from this Lodge is being thrown over Spain, and I see that from the old corpse of bigotry, superstition and credulity will be reared a temple of light which will unite its forces with that of America and Ireland, and from these three points I know that humanity shall be saved. This battle of light and darkness in our midst seems but small when I view the work before us, and the ends and prospects of our work shall stem the tide of this cruel and unworthy persecution. Under all of it, over it all, is the Master's hand; be sure that all is well for thee.

This is our centre here in America illuminated by the Lodge and protected by love. Send "Promise" out, but not yet; you can make what you will of "Promise," for the truthfulness of spirit and devotion to us that are there will make it a good instrument. But keep it well in the background. In outer work "Promise" is our mystery.

The foregoing "message" is followed by others of similar flavor. One from H.P.B. supposed to be dated

April 3, 1895, puts into her mouth the following, called by Mr. Hargrove "most weighty and momentous":

> How I yearn for the day when I can come myself and work. It is being put off by all this strife and bitterness. I WILL COME, AS I SAID, THROUGH "PROMISE." Every day they keep this up is another day of delay for that event.
>
> Had both ("Rajah" and "Promise") been free, you well, and ye met at the time I said, more and more wonderful phenomena would have happened than did with me.

The final "message" read by Mr. Hargrove to the meeting and given in the "minutes" in the pamphlet of April 3, is another "communication" declared to be from H.P.B. to Mr. Judge, apparently early in 1895:

> . . . your faculties begin to swell and a part of the connection is made. The moon and the place and water and "Promise" helped us. . . . When anything pushes you ahead it does the same for "Promise." . . .
>
> A year and over of probation was given by Master to those who do so madly try to destroy his work and his chela, yet they turn not from their evil ways.
>
> "Promise" through his hands will do some of my best work.

It is impossible to believe that any one soever could have treated these "messages" seriously on any theory of their inherent worth. Solely on the assumption that they were "phenomenal," were from the "Master," and from the discarnate H.P.B., does it seem possible that any one could give them a moment's respectful attention. But to regard them from that point of view is to do violence to all the Messages received from those very Masters through H.P.B. herself while she was alive—is to ignore and cast aside the repeated injunctions of Judge himself. *Philosophy and moral worth,* not *phenomena,* had been insistently held forth as the sole and only criterion of right judgment on any and all "messages" and conduct. Some light on the *glamour* enveloping these "messages" with a fictitious and phenomenal importance is thrown by Mr. Hargrove's closing remarks, after the reading of the "messages":

> This clearly shows that our only chance for the future lies in our trust in this light from the Lodge which is within us all, but which must also have a special centre of action to focus and distribute its rays. . . .
>
> Trust is our only salvation, but reason alone should show us that he *could not* have left that body if he had not had an occult heir and successor to take his place, for that is the law in the Lodge. This occult heir is the link between ourselves and him, and so on from the Rajah to H.P.B., to Masters and to the great Lodge. There must be that link; his papers showed us where to find it; we have found it, have tested it and verified it beyond all question, individually and unitedly.

These are the "proofs" that the circular of March 29 so positively informed the membership would be supplied them—"proofs" that were so "unmistakable" to Mr. Hargrove and his associates; yet "trust" and still more "trust" was affirmed by Mr. Hargrove as "our only chance for the future," as "our only salvation." Mr. Hargrove's closing remarks clearly show, clearly *prove*, not the claimed "successorship," but the attitude and state of mind with which he and his fellows approached their "examination." Their logic was: "Mr. Judge must have left a successor. He *could not* die without an occult heir. There must be a link. Where shall we find it? How shall we test it? By the philosophy of Theosophy, by the past statements of H.P.B. and Judge? No, by "messages" from him, from H.P.B., from Masters, through his "occult heir."

With such an attitude of mind, with such ideas of Theosophy, of Masters, of what was to be looked for, it was inevitable that they should find what they were looking for, receive the anticipated "messages," believe them, and accept as Mr. Judge's chosen Successor the one through whom they got their "confirmation," and should "continue to receive unmistakable proof."

After Mr. Hargrove's repeated positive assertions, one after another of the "Council" which sat with him upon the platform at the meeting of March 29, 1896, added his "solemn testimony" to the truth of what Mr. Hargrove had said. These statements are all reproduced *verbatim* in the pamphlet of April 3. Mr. Pryse said:

> We cannot be too careful of our words. So the little I have to say I have written down, simply for the sake of clearness. I endorse what Mr. Hargrove has said to you. And I wish to reiterate his request that in this critical time you should give us your confidence and unwavering support. Our position is not one to be envied. For myself I am here for only one reason: because our Chief desired it.

Mr. J. H. Fussell followed Mr. Pryse and declared:

> I wish first to say that I know of my own knowledge that what our Brother Ernest T. Hargrove has stated is true; that our Chief, the Rajah, is with us, and that he has not left us by the death of his worn-out body. But since the death of that body he has been, and is now, with us and the whole School, and he is still working along the same lines that he has worked hitherto; and will continue to so work and to lead us.

Mr. H. T. Patterson was as emphatic as those who preceded him:

> I realize the solemnity of this occasion. I realize the tremendous importance of the step we have taken. Were I doubtful I should not dare take the responsibility I have. I have no doubts. My certainty is due partly to knowledge held

> in common with these others; partly to my own independent knowledge; and partly to the writings of William Q. Judge which I myself have seen.

Mr. Claude Falls Wright spoke at some length and in his remarks will be found the unconscious disclosure of the source of the Tingley claim of successorship. Mr. Wright said:

> . . . what we are saying is in corroboration of the statements and documents laid before you by Mr. Hargrove. . . .
>
> For myself I will say that I have always believed and trusted in the aid of Higher Powers and the Masters, and I knew we should not be deserted. But a few weeks before the late body of the Rajah passed away I confess I became troubled a little about the future; such periods of gloom and darkness come to all. And then I received, no matter in what way, a message which at once removed all doubt and depression, and which I showed to many members present. . . .
>
> I met this Chela—"Promise"—several times in 1894 and 1895. Mr. Judge introduced me at a meeting of the Aryan T.S. in 1894, saying to me beforehand: "Here is some one I want you to look at closely; it is a particular person." He afterwards told me that "Promise" frequently was in touch with the Lodge. Later he sent me to a house where "Promise" was staying, and there this chela went into a trance and told me much of the future. . . .
>
> That we would not be deserted all of you must have felt sure. It is this trust . . . that has continued our school under the direct protection of the Masters and the Lodge. We on this platform have in the last few days had marvelous proofs of this.

It should be self-evident that if Mr. Judge had had anything to do with selecting his alleged successor, he would not have left the students dependent upon "messages," either before or after his death, which they would have no means of verifying, nor upon the verbal say-so of any, but would have left clear, indisputable evidence, in his own physical handwriting of his own opinion and advice. H.P.B. left no "successor," but she assuredly did leave abundant record in her own handwriting of how she regarded the various students, notably Mrs. Besant and Mr. Judge. That many came to regard Mrs. Besant as her successor was certainly no fault of H. P.B.'s, but due to Mrs. Besant's self-assertions and the natural credulity and misconceptions of human beings. It can be observed by any one who reads closely the assertions in the circular of March 29, and its "proof" in the pamphlet of April 3, 1896, that in no place is the specific statement made that any of the alleged "proofs" were in *Mr. Judge's own handwriting.* His "private papers" are freely spoken of, his "occult diary," his "instructions for the future management of the School" —but that is all. If Mr. Judge had *himself* left any such "unmistakable proofs," would not the "Council" and Mrs. Tingley have been first and foremost in proclaiming the fact and inviting the fullest and most rigid inspection of the alleged documents? The inference is irresistible. The surety is made doubly sure by the fact that from that day to this not one of those "private papers," or "instructions," or the "occult diary" has ever been produced. The weakness of Mr. Wright's statement of his conversations with Mr. Judge becomes the more evident the more it is examined from various aspects. If he had known since 1894 that Mrs. Tingley or "Promise" was in "communication with Masters," was a true "chela," was "frequently in touch with the Lodge"—was, in short, to be Mr. Judge's "successor"—why was he "troubled" just before Mr. Judge's death? If he received the "message" of which he spoke that "at once removed all doubt and depression," then it is evident that his "certainty" about "Promise" was not due to anything Mr. Judge had previously said to him about her. It seems not to have occurred to him or to any of the others that if Mr. Judge were, in fact, an "elder brother" in "high standing" with the "Lodge," an *"adept,"* perhaps Mr. Judge himself was able to see "much of the future" and was giving Mr. Wright an *occult hint to put him on his guard* against the future "successor" claim. If it were Mr. Judge who sent him later to see Mrs. Tingley, and if, as Mr. Wright says, she "went into a *trance,"* it only shows Mrs. Tingley to have been a medium, or "sensitive," *not a chela.* "Mediumship," wrote H.P.B. in "Isis Unveiled" (Volume 2, p. 588) "is the *opposite* of adeptship. And as to Mr. Wright's closing line as quoted, it is to be remarked that neither he nor any of the others went into any details on the "marvelous proofs" they had "continued to receive" after Mr. Judge's death.

Mrs. G. L. Griscom followed Mr. Wright in the meeting and said: "I wish most earnestly and emphatically to corroborate everything that has been said by Mr. Hargrove."

Her husband, Mr. C. A. Griscom, Jr., next stated:

> I have nothing to add to what has already been said except that I have followed step by step all that has led up to this meeting. And I bear my testimony to the absolute truthfulness of what has been said.

Mr. Neresheimer was the last to give his "solemn testimony." He said:

> I have a few remarks to make with regard to the Outer Head or chela of whom you have heard. Mr. Judge several years ago put me into communication with that person, and I think it is my duty to inform you of the fact. As you have heard, you will be made acquainted with the person after the expiration of one year.

Mr. Neresheimer then read a "communication from the Masters," which he said he had received "through this person" in March, 1895, assumedly in regard to the Boston Convention. Its last sentence is telltale. It reads: *"Under no circumstances must Mr. Judge know of this."* There is no doubt—since they both admitted it—that Mr. Neresheimer and Mr. Wright had been in the habit of "consulting" Mrs. Tingley, believed in her "powers," and accepted as "messages from the Masters" communications received through her, a year or more before Mr. Judge's death. Yet their "pledge" in the E.S.T. and the "Rules" of the "School," both absolutely forbade such intercourse. Like many another, they "wandered from the discipline" and inevitably reaped the consequences. To what state Mr. Neresheimer and the others had come in the few days following Mr. Judge's death is shown by Mr. Neresheimer's concluding remarks:

> It is the desire of the Rajah that those people who are on this platform, and others who have also been named by the Rajah are to be the Council of this movement in America. We are to receive our instructions, whatever there be, from the Outer Head, with whom, as I previously stated, I am acquainted and so are the others.

From all the foregoing it must be clear that the general membership not only had no knowledge of their own in regard to the "Successor," nor any means of verifying the alleged "proofs," even had such opportunity been afforded them, for the "unmistakable proofs" were all *phenomenal* and hung on "messages" from H.P.B. and "Masters." Equally must it be apparent that the membership relied wholly and absolutely on the "solemn testimony" of these eight witnesses and their direct assertions that all this was but carrying out Mr. Judge's directions. Those witnesses were all well-known Theosophists, all with good reputations, manifestly sincere in their point-blank declarations; hence their testimony as to super-mundane facts was accepted as unquestioningly as it might have been regarding the most ordinary everyday occurrences.

This brings the inquiry straight home to the eight witnesses themselves. The mass of the membership relied on them and their oaths. What did *they* rely on? The answer must be: On Mrs. Tingley and on "messages" received through her, not on any documents in the handwriting of William Q. Judge. Mr. Neresheimer and Mr. Wright, on their own confession, and the others by their indirect statements, showed they had attended *séances* with Mrs. Tingley before Mr. Judge's death, and certainly afterwards when all their "marvelous proofs" were received.

A reading of the pamplet of April 3 makes clear that some sort of consultations had been going on prior to the meeting of Sunday, March 29. What were they, and what reasons for secrecy and silence regarding them? No faintest intimation was suffered to leak out as to what took place in the interval between Mr. Judge's death, March 21, and the meeting of March 29, save and except the assertion that "we have been examining Mr. Judge's private papers." What were the facts thus kept purposely obscured?

This much is known: Almost at once after the funeral services, Messrs. Neresheimer and Griscom invaded the privacy of Mrs. Judge's grief and asked and obtained from her the keys to Mr. Judge's desk and to the safety-deposit box in which Mr. Judge kept his personal papers. Later on, when Mrs. Judge visited the headquarters she found no private papers of Mr. Judge in his desk, and on going to the safety-deposit box, found it absolutely empty. *What became of those papers?* They have never been produced to this day.

Next, it is known that Mr. Neresheimer went to Mrs. Tingley for "advice and instruction." That he received both abundantly is shown by the sequel—a sequel not disclosed for two years and then unwittingly as to its implications and bearings on the "successorship" claim. Mr. Neresheimer summoned to a private meeting at Mrs. Tingley's house on Thursday evening, March 26, the witnesses whose testimony the members afterwards relied on. There they were "told" *by Mrs. Tingley* that Mr.

Judge had "told" her in conversation in 1895 to appoint them as her "Council" in case of his death! On the strength of Mrs. Tingley's own rendition of this alleged "conversation" with Mr. Judge in 1895, and on the "messages" produced, assumedly from "H.P.B." and "the Masters," rests the whole myth that *Mr. Judge* appointed "Promise" his "occult heir and successor." The much-proclaimed and never-produced "private papers of Mr. Judge" bear a rather remarkable likeness to "private notes" of *Mrs. Tingley*.

It is from these "private notes" of *Mrs. Tingley* and other matter in *The Searchlight* for April, 1898, and Mr. Hargrove's admissions which drew them forth, that the final light is shed on the mysteries leading up to the E. S.T. meeting of March 29, 1896, and the pamphlet of April 3 following. *The Searchlight* itself was a rabidly pro-Tingley publication issued at irregular intervals during the throes of the fierce struggle that ensued in 1898 between Mrs. Tingley's supporters and those of Mr. Hargrove. To appreciate the bearings of *The Searchlight* revelations it is necessary to sketch briefly the intervening events.

The pamphlet of April 3, 1896, was followed at the end of April by the annual Convention of the T.S. in A. The active and controlling factor in the Society at large was, of course, the E.S.T. When the Convention met at New York City, it was already an open secret that "Promise" was Mrs. Tingley. On her "suggestion" Mr. Hargrove was enthusiastically elected President of the T.S. in A. He appointed Mr. Fussell as his private secretary and took charge of the editorial conduct of *The Path,* whose name had meantime been changed to *Theosophy*. Mr. Wright "called to more important work" as the private secretary of the "successor" to Mr. Judge, addressed the Convention and informed it that "the Masters" were "preparing to found a School for the Revival of the Lost Mysteries of Antiquity." Mrs. Tingley addressed the Convention on the same subject. Amidst unbounded enthusiasm a subscription list was opened for this "School" and a large sum quickly raised.

Following the Convention, on May 14, a "strictly private and confidential" circular was sent to all E.S.T. members and entitled "An Urgent Appeal." They were informed that a "CRUSADE has been directed by the Master," and all were urged to contribute. The circular included the following gem of inanity from the new "Outer Head":

> Today the needs of humanity are embodied in one great *call:* "Oh God, my God, is there no help for us?" All people should heed the call of the Master and help to belt the world within the compass of the "cable tow" of the crusaders, for in their force is a quality of the "golden promise"—the Light of the Lodge. It will radiate throughout the world, and with the aid of the widow's mite will make perfect the Master's plan.

This appeal of the "golden '*Promise*'—"the Light of the Lodge"—was joyfully responded to by the membership. Many thousands of dollars were raised and the "Crusaders," headed by Mrs. Tingley, prepared to carry the "message" around the world. Great meetings were held in Boston and New York City. Speeches were made, greetings were read from many noted Theosophists. By the middle of June, when the "Crusaders" departed for Europe on the first stage of their journey round the globe, Mrs. Tingley, whose "successorship" had meantime been publicly announced, was universally regarded by leaders and rank-and-file alike as the "Agent of the Masters." This feeling had been greatly strengthened by a seven-page circular issued in the E.S.T., written by Mr. Hargrove and sent out "with the consent and approval of the Council" on May 17, 1896. It was entitled "An Occultist's Life," and purported to give "certain facts" in the life of the new "Outer Head,"—"facts," says Mr. Hargrove, "which were well known to Judge during his lifetime." Mr. Judge's name thus having been lugged in to support his theme, Mr. Hargrove proceeds to tell of the "voices" and the "strange spirit" which accompanied "Promise" during her childhood; of her "fiery devotion to humanity"; of her being "at last allowed by the Master to separate herself from her [first] husband and to return to her father's home"; of her having been "directed to marry her present husband, on an unusual basis," after "throwing aside many more advantageous offers"; of her then becoming "more fully conscious of her true occult position"; of her using "her power as a psychometer"; of Mr. Judge's "approval of this work." Mr. Hargrove then declares that Mr. Judge told him that this "work" had been "carried on by Master's direction and under Master's supervision." Mr. Hargrove told how "'Promise' has suffered as very few have suffered," and concluded his panegyric:

> "Promise" reached Theosophy by degrees, and in the process of reaching it underwent a training and preparation even more rigid and comprehensive than that experienced by either H.P.B. or W.Q.J. Always guided by the Master, every event in her life had a meaning and a purpose: When the "moment of consummation" came, several years ago, known and recognized by Mr. Judge, the meaning and the purpose became clear at last. . . .
>
> Let us all bear this warning in mind: "Do not let us in any way throw the slightest obstacle in the path of our chosen leader. If we do, we shall regret it."

In prefacing this remarkable contribution Mr. Hargrove assured the members that it was sent out "unknown to the O[uter] H[ead]," and that the members "should use great discrimination in giving out the facts it contains." Those "facts" are unaccompanied by names, dates, verifiable references of any kind, and from first to last are such as could only have emanated from "Promise" herself.

Coincident with Mr. Hargrove's circular letter of May 17 to the E.S.T., there appeared in the *New York*

Tribune of May 18, an article of more than two full columns disclosing Mrs. Tingley's identity as the "Successor," and containing a long authorized "interview" with her. Under date of May 21, another "strictly private and confidential" circular was sent out to all members of the E.S.T., containing a "warning" against the "Black Powers"; a disclosure of "Promise's" identity as Mrs. Tingley, and enclosing a copy of the *Tribune* article.

Mr. Hargrove and Mr. Wright accompanied Mrs. Tingley on her "Crusade" from New York around the world. Mrs. Alice L. Cleather joined the party in Europe. From the departure in June, 1896, till the return to San Francisco in February, 1897, Mr. Hargrove kept *Theosophy* supplied with a monthly report of the wonders of the "Crusade." Mr. Fussell, Mr. Neresheimer, and others continued the propaganda in the United States. An E.S.T. circular was sent out, dated July 12, 1896, and signed "The Council," containing the text of a "message from H.P.B." received by the "Crusaders" in mid-ocean on June 15. During the eight months of the "Crusade" the pages of *Theosophy* witnessed from month to month the highly colored pictures painted for the edification and encouragement of the membership. On the return to America the "cornerstone" of the "School for the Revival of the Lost Mysteries of Antiquity" was laid with great *éclat* by Mrs. Tingley and her aides at Point Loma, near San Diego, California. "Warnings" were issued in E.S.T. circulars dated January 21, and May 4, 1897, of attacks upon the "Outer Head" and the "work." During the summer of 1897 the campaign of laudation of Mrs. Tingley as "successor" of Mr. Judge and as "Leader of the Theosophical Movement throughout the world," had reached the point where all lesser lights were eclipsed or shone as mere satellites.

Mr. Hargrove, despite his chief and most prominent part in these pyrotechnics, and in spite of being the President of the T.S.A. and editor of *Theosophy* would seem to have reached the conclusion that his rôle of Warwick, the King-maker, had been played entirely too successfully.

He found that Mr. Neresheimer as co-legatee of the publishing business under the will of Mr. Judge was disposed to overrule him in the editorial conduct of *Theosophy*. In the disputes which ensued, Mr. Hargrove, finding himself powerless, resigned the Presidency of the T.S. in A. and the conduct of *Theosophy*. Mutual felicitations were published, but the actual cause of controversy kept secret, as was the dissension between Mr. Neresheimer and "Jasper Niemand"—Mrs. Keightley—the other legatee. In the E.S.T. however, a circular was sent out, dated September 3, 1897. It was signed by Mrs. Tingley, and contains the admission that it was she who had "suggested" Mr. Hargrove for President in the first place, because, she said: "I knew at that crisis he was the only available man to fill the place." This circular was quickly followed by two additional communications to the E.S.T., both dated September 13, 1897, and both signed by Mrs. Tingley. As subsequently became clear, both these pamphlets were preparatory for the open battle which followed a little later. One of the pamphlets related to "The International Brotherhood League," organized by Mrs. Tingley immediately after the return from the "Crusade." The other was entitled "The Theosophical Movement." These were followed by the correspondence between Mr. Neresheimer and Mrs. Keightley, over the publishing business. Mrs. Keightley espoused the cause of Mr. Hargrove and Mr. Neresheimer was determined to support the cause of Mrs. Tingley. In November, Dr. Keightley resigned the Presidency of the affiliated Theosophical Society in England and the Presidency of the English E.S.T. "Council," without assigning any reasons.

By January, 1898, the internal rivalry had become so high-pitched that its echoes began to reach the ears of the general membership both of the T.S. in A., and of the E.S.T. On January 3, 1898, a highly laudatory pamphlet was distributed to the membership, recounting in detail the "great works" accomplished by Mrs. Tingley. It was signed by Mr. Fussell and others and was sent out "unofficially." This was followed by the perfecting of plans at a private conference held at Mrs. Tingley's home early in January for the organization of the "Universal Brotherhood" and the mergence in it of the T. S. in A. at the forthcoming annual Convention. This meeting was not made known at the time, but public official notice was sent out that the Convention would be held on February 18, 1898, at Chicago, instead of at the end of April, as had been the invariable custom from the beginning.

The proponents of Mr. Hargrove had meantime been active and vigilant. A circular was sent out by them, signed by Mrs. Keightley among others, and dated January 17, 1898, asking for signatures and support to elect Mr. Hargrove President at the coming Convention. As Mr. Neresheimer's name was proposed for Treasurer and as the circular proposed to create the old title of Corresponding Secretary and elect Mrs. Tingley to that office, the move was well calculated to appeal to peace-loving members. The pro-Tingley faction countered with a circular signed by Mr. Neresheimer as President of the T.S. in A., disavowing any connection with the scheme and calling for support of Mrs. Tingley. The Hargrove supporters re-issued their circular with a "Note" signed by Mr. A. H. Spencer and dated January 23, disclaiming any intention in the original circular of the 17th to make it appear that Mrs. Tingley was enlisted with the scheme. Another circular—undated—followed from the Hargrove faction declaring that "serious and obvious defects exist in the management of the Society" and, without naming her, arguing against the overwhelming authority exercised by Mrs. Tingley. This was followed by an E.S.T. circular issued by Mrs. Tingley, in which she tells the members:

> I have evidence from one or two places of absolute disloyalty to the Master and the School. Plans in embryo, indicating proposed action, which would be detrimental to the interests of the Theosophical Society, have come into my hands.

After invoking the names of H.P.B. and Mr. Judge, Mrs. Tingley gives the E.S.T. members the intimation of the program prepared for the Convention on February 18, in these words:

> Look for instructions which will open the door to those who wish to avail themselves of the opportunities of the new cycle, to be mailed on February 18, 1898, to Presidents of E.S.T. Groups for distribution to each Member.

The instructions referred to were duly distributed and advised the members of a New Lodge being formed under her direction, "to be the Guardians of the E.S.T.," and containing the usual warning against the "few who are working adversely at the present time to the interests of the School." She adds the significant words:

> When the report of the Convention of the Theosophical Society in America at Chicago shall have reached you, you will then better understand the deeper significance of one door closing and the other opening.

The Convention of the T.S. in A. duly met at Chicago on February 18, 1898. There was a large and enthusiastic attendance of delegates and visitors. There were placed in the hands of the delegates prepared and printed Resolutions, a Preamble and Constitution of the "Universal Brotherhood," and a "Proclamation to the Members of the Theosophical Society in America, by Katherine A. Tingley." Willingly, and with little short of unanimity, the Convention adopted the Resolutions, which provided for the turning over of the T.S. in A. to the "Universal Brotherhood" organization, and its future conduct as a department of that institution and under its Constitution. The Constitution of the "Universal Brotherhood" provided for various officers and a "Cabinet." Mrs. Tingley was constituted its "Leader and Official Head," and the same of the T.S. in A. department. Under the Constitution of both, as presented and adopted, all final authority vested in Mrs. Tingley. No action of any kind could be valid if disapproved of by her, and any action taken by her as "Leader and Official Head" was incontestable. It was provided that this "Constitution" might be amended by a two-thirds vote at any "Congress" of the organization, but such congress could be called only by the "Leader and Official Head," and "no amendment shall be of force until approved by the Leader and Official Head." Mrs. Tingley had the right to appoint or remove at pleasure any and all Officers, and supreme control over all Branches and Lodges coming under the new organization.

The Hargrove band of followers, few in number, met in another hall after the Tingley program was adopted by the Convention. Mr. Spencer presided and resolutions protesting against the action of the Convention were adopted. The meeting then proceeded to hold a "convention" of its own. Resolutions were passed affirming that the action of the Chicago Convention was illegal; electing Mr. Spencer acting President, appointing an Executive Committee, and reaffirming the Constitution of the T.S. in A. as originally adopted at Boston in April, 1895.

Thereafter an active and violent battle was waged to gain the adherence of the members of the T.S. in A. and of the E.S.T.—on the one hand by Mrs. Tingley's "Universal Brotherhood," and on the other by the Hargrove faction. More than 95 per cent of the membership accepted the action of the Chicago Convention. In all, some 200 members out of approximately 6,000 followed Mr. Hargrove and his associates. During the excitement which followed the Chicago Convention Mr. Hargrove issued a twenty-seven-page pamphlet entitled "E.S.T.," which was mailed to as many members as possible. It was dated March 1, 1898.

This "E.S.T." pamphlet of Mr. Hargrove's is, perhaps, the most remarkable of all the remarkable utterances put afloat by him during the entire period from the death of Mr. Judge onwards. It is in the form of "Minutes" of an "E.S.T. meeting" called by Mr. Hargrove at Chicago in the late afternoon of February 19, following the Chicago Convention and the dissentient meeting held by the "bolters" from the action taken by that Convention. At this meeting Mr. Hargrove read to those who answered his call, a series of letters addressed by him to Mrs. Tingley at various dates from January 19, 1898 up to and including noon of the date of the meeting—February 19. The pamphlet contains the full text of these letters, plus bracketed comments added by Mr. Hargrove, and containing also other letters addressed by him to Mrs. Tingley subsequent to the Convention and up to February 25, 1898. There can be no dispute regarding these letters, as they were published by Mr. Hargrove himself. In them he incidentally makes the most astonishing admissions as to the course of events immediately following Mr. Judge's death. If the reader will refer to the statements of Mr. Hargrove at the meeting of March 29, and those contained in the circulars of that date and of April 3, 1896, as given earlier in the present chapter, and compare them with the statements made in his letters to Mrs. Tingley as given in his "E.S.T." pamphlet of March 1, 1898, the nature of the fraud perpetrated on the membership in declaring Mrs. Tingley to have been the successor appointed by Mr. Judge, becomes at once apparent. For in his letter to Mrs. Tingley dated January 30, 1898, he says:

> Now, my dear friend, you have made an awful mess of it—that is the simple truth. *You were run in as O*(uter) *H*(ead) as the only person in sight who was ready to hand at the time. We were all of us heartily glad to welcome you, for you solved the problem which confronted us—who was to be O. H.; you were a sort of neutral centre around which we could congregate. And most of us fairly yelled with delight, for you solved our difficulty and we had ample proofs that some members of the Lodge were working through you and that you had high and rare mediumistic and psychic gifts and that you were

> a disciple of the Lodge. So things went swimmingly for a time.
>
> Our enthusiasm and anxiety to see all go well carried some of us too far—carried me too far to the extent of . . . leading me to use my personal influence with people to get them to accept you as O. H. I thought it was for the good of the work, but since then I have learned better.

In the course of his bracketed comments Mr. Hargrove refers to the *original* Minutes of the "Council" meeting at Mrs. Tingley's home following the death of Mr. Judge. This does not refer to the "general E.S.T. Meeting" of March 29, 1896, but to the secret gathering at Mrs. Tingley's home on Thursday evening, March 26, 1896. Mr. Hargrove quotes from page 2 of those Minutes: "After some speculation we finally, through E. T. H(argrove) were told that the Outer Head was Purple (Mrs. Tingley)." Mr. Hargrove adds a further reference to page 54 of the Minutes to show that it was *through him* that the other members of the Council "first heard of" Mrs. Tingley as the "Outer Head." His comments also show that a *revised* version of the original minutes of this meeting was later prepared *at Mrs. Tingley's direction.* Neither the "original" nor the "revised" version of what took place at that meeing has ever been made public, though Mr. Hargrove claimed in his comments that a certified copy of the original Minutes and the original of the *revised* version were in his possession.

That Mr. Hargrove, as well as Mrs. Tingley, had "high and rare mediumistic and psychic gifts" is indicated throughout his letters, for he tells Mrs. Tingley: "It is by Master's order that I write you"; "by order of the Master you have ceased to be the Outer Head of the E.S.T. in the interior and true sense"; "The Outer Head to follow you has already been appointed by the Master."

The circulation of Mr. Hargrove's pamphlet, the legal proceedings begun by him and his associates to test the validity of the action of the Chicago Convention, and the revival of the old *Theosophical Forum,* with its first number dated February, 1898, containing an account of the Chicago proceedings and the efforts of the "bolters" to continue on the old lines—all these were met by vigorous efforts on the part of the pro-Tingley majority. By the middle of April the first number of *The Searchlight*, to which we have referred, was out with forty large pages of fine print in an endeavor to counteract the feared effects of the Hargrove revelations. The combined matter of both sides, when sifted and related to the proceedings made public immediately after the death of Mr. Judge in the circulars of March 29 and April 3, 1896, establishes beyond all question that Mrs. Tingley's "successorship" was due, and due only, to the "messages" obtained by virtue of the "high and rare mediumistic and psychic gifts" of Mrs. Tingley, Mr. Hargrove, Mr. Wright, and others—"messages" from "Masters," from the *dead* H.P.B. and the *dead* W. Q. Judge—not to any "appointment" made by the *living* William Q. Judge in *his own physical handwriting.*

Completely inoculated with the virus of "apostolic succession," both the fragments of the parent Theosophical Society rapidly degenerated. To do more than sketch briefly the successive steps of that degeneracy would serve no useful purpose and would itself be foreign to the enduring work of the Movement.

After the Convention at Chicago in 1898 Mrs. Tingley carried with her, practically *in toto,* the American Theosophists. Her "Universal Brotherhood and Theosophical Society" soon removed its "international headquarters" to Point Loma, near San Diego, California. Disintegration began almost immediately. Silently, as disillusionment set in, the membership began to lapse, and within a few years the "society" became a mere "colony." Of the more than six thousand members of the T.S. in A. in 1896, less than as many hundred now regard the decaying stump at Point Loma as the Theosophical tree.

Mr. Hargrove and his group of recalcitrants fared no

better. Imbued with the same basic ideas, they substituted their revived "Theosophical Society in America" as the "successor" of the parent organization. In 1908 the name was changed to that of "The Theosophical Society." It has its own "chelas," its own "esoteric school," its own "messages from the Masters," and has become a mild and respectable Theosophical Episcopalianism, with particular emphasis on "the Master Jesus" and the "theosophy" of the "saints" of Catholic history. Its American membership has never exceeded from two to three hundred and its membership abroad has never been more than a handful.

Another offshoot of the break-up was the "Temple of the People." This began early in 1899 with a circular issued from Syracuse, New York, and signed by Dr. W. H. Dower and Frances J. Myers. Its particular "chela" was Mrs. Francia A. La Due, and her "messages from the Masters," given out under the pseudonym of "Blue Star," were its inspiration until her death in 1923. "The Temple" achieved a considerable following for several years. Many "Squares" (Branches) were established by ex-members of the "T.S. in A.," and the "Universal Brotherhood." Early in the present century Mrs. La Due was "ordered" to establish a "colony" at Halcyon, California. As other "initiates" offered new "messages from the Masters," the "Temple" became less and less frequented, and of this "successorship" but a forlorn remnant remains, as at Point Loma—sad relic of the collapse of the American fragment of the old Third Section.

"The Theosophical Society of New York" is still another attempt to resuscitate the work of the Third Section. This also began in 1899 and grew out of the long connection with Mr. Judge of Dr. J. H. Salisbury. Dr. Salisbury, with Mr. Donald Nicholson, managing editor of the *New York Tribune,* another early friend of H.P.B. and Mr. Judge, and Mr. Harold W. Percival, then a young man, gathered around them a small group. With this group became partly affiliated Dr. Alexander Wilder and Mrs. Laura Langford (Mrs. Laura Holloway), one of the "chela" authors of "Man: Fragments of Forgotten History." The work of this society was continued for many years, but its vitality was never great and it was subject to the same basic defects as the better known survivors of the old American Section. It has been practically dormant for years since the discontinuance of its organ, *The Word,* published by Mr. Percival.

Dr. J. D. Buck, one of the best known of the original generation of Theosophical students, a firm supporter of H.P.B. and Mr. Judge, and author of several books, was Vice-President of the T.S. in A. at the time of Mr. Judge's death. He, like the rest, accepted the Tingley "successorship" and was active in her support for two years. After the Chicago Convention in 1898, he followed Mr. Hargrove in secession from the action taken at that Convention. After a short adhesion to Mr. Hargrove's T.S. in A., Dr. Buck was attracted by Mrs. La Due's claims and joined the "Temple of the People." When "the T. K."—Richardson—and Mrs. Huntley began their "Great Work," the claims of "the T.K." to represent "the Masters" and to afford a "scientific formula" for "adeptship," presented an irresistible lure to Dr. Buck. He became one of the most ardent devotees of "the T. K." and did his utmost to secure the adhesion of his old time Theosophical associates to the new "messenger of the Masters." The fraud and exposure of "the T.K." broke his heart and Dr. Buck did not long survive.

Another Theosophist of the first generation, Mrs. Alice L. Cleather, accepted as unquestioningly as did the others Mrs. Tingley's "successorship." For two years Mrs. Cleather was one of the most ardent and active supporters of Mrs. Tingley. She quietly dropped out in 1899. In later years she gathered a group of "pupils" to whom she imparted her own version of Theosophical history and teachings. After traveling on the Continent from place to place she finally removed to India. When the dissensions regarding Mr. Leadbeater became once more acute in Mrs. Besant's society a few years ago, Mrs. Cleather emerged from the obscurity of her own "esoteric" retreat and work. Taking advantage of the occasion she wrote two booklets, ostensibly in "defense" of H.P.B. against the "successorship" and conduct of Mrs. Besant. In the course of these booklets Mrs. Cleather declared that Mr. Judge, not she and her one-time associates, had been deluded and dominated by Mrs. Tingley. Her declarations to that effect have been as readily and as unquestioningly accepted by many as her declarations to the contrary were formerly taken at face value. A Blavatsky Association was formed by followers of Mrs. Cleather to "perpetuate the memory and work" of H.P.B., to which members of Mrs. Besant's society are denied entrance.

Turning to the other fragment of the parent T.S.—that which adhered to Col. Olcott and Mrs. Besant after the split of 1895—it has, by contrast to the mutilated and dying *skandhas* of the old "American Section," achieved a far longer life and a far greater utilitarian success, with a correspondingly greater degradation of the original Objects and teachings enunciated by H.P.B. Various contributory factors have brought this about. In the beginning the great prestige and tradition attached to Col. Olcott as the President-Founder of the parent T.S. caused the whole of the Indian and Australasian membership to remain loyal to the fragment headed by him. In Great Britain, on the Continent, and, to a small extent, in the United States, the ability and reputation of Mrs. Besant, the secondary but powerful influence of Mr. Sinnett and other well-known writers and leaders, coupled with the fact that the Besant-Olcott wing were the accusers and not the accused, gave an initial great advantage before the public. The dogma of "successorship" can be applied equally to organizations as to persons, and many who might have remained indifferent to Mrs. Besant's own claims as "successor to H.P.B.," were undoubtedly influenced by the name "The Theosophical Society" and the venerable President-Founder's connection with it. The death of Mr. Judge in less than a year after the split left Col. Olcott for eleven years in the unique position of sole survivor of the original Three Founders of the parent T.S. and this was fully exploited.

The dissensions which almost at once sprang up among the survivors of the American fragment and the speedy collapse of the spectacular performances staged by Mrs. Tingley and her competitors for the mantle of Mr. Judge, left the Besant-Olcott combination with no real rival in the "successorship" rôle. In the summer of 1899, Mrs. Besant withdrew the pledge, *memorandum,* and instructions of H.P.B. and substituted a new "pledge" for her "esoteric" students. This was followed by "studies" and "instructions" of her own, and by the circulation in her "School" of the "clairvoyant investigations" of Mr. Leadbeater and herself which were later published as "Occult Chemistry." Mrs. Besant, Mr. Leadbeater, and Mr. Sinnett, along with a host of lesser lights, fed and fostered that hunger for the mysterious, the abnormal, and the "occult" which H.P.B. and Mr. Judge had so resolutely and so continually opposed and warned against. The "E.S.T.," which controlled absolutely the exoteric Society, speedily became a "hall of Occultism" and a "factory for the manufacture of initiates"—the very thing that the veritable *Mahatmas* had so insistently discountenanced in Their letters to Mr. Sinnett in 1880-82; letters whose complete text is now available to all students in "The Mahatma Letters to A. P. Sinnett."

In 1906 charges of infamous conduct and teaching to boys confided to his care were brought against Mr. Leadbeater. An inquiry into the matter was held by Col. Olcott at London. Mr. Leadbeater admitted the charges and resigned from the Society. Colonel Olcott, who had meantime come to distrust Mrs. Besant, had regarded Mr. Leadbeater as the "agent of the Masters," and the disclosures made undoubtedly hastened his death, which occurred early in 1907. Mr. Chakravarti and others had endeavored to procure the endorsement by Col. Olcott of Bertram Keightley to succeed to the Presidency, while those devoted to Mrs. Besant had done the same in her behalf. The mentally enfeebled and physically dying President-Founder was beset in this way till his parting moment. Immediately following his death

Mrs. Besant, on the strength of her own "visions" and the "clairvoyant" witness of Mrs. Marie Russak (Mrs. Hotchener), and Miss Renda, declared that the "Masters" had visited the headquarters and "impressed" her to be the "Successor" of Col. Olcott as she was already the "Successor" of H.P.B. These "Adyar manifestations" raised a great furore throughout the Society. Mr. Sinnett declared them to be anything but what they were claimed to be. Mr. Mead revolted. Even Mr. Fullerton rebelled. A great war of claims pro and con set in. Mrs. Besant, ever master of the strategy of partisan politics, issued a booklet, "H.P.B. and the Masters of the Wisdom." Ostensibly a "defense" of H.P.B. against the Coulomb-S.P.R. charges of more than twenty years earlier, it was in reality a clever move to picture Mrs. Besant in the frame of H.P.B.'s martyrdom, as its opening paragraphs abundantly testify. Mrs. Besant was overwhelmingly voted for by the members who believed her to have been "appointed by the Master."

Mrs. Besant at once began a campaign for the restoration of the repute of her colleague Mr. Leadbeater. He was soon invited to return to the Society and in the years that have gone on has become increasingly the "power behind the throne" in Mrs. Besant's Society. In due course came the "coming Christ" revelation, the order of the "Star in the East" to herald "His coming," and a long succession of adjunct and affiliated orders, organizations, and movements by Mrs. Besant and Mr. Leadbeater. Chief among these was the "Liberal Catholic Church." A quarrel broke out between Mrs. Besant and the father of "Krishnamurti," the assumed probable "vehicle" of the "Incarnation," over Mr. Leadbeater's influence on this Hindu boy. The series of incidents in connection with the "coming Christ" claims have led to increasing extravagances and increasing disturbances in Mrs. Besant's Society. In the thirty years of its history the lapses and withdrawals from Mrs. Besant's Society have been enormous. Only the most strenuous propagation of one new "revelation" after another and the pandering to the thirst for "occult preferment" have enabled it so far to withstand the immense drain of its losses which for more than twenty years have averaged annually some 15 per cent of the membership. Between the "coming Christ," the "Liberal Catholic Church," and the "Occultism" strenuously advocated by Mrs. Besant and Mr. Leadbeater and their imitators, the gulf that separates this fragment of the parent T.S. from the teachings of H.P.B. and Mr. Judge has grown so wide and deep that "Neo-theosophy" has been to all intents and purposes entirely substituted for the Theosophy recorded by H.P.B. as the Message of the Lodge of Masters. Not only has the Society itself become the reverse of the parent association whose name it bears, but the numerous segmentations from it have departed as widely from the original teachings and the original impulse of the Theosophical Movement.

Amongst these fractionations probably the most extensive was that due to Dr. Rudolph Steiner. Originally General Secretary of the German Section of Mrs. Besant's Society, his ability, his personal purity and earnestness, and his writings built up for him a very strong following. As his revelations of "Occultism" conflicted at many points with Mrs. Besant's inspiration, friction soon developed and with her usual methods Mrs. Besant set about forcing him into exile. Practically the entire German membership and many others throughout Europe followed Dr. Steiner when he organized his "Anthroposophical Society" which still numbers a very large membership and which depends entirely upon Dr. Steiner's "Occult" communications and instructions.

Mrs. Besant and Mr. Sinnett composed their differences over the "Adyar manifestations" and Mr. Sinnett accepted Mrs. Besant's invitation to resume the Vice-Presidency of her Society in which he remained till his death—as pathetic a figure as was Col. Olcott during his declining years.

Miss Mabel Collins was also sought out and invited back to membership in Mrs. Besant's Society. She, however, remained connected with it but a few years, and thereafter made various attempts to regain something of the prestige she enjoyed prior to the Coues-Collins attack on H.P.B. but with scant success.

Mr. Geo. R. S. Mead, after following Mrs. Besant's flag in the "case against W. Q. Judge," remained her devoted assistant till the death of the President-Founder and the "Adyar manifestations." He parted from her at that time, subsequently established "The Quest Society" and has since devoted his energies to it and its publication, *The Quest*. His society has gained a considerable and highly respectable membership, mostly in Great Britain, and is devoted almost entirely to comparative religions and psychical research.

Mr. Max Heindel, originally a member of Mrs. Besant's Society and a lecturer in its American Section, became interested early in Dr. Steiner's writings. After a due season of "initiation," Mr. Heindel blossomed forth on his own account with a "Rosicrucian Cosmo-Conception" and a "Rosicrucian" society. He established "headquarters" at Oceanside, California, and built up a flourishing association with numerous members throughout the world. Since his death the activities of this society have been directed by his wife, who survives him.

Aside from the foregoing, literally scores of "occult," "fraternal," "mystical," and "New Thought" groups and small followings have been established with varying appeals and fortunes, by ex-members of the old Theosophical Society and by renegade members of its Esoteric Section. Today it is a rare city indeed in Europe or America which is not the seat of from one to a dozen of these "successors" to the spoils of the Third Section of the Theosophical Movement.

CHAPTER XXXVI

PRESENT AND FUTURE OF THE THEOSOPHICAL MOVEMENT

HAS the Theosophical Movement of our times been a failure?

By many who have followed us thus far, this question will naturally be asked; perhaps by some as naturally decided in the affirmative. All such are asked to read again the Preface and the opening chapter, and then to consider the record made since 1875; not in the nature of an isolated phenomenon, but in the light of human history, even as known to us in a merely mundane sense. The story of civilization, as shown in the great empires of the world, is painted by their rise from savagery through many vicissitudes and, after reaching the culmination of their greatness, they descend again in accordance with the same law by which they ascended; till, having reached the lowest point, humanity reasserts itself and mounts once more, the height of its attainment being, by this law of ascending progression by Cycles, somewhat higher than the point from which it had before descended. As quoted in Chapter I, Mr. Henry Buckle, in his "History of Civilization in England," intuitively grasped this great truth and applied it to the rise and fall of religions and philosophies. The presence on earth at the same time with the highest civilization, of the most degraded and appalling savagery, or of the most abject superstition alongside and in the midst of the noblest ethical and philosophical culture, does not militate against this Law of Cycles—or Karma; it only illustrates one of its applications, for these Cycles do not affect all mankind instantly, or at one and the same time.

According to Theosophical teachings a centenary effort has been made in the West since the fourteenth century, and to its unseen and unrecognized influence has in fact been due the enormous acceleration of European and American progress in science, in political and religious liberty, in inter-racial and international intercourse. From this point of view the mission of H. P. Blavatsky was the fifth in an orderly and progressive series—all of them merely preparatory for that day when Adepts will appear in the West in *propria persona* and *demonstrate,* not merely teach, the reality of Their doctrines concerning Man and Nature. When one considers the appalling misuse and abuse made by men during the last five centuries of their power over their weaker and less endowed fellows, and of those powers wrested from Nature—powers that in every case *might* equally have been employed for universal benefit—he may perhaps appreciate the reticence of the Masters of the Wisdom-Religion in not putting prematurely before mankind the certain evidence of *occult* powers a thousand times more sinister and disastrous, in the hands of able but predatory and selfish men, than any merely physical instrumentations. Who can doubt, in view of what has been and what is, that mankind needs an immense philosophical and ethical preparation before its moral status is on a parity with its intellectual and physical progress? The ground having been plowed and harrowed and tilled in two fields—at what cost to humanity who runs can read, at what cost to the Lodge of Masters who can say? —remains yet to be achieved the far more onerous task of so arousing and promoting the Spiritual evolution of at least a choice minority of the race that a genuine *nucleus of Universal Brotherhood* shall be born to serve as a seed-bed for succeeding generations, before entrusting to it the rationale of those, to us, miraculous powers which, once acquired, may as easily be turned to satanic as to divine purposes. How the *Mahatmas* Themselves view the task before Them is set forth with terrible distinctness in the very first of Their *Letters* to Mr. Sinnett. Other Letters in the same series, now accessible to all who will, show something of the precautions taken by Them in every case of probationary and even accepted

interest indicated by the words religion, science, and philosophy.

No doubt today, as readily as half a century ago, orthodox opinion among leaders and laity alike in the established fields of religion, science, and philosophy still regards either as a delusion or a fraud the claimed Masters of H. P. Blavatsky, her Theosophy, and her phenomena. But when one examines present-day views and theories on Deity, Nature, and Man in contrast and comparison with the accepted ideas of half a century ago, and happens to be familiar with the actual aims and teachings of H. P. Blavatsky, he cannot fail to observe in every department of human interest the profound and far-reaching, if uncredited and unrecognized, influence she has exercised in the course of a single generation.

In the field of religion the orthodox has become the heterodox. "Fundamentalists" stand with their backs to the wall against the ever-increasing power of "Modernism" in religion. Serious writers like Edmond Holmes and Havelock Ellis, preachers like Dean Inge, Harry Emerson Fosdick, and scores of others, dramatists, poets, and essayists, like George Bernard Shaw, Algernon Blackwood, W. B. Yeats, George W. Russell, and Rabindranath Tagore, and popular writers for the press like Arthur Brisbane and Dr. Frank Crane, have been helped by, or have helped themselves to, the teachings of Madame Blavatsky to an enormous extent, both directly and indirectly. In turn, their output has had an immense effect upon the popular mind. That the source from which they have drawn or whence they have derived has not always been acknowledged or accredited does not alter the fact itself. Through such secondary channels her *ideas* have gained an enormous currency. Those who still believe in the Bible *literally,* and in a *carnalized* Christ, have been reduced to a minority in number and in influence, and placed on an apologetic defensive. The day when the clergy exercised a despotic authority over the public conscience has reached its gloaming. Among the clergy themselves the study of comparative religion in the endeavor to find the vital truths common to them all has largely taken the place of the former exclusive study of their own theological dogmas. Liberty of thought, freedom of conscience, the tolerance which goes with them, are everywhere in the air. Evolution, as applied to religion and religious convictions, instead of rigid and unyielding creeds and confessions, is very widely recognized and upheld as the law of the Spiritual Life.

In science the contrast is not less marked. Mr. Tyndall, as the mouthpiece of nineteenth-century science, wrote in his "Fragments": "We claim, and we shall wrest from theology, the entire domain of cosmological theory." What respectable exponent of the science of today would repeat his claim or his boast? If it is indubitably true that religion has become more scientific, it is not less, but even more the case, that science is becoming religious in a nearer spirit and truer sense than the theology of less than two generations since. Men like Thomas A. Edison, Prof. William Crookes, Sir Oliver Lodge, Camille Flammarion, Prof. Millikan, and Chunder Bose have, both by their discoveries and their writings, exercised a tremendous influence over the present and the future of the race at large. Their scientific theories and their views of life have been drawn in chief and large part directly or indirectly from the tenets of the Wisdom-Religion. Lesser but able and influential students of modern science by the hundred, influenced unconsciously to themselves by the Occultism of their awakening psychic faculties have practically overthrown the materialism which dominated the science of the middle of the nineteenth century. "Psychic research" is now a legitimate object of scientific inquiry. The recent investigations conducted by the foremost journal of its kind in the United States, *The Scientific American,* is typical of the new spirit in the scientific field. "Ectoplastic structure" is being seriously experimented with as the actual basis of mediumistic and other abnormal physical and psychological phenomena. This is simply the "astral body" of Theosophical teachings. Two of the greatest of the American universities, Harvard and

Columbia, are, in their departments of psychology, already entering upon the domain of "practical occultism" in their study of the workings of consciousness. Professor James, as his work and his writings show, was influenced by his acquaintance with many of the Theosophical teachings. In physics the old theory of "force and matter" is dead beyond resurrection—drowned by the progressive overflow of hypotheses and experiments directly in the line of the recorded statements and prophecies of H. P. Blavatsky. Science now *knows* that the essential basis of both force and matter is one and the same, and that that essence is electrical in its nature. Atomic and molecular structure and laws are recognized as identical with those that govern a solar system. When it is recognized that "ectoplasm" is the basis of all organic and inorganic action, the physics and the Occult doctrines of physical evolution outlined in the "Secret Doctrine" will have been completely, as they already are in two-thirds, vindicated by modern science itself. The Third Object of the Theosophical Movement is today the First Object of modern science, as its Second Object is the prime concern of Modernism in religion. Einstein has displaced Newton, and the 'science" of Tyndall, of Huxley, and of Haeckel is as much of an outcast today as were the teachings of Madame Blavatsky a single generation ago.

In philosophy, or what passes for philosophy among men of the times, the writings of Bergson, of Maeterlinck, generally, and of many others with particularized theories, show unmistakably that they have been derived and adapted from the ancient Oriental teachings once more brought to the West by Madame Blavatsky. The immense output of books, magazine and newspaper writings, impregnated by and colored with Theosophical ideas, and their ever-growing circulation and popularity, when contrasted with the utter dearth of similar literature prior to 1875, shows the enormous extent of the area watered by the Theosophical Movement, the enormous dissemination and reproduction of the seed brought by H.P.B.

Unrecognized though it be as among the results of the Theosophical Movement, all this is the success for which H.P.B. and Judge worked—the only object they hoped to accomplish, so far as concerned the mass of mankind in the West for the next one hundred years. In writing of the mission of H.P.B. in his *Path* for June, 1891, Mr. Judge stated both her aim and her mission to the world at large, in these words:

> Her aim was to elevate the race. Her method was to deal with the mind of the century as she found it, by trying to lead it on step by step; . . . to found a Society whose efforts—however small itself might be—would inject into the thought of the day the ideas, the doctrines, the nomenclature of the Wisdom-Religion, so that when the next century shall have seen its seventy-fifth year the new messenger coming again into the world would find the Society still at work, the ideas sown broadcast, the nomenclature ready to give expression and body to the immutable truth.

That she set herself no impossible task, that her Masters behind were under no illusions as to what could and what could not be accomplished by her mission, the prime obstacles she and They had to face, and the limitations under which Their work, no less than any other, has to be carried on, is set forth in the Letters of those very Masters Themselves to Mr. Sinnett and Mr. Hume in the earliest days of the Movement. Writing in 1880, the Master said:

> We never pretended to be able to draw nations in the mass to this or that crisis in spite of the general drift of the world's cosmic relations. The cycles must run their rounds. Periods of mental and moral light and darkness succeed each other as day does night. The major and minor cycles must be accomplished according to the natural order of things. And we, borne along

> on the mighty tide, can only modify and direct some of its minor currents. If we had the powers of the imaginary Personal God, and the universal and immutable laws were but toys to play with, then, indeed, might we have created conditions that would have turned this earth into an arcadia for lofty souls. But having to deal with an immutable law, being ourselves its creatures, we have had to do what we could, and rest thankful.

And what of the future of the Theosophical Movement? Will the mission of H. P. Blavatsky in time degenerate as did the mission of Krishna, of Buddha, of Jesus, into, at best, one more added to the number of "prevailing religions" at some future epoch?

It is possible; it is indeed, perhaps, probable, judging by the long record of the past, as that past is known to us. Yet, under the Law of Cycles, it is certain that its zenith is yet to come. The world-religions that have so long survived, and that still number among their adherents three-fourths of the earth's populations, have been in their decadence for many centuries. There are long periods during which the great Masters of the Wisdom-Religion not only do not put forth additions or restatements of Primeval Truths, but, knowing that "periods of mental and moral darkness must succeed each other as night follows day," they do their utmost to withdraw and conceal from the world of the profane every avenue of approach to the Mysteries. This is the opposite pole of that same Law of Spiritual and Intellectual evolution under which "from age to age They incarnate, for the preservation of the just, the destruction of the wicked, and the establishment of righteousness." These alternations are dimly indicated in the many myths of the "Flood," of the "Fall of Man," of the "Destruction of Atlantis," and of Saviours in the remote past, as well as of Avatars yet to come. All this has been extensively treated in the writings of H.P.B. herself, more particularly in her "Secret Doctrine."

The rise of Western civilization since the Middle Ages, the growth of modern science, with all its drawbacks taken into account, the rapid decline in the actual influence of Christian theological dogmas, the great strides in civil as well as religious freedom, the agnostic and inquiring spirit which is everywhere re-testing old measures of value so long esteemed fixed and inviolate—all these are visible and self-evident signs of the ascending arc of the Theosophical Movement among mankind at large. Read in the light of the successive efforts of the First and Second Sections in the last quarter of each of the five preceding centuries, their significance takes on an added augury. Each of these centenary efforts has its own cycle, and while, in the hundred-year cycle from 1875 to 1975, the effort of H.P.B. is at its nadir point in 1925, let it not be forgotten that the work she came to do, *she did.* There is never any failure on the part of the *Masters* of the First Section, or their Messengers and other agents of the Second Section. Her work was, first of all, to deliver a message. That message has been placed of imperishable record among men. Her work, second, was to set the example of true *chelaship* before her students of every degree—to show them how to live the life of utter and complete self-abnegation in the service of a Cause. Those who failed, failed because they tried to separate the Messenger from the message, to appropriate the fruits of her sacrifice without emulating that sacrifice itself. How could they know *her,* who did not live her life? In the third place, she came to reap the ripened harvest of former efforts of the same kind: to do her part in the forging of the final link for this cycle in the unending chain of accessions to the Great Lodge. Chelaship and Adeptship are not the product of one incarnation only, but of many lives devoted to the Path of Perfection, and each cycle completed, each link welded, sees some additions to the "Guardian Wall which shields mankind, since man is man, from other and far greater evils" than any of those known to our times. That this part of her mission did not fail is exemplified in the case of Damodar, of Mr. Judge, of the mysterious Unknown from whom emanated "Light on the Path," and of still others obscurely spoken of or hinted at in the pages of the old *Theosophist* and in "The Mahatma Letters to A. P. Sinnett." While, according to H.P.B., the "cycle of adeptship" closed with the last century for all those who were drawn into the orbit of her living activities, and while with her departure's twilight her Masters also withdrew from all direct contact with those who had not "opened up for themselves conscious communication with the *Guru,*" her mission has not closed, nor have the chelas of the Second Section, old and new, ceased their labors, albeit they work in "secrecy and silence" until 1975, so far as the "Third Section"—the world at large—is concerned.

Quite apart from the *Nirmanakayas,* so rarely spoken of, yet so inspiringly indicated to those in whom the divine spark of intuition is awake; quite apart from the continuous work of the Disciples of the Second Section amongst those to whom they are sent; quite apart from the recorded and abundant statements of H.P.B. that the Path is *never* closed, and can always be found by those who "knock in the right way"—there are those signs by which the thoughtful and reverent layman, the honest and earnest "man in the street," may recognize the unbroken continuity of even the Third Section of the Theosophical Movement.

Certainly those signs are not to be found in the literature or the activities of any of the "Theosophical" and "Occult" societies. In all these it is but too evident that the Master wrote prophetically as well as historically when he advised Mr. Sinnett that "the charlatans and the jugglers are the natural shields of the adepts." Today, as always, those who come to the Temple with unclean hearts are caught and held by the traders in the outer courts. "They have their reward," as Jesus is said to have taught—but perhaps it has been much overlooked that the "pure in heart" have *their* reward also; now, as much as in days of old. Even the traders have to gild their wares to find customers and victims—and the gold in the dross is quickly separated by those who have in them the "four requisites" to the gates of entrance of the inner Tabernacle: "doing service, strong search, questions, and humility." Thus, even during the darkest hours of the Theosophical Movement of our times, there are those who, when tested by the ancient Occult aphorism, "By their fruits shall ye know them," show by their *works* their allegiance without variableness or the shadow of turning to the direct line and the unbroken impulsion of the ageless Movement, as H.P.B. showed the unbroken consistency and undeviating accord of her work and wisdom with the Path of the Predecessors of all time.

A study, for example, of the originally anonymous "Creed of Buddha," and the subsequent writings of its author, Mr. Edmond Holmes, in "The Creed of Christ," and his work on Education, will show the same perception of fundamental Truth, the same grasp of the Eternal Verities, the same sane, wholesome, and practical application of those truths and verities to the problems of everyday life and action as so pre-eminently characterized the work of Mr. Judge. Who can measure the ever-widening influence of such writings as these upon an audience already rendered "porous to ideas and bibulous of thought" through the sacrifice of the Pioneers?

In India, "Motherland of my Master" as H.P.B. wrote, although the Theosophical influence by name has either withered or been turned into the grossest of corruptions—even in India, those who have observed and studied the antecedents and work of the *Angarika* Dharmapala for the revival on the soil of its ancient birthplace of primitive Buddhism, see one of the fruits of the Theosophical Movement. Dharmapala was long a student of H. P. Blavatsky's and close and true friend of Col. Olcott. Seeing the ruin of Theosophy as such in India, instead of folding his hands and waiting vainly for the Masters to do the appointed work of the true Theosophists, he bethought him of the statements of the Masters Themselves—"Col. Olcott works but for the revival of Buddhism," and, "Buddhism, stripped of its superstitions, *is* Eternal Truth itself"—and, undismayed and undisheartened, took upon himself the mighty task whose already visible structure is true to the Architecture of its Founder.

Out of India, too, has come to the West another true student of the wisdom of the "Secret Doctrine"—B. P. Wadia, member of an old and leading Parsi family of Bombay. This gentleman, given a copy of the "Secret Doctrine" in his youth, made it his constant guide during twenty years' work to restore its teachings to currency among the new generation of Theosophists in India, through the channel of the only Theosophical Society known in India—that of Mrs. Besant. Mr. Wadia's practical application of the Brotherhood of Theosophy in raising the status and labor conditions of the textile workers in the great mills of India, and in bringing about the recognition of the "Untouchables" by their fellow workmen, brought in its train a world-wide acquaintance with statesmen, economists, labor leaders, and governmental officials in Europe and America. Mr. Wadia came to the United States, first in 1919, and again in 1922, after a year and a half spent in Europe. Aware that in America the "forerunners" of the Sixth Root Race are appearing in the amalgamation now in process, and aware that the efforts since the fourteenth century have been in anticipation of, and parallel with that amalgamating process, he, in preparation for the future of the Movement in India, issued, in the summer of 1922, an Open Letter to his former associates and to all Theosophists. In this Letter he stated dispassionately and unargumentatively the results of his twenty years of study and work, and announced his resignation from all official and other connection with Mrs. Besant's Society. Hundreds of thoughtful members of that Society, aware of Wadia's history, and impressed by the force of the statements made, have followed it up with investigations of their own and have in turn withdrawn. Indirect results of Wadia's experience, coupled with their own knowledge of conditions, have led many others, notably Mr. Martyn of Australia, Mr. Prentice of New Zealand, Mr. Smythe of Canada, Dr. Stokes of Washington, D. C., Mr. H. Trevor Barker of England, and many other leading members of Mrs. Besant's society either into independent activities or into serious efforts to call attention to prevalent corruption of Theosophical teachings, and to restore that Society to the aims and writings of the Founders.

In Europe, the venerable Mrs. Julia Scott, a survivor of the parent Society and a faithful friend and pupil of H.P.B. and Mr. Judge, has labored for many years to assist and instruct a few in the teachings and practises originally ensouling the Third Section. First in England, then in Italy, and in recent years in Switzerland, her work has been carried on in the midst of many obstacles and despite ill-health and advancing years. Many owe to her their first Theosophical light in this incarnation, and many others their restoration to the lines that had been lost in the confusions following the death of H.P.B. and Mr. Judge.

In the United States, Mr. Robert Crosbie who entered the Movement coincidently with the foundation of *The Path*, and who for many years had the benefit of direct training and instruction from both H.P.B. and Mr. Judge, established in 1909 at Los Angeles, California, the parent United Lodge of Theosophists, after witnessing the final dissolution of the work left at Mr. Judge's death. Mr. Crosbie was imbued with the conviction that the model set in the *Preliminary Memorandum* by H.P.B., was the true and enduring modulus for Theosophical study and work after *her* heart. In 1912 Mr. Crosbie founded the magazine *Theosophy*, a re-incarnation of Mr. Judge's *Path*. He died in 1919, but during his entire period of active Theosophical work, he labored to restore the calumniated reputations of H.P.B. and Mr. Judge, convinced that until their unique status was recognized by Theosophists at large, no return to the Source of the Movement and no continuity of the original effort could succeed. From the very beginning Mr. Crosbie and his associates made no distinctions of organization and recognized "as Theosophists all who are engaged in